Essays
Essays: Second Series

A CHARLES E. MERRILL STANDARD EDITION

CHARLES E. MERRILL STANDARD EDITIONS

Under the General Editorship of
Matthew J. Bruccoli and Joseph Katz

Exact reprints, whenever possible facsimiles, of authoritative texts
of significant literary works. Each volume is introduced in an
appropriate manner by a major scholar, critic, or author.

Ralph Waldo Emerson

Essays
Essays: Second Series

Introduced by

Morse Peckham
University of South Carolina

CHARLES E. MERRILL PUBLISHING COMPANY
A Bell & Howell Company
Columbus, Ohio

These texts of Emerson's *Essays* and *Essays: Second Series* are facsimiles of the first printings in the McKissick Library, University of South Carolina.

Standard Book Number: 675-09389-9 Clothbound edition
675-09388-0 Paperbound edition

Library of Congress Catalog Number: 79-100634

1 2 3 4 5 6 7 8 9 10 — 78 77 76 75 74 73 72 71 70 69

Printed in the United States of America

Introduction

Morse Peckham

Ralph Waldo Emerson was the first to appear of that amazing sequence of literary intellects which emerged from the provincial darkness of the young American republic. Emerson (born in 1803), Hawthorne, Poe, Thoreau, Melville, Whitman — sooner or later they have all been accepted into that grand European culture which transcends and rises above the narrow considerations of nationalism; and it is from a supra-national European orientation that they are all best understood and best measured. In recent decades Emerson has not been so admired, at least in America, as he once was. Possibly his day is coming again. Certainly for some readers he has always been the greatest of that group, just as he was the inspiration and vital spark for almost all of them, even when they rebelled against him.

Of Emerson's various literary achievements, most of which began as lectures assembled from entries in the immense flowing Mississippi of his Journals, his greatest are the two series of *Essays*, published in 1844 and 1849. Within a decade of their publication in England they had become volumes which there every cultivated intellectual and literary figure found it necessary to know well. Matthew Arnold, a young man then, later said that Emerson, along with Goethe and J. H. Newman, was of central and utmost importance in his own development as a man and as a writer, and Arnold was above all other English writers the one who castigated the English for their failure to know and be interested in the literature and learning beyond the limits of their little island, particularly that of Continental Europe. His notion that a man should be a good European was taken up by Henry James and became the formative idea of the latter's life and literary career. To Arnold, the good European, Emerson belonged in the company of Goethe, the man who, more than any other great figure of the late eighteenth and early nineteenth century, insisted on the fundamental unity and internal coherence of European culture. Goethe was of the deepest importance to Emerson, and when the thirty-year-old American went to Scotland in 1833, he sought out Thomas Carlyle, who for nearly a decade had been struggling to bring the richness of Goethe and other German writers to the provincial English. Emerson's task, his mission, his goal, was to join America to supra-national Europe in a seamless continuum; it was a manifestation of his subtlety that one of his strategies was to endeavour to make his fellow Americans into good Europeans by making them exquisitely aware of what it meant to be an American, a matter on which there is still considerable confusion.

So Emerson flows from Europe and back to it again, and to think of him in exclusively American terms and categories is to miss much of his meaning and most of his greatness. Perhaps that is why to the young American of today, at a time when the weakest and least civilized of European cultural strata — those social and cultural strata which the most civilized Europeans have shamefully neglected — are themselves becoming so Americanized, Emerson's *Essays* may not be very appealing. If such a young American finds them pale, disjointed, wandering, faded, too optimistic, excessively bland, he will after all be but repeating the judgment of many of the critics and teachers but a generation or two older than himself. Yet for some men in their fifties and sixties, as they see death coming nearer, as — to borrow from Yeats what he has said better than anyone — they cast a colder eye on life, on death, as they increasingly take a half-concealed pleasure in watching the aggressive horseman of energy and achievement pass by, as they are increasingly torn between a certain contempt for men and an almost unendurable compassion for suffering and self-torturing mankind, the *Essays* of Emerson become always more satisfying and bracing. The affinities of Emerson, the bland optimist, with Schopenhauer, the most invigorating of pessimists, begin to become apparent. His affinities with Søren Kierkegaard, the Danish master of irony, become intriguing and engaging; ten years Emerson's junior, Kierkegaard wrote most of his works in the decade of the publishing of the older writer's *Essays*. The blandness, the optimism, fade away, and a vigor and intellectual toughness emerge which strike into the soul that iron in which the aging man delights. More than anything else, he has learned how to read Emerson. It is not easy.

Everyone knows that Emerson's style is aphoristic; everyone knows that the *Essays* were assembled from here and there in the Journals; everyone knows that they are disjointed, and that there is no particular reason why any sentence could not be omitted. It is easy enough to test this. Leaf through the volume of the essays, randomly selecting a dozen pages, and letting your eye strike any sentence by uncontrolled accident. You will find that almost any sentence you light on can be extracted from its context and savored or dismissed without reference to what precedes or follows it. In Emerson, it seems, there is no argument, no sustained discourse, philosophical or other kind, only a series of sentences stitched together under various grandiose titles of such a kind that almost any sentence could appear in almost any essay.

But that is not the only apparently damaging allegation that can be made against Emerson's style. As we read any *Essay* continuously, the connection between almost any of these aphoristic sentences and the one that follows it is by no means easy to grasp. Often the next sentence does not seem to follow at all. One of the gravest and most difficult philosophical problems is this: Given sentences *a* and *b*, how do you know that sentence *b* properly follows from sentence *a* except by sheer contiguity? Between any two sentences in any discourse lies, it would seem, an abyss, and the task of the man we call the good writer is to bridge the abyss, to give the reader at least the illusion, if nothing else, that sentence *b* really and truly follows from sentence *a*. This is what we expect when we start to read an essay, even the

essays of that most capricious of informal essayists, Charles Lamb.
After all, even Lamb does more to get his reader across the bridge
from *a* to *b* than does Emerson, at least much of the time. It is a
most interesting and instructive exercise to take any piece of
not remarkably good but of merely acceptable prose and explore
the devices used to get the reader from *a* to *b:* the hints, the
clues, the parallelisms, the contrasts, the quasi-logical connectives,
the pronouns with their antecedents in the previous sentence, the
conjunctions, the qualifying adverbs. The devices of style which
go into constructing the bridges across the abysses that lie between
sentences are innumerable, and every competent writer must
master them. Emerson neglects them. He does not build us
bridges; he makes us leap. And the matter is made worse by his
fusion of a capriciousness greater than Lamb's with the philosophical earnestness and moral seriousness of Plato, Montaigne,
Spinoza, Kant, Goethe, Carlyle. With the air of one bent on
absolute lucidity, he devotes himself to eluding us.

It is not in traditional discourse and expository prose or even
inspiriting rhetoric that we must look for a model for what Emerson is doing. It is not in prose at all, but in poetry. That model
is to be found in two kinds of poetry, the lyric poem and the poetic
drama. When we start to read a lyric we do not expect a continuous discourse with bridges carefully built from one sentence to
the next. Rather, we expect the speaker of the poem to fling
himself from one proposition to the next, at times to leap from
one proposition to the next like a predator flinging itself on its
victim; what we expect is the tingling exictement of subjectivity,
and when we respond adequately to the lyric poem we glow with
that same excitement. As Plato long ago said, poets cannot understand what they are talking about. He was quite right, but he
should have added that neither can anybody else. Since he was
a philosopher, he was scarcely performing a professional role that
would permit him to admit that truth. Lyric poets do not conceal
the abysses that divide sentences; they exploit them. Emerson is
a philosopher who writes like a lyric poet, and thinks like one.
His individual sentences are dazzling. How does he get from one
to another? He does not tell us, because he does not know. It is his
pride that he does not know. He refuses to submit to the universal
human illusion that we really know what we are doing while we
are doing it. One who does not grasp the immense and magnificently self-centered pride of Emerson, the pride of a Lucifer who
has fallen but knows that only in *his* kind of fall is there redemp-

tion, has not grasped an essential quality of the man and his writing.

The second model for Emerson's *Essays* is to be found in the speeches of the protagonists and other central characters of poetic drama, especially tragedy, and above all the tragedy of Shakespeare and his contemporaries. *Hamlet* is the greatest of tragedies because its central theme is what underlies the behavior of the heroes of all tragedy, and of all interesting non-comic characters whatever. It is the endless struggle of the hero to redefine himself. Each of us has a self-image and we have a similar image of each individual we know, for the images of both self and other are arrived at in the same way, by observing and making sense out of what we do and say. We can stabilize our world — ourselves, those we know, and the situations we live in — by making those images simple, coherent, and fixed. But we do this at the price of ignoring and repressing those bits and pieces of our behavior and the behavior of others which do not fit coherently and consistently into those images. In every tragic or serious work, the author puts his protagonist through a series of situations which shatters his self-image, and the images of those intimate with him, and of his world, which forces him to be aware of unexpected or hitherto unobserved and unassimilated aspects of his personality and of his social and natural environment. His image is shattered, and he must remake it, only to have it shattered again. Only when he has assimilated the unassimilated is he permitted to die, and he dies because to do that is in fact to do the impossible. The falsity of tragedy and the spurious comfort we gain from it rises from seeing the hero arrive at a self-understanding which no man in the real world, not in the illusory world of art, can ever have. Shakespeare, greatly daring, kills Hamlet without permitting him that spurious self-illumination. Hamlet, dying, tells Horatio to explain him, because the truth is that he cannot explain himself, nor can any man.

That is why Hamlet utters his great soliloquies; why these, not the conclusion, are the heart of the play. Shakespeare denies Hamlet self-illumination. Ever since, critics have been arguing about what ought to be a consistent image of Hamlet, and they have never agreed, and they never will agree, because Hamlet is inexplicable. Hamlet is Man, as no writer before or since has dared or had the genius to present him. Thus, to Emerson, Shakespeare was a great philosopher, and the model for Emerson's *Essays* are the soliloquies of Hamlet, of Shakespeare's other tragic heroes, and of those of Shakespeare's theatrical contemporaries. Hamlet's soliloquies emerge from dramatic situations in which self-image is shattered. Emerson's *Essays* emerge from a grander situation — the condition of man — which truly, apprehended, as it almost never is by anyone, shatters any man's self-image. That is why the first of the *Essays* is "History," which, Emerson tells us, is a spurious projection of our spurious self-images, and he shatters it. That is why the next essay is "Self-Reliance." To rely on oneself is to have the courage to doubt one's comforting self-image. This is the meaning of the famous statement, "A foolish consistency is the hobgoblin of little minds. . . . With consistency a great soul has simply nothing to do." A great soul may know that he must have a coherent and acceptable self-image to act at all, but he knows that at worst it is spurious and at best it is only an instrument.

The *Essays*, then, are a fusion of the lyric and the dramatic soliloquy. Emerson assembled them from here and there in his Journals because he knew that any self-image is an assemblage, not a coherent structure. Just as the lyric poet exploits the leap from sentence to sentence, so Emerson exploits the inconsistency of our personalities which our self-images endeavor to conceal. The tragic role he plays is that of Man acting his part on the stage of the World, and he sees that the personality of Man is an assemblage, the various bits and pieces of which come from he knows not where, and he does not conceal the fact. He glories in it; it is the source of his immense and magnificently self-centered pride.

A further genre of poetry can provide yet another model for reading Emerson's *Essays* — a kind of negative model. In the very decade of the essays, the 1840's, a younger contemporary of Emerson's, the Englishman Robert Browning, created the dramatic monologue. As with Emerson, his two sources were the lyric poem, and the soliloquy of the Elizabethan theater, of Shakespeare and his contemporaries. But Browning adds a twist neither in Shakespeare nor in Emerson. Browning's monologues emerge from situations which, though they do not shatter the self-images of his speakers, certainly threaten to shatter them; the monologist immediately throws himself into the effort to maintain his self-image. Consequently the reader sees through the self-image as the monologist does not. He sees that the speaker is making an assemblage out of the rags and tatters of his personality in order to preserve his self-esteem. He sees the threat which could shatter the self-image were it not for the defenses of the speaker. It is the process subsequent psychologists have come to call rationalization, and nowadays we know all about it, and perhaps can do it better because we do. It could be said, of course, that Shakespeare does the same thing in the soliloquies of such a villain as Iago, but that would be an error. Iago rationalizes because of a moral defect. Browning's monologists rationalize because they are human beings. Browning's twist is that we rationalize because we are human; rationalization is what we pay in order to exist. Rationalization is the price of the ticket of admission to the great theater of human society and culture. Emerson's *Essays*, then, can be profitably approached as dramatic monologues by a man who is doing his best not to rationalize. To be sure, we can say that he sometimes fails. To affirm that he always fails in an easy optimism is to miss the *Essays* almost completely, just as it is a total failure of comprehension to call Browning an easy optimist. We lie to ourselves in order to exist, to act, and since writing is a form of action, sometimes even Emerson lied to himself. But he knew, as Browning knew, that what we call honesty with ourselves is also a lie, because such honesty makes ourselves explicable, and we are inexplicable. Thus self-honesty is to ascribe to ourselves a moral defect which conceals from ourselves a condition of existence. And it must be added that in the 1850's Emerson became grimmer and developed something of the terrible insight of Browning.

Nevertheless, Emerson would not have been human had he not tried to justify his position and provide a rationale for his style. It cannot be denied that he succumbed to the philosophical temptation to explain the inexplicable. But then, not to have succumbed would have been consistent, and so inconsistent with his inconsistency. His tragic role is that of Man, and Man's struggle to achieve a consistent vision of his condition is a part of that role and cannot be avoided. Yet such a consistent vision, once achieved, can be denied and transcended; that is what the essay "Circles" is about. To think at all we must have a ground to our thinking, or, as those German philosophers of the time, whom Emerson knew directly and indirectly, liked to put it, there must be a ground to existence, if we are to exist. Yet there is no reason why we should not change that ground as often as we like — or can. That is why one cannot create a consistent philosophical position from Emerson's writings except by omitting a great deal.

In the fashion of his time he often used the terms *subject* and *object*, that is, the observing mind and what it observes. Ever since Kant it had been realized that the subject, or observing mind, observes what it wishes to observe, or, to put it more delicately, what it is its interest to observe; and we know this is so because the object, that which is observed, is always tripping up the observing mind. The instruments, or categories, of the observing mind, the subject, are never congruent with the world, the *ding-an-sich*, as Kant called it. We see not the real world, which is inaccessible to us, but the phenomenal world, the world as rearranged to our satisfaction, or dissatisfaction, as the case may be. Thus we have two images, that of the subject and that of the object, and they never match; or, to put it another way — and Emerson liked to put it both ways — the subject projects onto the world an image which falsifies the world. What the world really is we cannot know. In temporal terms, we are always just missing the bus, but then we are always just about to catch it. In more abstract terms, Emerson, like all the advanced thinkers of his time and ours — though today we would put it differently — was convinced that between subject and object there is an irresolvable tension. We do not perceive the world, we create it; or, in perceiving the world we create it. And this act of perceptual creation is man's deepest interest and satisfaction. Here is the most important reason for Emerson's style. Like so many of his contemporaries, to him the perception of a work of art or philosophy was as creative an act as creating it. Kierkegaard called writing which forces the reader to create, teaching by the indirect method. At any rate, from this irresolvable tension between subject and object emerges an odd paradox. Everybody interprets the world a little bit differently from everybody else, yet we all find our way around in it reasonably well; and these two facts can never be put together, or at least Emerson could not, except in a very special way. It is a way not completely acceptable to us today, but from it something of great significance can be rescued which reveals Emerson's modernity and relevance to our times.

In the essay "The Over-Soul" Emerson works out his position. To grasp it one must first seize vividly the way we ordinarily think about the relation of the mind to the world. To use non-Emersonian terms, our usual assumption is something like this: a stimulus or set of stimuli is fed into the brain by the nervous system. The brain processes these stimuli in various ways, usually called rational (*i.e.*, logical), irrational, and emotional, and the result of that processing, which we call mental activity, is the generation of some activity, including verbal activity. We identify ourselves with mental activity, and feel convinced that we are in control of it. "My mind," we say, "is my own." Now Emerson cannot accept this picture of what happens. Rather, he recommends that we stand aside from our own activity, watch ourselves generating activity, and sunder our usual identification of ourselves, that is, our awareness, with mental activity. If we do that, it then becomes apparent that the usual picture is quite false. Rather, a stimulus or set of stimuli is fed into the brain by the nervous system. The brain processes these stimuli in ways we canot possibly comprehend, and the result of that processing is our behavior, which is, therefore, inexplicable. Between stimulus and response lies a mystery, an abyss, the same abyss that lies between two sentences. Thus, if "mind" means awareness, or consciousness, then what happens between stimulus and response is not mind, is not mental activity. Or, if "mind" means what happens between stimulus and response, then awareness, or consciousness, is not mind. What happens in that abyss, Emerson thinks, is not only inexplicable; it is the source of everything that lends life its value. There, he thinks, subject and object are one; in that abyss, he believes, the divine enters the human.

It is interesting that in these very years in which Emerson was publishing the *Essays*, in Denmark, Søren Kierkegaard was working out a remarkably similar scheme. In human life he discerned three possible stages, or three levels of orientation towards the world. The first he called the aesthetic, the orientation which satisfies one with the sensuous and the imaginative. Should a man, however, discern that the values of such a life are incoherent and contradictory, he develops the ironic vision. As a result he comes to realize that he must choose among these values if he is to have a life more meaningful than the pure entertainment of the aesthetic orientation. Thus he arrives at the ethical stage, or orientation, in which he believes that he has his life in control, that he determines his life. Should he come to realize, however, that his life is not his own, that his behavior is actually inexplicable, he will, if fortunate, be amused that men should entertain the illusion that they know what they are doing, and that the sense that they make out of themselves and their experiences is anything more than, at the best, comforting. Thus humor precipitates him into a third stage, or orientation — the religious — in which he realizes that each of his acts is a leap from a previous act, a leap which he can only perform but cannot understand.

What sustains him in that leap is God, of whom, however, he can never hope to comprehend anything. Thus his position is remarkably like Emerson's.

It is worth noting that anyone who does not wish to employ the notion "God" in his thinking, can nevertheless find both Emerson's and Kierkegaard's schemes quite useful. It can be said that both, still dominated by something of traditional thinking, stripped the term "God" of all useful meaning and used it in order to have *something* to put into the gap between stimulus and response, the abyss over which man leaps from act to act. In the post-Freudian period Western culture is more inclined to use "unconscious" or "subconscious", but like "God" in the Emersonian and Kierkegaardian structures, these words simply mean that whatever is going on in that abyss — and we cannot know what it is — is very important, so important as to be the source of all value.

Although Emerson did not think in Kierkegaardian terms, the Dane's categories are helpful in understanding Emerson. Particularly they help us to understand what in Emerson has so often been condemned, especially by the terribly earnest, the irredeemably ethical, those moral bullies who are always trying to force themselves and everyone else to the irresistible choice, or what they fancy to be the irresistible choice, those who are so foolish as really to believe in reason and logic and man's self-possession as absolutes, not as dull and fragile instrument. What annoys such people is Emerson's radiant light-heartedness, which they think of as shallow optimism. It is nothing of the sort; it has gone beyond optimism. That is why Nietzsche so admired Emerson. If one reads Emerson's Journals, one comes to realize that Emerson achieved that light-heartedness only by paying a price of terrible strain and even suffering, a suffering which never left him. Emerson, like Kierkegaard, arrives at the religious stage through humor, and it is why among their many other virtues, the *Essays* are so amusing. The essay "Compensation" is an instance. Here he is not humorous but ironic. The universe, he tells us, is a system of justice; for every action there is a corresponding reaction; for every crime there is a punishment. At first glance it seems like a position that affirms that the universe is a harmonious and coherent unity. However, if for every action there is a corresponding reaction, then everything cancels out everything else. His point can be seen if we realize that when we talk about the importance of justice, we mean the importance of justice for other people, not ourselves. For ourselves we do not want justice, but favors, special consideration. We want the judges of *our* actions to render their judgments on our sins and errors with a full knowledge of the extenuating circumstances. But no, Emerson tells us, there are no extenuating circumstances; there are only our acts. Nevertheless he consoles us. In human life the compensation is that we transcend what we were, that we break through to a new vision of experience, we break down those defenses which preserve a spurious self-image and create a new one which is, hopefully, at least less spurious.

There is no doubt that Emerson, like Kierkegaard, was not an optimist but a redemptionist. The optimist thinks that the progress of the race is automatic. The redemptionist thinks that if man will truly understand his situation, he can redeem himself and the world, and permeate both with a radiant and permanent value. When Emerson was publishing the *Essays*, the young Karl Marx was struggling towards his vision of human redemption, of a society in which subject and object — for he thought in the same terms as Emerson and Kierkegaard — will be reconciled. But there is a difference between the German on the one hand and the American and the Dane on the other. Marx thought redemption could be achieved by the mass of mankind freeing itself from its oppressors, who had alienated from the individual the fruits of his labor. Emerson thought that the peculiar historical circumstances of his country might conceivably facilitate the achievement of individual redemption, which, like Browning, he thought could be but momentary and must constantly be achieved anew. Kierkegaard came to the conclusion that redemption could be achieved only by the individual, working in profound isolation, utterly separated from his fellow-man. Emerson, in the 1850's, moved in this direction, not Marx's.

The theme of alienation is common to all three. To Marx, economic oppression has alienated man from his happiness, the rewards of his work, those rewards being his natural right. To Marx the immediate task was to overthrow economic oppression and its political instruments so that man might enter at once upon his happiness. To Emerson, redemption was a spiritual achievement, and, like Kierkegaard, he came to see that it lay not in overcoming alienation but in plunging into alienation, with no assurance of what, if anything might lie beyond it. Thus what is often called the optimism of Emerson is closer to a sunny and cheerful indifference. Marx would resolve the inconsistencies of society and culture into a coherent value-laden society and culture; Emerson denied that society and culture could be coherent and value-laden. Value could be achieved by the individual only if he accepted his incoherence and his absurdity. For Marx the goal is to create a society in which all men are equally heroic in their common mastery of nature. For Emerson only the individual can be heroic, and only as an individual; and nature is not to be mastered but loved. To put it with excessive baldness, Marx thought that redemption could be realized only by bringing people together into a common cause and a social unity. Kierkegaard and Emerson and Browning thought that the only way was to keep people apart, and that one must begin by keeping oneself apart. Marx is the energetic horseman; but ultimately Emerson casts a cold eye.

These two ways, the Marxian and the Emersonian, are still the only ways of dealing with that alienation from society and culture which has been the experience of every modern and highly cultivated spirit of that last century and of this, our own. Which way is to be preferred? It was the problem of the 1840's, and it is the problem of today. Certainly Emerson, in his *Essays*, has illuminated that problem as have few writers then or since, and with a brilliance that one can never, finally, tire of.

ESSAYS.

ESSAYS:

BY

R. W. EMERSON.

———

BOSTON:
JAMES MUNROE AND COMPANY.
———
MDCCCXLI.

BOSTON:

PRINTED BY FREEMAN AND BOLLES,
WASHINGTON STREET.

CONTENTS.

CONTENTS.

HISTORY.

There is no great and no small
To the Soul that maketh all :
And where it cometh, all things are ;
And it cometh every where.

I am owner of the sphere,
Of the seven stars and the solar year,
Of Cæsar's hand, and Plato's brain,
Of Lord Christ's heart, and Shakspeare's strain.

ESSAY I.

HISTORY.

THERE is one mind common to all individual men. Every man is an inlet to the same and to all of the same. He that is once admitted to the right of reason is made a freeman of the whole estate. What Plato has thought, he may think; what a saint has felt, he may feel; what at any time has befallen any man, he can understand. Who hath access to this universal mind, is a party to all that is or can be done, for this is the only and sovereign agent.

Of the works of this mind history is the record. Its genius is illustrated by the entire series of days. Man is explicable by nothing less than all his history. Without hurry, without rest, the human spirit goes forth from the beginning to embody every faculty, every thought, every emotion, which belongs to it in appropriate events. But always the thought is prior to the fact; all the facts of history preëxist in the mind as laws. Each law in turn is made by circumstances predominant, and the limits of nature give power to but one at a time. A man is the whole encyclopædia of facts. The creation of a thousand forests is in one acorn, and Egypt, Greece, Rome, Gaul, Britain, America, lie folded already in the first man. Epoch after epoch, camp, kingdom, empire, republic, democracy, are merely the application of his manifold spirit to the manifold world.

This human mind wrote history and this must read it. The Sphinx must solve her own riddle. If the whole of history is in one man, it is all to be explained from individual experience. There is a relation between the hours of our life and the centuries of time. As the air I breathe is drawn from the great repositories of nature, as the light on my book is yielded by a star a hundred millions of miles distant, as the poise of my body depends on the equilibrium of centrifugal and centripetal forces, so the hours should be instructed by the ages, and the ages explained by the hours. Of the universal mind each individual man is one more incarnation. All its properties consist in him. Every step in his private experience flashes a light on what great bodies of men have done, and the crises of his life refer to national crises. Every revolution was first a thought in one man's mind, and when the same thought occurs to another man, it is the key to that era. Every reform was once a private opinion, and when it shall be a private opinion again, it will solve the problem of the age. The fact narrated must correspond to something in me to be credible or intelligible. We as we read must become Greeks, Romans, Turks, priest, and king, martyr and executioner, must fasten these images to some reality in our secret experience, or we shall see nothing, learn nothing, keep nothing. What befell Asdrubal or Cæsar Borgia, is as much an illustration of the mind's powers and depravations as what has befallen us. Each new law and political movement has meaning for you. Stand before each of its tablets and say, ' Here is one of my coverings. Under this fantastic, or odious, or graceful mask, did my Proteus nature hide itself.' This remedies the defect of our too great nearness to ourselves. This throws our own actions into perspective : and as crabs, goats, scorpions, the balance and the waterpot, lose all their meanness when hung as signs in the zodiack, so I can see my own vices without heat in the distant persons of Solomon, Alcibiades, and Catiline.

It is this universal nature which gives worth to particular men and things. Human life as containing this is mysterious and inviolable, and we hedge it round with penalties and laws. All laws derive hence their ultimate reason, all express at last reverence for some command of this supreme illimitable essence. Property also holds of the soul, covers great spiritual facts, and instinctively we at first hold to it with swords and laws, and wide and complex combinations. The obscure consciousness of this fact is the light of all our day, the claim of claims ; the plea for education, for justice, for charity, the foundation of friendship and love, and of the heroism and grandeur which belongs to acts of self-reliance. It is remarkable that involuntarily we always read as superior beings. Universal history, the poets, the romancers, do not in their stateliest pictures, — in the sacerdotal, the imperial palaces, in the triumphs of will, or of genius, anywhere lose our ear, anywhere make us feel that we intrude, that this is for our betters, but rather is it true that in their grandest strokes, there we feel most at home. All that Shakspeare says of the king, yonder slip of a boy that reads in the corner, feels to be true of himself. We sympathize in the great moments of history, in the great discoveries, the great resistances, the great prosperities of men ; — because there law was enacted, the sea was searched, the land was found, or the blow was struck *for us*, as we ourselves in that place would have done or applauded.

So is it in respect to condition and character. We honor the rich because they have externally the freedom, power and grace which we feel to be proper to man, proper to us. So all that is said of the wise man by stoic or oriental or modern essayist, describes to each man his own idea, describes his unattained but attainable self. All literature writes the character of the wise man. All books, monuments, pictures, conversation, are portraits in which the wise man finds the lineaments he is forming. The silent and the loud praise him, and accost him, and he is stimulated wherever he moves as by personal allusions. A wise and good soul, therefore, never needs look for allusions personal and laudatory in discourse. He hears the commendation, not of himself, but more sweet, of that character he seeks, in every word that is said concerning character, yea, further, in every fact that befalls, — in the running river, and the rustling corn. Praise is looked, homage tendered, love flows from mute nature, from the mountains and the lights of the firmament.

These hints, dropped as it were from sleep and night, let us use in broad day. The student is to read history actively and not passively ; to esteem his own life the text, and books the commentary. Thus compelled, the muse of history will utter oracles, as never to those who do not respect themselves. I have no expectation that any man will read history aright, who thinks that what was done in a remote age, by men whose names have resounded far, has any deeper sense than what he is doing to-day.

The world exists for the education of each man. There is no age or state of society or mode of action in history, to which there is not somewhat corresponding in his life. Every thing tends in a most wonderful manner to abbreviate itself and yield its whole virtue to him. He should see that he can live all history in his own person. He must sit at home with might and main, and not suffer himself to be bullied by kings or empires, but know that he is greater than all the geography and all the government of the world ; he must transfer the point of view from which history is commonly read, from Rome and Athens and London to himself, and not deny his conviction that he is the Court, and if England or Egypt have any thing to say to him, he will try the case ; if not, let them forever

be silent. He must attain and maintain that lofty
sight where facts yield their secret sense, and poetry
and annals are alike. The instinct of the mind, the
purpose of nature betrays itself in the use we make
of the signal narrations of history. Time dissipates
to shining ether the solid angularity of facts. No
anchor, no cable, no fences avail to keep a fact a
fact. Babylon and Troy and Tyre and even early
Rome are passing already into fiction. The Garden
of Eden, the Sun standing still in Gibeon, is poetry
thenceforward to all nations. Who cares what the
fact was, when we have thus made a constellation of
it to hang in heaven an immortal sign? London and
Paris and New York must go the same way. "What
is History," said Napoleon, " but a fable agreed
upon? ' This life of ours is stuck round with Egypt,
Greece, Gaul, England, War, Colonization, Church,
Court, and Commerce, as with so many flowers and
wild ornaments grave and gay. I will not make more
account of them. I believe in Eternity. I can find
Greece, Palestine, Italy, Spain, and the Islands, — the
genius and creative principle of each and of all eras
in my own mind.

We are always coming up with the facts that have
moved us in history in our private experience, and verifying them here. All history becomes subjective;
in other words, there is properly no History; only
Biography. Every soul must know the whole lesson
for itself — must go over the whole ground. What it
does not see, what it does not live, it will not know.
What the former age has epitomized into a formula

or rule for manipular convenience, it will lose all the good of verifying for itself, by means of the wall of that rule. Somewhere or other, some time or other, it will demand and find compensation for that loss by doing the work itself. Ferguson discovered many things in astronomy which had long been known. The better for him.

History must be this or it is nothing. Every law which the state enacts, indicates a fact in human nature ; that is all. We must in our own nature see the necessary reason for every fact, — see how it could and must be. So stand before every public, every private work ; before an oration of Burke, before a victory of Napoleon, before a martyrdom of Sir Thomas More, of Sidney, of Marmaduke Robinson, before a French Reign of Terror, and a Salem hanging of witches, before a fanatic Revival, and the Animal Magnetism in Paris, or in Providence. We assume that we under like influence should be alike affected, and should achieve the like ; and we aim to master intellectually the steps, and reach the same height or the same degradation that our fellow, our proxy has done.

All inquiry into antiquity, — all curiosity respecting the pyramids, the excavated cities, Stonehenge, the Ohio Circles, Mexico, Memphis, is the desire to do away this wild, savage and preposterous There or Then, and introduce in its place the Here and the Now. It is to banish the *Not me*, and supply the *Me*. It is to abolish difference and restore unity. Belzoni digs and measures in the mummy-

1*

pits and pyramids of Thebes, until he can see the end
of the difference between the monstrous work and
himself. When he has satisfied himself, in general
and in detail, that it was made by such a person
as himself, so armed and so motived, and to ends
to which he himself in given circumstances should
also have worked, the problem is then solved; his
thought lives along the whole line of temples and
sphinxes and catacombs, passes through them all like
a creative soul, with satisfaction, and they live again
to the mind, or are *now*.

A Gothic cathedral affirms that it was done by us,
and not done by us. Surely it was by man, but we
find it not in our man. But we apply ourselves to
the history of its production. We put ourselves into
the place and historical state of the builder. We remember the forest dwellers, the first temples, the adherence to the first type, and the decoration of it as
the wealth of the nation increased; the value which
is given to wood by carving led to the carving over
the whole mountain of stone of a cathedral. When
we have gone through this process, and added thereto
the Catholic Church, its cross, its music, its processions, its Saints' days and image-worship, we have, as
it were, been the man that made the minster; we
have seen how it could and must be. We have the
sufficient reason.

The difference between men is in their principle of
association. Some men classify objects by color and
size and other accidents of appearance; others by
intrinsic likeness, or by the relation of cause and

effect. The progress of the intellect consists in the clearer vision of causes, which overlooks surface differences. To the poet, to the philosopher, to the saint, all things are friendly and sacred, all events profitable, all days holy, all men divine. For the eye is fastened on the life, and slights the circumstance. Every chemical substance, every plant, every animal in its growth, teaches the unity of cause, the variety of appearance.

Why, being as we are surrounded by this all-creating nature, soft and fluid as a cloud or the air, should we be such hard pedants, and magnify a few forms ? Why should we make account of time, or of magnitude, or of form ? The soul knows them not, and genius, obeying its law, knows how to play with them as a young child plays with greybeards and in churches. Genius studies the causal thought, and far back in the womb of things, sees the rays parting from one orb, that diverge ere they fall by infinite diameters. Genius watches the monad through all his masks as he performs the metempsychosis of nature. Genius detects through the fly, through the caterpillar, through the grub, through the egg, the constant type of the individual; through countless individuals the fixed species; through many species the genus; through all genera the steadfast type; through all the kingdoms of organized life the eternal unity. Nature is a mutable cloud, which is always and never the same. She casts the same thought into troops of forms, as a poet makes twenty fables with one moral. Beautifully shines a spirit through the bruteness

and toughness of matter.   Alone omnipotent, it converts all things to its own end.   The adamant streams
into softest but precise form before it, but, whilst I
look at it, its outline and texture are changed altogether.   Nothing is so fleeting as form.   Yet never
does it quite deny itself.   In man we still trace the ru-
diments or hints of all that we esteem badges of servitude in the lower races, yet in him they enhance his
nobleness and grace ; as Io, in Æschylus, transformed
to a cow, offends the imagination, but how changed
when as Isis in Egypt she meets Jove, a beautiful
woman, with nothing of the metamorphosis left but the
lunar horns as the splendid ornament of her brows.

The identity of history is equally intrinsic, the
diversity equally obvious.   There is at the surface
infinite variety of things ; at the centre there is simplicity and unity of cause.   How many are the
acts of one man in which we recognise the same
character.   See the variety of the sources of our information in respect to the Greek genius.   Thus at
first we have the *civil history* of that people, as
Herodotus, Thucydides, Xenophon, Plutarch have
given it — a very sufficient account of what manner
of persons they were, and what they did.   Then we
have the same soul expressed for us again in their
literature ; in poems, drama, and philosophy : a very
complete form.   Then we have it once more in their
architecture, — the purest sensuous beauty, — the perfect medium never overstepping the limit of charming
propriety and grace.   Then we have it once more in
sculpture, — " the tongue on the balance of expres-

sion," those forms in every action, at every age of life, ranging through all the scale of condition, from god to beast, and never transgressing the ideal serenity, but in convulsive exertion the liege of order and of law. Thus, of the genius of one remarkable people, we have a fourfold representation, — the most various expression of one moral thing : and to the senses what more unlike than an ode of Pindar, a marble Centaur, the Peristyle of the Parthenon, and the last actions of Phocion ? Yet do these varied external expressions proceed from one national mind.

Every one must have observed faces and forms which, without any resembling feature, make a like impression on the beholder. A particular picture or copy of verses, if it do not awaken the same train of images, will yet superinduce the same sentiment as some wild mountain walk, although the resemblance is nowise obvious to the senses, but is occult and out of the reach of the understanding. Nature is an endless combination and repetition of a very few laws. She hums the old well known air through innumerable variations.

Nature is full of a sublime family likeness throughout her works. She delights in startling us with resemblances in the most unexpected quarters. I have seen the head of an old sachem of the forest, which at once reminded the eye of a bald mountain summit, and the furrows of the brow suggested the strata of the rock. There are men whose manners have the same essential splendor as the simple and awful sculpture on the friezes of the Parthenon,

and the remains of the earliest Greek art.   And
there are compositions of the same strain to be found
in the books of all ages.   What is Guido's Ros-
pigliosi Aurora but a morning thought, as the horses
in it are only a morning cloud.   If any one will but
take pains to observe the variety of actions to which
he is equally inclined in certain moods of mind, and
those to which he is averse, he will see how deep is
the chain of affinity.

A painter told me that nobody could draw a tree
without in some sort becoming a tree; or draw a
child by studying the outlines of its form merely, —
but, by watching for a time his motions and plays, the
painter enters into his nature, and can then draw him
at will in every attitude.   So Roos " entered into the
inmost nature of a sheep."   I knew a draughtsman
employed in a public survey, who found that he could
not sketch the rocks until their geological structure
was first explained to him.

What is to be inferred from these facts but this;
that in a certain state of thought is the common origin of very diverse works?   It is the spirit and not
the fact that is identical.   By descending far down
into the depths of the soul, and not primarily by a
painful acquisition of many manual skills, the artist
attains the power of awakening other souls to a given
activity.

It has been said that " common souls pay with
what they do; nobler souls with that which they are."
And why ? Because a soul, living from a great depth
of being, awakens in us by its actions and words, by

its very looks and manners, the same power and beauty that a gallery of sculpture, or of pictures, are wont to animate.

Civil history, natural history, the history of art, and the history of literature, — all must be explained from individual history, or must remain words. There is nothing but is related to us, nothing that does not interest us — kingdom, college, tree, horse, or iron shoe, the roots of all things are in man. It is in the soul that architecture exists. Santa Croce and the Dome of St. Peter's are lame copies after a divine model. Strasburg Cathedral is a material counterpart of the soul of Erwin of Steinbach. The true poem is the poet's mind ; the true ship is the ship-builder. In the man, could we lay him open, we should see the sufficient reason for the last flourish and tendril of his work, as every spine and tint in the sea-shell preëxist in the secreting organs of the fish. The whole of heraldry and of chivalry is in courtesy. A man of fine manners shall pronounce your name with all the ornament that titles of nobility could ever add.

The trivial experience of every day is always verifying some old prediction to us, and converting into things for us also the words and signs which we had heard and seen without heed. Let me add a few examples, such as fall within the scope of every man's observation, of trivial facts which go to illustrate great and conspicuous facts.

A lady, with whom I was riding in the forest, said to me, that the woods always seemed to her *to wait*, as if the genii who inhabit them suspended their deeds until the wayfarer has passed onward. This is precisely the thought which poetry has celebrated in the dance of the fairies which breaks off on the approach of human feet. The man who has seen the rising moon break out of the clouds at midnight, has been present like an archangel at the creation of light and of the world. I remember that being abroad one summer day, my companion pointed out to me a broad cloud, which might extend a quarter of a mile parallel to the horizon, quite accurately in the form of a cherub as painted over churches, — a round block in the centre which it was easy to animate with eyes and mouth, supported on either side by wide stretched symmetrical wings. What appears once in the atmosphere may appear often, and it was undoubtedly the archetype of that familiar ornament. I have seen in the sky a chain of summer lightning which at once revealed to me that the Greeks drew from nature when they painted the thunderbolt in the hand of Jove. I have seen a snow-drift along the sides of the stone wall which obviously gave the idea of the common architectural scroll to abut a tower.

By simply throwing ourselves into new circum-stances we do continually invent anew the orders and the ornaments of architecture, as we see how each people merely decorated its primitive abodes. The Doric temple still presents the semblance of the wooden cabin in which the Dorian dwelt. The Chinese pagoda is plainly a Tartar tent. The Indian and Egyptian temples still betray the mounds and subterranean houses of their forefathers. " The custom of making houses and tombs in the living rock," (says Heeren, in his Researches on the Ethiopians) " determined very naturally the principal character of the Nubian Egyptian architecture to the colossal form which it assumed. In these caverns already prepared by nature, the eye was accustomed to dwell on huge shapes and masses, so that when art came to the assistance of nature, it could not move on a small scale without degrading itself. What would statues of the usual size, or neat porches and wings have been, associated with those gigantic halls before which only Colossi could sit as watchmen, or lean on the pillars of the interior ?"

The Gothic church plainly originated in a rude adaptation of the forest trees with all their boughs to a festal or solemn arcade, as the bands about the cleft pillars still indicate the green withes that tied them. No one can walk in a road cut through pine woods, without being struck with the architectural appearance of the grove, especially in winter, when the bareness of all other trees shows the low arch of the Saxons. In the woods in a winter afternoon one will see as readily the origin of the stained glass window with which the Gothic cathedrals are adorned, in the colors of the western sky seen through the bare and crossing branches of the forest. Nor can any lover of nature enter the old piles of Oxford and the English cathedrals without feeling that the forest overpowered the mind of the builder, and that his chisel, his saw, and plane still reproduced its ferns, its spikes of flowers, its locust, its pine, its oak, its fir, its spruce.

The Gothic cathedral is a blossoming in stone subdued by the insatiable demand of harmony in man. The mountain of granite blooms into an eternal flower with the lightness and delicate finish as well as the aerial proportions and perspective of vegetable beauty.

In like manner all public facts are to be individualized, all private facts are to be generalized. Then at once History becomes fluid and true, and Biography deep and sublime. As the Persian imitated in the slender shafts and capitals of his architecture the stem and flower of the lotus and palm, so the Persian Court in its magnificent era never gave over the Nomadism of its barbarous tribes, but travelled from Ecbatana, where the spring was spent, to Susa in summer, and to Babylon for the winter.

In the early history of Asia and Africa, Nomadism and Agriculture are the two antagonist facts. The geography of Asia and of Africa necessitated a nomadic life. But the nomads were the terror of all those whom the soil or the advantages of a market had induced to build towns. Agriculture therefore was a religious injunction because of the perils of the state from nomadism. And in these late and civil countries of England and America, the contest of these propensities still fights out the old battle in each individual. We are all rovers and all fixtures by turns, and pretty rapid turns. The nomads of Africa are constrained to wander by the attacks of the gadfly, which drives the cattle mad, and so compels the tribe to emigrate in the rainy season and drive off the cattle to the higher sandy regions. The nomads of Asia follow the pasturage from month to month. In America and Europe the nomadism is of trade and curiosity. A progress certainly from the gad-fly of Astaboras to the Anglo and Italo-mania of Boston Bay. The difference between men in this respect is the faculty of rapid domestication, the power to find his chair and bed everywhere, which one man has, and another has not. Some men have so much of the Indian left, have constitutionally such habits of accommodation, that at sea, or in the forest, or in the snow, they sleep as warm, and dine with as good appetite, and associate as happily, as in their own house. And to push this old fact still one degree nearer, we may find it a representative of a permanent fact in human nature. The intellectual nomadism is the faculty of objectiveness or of eyes which everywhere feed themselves. Who hath such eyes, everywhere falls into easy relations with his fellow-men. Every man, every thing is a prize, a study, a property to him, and this love smooths his brow, joins him to men and makes him beautiful and beloved in their sight. His house is a wagon ; he roams through all latitudes as easily as a Calmuc.

Every thing the individual sees without him, corresponds to his states of mind, and every thing is in turn intelligible to him, as his onward thinking leads him into the truth to which that fact or series belongs.

The primeval world, the Fore-World, as the Germans say,— I can dive to it in myself as well as grope for it with researching fingers in catacombs, libraries, and the broken reliefs and torsos of ruined villas.

What is the foundation of that interest all men feel
in Greek history, letters, art and poetry, in all its periods, from the heroic or Homeric age, down to
the domestic life of the Athenians and Spartans, four
or five centuries later ? This period draws us because
we are Greeks. It is a state through which every man
in some sort passes. The Grecian state is the era of
the bodily nature, the perfection of the senses, — of
the spiritual nature unfolded in strict unity with the
body. In it existed those human forms which supplied the sculptor with his models of Hercules, Phœbus, and Jove ; not like the forms abounding in the
streets of modern cities, wherein the face is a confused blur of features, but composed of incorrupt,
sharply defined and symmetrical features, whose eye-
sockets are so formed that it would be impossible for
such eyes to squint, and take furtive glances on this
side and on that, but they must turn the whole head.

The manners of that period are plain and fierce.
The reverence exhibited is for personal qualities,
courage, address, self-command, justice, strength,
swiftness, a loud voice, a broad chest. Luxury is not
known, nor elegance. A sparse population and want
make every man his own valet, cook, butcher, and
soldier, and the habit of supplying his own needs
educates the body to wonderful performances. Such
are the Agamemnon and Diomed of Homer, and not far
different is the picture Xenophon gives of himself and
his compatriots in the Retreat of the Ten Thousand.
" After the army had crossed the river Teleboas in
Armenia, there fell much snow, and the troops lay

miserably on the ground, covered with it. But Xenophon arose naked, and taking an axe, began to split
wood ; whereupon others rose and did the like."
Throughout his army seemed to be a boundless liberty of speech. They quarrel for plunder, they
wrangle with the generals on each new order, and
Xenophon is as sharp-tongued as any, and sharper-
tongued than most, and so gives as good as he gets.
Who does not see that this is a gang of great boys
with such a code of honor and such lax discipline as
great boys have ?

The costly charm of the ancient tragedy and indeed of all the old literature is, that the persons speak
simply, — speak as persons who have great good
sense without knowing it, before yet the reflective
habit has become the predominant habit of the mind.
Our admiration of the antique is not admiration of the
old, but of the natural. The Greeks are not reflective
but perfect in their senses, perfect in their health,
with the finest physical organization in the world.
Adults acted with the simplicity and grace of boys.
They made vases, tragedies, and statues such as
healthy senses should — that is, in good taste. Such
things have continued to be made in all ages, and are
now, wherever a healthy physique exists, but, as a class,
from their superior organization, they have surpassed
all. They combine the energy of manhood with the engaging unconsciousness of childhood. Our reverence
for them is our reverence for childhood. Nobody
can reflect upon an unconscious act with regret or
contempt. Bard or hero cannot look down on the

word or gesture of a child. It is as great as they. The attraction of these manners is, that they belong to man, and are known to every man in virtue of his being once a child ; beside that always there are individuals who retain these characteristics. A person of childlike genius and inborn energy is still a Greek, and revives our love of the muse of Hellas. A great boy, a great girl, with good sense, is a Greek. Beautiful is the love of nature in the Philoctetes. But in reading those fine apostrophes to sleep, to the stars, rocks, mountains, and waves, I feel time passing away as an ebbing sea. I feel the eternity of man, the identity of his thought. The Greek had, it seems, the same fellow beings as I. The sun and moon, water and fire, met his heart precisely as they meet mine. Then the vaunted distinction between Greek and English, between Classic and Romantic schools seems superficial and pedantic. When a thought of Plato becomes a thought to me, — when a truth that fired the soul of Pindar fires mine, time is no more. When I feel that we two meet in a perception, that our two souls are tinged with the same hue, and do, as it were, run into one, why should I measure degrees of latitude, why should I count Egyptian years ?

The student interprets the age of chivalry by his own age of chivalry, and the days of maritime adventure and circumnavigation by quite parallel miniature experiences of his own. To the sacred history of the world, he has the same key. When the voice of a prophet out of the deeps of antiquity merely echoes to him a sentiment of his infancy, a prayer of his youth, he then pierces to the truth through all the confusion of tradition and the caricature of institutions.

Rare, extravagant spirits come by us at intervals, who disclose to us new facts in nature. I see that men of God have always, from time to time, walked among men and made their commission felt in the heart and soul of the commonest hearer. Hence, evidently, the tripod, the priest, the priestess inspired by the divine afflatus.

Jesus astonishes and overpowers sensual people. They cannot unite him to history or reconcile him with themselves. As they come to revere their intuitions and aspire to live holily, their own piety explains every fact, every word.

How easily these old worships of Moses, of Zoroaster, of Menu, of Socrates, domesticate themselves in the mind. I cannot find any antiquity in them. They are mine as much as theirs.

Then I have seen the first monks and anchorets without crossing seas or centuries. More than once some individual has appeared to me with such negligence of labor and such commanding contemplation, a haughty beneficiary, begging in the name of God, as made good to the nineteenth century Simeon the Stylite, the Thebais, and the first Capuchins.

The priestcraft of the East and West, of the Magian, Brahmin, Druid and Inca, is expounded in the individual's private life. The cramping influence of a hard formalist on a young child in repressing his

spirits and courage, paralyzing the understanding, and
that without producing indignation, but only fear and
obedience, and even much sympathy with the tyranny, — is a familiar fact explained to the child when he
becomes a man, only by seeing that the oppressor of
his youth is himself a child tyrannized over by those
names and words and forms, of whose influence he
was merely the organ to the youth.　The fact teaches
him how Belus was worshipped, and how the pyramids were built, better than the discovery by Cham-
pollion of the names of all the workmen and the cost of
every tile.　He finds Assyria and the Mounds of
Cholula at his door, and himself has laid the courses.

Again, in that protest which each considerate person makes against the superstition of his times, he
reacts step for step the part of old reformers, and in
the search after truth finds like them new perils to
virtue.　He learns again what moral vigor is needed to
supply the girdle of a superstition.　A great licen-
tiousness treads on the heels of a reformation.　How
many times in the history of the world has the Luther of the day had to lament the decay of piety in
his own household.　"Doctor," said his wife to Mar-
tin Luther one day, "how is it that whilst subject to
papacy, we prayed so often and with such fervor,
whilst now we pray with the utmost coldness and very
seldom ? "

The advancing man discovers how deep a property
he hath in all literature, — in all fable as well as in
all history.　He finds that the poet was no odd fellow
who described strange and impossible situations, but

that universal man wrote by his pen a confession true for one and true for all. His own secret biography he finds in lines wonderfully intelligible to him, yet dotted down before he was born. One after another he comes up in his private adventures with every fable of Æsop, of Homer, of Hafiz, of Ariosto, of Chaucer, of Scott, and verifies them with his own head and hands.

The beautiful fables of the Greeks, being proper creations of the Imagination and not of the Fancy, are universal verities. What a range of meanings and what perpetual pertinence has the story of Prometheus! Beside its primary value as the first chapter of the history of Europe, (the mythology thinly veiling authentic facts, the invention of the mechanic arts, and the migration of colonies,) it gives the history of religion with some closeness to the faith of later ages. Prometheus is the Jesus of the old mythology. He is the friend of man; stands between the unjust 'justice' of the Eternal Father, and the race of mortals; and readily suffers all things on their account. But where it departs from the Calvinistic Christianity, and exhibits him as the defier of Jove, it represents a state of mind which readily appears wherever the doctrine of Theism is taught in a crude, objective form, and which seems the self-defence of man against this untruth, namely, a discontent with the believed fact that a God exists, and a feeling that the obligation of reverence is onerous. It would steal, if it could, the fire of the Creator, and live apart from him, and independent of him. The Prome-

2

theus Vinctus is the romance of skepticism. Not less
true to all time are all the details of that stately apologue. Apollo kept the flocks of Admetus, said the
poets. Every man is a divinity in disguise, a god
playing the fool. It seems as if heaven had sent its insane angels into our world as to an asylum, and
here they will break out into their native music and
utter at intervals the words they have heard in heaven ;
then the mad fit returns, and they mope and wallow
like dogs. When the gods come among men, they
are not known. Jesus was not ; Socrates and Shakspeare were not. Antæus was suffocated by the
gripe of Hercules, but every time he touched his
mother earth, his strength was renewed. Man is the
broken giant, and in all his weakness, both his body
and his mind are invigorated by habits of conversation with nature. The power of music, the power
of poetry to unfix, and as it were, clap wings to all
solid nature, interprets the riddle of Orpheus, which
was to his childhood an idle tale. The philosophical
perception of identity through endless mutations of
form, makes him know the Proteus. What else am
I who laughed or wept yesterday, who slept last
night like a corpse, and this morning stood and ran ?
And what see I on any side but the transmigrations
of Proteus ? I can symbolize my thought by using
the name of any creature, of any fact, because every
creature is man agent, or patient. Tantalus is but
a name for you and me. Tantalus means the impossibility of drinking the waters of thought which are
always gleaming and waving within sight of the soul.

The transmigration of souls: that too is no fable.
I would it were; but men and women are only half
human. Every animal of the barn-yard, the field and
the forest, of the earth and of the waters that are under the earth, has contrived to get a footing and to
leave the print of its features and form in some one
or other of these upright, heaven-facing speakers.
Ah, brother, hold fast to the man and awe the beast;
stop the ebb of thy soul — ebbing downward into
the forms into whose habits thou hast now for many
years slid. As near and proper to us is also that old
fable of the Sphinx, who was said to sit in the roadside and put riddles to every passenger. If the man
could not answer she swallowed him alive. If he
could solve the riddle, the Sphinx was slain. What
is our life but an endless flight of winged facts or
events! In splendid variety these changes come, all
putting questions to the human spirit. Those men
who cannot answer by a superior wisdom these facts
or questions of time, serve them. Facts encumber
them, tyrannize over them, and make the men of routine, the men of *sense*, in whom a literal obedience to
facts has extinguished every spark of that light by
which man is truly man. But if the man is true to
his better instincts or sentiments, and refuses the dominion of facts, as one that comes of a higher race,
remains fast by the soul and sees the principle, then
the facts fall aptly and supple into their places; they
know their master, and the meanest of them glo-
rifies him.

See in Goethe's Helena the same desire that every

word should be a thing. These figures, he would say, these Chirons, Griffins, Phorkyas, Helen, and Leda, are somewhat, and do exert a specific influence on the mind. So far then are they eternal entities, as real to-day as in the first Olympiad. Much revolving them, he writes out freely his humor, and gives them body to his own imagination. And although that poem be as vague and fantastic as a dream, yet is it much more attractive than the more regular dramatic pieces of the same author, for the reason that it operates a wonderful relief to the mind from the routine of customary images, — awakens the reader's invention and fancy by the wild freedom of the design, and by the unceasing succession of brisk shocks of surprise.

The universal nature, too strong for the petty nature of the bard, sits on his neck and writes through his hand ; so that when he seems to vent a mere caprice and wild romance, the issue is an exact allegory. Hence Plato said that " poets utter great and wise things which they do not themselves understand." All the fictions of the Middle Age explain themselves as a masked or frolic expression of that which in grave earnest the mind of that period toiled to achieve. Magic, and all that is ascribed to it, is manifestly a deep presentiment of the powers of science. The shoes of swiftness, the sword of sharpness, the power of subduing the elements, of using the secret virtues of minerals, of understanding the voices of birds, are the obscure efforts of the mind in a right direction. The preternatural prowess of the hero, the gift of perpetual youth, and the like, are alike the endeavor of the human spirit " to bend the shows of things to the desires of the mind."

In Perceforest and Amadis de Gaul, a garland and a rose bloom on the head of her who is faithful, and fade on the brow of the inconstant. In the story of the Boy and the Mantle, even a mature reader may be surprised with a glow of virtuous pleasure at the triumph of the gentle Genelas; and indeed, all the postulates of elfin annals, that the Fairies do not like to be named; that their gifts are capricious and not to be trusted; that who seeks a treasure must not speak; and the like, I find true in Concord, however they might be in Cornwall or Bretagne.

Is it otherwise in the newest romance? I read the Bride of Lammermoor. Sir William Ashton is a mask for a vulgar temptation, Ravenswood Castle, a fine name for proud poverty, and the foreign mission of state only a Bunyan disguise for honest industry. We may all shoot a wild bull that would toss the good and beautiful, by fighting down the unjust and sensual. Lucy Ashton is another name for fidelity, which is always beautiful and always liable to calamity in this world.

But along with the civil and metaphysical history of man, another history goes daily forward — that of the external world, — in which he is not less strictly implicated. He is the compend of time : he is also the correlative of nature. The power of man consists in the multitude of his affinities, in the fact that his life is intertwined with the whole chain of organic

and inorganic being.   In the age of the Cæsars, out
from the Forum at Rome proceeded the great highways north, south, east, west, to the centre of every province of the empire, making each market-
town of Persia, Spain and Britain, pervious to the sol-
diers of the capital : so out of the human heart go, as
it were, highways to the heart of every object in nature, to reduce it under the dominion of man.   A
man is a bundle of relations, a knot of roots, whose
flower and fruitage is the world.   All his faculties refer to natures out of him.   All his faculties predict
the world he is to inhabit, as the fins of the fish foreshow that water exists, or the wings of an eagle in
the egg presuppose a medium like air.   Insulate and
you destroy him.   He cannot live without a world.
Put Napoleon in an island prison, let his faculties
find no men to act on, no Alps to climb, no stake
to play for, and he would beat the air and appear
stupid.   Transport him to large countries, dense population, complex interests, and antagonist power,
and you shall see that the man Napoleon, bounded,
that is, by such a profile and outline, is not the virtual Napoleon.   This is but Talbot's shadow ;

> His substance is not here :
> For what you see is but the smallest part,
> And least proportion of humanity ;
> But were the whole frame here,
> It is of such a spacious, lofty pitch,
> Your roof were not sufficient to contain it.
>
> *Henry VI.*

Columbus needs a planet to shape his course upon.
Newton and Laplace need myriads of ages and thick-

strown celestial areas.   One may say a gravitating solar system is already prophesied in the nature of Newton's mind.   Not less does the brain of Davy and Gay Lussac from childhood exploring always the affinities and repulsions of particles, anticipate the laws of organization.   Does not the eye of the human embryo predict the light ? the ear of Handel predict the witchcraft of harmonic sound ?   Do not the constructive fingers of Watt, Fulton, Whittemore, Arkwright predict the fusible, hard, and temperable texture of metals, the properties of stone, water and wood ? the lovely attributes of the maiden child predict the refinements and decorations of civil society ? Here also we are reminded of the action of man on man.   A mind might ponder its thought for ages, and not gain so much self-knowledge as the passion of love shall teach it in a day.   Who knows himself before he has been thrilled with indignation at an outrage, or has heard an eloquent tongue, or has shared the throb of thousands in a national exultation or alarm ?   No man can antedate his experience, or guess what faculty or feeling a new object shall unlock, any more than he can draw to-day the face of a person whom he shall see to-morrow for the first time.

I will not now go behind the general statement to explore the reason of this correspondency.   Let it suffice that in the light of these two facts, namely, that the mind is One ; and that nature is its correlative, history is to be read and written.

Thus in all ways does the soul concentrate and

reproduce its treasures for each pupil, for each
new-born man. He, too, shall pass through the whole
cycle of experience. He shall collect into a focus
the rays of nature. History no longer shall be a dull
book. It shall walk incarnate in every just and wise
man. You shall not tell me by languages and titles a
catalogue of the volumes you have read. You shall
make me feel what periods you have lived. A man
shall be the Temple of Fame. He shall walk, as the
poets have described that goddess, in a robe painted
all over with wonderful events and experiences ;—
his own form and features by their exalted intelligence
shall be that variegated vest. I shall find in him the
Foreworld ; in his childhood the Age of Gold ; the
Apples of Knowledge ; the Argonautic Expedition ;
the calling of Abraham ; the building of the Temple ;
the Advent of Christ ; Dark Ages ; the Revival of
Letters ; the Reformation ; the discovery of new
lands, the opening of new sciences , and new regions
in man. He shall be the priest of Pan, and bring
with him into humble cottages the blessing of the
morning stars and all the recorded benefits of heaven
and earth.

Is there somewhat overweening in this claim ?
Then I reject all I have written, for what is the use of
pretending to know what we know not ? But it is the
fault of our rhetoric that we cannot strongly state one
fact without seeming to belie some other. I hold our
actual knowledge very cheap. Hear the rats in the
wall, see the lizard on the fence, the fungus under
foot, the lichen on the log. What do I know sym-

pathetically, morally, of either of these worlds of life ? As long as the Caucasian man — perhaps longer — these creatures have kept their counsel beside him, and there is no record of any word or sign that has passed from one to the other. Nay, what does history yet record of the metaphysical annals of man ? What light does it shed on those mysteries which we hide under the names Death and Immortality ? Yet every history should be written in a wisdom which divined the range of our affinities and looked at facts as symbols. I am ashamed to see what a shallow village tale our so-called History is. How many times we must say Rome, and Paris, and Constantinople. What does Rome know of rat and lizard ? What are Olympiads and Consulates to these neighboring systems of being ? Nay, what food or experience or succor have they for the Esquimaux seal-hunter, for the Kanàka in his canoe, for the fisherman, the stevedore, the porter ?

Broader and deeper we must write our annals — from an ethical reformation, from an influx of the ever new, ever sanative conscience, — if we would truelier express our central and wide-related nature, instead of this old chronology of selfishness and pride to which we have too long lent our eyes. Already that day exists for us, shines in on us at unawares, but the path of science and of letters is not the way into nature, but from it, rather. The idiot, the Indian, the child, and unschooled farmer's boy, come much nearer to these, — understand them better than the dissector or the antiquary.

2*

SELF-RELIANCE.

Ne te quæsiveris extra.

" Man is his own star, and the soul that can
Render an honest and a perfect man,
Command all light, all influence, all fate,
Nothing to him falls early or too late.
Our acts our angels are, or good or ill,
Our fatal shadows that walk by us still."

Epilogue to Beaumont and Fletcher's Honest Man's Fortune.

Cast the bantling on the rocks,
Suckle him with the she-wolf's teat:
Wintered with the hawk and fox,
Power and speed be hands and feet.

ESSAY II.

SELF-RELIANCE.

I READ the other day some verses written by an eminent painter which were original and not conventional. Always the soul hears an admonition in such lines, let the subject be what it may. The sentiment they instil is of more value than any thought they may contain. To believe your own thought, to believe that what is true for you in your private heart, is true for all men, — that is genius. Speak your latent conviction and it shall be the universal sense ; for always the inmost becomes the outmost, — and our first thought is rendered back to us by the trumpets of the Last Judgment. Familiar as the voice of the mind is to each, the highest merit we ascribe to Moses, Plato, and Milton, is that they set at naught books and traditions, and spoke not what men but what they thought. A man should learn to detect and watch that gleam of light which flashes across his mind from within, more than the lustre of the firmament of bards and sages. Yet he dismisses without notice his thought, because it is his. In every work of genius we recognise our own rejected thoughts : they come back to us with a certain alienated majesty. Great works of art have no more affecting lesson for us than this. They teach us to abide by our spontaneous impression with good humored inflexibility then most when the whole cry of voices is on the other side. Else, to-morrow a stranger will say with masterly good sense precisely what we have thought and felt all the time, and we shall be forced to take with shame our own opinion from another.

There is a time in every man's education when he arrives at the conviction that envy is ignorance ; that imitation is suicide ; that he must take himself for better, for worse, as his portion ; that though the wide universe is full of good, no kernel of nourishing corn can come to him but through his toil bestowed on that plot of ground which is given to him to till. The power which resides in him is new in nature, and none but he knows what that is which he can do, nor does he know until he has tried. Not for nothing one face, one character, one fact makes much impression on him, and another none. It is not without preëstab-lished harmony, this sculpture in the memory. The eye was placed where one ray should fall, that it might testify of that particular ray. Bravely let him speak the utmost syllable of his confession. We but half express ourselves, and are ashamed of that di-vine idea which each of us represents. It may be safely trusted as proportionate and of good issues, so it be faithfully imparted, but God will not have his work made manifest by cowards. It needs a divine man to exhibit any thing divine. A man is relieved and gay when he has put his heart into his work and done his best ; but what he has said or done otherwise, shall give him no peace. It is a deliverance which does not deliver. In the attempt his genius deserts him ; no muse befriends ; no invention, no hope.

Trust thyself: every heart vibrates to that iron string. Accept the place the divine Providence has found for you ; the society of your contemporaries, the connexion of events. Great men have always done so and confided themselves childlike to the genius of their age, betraying their perception that the Eternal was stirring at their heart, working through their hands, predominating in all their being. And we are now men, and must accept in the highest mind the same transcendent destiny ; and not pinched in a corner, not cowards fleeing before a revolution, but redeemers and benefactors, pious aspirants to be noble clay plastic under the Almighty effort, let us advance and advance on Chaos and the Dark.

What pretty oracles nature yields us on this text in the face and behavior of children, babes and even brutes. That divided and rebel mind, that distrust of a sentiment because our arithmetic has computed the strength and means opposed to our purpose, these have not. Their mind being whole, their eye is as yet unconquered, and when we look in their faces, we are disconcerted. Infancy conforms to nobody : all conform to it, so that one babe commonly makes four

or five out of the adults who prattle and play to it.
So God has armed youth and puberty and manhood
no less with its own piquancy and charm, and made it
enviable and gracious and its claims not to be put by,
if it will stand by itself.   Do not think the youth has
no force because he cannot speak to you and me.
Hark ! in the next room, who spoke so clear and emphatic ? Good Heaven ! it is he ! it is that very lump of
bashfulness and phlegm which for weeks has done
nothing but eat when you were by, that now rolls out
these words like bell-strokes. It seems he knows how
to speak to his contemporaries.   Bashful or bold, then,
he will know how to make us seniors very unnecessary.

The nonchalance of boys who are sure of a dinner, and would disdain as much as a lord to do or say
aught to conciliate one, is the healthy attitude of human nature.   How is a boy the master of society ; independent, irresponsible, looking out from his corner
on such people and facts as pass by, he tries and sentences them on their merits, in the swift summary
way of boys, as good, bad, interesting, silly, eloquent,
troublesome.   He cumbers himself never about consequences, about interests : he gives an independent,
genuine verdict.   You must court him : he does not
court you.   But the man is, as it were, clapped into
jail by his consciousness.   As soon as he has once
acted or spoken with eclat, he is a committed person,
watched by the sympathy or the hatred of hundreds
whose affections must now enter into his account.
There is no Lethe for this.   Ah, that he could pass

again into his neutral, godlike independence ! Who can thus lose all pledge, and having observed, observe again from the same unaffected, unbiased, unbribable, unaffrighted innocence, must always be formidable, must always engage the poet's and the man's regards. Of such an immortal youth the force would be felt. He would utter opinions on all passing affairs, which being seen to be not private but necessary, would sink like darts into the ear of men, and put them in fear.

These are the voices which we hear in solitude, but they grow faint and inaudible as we enter into the world. Society everywhere is in conspiracy against the manhood of every one of its members. Society is a joint-stock company in which the members agree for the better securing of his bread to each shareholder, to surrender the liberty and culture of the eater. The virtue in most request is conformity. Self-reliance is its aversion. It loves not realities and creators, but names and customs.

Whoso would be a man must be a nonconformist. He who would gather immortal palms must not be hindered by the name of goodness, but must explore if it be goodness. Nothing is at last sacred but the integrity of our own mind. Absolve you to yourself, and you shall have the suffrage of the world. I remember an answer which when quite young I was prompted to make to a valued adviser who was wont to importune me with the dear old doctrines of the church. On my saying, What have I to do with the sacredness of traditions, if I live wholly from within ? my friend suggested — "But these impulses may be from below, not from above." I replied, 'They do not seem to me to be such; but if I am the devil's child, I will live then from the devil.' No law can be sacred to me but that of my nature. Good and bad are but names very readily transferable to that or this; the only right is what is after my constitution, the only wrong what is against it. A man is to carry himself in the presence of all opposition as if every thing were titular and ephemeral but he. I am ashamed to think how easily we capitulate to badges and names, to large societies and dead institutions. Every decent and well-spoken individual affects and sways me more than is right. I ought to go upright and vital, and speak the rude truth in all ways. If malice and vanity wear the coat of philanthropy, shall that pass? If an angry bigot assumes this bountiful cause of Abolition, and comes to me with his last news from Barbadoes, why should I not say to him, ' Go love thy infant; love thy wood-chopper: be good-natured and modest: have that grace; and never varnish your hard, uncharitable ambition with this incredible tenderness for black folk a thousand miles off. Thy love afar is spite at home.' Rough and graceless would be such greeting, but truth is handsomer than the affectation of love. Your goodness must have some edge to it — else it is none. The doctrine of hatred must be preached as the coun-teraction of the doctrine of love when that pules and whines. I shun father and mother and wife and bro-ther, when my genius calls me. I would write on the lintels of the door-post, *Whim.* I hope it is somewhat better than whim at last, but we cannot spend the day in explanation. Expect me not to show cause why I seek or why I exclude company. Then, again, do not tell me, as a good man did to-day, of my obligation to put all poor men in good situations. Are they *my* poor ? I tell thee, thou foolish philanthropist, that I grudge the dollar, the dime, the cent I give to such men as do not belong to me and to whom I do not belong. There is a class of persons to whom by all spiritual affinity I am bought and sold ; for them I will go to prison, if need be ; but your miscellaneous popular charities ; the education at college of fools ; the building of meeting-houses to the vain end to which many now stand ; alms to sots ; and the thousandfold Relief Societies ; — though I confess with shame I sometimes succumb and give the dollar, it is a wicked dollar which by-and-by I shall have the manhood to withhold.

Virtues are in the popular estimate rather the exception than the rule. There is the man *and* his virtues. Men do what is called a good action, as some piece of courage or charity, much as they would pay a fine in expiation of daily non-appearance on parade. Their works are done as an apology or extenuation of their living in the world, — as invalids and the insane pay a high board. Their virtues are penances. I do not wish to expiate, but to live. My life is not an apology, but a life. It is for itself and not for a spectacle. I much prefer that it should be of a lower strain, so it be genuine and equal, than that it should be glittering and unsteady. I wish it to be sound and sweet, and not to need diet and bleeding.

My life should be unique ; it should be an alms, a battle, a conquest, a medicine. I ask primary evidence that you are a man, and refuse this appeal from the man to his actions. I know that for myself it makes no difference whether I do or forbear those actions which are reckoned excellent. I cannot consent to pay for a privilege where I have intrinsic right. Few and mean as my gifts may be, I actually am, and do not need for my own assurance or the assurance of my fellows any secondary testimony.

What I must do, is all that concerns me, not what the people think. This rule, equally arduous in actual and in intellectual life, may serve for the whole distinction between greatness and meanness. It is the harder, because you will always find those who think they know what is your duty better than you know it. It is easy in the world to live after the world's opinion ; it is easy in solitude to live after our own ; but the great man is he who in the midst of the crowd keeps with perfect sweetness the independence of solitude.

The objection to conforming to usages that have become dead to you, is, that it scatters your force. It loses your time and blurs the impression of your character. If you maintain a dead church, contribute to a dead Bible-Society, vote with a great party either for the Government or against it, spread your table like base housekeepers, — under all these screens, I have difficulty to detect the precise man you are. And, of course, so much force is withdrawn from your proper life. But do your thing, and I shall know you. Do your work, and you shall re-inforce yourself. A man must consider what a blind-man's-buff is this game of conformity. If I know your sect, I anticipate your argument. I hear a preacher announce for his text and topic the expedi-ency of one of the institutions of his church. Do I not know beforehand that not possibly can he say a new and spontaneous word ? Do I not know that with all this ostentation of examining the grounds of the institution, he will do no such thing ? Do I not know that he is pledged to himself not to look but at one side ; the permitted side, not as a man, but as a parish minister ? He is a retained attorney, and these airs of the bench are the emptiest affectation. Well, most men have bound their eyes with one or another handkerchief, and attached themselves to some one of these communities of opinion. This conformity makes them not false in a few particulars, authors of a few lies, but false in all particulars. Their every truth is not quite true. Their two is not the real two, their four not the real four : so that every word they say chagrins us, and we know not where to begin to set them right. Meantime nature is not slow to equip us in the prison-uniform of the party to which we adhere. We come to wear one cut of face and fig-ure, and acquire by degrees the gentlest asinine ex-pression. There is a mortifying experience in par-ticular which does not fail to wreak itself also in the general history ; I mean, " the foolish face of praise," the forced smile which we put on in company where we do not feel at ease in answer to conversation which does not interest us. The muscles, not spontaneously moved, but moved by a low usurping wilfulness, grow tight about the outline of the face and make the most disagreeable sensation, a sensation of rebuke and warning which no brave young man will suffer twice.

For non-conformity the world whips you with its displeasure. And therefore a man must know how to estimate a sour face. The bystanders look askance on him in the public street or in the friend's parlor. If this aversation had its origin in contempt and resistance like his own, he might well go home with a sad countenance; but the sour faces of the multitude, like their sweet faces, have no deep cause, — disguise no god, but are put on and off as the wind blows, and a newspaper directs. Yet is the discontent of the multitude more formidable than that of the senate and the college. It is easy enough for a firm man who knows the world to brook the rage of the cultivated classes. Their rage is decorous and prudent, for they are timid as being very vulnerable themselves. But when to their feminine rage the indignation of the people is added, when the ignorant and the poor are aroused, when the unintelligent brute force that lies at the bottom of society is made to growl and mow, it needs the habit of magnanimity and religion to treat it godlike as a trifle of no concernment.

The other terror that scares us from self-trust is our consistency; a reverence for our past act or word, because the eyes of others have no other data for computing our orbit than our past acts, and we are loath to disappoint them.

But why should you keep your head over your shoulder? Why drag about this monstrous corpse of your memory, lest you contradict somewhat you have stated in this or that public place? Suppose you should contradict yourself; what then? It seems to be a rule of wisdom never to rely on your memory alone, scarcely even in acts of pure memory, but bring the past for judgment into the thousand-eyed present, and live ever in a new day. Trust your emotion. In your metaphysics you have denied personality to the Deity : yet when the devout motions of the soul come, yield to them heart and life, though they should clothe God with shape and color. Leave your theory as Joseph his coat in the hand of the harlot, and flee.

A foolish consistency is the hobgoblin of little minds, adored by little statesmen and philosophers and divines. With consistency a great soul has simply nothing to do. He may as well concern himself with his shadow on the wall. Out upon your guarded lips! Sew them up with packthread, do. Else, if you would be a man, speak what you think to-day in words as hard as cannon balls, and to-morrow speak what to-morrow thinks in hard words again, though it contradict every thing you said to-day. Ah, then, exclaim the aged ladies, you shall be sure to be misunderstood. Misunderstood! It is a right fool's word. Is it so bad then to be misunderstood? Pythagoras was misunderstood, and Socrates, and Jesus, and Luther, and Copernicus, and Galileo, and Newton, and every pure and wise spirit that ever took flesh. To be great is to be misunderstood.

I suppose no man can violate his nature. All the sallies of his will are rounded in by the law of his being as the inequalities of Andes and Himmaleh are insignificant in the curve of the sphere. Nor does it matter how you guage and try him. A character is like an acrostic or Alexandrian stanza ; — read it forward, backward, or across, it still spells the same thing. In this pleasing contrite wood-life which God allows me, let me record day by day my honest thought without prospect or retrospect, and, I cannot doubt, it will be found symmetrical, though I mean it not, and see it not. My book should smell of pines and resound with the hum of insects. The swallow over my window should interweave that thread or straw he carries in his bill into my web also. We pass for what we are. Character teaches above our wills. Men imagine that they communicate their virtue or vice only by overt actions and do not see that virtue or vice emit a breath every moment.

Fear never but you shall be consistent in whatever variety of actions, so they be each honest and natural in their hour. For of one will, the actions will be harmonious, however unlike they seem. These varieties are lost sight of when seen at a little distance, at a little height of thought. One tendency unites them all. The voyage of the best ship is a zigzag line of a hundred tacks. This is only microscopic criticism. See the line from a sufficient distance, and it straightens itself to the average tendency. Your genuine action will explain itself and will explain your other genuine actions. Your conformity explains nothing. Act sin-

gly, and what you have already done singly, will justify
you now. Greatness always appeals to the future.
If I can be great enough now to do right and scorn
eyes, I must have done so much right before, as to defend me now. Be it how it will, do right now. Always scorn appearances, and you always may. The
force of character is cumulative. All the foregone
days of virtue work their health into this. What
makes the majesty of the heroes of the senate and the
field, which so fills the imagination? The consciousness of a train of great days and victories behind.
There they all stand and shed an united light on the
advancing actor. He is attended as by a visible es-
cort of angels to every man's eye. That is it which
throws thunder into Chatham's voice, and dignity into
Washington's port, and America into Adams's eye.
Honor is venerable to us because it is no ephemeris.
It is always ancient virtue. We worship it to-day, because it is not of to-day. We love it and pay it homage, because it is not a trap for our love and homage,
but is self-dependent, self-derived, and therefore of an
old immaculate pedigree, even if shown in a young
person.

I hope in these days we have heard the last of conformity and consistency. Let the words be gazetted
and ridiculous henceforward. Instead of the gong for
dinner, let us hear a whistle from the Spartan fife.
Let us bow and apologize never more. A great man
is coming to eat at my house. I do not wish to please
him : I wish that he should wish to please me. I will
stand here for humanity, and though I would make it

kind, I would made it true. Let us affront and repri-
mand the smooth mediocrity and squalid contentment
of the times, and hurl in the face of custom, and trade,
and office, the fact which is the upshot of all history,
that there is a great responsible Thinker and Actor
moving wherever moves a man ; that a true man belongs to no other time or place, but is the centre of
things. Where he is, there is nature. He measures
you, and all men, and all events. You are constrained
to accept his standard. Ordinarily every body in society reminds us of somewhat else or of some other
person. Character, reality, reminds you of nothing
else. It takes place of the whole creation. The man
must be so much that he must make all circumstances
indifferent, — put all means into the shade. This all
great men are and do. Every true man is a cause, a
country, and an age ; requires infinite spaces and numbers and time fully to accomplish his thought ; — and
posterity seem to follow his steps as a procession. A
man Cæsar is born, and for ages after, we have a Roman Empire. Christ is born, and millions of minds
so grow and cleave to his genius, that he is confound-
ed with virtue and the possible of man. An institution
is the lengthened shadow of one man ; as, the Reformation, of Luther ; Quakerism, of Fox ; Methodism,
of Wesley ; Abolition, of Clarkson. Scipio, Milton
called " the height of Rome ;" and all history resolves
itself very easily into the biography of a few stout and
earnest persons.

Let a man then know his worth, and keep things under his feet. Let him not peep or steal, or skulk up

and down with the air of a charity-boy, a bastard, or an interloper, in the world which exists for him. But the man in the street finding no worth in himself which corresponds to the force which built a tower or sculptured a marble god, feels poor when he looks on these. To him a palace, a statue, or a costly book have an alien and forbidding air, much like a gay equipage, and seem to say like that, ' Who are you, sir ?' Yet they all are his, suitors for his notice, petitioners to his faculties that they will come out and take possession. The picture waits for my verdict : it is not to command me, but I am to settle its claims to praise. That popular fable of the sot who was picked up dead drunk in the street, carried to the duke's house, washed and dressed and laid in the duke's bed, and, on his waking, treated with all obsequious ceremony like the duke, and assured that he had been insane, — owes its popularity to the fact, that it symbolizes so well the state of man, who is in the world a sort of sot, but now and then wakes up, exercises his reason, and finds himself a true prince.

Our reading is mendicant and sycophantic. In history, our imagination makes fools of us, plays us false. Kingdom and lordship, power and estate are a gaudier vocabulary than private John and Edward in a small house and common day's work : but the things of life are the same to both : the sum total of both is the same. Why all this deference to Alfred, and Scanderbeg, and Gustavus ? Suppose they were virtuous : did they wear out virtue ? As great a stake depends on your private act to-day, as followed their public and

renowned steps.   When private men shall act with
vast views, the lustre will be transferred from the actions of kings to those of gentlemen.

The world has indeed been instructed by its kings,
who have so magnetized the eyes of nations.   It has
been taught by this colossal symbol the mutual reverence that is due from man to man.   The joyful loyalty with which men have every where suffered the
king, the noble, or the great proprietor to walk among
them by a law of his own, make his own scale of men
and things, and reverse theirs, pay for benefits not with
money but with honor, and represent the Law in his
person, was the hieroglyphic by which they obscurely
signified their consciousness of their own right and
comeliness, the right of every man.

The magnetism which all original action exerts is
explained when we inquire the reason of self-trust.
Who is the Trustee ?   What is the aboriginal Self on
which a universal reliance may be grounded ?   What
is the nature and power of that science-baffling star,
without parallax, without calculable elements, which
shoots a ray of beauty even into trivial and impure
actions, if the least mark of independence appear ?
The inquiry leads us to that source, at once the essence
of genius, the essence of virtue, and the essence of life,
which we call Spontaneity or Instinct.   We denote
this primary wisdom as Intuition, whilst all later teach-
ings are tuitions.   In that deep force, the last fact behind which analysis cannot go, all things find their
common origin.   For the sense of being which in
calm hours rises, we know not how, in the soul, is not

diverse from things, from space, from light, from time, from man, but one with them, and proceedeth obviously from the same source whence their life and being also proceedeth. We first share the life by which things exist, and afterwards see them as appearances in nature, and forget that we have shared their cause. Here is the fountain of action and the fountain of thought. Here are the lungs of that inspiration which giveth man wisdom, of that inspiration of man which cannot be denied without impiety and atheism. We lie in the lap of immense intelligence, which makes us organs of its activity and receivers of its truth. When we discern justice, when we discern truth, we do nothing of ourselves, but allow a passage to its beams. If we ask whence this comes, if we seek to pry into the soul that causes, — all metaphysics, all philosophy is at fault. Its presence or its absence is all we can affirm. Every man discerns between the voluntary acts of his mind, and his involuntary perceptions. And to his involuntary perceptions, he knows a perfect respect is due. He may err in the expression of them, but he knows that these things are so, like day and night, not to be disputed. All my wilful actions and acquisitions are but roving; — the most trivial reverie, the faintest native emotion are domestic and divine. Thoughtless people contradict as readily the statement of perceptions as of opinions, or rather much more readily ; for, they do not distinguish between perception and notion. They fancy that I choose to see this or that thing. But perception is not whimsical, but fatal. If I see a trait, my children will see it after me, and in course of time, all mankind, — although it may chance that no one has seen it before me. For my perception of it is as much a fact as the sun.

The relations of the soul to the divine spirit are so pure that it is profane to seek to interpose helps. It must be that when God speaketh, he should communicate not one thing, but all things; should fill the world with his voice; should scatter forth light, nature, time, souls, from the centre of the present thought; and new date and new create the whole. Whenever a mind is simple, and receives a divine wisdom, then old things pass away, — means, teachers, texts, temples fall; it lives now and absorbs past and future into the present hour. All things are made sacred by relation to it, — one thing as much as another. All things are dissolved to their centre by their cause, and in the universal miracle petty and particular miracles disappear. This is and must be. If, therefore, a man claims to know and speak of God, and carries you backward to the phraseology of some old mouldered nation in another country, in another world, believe him not. Is the acorn better than the oak which is its fulness and completion? Is the parent better than the child into whom he has cast his ripened being? Whence then this worship of the past? The centuries are conspirators against the sanity and majesty of the soul. Time and space are but physiological colors which the eye maketh, but the soul is light; where it is, is day; where it was, is night; and history is an impertinence and an injury, if it be anything more than a cheerful apologue or parable of my being and becoming.

Man is timid and apologetic. He is no longer upright. He dares not say ' I think,' ' I am,' but quotes
some saint or sage. He is ashamed before the blade
of grass or the blowing rose. These roses under my
window make no reference to former roses or to better ones ; they are for what they are ; they exist with
God to-day. There is no time to them. There is
simply the rose ; it is perfect in every moment of its
existence. Before a leaf-bud has burst, its whole life
acts ; in the full-blown flower, there is no more ; in
the leafless root, there is no less. Its nature is satisfied, and it satisfies nature, in all moments alike. There
is no time to it. But man postpones or remembers ;
he does not live in the present, but with reverted eye
laments the past, or, heedless of the riches that sur-
round him, stands on tiptoe to foresee the future. He
cannot be happy and strong until he too lives with
nature in the present, above time.

This should be plain enough. Yet see what strong
intellects dare not yet hear God himself, unless he speak
the phraseology of I know not what David, or Jeremi-
ah, or Paul. We shall not always set so great a price
on a few texts, on a few lives. We are like children
who repeat by rote the sentences of grandames and
tutors, and, as they grow older, of the men of talents
and character they chance to see, — painfully recol-
lecting the exact words they spoke ; afterwards, when
they come into the point of view which those had who
uttered these sayings, they understand them, and are
willing to let the words go ; for, at any time, they can
use words as good, when occasion comes. So was it

with us, so will it be, if we proceed. If we live truly, we shall see truly. It is as easy for the strong man to be strong, as it is for the weak to be weak. When we have new perception, we shall gladly disburthen the memory of its hoarded treasures as old rubbish. When a man lives with God, his voice shall be as sweet as the murmur of the brook and the rustle of the corn.

And now at last the highest truth on this subject remains unsaid; probably, cannot be said; for all that we say is the far off remembering of the intuition. That thought, by what I can now nearest approach to say it, is this. When good is near you, when you have life in yourself, — it is not by any known or appointed way; you shall not discern the foot-prints of any other; you shall not see the face of man; you shall not hear any name; — the way, the thought, the good shall be wholly strange and new. It shall exclude all other being. You take the way from man not to man. All persons that ever existed are its fugitive ministers. There shall be no fear in it. Fear and hope are alike beneath it. It asks nothing. There is somewhat low even in hope. We are then in vision. There is nothing that can be called gratitude nor properly joy. The soul is raised over passion. It seeth identity and eternal causation. It is a perceiving that Truth and Right are. Hence it becomes a Tranquillity out of the knowing that all things go well. Vast spaces of nature; the Atlantic Ocean, the South Sea; vast intervals of time, years, centuries, are of no account. This which I think and feel, underlay that former state of life and circumstances, as it does underlie my present, and will always all circumstance, and what is called life, and what is called death.

Life only avails, not the having lived. Power ceases in the instant of repose ; it resides in the moment of transition from a past to a new state ; in the shooting of the gulf ; in the darting to an aim. This one fact the world hates, that the soul *becomes ;* for, that forever degrades the past ; turns all riches to poverty ; all reputation to a shame ; confounds the saint with the rogue ; shoves Jesus and Judas equally aside. Why then do we prate of self-reliance ? Inasmuch as the soul is present, there will be power not confident but agent. To talk of reliance, is a poor external way of speaking. Speak rather of that which relies, because it works and is. Who has more soul than I, masters me, though he should not raise his finger. Round him I must revolve by the gravitation of spirits ; who has less, I rule with like facility. We fancy it rhetoric when we speak of eminent virtue. We do not yet see that virtue is Height, and that a man or a company of men plastic and permeable to principles, by the law of nature must overpower and ride all cities, nations, kings, rich men, poets, who are not.

This is the ultimate fact which we so quickly reach on this as on every topic, the resolution of all into the ever blessed ONE. Virtue is the governor, the creator, the reality. All things real are so by so much of virtue as they contain. Hardship, husbandry, hunting, whaling, war, eloquence, personal weight, are some-

3*

what, and engage my respect as examples of the
soul's presence and impure action. I see the same
law working in nature for conservation and growth.
The poise of a planet, the bended tree recovering itself from the strong wind, the vital resources of every
vegetable and animal, are also demonstrations of the
self-sufficing, and therefore self-relying soul. All history from its highest to its trivial passages is the various record of this power.

Thus all concentrates ; let us not rove ; let us sit at
home with the cause. Let us stun and astonish the intruding rabble of men and books and institutions by a
simple declaration of the divine fact. Bid them take the
shoes from off their feet, for God is here within. Let our
simplicity judge them, and our docility to our own law
demonstrate the poverty of nature and fortune beside
our native riches.

But now we are a mob. Man does not stand in awe
of man, nor is the soul admonished to stay at home,
to put itself in communication with the internal ocean,
but it goes abroad to beg a cup of water of the urns
of men. We must go alone. Isolation must pre-
cede true society. I like the silent church before the
service begins, better than any preaching. How far
off, how cool, how chaste the persons look, begirt
each one with a precinct or sanctuary. So let us
always sit. Why should we assume the faults of our
friend, or wife, or father, or child, because they sit
around our hearth, or are said to have the same blood ?
All men have my blood, and I have all men's. Not
for that will I adopt their petulance or folly, even to

the extent of being ashamed of it. But your isolation must not be mechanical, but spiritual, that is, must
be elevation. At times the whole world seems to be
in conspiracy to importune you with emphatic trifles.
Friend, client, child, sickness, fear, want, charity, all
knock at once at thy closet door and say, ' Come out
unto us.' — Do not spill thy soul ; do not all descend ;
keep thy state ; stay at home in thine own heaven ;
come not for a moment into their facts, into their hub-
bub of conflicting appearances, but let in the light of
thy law on their confusion. The power men possess
to annoy me, I give them by a weak curiosity. No man
can come near me but through my act. " What we
love that we have, but by desire we bereave ourselves of the love."

If we cannot at once rise to the sanctities of obedience and faith, let us at least resist our temptations,
let us enter into the state of war, and wake Thor and
Woden, courage and constancy in our Saxon breasts.
This is to be done in our smooth times by speaking
the truth. Check this lying hospitality and lying affection. Live no longer to the expectation of these
deceived and deceiving people with whom we converse. Say to them, O father, O mother, O wife,
O brother, O friend, I have lived with you after appearances hitherto. Henceforward I am the truth's.
Be it known unto you that henceforward I obey no
law less than the eternal law. I will have no covenants but proximities. I shall endeavor to nourish my
parents, to support my family, to be the chaste hus-
band of one wife, — but these relations I must fill after

a new and unprecedented way. I appeal from your customs. I must be myself. I cannot break myself any longer for you, or you. If you can love me for what I am, we shall be the happier. If you cannot, I will still seek to deserve that you should. I must be myself. I will not hide my tastes or aversions. I will so trust that what is deep is holy, that I will do strongly before the sun and moon whatever inly rejoices me, and the heart appoints. If you are noble, I will love you; if you are not, I will not hurt you and myself by hypocritical attentions. If you are true, but not in the same truth with me, cleave to your companions; I will seek my own. I do this not selfishly, but humbly and truly. It is alike your interest and mine and all men's, however long we have dwelt in lies, to live in truth. Does this sound harsh to-day? You will soon love what is dictated by your nature as well as mine, and if we follow the truth, it will bring us out safe at last. — But so you may give these friends pain. Yes, but I cannot sell my liberty and my power, to save their sensibility. Besides, all persons have their moments of reason when they look out into the region of absolute truth; then will they justify me and do the same thing.

The populace think that your rejection of popular standards is a rejection of all standard, and mere antinomianism; and the bold sensualist will use the name of philosophy to gild his crimes. But the law of consciousness abides. There are two confessionals, in one or the other of which we must be shriven. You may fulfil your round of duties by clearing yourself in the *direct*, or, in the *reflex* way. Consider whether you have satisfied your relations to father, mother, cousin, neighbor, town, cat, and dog; whether any of these can upbraid you. But I may also neglect this reflex standard, and absolve me to myself. I have my own stern claims and perfect circle. It denies the name of duty to many offices that are called duties. But if I can discharge its debts, it enables me to dispense with the popular code. If any one imagines that this law is lax, let him keep its commandment one day.

And truly it demands something godlike in him who has cast off the common motives of humanity, and has ventured to trust himself for a task-master. High be his heart, faithful his will, clear his sight, that he may in good earnest be doctrine, society, law to himself, that a simple purpose may be to him as strong as iron necessity is to others.

If any man consider the present aspects of what is called by distinction *society*, he will see the need of these ethics. The sinew and heart of man seem to be drawn out, and we are become timorous desponding whimperers. We are afraid of truth, afraid of fortune, afraid of death, and afraid of each other. Our age yields no great and perfect persons. We want men and women who shall renovate life and our social state, but we see that most natures are insolvent; cannot satisfy their own wants, have an ambition out of all proportion to their practical force, and so do lean and beg day and night continually. Our housekeeping is mendicant, our arts, our occupations, our marriages, our religion we have not chosen, but society has chosen for us. We are parlor soldiers. The rugged battle of fate, where strength is born, we shun.

If our young men miscarry in their first enterprizes, they lose all heart. If the young merchant fails, men say he is *ruined*. If the finest genius studies at one of our colleges, and is not installed in an office within one year afterwards in the cities or suburbs of Boston or New York, it seems to his friends and to himself that he is right in being disheartened and in complaining the rest of his life. A sturdy lad from New Hampshire or Vermont, who in turn tries all the professions, who *teams it, farms it, peddles*, keeps a school, preaches, edits a newspaper, goes to Congress, buys a township, and so forth, in successive years, and always, like a cat, falls on his feet, is worth a hundred of these city dolls. He walks abreast with his days, and feels no shame in not ' studying a profession,' for he does not postpone his life, but lives already. He has not one chance, but a hundred chances. Let a stoic arise who shall reveal the resources of man, and tell men they are not leaning willows, but can and must detach themselves ; that with the exercise of self-trust, new powers shall appear ; that a man is the word made flesh, born to shed healing to the nations, that he should be ashamed of our compassion, and that the moment he acts from himself, tossing the laws, the books, idolatries, and customs out of the window, — we pity him no more but thank and revere him, — and that teacher shall restore the life of man to splendor, and make his name dear to all History.

It is easy to see that a greater self-reliance, — a new respect for the divinity in man, — must work a revolution in all the offices and relations of men ; in their religion ; in their education ; in their pursuits ; their modes of living ; their association ; in their property ; in their speculative views.

1. In what prayers do men allow themselves ! That which they call a holy office, is not so much as brave and manly. Prayer looks abroad and asks for some foreign addition to come through some foreign virtue, and loses itself in endless mazes of natural and supernatural, and mediatorial and miraculous. Prayer that craves a particular commodity — any thing less than all good, is vicious. Prayer is the contemplation of the facts of life from the highest point of view. It is the soliloquy of a beholding and jubilant soul. It is the spirit of God pronouncing his works good. But prayer as a means to effect a private end, is theft and meanness. It supposes dualism and not unity in nature and consciousness. As soon as the man is at one with God, he will not beg. He will then see prayer in all action. The prayer of the farmer kneeling in his field to weed it, the prayer of the rower kneeling with the stroke of his oar, are true prayers heard throughout nature, though for cheap ends. Caratach, in Fletcher's Bonduca, when admonished to inquire the mind of the god Audate, replies,

" His hidden meaning lies in our endeavors,
Our valors are our best gods."

Another sort of false prayers are our regrets.
Discontent is the want of self-reliance : it is infirmity of will. Regret calamities, if you can thereby
help the sufferer ; if not, attend your own work, and
already the evil begins to be repaired. Our sympathy is just as base. We come to them who weep
foolishly, and sit down and cry for company, instead
of imparting to them truth and health in rough electric shocks, putting them once more in communication with the soul. The secret of fortune is joy in
our hands. Welcome evermore to gods and men is
the self-helping man. For him all doors are flung
wide. Him all tongues greet, all honors crown, all
eyes follow with desire. Our love goes out to him
and embraces him, because he did not need it. We
solicitously and apologetically caress and celebrate
him, because he held on his way and scorned our dis-
approbation. The gods love him because men hated
him. " To the persevering mortal," said Zoroaster,
" the blessed Immortals are swift."

As men's prayers are a disease of the will, so are
their creeds a disease of the intellect. They say
with those foolish Israelites, ' Let not God speak to us,
lest we die. Speak thou, speak any man with us,
and we will obey.' Everywhere I am bereaved of
meeting God in my brother, because he has shut his
own temple doors, and recites fables merely of his
brother's, or his brother's brother's God. Every new
mind is a new classification. If it prove a mind of

uncommon activity and power, a Locke, a Lavoisier, a Hutton, a Bentham, a Spurzheim, it imposes its classification on other men, and lo! a new system. In proportion always to the depth of the thought, and so to the number of the objects it touches and brings within reach of the pupil, is his complacency. But chiefly is this apparent in creeds and churches, which are also classifications of some powerful mind acting on the great elemental thought of Duty, and man's relation to the Highest. Such is Calvinism, Quakerism, Swedenborgianism. The pupil takes the same delight in subordinating every thing to the new terminology that a girl does who has just learned botany, in seeing a new earth and new seasons thereby. It will happen for a time, that the pupil will feel a real debt to the teacher, — will find his intellectual power has grown by the study of his writings. This will continue until he has exhausted his master's mind. But in all unbalanced minds, the classification is idolized, passes for the end, and not for a speedily exhaustible means, so that the walls of the system blend to their eye in the remote horizon with the walls of the universe; the luminaries of heaven seem to them hung on the arch their master built. They cannot imagine how you aliens have any right to see, — how you can see; 'It must be somehow that you stole the light from us.' They do not yet perceive, that, light unsystematic, indomitable, will break into any cabin, even into theirs. Let them chirp awhile and call it their own. If they are honest and do well, presently their neat new pinfold will be too

strait and low, will crack, will lean, will rot and vanish, and the immortal light, all young and joyful,
million-orbed, million-colored, will beam over the
universe as on the first morning.

2. It is for want of self-culture that the idol of Travelling, the idol of Italy, of England, of Egypt, remains for all educated Americans. They who made
England, Italy, or Greece venerable in the imagination, did so not by rambling round creation as a moth
round a lamp, but by sticking fast where they were,
like an axis of the earth. In manly hours, we feel
that duty is our place, and that the merrymen of circumstance should follow as they may. The soul is
no traveller: the wise man stays at home with the
soul, and when his necessities, his duties, on any occasion call him from his house, or into foreign lands,
he is at home still, and is not gadding abroad from
himself, and shall make men sensible by the expression of his countenance, that he goes the missionary
of wisdom and virtue, and visits cities and men like a
sovereign, and not like an interloper or a valet.

I have no churlish objection to the circumnavigation
of the globe, for the purposes of art, of study, and
benevolence, so that the man is first domesticated, or
does not go abroad with the hope of finding somewhat greater than he knows. He who travels to be
amused, or to get somewhat which he does not carry,
travels away from himself, and grows old even in
youth among old things. In Thebes, in Palmyra, his
will and mind have become old and dilapidated as
they. He carries ruins to ruins.

Travelling is a fool's paradise. We owe to our first journeys the discovery that place is nothing. At home I dream that at Naples, at Rome, I can be intoxicated with beauty, and lose my sadness. I pack my trunk, embrace my friends, embark on the sea, and at last wake up in Naples, and there beside me is the stern Fact, the sad self, unrelenting, identical, that I fled from. I seek the Vatican, and the palaces. I affect to be intoxicated with sights and suggestions, but I am not intoxicated. My giant goes with me wherever I go.

3. But the rage of travelling is itself only a symptom of a deeper unsoundness affecting the whole intellectual action. The intellect is vagabond, and the universal system of education fosters restlessness. Our minds travel when our bodies are forced to stay at home. We imitate; and what is imitation but the travelling of the mind? Our houses are built with foreign taste; our shelves are garnished with foreign ornaments; our opinions, our tastes, our whole minds lean, and follow the Past and the Distant, as the eyes of a maid follow her mistress. The soul created the arts wherever they have flourished. It was in his own mind that the artist sought his model. It was an application of his own thought to the thing to be done and the conditions to be observed. And why need we copy the Doric or the Gothic model? Beauty, convenience, grandeur of thought, and quaint expression are as near to us as to any, and if the American artist will study with hope and love the precise thing to be done by him, considering the cli-

mate, the soil, the length of the day, the wants of the people, the habit and form of the government, he will create a house in which all these will find themselves fitted, and taste and sentiment will be satisfied also.

Insist on yourself; never imitate. Your own gift you can present every moment with the cumulative force of a whole life's cultivation; but of the adopted talent of another, you have only an extemporaneous, half possession. That which each can do best, none but his Maker can teach him. No man yet knows what it is, nor can, till that person has exhibited it. Where is the master who could have taught Shakspeare? Where is the master who could have instructed Franklin, or Washington, or Bacon, or Newton. Every great man is an unique. The Scipionism of Scipio is precisely that part he could not borrow. If any body will tell me whom the great man imitates in the original crisis when he performs a great act, I will tell him who else than himself can teach him. Shakspeare will never be made by the study of Shakspeare. Do that which is assigned thee, and thou canst not hope too much or dare too much. There is at this moment, there is for me an utterance bare and grand as that of the colossal chisel of Phidias, or trowel of the Egyptians, or the pen of Moses, or Dante, but different from all these. Not possibly will the soul all rich, all eloquent, with thousand-cloven tongue, deign to repeat itself; but if I can hear what these patriarchs say, surely I can reply to them in the same pitch of voice: for the ear and the tongue are

two organs of one nature. Dwell up there in the simple and noble regions of thy life, obey thy heart, and
thou shalt reproduce the Foreworld again.

4. As our Religion, our Education, our Art look
abroad, so does our spirit of society. All men
plume themselves on the improvement of society, and
no man improves.

Society never advances. It recedes as fast on one
side as it gains on the other. Its progress is only apparent, like the workers of a treadmill. It undergoes
continual changes : it is barbarous, it is civilized, it is
christianized, it is rich, it is scientific ; but this change
is not amelioration. For every thing that is given,
something is taken. Society acquires new arts and
loses old instincts. What a contrast between the well-
clad, reading, writing, thinking American, with a
watch, a pencil, and a bill of exchange in his pocket,
and the naked New Zealander, whose property is a
club, a spear, a mat, and an undivided twentieth of a
shed to sleep under. But compare the health of the two
men, and you shall see that his aboriginal strength the
white man has lost. If the traveller tell us truly,
strike the savage with a broad axe, and in a day or
two the flesh shall unite and heal as if you struck
the blow into soft pitch, and the same blow shall send
the white to his grave.

The civilized man has built a coach, but has lost the
use of his feet. He is supported on crutches, but
loses so much support of muscle. He has got a fine
Geneva watch, but he has lost the skill to tell the hour
by the sun. A Greenwich nautical almanac he has,

and so being sure of the information when he wants it, the man in the street does not know a star in the sky. The solstice he does not observe ; the equinox he knows as little ; and the whole bright calendar of the year is without a dial in his mind. His note-books impair his memory ; his libraries overload his wit ; the insurance office increases the number of accidents ; and it may be a question whether machinery does not encumber ; whether we have not lost by refinement some energy, by a christianity entrenched in establishments and forms, some vigor of wild virtue. For every stoic was a stoic ; but in Christendom where is the Christian ?

There is no more deviation in the moral standard than in the standard of height or bulk. No greater men are now than ever were. A singular equality may be observed between the great men of the first and of the last ages ; nor can all the science, art, religion and philosophy of the nineteenth century avail to educate greater men than Plutarch's heroes, three or four and twenty centuries ago. Not in time is the race progressive. Phocion, Socrates, Anaxagoras, Diogenes, are great men, but they leave no class. He who is really of their class will not be called by their name, but be wholly his own man, and, in his turn the founder of a sect. The arts and inventions of each period are only its costume, and do not invigorate men. The harm of the improved machinery may compensate its good. Hudson and Behring accomplished so much in their fishing-boats, as to astonish Parry and Franklin, whose equipment exhaust-

ed the resources of science and art. Galileo, with
an opera-glass, discovered a more splendid series of
facts than any one since. Columbus found the New
World in an undecked boat. It is curious to see the
periodical disuse and perishing of means and machinery which were introduced with loud laudation,
a few years or centuries before. The great genius
returns to essential man. We reckoned the improve-
ments of the art of war among the triumphs of science, and yet Napoleon conquered Europe by the
Bivouac, which consisted of falling back on naked
valor, and disencumbering it of all aids. The Emperor held it impossible to make a perfect army,
says Las Casas, " without abolishing our arms, magazines, commissaries, and carriages, until in imitation
of the Roman custom, the soldier should receive his
supply of corn, grind it in his hand-mill, and bake his
bread himself."

Society is a wave. The wave moves onward, but
the water of which it is composed, does not. The
same particle does not rise from the valley to the
ridge. Its unity is only phenomenal. The persons
who make up a nation to-day, next year die, and
their experience with them.

And so the reliance on Property, including the reliance on governments which protect it, is the want
of self-reliance. Men have looked away from themselves and at things so long, that they have come to
esteem what they call the soul's progress, namely,
the religious, learned, and civil institutions, as guards
of property, and they deprecate assaults on these,

because they feel them to be assaults on property
They measure their esteem of each other, by what each
has, and not by what each is. But a cultivated man
becomes ashamed of his property, ashamed of what
he has, out of new respect for his being. Especially
he hates what he has, if he see that it is accidental, —
came to him by inheritance, or gift, or crime ; then
he feels that it is not having ; it does not belong to
him, has no root in him, and merely lies there, because no revolution or no robber takes it away. But
that which a man is, does always by necessity acquire, and what the man acquires is permanent and
living property, which does not wait the beck of rulers, or mobs, or revolutions, or fire, or storm, or
bankruptcies, but perpetually renews itself wherever
the man is put. " Thy lot or portion of life," said
the Caliph Ali, " is seeking after thee ; therefore be
at rest from seeking after it." Our dependence on
these foreign goods leads us to our slavish respect for
numbers. The political parties meet in numerous
conventions ; the greater the concourse, and with
each new uproar of announcement, The delega-
tion from Essex ! The Democrats from New Hampshire ! The Whigs of Maine ! the young patriot feels
himself stronger than before by a new thousand of
eyes and arms. In like manner the reformers sum-
mon conventions, and vote and resolve in multitude.
But not so, O friends ! will the God deign to enter
and inhabit you, but by a method precisely the reverse. It is only as a man puts off from himself all
external support, and stands alone, that I see him to

be strong and to prevail. He is weaker by every recruit to his banner. Is not a man better than a town ? Ask nothing of men, and in the endless mutation, thou only firm column must presently appear the upholder of all that surrounds thee. He who knows that power is in the soul, that he is weak only because he has looked for good out of him and elsewhere, and so perceiving, throws himself unhesitatingly on his thought, instantly rights himself, stands in the erect position, commands his limbs, works miracles ; just as a man who stands on his feet is stronger than a man who stands on his head.

So use all that is called Fortune. Most men gamble with her, and gain all, and lose all, as her wheel rolls. Bu tdo thou leave as unlawful these winnings, and deal with Cause and Effect, the chancellors of God. In the Will work and acquire, and thou hast chained the wheel of Chance, and shalt always drag her after thee. A political victory, a rise of rents, the recovery of your sick, or the return of your absent friend, or some other quite external event, raises your spirits, and you think good days are preparing for you. Do not believe it. It can never be so. Nothing can bring you peace but yourself. Nothing can bring you peace but the triumph of principles.

4

COMPENSATION.

ESSAY III.

COMPENSATION.

_____

EVER since I was a boy, I have wished to write a discourse on Compensation : for, it seemed to me when very young, that, on this subject, Life was ahead of theology, and the people knew more than the preachers taught. The documents too, from which the doctrine is to be drawn, charmed my fancy by their endless variety, and lay always before me, even in sleep ; for they are the tools in our hands, the bread in our basket, the transactions of the street, the farm, and the dwelling-house, the greetings, the relations, the debts and credits, the influence of character, the nature and endowment of all men. It seemed to me also that in it might be shown men a ray of divinity, the present action of the Soul of this world, clean from all vestige of tradition, and so the heart of man might be bathed by an inundation of eternal love, conversing with that which he knows was always and always must be, because it really is now. It appeared, moreover, that if this doctrine could be stated in terms with any resemblance to those bright intuitions in which this truth is sometimes revealed to us, it would be a star in many dark hours and crooked passages in our journey that would not suffer us to lose our way.

I was lately confirmed in these desires by hearing a sermon at church. The preacher, a man esteemed for his orthodoxy, unfolded in the ordinary manner the doctrine of the Last Judgment. He assumed that judgment is not executed in this world; that the wicked are successful; that the good are miserable; and then urged from reason and from Scripture a compensation to be made to both parties in the next life. No offence appeared to be taken by the congregation at this doctrine. As far as I could observe, when the meeting broke up, they separated without remark on the sermon.

Yet what was the import of this teaching? What did the preacher mean by saying that the good are miserable in the present life? Was it that houses and lands, offices, wine, horses, dress, luxury, are had by unprincipled men, whilst the saints are poor and despised; and that a compensation is to be made to these last hereafter, by giving them the like gratifications another day, — bank-stock and doubloons, venison and champagne? This must be the compensation intended; for, what else? Is it that they are to have leave to pray and praise? to love and serve men? Why, that they can do now. The

legitimate inference the disciple would draw, was ;
' We are to have *such* a good time as the sinners have
now ;' — or, to push it to its extreme import, — ' You
sin now; we shall sin by-and-by ; we would sin
now, if we could ; not being successful, we expect
our revenge tomorrow.'

The fallacy lay in the immense concession that the
bad are successful ; that justice is not done now.
The blindness of the preacher consisted in deferring
to the base estimate of the market of what constitutes
a manly success, instead of confronting and convict-
ing the world from the truth ; announcing the Presence
of the Soul ; the omnipotence of the Will : and so
establishing the standard of good and ill, of success
and falsehood, and summoning the dead to its present
tribunal.

I find a similar base tone in the popular religious
works of the day, and the same doctrines assumed by
the literary men when occasionally they treat the related topics. I think that our popular theology has
gained in decorum, and not in principle, over the superstitions it has displaced. But men are better than
this theology. Their daily life gives it the lie.
Every ingenuous and aspiring soul leaves the doctrine behind him in his own experience ; and all men
feel sometimes the falsehood which they cannot demonstrate. For men are wiser than they know.
That which they hear in schools and pulpits without
afterthought, if said in conversation, would probably
be questioned in silence. If a man dogmatize in a
mixed company on Providence and the divine laws,

he is answered by a silence which conveys well enough to an observer the dissatisfaction of the hearer, but his incapacity to make his own statement.

I shall attempt in this and the following chapter to record some facts that indicate the path of the law of Compensation; happy beyond my expectation, if I shall truly draw the smallest arc of this circle.

POLARITY, or action and reaction, we meet in every part of nature; in darkness and light; in heat and cold; in the ebb and flow of waters; in male and female; in the inspiration and expiration of plants and animals; in the systole and diastole of the heart; in the undulations of fluids, and of sound; in the centrifugal and centripetal gravity; in electricity, galvanism, and chemical affinity. Superinduce magnetism at one end of a needle; the opposite magnetism takes place at the other end. If the south attracts, the north repels. To empty here, you must condense there. An inevitable dualism bisects nature, so that each thing is a half, and suggests another thing to make it whole; as spirit, matter; man, woman; subjective, objective; in, out; upper, under; motion, rest; yea, nay.

Whilst the world is thus dual, so is every one of its parts. The entire system of things gets represented in every particle. There is somewhat that resembles the ebb and flow of the sea, day and night, man and woman, in a single needle of the pine, in a kernel of corn, in each individual of every animal tribe. The reaction so grand in the elements, is repeated within these small boundaries. For example, in the animal kingdom, the physiologist has observed that no creatures are favorites, but a certain compensation balances every gift and every defect. A surplusage given to one part is paid out of a reduction from another part of the same creature. If the head and neck are enlarged, the trunk and extremities are cut short.

The theory of the mechanic forces is another example. What we gain in power is lost in time ; and the converse. The periodic or compensating errors of the planets, is another instance. The influences of climate and soil in political history are another. The cold climate invigorates. The barren soil does not breed fevers, crocodiles, tigers, or scorpions.

The same dualism underlies the nature and condition of man. Every excess causes a defect ; every defect an excess. Every sweet hath its sour ; every evil its good. Every faculty which is a receiver of pleasure, has an equal penalty put on its abuse. It is to answer for its moderation with its life. For every grain of wit there is a grain of folly. For every thing you have missed, you have gained something else ; and for every thing you gain, you lose something. If riches increase, they are increased that use them. If the gatherer gathers too much, nature takes out of the man what she puts into his chest ; swells the estate, but kills the owner. Nature hates monopolies and exceptions. The waves of the sea do not more speedily seek a level from their loftiest tossing, than the varieties of condition tend to equalize themselves. There is always some levelling circumstance that puts down the

4*

overbearing, the strong, the rich, the fortunate, sub-
stantially on the same ground with all others. Is a
man too strong and fierce for society, and by temper
and position a bad citizen, — a morose ruffian with a
dash of the pirate in him ; — nature sends him a
troop of pretty sons and daughters who are getting
along in the dame's classes at the village school, and
love and fear for them smooths his grim scowl to courtesy. Thus she contrives to intenerate the granite
and felspar, takes the boar out and puts the lamb in,
and keeps her balance true.

The farmer imagines power and place are fine
things. But the President has paid dear for his White
House. It has commonly cost him all his peace and
the best of his manly attributes. To preserve for a
short time so conspicuous an appearance before the
world, he is content to eat dust before the real masters who stand erect behind the throne. Or, do men
desire the more substantial and permanent grandeur of
genius ? Neither has this an immunity. He who by
force of will or of thought is great, and overlooks
thousands, has the responsibility of overlooking.
With every influx of light, comes new danger.
Has he light ? he must bear witness to the light,
and always outrun that sympathy which gives him
such keen satisfaction, by his fidelity to new revelations of the incessant soul. He must hate father
and mother, wife and child. Has he all that the
world loves and admires and covets? — he must
cast behind him their admiration, and afflict them by
faithfulness to his truth, and become a by-word and
a hissing.

This Law writes the laws of cities and nations. It will not be baulked of its end in the smallest iota. It is in vain to build or plot or combine against it. Things refuse to be mismanaged long. *Res nolunt diu male administrari.* Though no checks to a new evil appear, the checks exist and will appear. If the government is cruel, the governor's life is not safe. If you tax too high, the revenue will yield nothing. If you make the criminal code sanguinary, juries will not convict. Nothing arbitrary, nothing artificial can endure. The true life and satisfactions of man seem to elude the utmost rigors or felicities of condition, and to establish themselves with great indifferency under all varieties of circumstance. Under all governments the influence of character remains the same, — in Turkey and in New England about alike. Under the primeval despots of Egypt, history honestly confesses that man must have been as free as culture could make him.

These appearances indicate the fact that the universe is represented in every one of its particles. Every thing in nature contains all the powers of nature. Every thing is made of one hidden stuff; as the naturalist sees one type under every metamorphosis, and regards a horse as a running man, a fish as a swimming man, a bird as a flying man, a tree as a rooted man. Each new form repeats not only the main character of the type, but part for part all the details, all the aims, furtherances, hindrances, energies, and whole system of every other. Every occupation, trade, art, transaction, is a compend of the world, and a correlative of every other. Each one is an entire emblem of human life ; of its good and ill, its trials, its enemies, its course and its end. And each one must somehow accommodate the whole man, and recite all his destiny.

The world globes itself in a drop of dew. The microscope cannot find the animalcule which is less perfect for being little. Eyes, ears, taste, smell, motion, resistance, appetite, and organs of reproduction that take hold on eternity, — all find room to consist in the small creature. So do we put our life into every act. The true doctrine of omnipresence is, that God reappears with all his parts in every moss and cobweb. The value of the universe contrives to throw itself into every point. If the good is there, so is the evil ; if the affinity, so the repulsion ; if the force, so the limitation.

Thus is the universe alive. All things are moral. That soul which within us is a sentiment, outside of us is a law. We feel its inspirations ; out there in history we can see its fatal strength. It is almighty. All nature feels its grasp. " It is in the world and the world was made by it." It is eternal, but it enacts itself in time and space. Justice is not postponed A perfect equity adjusts its balance in all parts of life. *Οἱ κυβοι Διος ἀει εὐπίπτυσι.* The dice of God are always loaded. The world looks like a multiplication-table or a mathematical equation, which, turn it how you will, balances itself. Take what figure you will, its exact value, nor more nor less, still returns to you. Every secret is told, every crime is punished, every virtue rewarded, every wrong redressed, in silence and certainty. What we call retribution, is the universal necessity by which the whole appears wherever a part appears. If you see smoke, there must be fire. If you see a hand or a limb, you know that the trunk to which it belongs, is there behind.

Every act rewards itself, or, in other words, integrates itself, in a twofold manner; first, in the thing, or, in real nature; and secondly, in the circumstance, or, in apparent nature. Men call the circumstance the retribution. The causal retribution is in the thing, and is seen by the soul. The retribution in the circumstance, is seen by the understanding; it is inseparable from the thing, but is often spread over a long time, and so does not become distinct until after many years. The specific stripes may follow late after the offence, but they follow because they accompany it. Crime and punishment grow out of one stem. Punishment is a fruit that unsuspected ripens within the flower of the pleasure which concealed it. Cause and effect, means and ends, seed and fruit, cannot be severed; for the effect already blooms in the cause, the end preëxists in the means, the fruit in the seed.

Whilst thus the world will be whole, and refuses to be disparted, we seek to act partially; to sunder; to appropriate; for example, — to gratify the senses, we sever the pleasure of the senses from the needs of the character. The ingenuity of man has been dedicated always to the solution of one problem, — how to detach the sensual sweet, the sensual strong, the sensual bright, &c. from the moral sweet, the moral deep, the

moral fair ; that is, again, to contrive to cut clean off
this upper surface so thin as to leave it bottomless ;
to get a *one end*, without an *other end*. The soul
says, Eat ; the body would feast. The soul says, The
man and woman shall be one flesh and one soul ; the
body would join the flesh only. The soul says, Have
dominion over all things to the ends of virtue ; the
body would have the power over things to its own
ends.

The soul strives amain to live and work through
all things. It would be the only fact. All things
shall be added unto it, — power, pleasure, knowledge,
beauty. The particular man aims to be somebody ;
to set up for himself ; to truck and higgle for a private good ; and, in particulars, to ride, that he may
ride ; to dress, that he may be dressed ; to eat, that he
may eat ; and to govern that he may be seen. Men
seek to be great ; they would have offices, wealth,
power and fame. They think that to be great is to
get only one side of nature — the sweet, without the
other side — the bitter.

Steadily is this dividing and detaching counteracted.
Up to this day, it must be owned, no projector has
had the smallest success. The parted water re-unites
behind our hand. Pleasure is taken out of pleasant
things, profit out of profitable things, power out of
strong things, the moment we seek to separate them
from the whole. We can no more halve things and
get the sensual good, by itself, than we can get an inside that shall have no outside, or a light without a
shadow. "Drive out nature with a fork, she comes
running back."

Life invests itself with inevitable conditions, which the unwise seek to dodge, which one and another brags that he does not know; brags that they do not touch him; — but the brag is on his lips, the conditions are in his soul. If he escapes them in one part, they attack him in another more vital part. If he has escaped them in form, and in the appearance, it is that he has resisted his life, and fled from himself, and the retribution is so much death. So signal is the failure of all attempts to make this separation of the good from the tax, that the experiment would not be tried, — since to try it is to be mad, — but for the circumstance, that when the disease began in the will, of rebellion and separation, the intellect is at once infected, so that the man ceases to see God whole in each object, but is able to see the sensual allurement of an object, and not see the sensual hurt; he sees the mermaid's head, but not the dragon's tail; and thinks he can cut off that which he would have, from that which he would not have. "How secret art thou who dwellest in the highest heavens in silence, O thou only great God, sprinkling with an unwearied Providence certain penal blindnesses upon such as have unbridled desires!"*

The human soul is true to these facts in the painting of fable, of history, of law, of proverbs, of conversation. It finds a tongue in literature unawares. Thus the Greeks called Jupiter, Supreme Mind; but having traditionally ascribed to him many base actions,

---

* St. Augustine: Confessions, B. I.

they involuntarily made amends to Reason, by tying
up the hands of so bad a god.   He is made as helpless as a king of England.   Prometheus knows one secret, which Jove must bargain for ; Minerva, another.
He cannot get his own thunders ; Minerva keeps the
key of them.

> " Of all the gods I only know the keys
>   That ope the solid doors within whose vaults
>   His thunders sleep."

A plain confession of the in-working of the All,
and of its moral aim.   The Indian mythology ends
in the same ethics ; and indeed it would seem impossible for any fable to be invented and get any currency
which was not moral.   Aurora forgot to ask youth
for her lover, and so though Tithonus is immortal,
he is old.   Achilles is not quite invulnerable ; for
Thetis held him by the heel when she dipped him in
the Styx, and the sacred waters did not wash that
part.   Siegfried, in the Nibelungen, is not quite immortal, for a leaf fell on his back whilst he was bath-
ing in the Dragon's blood, and that spot which it cov-
ered is mortal.   And so it always is.   There is a
crack in every thing God has made.   Always, it would
seem, there is this vindictive circumstance stealing in
at unawares, even into the wild poesy in which the
human fancy attempted to make bold holiday, and to
shake itself free of the old laws, — this back-stroke,
this kick of the gun, certifying that the law is fatal ;
that in Nature, nothing can be given, all things are
sold.

This is that ancient doctrine of Nemesis, who keeps watch in the Universe, and lets no offence go unchastised. The Furies, they said, are attendants on Justice, and if the sun in heaven should transgress his path, they would punish him. The poets related that stone walls, and iron swords, and leathern thongs had an occult sympathy with the wrongs of their owners; that the belt which Ajax gave Hector, dragged the Trojan hero over the field at the wheels of the car of Achilles; and the sword which Hector gave Ajax, was that on whose point Ajax fell. They recorded that when the Thasians erected a statue to Theogenes, a victor in the games, one of his rivals went to it by night, and endeavored to throw it down by repeated blows, until at last he moved it from its pedestal and was crushed to death beneath its fall.

This voice of fable has in it somewhat divine. It came from thought above the will of the writer. That is the best part of each writer, which has nothing private in it. That is the best part of each, which he does not know, that which flowed out of his constitution, and not from his too active invention; that which in the study of a single artist you might not easily find, but in the study of many, you would abstract as the spirit of them all. Phidias it is not, but the work of man in that early Hellenic world, that I would know. The name and circumstance of Phidias, however convenient for history, embarrasses when we come to the highest criticism. We are to see that which man was tending to do in a given period, and was hindered, or, if you will, modified in doing, by the interfering volitions of Phidias, of Dante, of Shakspeare, the organ whereby man at the moment wrought.

Still more striking is the expression of this fact in the proverbs of all nations, which are always the literature of Reason, or the statements of an absolute truth, without qualification. Proverbs, like the sacred books of each nation, are the sanctuary of the Intuitions. That which the droning world, chained to appearances, will not allow the realist to say in his own words, it will suffer him to say in proverbs without contradiction. And this law of laws which the pulpit, the senate and the college deny, is hourly preached in all markets and all languages by flights of proverbs, whose teaching is as true and as omnipresent as that of birds and flies.

All things are double, one against another. — Tit for tat; an eye for an eye; a tooth for a tooth; blood for blood; measure for measure; love for love. — Give and it shall be given you. — He that watereth shall be watered himself. — What will you have? quoth God; pay for it and take it. — Nothing venture, nothing have. — Thou shalt be paid exactly for what thou hast done, no more, no less. — Who doth not work shall not eat. — Harm watch, harm catch. — Curses always recoil on the head of him who imprecates them. — If you put a chain around the neck of a slave, the other end fastens itself around your own. — Bad counsel confounds the adviser. — The devil is an ass.

It is thus written, because it is thus in life. Our action is overmastered and characterised above our will by the law of nature. We aim at a petty end quite aside from the public good, but our act arranges itself by irresistible magnetism in a line with the poles of the world.

A man cannot speak but he judges himself. With his will, or against his will, he draws his portrait to the eye of his companions by every word. Every opinion reacts on him who utters it. It is a thread-ball thrown at a mark, but the other end remains in the thrower's bag. Or, rather, it is a harpoon thrown at the whale, unwinding, as it flies, a coil of cord in the boat, and if the harpoon is not good, or not well thrown, it will go nigh to cut the steersman in twain, or to sink the boat.

You cannot do wrong without suffering wrong. "No man had ever a point of pride that was not injurious to him," said Burke. The exclusive in fashionable life does not see that he excludes himself from enjoyment, in the attempt to appropriate it. The exclusionist in religion does not see that he shuts the door of heaven on himself, in striving to shut out others. Treat men as pawns and ninepins, and you shall suffer as well as they. If you leave out their heart, you shall lose your own. The senses would make things of all persons ; of women, of children, of the poor. The vulgar proverb, " I will get it from his purse or get it from his skin, " is sound philosophy.

All infractions of love and equity in our social relations are speedily punished. They are punished by Fear. Whilst I stand in simple relations to my fellow man, I have no displeasure in meeting him. We meet as water meets water, or a current of air meets another, with perfect diffusion and interpenetration of nature. But as soon as there is any departure from simplicity, and attempt at halfness, or good for me that is not good for him, my neighbor feels the wrong ; he shrinks from me as far as I have shrunk from him ; his eyes no longer seek mine ; there is war between us ; there is hate in him and fear in me.

All the old abuses in society, the great and universal and the petty and particular, all unjust accumulations of property and power, are avenged in the same manner. Fear is an instructer of great sagacity, and the herald of all revolutions. One thing he always teaches, that there is rottenness where he appears. He is a carrion crow, and though you see not well what he hovers for, there is death somewhere. Our property is timid, our laws are timid, our cultivated classes are timid. Fear for ages has boded and mowed and gibbered over government and property. That obscene bird is not there for nothing. He indicates great wrongs which must be revised.

Of the like nature is that expectation of change which instantly follows the suspension of our voluntary activity. The terror of cloudless noon, the emerald of Polycrates, the awe of prosperity, the instinct which leads every generous soul to impose on itself tasks of a noble asceticism and vicarious virtue, are the tremblings of the balance of justice through the heart and mind of man.

Experienced men of the world know very well

that it is always best to pay scot and lot as they go along, and that a man often pays dear for a small frugality. The borrower runs in his own debt. Has a man gained any thing who has received a hundred favors and rendered none? Has he gained by borrowing, through indolence or cunning, his neighbor's wares, or horses, or money? There arises on the deed the instant acknowledgment of benefit on the one part, and of debt on the other; that is, of superiority and inferiority. The transaction remains in the memory of himself and his neighbor; and every new transaction alters, according to its nature, their relation to each other. He may soon come to see that he had better have broken his own bones than to have ridden in his neighbor's coach, and that " the highest price he can pay for a thing is to ask for it."

A wise man will extend this lesson to all parts of life, and know that it is always the part of prudence to face every claimant, and pay every just demand on your time, your talents, or your heart. Always pay; for, first or last, you must pay your entire debt. Persons and events may stand for a time between you and justice, but it is only a postponement. You must pay at last your own debt. If you are wise, you will dread a prosperity which only loads you with more. Benefit is the end of nature. But for every benefit which you receive, a tax is levied. He is great who confers the most benefits. He is base, — and that is the one base thing in the universe, — to receive favors and render none. In the order of nature we cannot render benefits to those from whom we receive

them, or only seldom.   But the benefit we receive
must be rendered again, line for line, deed for deed,
cent for cent, to somebody.   Beware of too much
good staying in your hand.   It will fast corrupt and
worm worms.   Pay it away quickly in some sort.

Labor is watched over by the same pitiless laws.
Cheapest, say the prudent, is the dearest labor.   What
we buy in a broom, a mat, a wagon, a knife, is some
application of good sense to a common want.   It
is best to pay in your land a skilful gardener, or
to buy good sense applied to gardening ; in your
sailor, good sense applied to navigation ; in the house,
good sense applied to cooking, sewing, serving ; in
your agent, good sense applied to accounts and affairs.   So do you multiply your presence, or spread
yourself throughout your estate.   But because of the
dual constitution of all things, in labor as in life there
can be no cheating.   The thief steals from himself.
The swindler swindles himself.   For the real price of
labor is knowledge and virtue, whereof wealth and
credit are signs.   These signs, like paper money, may
be counterfeited or stolen, but that which they represent, namely, knowledge and virtue, cannot be counterfeited or stolen.   These ends of labor cannot be
answered but by real exertions of the mind, and
in obedience to pure motives.   The cheat, the de-
faulter, the gambler cannot extort the benefit, cannot
extort the knowledge of material and moral nature
which his honest care and pains yield to the operative.
The law of nature is, Do the thing, and you shall
have the power : but they who do not the thing have
not the power.

Human labor, through all its forms, from the sharpening of a stake to the construction of a city or an epic, is one immense illustration of the perfect compensation of the universe. Every where and always this law is sublime. The absolute balance of Give and Take, the doctrine that every thing has its price ; and if that price is not paid, not that thing but something else is obtained, and that it is impossible to get any thing without its price, — this doctrine is not less sublime in the columns of a leger than in the budgets of states, in the laws of light and darkness, in all the action and reaction of nature. I cannot doubt that the high laws which each man sees ever implicated in those processes with which he is conversant, the stern ethics which sparkle on his chisel-edge, which are measured out by his plumb and foot-rule, which stand as manifest in the footing of the shop-bill as in the history of a state, — do recommend to him his trade, and though seldom named, exalt his business to his imagination.

The league between virtue and nature engages all things to assume a hostile front to vice. The beautiful laws and substances of the world persecute and whip the traitor. He finds that things are arranged for truth and benefit, but there is no den in the wide world to hide a rogue. There is no such thing as concealment. Commit a crime, and the earth is made of glass. Commit a crime, and it seems as if a coat of snow fell on the ground, such as reveals in the woods the track of every partridge and fox and squirrel and mole. You cannot recall the spoken word.

you cannot wipe out the foot-track, you cannot draw up the ladder, so as to leave no inlet or clew. Always some damning circumstance transpires. The laws and substances of nature, water, snow, wind, gravitation, become penalties to the thief.

On the other hand, the law holds with equal sureness for all right action. Love, and you shall be loved. All love is mathematically just, as much as the two sides of an algebraic equation. The good man has absolute good, which like fire turns every thing to its own nature, so that you cannot do him any harm ; but as the royal armies sent against Napoleon, when he approached, cast down their colors and from enemies became friends, so do disasters of all kinds, as sickness, offence, poverty, prove benefactors.

> " Winds blow and waters roll
> Strength to the brave, and power and deity,
> Yet in themselves are nothing."

The good are befriended even by weakness and defect. As no man had ever a point of pride that was not injurious to him, so no man had ever a defect that was not somewhere made useful to him. The stag in the fable admired his horns and blamed his feet, but when the hunter came, his feet saved him, and afterwards, caught in the thicket, his horns destroyed him. Every man in his lifetime needs to thank his faults. As no man thoroughly understands a truth until first he has contended against it, so no man has a thorough acquaintance with the hindrances or talents of men, until he has suffered from the one, and seen the triumph of the other over his own want of the same. Has he a defect of temper that unfits him to live in society? Thereby he is driven to entertain himself alone, and acquire habits of self-help; and thus, like the wounded oyster, he mends his shell with pearl.

Our strength grows out of our weakness. Not until we are pricked and stung and sorely shot at, awakens the indignation which arms itself with secret forces. A great man is always willing to be little. Whilst he sits on the cushion of advantages, he goes to sleep. When he is pushed, tormented, defeated, he has a chance to learn something; he has been put on his wits, on his manhood; he has gained facts; learns his ignorance; is cured of the insanity of conceit; has got moderation and real skill. The wise man always throws himself on the side of his assailants. It is more his interest than it is theirs to find his weak point. The wound cicatrizes and falls off from him, like a dead skin, and when they would triumph, lo! he has passed on invulnerable. Blame is safer than praise. I hate to be defended in a newspaper. As long as all that is said, is said against me, I feel a certain assurance of success. But as soon as honied words of praise are spoken for me, I feel as one that lies unprotected before his enemies. In general, every evil to which we do not succumb, is a benefactor. As the Sandwich Islander believes that the strength and valor of the enemy he kills, passes into himself, so we gain the strength of the temptation we resist.

5

The same guards which protect us from disaster, defect, and enmity, defend us, if we will, from selfishness and fraud. Bolts and bars are not the best of our institutions, nor is shrewdness in trade a mark of wisdom. Men suffer all their life long, under the foolish superstition that they can be cheated. But it is as impossible for a man to be cheated by any one but himself, as for a thing to be, and not to be, at the same time. There is a third silent party to all our bargains. The nature and soul of things takes on itself the guaranty of the fulfilment of every contract, so that honest service cannot come to loss. If you serve an ungrateful master, serve him the more. Put God in your debt. Every stroke shall be repaid. The longer the payment is withholden, the better for you; for compound interest on compound interest is the rate and usage of this exchequer.

The history of persecution is a history of endeavors to cheat nature, to make water run up hill, to twist a rope of sand. It makes no difference whether the actors be many or one, a tyrant or a mob. A mob is a society of bodies voluntarily bereaving themselves of reason and traversing its work. The mob is man voluntarily descending to the nature of the beast. Its fit hour of activity is night. Its actions are insane like its whole constitution. It persecutes a principle; it would whip a right; it would tar and feather justice, by inflicting fire and outrage upon the houses and persons of those who have these. It resembles the prank of boys who run with fire-engines to put out the ruddy aurora streaming to the stars. The inviolate spirit turns their spite against the wrong doers. The martyr cannot be dishonored. Every lash inflicted is a tongue of fame; every prison a more illustrious abode; every burned book or house enlightens the world; every suppressed or expunged word reverberates through the earth from side to side. The minds of men are at last aroused; reason looks out and justifies her own, and malice finds all her work vain. It is the whipper who is whipped, and the tyrant who is undone.

Thus do all things preach the indifferency of circumstances. The man is all. Every thing has two sides, a good and an evil. Every advantage has its tax. I learn to be content. But the doctrine of compensation is not the doctrine of indifferency. The thoughtless say, on hearing these representations, — What boots it to do well? there is one event to good and evil; if I gain any good, I must pay for it; if I lose any good, I gain some other; all actions are indifferent.

There is a deeper fact in the soul than compensation, to wit, its own nature. The soul is not a compensation, but a life. The soul *is*. Under all this running sea of circumstance, whose waters ebb and flow with perfect balance, lies the aboriginal abyss of real Being. Existence, or God, is not a relation, or a part, but the whole. Being is the vast affirmative, excluding negation, self-balanced, and swallowing up all relations, parts and times, within itself. Nature, truth, virtue are the influx from thence. Vice is the

absence or departure of the same. Nothing, Falsehood, may indeed stand as the great Night or shade,
on which, as a back-ground, the living universe paints
itself forth; but no fact is begotten by it; it cannot
work; for it is not. It cannot work any good; it
cannot work any harm. It is harm inasmuch as it is
worse not to be than to be.

We feel defrauded of the retribution due to evil
acts, because the criminal adheres to his vice and con-
tumacy, and does not come to a crisis or judgment
any where in visible nature. There is no stunning
confutation of his nonsense before men and angels.
Has he therefore outwitted the law? Inasmuch as he
carries the malignity and the lie with him, he so far
deceases from nature. In some manner there will be
a demonstration of the wrong to the understanding
also; but should we not see it, this deadly deduction makes square the eternal account.

Neither can it be said, on the other hand, that the
gain of rectitude must be bought by any loss. There
is no penalty to virtue; no penalty to wisdom; they
are proper additions of being. In a virtuous action,
I properly *am*; in a virtuous act, I add to the world;
I plant into deserts conquered from Chaos and Nothing, and see the darkness receding on the limits of the
horizon. There can be no excess to love; none to
knowledge; none to beauty, when these attributes
are considered in the purest sense. The soul refuses
all limits. It affirms in man always an Optimism,
never a Pessimism.

His life is a progress, and not a station. His instinct

is trust. Our instinct uses " more " and " less " in application to man, always of the *presence of the soul*, and not of its absence ; the brave man is greater than the coward ; the true, the benevolent, the wise, is more a man and not less, than the fool and knave. There is, therefore, no tax on the good of virtue ; for, that is the incoming of God himself, or absolute existence, without any comparative. All external good has its tax, and if it came without desert or sweat, has no root in me and the next wind will blow it away. But all the good of nature is the soul's, and may be had, if paid for in nature's lawful coin, that is, by labor which the heart and the head allow. I no longer wish to meet a good I do not earn, for example, to find a pot of buried gold, knowing that it brings with it new responsibility. I do not wish more external goods, — neither possessions, nor honors, nor powers, nor persons. The gain is apparent : the tax is certain. But there is no tax on the knowledge that the compensation exists, and that it is not desirable to dig up treasure. Herein I rejoice with a serene eternal peace. I contract the boundaries of possible mischief. I learn the wisdom of St. Bernard, " Nothing can work me damage except myself ; the harm that I sustain, I carry about with me, and never am a real sufferer but by my own fault."

In the nature of the soul is the compensation for the inequalities of condition. The radical tragedy of nature seems to be the distinction of More and Less. How can Less not feel the pain ; how not feel indignation or malevolence towards More ? Look at those

who have less faculty, and one feels sad, and knows
not well what to make of it. Almost he shuns their
eye ; almost he fears they will upbraid God. What
should they do ? It seems a great injustice. But
face the facts, and see them nearly, and these moun-
tainous inequalities vanish. Love reduces them all, as
the sun melts the iceberg in the sea. The heart and
soul of all men being one, this bitterness of *His* and
Mine ceases. His is mine. I am my brother, and
my brother is me. If I feel overshadowed and outdone by great neighbors, I can yet love ; I can still
receive ; and he that loveth, maketh his own the grandeur he loves. Thereby I make the discovery that
my brother is my guardian, acting for me with the
friendliest designs, and the estate I so admired and
envied, is my own. It is the eternal nature of the soul
to appropriate and make all things its own. Jesus and
Shakspeare are fragments of the soul, and by love I
conquer and incorporate them in my own conscious
domain. His virtue, — is not that mine ? His wit, —
if it cannot be made mine, it is not wit.

Such, also, is the natural history of calamity. The
changes which break up at short intervals the prosperity of men, are advertisements of a nature whose law
is growth. Evermore it is the order of nature to
grow, and every soul is by this intrinsic necessity quit-
ting its whole system of things, its friends, and home,
and laws, and faith, as the shell-fish crawls out of its
beautiful but stony case, because it no longer admits of
its growth, and slowly forms a new house. In proportion to the vigor of the individual, these revolu-

tions are frequent, until in some happier mind they are incessant, and all worldly relations hang very loosely about him, becoming, as it were, a transparent fluid membrane through which the form is alway seen, and not as in most men an indurated heterogeneous fabric of many dates, and of no settled character, in which the man is imprisoned. Then there can be enlargement, and the man of to-day scarcely recognises the man of yesterday. And such should be the outward biography of man in time, a putting off of dead circumstances day by day, as he renews his raiment day by day. But to us, in our lapsed estate, resting not advancing, resisting not coöperating with the divine expansion, this growth comes by shocks.

We cannot part with our friends. We cannot let our angels go. We do not see that they only go out, that archangels may come in. We are idolaters of the old. We do not believe in the riches of the soul, in its proper eternity and omnipresence. We do not believe there is any force in to-day to rival or re-create that beautiful yesterday. We linger in the ruins of the old tent, where once we had bread and shelter and organs, nor believe that the spirit can feed, cover, and nerve us again. We cannot again find aught so dear, so sweet, so graceful. But we sit and weep in vain. The voice of the Almighty saith, ' Up and onward forevermore ! ' We cannot stay amid the ruins. Neither will we rely on the New ; and so we walk ever with reverted eyes, like those monsters who look backwards.

And yet the compensations of calamity are made

apparent to the understanding also, after long intervals
of time.   A fever, a mutilation, a cruel disappointment, a loss of wealth, a loss of friends seems at the
moment unpaid loss, and unpayable.   But the sure
years reveal the deep remedial force that underlies
all facts.   The death of a dear friend, wife, brother,
lover, which seemed nothing but privation, somewhat
later assumes the aspect of a guide or genius ; for it
commonly operates revolutions in our way of life,
terminates an epoch of infancy or of youth which
was waiting to be closed, breaks up a wonted occupation, or a household, or style of living, and allows the
formation of new ones more friendly to the growth of
character.   It permits or constrains the formation of
new acquaintances, and the reception of new influences that prove of the first importance to the next
years ; and the man or woman who would have remained a sunny garden flower, with no room for its
roots and too much sunshine for its head, by the falling of the walls and the neglect of the gardener, is
made the banian of the forest, yielding shade and
fruit to wide neighborhoods of men.

SPIRITUAL LAWS.

5*

ESSAY IV.

SPIRITUAL LAWS.

WHEN the act of reflection takes place in the mind, when we look at ourselves in the light of thought, we discover that our life is embosomed in beauty. Behind us, as we go, all things assume pleasing forms, as clouds do far off. Not only things familiar and stale, but even the tragic and terrible are comely, as they take their place in the pictures of memory. The river-bank, the weed at the water-side, the old house, the foolish person, — however neglected in the passing, — have a grace in the past. Even the corpse that has lain in the chambers has added a solemn ornament to the house. The soul will not know either deformity or pain. If in the hours of clear reason we should speak the severest truth, we should say, that we had never made a sacrifice. In these hours the mind seems so great, that nothing can be

taken from us that seems much.   All loss, all pain is
particular : the universe remains to the heart unhurt.
Distress never, trifles never abate our trust.   No man
ever stated his griefs as lightly as he might.   Allow
for exaggeration in the most patient and sorely ridden
hack that ever was driven.   For it is only the finite
that has wrought and suffered ; the infinite lies
stretched in smiling repose.

The intellectual life may be kept clean and healthful, if man will live the life of nature, and not import
into his mind difficulties which are none of his.   No
man need be perplexed in his speculations.   Let him
do and say what strictly belongs to him, and though
very ignorant of books, his nature shall not yield him
any intellectual obstructions and doubts.   Our young
people are diseased with the theological problems of
original sin, origin of evil, predestination, and the
like.   These never presented a practical difficulty to
any man, — never darkened across any man's road,
who did not go out of his way to seek them.   These
are the soul's mumps and measles, and whooping-
coughs, and those who have not caught them, cannot
describe their health or prescribe the cure.   A simple
mind will not know these enemies.   It is quite another thing that he should be able to give account of
his faith, and expound to another the theory of his self-
union and freedom.   This requires rare gifts.   Yet
without this self-knowledge, there may be a sylvan
strength and integrity in that which he is.   " A few
strong instincts and a few plain rules " suffice us.

My will never gave the images in my mind the rank

they now take. The regular course of studies, the years of academical and professional education have not yielded me better facts than some idle books under the bench at the Latin school. What we do not call education is more precious than that which we call so. We form no guess at the time of receiving a thought, of its comparative value. And education often wastes its effort in attempts to thwart and baulk this natural magnetism which with sure discrimination selects its own.

In like manner, our moral nature is vitiated by any interference of our will. People represent virtue as a struggle, and take to themselves great airs upon their attainments, and the question is every where vexed, when a noble nature is commended, Whether the man is not better who strives with temptation? But there is no merit in the matter. Either God is there, or he is not there. We love characters in proportion as they are impulsive and spontaneous. The less a man thinks or knows about his virtues, the better we like him. Timoleon's victories are the best victories; which ran and flowed like Homer's verses, Plutarch said. When we see a soul whose acts are all regal, graceful and pleasant as roses, we must thank God that such things can be and are, and not turn sourly on the angel, and say, ' Crump is a better man with his grunting resistance to all his native devils.'

Not less conspicuous is the preponderance of nature over will in all practical life. There is less intention in history than we ascribe to it. We impute deep-laid, far-sighted plans to Cæsar and Napoleon;

but the best of their power was in nature, not in them.
Men of an extraordinary success, in their honest moments, have always sung, ' Not unto us, not unto us.'
According to the faith of their times, they have built
altars to Fortune or to Destiny, or to St. Julian. Their
success lay in their parallelism to the course of thought,
which found in them an unobstructed channel ; and
the wonders of which they were the visible conductors, seemed to the eye their deed.   Did the wires generate the galvanism ?   It is even true that there
was less in them on which they could reflect, than
in another ; as the virtue of a pipe is to be smooth
and hollow.   That which externally seemed will and
immovableness, was willingness and self-annihilation.
Could Shakspeare give a theory of Shakspeare ?
Could ever a man of prodigious mathematical genius convey to others any insight into his methods ? If
he could communicate that secret, instantly it would
lose all its exaggerated value, blending with the day-
light and the vital energy, the power to stand and to go.

The lesson is forcibly taught by these observations
that our life might be much easier and simpler than
we make it, that the world might be a happier place
than it is, that there is no need of struggles, convulsions, and despairs, of the wringing of the hands and
the gnashing of the teeth ; that we miscreate our own
evils.   We interfere with the optimism of nature, for,
whenever we get this vantage ground of the past,
or of a wiser mind in the present, we are able to
discern that we are begirt with spiritual laws which execute themselves.

The face of external nature teaches the same lesson with calm superiority. Nature will not have us fret and fume. She does not like our benevolence or our learning, much better than she likes our frauds and wars. When we come out of the caucus, or the bank, or the Abolition convention, or the Temperance meeting, or the Transcendental club, into the fields and woods, she says to us, " So hot ? my little sir."

We are full of mechanical actions. We must needs intermeddle, and have things in our own way, until the sacrifices and virtues of society are odious. Love should make joy; but our benevolence is unhappy. Our Sunday schools and churches and pauper-societies are yokes to the neck. We pain ourselves to please nobody. There are natural ways of arriving at the same ends at which these aim, but do not arrive. Why should all virtue work in one and the same way ? Why should all give dollars ? It is very inconvenient to us country folk, and we do not think any good will come of it. We have not dollars. Merchants have. Let them give them. Farmers will give corn. Poets will sing. Women will sew. Laborers will lend a hand. The children will bring flowers. And why drag this dead weight of a Sunday school over the whole Christendom ? It is natural and beautiful that childhood should inquire, and maturity should teach ; but it is time enough to answer questions, when they are asked. Do not shut up the young people against their will in a pew, and force the children to ask them questions for an hour against their will.

If we look wider, things are all alike ; laws, and

letters, and creeds and modes of living, seem a tra-
vestie of truth. Our society is encumbered by ponderous machinery which resembles the endless aque-
ducts which the Romans built over hill and dale, and
which are superseded by the discovery of the law that
water rises to the level of its source. It is a Chinese
wall which any nimble Tartar can leap over. It is a
standing army, not so good as a peace. It is a graduated, titled, richly appointed Empire, quite superfluous when Town-meetings are found to answer just as
well.

Let us draw a lesson from nature, which always
works by short ways. When the fruit is ripe, it falls.
When the fruit is despatched, the leaf falls. The
circuit of the waters is mere falling. The walking
of man and all animals is a falling forward. All
our manual labor and works of strength, as prying,
splitting, digging, rowing, and so forth, are done by
dint of continual falling, and the globe, earth, moon,
comet, sun, star, fall forever and ever.

The simplicity of the universe is very different from
the simplicity of a machine. He who sees moral
nature out and out, and thoroughly knows how
knowledge is acquired and character formed, is a pe-
dant. The simplicity of nature is not that which may
easily be read, but is inexhaustible. The last analysis can no wise be made. We judge of a man's wisdom by his hope, knowing that the perception of the
inexhaustibleness of nature is an immortal youth.
The wild fertility of nature is felt in comparing our
rigid names and reputations with our fluid conscious-

ness. We pass in the world for sects and schools, for erudition and piety, and we are all the time jejune babes. One sees very well how Pyrrhonism grew up. Every man sees that he is that middle point whereof every thing may be affirmed and denied with equal reason. He is old, he is young, he is very wise, he is altogether ignorant. He hears and feels what you say of the seraphim, and of the tin-pedlar. There is no permanent wise man, except in the figment of the stoics. We side with the hero, as we read or paint, against the coward and the robber; but we have been ourselves that coward and robber, and shall be again, not in the low circumstance, but in comparison with the grandeurs possible to the soul.

A little consideration of what takes place around us every day, would show us that a higher law, than that of our will, regulates events; that our painful labors are very unnecessary, and altogether fruitless; that only in our easy, simple, spontaneous action are we strong, and by contenting ourselves with obedience we become divine. Belief and love, — a believing love will relieve us of a vast load of care. O myb rothers, God exists. There is a soul at the centre of nature, and over the will of every man, so that none of us can wrong the universe. It has so infused its strong enchantment into nature, that we prosper when we accept its advice, and when we struggle to wound its creatures, our hands are glued to our sides, or they beat our own breasts. The whole course of things goes to teach us faith. We need

only obey.   There is guidance for each of us, and by
lowly listening we shall hear the right word.   Why
need you choose so painfully your place, and occupation, and associates, and modes of action, and of entertainment ? Certainly there is a possible right for
you that precludes the need of balance and wilful
election.   For you there is a reality, a fit place and
congenial duties.   Place yourself in the middle of
the stream of power and wisdom which flows into
you as life, place yourself in the full centre of that
flood, then you are without effort impelled to truth, to
right, and a perfect contentment.   Then you put all
gainsayers in the wrong.   Then you are the world,
the measure of right, of truth, of beauty.   If we will
not be mar-plots with our miserable interferences,
the work, the society, letters, arts, science, religion
of men, would go on far better than now, and the
Heaven predicted from the beginning of the world,
and still predicted from the bottom of the heart, would
organize itself, as do now the rose and the air and the
sun.

   I say, *do not choose ;* but that is a figure of speech
by which I would distinguish what is commonly called
choice among men, and which is a partial act, the
choice of the hands, of the eyes, of the appetites,
and not a whole act of the man.   But that which I
call right or goodness, is the choice of my constitution ;
and that which I call heaven, and inwardly aspire
after, is the state or circumstance desirable to my
constitution ; and the action which I in all my years
tend to do, is the work for my faculties.   We must

hold a man amenable to reason for the choice of his daily craft or profession. It is not an excuse any longer for his deeds that they are the custom of his trade. What business has he with an evil trade? Has he not a *calling* in his character.

Each man has his own vocation. The talent is the call. There is one direction in which all space is open to him. He has faculties silently inviting him thither to endless exertion. He is like a ship in a river; he runs against obstructions on every side but one; on that side, all obstruction is taken away, and he sweeps serenely over God's depths into an infinite sea. This talent and this call depend on his organization, or the mode in which the general soul incarnates itself in him. He inclines to do something which is easy to him, and good when it is done, but which no other man can do. He has no rival. For the more truly he consults his own powers, the more difference will his work exhibit from the work of any other. When he is true and faithful, his ambition is exactly proportioned to his powers. The height of the pinnacle is determined by the breadth of the base. Every man has this call of the power to do somewhat unique, and no man has any other call. The pretence that he has another call, a summons by name and personal election and outward " signs that mark him extraordinary, and not in the roll of common men," is fanaticism, and betrays obtuseness to perceive that there is one mind in all the individuals, and no respect of persons therein.

By doing his work, he makes the need felt which

he can supply. He creates the taste by which he is enjoyed. He provokes the wants to which he can minister. By doing his own work, he unfolds himself. It is the vice of our public speaking, that it has not abandonment. Somewhere, not only every orator but every man should let out all the length of all the reins ; should find or make a frank and hearty expression of what force and meaning is in him. The common experience is, that the man fits himself as well as he can to the customary details of that work or trade he falls into, and tends it as a dog turns a spit. Then is he a part of the machine he moves ; the man is lost. Until he can manage to communicate himself to others in his full stature and proportion as a wise and good man, he does not yet find his vocation. He must find in that an outlet for his character, so that he may justify himself to their eyes for doing what he does. If the labor is trivial, let him by his thinking and character, make it liberal. Whatever he knows and thinks, whatever in his apprehension is worth doing, that let him communicate, or men will never know and honor him aright. Foolish, whenever you take the meanness and formality of that thing you do, instead of converting it into the obedient spiracle of your character and aims.

We like only such actions as have already long had the praise of men, and do not perceive that any thing man can do, may be divinely done. We think greatness entailed or organized in some places or duties, in certain offices or occasions, and do not see that Paganini can extract rapture from a catgut, and

Eulenstein from a jews-harp, and a nimble-fingered lad out of shreds of paper with his scissors ; and Landseer out of swine, and the hero out of the pitiful habitation and company in which he was hidden. What we call obscure condition or vulgar society, is that condition and society whose poetry is not yet written, but which you shall presently make as enviable and renowned as any. Accept your genius, and say what you think. In our estimates, let us take a lesson from kings. The parts of hospitality, the connection of families, the impressiveness of death, and a thousand other things, royalty makes its own estimate of, and a royal mind will. To make habitually a new estimate, — that is elevation.

What a man does, that he has. What has he to do with hope or fear ? In himself is his might. Let him regard no good as solid, but that which is in his nature, and which must grow out of him as long as he exists. The goods of fortune may come and go like summer leaves ; let him play with them, and scatter them on every wind as the momentary signs of his infinite productiveness.

He may have his own. A man's genius, the quality that differences him from every other, the susceptibility to one class of influences, the selection of what is fit for him, the rejection of what is unfit, determines for him the character of the universe. As a man thinketh, so is he, and as a man chooseth, so is he and so is nature. A man is a method, a progressive arrangement ; a selecting principle, gathering his like to him, wherever he goes. He takes only his own,

out of the multiplicity that sweeps and circles round
him. He is like one of those booms which are set
out from the shore on rivers to catch drift-wood, or
like the loadstone amongst splinters of steel.

Those facts, words, persons which dwell in his memory without his being able to say why, remain, because they have a relation to him not less real for being as yet unapprehended. They are symbols of
value to him, as they can interpret parts of his consciousness which he would vainly seek words for in
the conventional images of books and other minds.
What attracts my attention shall have it, as I will go
to the man who knocks at my door, whilst a thousand
persons, as worthy, go by it, to whom I give no regard.
It is enough that these particulars speak to me. A
few anecdotes, a few traits of character, manners,
face, a few incidents have an emphasis in your memory out of all proportion to their apparent significance, if you measure them by the ordinary standards. They relate to your gift. Let them have their
weight, and do not reject them and cast about for
illustration and facts more usual in literature. Respect them, for they have their origin in deepest nature. What your heart thinks great, is great. The
soul's emphasis is always right.

Over all things that are agreeable to his nature and
genius, the man has the highest right. Every where
he may take what belongs to his spiritual estate, nor
can he take any thing else, though all doors were
open, nor can all the force of men hinder him from
taking so much. It is vain to attempt to keep a se-

cret from one who has a right to know it. It will tell itself. That mood into which a friend can bring us, is his dominion over us. To the thoughts of that state of mind, he has a right. All the secrets of that state of mind, he can compel. This is a law which statesmen use in practice. All the terrors of the French Republic, which held Austria in awe, were unable to command her diplomacy. But Napoleon sent to Vienna M. de Narbonne, one of the old noblesse, with the morals, manners and name of that interest, saying, that it was indispensable to send to the old aristocracy of Europe, men of the same connexion, which, in fact, constitutes a sort of free-masonry. M. Narbonne, in less than a fortnight, penetrated all the secrets of the Imperial Cabinet.

A mutual understanding is ever the firmest chain. Nothing seems so easy as to speak and to be understood. Yet a man may come to find *that* the strongest of defences and of ties, — that he has been understood ; and he who has received an opinion, may come to find it the most inconvenient of bonds.

If a teacher have any opinion which he wishes to conceal, his pupils will become as fully indoctrinated into that as into any which he publishes. If you pour water into a vessel twisted into coils and angles, it is vain to say, I will pour it only into this or that ; — it will find its own level in all. Men feel and act the consequences of your doctrine, without being able to show how they follow. Show us an arc of the curve, and a good mathematician will find out the whole figure. We are always reasoning from the seen to the unseen.

Hence the perfect intelligence that subsists between wise men of remote ages. A man cannot bury his meanings so deep in his book, but time and like-minded men will find them. Plato had a secret doctrine, had he? What secret can he conceal from the eyes of Bacon? of Montaigne? of Kant? Therefore, Aristotle said of his works, "They are published and not published."

No man can learn what he has not preparation for learning, however near to his eyes is the object. A chemist may tell his most precious secrets to a carpenter, and he shall be never the wiser, — the secrets he would not utter to a chemist for an estate. God screens us evermore from premature ideas. Our eyes are holden that we cannot see things that stare us in the face, until the hour arrives when the mind is ripened, — then we behold them, and the time when we saw them not, is like a dream.

Not in nature but in man is all the beauty and worth he sees. The world is very empty, and is indebted to this gilding, exalting soul for all its pride. " Earth fills her lap with splendors " *not her own.* The vale of Tempe, Tivoli, and Rome are earth and water, rocks and sky. There are as good earth and water in a thousand places, yet how unaffecting!

People are not the better for the sun and moon, the horizon and the trees; as it is not observed that the keepers of Roman galleries, or the valets of painters have any elevation of thought, or that librarians are wiser men than others. There are graces in the demeanor of a polished and noble person, which are lost upon the eye of a churl. These are like the stars whose light has not yet reached us.

He may see what he maketh. Our dreams are the sequel of our waking knowledge. The visions of the night always bear some proportion to the visions of the day. Hideous dreams are only exaggerations of the sins of the day. We see our own evil affections embodied in bad physiognomies. On the Alps, the traveller sometimes sees his own shadow magnified to a giant, so that every gesture of his hand is terrific. " My children," said an old man to his boys scared by a figure in the dark entry, " my children, you will never see any thing worse than yourselves." As in dreams, so in the scarcely less fluid events of the world, every man sees himself in colossal, without knowing that it is himself that he sees. The good which he sees, compared to the evil which he sees, is as his own good to his own evil. Every quality of his mind is magnified in some one acquaintance, and every emotion of his heart in some one. He is like a quincunx of trees, which counts five, east, west, north, or south ; or, an initial, medial, and terminal acrostic. And why not ? He cleaves to one person, and avoids another, according to their likeness or unlikeness to himself, truly seeking himself in his associates, and moreover in his trade, and habits, and gestures, and meats, and drinks ; and comes at last to be faithfully represented by every view you take of his circumstances.

He may read what he writeth. What can we see or acquire, but what we are ? You have seen a skilful
6

man reading Virgil. Well, that author is a thousand books to a thousand persons. Take the book into your two hands, and read your eyes out; you will never find what I find. If any ingenious reader would have a monopoly of the wisdom or delight he gets, he is as secure now the book is Englished, as if it were imprisoned in the Pelews tongue. It is with a good book as it is with good company. Introduce a base person among gentlemen : it is all to no purpose : he is not their fellow. Every society protects itself. The company is perfectly safe, and he is not one of them, though his body is in the room.

What avails it to fight with the eternal laws of mind, which adjust the relation of all persons to each other, by the mathematical measure of their havings and beings ? Gertrude is enamored of Guy; how high, how aristocratic, how Roman his mien and manners ! to live with him were life indeed : and no purchase is too great ; and heaven and earth are moved to that end. Well, Gertrude has Guy : but what now avails how high, how aristocratic, how Roman his mien and manners, if his heart and aims are in the senate, in the theatre, and in the billiard room, and she has no aims, no conversation that can enchant her graceful lord ?

He shall have his own society. We can love nothing but nature. The most wonderful talents, the most meritorious exertions really avail very little with us ; but nearness or likeness of nature, — how beautiful is the ease of its victory ! Persons approach us famous for their beauty, for their accomplishments, worthy of all wonder for their charms and gifts: they dedicate their whole skill to the hour and the company; with very imperfect result. To be sure, it would be very ungrateful in us not to praise them very loudly. Then, when all is done, a person of related mind, a brother or sister by nature, comes to us so softly and easily, so nearly and intimately, as if it were the blood in our proper veins, that we feel as if some one was gone, instead of another having come : we are utterly relieved and refreshed : it is a sort of joyful solitude. We foolishly think, in our days of sin, that we must court friends by compliance to the customs of society, to its dress, its breeding and its estimates. But later, if we are so happy, we learn that only that soul can be my friend, which I encounter on the line of my own march, that soul to which I do not decline, and which does not decline to me, but, native of the same celestial latitude, repeats in its own all my experience. The scholar and the prophet forget themselves, and ape the customs and costumes of the man of the world, to deserve the smile of beauty. He is a fool and follows some giddy girl, and not with religious, ennobling passion, a woman with all that is serene, oracular and beautiful in her soul. Let him be great, and love shall follow him. Nothing is more deeply punished than the neglect of the affinities by which alone society should be formed, and the insane levity of choosing associates by others' eyes.

He may set his own rate. It is an universal maxim worthy of all acceptation, that a man may have that allowance he takes. Take the place and attitude to which you see your unquestionable right, and all men acquiesce. The world must be just. It always leaves every man with profound unconcern to set his own rate. Hero or driveller, it meddles not in the matter. It will certainly accept your own measure of your doing and being, whether you sneak about and deny your own name, or, whether you see your work produced to the concave sphere of the heavens, one with the revolution of the stars.

The same reality pervades all teaching. The man may teach by doing, and not otherwise. If he can communicate himself, he can teach, but not by words. He teaches who gives, and he learns who receives. There is no teaching until the pupil is brought into the same state or principle in which you are ; a transfusion takes place : he is you, and you are he ; then is a teaching, and by no unfriendly chance or bad company can he ever quite lose the benefit. But your propositions run out of one ear as they ran in at the other. We see it advertised that Mr. Grand will deliver an oration on the Fourth of July, and Mr. Hand before the Mechanics' Association, and we do not go thither, because we know that these gentlemen will not communicate their own character and being to the audience. If we had reason to expect such a communication, we should go through all inconvenience and opposition. The sick would be carried in litters. But a public oration is an escapade, a noncommittal, an apology, a gag, and not a communication, not a speech, not a man.

A like Nemesis presides over all intellectual works. We have yet to learn, that the thing uttered in words is not therefore affirmed. It must affirm itself, or no forms of grammar and no plausibility can give it evidence, and no array of arguments. The sentence must also contain its own apology for being spoken.

The effect of any writing on the public mind is mathematically measurable by its depth of thought. How much water does it draw? If it awaken you to think; if it lift you from your feet with the great voice of eloquence; then the effect is to be wide, slow, permanent, over the minds of men; if the pages instruct you not, they will die like flies in the hour. The way to speak and write what shall not go out of fashion, is, to speak and write sincerely. The argument which has not power to reach my own practice, I may well doubt, will fail to reach yours. But take Sidney's maxim: " Look in thy heart, and write." He that writes to himself, writes to an eternal public. That statement only is fit to be made public which you have come at in attempting to satisfy your own curiosity. The writer who takes his subject from his ear and not from his heart, should know that he has lost as much as he seems to have gained, and when the empty book has gathered all its praise, and half the people say — ' what poetry ! what genius !' it still needs fuel to make fire. That only profits which is profitable. Life alone can impart life ; and though we should burst, we can only be valued as we make ourselves valuable. There is no luck in literary reputation. They who make up the final verdict upon every book, are not the partial and noisy readers of the hour when it appears ; but a court as of angels, a public not to be bribed, not to be entreated, and not to be overawed, decides upon every man's title to fame. Only those books come down which deserve to last. All the gilt edges and vellum and morocco, all the presentation-copies to all the libraries will not preserve a book in circulation beyond its intrinsic date. It must go with all Walpole's Noble and Royal Authors to its fate. Blackmore, Kotzebue, or Pollok may endure for a night, but Moses and Homer stand forever. There are not in the world at any one time more than a dozen persons who read and understand Plato : — never enough to pay for an edition of his works ; yet to every generation these come duly down, for the sake of those few persons, as if God brought them in his hand. " No book," said Bentley, " was ever written down by any but itself." The permanence of all books is fixed by no effort friendly or hostile, but by their own specific gravity, or the intrinsic importance of their contents to the constant mind of man. " Do not trouble yourself too much about the light on your statue," said Michael Angelo to the young sculptor ; " the light of the public square will test its value."

In like manner the effect of every action is measured by the depth of the sentiment from which it proceeds. The great man knew not that he was great. It took a century or two, for that fact to appear. What he did, he did because he must : he used no election : it was the most natural thing in the world, and grew out of the circumstances of the moment. But now, every thing he did, even to the lifting of his finger, or the eating of bread, looks large, all-related, and is called an institution.

These are the demonstrations in a few particulars of the genius of nature : they show the direction of the stream. But the stream is blood : every drop is alive. Truth has not single victories : all things are its organs, not only dust and stones, but errors and lies. The laws of disease, physicians say, are as beautiful as the laws of health. Our philosophy is affirmative, and readily accepts the testimony of negative facts, as every shadow points to the sun. By a divine necessity, every fact in nature is constrained to offer its testimony.

Human character does evermore publish itself. It will not be concealed. It hates darkness, — it rushes into light. The most fugitive deed and word, the mere air of doing a thing, the intimated purpose, expresses character. If you act, you show character ; if you sit still, you show it ; if you sleep, you show it. You think because you have spoken nothing, when others spoke, and have given no opinion on the times, on the church, on slavery, on the college, on parties and persons, that your verdict is still expected with curiosity as a reserved wisdom. Far otherwise ; your silence answers very loud. You have no oracle to utter, and your fellow men have learned that you cannot help them ; for, oracles speak. Doth not wisdom cry, and understanding put forth her voice ?

Dreadful limits are set in nature to the powers of

dissimulation. Truth tyrannizes over the unwilling members of the body. Faces never lie, it is said. No man need be deceived, who will study the changes of expression. When a man speaks the truth in the spirit of truth, his eye is as clear as the heavens. When he has base ends, and speaks falsely, the eye is muddy and sometimes asquint.

I have heard an experienced counsellor say, that he feared never the effect upon a jury, of a lawyer who does not believe in his heart that his client ought to have a verdict. If he does not believe it, his unbelief will appear to the jury, despite all his protestations, and will become their unbelief. This is that law whereby a work of art, of whatever kind, sets us in the same state of mind wherein the artist was, when he made it. That which we do not believe, we cannot adequately say, though we may repeat the words never so often. It was this conviction which Swedenborg expressed, when he described a group of persons in the spiritual world endeavoring in vain to articulate a proposition which they did not believe : but they could not, though they twisted and folded their lips even to indignation.

A man passes for that he is worth. Very idle is all curiosity concerning other people's estimate of us, and idle is all fear of remaining unknown. If a man know that he can do any thing, — that he can do it better than any one else, — he has a pledge of the acknowledgment of that fact by all persons. The world is full of judgment days, and into every assembly that a man enters, in every action he attempts, he is guaged and stamped. In every troop of boys that whoop and run in each yard and square, a new comer is as well and accurately weighed in the balance, in the course of a few days, and stamped with his right number, as if he had undergone a formal trial of his strength, speed, and temper. A stranger comes from a distant school, with better dress, with trinkets in his pockets, with airs, and pretension : an old boy sniffs thereat, and says to himself, 'It 's of no use : we shall find him out tomorrow.' ' What hath he done ? ' is the divine question which searches men, and transpierces every false reputation. A fop may sit in any chair of the world, nor be distinguished for his hour from Homer and Washington ; but there can never be any doubt concerning the respective ability of human beings, when we seek the truth. Pretension may sit still, but cannot act. Pretension never feigned an act of real greatness. Pretension never wrote an Iliad, nor drove back Xerxes, nor christianized the world, nor abolished slavery.

Always as much virtue as there is, so much appears ; as much goodness as there is, so much reverence it commands. All the devils respect virtue. The high, the generous, the self-devoted sect will always instruct and command mankind. Never a sincere word was utterly lost. Never a magnanimity fell to the ground. Always the heart of man greets and accepts it unexpectedly. A man passes for that he is worth. What he is, engraves itself on his face, on his form, on his fortunes, in letters of light which all men may read but himself. Concealment avails

6*

him nothing ; boasting, nothing. There is confession in the glances of our eyes ; in our smiles ; in salutations ; and the grasp of hands. His sin bedaubs him, mars all his good impression. Men know not why they do not trust him ; but they do not trust him. His vice glasses his eye, demeans his cheek, pinches the nose, sets the mark of the beast on the back of the head, and writes O fool ! fool ! on the forehead of a king.

If you would not be known to do any thing, never do it. A man may play the fool in the drifts of a desert, but every grain of sand shall seem to see. He may be a solitary eater, but he cannot keep his foolish counsel. A broken complexion, a swinish look, ungenerous acts, and the want of due knowledge, — all blab. Can a cook, a Chiffinch, an Iach-imo be mistaken for Zeno or Paul ? Confucius exclaimed, " How can a man be concealed ! How can a man be concealed ! "

On the other hand, the hero fears not, that if he withhold the avowal of a just and brave act, it will go unwitnessed and unloved. One knows it, — himself, — and is pledged by it to sweetness of peace, and to nobleness of aim, which will prove in the end a better proclamation of it than the relating of the incident. Virtue is the adherence in action to the nature of things, and the nature of things makes it prevalent. It consists in a perpetual substitution of being for seeming, and with sublime propriety God is described as saying, I AM.

The lesson which all these observations convey, is,

Be and not seem. Let us acquiesce. Let us take our bloated nothingness out of the path of the divine circuits. Let us unlearn our wisdom of the world. Let us lie low in the Lord's power, and learn that truth alone makes rich and great.

If you visit your friend, why need you apologize for not having visited him, and waste his time and deface your own act? Visit him now. Let him feel that the highest love has come to see him, in thee its lowest organ. Or why need you torment yourself and friend by secret self-reproaches that you have not assisted him or complimented him with gifts and salutations heretofore? Be a gift and a benediction. Shine with real light, and not with the borrowed reflection of gifts. Common men are apologies for men; they bow the head, they excuse themselves with prolix reasons, they accumulate appearances, because the substance is not.

We are full of these superstitions of sense, the worship of magnitude. God loveth not size : whale and minnow are of like dimension. But we call the poet inactive, because he is not a president, a merchant, or a porter. We adore an institution, and do not see that it is founded on a thought which we have. But real action is in silent moments. The epochs of our life are not in the visible facts of our choice of a calling, our marriage, our acquisition of an office, and the like, but in a silent thought by the way-side as we walk ; in a thought which revises our entire manner of life, and says, ' Thus hast thou done, but it were better thus.' And all our after years, like menials, do serve and wait on this, and, according to their ability, do execute its will. This revisal or correction is a constant force, which, as a tendency, reaches through our lifetime. The object of the man, the aim of these moments is to make daylight shine through him, to suffer the law to traverse his whole being without obstruction, so that, on what point soever of his doing your eye falls, it shall report truly of his character, whether it be his diet, his house, his religious forms, his society, his mirth, his vote, his opposition. Now he is not homogeneous, but heterogeneous, and the ray does not traverse; there are no thorough lights: but the eye of the beholder is puzzled, detecting many unlike tendencies, and a life not yet at one.

Why should we make it a point with our false modesty to disparage that man we are, and that form of being assigned to us? A good man is contented. I love and honor Epaminondas, but I do not wish to be Epaminondas. I hold it more just to love the world of this hour, than the world of his hour. Nor can you, if I am true, excite me to the least uneasiness by saying, ' he acted, and thou sittest still.' I see action to be good, when the need is, and sitting still to be also good. Epaminondas, if he was the man I take him for, would have sat still with joy and peace, if his lot had been mine. Heaven is large, and affords space for all modes of love and fortitude. Why should we be busy-bodies and superserviceable? Action and inaction are alike to the true. One piece of the tree is cut for a weathercock, and one for the sleeper of a bridge; the virtue of the wood is apparent in both.

I desire not to disgrace the soul. The fact that I am here, certainly shows me that the soul had need of an organ here. Shall I not assume the post? Shall I skulk and dodge and duck with my unseasonable apologies and vain modesty, and imagine my being here impertinent? less pertinent than Epaminondas or Homer being there? and that the soul did not know its own needs? Besides, without any reasoning on the matter, I have no discontent. The good soul nourishes me alway, unlocks new magazines of power and enjoyment to me every day. I will not meanly decline the immensity of good, because I have heard that it has come to others in another shape.

Besides, why should we be cowed by the name of Action? 'T is a trick of the senses, — no more. We know that the ancestor of every action is a thought. The poor mind does not seem to itself to be any thing, unless it have an outside badge, — some Gentoo diet, or Quaker coat, or Calvinistic prayer-meeting, or philanthropic society, or a great donation, or a high office, or, any how, some wild contrasting action to testify that it is somewhat. The rich mind lies in the sun and sleeps, and is Nature. To think is to act.

Let us, if we must have great actions, make our own so. All action is of an infinite elasticity, and the least admits of being inflated with the celestial air until it eclipses the sun and moon. Let us seek *one* peace by fidelity. Let me do my duties. Why need I go gadding into the scenes and philosophy of Greek and Italian history, before I have washed my own face, or justified myself to my own benefactors? How dare I read Washington's campaigns, when I have not answered the letters of my own correspondents? Is not that a just objection to much of our reading? It is a pusillanimous desertion of our work to gaze after our neighbors. It is peeping. Byron says of Jack Bunting,

" He knew not what to say, and so, he swore."

I may say it of our preposterous use of books: He knew not what to do, and so, *he read.* I can think of nothing to fill my time with, and so, without any constraint, I find the Life of Brant. It is a very extravagant compliment to pay to Brant, or to General Schuyler, or to General Washington. My time should be as good as their time : my world, my facts, all my net of relations as good as theirs, or either of theirs. Rather let me do my work so well that other idlers, if they choose, may compare my texture with the texture of these and find it identical with the best.

This over-estimate of the possibilities of Paul and Pericles, this under-estimate of our own, comes from a neglect of the fact of an identical nature. Bonaparte knew but one Merit, and rewarded in one and the same way the good soldier, the good astronomer, the good poet, the good player. Thus he signified his sense of a great fact. The poet uses the names of Cæsar, of Tamerlane, of Bonduca, of Belisarius ; the painter uses the conventional story of the Virgin Mary, of Paul, of Peter. He does not, therefore, defer to the nature of these accidental men, of these stock heroes. If the poet write a true drama, then he is Cæsar, and not the player of Cæsar ; then the self-same strain of thought, emotion as pure, wit as subtle, motions as swift, mounting, extravagant, and a heart as great, self-sufficing, dauntless, which on the waves of its love and hope can uplift all that is reckoned solid and precious in the world, palaces, gardens, money, navies, kingdoms, — marking its own incomparable worth by the slight it casts on these gauds of men, — these all are his, and by the power of these he rouses the nations. But the great names cannot stead him, if he have not life himself. Let a man believe in God, and not in names and places and persons. Let the great soul incarnated in some woman's form, poor and sad and single, in some Dolly or Joan, go out to service, and sweep chambers and scour floors, and its effulgent day-beams cannot be muffled or hid, but to sweep and scour will instantly appear supreme and beautiful actions, the top and radiance of human life, and all people will get mops and brooms ; until, lo, suddenly the great soul has enshrined itself in some other form, and done some other deed, and that is now the flower and head of all living nature.

We are the photometers, we the irritable goldleaf and tinfoil that measure the accumulations of the subtle element. We know the authentic effects of the true fire through every one of its million disguises.

LOVE.

ESSAY V.

LOVE.

Every soul is a celestial Venus to every other soul.
The heart has its sabbaths and jubilees, in which the
world appears as a hymeneal feast, and all natural
sounds and the circle of the seasons are erotic odes
and dances.   Love is omnipresent in nature as motive
and reward.   Love is our highest word, and the sy-
nonym of God.   Every promise of the soul has
innumerable fulfilments : each of its joys ripens into
a new want.   Nature, uncontainable, flowing, forelooking, in the first sentiment of kindness anticipates
already a benevolence which shall lose all particular
regards in its general light.   The introduction to this
felicity is in a private and tender relation of one to
one, which is the enchantment of human life ; which,
like a certain divine rage and enthusiasm, seizes on
man at one period, and works a revolution in his mind
and body ; unites him to his race, pledges him to the

domestic and civic relations, carries him with new sympathy into nature, enhances the power of the senses, opens the imagination, adds to his character heroic and sacred attributes, establishes marriage, and gives permanence to human society.

The natural association of the sentiment of love with the heyday of the blood, seems to require that in order to portray it in vivid tints which every youth and maid should confess to be true to their throbbing experience, one must not be too old. The delicious fancies of youth reject the least savor of a mature philosophy, as chilling with age and pedantry their purple bloom. And, therefore, I know I incur the imputation of unnecessary hardness and stoicism from those who compose the Court and Parliament of Love. But from these formidable censors I shall appeal to my seniors. For, it is to be considered that this passion of which we speak, though it begin with the young, yet forsakes not the old, or rather suffers no one who is truly its servant to grow old, but makes the aged participators of it, not less than the tender maiden, though in a different and nobler sort. For, it is a fire that kindling its first embers in the narrow nook of a private bosom, caught from a wandering spark out of another private heart, glows and enlarges until it warms and beams upon multitudes of men and women, upon the universal heart of all, and so lights up the whole world and all nature with its generous flames. It matters not, therefore, whether we attempt to describe the passion at twenty, at thirty, or at eighty years. He who paints it at the first period, will lose some of its later, he who paints it at the last, some of its earlier traits. Only it is to be hoped that by patience and the muses' aid, we may attain to that inward view of the law, which shall describe a truth ever young, ever beautiful, so central that it shall commend itself to the eye at whatever angle beholden.

And the first condition is, that we must leave a too close and lingering adherence to the actual, to facts, and study the sentiment as it appeared in hope and not in history. For, each man sees his own life defaced and disfigured, as the life of man is not, to his imagination. Each man sees over his own experience a certain slime of error, whilst that of other men looks fair and ideal. Let any man go back to those delicious relations which make the beauty of his life, which have given him sincerest instruction and nourishment, he will shrink and shrink. Alas! I know not why, but infinite compunctions embitter in mature life all the remembrances of budding sentiment, and cover every beloved name. Every thing is beautiful seen from the point of the intellect, or as truth. But all is sour, if seen as experience. Details are always melancholy; the plan is seemly and noble. It is strange how painful is the actual world, — the painful kingdom of time and place. There dwells care and canker and fear. With thought, with the ideal, is immortal hilarity, the rose of joy. Round it all the muses sing. But with names and persons and the partial interests of to-day and yesterday, is grief.

The strong bent of nature is seen in the proportion which this topic of personal relations usurps in the conversation of society. What do we wish to know of any worthy person so much as how he has sped in the history of this sentiment? What books in the circulating libraries circulate? How we glow over these novels of passion, when the story is told with any spark of truth and nature! And what fastens attention, in the intercourse of life, like any passage betraying affection between two parties? Perhaps we never saw them before, and never shall meet them again. But we see them exchange a glance, or betray a deep emotion, and we are no longer strangers. We understand them, and take the warmest interest in the development of the romance. All mankind love a lover. The earliest demonstrations of complacency and kindness are nature's most winning pictures. It is the dawn of civility and grace in the coarse and rustic. The rude village boy teazes the girls about the school house door; — but to-day he comes running into the entry, and meets one fair child arranging her satchel : he holds her books to help her, and instantly it seems to him as if she removed herself from him infinitely, and was a sacred precinct. Among the throng of girls he runs rudely enough, but one alone distances him : and these two little neighbors that were so close just now, have learned to respect each other's personality. Or who can avert his eyes from the engaging, half-artful, half-artless ways of school girls who go into the country shops to buy a skein of silk or a sheet of paper, and talk half an hour about nothing, with the broad-faced, good-natured shop-boy. In the village, they are on a perfect equal-

ity, which love delights in, and without any coquetry
the happy, affectionate nature of woman flows out in
this pretty gossip.   The girls may have little beauty,
yet plainly do they establish between them and the
good boy the most agreeable, confiding relations,
what with their fun and their earnest, about Edgar,
and Jonas, and Almira, and who was invited to the
party, and who danced at the dancing school, and
when the singing school would begin, and other no-
things concerning which the parties cooed.   By-and-
by that boy wants a wife, and very truly and heartily
will he know where to find a sincere and sweet mate,
without any risk such as Milton deplores as incident to
scholars and great men.

I have been told that my philosophy is unsocial, and,
that in public discourses, my reverence for the intellect
makes me unjustly cold to the personal relations.   But
now I almost shrink at the remembrance of such dispar-
aging words.   For persons are love's world, and the
coldest philosopher cannot recount the debt of the young
soul wandering here in nature to the power of love, without being tempted to unsay as treasonable to nature,
aught derogatory to the social instincts.   For, though the
celestial rapture falling out of heaven seizes only upon
those of tender age, and although a beauty overpowering all analysis or comparison, and putting us quite
beside ourselves, we can seldom see after thirty years,
yet the remembrance of these visions outlasts all other
remembrances, and is a wreath of flowers on the
oldest brows.   But here is a strange fact; it may
seem to many men in revising their experience, that

they have no fairer page in their life's book than the delicious memory of some passages wherein affection contrived to give a witchcraft surpassing the deep attraction of its own truth to a parcel of accidental and trivial circumstances. In looking backward, they may find that several things which were not the charm, have more reality to this groping memory than the charm itself which embalmed them. But be our experience in particulars what it may, no man ever forgot the visitations of that power to his heart and brain, which created all things new ; which was the dawn in him of music, poetry and art ; which made the face of nature radiant with purple light, the morning and the night varied enchantments ; when a single tone of one voice could make the heart beat, and the most trivial circumstance associated with one form, is put in the amber of memory : when we became all eye when one was present, and all memory when one was gone ; when the youth becomes a watcher of windows, and studious of a glove, a veil, a ribbon, or the wheels of a carriage ; when no place is too solitary, and none too silent for him who has richer company and sweeter conversation in his new thoughts, than any old friends, though best and purest, can give him ; for, the figures, the motions, the words of the beloved object are not like other images written in water, but, as Plutarch said, " enamelled in fire," and make the study of midnight.

" Thou art not gone being gone, where e'er thou art,
  Thou leav'st in him thy watchful eyes, in him thy loving
      heart."

In the noon and the afternoon of life, we still throb at the recollection of days when happiness was not happy enough, but must be drugged with the relish of pain and fear ; for he touched the secret of the matter, who said of love,

" All other pleasures are not worth its pains : "

and when the day was not long enough, but the night too must be consumed in keen recollections; when the head boiled all night on the pillow with the generous deed it resolved on ; when the moonlight was a pleasing fever, and the stars were letters, and the flowers ciphers, and the air was coined into song; when all business seemed an impertinence, and all the men and women running to and fro in the streets, mere pictures.

The passion re-makes the world for the youth. It makes all things alive and significant. Nature grows conscious. Every bird on the boughs of the tree sings now to his heart and soul. Almost the notes are articulate. The clouds have faces, as he looks on them. The trees of the forest, the waving grass and the peeping flowers have grown intelligent; and almost he fears to trust them with the secret which they seem to invite. Yet nature soothes and sympathizes. In the green solitude he finds a dearer home than with men.

"Fountain heads and pathless groves,
Places which pale passion loves,
Moonlight walks, when all the fowls
Are safely housed, save bats and owls,
A midnight bell, a passing groan,
These are the sounds we feed upon."

7

Behold there in the wood the fine madman! He
is a palace of sweet sounds and sights; he dilates;
he is twice a man; he walks with arms akimbo; he
soliloquizes; he accosts the grass and the trees; he
feels the blood of the violet, the clover and the lily in
his veins; and he talks with the brook that wets his
foot.

The causes that have sharpened his perceptions of
natural beauty, have made him love music and verse.
It is a fact often observed, that men have written good
verses under the inspiration of passion, who cannot
write well under any other circumstances.

The like force has the passion over all his nature.
It expands the sentiment; it makes the clown gentle,
and gives the coward heart. Into the most pitiful and
abject it will infuse a heart and courage to defy the
world, so only it have the countenance of the beloved
object. In giving him to another, it still more gives
him to himself. He is a new man, with new perceptions, new and keener purposes, and a religious solemnity of character and aims. He does not longer
appertain to his family and society. *He* is somewhat.
He is a person. *He* is a soul.

And here let us examine a little nearer the nature
of that influence which is thus potent over the human
youth. Let us approach and admire Beauty, whose
revelation to man we now celebrate, — beauty, welcome as the sun wherever it pleases to shine, which
pleases everybody with it and with themselves. Wonderful is its charm. It seems sufficient to itself. The
lover cannot paint his maiden to his fancy poor and

solitary. Like a tree in flower, so much soft, budding, informing loveliness is society for itself, and she teaches his eye why Beauty was ever painted with Loves and Graces attending her steps. Her existence makes the world rich. Though she extrudes all other persons from his attention as cheap and unworthy, yet she indemnifies him by carrying out her own being into somewhat impersonal, large, mundane, so that the maiden stands to him for a representative of all select things and virtues. For that reason the lover sees never personal resemblances in his mistress to her kindred or to others. His friends find in her a likeness to her mother, or her sisters, or to persons not of her blood. The lover sees no resemblance except to summer evenings and diamond mornings, to rainbows and the song of birds.

Beauty is ever that divine thing the ancients esteemed it. It is, they said, the flowering of virtue. Who can analyze the nameless charm which glances from one and another face and form ? We are touched with emotions of tenderness and complacency, but we cannot find whereat this dainty emotion, this wandering gleam point. It is destroyed for the imagination by any attempt to refer it to organization. Nor does it point to any relations of friendship or love that society knows and has, but, as it seems to me, to a quite other and unattainable sphere, to relations of transcendant delicacy and sweetness, a true faerie land ; to what roses and violets hint and foreshow. We cannot get at beauty. Its nature is like opaline doves'-neck lustres, hovering and evanescent. Herein it re-

sembles the most excellent things, which all have this
rainbow character, defying all attempts at appropriation and use.   What else did Jean Paul Richter signify, when he said to music, " Away ! away ! thou
speakest to me of things which in all my endless life
I have found not, and shall not find."   The same fact
may be observed in every work of the plastic arts.
The statue is then beautiful, when it begins to be in-
comprehensible, when it is passing out of criticism,
and can no longer be defined by compass and measuring wand, but demands an active imagination to go
with it, and to say what it is in the act of doing.   The
god or hero of the sculptor is always represented in a
transition *from* that which is representable to the
senses, *to* that which is not.   Then first it ceases to
be a stone.   The same remark holds of painting.
And of poetry, the success is not attained when it lulls
and satisfies, but when it astonishes and fires us with
new endeavors after the unattainable.   Concerning it,
Landor inquires " whether it is not to be referred to
some purer state of sensation and existence."

So must it be with personal beauty, which love worships.   Then first is it charming and itself, when it
dissatisfies us with any end ; when it becomes a story
without an end ; when it suggests gleams and visions,
and not earthly satisfactions ; when it seems

> " too bright and good,
> For human nature's daily food ; "

when it makes the beholder feel his unworthiness;
when he cannot feel his right to it, though he were

Cæsar; he cannot feel more right to it, than to the firmament and the splendors of a sunset.

Hence arose the saying, " If I love you, what is that to you?" We say so, because we feel that what we love, is not in your will, but above it. It is the radiance of you and not you. It is that which you know not in yourself, and can never know.

This agrees well with that high philosophy of Beauty which the ancient writers delighted in ; for they said, that the soul of man, embodied here on earth, went roaming up and down in quest of that other world of its own, out of which it came into this, but was soon stupefied by the light of the natural sun, and unable to see any other objects than those of this world, which are but shadows of real things. Therefore, the Deity sends the glory of youth before the soul, that it may avail itself of beautiful bodies as aids to its recollection of the celestial good and fair ; and the man beholding such a person in the female sex, runs to her, and finds the highest joy in contemplating the form, movement, and intelligence of this person, because it suggests to him the presence of that which indeed is within the beauty, and the cause of the beauty.

If, however, from too much conversing with material objects, the soul was gross, and misplaced its satisfaction in the body, it reaped nothing but sorrow ; body being unable to fulfil the promise which beauty holds out; but if, accepting the hint of these visions and suggestions which beauty makes to his mind, the soul passes through the body, and falls to admire strokes of character, and the lovers contemplate one another in their discourses and their actions, then, they pass to the true palace of Beauty, more and more inflame their love of it, and by this love extinguishing the base affection, as the sun puts out the fire by shining on the hearth, they become pure and hallowed. By conversation with that which is in itself excellent, magnanimous, lowly and just, the lover comes to a warmer love of these nobilities, and a quicker apprehension of them. Then, he passes from loving them in one, to loving them in all, and so is the one beautiful soul only the door through which he enters to the society of all true and pure souls. In the particular society of his mate, he attains a clearer sight of any spot, any taint, which her beauty has contracted from this world, and is able to point it out, and this with mutual joy that they are now able without offence to indicate blemishes and hindrances in each other, and give to each all help and comfort in curing the same. And, beholding in many souls the traits of the divine beauty, and separating in each soul that which is divine from the taint which they have contracted in the world, the lover ascends ever to the highest beauty, to the love and knowledge of the Divinity, by steps on this ladder of created souls.

Somewhat like this have the truly wise told us of love in all ages. The doctrine is not old, nor is it new. If Plato, Plutarch and Apuleius taught it, so have Petrarch, Angelo, and Milton. It awaits a truer unfolding in opposition and rebuke to that subterranean prudence which presides at marriages with

words that take hold of the upper world, whilst one
eye is eternally boring down into the cellar, so that
its gravest discourse has ever a slight savor of hams
and powdering-tubs. Worst, when the snout of this
sensualism intrudes into the education of young women, and withers the hope and affection of human
nature, by teaching, that marriage signifies nothing but
a housewife's thrift, and that woman's life has no
other aim.

But this dream of love, though beautiful, is only
one scene in our play. In the procession of the soul
from within outward, it enlarges its circles ever, like
the pebble thrown into the pond, or the light proceeding from an orb. The rays of the soul alight first on
things nearest, on every utensil and toy, on nurses
and domestics, on the house and yard and passengers,
on the circle of household acquaintance, on politics,
and geography, and history. But by the necessity of
our constitution, things are ever grouping themselves
according to higher or more interior laws. Neighborhood, size, numbers, habits, persons, lose by degrees their power over us. Cause and effect, real
affinities, the longing for harmony between the soul
and the circumstance, the high progressive idealizing
instinct, these predominate later, and ever the step
backward from the higher to the lower relations is
impossible. Thus even love, which is the deification
of persons, must become more impersonal every day.
Of this at first it gives no hint. Little think the youth
and maiden who are glancing at each other across
crowded rooms, with eyes so full of mutual intelli-

gence, — of the precious fruit long hereafter to proceed from this new, quite external stimulus. The
work of vegetation begins first in the irritability of
the bark and leaf-buds. From exchanging glances,
they advance to acts of courtesy, of gallantry, then
to fiery passion, to plighting troth and marriage.
Passion beholds its object as a perfect unit. The soul
is wholly embodied, and the body is wholly ensouled.

> " Her pure and eloquent blood
> Spoke in her cheeks, and so distinctly wrought,
> That one might almost say her body thought."

Romeo, if dead, should be cut up into little stars to
make the heavens fine. Life, with this pair, has no
other aim, asks no more than Juliet, — than Romeo.
Night, day, studies, talents, kingdoms, religion, are all
contained in this form full of soul, in this soul which
is all form. The lovers delight in endearments, in
avowals of love, in comparisons of their regards.
When alone, they solace themselves with the remembered image of the other. Does that other see the
same star ; the same melting cloud, read the same
book, feel the same emotion that now delight me ?
They try and weigh their affection, and adding up all
costly advantages, friends, opportunities, properties,
exult in discovering that willingly, joyfully, they
would give all as a ransom for the beautiful, the beloved head, not one hair of which shall be harmed.
But the lot of humanity is on these children. Danger, sorrow, and pain arrive to them, as to all. Love
prays. It makes covenants with Eternal Power, in
behalf of this dear mate. The union which is thus

effected, and which adds a new value to every atom
in nature, for it transmutes every thread throughout
the whole web of relation into a golden ray, and bathes
the soul in a new and sweeter element, is yet a temporary state.   Not always can flowers, pearls, poetry,
protestations, nor even home in another heart, content
the awful soul that dwells in clay.   It arouses itself
at last from these endearments, as toys, and puts on
the harness, and aspires to vast and universal aims.
The soul which is in the soul of each, craving for a
perfect beatitude, detects incongruities, defects, and
disproportion in the behavior of the other.   Hence
arises surprise, expostulation, and pain.   Yet that
which drew them to each other was signs of loveliness, signs of virtue : and these virtues are there,
however eclipsed.   They appear and reappear, and
continue to attract ; but the regard changes, quits the
sign, and attaches to the substance.   This repairs the
wounded affection.   Meantime, as life wears on, it
proves a game of permutation and combination of all
possible positions of the parties, to extort all the resources of each, and acquaint each with the whole
strength and weakness of the other.   For, it is the
nature and end of this relation, that they should represent the human race to each other.   All that is in
the world which is or ought to be known, is cunningly wrought into the texture of man, of woman.

> " The person love does to us fit,
> Like manna, has the taste of all in it."

The world rolls : the circumstances vary, every
hour.   All the angels that inhabit this temple of the

body appear at the windows, and all the gnomes and vices also. By all the virtues, they are united. If there be virtue, all the vices are known as such ; they confess and flee. Their once flaming regard is sobered by time in either breast, and losing in violence what it gains in extent, it becomes a thorough good understanding. They resign each other, without complaint, to the good offices which man and woman are severally appointed to discharge in time, and exchange the passion which once could not lose sight of its object, for a cheerful, disengaged furtherance, whether present or absent, of each other's designs. At last they discover that all which at first drew them together, — those once sacred features, that magical play of charms, — was deciduous, had a prospective end, like the scaffolding by which the house was built ; and the purification of the intellect and the heart, from year to year, is the real marriage, foreseen and prepared from the first, and wholly above their consciousness. Looking at these aims with which two persons, a man and a woman, so variously and correlatively gifted, are shut up in one house to spend in the nuptial society forty or fifty years, I do not wonder at the emphasis with which the heart prophesies this crisis from early infancy, at the profuse beauty with which the instincts deck the nuptial bower, and nature and intellect and art emulate each other in the gifts and the melody they bring to the epithalamium.

Thus are we put in training for a love which knows not sex, nor person, nor partiality, but which seeketh virtue and wisdom every where, to the end of increasing virtue and wisdom. We are by nature observers, and thereby learners. That is our permanent state. But we are often made to feel that our affections are but tents of a night. Though slowly and with pain, the objects of the affections change, as the objects of thought do. There are moments when the affections rule and absorb the man, and make his happiness dependent on a person or persons. But in health the mind is presently seen again, — its overarching vault, bright with galaxies of immutable lights, and the warm loves and fears that swept over us as clouds, must lose their finite character, and blend with God, to attain their own perfection. But we need not fear that we can lose any thing by the progress of the soul. The soul may be trusted to the end. That which is so beautiful and attractive as these relations, must be succeeded and supplanted only by what is more beautiful, and so on for ever.

FRIENDSHIP.

ESSAY VI.

FRIENDSHIP.

––––––

We have a great deal more kindness than is ever spoken. Maugre all the selfishness that chills like east winds the world, the whole human family is bathed with an element of love like a fine ether. How many persons we meet in houses, whom we scarcely speak to, whom yet we honor, and who honor us! How many we see in the street, or sit with in church, whom, though silently, we warmly rejoice to be with! Read the language of these wandering eye-beams. The heart knoweth.

The effect of the indulgence of this human affection is a certain cordial exhilaration. In poetry, and in common speech, the emotions of benevolence and complacency which are felt towards others, are likened to the material effects of fire ; so swift, or much more swift, more active, more cheering are these fine inward irradiations. From the highest

degree of passionate love, to the lowest degree of
good will, they make the sweetness of life.

Our intellectual and active powers increase with
our affection. The scholar sits down to write, and all
his years of meditation do not furnish him with one
good thought or happy expression ; but it is necessary
to write a letter to a friend, — and, forthwith, troops of
gentle thoughts invest themselves, on every hand, with
chosen words. See in any house where virtue and
self-respect abide, the palpitation which the approach
of a stranger causes. A commended stranger is expected and announced, and an uneasiness betwixt
pleasure and pain invades all the hearts of a household. His arrival almost brings fear to the good
hearts that would welcome him. The house is dusted,
all things fly into their places, the old coat is exchanged for the new, and they must get up a dinner if
they can. Of a commended stranger, only the good
report is told by others, only the good and new is
heard by us. He stands to us for humanity. He is,
what we wish. Having imagined and invested him,
we ask how we should stand related in conversation
and action with such a man, and are uneasy with
fear. The same idea exalts conversation with him.
We talk better than we are wont. We have the
nimblest fancy, a richer memory, and our dumb
devil has taken leave for the time. For long hours
we can continue a series of sincere, graceful, rich
communications, drawn from the oldest, secretest experience, so that they who sit by, of our own kins-
folk and acquaintance, shall feel a lively surprise at

our unusual powers. But as soon as the stranger begins to intrude his partialities, his definitions, his defects, into the conversation, it is all over. He has
heard the first, the last and best, he will ever hear
from us. He is no stranger now. Vulgarity, ignorance, misapprehension, are old acquaintances. Now,
when he comes, he may get the order, the dress, and
the dinner, — but the throbbing of the heart, and the
communications of the soul, no more.

Pleasant are these jets of affection which relume
a young world for me again. Delicious is a just and
firm encounter of two, in a thought, in a feeling.
How beautiful, on their approach to this beating heart,
the steps and forms of the gifted and the true ! The
moment we indulge our affections, the earth is meta-
morphosed : there is no winter, and no night : all
tragedies, all ennuis vanish ; — all duties even ; nothing fills the proceeding eternity but the forms all
radiant of beloved persons. Let the soul be assured
that somewhere in the universe it should rejoin its
friend, and it would be content and cheerful alone for
a thousand years.

I awoke this morning with devout thanksgiving for
my friends, the old and the new. Shall I not call
God, the Beautiful, who daily showeth himself so to
me in his gifts ? I chide society, I embrace solitude,
and yet I am not so ungrateful as not to see the wise,
the lovely, and the noble-minded, as from time to
time they pass my gate. Who hears me, who understands me, becomes mine, — a possession for all time.
Nor is nature so poor, but she gives me this joy seve-

ral times, and thus we weave social threads of our
own, a new web of relations ; and, as many thoughts
in succession substantiate themselves, we shall by-and-
by stand in a new world of our own creation, and no
longer strangers and pilgrims in a traditionary globe.
My friends have come to me unsought. The great
God gave them to me. By oldest right, by the divine
affinity of virtue with itself, I find them, or rather,
not I, but the Deity in me and in them, both deride
and cancel the thick walls of individual character, relation, age, sex and circumstance, at which he usually
connives, and now makes many one. High thanks I
owe you, excellent lovers, who carry out the world
for me to new and noble depths, and enlarge the
meaning of all my thoughts. These are not stark
and stiffened persons, but the new-born poetry of
God, — poetry without stop, — hymn, ode, and epic,
poetry still flowing, and not yet caked in dead books
with annotation and grammar, but Apollo and the
Muses chanting still. Will these too separate themselves from me again, or some of them ? I know
not, but I fear it not ; for my relation to them is so
pure, that we hold by simple affinity, and the Genius
of my life being thus social, the same affinity will
exert its energy on whomsoever is as noble as these
men and women, wherever I may be.

I confess to an extreme tenderness of nature on
this point. It is almost dangerous to me to " crush
the sweet poison of misused wine " of the affections.
A new person is to me always a great event, and
hinders me from sleep. I have had such fine fancies

lately about two or three persons, as have given me delicious hours ; but the joy ends in the day : it yields no fruit. Thought is not born of it ; my action is very little modified. I must feel pride in my friend's accomplishments as if they were mine, — wild, delicate, throbbing property in his virtues. I feel as warmly when he is praised, as the lover when he hears applause of his engaged maiden. We over-estimate the conscience of our friend. His goodness seems better than our goodness, his nature finer, his temptations less. Every thing that is his, his name, his form, his dress, books, and instruments, fancy en-hances. Our own thought sounds new and larger from his mouth.

Yet the systole and diastole of the heart are not without their analogy in the ebb and flow of love. Friendship, like the immortality of the soul, is too good to be believed. The lover, beholding his maid-en, half knows that she is not verily that which he worships ; and in the golden hour of friendship, we are surprised with shades of suspicion and unbelief. We doubt that we bestow on our hero the virtues in which he shines, and afterwards worship the form to which we have ascribed this divine inhabitation. In strictness, the soul does not respect men as it respects itself. In strict science, all persons underlie the same condition of an infinite remoteness. Shall we fear to cool our love by facing the fact, by mining for the me-taphysical foundation of this Elysian temple ? Shall I not be as real as the things I see ? If I am, I shall not fear to know them for what they are. Their essence is not less beautiful than their appearance, though it needs finer organs for its apprehension. The root of the plant is not unsightly to science, though for chaplets and festoons we cut the stem short. And I must hazard the production of the bald fact amidst these pleasing reveries, though it should prove an Egyptian skull at our banquet. A man who stands united with his thought, conceives magnificently of himself. He is conscious of a universal success, even though bought by uniform particular failures. No advantages, no powers, no gold or force can be any match for him. I cannot choose but rely on my own poverty, more than on your wealth. I cannot make your consciousness tantamount to mine. Only the star dazzles ; the planet has a faint, moon-like ray. I hear what you say of the admirable parts and tried temper of the party you praise, but I see well that for all his purple cloaks I shall not like him, unless he is at last a poor Greek like me. I cannot deny it, O friend, that the vast shadow of the Phenomenal includes thee, also, in its pied and painted immensity, — thee, also, compared with whom all else is shadow. Thou art not Being, as Truth is, as Justice is, — thou art not my soul, but a picture and effigy of that. Thou hast come to me lately, and already thou art seizing thy hat and cloak. Is it not that the soul puts forth friends, as the tree puts forth leaves, and presently, by the germination of new buds, extrudes the old leaf? The law of nature is alternation forevermore. Each electrical state superinduces the opposite. The soul environs itself with friends, that it may enter into a grander self-acquaintance or solitude ; and it goes alone, for a season, that it may exalt its conversation or society. This method betrays itself along the whole history of our personal relations. Ever the instinct of affection revives the hope of union with our mates, and ever the returning sense of insulation recalls us from the chase. Thus every man passes his life in the search after friendship, and if he should record his true sentiment, he might write a letter like this, to each new candidate for his love.

DEAR FRIEND,

If I was sure of thee, sure of thy capacity, sure to match my mood with thine, I should never think again of trifles, in relation to thy comings and goings. I am not very wise : my moods are quite attainable : and I respect thy genius : it is to me as yet unfathomed ; yet dare I not presume in thee a perfect intelligence of me, and so thou art to me a delicious torment. Thine ever, or never.

Yet these uneasy pleasures and fine pains are for curiosity, and not for life. They are not to be indulged. This is to weave cobweb, and not cloth. Our friendships hurry to short and poor conclusions, because we have made them a texture of wine and dreams, instead of the tough fibre of the human heart. The laws of friendship are great, austere, and eternal, of one web with the laws of nature and of morals. But we have aimed at a swift and petty benefit, to suck a sudden sweetness. We snatch at the slow-est fruit in the whole garden of God, which many summers and many winters must ripen. We seek our friend not sacredly, but with an adulterate passion which would appropriate him to ourselves. In vain. We are armed all over with subtle antagonisms, which, as soon as we meet, begin to play, and translate all poetry into stale prose. Almost all people descend to meet. All association must be a compromise, and, what is worst, the very flower and aroma of the flower of each of the beautiful natures disappears as they approach each other. What a perpetual disappointment is actual society, even of the virtuous and gifted! After interviews have been compassed with long foresight, we must be tormented presently by baffled blows, by sudden, unseasonable apathies, by epilepsies of wit and of animal spirits, in the hey-day of friendship and thought. Our faculties do not play us true, and both parties are relieved by solitude.

I ought to be equal to every relation. It makes no difference how many friends I have, and what content I can find in conversing with each, if there be one to whom I am not equal. If I have shrunk unequal from one contest, instantly the joy I find in all the rest becomes mean and cowardly. I should hate myself, if then I made my other friends my asylum.

> "The valiant warrior famoused for fight,
> After a hundred victories, once foiled,
> Is from the book of honor razed quite,
> And all the rest forgot for which he toiled."

Our impatience is thus sharply rebuked. Bashfulness and apathy are a tough husk in which a delicate organization is protected from premature ripening. It would be lost if it knew itself before any of the best souls were yet ripe enough to know and own it. Respect the *naturlangsamkeit* which hardens the ruby in a million years, and works in duration, in which Alps and Andes come and go as rainbows. The good spirit of our life has no heaven which is the price of rashness. Love, which is the essence of God, is not for levity, but for the total worth of man. Let us not have this childish luxury in our regards ; but the austerest worth ; let us approach our friend with an audacious trust in the truth of his heart, in the breadth, impossible to be overturned, of his foundations.

The attractions of this subject are not to be resisted, and I leave, for the time, all account of subordinate social benefit, to speak of that select and sacred relation which is a kind of absolute, and which even leaves the language of love suspicious and common, so much is this purer, and nothing is so much divine.

I do not wish to treat friendships daintily, but with roughest courage. When they are real, they are not glass threads or frost-work, but the solidest thing we know. For now, after so many ages of experience, what do we know of nature, or of ourselves? Not one step has man taken toward the solution of the problem of his destiny. In one condemnation of folly stand the whole universe of men. But the sweet sincerity of joy and peace, which I draw from this alliance with my brother's soul, is the nut itself

whereof all nature and all thought is but the husk and
shell.   Happy is the house that shelters a friend !   It
might well be built, like a festal bower or arch, to entertain him a single day.   Happier, if he know the
solemnity of that relation, and honor its law ! It is no
idle band, no holiday engagement.   He who offers
himself a candidate for that covenant, comes up, like an
Olympian, to the great games, where the first-born of the
world are the competitors.   He proposes himself for
contests where Time, Want, Danger are in the lists,
and he alone is victor who has truth enough in his
constitution to preserve the delicacy of his beauty
from the wear and tear of all these.   The gifts of fortune may be present or absent, but all the hap in that
contest depends on intrinsic nobleness, and the contempt of trifles.   There are two elements that go to
the composition of friendship, each so sovereign, that
I can detect no superiority in either, no reason why
either should be first named.   One is Truth.   A
friend is a person with whom I may be sincere.   Before him, I may think aloud.   I am arrived at last in
the presence of a man so real and equal, that I may
drop even those undermost garments of dissimulation,
courtesy, and second thought, which men never put
off, and may deal with him with the simplicity and
wholeness, with which one chemical atom meets another.   Sincerity is the luxury allowed, like diadems
and authority, only to the highest rank, *that* being permitted to speak truth, as having none above it to court
or conform unto.   Every man alone is sincere.   At
the entrance of a second person, hypocrisy begins.

We parry and fend the approach of our fellow man by compliments, by gossip, by amusements, by affairs. We cover up our thought from him under a hundred folds. I knew a man who, under a certain religious frenzy, cast off this drapery, and omitting all compliment and commonplace, spoke to the conscience of every person he encountered, and that with great insight and beauty. At first he was resisted, and all men agreed he was mad. But persisting, as indeed he could not help doing, for some time in this course, he attained to the advantage of bringing every man of his acquaintance into true relations with him. No man would think of speaking falsely with him, or of putting him off with any chat of markets or reading-rooms. But every man was constrained by so much sincerity to face him, and what love of nature, what poetry, what symbol of truth he had, he did certainly show him. But to most of us society shows not its face and eye, but its side and its back. To stand in true relations with men in a false age, is worth a fit of insanity, is it not? We can seldom go erect. Almost every man we meet requires some civility, requires to be humored; — he has some fame, some talent, some whim of religion or philanthropy in his head that is not to be questioned, and so spoils all conversation with him. But a friend is a sane man who exercises not my ingenuity but me. My friend gives me entertainment without requiring me to stoop, or to lisp, or to mask myself. A friend, therefore, is a sort of paradox in nature. I who alone am, I who see nothing in nature

8

whose existence I can affirm with equal evidence to
my own, behold now the semblance of my being in
all its height, variety and curiosity, reiterated in a foreign form ; so that a friend may well be reckoned
the masterpiece of nature.

The other element of friendship is Tenderness.
We are holden to men by every sort of tie, by blood,
by pride, by fear, by hope, by lucre, by lust, by hate,
by admiration, by every circumstance and badge and
trifle, but we can scarce believe that so much character can subsist in another as to draw us by love. Can
another be so blessed, and we so pure, that we can offer
him tenderness ?   When a man becomes dear to me,
I have touched the goal of fortune.   I find very little
written directly to the heart of this matter in books.
And yet I have one text which I cannot choose but
remember.   My author says, " I offer myself faintly
and bluntly to those whose I effectually am, and tender myself least to him to whom I am the most devoted."   I wish that friendship should have feet, as
well as eyes and eloquence.   It must plant itself on
the ground, before it walks over the moon.   I wish it
to be a little of a citizen, before it is quite a cherub.
We chide the citizen because he makes love a commodity.   It is an exchange of gifts, of useful loans ;
it is good neighborhood ; it watches with the sick ; it
holds the pall at the funeral ; and quite loses sight of
the delicacies and nobility of the relation.   But
though we cannot find the god under this disguise of
a sutler, yet, on the other hand, we cannot forgive
the poet if he spins his thread too fine, and does not

substantiate his romance by the municipal virtues of justice, punctuality, fidelity and pity. I hate the prostitution of the name of friendship to signify modish and worldly alliances. I much prefer the company of plough-boys and tin-pedlars, to the silken and perfumed amity which only celebrates its days of encounter by a frivolous display, by rides in a curricle, and dinners at the best taverns. The end of friendship is a commerce the most strict and homely that can be joined ; more strict than any of which we have experience. It is for aid and comfort through all the relations and passages of life and death. It is fit for serene days, and graceful gifts, and country rambles, but also for rough roads and hard fare, shipwreck, poverty, and persecution. It keeps company with the sallies of the wit and the trances of religion. We are to dignify to each other the daily needs and offices of man's life, and embellish it by courage, wisdom and unity. It should never fall into something usual and settled, but should be alert and inventive, and add rhyme and reason to what was drudgery.

For perfect friendship it may be said to require natures so rare and costly, so well tempered each, and so happily adapted, and withal so circumstanced, (for even in that particular, a poet says, love demands that the parties be altogether paired,) that very seldom can its satisfaction be realized. It cannot subsist in its perfection, say some of those who are learned in this warm lore of the heart, betwixt more than two. I am not quite so strict in my terms, perhaps because I have never known so high a fellowship as others. I please my imagination more with a circle of godlike men and women variously related to each other, and between whom subsists a lofty intelligence. But I find this law of *one to one*, peremptory for conversation, which is the practice and consummation of friendship. Do not mix waters too much. The best mix as ill as good and bad. You shall have very useful and cheering discourse at several times with two several men, but let all three of you come together, and you shall not have one new and hearty word. Two may talk and one may hear, but three cannot take part in a conversation of the most sincere and searching sort. In good company there is never such discourse between two, across the table, as takes place when you leave them alone. In good company, the individuals at once merge their egotism into a social soul exactly cöextensive with the several consciousnesses there present. No partialities of friend to friend, no fondnesses of brother to sister, of wife to husband, are there pertinent, but quite otherwise. Only he may then speak who can sail on the common thought of the party, and not poorly limited to his own. Now this convention, which good sense demands, destroys the high freedom of great conversation, which requires an absolute running of two souls into one.

No two men but being left alone with each other, enter into simpler relations. Yet it is affinity that determines *which* two shall converse. Unrelated men give little joy to each other ; will never suspect the latent powers of each. We talk sometimes of a great talent for conversation, as if it were a permanent property in some individuals. Conversation is an evanescent relation, — no more. A man is reputed to have thought and eloquence ; he cannot, for all that, say a word to his cousin or his uncle. They accuse his silence with as much reason as they would blame the insignificance of a dial in the shade. In the sun it will mark the hour. Among those who enjoy his thought, he will regain his tongue.

Friendship requires that rare mean betwixt likeness and unlikeness, that piques each with the presence of power and of consent in the other party. Let me be alone to the end of the world, rather than that my friend should overstep by a word or a look his real sympathy. I am equally baulked by antagonism and by compliance. Let him not cease an instant to be himself. The only joy I have in his being mine, is that the *not mine* is *mine*. It turns the stomach, it blots the daylight ; where I looked for a manly furtherance, or at least a manly resistance, to find a mush of concession. Better be a nettle in the side of your friend than his echo. The condition which high friendship demands, is, ability to do without it. To be capable of that high office, requires great and sublime parts. There must be very two, before there can be very one. Let it be an alliance of two large formidable natures, mutually beheld, mutually feared, before yet they recognise the deep identity which beneath these disparities unites them.

He only is fit for this society who is magnanimous. He must be so, to know its law. He must be one who is sure that greatness and goodness are always

economy. He must be one who is not swift to intermeddle with his fortunes. Let him not dare to intermeddle with this. Leave to the diamond its ages to
grow, nor expect to accelerate the births of the eternal. Friendship demands a religious treatment. We
must not be wilful, we must not provide. We talk of
choosing our friends, but friends are self-elected.
Reverence is a great part of it. Treat your friend as
a spectacle. Of course, if he be a man, he has
merits that are not yours, and that you cannot honor,
if you must needs hold him close to your person.
Stand aside. Give those merits room. Let them
mount and expand. Be not so much his friend that
you can never know his peculiar energies, like fond
mammas who shut up their boy in the house until he
is almost grown a girl. Are you the friend of your
friend's buttons, or of his thought? To a great heart
he will still be a stranger in a thousand particulars,
that he may come near in the holiest ground. Leave
it to girls and boys to regard a friend as property, and
to suck a short and all-confounding pleasure instead
of the pure nectar of God.

Let us buy our entrance to this guild by a long probation. Why should we desecrate noble and beautiful souls by intruding on them? Why insist on rash
personal relations with your friend? Why go to his
house, or know his mother and brother and sisters?
Why be visited by him at your own? Are these
things material to our covenant? Leave this touch-
ing and clawing. Let him be to me a spirit. A mes-
sage, a thought, a sincerity, a glance from him, I

want, but not news, nor pottage. I can get politics, and chat, and neighborly conveniences, from cheaper companions. Should not the society of my friend be to me poetic, pure, universal, and great as nature itself? Ought I to feel that our tie is profane in comparison with yonder bar of cloud that sleeps on the horizon, or that clump of waving grass that divides the brook? Let us not vilify but raise it to that standard. That great defying eye, that scornful beauty of his mien and action, do not pique yourself on reducing, but rather fortify and enhance. Worship his superiorities. Wish him not less by a thought, but hoard and tell them all. Guard him as thy great counterpart; have a princedom to thy friend. Let him be to thee forever a sort of beautiful enemy, untamable, devoutly revered, and not a trivial conveniency to be soon outgrown and cast aside. The hues of the opal, the light of the diamond, are not to be seen, if the eye is too near. To my friend I write a letter, and from him I receive a letter. That seems to you a little. Me it suffices. It is a spiritual gift worthy of him to give and of me to receive. It profanes nobody. In these warm lines the heart will trust itself, as it will not to the tongue, and pour out the prophecy of a godlier existence than all the annals of heroism have yet made good.

Respect so far the holy laws of this fellowship as not to prejudice its perfect flower by your impatience for its opening. We must be our own, before we can be another's. There is at least this satisfaction in crime, according to the Latin proverb; you can speak to your accomplice on even terms. *Crimen quos inquinat, æquat.* To those whom we admire and love, at first we cannot. Yet the least defect of self-possession vitiates, in my judgment, the entire relation. There can never be deep peace between two spirits, never mutual respect until, in their dialogue, each stands for the whole world.

What is so great as friendship, let us carry with what grandeur of spirit we can. Let us be silent, — so we may hear the whisper of the gods. Let us not interfere. Who set you to cast about what you should say to the select souls, or to say any thing to such? No matter how ingenious, no matter how graceful and bland. There are innumerable degrees of folly and wisdom, and for you to say aught is to be frivolous. Wait, and thy soul shall speak. Wait until the necessary and everlasting overpowers you, until day and night avail themselves of your lips. The only money of God is God. He pays never with any thing less or any thing else. The only reward of virtue, is virtue: the only way to have a friend, is to be one. Vain to hope to come nearer a man by getting into his house. If unlike, his soul only flees the faster from you, and you shall catch never a true glance of his eye. We see the noble afar off, and they repel us; why should we intrude? Late — very late — we perceive that no arrangements, no introductions, no consuetudes, or habits of society, would be of any avail to establish us in such relations with them as we desire, — but solely the uprise of nature in us to the same degree it is in them: then shall we meet as water with water : and if we should not meet them then, we shall not want them, for we are already they. In the last analysis, love is only the reflection of a man's own worthiness from other men. Men have sometimes exchanged names with their friends, as if they would signify that in their friend each loved his own soul.

The higher the style we demand of friendship, of course the less easy to establish it with flesh and blood. We walk alone in the world. Friends, such as we desire, are dreams and fables. But a sublime hope cheers ever the faithful heart, that elsewhere, in other regions of the universal power, souls are now acting, enduring, and daring, which can love us, and which we can love. We may congratulate ourselves that the period of nonage, of follies, of blunders, and of shame, is passed in solitude, and when we are finished men, we shall grasp heroic hands in heroic hands. Only be admonished by what you already see, not to strike leagues of friendship with cheap persons, where no friendship can be. Our impatience betrays us into rash and foolish alliances which no God attends. By persisting in your path, though you forfeit the little, you gain the great. You become pronounced. You demonstrate yourself, so as to put yourself out of the reach of false relations, and you draw to you the first-born of the world, — those rare pilgrims whereof only one or two wander in nature at once, and before whom the vulgar great, show as spectres and shadows merely.

It is foolish to be afraid of making our ties too

8*

spiritual, as if so we could lose any genuine love. Whatever correction of our popular views we make from insight, nature will be sure to bear us out in, and though it seem to rob us of some joy, will repay us with a greater. Let us feel, if we will, the absolute insulation of man. We are sure that we have all in us. We go to Europe, or we pursue persons, or we read books, in the instinctive faith that these will call it out and reveal us to ourselves. Beggars all. The persons are such as we ; the Europe, an old faded garment of dead persons ; the books, their ghosts. Let us drop this idolatry. Let us give over this mendicancy. Let us even bid our dearest friends farewell, and defy them, saying, ' Who are you ? Unhand me : I will be dependent no more.' Ah ! seest thou not, O brother, that thus we part only to meet again on a higher platform, and only be more each other's, because we are more our own ? A friend is Janusfaced : he looks to the past and the future. He is the child of all my foregoing hours, the prophet of those to come. He is the harbinger of a greater friend. It is the property of the divine to be reproductive.

I do then with my friends as I do with my books. I would have them where I can find them, but I seldom use them. We must have society on our own terms, and admit or exclude it on the slightest cause. I cannot afford to speak much with my friend. If he is great, he makes me so great that I cannot descend to converse. In the great days, presentiments hover before me, far before me in the firmament. I ought then to dedicate myself to them. I go in that I may seize them, I go out that I may seize them. I fear only that I may lose them receding into the sky in which now they are only a patch of brighter light. Then, though I prize my friends, I cannot afford to talk with them and study their visions, lest I lose my own. It would indeed give me a certain household joy to quit this lofty seeking, this spiritual astronomy, or search of stars, and come down to warm sympathies with you; but then I know well I shall mourn always the vanishing of my mighty gods. It is true, next week I shall have languid times, when I can well afford to occupy myself with foreign objects; then I shall regret the lost literature of your mind, and wish you were by my side again. But if you come, perhaps you will fill my mind only with new visions, not with yourself but with your lustres, and I shall not be able any more than now to converse with you. So I will owe to my friends this evanescent intercourse. I will receive from them not what they have, but what they are. They shall give me that which properly they cannot give me, but which radiates from them. But they shall not hold me by any relations less subtle and pure. We will meet as though we met not, and part as though we parted not.

It has seemed to me lately more possible than I knew, to carry a friendship greatly, on one side, without due correspondence on the other. Why should I cumber myself with the poor fact that the receiver is not capacious? It never troubles the sun that some of his rays fall wide and vain into ungrateful space, and only a small part on the reflecting planet. Let your greatness educate the crude and cold companion. If he is unequal, he will presently pass away, but thou art enlarged by thy own shining ; and, no longer a mate for frogs and worms, dost soar and burn with the gods of the empyrean. It is thought a disgrace to love unrequited. But the great will see that true love cannot be unrequited. True love transcends instantly the unworthy object, and dwells and broods on the eternal, and when the poor, interposed mask crumbles, it is not sad, but feels rid of so much earth, and feels its independency the surer. Yet these things may hardly be said without a sort of treachery to the relation. The essence of friendship is entireness, a total magnanimity and trust. It must not surmise or provide for infirmity. It treats its object as a god, that it may deify both.

PRUDENCE.

ESSAY VII.

PRUDENCE.

WHAT right have I to write on Prudence, whereof I
have little, and that of the negative sort? My prudence consists in avoiding and going without, not in
the inventing of means and methods, not in adroit
steering, not in gentle repairing. I have no skill to
make money spend well, no genius in my economy,
and whoever sees my garden, discovers that I must
have some other garden. Yet I love facts, and hate
lubricity, and people without perception. Then I
have the same title to write on prudence, that I have
to write on poetry or holiness. We write from
aspiration and antagonism, as well as from experience. We paint those qualities which we do not
possess. The poet admires the man of energy and
tactics; the merchant breeds his son for the church
or the bar: and where a man is not vain and egotis-
tic, you shall find what he has not, by his praise.

Moreover, it would be hardly honest in me not to balance these fine lyric words of Love and Friendship with words of coarser sound, and whilst my debt to my senses is real and constant, not to own it in passing.

Prudence is the virtue of the senses. It is the science of appearances. It is the outmost action of the inward life. It is God taking thought for oxen. It moves matter after the laws of matter. It is content to seek health of body by complying with physical conditions, and health of mind by the laws of the intellect.

The world of the senses is a world of shows ; it does not exist for itself, but has a symbolic character ; and a true prudence or law of shows, recognises the co-presence of other laws ; and knows that its own office is subaltern ; knows that it is surface and not centre where it works. Prudence is false when detached. It is legitimate when it is the Natural History of the soul incarnate ; when it unfolds the beauty of laws within the narrow scope of the senses.

There are all degrees of proficiency in knowledge of the world. It is sufficient, to our present purpose, to indicate three. One class lives to the utility of the symbol ; esteeming health and wealth a final good. Another class live above this mark to the beauty of the symbol ; as the poet, and artist, and the naturalist, and man of science. A third class live above the beauty of the symbol to the beauty of the thing signified ; these are wise men. The first class have common sense ; the second, taste ; and the third, spiritual perception. Once in a long time, a man traverses the whole scale, and sees and enjoys the symbol solidly ; then also has a clear eye for its beauty, and, lastly, whilst he pitches his tent on this sacred volcanic isle of nature, does not offer to build houses and barns thereon, reverencing the splendor of the God which he sees bursting through each chink and cranny.

The world is filled with the proverbs and acts and winkings of a base prudence, which is a devotion to matter as if we possessed no other faculties than the palate, the nose, the touch, the eye and ear ; a prudence which adores the Rule of Three, which never subscribes, which gives never, which lends seldom, and asks but one question of any project — Will it bake bread ? This is a disease like a thickening of the skin until the vital organs are destroyed. But culture, revealing the high origin of the apparent world, and aiming at the perfection of the man as the end, degrades every thing else, as health and bodily life, into means. It sees prudence not to be a several faculty, but a name for wisdom and virtue conversing with the body and its wants. Cultivated men always feel and speak so, as if a great fortune, the achievement of a civil or social measure, great personal influence, a graceful and commanding address had their value as proofs of the energy of the spirit. If a man lose his balance, and immerse himself in any trades or pleasures for their own sake, he may be a good wheel or pin, but he is not a cultivated man.

The spurious prudence, making the senses final, is the god of sots and cowards, and is the subject of

all comedy. It is nature's joke, and therefore literature's. The true prudence limits this sensualism by
admitting the knowledge of an internal and real
world. This recognition once made, — the order of
the world and the distribution of affairs and times being studied with the co-perception of their subordinate
place, will reward any degree of attention. For, our
existence thus apparently attached in nature to the
sun and the returning moon and the periods which
they mark ; so susceptible to climate and to country,
so alive to social good and evil, so fond of splendor,
and so tender to hunger and cold and debt, — reads
all its primary lessons out of these books.

Prudence does not go behind nature, and ask,
whence it is ? It takes the laws of the world whereby
man's being is conditioned, as they are, and keeps
these laws, that it may enjoy their proper good. It
respects space and time, climate, want, sleep, the law
of polarity, growth and death. There revolve to
give bound and period to his being, on all sides, the
sun and moon, the great formalists in the sky : here
lies stubborn matter, and will not swerve from its
chemical routine. Here is a planted globe, pierced
and belted with natural laws, and fenced and distributed externally with civil partitions and properties
which impose new restraints on the young inhabitant.

We eat of the bread which grows in the field.
We live by the air which blows around us, and we
are poisoned by the air that is too cold or too hot,
too dry or too wet. Time, which shows so vacant, indivisible and divine in its coming, is slit and

peddled into trifles and tatters. A door is to be painted, a lock to be repaired. I want wood, or oil, or meal, or salt; the house smokes, or I have a head ache; then the tax; and an affair to be transacted with a man without heart or brains; and the stinging recollection of an injurious or very awkward word, — these eat up the hours. Do what we can, summer will have its flies. If we walk in the woods, we must feed musquitoes. If we go a fishing, we must expect a wet coat. Then climate is a great impediment to idle persons. We often resolve to give up the care of the weather, but still we regard the clouds and the rain.

We are instructed by these petty experiences which usurp the hours and years. The hard soil and four months of snow make the inhabitant of the northern temperate zone wiser and abler than his fellow who enjoys the fixed smile of the tropics. The islander may ramble all day at will. At night, he may sleep on a mat under the moon, and wherever a wild date-tree grows, nature has, without a prayer even, spread a table for his morning meal. The northerner is perforce a householder. He must brew, bake, salt and preserve his food. He must pile wood and coal. But as it happens that not one stroke can labor lay to, without some new acquaintance with nature; and as nature is inexhaustibly significant, the inhabitants of these climates have always excelled the southerner in force. Such is the value of these matters, that a man who knows other things, can never know too much of these. Let him have accurate perceptions. Let him, if he have hands, handle ; if eyes, measure and discriminate ; let him accept and hive every fact of chemistry, natural history, and economics ; the more he has, the less is he willing to spare any one. Time is always bringing the occasions that disclose their value. Some wisdom comes out of every natural and innocent action. The domestic man, who loves no music so well as his kitchen clock, and the airs which the logs sing to him as they burn on the hearth, has solaces which others never dream of. The application of means to ends, ensures victory and the songs of victory not less in a farm or a shop, than in the tactics of party, or of war. The good husband finds method as efficient in the packing of fire-wood in a shed, or in the harvesting of fruits in the cellar, as in Peninsular campaigns or the files of the Department of State. In the rainy day he builds a work-bench, or gets his tool-box set in the corner of the barn-chamber, and stored with nails, gimlet, pincers, screwdriver, and chisel. Herein he tastes an old joy of youth and childhood, the cat-like love of garrets, presses, and corn-chambers, and of the conveniences of long housekeeping. His garden or his poultry-yard, — very paltry places, it may be, — tell him many pleasant anecdotes. One might find argument for optimism, in the abundant flow of this saccharine element of pleasure, in every suburb and extremity of the good world. Let a man keep the law, — any law, — and his way will be strown with satisfactions. There is more difference in the quality of our pleasures than in the amount.

On the other hand, nature punishes any neglect of

prudence. If you think the senses final, obey their law. If you believe in the soul, do not clutch at sensual sweetness before it is ripe on the slow tree of cause and effect. It is vinegar to the eyes, to deal with men of loose and imperfect perception. Dr. Johnson is reported to have said, "If the child says, he looked out of this window, when he looked out of that, — whip him." Our American character is marked by a more than average delight in accurate perception, which is shown by the currency of the by-word, "No mistake." But the discomfort of unpunctuality, of confusion of thought about facts, of inattention to the wants of to-morrow, is of no nation. The beautiful laws of time and space once dislocated by our inaptitude, are holes and dens. If the hive be disturbed by rash and stupid hands, instead of honey, it will yield us bees. Our words and actions to be fair, must be timely. A gay and pleasant sound is the whetting of the scythe in the mornings of June ; yet what is more lonesome and sad than the sound of a whetstone or mower's rifle, when it is too late in the season to make hay ? Scatter-brained and "afternoon men" spoil much more than their own affair, in spoiling the temper of those who deal with them. I have seen a criticism on some paintings, of which I am reminded, when I see the shiftless and unhappy men who are not true to their senses. The last Grand Duke of Weimar, a man of superior understanding, said ; "I have sometimes remarked in the presence of great works of art, and just now especially, in Dresden, how much a certain property contributes to the effect which gives life to the figures, and to the life an irresistible truth. This property is the hitting, in all the figures we draw, the right centre of gravity. I mean, the placing the figures firm upon their feet, making the hands grasp, and fastening the eyes on the spot where they should look. Even life-less figures, as vessels and stools, — let them be drawn ever so correctly, — lose all effect so soon as they lack the resting upon their centre of gravity, and have a certain swimming and oscillating appearance. The Raphael, in the Dresden gallery, (the only greatly affecting picture which I have seen), is the quietest and most passionless piece you can imagine ; a couple of saints who worship the Virgin and child. Nevertheless, it awakens a deeper impression than the contortions of ten crucified martyrs. For, beside all the resistless beauty of form, it possesses in the highest degree the property of the perpendicularity of all the figures." — This perpendicularity we demand of all the figures in this picture of life. Let them stand on their feet, and not float and swing. Let us know where to find them. Let them discriminate between what they remember, and what they dreamed. Let them call a spade a spade. Let them give us facts, and honor their own senses with trust.

But what man shall dare tax another with imprudence ? Who is prudent ? The men we call greatest are least in this kingdom. There is a certain fatal dislocation in our relation to nature, distorting all our modes of living, and making every law our enemy, which seems at last to have aroused all the wit and

virtue in the world to ponder the question of Reform.
We must call the highest prudence to counsel, and
ask why health and beauty and genius should now be
the exception, rather than the rule of human nature ?
We do not know the properties of plants and animals
and the laws of nature through our sympathy with
the same ; but this remains the dream of poets. Poetry and prudence should be coincident. Poets should
be lawgivers ; that is, the boldest lyric inspiration
should not chide and insult, but should announce and
lead the civil code, and the day's work. But now
the two things seem irreconcilably parted. We have
violated law upon law, until we stand amidst ruins,
and when by chance we espy a coincidence between
reason and the phenomena, we are surprised. Beauty
should be the dowry of every man and woman, as invariably as sensation ; but it is rare. Health or sound
organization should be universal. Genius should be
the child of genius, and every child should be inspired ; but now it is not to be predicted of any child,
and nowhere is it pure. We call partial half-lights,
by courtesy, genius; talent which converts itself to
money, talent which glitters to-day, that it may dine
and sleep well to-morrow ; and society is officered by
men of parts, as they are properly called, and not by
divine men. These use their gifts to refine luxury,
not to abolish it. Genius is always ascetic ; and piety
and love. Appetite shows to the finer souls as a disease, and they find beauty in rites and bounds that
resist it.

We have found out fine names to cover our sensu-

ality withal, but no gifts can raise intemperance.
The man of talent affects to call his transgressions of
the laws of the senses trivial, and to count them nothing
considered with his devotion to his art. His art rebukes
him. That never taught him lewdness, nor the love
of wine, nor the wish to reap where he had not sowed.
His art is less for every deduction from his holiness,
and less for every defect of common sense. On him
who scorned the world, as he said, the scorned world
wreaks its revenge. He that despiseth small things,
will perish by little and little. Goethe's Tasso is very
likely to be a pretty fair historical portrait, and that is
true tragedy. It does not seem to me so genuine
grief when some tyrannous Richard III. oppresses
and slays a score of innocent persons, as when An-
tonio and Tasso, both apparently right, wrong each
other. One living after the maxims of this world,
and consistent and true to them, the other fired with
all divine sentiments, yet grasping also at the pleasures of sense, without submitting to their law. That
is a grief we all feel, a knot we cannot untie. Tasso's
is no infrequent case in modern biography. A man
of genius, of an ardent temperament, reckless of physical laws, self-indulgent, becomes presently unfortu-
nate, querulous, a " discomfortable cousin," a thorn
to himself and to others.

The scholar shames us by his bifold life. Whilst
something higher than prudence is active, he is admirable ; when common sense is wanted, he is an in-
cumbrance. Yesterday, Cæsar was not so great ;
to-day, Job not so miserable. Yesterday, radiant

with the light of an ideal world, in which he lives, the first of men, and now oppressed by wants, and by sickness, for which he must thank himself, none is so poor to do him reverence. He resembles the opium eaters, whom travellers describe as frequenting the bazaars of Constantinople, who skulk about all day, the most pitiful drivellers, yellow, emaciated, ragged, and sneaking ; then, at evening, when the bazaars are open, they slink to the opium shop, swallow their morsel, and become tranquil, glorious, and great. And who has not seen the tragedy of imprudent genius, struggling for years with paltry pecuniary difficulties, at last sinking, chilled, exhausted, and fruitless, like a giant slaughtered by pins ?

Is it not better that a man should accept the first pains and mortifications of this sort, which nature is not slack in sending him, as hints that he must expect no other good than the just fruit of his own labor and self-denial ? Health, bread, climate, social position, have their importance, and he will give them their due. Let him esteem Nature a perpetual counsellor, and her perfections the exact measure of our deviations. Let him make the night, night, and the day, day. Let him control the habit of expense. Let him see that as much wisdom may be expended on a private economy, as on an empire, and as much wisdom may be drawn from it. The laws of the world are written out for him on every piece of money in his hand. There is nothing he will not be the better for knowing, were it only the wisdom of Poor Richard ; or the State-street prudence of buying by the acre, to sell by the foot; or the thrift of the agriculturist, to stick a tree between whiles, because it will grow whilst he sleeps; or the prudence which consists in husbanding little strokes of the tool, little portions of time, particles of stock, and small gains. The eye of prudence may never shut. Iron, if kept at the ironmonger's, will rust. Beer, if not brewed in the right state of the atmosphere, will sour. Timber of ships will rot at sea, or, if laid up high and dry, will strain, warp, and dry-rot. Money, if kept by us, yields no rent, and is liable to loss; if invested, is liable to depreciation of the particular kind of stock. Strike, says the smith, the iron is white. Keep the rake, says the haymaker, as nigh the scythe as you can, and the cart as nigh the rake. Our Yankee trade is reputed to be very much on the extreme of this prudence. It saves itself by its activity. It takes bank notes — good, bad, clean, ragged, and saves itself by the speed with which it passes them off. Iron cannot rust, nor beer sour, nor timber rot, nor calicoes go out of fashion, nor money stocks depreciate, in the few swift moments which the Yankee suffers any one of them to remain in his possession. In skating over thin ice, our safety is in our speed.

Let him learn a prudence of a higher strain. Let him learn that every thing in nature, even motes and feathers, go by law and not by luck, and that what he sows, he reaps. By diligence and self-command, let him put the bread he eats at his own disposal, and not at that of others, that he may not stand in bitter and false relations to other men; for the best good of wealth is freedom. Let him practise the minor virtues. How much of human life is lost in waiting! Let him not make his fellow creatures wait. How many words and promises are promises of conversation! Let his be words of fate. When he sees a folded and sealed scrap of paper float round the globe in a pine ship, and come safe to the eye for which it was written, amidst a swarming population; let him likewise feel the admonition to integrate his being across all these distracting forces, and keep a slender human word among the storms, distances, and accidents, that drive us hither and thither, and, by persistency, make the paltry force of one man reappear to redeem its pledge, after months and years, in the most distant climates.

We must not try to write the laws of any one virtue, looking at that only. Human nature loves no contradictions, but is symmetrical. The prudence which secures an outward well-being, is not to be studied by one set of men, whilst heroism and holiness are studied by another, but they are reconcilable. Prudence concerns the present time, persons, property, and existing forms. But as every fact hath its roots in the soul, and if the soul were changed, would cease to be, or would become some other thing, therefore, the proper administration of outward things will always rest on a just apprehension of their cause and origin, that is, the good man will be the wise man, and the single-hearted, the politic man. Every violation of truth is not only a sort of suicide in the liar, but is a stab at the health of human society.

On the most profitable lie, the course of events presently lays a destructive tax ; whilst frankness proves to be the best tactics, for it invites frankness, puts the parties on a convenient footing, and makes their business a friendship. Trust men, and they will be true to you ; treat them greatly, and they will show themselves great, though they make an exception in your favor to all their rules of trade.

So, in regard to disagreeable and formidable things, prudence does not consist in evasion, or in flight, but in courage. He who wishes to walk in the most peaceful parts of life with any serenity, must screw himself up to resolution. Let him front the object of his worst apprehension, and his stoutness will commonly make his fear groundless. The Latin proverb says, that " in battles, the eye is first overcome." The eye is daunted, and greatly exaggerates the perils of the hour. Entire self-possession may make a battle very little more dangerous to life than a match at foils or at foot-ball. Examples are cited by soldiers, of men who have seen the cannon pointed, and the fire given to it, and who have stepped aside from the path of the ball. The terrors of the storm are chiefly confined to the parlor and the cabin. The drover, the sailor, buffets it all day, and his health renews itself at as vigorous a pulse under the sleet, as under the sun of June.

In the occurrence of unpleasant things among neighbors, fear comes readily to heart, and magnifies the consequence of the other party ; but it is a bad counsellor. Every man is actually weak, and apparently strong. To himself, he seems weak ; to others, formidable. You are afraid of Grim ; but Grim also is afraid of you. You are solicitous of the good will of the meanest person, uneasy at his ill will. But the sturdiest offender of your peace and of the neighborhood, if you rip up *his* claims, is as thin and timid as any ; and the peace of society is often kept, because, as children say, one is afraid, and the other dares not. Far off, men swell, bully, and threaten : bring them hand to hand, and they are a feeble folk.

It is a proverb, that ' courtesy costs nothing ;' but calculation might come to value love for its profit. Love is fabled to be blind ; but kindness is necessary to perception ; love is not a hood, but an eye-water. If you meet a sectary, or a hostile partisan, never recognise the dividing lines ; but meet on what common ground remains, — if only that the sun shines, and the rain rains for both, — the area will widen very fast, and ere you know it, the boundary mountains, on which the eye had fastened, have melted into air. If he set out to contend, almost St. Paul will lie, almost St. John will hate. What low, poor, paltry, hypocritical people, an argument on religion will make of the pure and chosen souls. Shuffle they will, and crow, crook, and hide, feign to confess here, only that they may brag and conquer there, and not a thought has enriched either party, and not an emotion of bravery, modesty, or hope. So neither should you put yourself in a false position to your contemporaries, by indulging a vein of hostility and bitterness. Though your views are in straight antag-

onism to theirs, assume an identity of sentiment, assume that you are saying precisely that which all
think, and in the flow of wit and love, roll out your
paradoxes in solid column, with not the infirmity of
a doubt.   So at least shall you get an adequate deliverance.   The natural motions of the soul are so much
better than the voluntary ones, that you will never do
yourself justice in dispute.   The thought is not then
taken hold of by the right handle, does not show itself
proportioned, and in its true bearings, but bears extorted,
hoarse, and half witness.   But assume a consent, and
it shall presently be granted, since, really, and underneath all their external diversities, all men are of one
heart and mind.

Wisdom will never let us stand with any man or
men, on an unfriendly footing.   We refuse sympathy
and intimacy with people, as if we waited for some
better sympathy and intimacy to come.   But whence
and when ?   To-morrow will be like to-day.   Life
wastes itself whilst we are preparing to live.   Our
friends and fellow-workers die off from us.   Scarcely
can we say, we see new men, new women approaching us.   We are too old to regard fashion, too old to
expect patronage of any greater, or more powerful.
Let us suck the sweetness of those affections and
consuetudes that grow near us.   These old shoes are
easy to the feet.   Undoubtedly, we can easily pick
faults in our company, can easily whisper names
prouder, and that tickle the fancy more.   Every
man's imagination hath its friends ; and pleasant
would life be with such companions.   But, if you

cannot have them on good mutual terms, you cannot have them. If not the Deity, but our ambition hews and shapes the new relations, their virtue escapes, as strawberries lose their flavor in garden beds.

Thus truth, frankness, courage, love, humility, and all the virtues range themselves on the side of prudence, or the art of securing a present well-being. I do not know if all matter will be found to be made of one element, as oxygen or hydrogen, at last, but the world of manners and actions is wrought of one stuff, and begin where we will, we are pretty sure in a short space, to be mumbling our ten commandments.

HEROISM.

" Paradise is under the shadow of swords."
Mahomet.

9*

ESSAY VIII.

HEROISM.

––––––

In the elder English dramatists, and mainly in the plays of Beaumont and Fletcher, there is a constant recognition of gentility, as if a noble behavior were as easily marked in the society of their age, as color is in our American population. When any Rodrigo, Pedro, or Valerio enters, though he be a stranger, the duke or governor exclaims, This is a gentleman, — and proffers civilities without end; but all the rest are slag and refuse. In harmony with this delight in personal advantages, there is in their plays a certain heroic cast of character and dialogue, — as in Bonduca, Sophocles, the Mad Lover, the Double Marriage, — wherein the speaker is so earnest and cordial, and on such deep grounds of character, that the dialogue, on the slightest additional incident in the plot, rises naturally into poetry. Among many texts, take the following. The Roman Martius has conquered Athens, —

all but the invincible spirits of Sophocles, the duke of
Athens, and Dorigen, his wife. The beauty of the
latter inflames Martius, and he seeks to save her hus-
band ; but Sophocles will not ask his life, although
assured that a word will save him, and the execution
of both proceeds.

> *Valerius.* Bid thy wife farewell.
> *Soph.* No, I will take no leave. My Dorigen,
> Yonder, above, 'bout Ariadne's crown,
> My spirit shall hover for thee. Prithee, haste.
> *Dor.* Stay, Sophocles, — with this, tie up my sight ;
> Let not soft nature so transformed be,
> And lose her gentler sexed humanity,
> To make me see my lord bleed. So, 't is well ;
> Never one object underneath the sun
> Will I behold before my Sophocles :
> Farewell; now teach the Romans how to die.
> *Mar.* Dost know what 't is to die ?
> *Soph.* Thou dost not, Martius,
> And therefore, not what 't is to live ; to die
> Is to begin to live. It is to end
> An old, stale, weary work, and to commence
> A newer, and a better. 'T is to leave
> Deceitful knaves for the society
> Of gods and goodness. Thou, thyself, must part
> At last, from all thy garlands, pleasures, triumphs,
> And prove thy fortitude what then 't will do.
> *Val.* But art not grieved nor vexed to leave thy life thus ?
> *Soph.* Why should I grieve or vex for being sent
> To them I ever loved best ? Now I 'll kneel,
> But with my back toward thee ; ' tis the last duty
> This trunk can do the gods.
> *Mar.* Strike, strike, Valerius,
> Or Martius' heart will leap out at his mouth :
> This is a man, a woman ! Kiss thy lord,
> And live with all the freedom you were wont.

O love ! thou doubly hast afflicted me
With virtue and with beauty.   Treacherous heart,
My hand shall cast thee quick into my urn,
Ere thou transgress this knot of piety.
  Val.   What ails my brother ?
  Soph.   Martius, oh Martius,
Thou now hast found a way to conquer me.
  Dor.   O star of Rome ! what gratitude can speak
Fit words to follow such a deed as this ?
  Mar.   This admirable duke, Valerius,
With his disdain of fortune and of death,
Captived himself, has captivated me,
And though my arm hath ta'en his body here,
His soul hath subjugated Martius' soul.
By Romulus, he is all soul, I think ;
He hath no flesh, and spirit cannot be gyved ;
Then we have vanquished nothing ; he is free,
And Martius walks now in captivity.

I do not readily remember any poem, play, sermon, novel, or oration, that our press vents in the last few years, which goes to the same tune.   We have a great many flutes and flageolets, but not often the sound of any fife.   Yet, Wordsworth's Laodamia, and the ode of " Dion," and some sonnets, have a certain noble music ; and Scott will sometimes draw a stroke like the portrait of Lord Evandale, given by Balfour of Burley.   Thomas Carlyle, with his natural taste for what is manly and daring in character, has suffered no heroic trait in his favorites to drop from his biographical and historical pictures.   Earlier, Robert Burns has given us a song or two.   In the Harleian Miscellanies, there is an account of the battle of Lutzen, which deserves to be read.   And Simon Ockley's History of the Saracens, recounts the

prodigies of individual valor with admiration, all
the more evident on the part of the narrator, that he
seems to think that his place in Christian Oxford
requires of him some proper protestations of abhorrence.   But if we explore the literature of Heroism,
we shall quickly come to Plutarch, who is its Doctor
and historian.   To him we owe the Brasidas, the
Dion, the Epaminondas, the Scipio of old, and I must
think we are more deeply indebted to him than to all
the ancient writers.   Each of his " Lives " is a refu-
tation to the despondency and cowardice of our religious and political theorists.   A wild courage, a stoicism not of the schools, but of the blood, shines in
every anecdote, and has given that book its immense
fame.

We need books of this tart cathartic virtue, more
than books of political science, or of private economy.
Life is a festival only to the wise.   Seen from the
nook and chimney-side of prudence, it wears a ragged and dangerous front.   The violations of the laws
of nature by our predecessors and our contemporaries, are punished in us also.   The disease and deformity around us, certify the infraction of natural,
intellectual, and moral laws, and often violation on
violation to breed such compound misery.   A lock-
jaw, that bends a man's head back to his heels, hydro-
phobia, that makes him bark at his wife and babes,
insanity, that makes him eat grass; war, plague,
cholera, famine, indicate a certain ferocity in nature,
which, as it had its inlet by human crime, must have
its outlet by human suffering.   Unhappily, almost no

man exists, who has not in his own person, become to some amount, a stockholder in the sin, and so made himself liable to a share in the expiation.

Our culture, therefore, must not omit the arming of the man. Let him hear in season, that he is born into the state of war, and that the commonwealth and his own well-being, require that he should not go dancing in the weeds of peace, but warned, self-collected, and neither defying nor dreading the thunder, let him take both reputation and life in his hand, and with perfect urbanity, dare the gibbet and the mob by the absolute truth of his speech, and the rectitude of his behavior.

Towards all this external evil, the man within the breast assumes a warlike attitude, and affirms his ability to cope single-handed with the infinite army of enemies. To this military attitude of the soul, we give the name of Heroism. Its rudest form is the contempt for safety and ease, which makes the attractiveness of war. It is a self-trust which slights the restraints of prudence in the plenitude of its energy and power to repair the harms it may suffer. The hero is a mind of such balance that no disturbances can shake his will, but pleasantly, and, as it were, merrily, he advances to his own music, alike in frightful alarms, and in the tipsy mirth of universal dissoluteness. There is somewhat not philosophical in heroism ; there is somewhat not holy in it : it seems not to know that other souls are of one texture with it ; it hath pride ; it is the extreme of individual nature. Nevertheless, we must profoundly revere it.

There is somewhat in great actions, which does not allow us to go behind them. Heroism feels and never reasons, and therefore is always right, and, although a different breeding, different religion, and greater intellectual activity, would have modified, or even reversed the particular action, yet for the hero, that thing he does, is the highest deed, and is not open to the censure of philosophers or divines. It is the avowal of the unschooled man, that he finds a quality in him that is negligent of expense, of health, of life, of danger, of hatred, of reproach, and that he knows that his will is higher and more excellent than all actual and all possible antagonists.

Heroism works in contradiction to the voice of mankind, and in contradiction, for a time, to the voice of the great and good. Heroism is an obedience to a secret impulse of an individual's character. Now to no other man can its wisdom appear as it does to him, for every man must be supposed to see a little farther on his own proper path, than any one else. Therefore, just and wise men take umbrage at his act, until after some little time be past : then, they see it to be in unison with their acts. All prudent men see that the action is clean contrary to a sensual prosperity ; for every heroic act measures itself by its contempt of some external good. But it finds its own success at last, and then the prudent also extol.

Self-trust is the essence of heroism. It is the state of the soul at war, and its ultimate objects are the last defiance of falsehood and wrong, and the power to bear all that can be inflicted by evil agents. It speaks the truth, and it is just. It is generous, hospitable, temperate, scornful of petty calculations, and scornful of being scorned. It persists ; it is of an undaunted boldness, and of a fortitude not to be wearied out. Its jest is the littleness of common life. That false prudence which dotes on health and wealth, is the foil, the butt and merriment of heroism. Heroism, like Plotinus, is almost ashamed of its body. What shall it say, then, to the sugar-plums, and cats'-cradles, to the toilet, compliments, quarrels, cards, and custard, which rack the wit of all human society. What joys has kind nature provided for us dear creatures ! There seems to be no interval between greatness and meanness. When the spirit is not master of the world, then is it its dupe. Yet the little man takes the great hoax so innocently, works in it so headlong and believing, is born red, and dies gray, arranging his toilet, attending on his own health, laying traps for sweet food and strong wine, setting his heart on a horse or a rifle, made happy with a little gossip, or a little praise, that the great soul cannot choose but laugh at such earnest nonsense. " Indeed, these humble considerations make me out of love with greatness. What a disgrace is it to me to take note how many pairs of silk stockings thou hast, namely, these and those that were the peach-colored ones, or to bear the inventory of thy shirts, as one for superfluity, and one other for use."

Citizens, thinking after the laws of arithmetic, consider the inconvenience of receiving strangers at their fireside, reckon narrowly the loss of time and the unusual display : the soul of a better quality thrusts back the unseasonable economy into the vaults of life, and says, I will obey the God, and the sacrifice and the fire he will provide. Ibn Hankal, the Arabian geographer, describes a heroic extreme in the hospitality of Sogd, in Bukharia. " When I was in Sogd, I saw a great building, like a palace, the gates of which were open and fixed back to the wall with large nails. I asked the reason, and was told that the house had not been shut night or day, for a hundred years. Strangers may present themselves at any hour, and in whatever number ; the master has amply provided for the reception of the men and their animals, and is never happier than when they tarry for some time. Nothing of the kind have I seen in any other country." The magnanimous know very well that they who give time, or money, or shelter, to the stranger — so it be done for love, and not for ostentation — do, as it were, put God under obligation to them, so perfect are the compensations of the universe. In some way, the time they seem to lose, is redeemed, and the pains they seem to take, remunerate themselves. These men fan the flame of human love and raise the standard of civil virtue among mankind. But hospitality must be for service, and not for show, or it pulls down the host. The brave soul rates itself too high to value itself by the splendor of its table and draperies. It gives what it hath, and all it hath, but its own majesty can lend a better grace to bannocks and fair water, than belong to city feasts.

The temperance of the hero, proceeds from the same wish to do no dishonor to the worthiness he has. But he loves it for its elegancy, not for its austerity. It seems not worth his while to be solemn, and denounce with bitterness flesh-eating, or wine-drinking, the use of tobacco, or opium, or tea, or silk, or gold. A great man scarcely knows how he dines, how he dresses, but without railing or precision, his living is natural and poetic. John Eliot, the Indian Apostle, drank water, and said of wine, " It is a noble, generous liquor, and we should be humbly thankful for it, but, as I remember, water was made before it." Better still, is the temperance of king David, who poured out on the ground unto the Lord, the water which three of his warriors had brought him to drink, at the peril of their lives.

It is told of Brutus, that when he fell on his sword, after the battle of Philippi, he quoted a line of Euripides, " O virtue, I have followed thee through life, and I find thee at last but a shade." I doubt not the hero is slandered by this report. The heroic soul does not sell its justice and its nobleness. It does not ask to dine nicely, and to sleep warm. The essence of greatness is the perception that virtue is enough. Poverty is its ornament. Plenty, it does not need, and can very well abide its loss.

But that which takes my fancy most, in the heroic class, is the good humor and hilarity they exhibit. It is a height to which common duty can very well attain, to suffer and to dare with solemnity. But these rare souls set opinion, success, and life, at so cheap a

rate, that they will not soothe their enemies by peti-
tions, or the show of sorrow, but wear their own
habitual greatness.   Scipio, charged with peculation,
refuses to do himself so great a disgrace, as to wait
for justification, though he had the scroll of his accounts in his hands, but tears it to pieces before the
tribunes.   Socrates' condemnation of himself to be
maintained in all honor in the Prytaneum, during his
life, and Sir Thomas More's playfulness at the scaffold,
are of the same strain.   In Beaumont and Fletcher's
" Sea Voyage," Juletta tells the stout captain and his
company,

> *Jul.*   Why, slaves, 't is in our power to hang ye.
> *Master*.   Very likely,
> 'T is in our powers, then, to be hanged, and scorn ye.

These replies are sound and whole.   Sport is the
bloom and glow of a perfect health.   The great
will not condescend to take any thing seriously ;
all must be as gay as the song of a canary, though
it were the building of cities or the eradication of
old and foolish churches and nations, which have
cumbered the earth long thousands of years.   Simple hearts put all the history and customs of this
world behind them, and play their own play in innocent defiance of the Blue-Laws of the world ; and
such would appear, could we see the human race assembled in vision, like little children frolicking together,
though, to the eyes of mankind at large, they wear a
stately and solemn garb of works and influences.

The interest these fine stories have for us, the

power of a romance over the boy who grasps the forbidden book under his bench at school, our delight in the hero, is the main fact to our purpose. All these great and transcendent properties are ours. If we dilate in beholding the Greek energy, the Roman pride, it is that we are already domesticating the same sentiment. Let us find room for this great guest in our small houses. The first step of worthiness will be to disabuse us of our superstitious associations with places and times, with number and size. Why should these words, Athenian, Roman, Asia, and England, so tingle in the ear. Let us feel that where the heart is, there the muses, there the gods sojourn, and not in any geography of fame. Massachusetts, Connecticut River, and Boston Bay, you think paltry places, and the ear loves names of foreign and classic topography. But here we are ; — that is a great fact, and, if we will tarry a little, we may come to learn that here is best. See to it, only that thyself is here ; — and art and nature, hope and dread, friends, angels, and the Supreme Being, shall not be absent from the chamber where thou sittest. Epaminondas, brave and affectionate, does not seem to us to need Olympus to die upon, nor the Syrian sunshine. He lies very well where he is. The Jerseys were handsome ground enough for Washington to tread, and London streets for the feet of Milton. A great man illustrates his place, makes his climate genial in the imagination of men, and its air the beloved element of all delicate spirits. That country is the fairest, which is inhabited by the noblest minds. The pictures which fill the imagination in reading the actions of Pericles, Xenophon, Columbus, Bayard, Sidney, Hampden, teach us how needlessly mean our life is, that we, by the depth of our living, should deck it with more than regal or national splendor, and act on principles that should interest man and nature in the length of our days.

We have seen or heard of many extraordinary young men, who never ripened, or whose performance in actual life, was not extraordinary. When we see their air and mien, when we hear them speak of society, of books, of religion, we admire their superiority, they seem to throw contempt on the whole state of the world ; theirs is the tone of a youthful giant, who is sent to work revolutions. But they enter an active profession, and the forming Colossus shrinks to the common size of man. The magic they used, was the ideal tendencies, which always make the Actual ridiculous ; but the tough world had its revenge the moment they put their horses of the sun to plough in its furrow. They found no example and no companion, and their heart fainted. What then ? The lesson they gave in their first aspirations, is yet true, and a better valor, and a purer truth, shall one day execute their will, and put the world to shame. Or why should a woman liken herself to any historical woman, and think, because Sappho, or Sévigné, or De Staël, or the cloistered souls who have had genius and cultivation, do not satisfy the imagination, and the serene Themis, none can, — certainly not she. Why not ? She has a new and unattempted problem to solve, perchance that of the happiest nature that ever bloomed. Let the maiden, with erect soul, walk serenely on her way, accept the hint of each new experience, try, in turn, all the gifts God offers her, that she may learn the power and the charm, that like a new dawn radiating out of the deep of space, her new-born being is. The fair girl, who repels interference by a decided and proud choice of influences, so careless of pleasing, so wilful and lofty, inspires every beholder with somewhat of her own nobleness. The silent heart encourages her ; O friend, never strike sail to a fear. Come into port greatly, or sail with God the seas. Not in vain you live, for every passing eye is cheered and refined by the vision.

The characteristic of a genuine heroism is its persistency. All men have wandering impulses, fits and starts of generosity. But when you have resolved to be great, abide by yourself, and do not weakly try to reconcile yourself with the world. The heroic cannot be the common, nor the common the heroic. Yet we have the weakness to expect the sympathy of people in those actions whose excellence is that they outrun sympathy, and appeal to a tardy justice. If you would serve your brother, because it is fit for you to serve him, do not take back your words when you find that prudent people do not commend you. Be true to your own act, and congratulate yourself if you have done something strange and extravagant, and broken the monotony of a decorous age. It was a high counsel that I once heard given to a young per-

son, " Always do what you are afraid to do." A
simple manly character need never make an apology,
but should regard its past action with the calmness of
Phocion, when he admitted that the event of the battle
was happy, yet did not regret his dissuasion from the
battle.

There is no weakness or exposure for which we
cannot find consolation in the thought, — this is a part
of my constitution, part of my relation and office to
my fellow creature.   Has nature covenanted with me
that I should never appear to disadvantage, never
make a ridiculous figure ?   Let us be generous of
our dignity, as well as of our money.   Greatness
once and forever has done with opinion.   We tell our
charities, not because we wish to be praised for them,
not because we think they have great merit, but for
our justification.   It is a capital blunder ; as you discover, when another man recites his charities.

To speak the truth, even with some austerity, to
live with some rigor of temperance, or some extremes
of generosity, seems to be an asceticism which common good nature would appoint to those who are at
ease and in plenty, in sign that they feel a brotherhood with the great multitude of suffering men.   And
not only need we breathe and exercise the soul by
assuming the penalties of abstinence, of debt, of solitude, of unpopularity, but it behoves the wise man
to look with a bold eye into those rarer dangers which
sometimes invade men, and to familiarize himself with
disgusting forms of disease, with sounds of execra-
tion, and the vision of violent death.

Times of heroism are generally times of terror,
but the day never shines, in which this element may
not work. The circumstances of man, we say, are
historically somewhat better in this country, and at
this hour, than perhaps ever before. More freedom
exists for culture. It will not now run against an axe,
at the first step out of the beaten track of opinion.
But whoso is heroic, will always find crises to try his
edge. Human virtue demands her champions and
martyrs, and the trial of persecution always proceeds.
It is but the other day, that the brave Lovejoy gave
his breast to the bullets of a mob, for the rights of
free speech and opinion, and died when it was better
not to live.

I see not any road of perfect peace, which a man
can walk but to take counsel of his own bosom. Let
him quit too much association, let him go home much,
and stablish himself in those courses he approves.
The unremitting retention of simple and high sentiments in obscure duties, is hardening the character to
that temper which will work with honor, if need be,
in the tumult, or on the scaffold. Whatever outrages
have happened to men, may befall a man again : and
very easily in a republic, if there appear any signs
of a decay of religion. Coarse slander, fire, tar and
feathers, and the gibbet, the youth may freely bring
home to his mind, and with what sweetness of temper
he can, and inquire how fast he can fix his sense of
duty, braving such penalties, whenever it may please
the next newspaper, and a sufficient number of his
neighbors to pronounce his opinions incendiary.

10

It may calm the apprehension of calamity in the most susceptible heart, to see how quick a bound nature has set to the utmost infliction of malice. We rapidly approach a brink over which no enemy can follow us.

> " Let them rave :
> Thou art quiet in thy grave."

In the gloom of our ignorance of what shall be, in the hour when we are deaf to the higher voices, who does not envy them who have seen safely to an end their manful endeavor ? Who that sees the meanness of our politics, but inly congratulates Washington, that he is long already wrapped in his shroud, and forever safe ; that he was laid sweet in his grave, the hope of humanity not yet subjugated in him ? Who does not sometimes envy the good and brave, who are no more to suffer from the tumults of the natural world, and await with curious complacency the speedy term of his own conversation with finite nature ? And yet the love that will be annihilated sooner than treacherous, has already made death impossible, and affirms itself no mortal, but a native of the deeps of absolute and inextinguishable being.

THE OVER-SOUL.

"But souls that of his own good life partake,
He loves as his own self; dear as his eye
They are to Him: He 'll never them forsake :
When they shall die, then God himself shall die :
They live, they live in blest eternity."

Henry More.

ESSAY IX.

THE OVER-SOUL.

THERE is a difference between one and another hour
of life, in their authority and subsequent effect. Our
faith comes in moments ; our vice is habitual. Yet
is there a depth in those brief moments, which constrains us to ascribe more reality to them than to all
other experiences. For this reason, the argument,
which is always forthcoming to silence those who
conceive extraordinary hopes of man, namely, the
appeal to experience, is forever invalid and vain. A
mightier hope abolishes despair. We give up the
past to the objector, and yet we hope. He must explain this hope. We grant that human life is mean ;
but how did we find out that it was mean ? What is
the ground of this uneasiness of ours ; of this old
discontent ? What is the universal sense of want and
ignorance, but the fine inuendo by which the great
soul makes its enormous claim ? Why do men feel

that the natural history of man has never been written, but always he is leaving behind what you have
said of him, and it becomes old, and books of metaphysics worthless ?   The philosophy of six thousand
years has not searched the chambers and magazines
of the soul.   In its experiments there has always remained, in the last analysis, a residuum it could not
resolve.   Man is a stream whose source is hidden.
Always our being is descending into us from we know
not whence.   The most exact calculator has no pre-
science that somewhat incalculable may not baulk the
very next moment.   I am constrained every moment
to acknowledge a higher origin for events than the
will I call mine.

As with events, so is it with thoughts.   When I
watch that flowing river, which, out of regions I see
not, pours for a season its streams into me, — I see
that I am a pensioner, — not a cause, but a surprised
spectator of this ethereal water ; that I desire and look
up, and put myself in the attitude of reception, but
from some alien energy the visions come.

The Supreme Critic on all the errors of the past
and the present, and the only prophet of that which
must be, is that great nature in which we rest, as the
earth lies in the soft arms of the atmosphere ; that
Unity, that Over-Soul, within which every man's particular being is contained and made one with all other ;
that common heart, of which all sincere conversation
is the worship, to which all right action is submission ;
that overpowering reality which confutes our tricks
and talents, and constrains every one to pass for what

he is, and to speak from his character and not from his tongue ; and which evermore tends and aims to pass into our thought and hand, and become wisdom, and virtue, and power, and beauty. We live in succession, in division, in parts, in particles. Meantime within man is the soul of the whole ; the wise silence ; the universal beauty, to which every part and particle is equally related ; the eternal ONE. And this deep power in which we exist, and whose beatitude is all accessible to us, is not only self-sufficing and perfect in every hour, but the act of seeing, and the thing seen, the seer and the spectacle, the subject and the object, are one. We see the world piece by piece, as the sun, the moon, the animal, the tree ; but the whole, of which these are the shining parts, is the soul. It is only by the vision of that Wisdom, that the horoscope of the ages can be read, and it is only by falling back on our better thoughts, by yielding to the spirit of prophecy which is innate in every man, that we can know what it saith. Every man's words, who speaks from that life, must sound vain to those who do not dwell in the same thought on their own part. I dare not speak for it. My words do not carry its august sense ; they fall short and cold. Only itself can inspire whom it will, and behold ! their speech shall be lyrical, and sweet, and universal as the rising of the wind. Yet I desire, even by profane words, if sacred I may not use, to indicate the heaven of this deity, and to report what hints I have collected of the transcendent simplicity and energy of the Highest Law.

If we consider what happens in conversation, in reveries, in remorse, in times of passion, in surprises, in the instructions of dreams wherein often we see ourselves in masquerade, — the droll disguises only magnifying and enhancing a real element, and forcing it on our distinct notice, — we shall catch many hints that will broaden and lighten into knowledge of the secret of nature. All goes to show that the soul in man is not an organ, but animates and exercises all the organs ; is not a function, like the power of memory, of calculation, of comparison, —but uses these as hands and feet; is not a faculty, but a light ; is not the intellect or the will, but the master of the intellect and the will ;— is the vast back-ground of our being, in which they lie, — an immensity not possessed and that cannot be possessed. From within or from behind, a light shines through us upon things, and makes us aware that we are nothing, but the light is all. A man is the façade of a temple wherein all wisdom and all good abide. What we commonly call man, the eating, drinking, planting, counting man, does not, as we know him, represent himself, but misrepresents himself. Him we do not respect, but the soul, whose organ he is, would he let it appear through his action, would make our knees bend. When it breathes through his intellect, it is genius ; when it breathes through his will, it is virtue ; when it flows through his affection, it is love. And the blindness of the intellect begins, when it would be something of itself. The weakness of the will begins when the individual would be something of himself.' All re-

form aims, in some one particular, to let the great soul
have its way through us ; in other words, to engage
us to obey.

Of this pure nature every man is at some time
sensible. Language cannot paint it with his colors.
It is too subtle. It is undefinable, unmeasureable, but
we know that it pervades and contains us. We know
that all spiritual being is in man. A wise old proverb says, " God comes to see us without bell : "
that is, as there is no screen or ceiling between our
heads and the infinite heavens, so is there no bar or
wall in the soul where man, the effect, ceases, and
God, the cause, begins. The walls are taken away.
We lie open on one side to the deeps of spiritual nature, to all the attributes of God. Justice we see and
know, Love, Freedom, Power. These natures no
man ever got above, but always they tower over us,
and most in the moment when our interests tempt us
to wound them.

The sovereignty of this nature whereof we speak,
is made known by its independency of those limitations which circumscribe us on every hand. The
soul circumscribeth all things. As I have said, it contradicts all experience. In like manner it abolishes
time and space. The influence of the senses has, in
most men, overpowered the mind to that degree, that
the walls of time and space have come to look solid,
real and insurmountable ; and to speak with levity
of these limits, is, in the world, the sign of insanity.
Yet time and space are but inverse measures of the

10*

force of the soul.　A man is capable of abolishing them both.　The spirit sports with time —

" Can crowd eternity into an hour,
　Or stretch an hour to eternity."

We are often made to feel that there is another youth and age than that which is measured from the year of our natural birth.　Some thoughts always find us young and keep us so.　Such a thought is the love of the universal and eternal beauty.　Every man parts from that contemplation with the feeling that it rather belongs to ages than to mortal life.　The least activity of the intellectual powers redeems us in a degree from the influences of time.　In sickness, in languor, give us a strain of poetry or a profound sentence, and we are refreshed ; or produce a volume of Plato, or Shakspeare, or remind us of their names, and instantly we come into a feeling of longevity.　See how the deep, divine thought demolishes centuries, and millenniums, and makes itself present through all ages.　Is the teaching of Christ less effective now than it was when first his mouth was opened ?　The emphasis of facts and persons to my soul has nothing to do with time.　And so, always, the soul's scale is one ; the scale of the senses and the understanding is another.　Before the great revelations of the soul, Time, Space and Nature shrink away.　In common speech, we refer all things to time, as we habitually refer the immensely sundered stars to one concave sphere.　And so we say that the Judgment is distant or near, that the Millennium approaches, that a day of certain political, moral, social reforms is at hand, and the like, when we mean, that in the nature of things, one of the facts we contemplate is external and fugitive, and the other is permanent and connate with the soul. The things we now esteem fixed, shall, one by one, detach themselves, like ripe fruit, from our experience, and fall. The wind shall blow them none knows whither. The landscape, the figures, Boston, London, are facts as fugitive as any institution past, or any whiff of mist or smoke, and so is society, and so is the world. The soul looketh steadily forwards, creating a world alway before her, and leaving worlds alway behind her. She has no dates, nor rites, nor persons, nor specialties, nor men. The soul knows only the soul. All else is idle weeds for her wearing.

After its own law and not by arithmetic is the rate of its progress to be computed. The soul's advances are not made by gradation, such as can be represented by motion in a straight line ; but rather by ascension of state, such as can be represented by metamorphosis, — from the egg to the worm, from the worm to the fly. The growths of genius are of a certain *total* character, that does not advance the elect individual first over John, then Adam, then Richard, and give to each the pain of discovered inferiority, but by every throe of growth, the man expands there where he works, passing, at each pulsation, classes, populations of men. With each divine impulse the mind rends the thin rinds of the visible and finite, and comes out into eternity, and inspires and expires its air. It converses with truths that have always been spoken in the world, and becomes conscious of a closer sympathy with Zeno and Arrian, than with persons in the house.

This is the law of moral and of mental gain. The simple rise as by specific levity, not into a particular virtue, but into the region of all the virtues. They are in the spirit which contains them all. The soul is superior to all the particulars of merit. The soul requires purity, but purity is not it ; requires justice, but justice is not that ; requires beneficence, but is somewhat better : so that there is a kind of descent and accommodation felt when we leave speaking of moral nature, to urge a virtue which it enjoins. For, to the soul in her pure action, all the virtues are natural, and not painfully acquired. Speak to his heart, and the man becomes suddenly virtuous.

Within the same sentiment is the germ of intellectual growth, which obeys the same law. Those who are capable of humility, of justice, of love, of aspiration, are already on a platform that commands the sciences and arts, speech and poetry, action and grace. For whoso dwells in this moral beatitude, does already anticipate those special powers which men prize so highly ; just as love does justice to all the gifts of the object beloved. The lover has no talent, no skill, which passes for quite nothing with his enamored maiden, however little she may possess of related faculty. And the heart, which abandons itself to the Supreme Mind, finds itself related to all its works and will travel a royal road to particular knowledges and powers. For, in ascending to this primary and aboriginal sentiment, we have come from our remote sta-

tion on the circumference instantaneously to the centre of the world, where, as in the closet of God, we
see causes, and anticipate the universe, which is but
a slow effect.

One mode of the divine teaching is the incarnation
of the spirit in a form, — in forms, like my own. I
live in society ; with persons who answer to thoughts
in my own mind, or outwardly express to me a certain
obedience to the great instincts to which I live. I see
its presence to them. I am certified of a common
nature ; and so these other souls, these separated
selves, draw me as nothing else can. They stir in
me the new emotions we call passion ; of love, hatred,
fear, admiration, pity ; thence comes conversation,
competition, persuasion, cities, and war. Persons are
supplementary to the primary teaching of the soul.
In youth we are mad for persons. Childhood and
youth see all the world in them. But the larger experience of man discovers the identical nature appearing through them all. Persons themselves acquaint us with the impersonal. In all conversation between two persons, tacit reference is made as to a
third party, to a common nature. That third party
or common nature is not social ; it is impersonal ; is
God. And so in groups where debate is earnest, and
especially on great questions of thought, the company
become aware of their unity ; aware that the thought
rises to an equal height in all bosoms, that all have a
spiritual property in what was said, as well as the
sayer. They all wax wiser than they were. It
arches over them like a temple, this unity of thought,

in which every heart beats with nobler sense of power
and duty, and thinks and acts with unusual solemnity.
All are conscious of attaining to a higher self-possession.   It shines for all.   There is a certain wisdom of
humanity which is common to the greatest men with
the lowest, and which our ordinary education often
labors to silence and obstruct.   The mind is one, and
the best minds who love truth for its own sake, think
much less of property in truth.   Thankfully they accept it everywhere, and do not label or stamp it with
any man's name, for it is theirs long beforehand.   It
is theirs from eternity.   The learned and the studious
of thought have no monopoly of wisdom.   Their violence of direction in some degree disqualifies them to
think truly.   We owe many valuable observations to
people who are not very acute or profound, and who
say the thing without effort, which we want and have
long been hunting in vain.   The action of the soul is
oftener in that which is felt and left unsaid, than in
that which is said in any conversation.   It broods over
every society, and they unconsciously seek for it in
each other.   We know better than we do.   We do
not yet possess ourselves, and we know at the same
time that we are much more.   I feel the same truth
how often in my trivial conversation with my neighbors, that somewhat higher in each of us overlooks this
by-play, and Jove nods to Jove from behind each of us.
    Men descend to meet.   In their habitual and mean
service to the world, for which they forsake their native nobleness, they resemble those Arabian Sheikhs,
who dwell in mean houses and affect an external po-

verty, to escape the rapacity of the Pacha, and reserve all their display of wealth for their interior and guarded retirements.

As it is present in all persons, so it is in every period of life. It is adult already in the infant man. In my dealing with my child, my Latin and Greek, my accomplishments and my money, stead me nothing. They are all lost on him : but as much soul as I have, avails. If I am merely wilful, he gives me a Rowland for an Oliver, sets his will against mine, one for one, and leaves me, if I please, the degradation of beating him by my superiority of strength. But if I renounce my will, and act for the soul, setting that up as umpire between us two, out of his young eyes looks the same soul; he reveres and loves with me.

The soul is the perceiver and revealer of truth. We know truth when we see it, let skeptic and scoffer say what they choose. Foolish people ask you, when you have spoken what they do not wish to hear, ' How do you know it is truth, and not an error of your own?' We know truth when we see it, from opinion, as we know when we are awake that we are awake. It was a grand sentence of Emanuel Swedenborg, which would alone indicate the greatness of that man's perception, — " It is no proof of a man's understanding to be able to affirm whatever he pleases, but to be able to discern that what is true is true, and that what is false is false, this is the mark and character of intelligence." In the book I read, the good thought returns to me, as every truth will, the image of the whole soul. To the bad thought which I find

in it, the same soul becomes a discerning, separating
sword and lops it away. We are wiser than we know.
If we will not interfere with our thought, but will act
entirely, or see how the thing stands in God, we know
the particular thing, and every thing, and every man.
For, the Maker of all things and all persons, stands
behind us, and casts his dread omniscience through us
over things.

But beyond this recognition of its own in particular
passages of the individual's experience, it also reveals
truth.   And here we should seek to reinforce ourselves
by its very presence, and to speak with a worthier,
loftier strain of that advent.   For the soul's communication of truth is the highest event in nature, for it
then does not give somewhat from itself, but it gives
itself, or passes into and becomes that man whom it
enlightens ; or in proportion to that truth he receives,
it takes him to itself.

We distinguish the announcements of the soul, its
manifestations of its own nature, by the term *Revelation.*   These are always attended by the emotion of
the sublime.   For this communication is an influx
of the Divine mind into our mind.   It is an ebb of the
individual rivulet before the flowing surges of the sea
of life.   Every distinct apprehension of this central
commandment agitates men with awe and delight.   A
thrill passes through all men at the reception of new
truth, or at the performance of a great action, which
comes out of the heart of nature.   In these communications, the power to see, is not separated from
the will to do, but the insight proceeds from obedi-

ence, and the obedience proceeds from a joyful perception. Every moment when the individual feels himself invaded by it, is memorable. Always, I believe, by the necessity of our constitution, a certain enthusiasm attends the individual's consciousness of that divine presence. The character and duration of this enthusiasm varies with the state of the individual, from an extasy and trance and prophetic inspiration, — which is its rarer appearance, to the faintest glow of virtuous emotion, in which form it warms, like our household fires, all the families and associations of men, and makes society possible. A certain tendency to insanity has always attended the opening of the religious sense in men, as if " blasted with excess of light." The trances of Socrates ; the " union " of Plotinus ; the vision of Porphyry ; the conversion of Paul ; the aurora of Behmen ; the convulsions of George Fox and his Quakers ; the illumination of Swedenborg ; are of this kind. What was in the case of these remarkable persons a ravishment, has, in innumerable instances in common life, been exhibited in less striking manner. Everywhere the history of religion betrays a tendency to enthusiasm. The rapture of the Moravian and Quietist ; the opening of the internal sense of the Word, in the language of the New Jerusalem Church ; the revival of the Calvinistic Churches ; the experiences of the Methodists, are varying forms of that shudder of awe and delight with which the individual soul always mingles with the universal soul.

The nature of these revelations is always the same : they are perceptions of the absolute law. They are solutions of the soul's own questions. They do not answer the questions which the understanding asks. The soul answers never by words, but by the thing itself that is inquired after.

Revelation is the disclosure of the soul. The popular notion of a revelation, is, that it is a telling of fortunes. In past oracles of the soul, the understanding seeks to find answers to sensual questions, and undertakes to tell from God how long men shall exist, what their hands shall do, and who shall be their company, adding even names, and dates and places. But we must pick no locks. We must check this low curiosity. An answer in words is delusive ; it is really no answer to the questions you ask. Do not ask a description of the countries towards which you sail. The description does not describe them to you, and to-morrow you arrive there, and know them by inhabiting them. Men ask of the immortality of the soul, and the employments of heaven, and the state of the sinner, and so forth. They even dream that Jesus has left replies to precisely these interrogatories. Never a moment did that sublime spirit speak in their *patois*. To truth, justice, love, the attributes of the soul, the idea of immutableness is essentially associated. Jesus, living in these moral sentiments, heedless of sensual fortunes, heeding only the manifestations of these, never made the separation of the idea of duration from the essence of these attributes ; never uttered a syllable concerning the duration of the soul. It was left to his disciples to sever duration from the moral elements and to teach the immortality of the soul as a doctrine, and maintain it by evidences. The moment the doctrine of the immortality is separately taught, man is already fallen. In the flowing of love, in the adoration of humility, there is no question of continuance. No inspired man ever asks this question, or condescends to these evidences. For the soul is true to itself, and the man in whom it is shed abroad, cannot wander from the present, which is infinite, to a future, which would be finite.

These questions which we lust to ask about the future, are a confession of sin. God has no answer for them. No answer in words can reply to a question of things. It is not in an arbitrary " decree of God," but in the nature of man that a veil shuts down on the facts of to-morrow : for the soul will not have us read any other cipher but that of cause and effect. By this veil, which curtains events, it instructs the children of men to live in to-day. The only mode of obtaining an answer to these questions of the senses, is, to forego all low curiosity, and, accepting the tide of being which floats us into the secret of nature, work and live, work and live, and all unawares, the advancing soul has built and forged for itself a new condition, and the question and the answer are one.

Thus is the soul the perceiver and revealer of truth. By the same fire, serene, impersonal, perfect, which burns until it shall dissolve all things into the waves and surges of an ocean of light, — we see and know each other, and what spirit each is of. Who can tell the grounds of his knowledge of the character of the several individuals in his circle of friends ?

No man. Yet their acts and words do not disappoint him. In that man, though he knew no ill of him, he put no trust. In that other, though they had seldom met, authentic signs had yet passed, to signify that he might be trusted as one who had an interest in his own character. We know each other very well, — which of us has been just to himself, and whether that which we teach or behold, is only an aspiration, or is our honest effort also.

We are all discerners of spirits. That diagnosis lies aloft in our life or unconscious power, not in the understanding. The whole intercourse of society, its trade, its religion, its friendships, its quarrels, — is one wide, judicial investigation of character. In full court, or in small committee, or confronted face to face, accuser and accused, men offer themselves to be judged. Against their will they exhibit those decisive trifles by which character is read. But who judges ? and what ? Not our understanding. We do not read them by learning or craft. No ; the wisdom of the wise man consists herein, that he does not judge them ; he lets them judge themselves, and merely reads and records their own verdict.

By virtue of this inevitable nature, private will is overpowered, and, maugre our efforts, or our imperfections, your genius will speak from you, and mine from me. That which we are, we shall teach, not voluntarily, but involuntarily. Thoughts come into our minds by avenues which we never left open, and thoughts go out of our minds through avenues which we never voluntarily opened. Character teaches over our head. The infallible index of true progress is found in the tone the man takes. Neither his age, nor his breeding, nor company, nor books, nor actions, nor talents, nor all together, can hinder him from being deferential to a higher spirit than his own. If he have not found his home in God, his manners, his forms of speech, the turn of his sentences, the build, shall I say, of all his opinions will involuntarily confess it, let him brave it out how he will. If he have found his centre, the Deity will shine through him, through all the disguises of ignorance, of ungenial temperament, of unfavorable circumstance. The tone of seeking, is one, and the tone of having is another.

The great distinction between teachers sacred or literary ; between poets like Herbert, and poets like Pope ; between philosophers like Spinoza, Kant, and Coleridge, — and philosophers like Locke, Paley, Mackintosh, and Stewart ; between men of the world who are reckoned accomplished talkers, and here and there a fervent mystic, prophesying half-insane under the infinitude of his thought, is, that one class speak *from within*, or from experience, as parties and possessors of the fact ; and the other class, *from without*, as spectators merely, or perhaps as acquainted with the fact, on the evidence of third persons. It is of no use to preach to me from without. I can do that too easily myself. Jesus speaks always from within, and in a degree that transcends all others. In that, is the miracle. That includes the miracle. My soul believes beforehand that it ought so to be. All men stand continually in the expectation of the appearance of such a teacher. But if a man do not speak from within the veil, where the word is one with that it tells of, let him lowly confess it.

The same Omniscience flows into the intellect, and makes what we call genius. Much of the wisdom of the world is not wisdom, and the most illuminated class of men are no doubt superior to literary fame, and are not writers. Among the multitude of scholars and authors, we feel no hallowing presence; we are sensible of a knack and skill rather than of inspiration; they have a light, and know not whence it comes, and call it their own: their talent is some exaggerated faculty, some overgrown member, so that their strength is a disease. In these instances, the intellectual gifts do not make the impression of virtue, but almost of vice; and we feel that a man's talents stand in the way of his advancement in truth. But genius is religious. It is a larger imbibing of the common heart. It is not anomalous, but more like, and not less like other men. There is in all great poets, a wisdom of humanity, which is superior to any talents they exercise. The author, the wit, the partisan, the fine gentleman, does not take place of the man. Humanity shines in Homer, in Chaucer, in Spenser, in Shakspeare, in Milton. They are content with truth. They use the positive degree. They seem frigid and phlegmatic to those who have been spiced with the frantic passion and violent coloring of inferior, but popular writers. For, they are poets by the free course which they allow to the informing soul, which,

though their eyes beholdeth again, and blesseth the
things which it hath made. The soul is superior to
its knowledge ; wiser than any of its works. The
great poet makes us feel our own wealth, and then
we think less of his compositions. His greatest communication to our mind, is, to teach us to despise all
he has done. Shakspeare carries us to such a lofty
strain of intelligent activity, as to suggest a wealth
which beggars his own ; and we then feel that the
splendid works which he has created, and which in
other hours, we extol as a sort of self-existent poetry,
take no stronger hold of real nature than the shadow
of a passing traveller on the rock. The inspiration
which uttered itself in Hamlet and Lear, could utter
things as good from day to day, forever. Why then
should I make account of Hamlet and Lear, as if we
had not the soul from which they fell as syllables
from the tongue ?

This energy does not descend into individual life,
on any other condition than entire possession. It
comes to the lowly and simple ; it comes to whomsoever will put off what is foreign and proud ; it comes
as insight ; it comes as serenity and grandeur. When
we see those whom it inhabits, we are apprised of
new degrees of greatness. From that inspiration
the man comes back with a changed tone. He does
not talk with men, with an eye to their opinion. He
tries them. It requires of us to be plain and true.
The vain traveller attempts to embellish his life by
quoting my Lord, and the Prince, and the Countess,
who thus said or did to *him*. The ambitious vulgar,

show you their spoons, and brooches, and rings, and preserve their cards and compliments. The more cultivated, in their account of their own experience, cull out the pleasing poetic circumstance ; the visit to Rome ; the man of genius they saw ; the brilliant friend they know ; still further on, perhaps, the gorgeous landscape, the mountain lights, the mountain thoughts, they enjoyed yesterday, — and so seek to throw a romantic color over their life. But the soul that ascendeth to worship the great God, is plain and true ; has no rose color ; no fine friends ; no chivalry ; no adventures ; does not want admiration ; dwells in the hour that now is, in the earnest experience of the common day, — by reason of the present moment, and the mere trifle having become porous to thought, and bibulous of the sea of light.

Converse with a mind that is grandly simple, and literature looks like word-catching. The simplest utterances are worthiest to be written, yet are they so cheap, and so things of course, that in the infinite riches of the soul, it is like gathering a few pebbles off the ground, or bottling a little air in a phial, when the whole earth, and the whole atmosphere are ours. The mere author, in such society, is like a pickpocket among gentlemen, who has come in to steal a gold button or a pin. Nothing can pass there, or make you one of the circle, but the casting aside your trappings, and dealing man to man in naked truth, plain confession and omniscient affirmation.

Souls, such as these, treat you as gods would ; walk as gods in the earth, accepting without any admiration, your wit, your bounty, your virtue, even, say rather your act of duty, for your virtue they own as their proper blood, royal as themselves, and over-royal, and the father of the gods. But what rebuke their plain fraternal bearing casts on the mutual flattery with which authors solace each other, and wound themselves! These flatter not. I do not wonder that these men go to see Cromwell, and Christina, and Charles II., and James I., and the Grand Turk. For they are in their own elevation, the fellows of kings, and must feel the servile tone of conversation in the world. They must always be a godsend to princes, for they confront them, a king to a king, without ducking or concession, and give a high nature the refreshment and satisfaction of resistance, of plain humanity, of even companionship, and of new ideas. They leave them wiser and superior men. Souls like these make us feel that sincerity is more excellent than flattery. Deal so plainly with man and woman, as to constrain the utmost sincerity, and destroy all hope of trifling with you. It is the highest compliment you can pay. Their " highest praising," said Milton, " is not flattery, and their plainest advice is a kind of praising."

Ineffable is the union of man and God in every act of the soul. The simplest person, who in his integrity worships God, becomes God; yet forever and ever the influx of this better and universal self is new and unsearchable. Ever it inspires awe and astonishment. How dear, how soothing to man, arises the idea of God, peopling the lonely place, effacing the

11

scars of our mistakes and disappointments! When
we have broken our god of tradition, and ceased from
our god of rhetoric, then may God fire the heart with
his presence. It is the doubling of the heart itself, nay,
the infinite enlargement of the heart with a power of
growth to a new infinity on every side. It inspires in man
an infallible trust. He has not the conviction, but the
sight that the best is the true, and may in that thought
easily dismiss all particular uncertainties and fears,
and adjourn to the sure revelation of time, the solution of his private riddles. He is sure that his wel-
fare is dear to the heart of being. In the presence
of law to his mind, he is overflowed with a reliance
so universal, that it sweeps away all cherished hopes
and the most stable projects of mortal condition in its
flood. He believes that he cannot escape from his
good. The things that are really for thee, gravitate
to thee. You are running to seek your friend. Let
your feet run, but your mind need not. If you do
not find him, will you not acquiesce that it is best you
should not find him? for there is a power, which, as
it is in you, is in him also, and could therefore very
well bring you together, if it were for the best. You
are preparing with eagerness to go and render a service to which your talent and your taste invite you,
the love of men, and the hope of fame. Has it not
occurred to you, that you have no right to go, unless
you are equally willing to be prevented from going?
O believe, as thou livest, that every sound that is spoken over the round world, which thou oughtest to hear,
will vibrate on thine ear. Every proverb, every book,

every by-word that belongs to thee for aid or comfort, shall surely come home through open or winding passages. Every friend whom not thy fantastic will, but the great and tender heart in thee craveth, shall lock thee in his embrace. And this, because the heart in thee is the heart of all; not a valve, not a wall, not an intersection is there any where in nature, but one blood rolls uninterruptedly, an endless circulation through all men, as the water of the globe is all one sea, and, truly seen, its tide is one.

Let man then learn the revelation of all nature, and all thought to his heart; this, namely; that the Highest dwells with him; that the sources of nature are in his own mind, if the sentiment of duty is there. But if he would know what the great God speaketh, he must 'go into his closet and shut the door,' as Jesus said. God will not make himself manifest to cowards. He must greatly listen to himself, withdrawing himself from all the accents of other men's devotion. Their prayers even are hurtful to him, until he have made his own. The soul makes no appeal from itself. Our religion vulgarly stands on numbers of believers. Whenever the appeal is made, — no matter how indirectly, — to numbers, proclamation is then and there made, that religion is not. He that finds God a sweet, enveloping thought to him, never counts his company. When I sit in that presence, who shall dare to come in? When I rest in perfect humility, when I burn with pure love, — what can Calvin or Swedenborg say?

It makes no difference whether the appeal is to

numbers or to one. The faith that stands on authority is not faith. The reliance on authority, measures the decline of religion, the withdrawal of the soul. The position men have given to Jesus, now for many centuries of history, is a position of authority. It characterizes themselves. It cannot alter the eternal facts. Great is the soul, and plain. It is no flatterer, it is no follower ; it never appeals from itself. It always believes in itself. Before the immense possibilities of man, all mere experience, all past biography, however spotless and sainted, shrinks away. Before that holy heaven which our presentiments foreshow us, we cannot easily praise any form of life we have seen or read of. We not only affirm that we have few great men, but absolutely speaking, that we have none ; that we have no history, no record of any character or mode of living, that entirely contents us. The saints and demigods whom history worships, we are constrained to accept with a grain of allowance. Though in our lonely hours, we draw a new strength out of their memory, yet pressed on our attention, as they are by the thoughtless and customary, they fatigue and invade. The soul gives itself alone, original, and pure, to the Lonely, Original and Pure, who, on that condition, gladly inhabits, leads, and speaks through it. Then is it glad, young, and nimble. It is not wise, but it sees through all things. It is not called religious, but it is innocent. It calls the light its own, and feels that the grass grows, and the stone falls by a law inferior to, and dependent on its nature. Behold, it saith, I am born into the great, the universal mind. I the imperfect, adore my own Perfect. I am somehow receptive of the great soul, and thereby I do overlook the sun and the stars, and feel them to be but the fair accidents and effects which change and pass. More and more the surges of everlasting nature enter into me, and I become public and human in my regards and actions. So come I to live in thoughts, and act with energies which are immortal. Thus revering the soul, and learning, as the ancient said, that " its beauty is immense," man will come to see that the world is the perennial miracle which the soul worketh, and be less astonished at particular wonders ; he will learn that there is no profane history ; that all history is sacred ; that the universe is represented in an atom, in a moment of time. He will weave no longer a spotted life of shreds and patches, but he will live with a divine unity. He will cease from what is base and frivolous in his own life, and be content with all places and any service he can render. He will calmly front the morrow in the negligency of that trust which carries God with it, and so hath already the whole future in the bottom of the heart.

CIRCLES.

ESSAY X.

CIRCLES.

———

THE eye is the first circle; the horizon which it forms is the second; and throughout nature this primary figure is repeated without end. It is the highest emblem in the cipher of the world. St. Augustine described the nature of God as a circle whose centre was everywhere, and its circumference nowhere. We are all our lifetime reading the copious sense of this first of forms. One moral we have already deduced in considering the circular or compensatory character of every human action. Another analogy we shall now trace; that every action admits of being outdone. Our life is an apprenticeship to the truth, that around every circle another can be drawn; that there is no end in nature, but every end is a beginning; that there is always another dawn risen on mid-noon, and under every deep a lower deep opens.

This fact, as far as it symbolizes the moral fact of

11*

the Unattainable, the flying Perfect, around which the
hands of man can never meet, at once the inspirer
and the condemner of every success, may conven-
iently serve us to connect many illustrations of human power in every department.

There are no fixtures in nature. The universe is
fluid and volatile. Permanence is but a word of degrees. Our globe seen by God, is a transparent law,
not a mass of facts. The law dissolves the fact and
holds it fluid. Our culture is the predominance of an
idea which draws after it all this train of cities and
institutions. Let us rise into another idea : they will
disappear. The Greek sculpture is all melted away,
as if it had been statues of ice : here and there a
solitary figure or fragment remaining, as we see
flecks and scraps of snow left in cold dells and mountain clefts, in June and July. For, the genius that
created it, creates now somewhat else. The Greek
letters last a little longer, but are already passing under the same sentence, and tumbling into the inevitable pit which the creation of new thought opens for
all that is old. The new continents are built out of
the ruins of an old planet : the new races fed out of
the decomposition of the foregoing. New arts destroy the old. See the investment of capital in aque-
ducts, made useless by hydraulics ; fortifications, by
gunpowder ; roads and canals, by railways ; sails, by
steam ; steam by electricity.

You admire this tower of granite, weathering the
hurts of so many ages. Yet a little waving hand built
this huge wall, and that which builds, is better than

that which is built. The hand that built, can topple it down much faster. Better than the hand, and nimbler, was the invisible thought which wrought through it, and thus ever behind the coarse effect, is a fine cause, which, being narrowly seen, is itself the effect of a finer cause. Every thing looks permanent until its secret is known. A rich estate appears to women and children, a firm and lasting fact ; to a merchant, one easily created out of any materials, and easily lost. An orchard, good tillage, good grounds, seem a fixture, like a gold mine, or a river, to a citizen, but to a large farmer, not much more fixed than the state of the crop. Nature looks provokingly stable and secular, but it has a cause like all the rest ; and when once I comprehend that, will these fields stretch so immovably wide, these leaves hang so individually considerable ? Permanence is a word of degrees. Every thing is medial. Moons are no more bounds to spiritual power than bat-balls.

The key to every man is his thought. Sturdy and defying though he look, he has a helm which he obeys, which is, the idea after which all his facts are classified. He can only be reformed by showing him a new idea which commands his own. The life of man is a self-evolving circle, which, from a ring imperceptibly small, rushes on all sides outwards to new and larger circles, and that without end. The extent to which this generation of circles, wheel without wheel will go, depends on the force or truth of the individual soul. For, it is the inert effort of each thought having formed itself into a circular wave of circumstance, as, for instance, an empire, rules of an art, a local usage, a religious rite, to heap itself on that ridge, and to solidify, and hem in the life. But if the soul is quick and strong, it bursts over that boundary on all sides, and expands another orbit on the great deep, which also runs up into a high wave, with attempt again to stop and to bind. But the heart refuses to be imprisoned ; in its first and narrowest pulses, it already tends outward with a vast force, and to immense and innumerable expansions.

Every ultimate fact is only the first of a new series. Every general law only a particular fact of some more general law presently to disclose itself. There is no outside, no enclosing wall, no circumference to us. The man finishes his story, — how good ! how final ! how it puts a new face on all things ! He fills the sky. Lo, on the other side, rises also a man, and draws a circle around the circle we had just pronounced the outline of the sphere. Then already is our first speaker, not man, but only a first speaker. His only redress is forthwith to draw a circle outside of his antagonist. And so men do by themselves. The result of to-day which haunts the mind and cannot be escaped, will presently be abridged into a word, and the principle that seemed to explain nature, will itself be included as one example of a bolder generalization. In the thought of tomorrow there is a power to upheave all thy creed, all the creeds, all the literatures of the nations, and marshal thee to a heaven which no epic dream has yet depicted. Every man is not so much a workman in

the world, as he is a suggestion of that he should be.
Men walk as prophecies of the next age.

Step by step we scale this mysterious ladder : the
steps are actions ; the new prospect is power. Every
several result is threatened and judged by that which
follows. Every one seems to be contradicted by the
new ; it is only limited by the new. The new statement is always hated by the old, and, to those dwell-
ing in the old, comes like an abyss of skepticism.
But the eye soon gets wonted to it, for the eye and it
are effects of one cause ; then its innocency and benefit
appear, and, presently, all its energy spent, it pales
and dwindles before the revelation of the new hour.

Fear not the new generalization. Does the fact look
crass and material, threatening to degrade thy theory
of spirit ? Resist it not ; it goes to refine and raise
thy theory of matter just as much.

There are no fixtures to men, if we appeal to consciousness. Every man supposes himself not to be
fully understood ; and if there is any truth in him, if
he rests at last on the divine soul, I see not how it
can be otherwise. The last chamber, the last closet,
he must feel, was never opened ; there is always a
residuum unknown, unanalyzable. That is, every
man believes that he has a greater possibility.

Our moods do not believe in each other. To-day,
I am full of thoughts, and can write what I please. I
see no reason why I should not have the same thought,
the same power of expression to-morrow. What I
write, whilst I write it, seems the most natural thing in
the world : but, yesterday, I saw a dreary vacuity in

this direction in which now I see so much ; and a month
hence, I doubt not, I shall wonder who he was that
wrote so many continuous pages.   Alas for this infirm
faith, this will not strenuous, this vast ebb of a vast
flow !   I am God in nature ; I am a weed by the
wall.

The continual effort to raise himself above himself,
to work a pitch above his last height, betrays itself in
a man's relations. We thirst for approbation, yet cannot forgive the approver.   The sweet of nature is
love ; yet if I have a friend, I am tormented by my
imperfections.   The love of me accuses the other
party.   If he were high enough to slight me, then
could I love him, and rise by my affection to new
heights.   A man's growth is seen in the successive
choirs of his friends.   For every friend whom he
loses for truth, he gains a better.   I thought, as I
walked in the woods and mused on my friends, why
should I play with them this game of idolatry ?   I
know and see too well, when not voluntarily blind,
the speedy limits of persons called high and worthy.
Rich, noble, and great they are by the liberality of
our speech, but truth is sad.   O blessed Spirit, whom
I forsake for these, they are not thee !   Every personal consideration that we allow, costs us heavenly
state.   We sell the thrones of angels for a short and
turbulent pleasure.

How often must we learn this lesson ?   Men cease
to interest us when we find their limitations.   The
only sin is limitation.   As soon as you once come up
with a man's limitations, it is all over with him.   Has

he talents ? has he enterprises ? has he knowledge ?
it boots not. Infinitely alluring and attractive was he
to you yesterday, a great hope, a sea to swim in ;
now, you have found his shores, found it a pond, and
you care not if you never see it again.

Each new step we take in thought reconciles twenty
seemingly discordant facts, as expressions of one law.
Aristotle and Plato are reckoned the respective heads
of two schools. A wise man will see that Aristotle
Platonizes. By going one step farther back in thought,
discordant opinions are reconciled, by being seen to
be two extremes of one principle, and we can never
go so far back as to preclude a still higher vision.

Beware when the great God lets loose a thinker on
this planet. Then all things are at risk. It is as
when a conflagration has broken out in a great city,
and no man knows what is safe, or where it will end.
There is not a piece of science, but its flank may be
turned to-morrow ; there is not any literary reputation, not the so-called eternal names of fame, that
may not be revised and condemned. The very hopes
of man, the thoughts of his heart, the religion of nations, the manners and morals of mankind, are all at
the mercy of a new generalization. Generalization
is always a new influx of the divinity into the mind.
Hence the thrill that attends it.

Valor consists in the power of self-recovery, so that
a man cannot have his flank turned, cannot be out-
generaled, but put him where you will, he stands.
This can only be by his preferring truth to his past
apprehension of truth ; and his alert acceptance of it

from whatever quarter; the intrepid conviction that his laws, his relations to society, his christianity, his world, may at any time be superseded and decease.

There are degrees in idealism. We learn first to play with it academically, as the magnet was once a toy. Then we see in the heyday of youth and poetry that it may be true, that it is true in gleams and fragments. Then, its countenance waxes stern and grand, and we see that it must be true. It now shows itself ethical and practical. We learn that God is ; that he is in me ; and that all things are shadows of him. The idealism of Berkeley is only a crude statement of the idealism of Jesus, and that, again, is a crude statement of the fact that all nature is the rapid efflux of goodness executing and organizing itself. Much more obviously is history and the state of the world at any one time, directly dependent on the intellectual classification then existing in the minds of men. The things which are dear to men at this hour, are so on account of the ideas which have emerged on their mental horizon, and which cause the present order of things as a tree bears its apples. A new degree of culture would instantly revolutionize the entire system of human pursuits.

Conversation is a game of circles. In conversation we pluck up the *termini* which bound the common of silence on every side. The parties are not to be judged by the spirit they partake and even express under this Pentecost. To-morrow they will have receded from this high-water mark. To-morrow you shall find them stooping under the old packsaddles.

Yet let us enjoy the cloven flame whilst it glows on our walls. When each new speaker strikes a new light, emancipates us from the oppression of the last speaker, to oppress us with the greatness and exclusiveness of his own thought, then yields us to another redeemer, we seem to recover our rights, to become men. O what truths profound and executable only in ages and orbs, are supposed in the announcement of every truth ! In common hours, society sits cold and statuesque. We all stand waiting, empty, — knowing, possibly, that we can be full, surrounded by mighty symbols which are not symbols to us, but prose and trivial toys. Then cometh the god, and converts the statues into fiery men, and by a flash of his eye burns up the veil which shrouded all things, and the meaning of the very furniture, of cup and saucer, of chair and clock and tester, is manifest. The facts which loomed so large in the fogs of yesterday, — property, climate, breeding, personal beauty, and the like, have strangely changed their proportions. All that we reckoned settled, shakes now and rattles ; and literatures, cities, climates, religions, leave their foundations, and dance before our eyes. And yet here again see the swift circumscription. Good as is discourse, silence is better, and shames it. The length of the discourse indicates the distance of thought betwixt the speaker and the hearer. If they were at a perfect understanding in any part, no words would be necessary thereon. If at one in all parts, no words would be suffered.

Literature is a point outside of our hodiernal circle,

through which a new one may be described. The use of literature is to afford us a platform whence we may command a view of our present life, a purchase by which we may move it. We fill ourselves with ancient learning; install ourselves the best we can in Greek, in Punic, in Roman houses, only that we may wiselier see French, English, and American houses and modes of living. In like manner, we see literature best from the midst of wild nature, or from the din of affairs, or from a high religion. The field cannot be well seen from within the field. The astronomer must have his diameter of the earth's orbit as a base to find the parallax of any star.

Therefore, we value the poet. All the argument, and all the wisdom, is not in the encyclopedia, or the treatise on metaphysics, or the Body of Divinity, but in the sonnet or the play. In my daily work I incline to repeat my old steps, and do not believe in remedial force, in the power of change and reform. But some Petrarch or Ariosto, filled with the new wine of his imagination, writes me an ode, or a brisk romance, full of daring thought and action. He smites and arouses me with his shrill tones, breaks up my whole chain of habits, and I open my eye on my own possibilities. He claps wings to the sides of all the solid old lumber of the world, and I am capable once more of choosing a straight path in theory and practice.

We have the same need to command a view of the religion of the world. We can never see christianity from the catechism : — from the pastures, from a boat in the pond, from amidst the songs of wood-birds, we possibly may. Cleansed by the elemental light and wind, steeped in the sea of beautiful forms which the field offers us, we may chance to cast a right glance back upon biography. Christianity is rightly dear to the best of mankind ; yet was there never a young philosopher whose breeding had fallen into the christian church, by whom that brave text of Paul's, was not specially prized, " Then shall also the Son be subject unto Him who put all things under him, that God may be all in all." Let the claims and virtues of persons be never so great and welcome, the instinct of man presses eagerly onward to the impersonal and illimitable, and gladly arms itself against the dogmatism of bigots with this generous word, out of the book itself.

The natural world may be conceived of as a system of concentric circles, and we now and then detect in nature slight dislocations, which apprize us that this surface on which we now stand, is not fixed, but sliding. These manifold tenacious qualities, this chemistry and vegetation, these metals and animals, which seem to stand there for their own sake, are means and methods only, are words of God, and as fugitive as other words. Has the naturalist or chemist learned his craft, who has explored the gravity of atoms and the elective affinities, who has not yet discerned the deeper law whereof this is only a partial or approximate statement, namely, that like draws to like ; and that the goods which belong to you, gravitate to you, and need not be pursued with pains and cost ? Yet is that statement approximate also, and not final.

Omnipresence is a higher fact. Not through subtle, subterranean channels, need friend and fact be drawn to their counterpart, but, rightly considered, these things proceed from the eternal generation of the soul. Cause and effect are two sides of one fact.

The same law of eternal procession ranges all that we call the virtues, and extinguishes each in the light of a better. The great man will not be prudent in the popular sense ; all his prudence will be so much deduction from his grandeur. But it behoves each to see when he sacrifices prudence, to what god he devotes it ; if to ease and pleasure, he had better be prudent still : if to a great trust, he can well spare his mule and panniers, who has a winged chariot instead. Geoffrey draws on his boots to go through the woods, that his feet may be safer from the bite of snakes ; Aaron never thinks of such a peril. In many years, neither is harmed by such an accident. Yet it seems to me that with every precaution you take against such an evil, you put yourself into the power of the evil. I suppose that the highest prudence is the lowest prudence. Is this too sudden a rushing from the centre to the verge of our orbit ? Think how many times we shall fall back into pitiful calculations, before we take up our rest in the great sentiment, or make the verge of to-day the new centre. Besides, your bravest sentiment is familiar to the humblest men. The poor and the low have their way of expressing the last facts of philosophy as well as you. " Blessed be nothing," and " the worse things are, the better they are," are proverbs which express the transcendentalism of common life.

One man's justice is another's injustice ; one man's beauty, another's ugliness ; one man's wisdom, another's folly, as one beholds the same objects from a higher point of view. One man thinks justice consists in paying debts, and has no measure in his abhorrence of another who is very remiss in this duty, and makes the creditor wait tediously. But that second man has his own way of looking at things ; asks himself, which debt must I pay first, the debt to the rich, or the debt to the poor ? the debt of money, or the debt of thought to mankind, of genius to nature ? For you, O broker, there is no other principle but arithmetic. For me, commerce is of trivial import ; love, faith, truth of character, the aspiration of man, these are sacred : nor can I detach one duty, like you, from all other duties, and concentrate my forces mechanically on the payment of moneys. Let me live onward : you shall find that, though slower, the progress of my character will liquidate all these debts without injustice to higher claims. If a man should dedicate himself to the payment of notes, would not this be injustice ? Owes he no debt but money ? And are all claims on him to be postponed to a landlord's or a banker's ?

There is no virtue which is final ; all are initial. The virtues of society are vices of the saint. The terror of reform is the discovery that we must cast away our virtues, or what we have always esteemed such, into the same pit that has consumed our grosser vices.

" Forgive his crimes, forgive his virtues too,
   Those smaller faults, half converts to the right."

It is the highest power of divine moments that they abolish our contritions also. I accuse myself of sloth and unprofitableness, day by day ; but when these waves of God flow into me, I no longer reckon lost time. I no longer poorly compute my possible achievement by what remains to me of the month or the year ; for these moments confer a sort of omnipresence and omnipotence, which asks nothing of duration, but sees that the energy of the mind is commensurate with the work to be done, without time.

And thus, O circular philosopher, I hear some reader exclaim, you have arrived at a fine pyrrhonism, at an equivalence and indifferency of all actions, and would fain teach us, that, *if we are true*, forsooth, our crimes may be lively stones out of which we shall construct the temple of the true God.

I am not careful to justify myself. I own I am gladdened by seeing the predominance of the saccharine principle throughout vegetable nature, and not less by beholding in morals that unrestrained inundation of the principle of good into every chink and hole that selfishness has left open, yea, into selfishness and sin itself ; so that no evil is pure ; nor hell itself without its extreme satisfactions. But lest I should mislead any when I have my own head, and obey my whims, let me remind the reader that I am only an experimenter. Do not set the least value on what I do, or the least discredit on what I do not, as if I pretended to settle anything as true or false. I unsettle all things. No facts are to me sacred ; none are profane ; I simply experiment, an endless seeker, with no Past at my back.

Yet this incessant movement and progression, which all things partake, could never become sensible to us, but by contrast to some principle of fixture or stability in the soul. Whilst the eternal generation of circles proceeds, the eternal generator abides. That central life is somewhat superior to creation, superior to knowledge and thought, and contains all its circles. Forever it labors to create a life and thought as large and excellent as itself; but in vain; for that which is made, instructs how to make a better.

Thus there is no sleep, no pause, no preservation, but all things renew, germinate, and spring. Why should we import rags and relics into the new hour? Nature abhors the old, and old age seems the only disease: all others run into this one. We call it by many names, fever, intemperance, insanity, stupidity, and crime: they are all forms of old age: they are rest, conservatism, appropriation, inertia, not new- ness, not the way onward. We grizzle every day. I see no need of it. Whilst we converse with what is above us, we do not grow old, but grow young. Infancy, youth, receptive, aspiring, with religious eye looking upward, counts itself nothing, and aban- dons itself to the instruction flowing from all sides. But the man and woman of seventy, assume to know all; throw up their hope; renounce aspiration; ac- cept the actual for the necessary; and talk down to the young. Let them then become organs of the Holy Ghost; let them be lovers; let them behold truth; and their eyes are uplifted, their wrinkles smoothed, they are perfumed again with hope and power. This old age ought not to creep on a human mind. In nature, every moment is new ; the past is always swallowed and forgotten ; the coming only is sacred. Nothing is secure but life, transition, the energizing spirit. No love can be bound by oath or covenant to secure it against a higher love. No truth so sublime but it may be trivial tomorrow in the light of new thoughts. People wish to be settled : only as far as they are unsettled, is there any hope for them.

Life is a series of surprises. We do not guess today the mood, the pleasure, the power of to-morrow, when we are building up our being. Of lower states, — of acts of routine and sense, we can tell somewhat, but the masterpieces of God, the total growths, and universal movements of the soul, he hideth ; they are incalculable. I can know that truth is divine and helpful, but how it shall help me, I can have no guess, for, *so to be* is the sole inlet of *so to know*. The new position of the advancing man has all the powers of the old, yet has them all new. It carries in its bosom all the energies of the past, yet is itself an exhalation of the morning. I cast away in this new moment all my once hoarded knowledge, as vacant and vain. Now, for the first time, seem I to know any thing rightly. The simplest words, — we do not know what they mean, except when we love and aspire.

The difference between talents and character is adroitness to keep the old and trodden round, and power and courage to make a new road to new and better goals. Character makes an overpowering present, a cheerful, determined hour, which fortifies all the company, by making them see that much is possible and excellent, that was not thought of. Character dulls the impression of particular events. When we see the conqueror, we do not think much of any one battle or success. We see that we had exaggerated the difficulty. It was easy to him. The great man is not convulsible or tormentable. He is so much, that events pass over him without much impression. People say sometimes, ' See what I have overcome ; see how cheerful I am ; see how completely I have triumphed over these black events.' Not if they still remind me of the black event, — they have not yet conquered. Is it conquest to be a gay and decorated sepulchre, or a half-crazed widow hysterically laughing ? True conquest is the causing the black event to fade and disappear as an early cloud of insignificant result in a history so large and advancing.

The one thing which we seek with insatiable desire, is to forget ourselves, to be surprised out of our propriety, to lose our sempiternal memory, and to do something without knowing how or why ; in short, to draw a new circle. Nothing great was ever achieved without enthusiasm. The way of life is wonderful. It is by abandonment. The great moments of history are the facilities of performance through the strength of ideas, as the works of genius and religion. " A man," said Oliver Cromwell, " never rises so high as when he knows not whither he is going." Dreams and drunkenness, the use of opium and alcohol are

12

the semblance and counterfeit of this oracular genius,
and hence their dangerous attraction for men.   For the
like reason, they ask the.aid of wild passions, as in
gaming and war, to ape in some manner these flames
and generosities of the heart.

INTELLECT.

ESSAY XI.

INTELLECT.

––––––

EVERY substance is negatively electric to that which stands above it in the chemical tables, positively to that which stands below it. Water dissolves wood and stone, and salt; air dissolves water; electric fire dissolves air, but the intellect dissolves fire, gravity, laws, method, and the subtlest unnamed relations of nature in its resistless menstruum. Intellect lies behind genius, which is intellect constructive. Intellect is the simple power anterior to all action or construction. Gladly would I unfold in calm degrees a natural history of the intellect, but what man has yet been able to mark the steps and boundaries of that transparent essence? The first questions are always to be asked, and the wisest doctor is gravelled by the inquisitiveness of a child. How can we speak of the action of the mind under any divisions, as, of its knowledge, of its ethics, of its works, and so forth,

since it melts will into perception, knowledge into act?
Each becomes the other. Itself alone is. Its vision
is not like the vision of the eye, but is union with the
things known.

Intellect and intellection signify, to the common ear
consideration of abstract truth. The consideration of
time and place, of you and me, of profit and hurt,
tyrannize over most men's minds. Intellect separates
the fact considered from *you*, from all local and personal reference, and discerns it as if it existed for its
own sake. Heraclitus looked upon the affections as
dense and colored mists. In the fog of good and
evil affections, it is hard for man to walk forward in
a straight line. Intellect is void of affection, and
sees an object as it stands in the light of science, cool
and disengaged. The intellect goes out of the individual, floats over its own personality, and regards it
as a fact, and not as *I* and *mine*. He who is immersed
in what concerns person or place, cannot see the problem of existence. This the intellect always ponders.
Nature shows all things formed and bound. The intellect pierces the form, overleaps the wall, detects
intrinsic likeness between remote things, and reduces
all things into a few principles.

The making a fact the subject of thought, raises it.
All that mass of mental and moral phenomena which
we do not make objects of voluntary thought, come
within the power of fortune; they constitute the circumstance of daily life; they are subject to change,
to fear, and hope. Every man beholds his human
condition with a degree of melancholy. As a ship

aground is battered by the waves, so man, imprisoned in mortal life, lies open to the mercy of coming events. But a truth, separated by the intellect, is no longer a subject of destiny. We behold it as a god upraised above care and fear. And so any fact in our life, or any record of our fancies or reflections, disentangled from the web of our unconsciousness, becomes an object impersonal and immortal. It is the past restored, but embalmed. A better art than that of Egypt has taken fear and corruption out of it. It is eviscerated of care. It is offered for science. What is addressed to us for contemplation does not threaten us, but makes us intellectual beings.

The growth of the intellect is spontaneous in every step. The mind that grows could not predict the times, the means, the mode of that spontaneity. God enters by a private door into every individual. Long prior to the age of reflection, is the thinking of the mind. Out of darkness, it came insensibly into the marvellous light of to-day. Over it always reigned a firm law. In the period of infancy it accepted and disposed of all impressions from the surrounding creation after its own way. Whatever any mind doth or saith, is after a law. It has no random act or word. And this native law remains over it after it has come to reflection or conscious thought. In the most worn, pedantic, introverted, self-tormentor's life, the greatest part is incalculable by him, unforeseen, unimaginable, and must be, until he can take himself up by his own ears. What am I? What has my will done to make me that I am? Nothing. I have been floated into this thought, this hour, this connection of events, by might and mind sublime, and my ingenuity and wilfulness have not thwarted, have not aided to an appreciable degree.

Our spontaneous action is always the best. You cannot, with your best deliberation and heed, come so close to any question as your spontaneous glance shall bring you, whilst you rise from your bed, or walk abroad in the morning after meditating the matter before sleep, on the previous night. Always our thinking is a pious reception. Our truth of thought is therefore vitiated as much by too violent direction given by our will, as by too great negligence. We do not determine what we will think. We only open our senses, clear away, as we can, all obstruction from the fact, and suffer the intellect to see. We have little control over our thoughts. We are the prisoners of ideas. They catch us up for moments into their heaven, and so fully engage us, that we take no thought for the morrow, gaze like children, without an effort to make them our own. By-and-by we fall out of that rapture, bethink us where we have been, what we have seen, and repeat, as truly as we can, what we have beheld. As far as we can recall these extasies, we carry away in the ineffaceable memory, the result, and all men and all the ages confirm it. It is called Truth. But the moment we cease to report, and attempt to correct and contrive, it is not truth.

If we consider what persons have stimulated and profited us, we shall perceive the superiority of the spontaneous or intuitive principle over the arithmetical or logical. The first always contains the second, but virtual and latent. We want, in every man, a long logic ; we cannot pardon the absence of it, but it must not be spoken. Logic is the procession or proportionate unfolding of the intuition ; but its virtue is as silent method ; the moment it would appear as propositions, and have a separate value, it is worthless.

In every man's mind, some images, words, and facts remain, without effort on his part to imprint them, which others forget, and afterwards these illustrate to him important laws. All our progress is an unfolding, like the vegetable bud. You have first an instinct, then an opinion, then a knowledge, as the plant has root, bud, and fruit. Trust the instinct to the end, though you can render no reason. It is vain to hurry it. By trusting it to the end, it shall ripen into truth, and you shall know why you believe.

Each mind has its own method. A true man never acquires after college rules. What you have aggregated in a natural manner, surprizes and delights when it is produced. For we cannot oversee each other's secret. And hence the differences between men in natural endowment are insignificant in comparison with their common wealth. Do you think the porter and the cook have no anecdotes, no experiences, no wonders for you? Every body knows as much as the savant. The walls of rude minds are scrawled all over with facts, with thoughts. They shall one day bring a lantern and read the inscriptions. Every man, in the degree in which he has wit and culture, finds his curiosity inflamed concerning

12*

the modes of living and thinking of other men, and especially of those classes whose minds have not been subdued by the drill of school education.

This instinctive action never ceases in a healthy mind, but becomes richer and more frequent in its informations through all states of culture. At last comes the era of reflection, when we not only observe, but take pains to observe ; when we of set purpose, sit down to consider an abstract truth ; when we keep the mind's eye open, whilst we converse, whilst we read, whilst we act, intent to learn the secret law of some class of facts.

What is the hardest task in the world ? To think. I would put myself in the attitude to look in the eye an abstract truth, and I cannot. I blench and withdraw on this side and on that. I seem to know what he meant, who said, No man can see God face to face and live. For example, a man explores the basis of civil government. Let him intend his mind without respite, without rest, in one direction. His best heed long time avails him nothing. Yet thoughts are flitting before him. We all but apprehend, we dimly forebode the truth. We say, I will walk abroad, and the truth will take form and clearness to me. We go forth, but cannot find it. It seems as if we needed only the stillness and composed attitude of the library, to seize the thought. But we come in, and are as far from it as at first. Then, in a moment, and unannounced, the truth appears. A certain, wandering light appears, and is the distinction, the principle we wanted. But the oracle comes, because we had previously laid siege to the shrine. It seems as if the law of the intellect resembled that law of nature by which we now inspire, now expire the breath ; by which the heart now draws in, then hurls out the blood, — the law of undulation. So now you must labor with your brains, and now you must forbear your activity, and see what the great Soul showeth.

Our intellections are mainly prospective. The immortality of man is as legitimately preached from the intellections as from the moral volitions. Every intellection is mainly prospective. Its present value is its least. It is a little seed. Inspect what delights you in Plutarch, in Shakspeare, in Cervantes. Each truth that a writer acquires, is a lantern which he instantly turns full on what facts and thoughts lay already in his mind, and behold, all the mats and rubbish which had littered his garret, become precious. Every trivial fact in his private biography becomes an illustration of this new principle, revisits the day, and delights all men by its piquancy and new charm. Men say, where did he get this ? and think there was something divine in his life. But no ; they have myriads of facts just as good, would they only get a lamp to ransack their attics withal.

We are all wise. The difference between persons is not in wisdom but in art. I knew, in an academical club, a person who always deferred to me, who, seeing my whim for writing, fancied that my experiences had somewhat superior ; whilst I saw that his experiences were as good as mine. Give them to me, and I would make the same use of them. He held the old ; he holds the new ; I had the habit of tacking together the old and the new, which he did not use to exercise. This may hold in the great examples. Perhaps if we should meet Shakspeare, we should not be conscious of any steep inferiority ; no : but of a great equality, — only that he possessed a strange skill of using, of classifying his facts, which we lacked. For, notwithstanding our utter incapacity to produce anything like Hamlet and Othello, see the perfect reception this wit, and immense knowledge of life, and liquid eloquence find in us all.

If you gather apples in the sunshine, or make hay, or hoe corn, and then retire within doors, and shut your eyes, and press them with your hand, you shall still see apples hanging in the bright light, with boughs and leaves thereto, or the tasselled grass, or the cornflags, and this for five or six hours afterwards. There lie the impressions on the retentive organ, though you knew it not. So lies the whole series of natural images with which your life has made you acquainted, in your memory, though you know it not, and a thrill of passion flashes light on their dark chamber, and the active power seizes instantly the fit image, as the word of its momentary thought.

It is long ere we discover how rich we are. Our history, we are sure, is quite tame. We have nothing to write, nothing to infer. But our wiser years still run back to the despised recollections of childhood, and always we are fishing up some wonderful article out of that pond ; until, by-and-by, we begin to suspect that the biography of the one foolish person we know,

is, in reality, nothing less than the miniature para-
phrase of the hundred volumes of the Universal
History.

In the intellect constructive, which we popularly
designate by the word Genius, we observe the same
balance of two elements, as in intellect receptive.
The constructive intellect produces thoughts, sentences, poems, plans, designs, systems. It is the generation of the mind, the marriage of thought with
nature. To genius must always go two gifts, the
thought and the publication. The first is revelation,
always a miracle, which no frequency of occurrence,
or incessant study can ever familiarize, but which
must always leave the inquirer stupid with wonder.
It is the advent of truth into the world, a form of
thought now, for the first time, bursting into the universe, a child of the old eternal soul, a piece of genuine and immeasurable greatness. It seems, for the
time, to inherit all that has yet existed, and to dictate
to the unborn. It affects every thought of man, and
goes to fashion every institution. But to make it
available, it needs a vehicle or art by which it is conveyed to men. To be communicable, it must become
picture or sensible object. We must learn the language of facts. The most wonderful inspirations die
with their subject, if he has no hand to paint them to
the senses. The ray of light passes invisible through
space, and only when it falls on an object is it seen.
When the spiritual energy is directed on something
outward, then is it a thought. The relation between
it and you, first makes you, the value of you, apparent

to me. The rich, inventive genius of the painter must be smothered and lost for want of the power of drawing, and in our happy hours, we should be inexhaustible poets, if once we could break through the silence into adequate rhyme. As all men have some access to primary truth, so all have some art or power of communication in their head, but only in the artist does it descend into the hand. There is an inequality whose laws we do not yet know, between two men and between two moments of the same man, in respect to this faculty. In common hours, we have the same facts as in the uncommon or inspired, but they do not sit for their portraits, they are not detached, but lie in a web. The thought of genius is spontaneous; but the power of picture or expression, in the most enriched and flowing nature, implies a mixture of will, a certain control over the spontaneous states, without which no production is possible. It is a conversion of all nature into the rhetoric of thought, under the eye of judgment, with a strenuous exercise of choice. And yet the imaginative vocabulary seems to be spontaneous also. It does not flow from experience only or mainly, but from a richer source. Not by any conscious imitation of particular forms are the grand strokes of the painter executed, but by repairing to the fountain-head of all forms in his mind. Who is the first drawing-master? Without instruction we know very well the ideal of the human form. A child knows if an arm or a leg be distorted in a picture, if the attitude be natural, or grand, or mean, though he has never received any instruction in drawing, or heard any conversation on the subject, nor can himself draw with correctness a single feature. A good form strikes all eyes pleasantly, long before they have any science on the subject, and a beautiful face sets twenty hearts in palpitation, prior to all consideration of the mechanical proportions of the features and head. We may owe to dreams some light on the fountain of this skill ; for, as soon as we let our will go, and let the unconscious states ensue, see what cunning draughtsmen we are! We entertain ourselves with wonderful forms of men, of women, of animals, of gardens, of woods, and of monsters, and the mystic pencil wherewith we then draw, has no awkwardness or inexperience, no meagreness or poverty ; it can design well, and group well ; its composition is full of art, its colors are well laid on, and the whole canvass which it paints, is life-like, and apt to touch us with terror, with tenderness, with desire, and with grief. Neither are the artist's copies from experience, ever mere copies, but always touched and softened by tints from this ideal domain.

The conditions essential to a constructive mind, do not appear to be so often combined but that a good sentence or verse remains fresh and memorable for a long time. Yet when we write with ease, and come out into the free air of thought, we seem to be assured that nothing is easier than to continue this communication at pleasure. Up, down, around, the kingdom of thought has no enclosures, but the Muse makes us free of her city. Well, the world has a million writers. One would think, then, that good thought would

be as familiar as air and water, and the gifts of each
new hour would exclude the last. Yet we can count
all our good books ; nay, I remember any beautiful
verse for twenty years. It is true that the discerning
intellect of the world is always greatly in advance of
the creative, so that always there are many competent judges of the best book, and few writers of the
best books. But some of the conditions of intellectual
construction are of rare occurrence. The intellect is
a whole, and demands integrity in every work. This
is resisted equally by a man's devotion to a single
thought, and by his ambition to combine too many.

Truth is our element of life, yet if a man fasten
his attention on a single aspect of truth, and apply
himself to that alone for a long time, the truth becomes
distorted and not itself, but falsehood ; herein resembling the air, which is our natural element, and the
breath of our nostrils, but if a stream of the same be
directed on the body for a time, it causes cold, fever,
and even death. How wearisome the grammarian,
the phrenologist, the political or religious fanatic, or
indeed any possessed mortal, whose balance is lost
by the exaggeration of a single topic. It is incipient
insanity. Every thought is a prison also. I cannot
see what you see, because I am caught up by a strong
wind and blown so far in one direction, that I am out
of the hoop of your horizon.

Is it any better, if the student, to avoid this offence,
and to liberalize himself, aims to make a mechanical
whole, of history, or science, or philosophy, by a numerical addition of all the facts that fall within his

vision ? The world refuses to be analyzed by addition and subtraction. When we are young, we spend much time and pains in filling our note-books with all definitions of Religion, Love, Poetry, Politics, Art, in the hope that in the course of a few years, we shall have condensed into our encyclopedia, the net value of all the theories at which the world has yet arrived. But year after year our tables get no completeness, and at last we discover that our curve is a parabola, whose arcs will never meet.

Neither by detachment, neither by aggregation, is the integrity of the intellect transmitted to its works, but by a vigilance which brings the intellect in its greatness and best state to operate every moment. It must have the same wholeness which nature has. Although no diligence can rebuild the universe in a model, by the best accumulation or disposition of details, yet does the world reappear in miniature in every event, so that all the laws of nature may be read in the smallest fact. The intellect must have the like perfection in its apprehension, and in its works. For this reason, an index or mercury of intellectual proficiency is the perception of identity. We talk with accomplished persons who appear to be strangers in nature. The cloud, the tree, the turf, the bird are not theirs, have nothing of them : the world is only their lodging and table. But the poet, whose verses are to be spheral and complete, is one whom nature cannot deceive, whatsoever face of strangeness she may put on. He feels a strict consanguinity, and detects more likeness than variety in all her changes.

We are stung by the desire for new thought, but when we receive a new thought, it is only the old thought with a new face, and though we make it our own, we instantly crave another ; we are not really enriched. For the truth was in us, before it was reflected to us from natural objects ; and the profound genius will cast the likeness of all creatures into every product of his wit.

But if the constructive powers are rare, and it is given to few men to be poets, yet every man is a receiver of this descending holy ghost, and may well study the laws of its influx. Exactly parallel is the whole rule of intellectual duty, to the rule of moral duty. A self-denial, no less austere than the saint's, is demanded of the scholar. He must worship truth, and forego all things for that, and choose defeat and pain, so that his treasure in thought is thereby augmented.

God offers to every mind its choice between truth and repose. Take which you please, — you can never have both. Between these, as a pendulum, man oscillates ever. He in whom the love of repose predominates, will accept the first creed, the first philosophy, the first political party he meets, — most likely, his father's. He gets rest, commodity, and reputation ; but he shuts the door of truth. He in whom the love of truth predominates, will keep himself aloof from all moorings and afloat. He will abstain from dogmatism, and recognise all the opposite negations between which, as walls, his being is swung. He submits to the inconvenience of suspense and imperfect opinion, but he is a candidate for truth, as the other is not, and respects the highest law of his being.

The circle of the green earth he must measure with his shoes, to find the man who can yield him truth. He shall then know that there is somewhat more blessed and great in hearing than in speaking. Happy is the hearing man : unhappy the speaking man. As long as I hear truth, I am bathed by a beautiful element, and am not conscious of any limits to my nature. The suggestions are thousandfold that I hear and see. The waters of the great deep have ingress and egress to the soul. But if I speak, I define, I confine, and am less. When Socrates speaks, Lysis and Menexenus are afflicted by no shame that they do not speak. They also are good. He likewise defers to them, loves them, whilst he speaks. Because a true and natural man contains and is the same truth which an eloquent man articulates : but in the eloquent man, because he can articulate it, it seems something the less to reside, and he turns to these silent beautiful with the more inclination and respect. The ancient sentence said, Let us be silent, for so are the gods. Silence is a solvent that destroys personality, and gives us leave to be great and universal. Every man's progress is through a succession of teachers, each of whom seems at the time to have a superlative influence, but it at last gives place to a new. Frankly let him accept it all. Jesus says, Leave father, mother, house and lands, and follow me. Who leaves all, receives more. This is as true intellectually, as morally. Each new mind we approach, seems to require an abdication of all our past and present possessions. A new doctrine seems, at first, a subversion of all our opinions, tastes, and manner of living. Such has Swedenborg, such has Kant, such has Coleridge, such has Cousin seemed to many young men in this country. Take thankfully and heartily all they can give. Exhaust them, wrestle with them, let them not go until their blessing be won, and after a short season, the dismay will be overpast, the excess of influence withdrawn, and they will be no longer an alarming meteor, but one more bright star shining serenely in your heaven, and blending its light with all your day.

But whilst he gives himself up unreservedly to that which draws him, because that is his own, he is to refuse himself to that which draws him not, whatsoever fame and authority may attend it, because it is not his own. Entire self-reliance belongs to the intellect. One soul is a counterpoise of all souls, as a capillary column of water is a balance for the sea. It must treat things, and books, and sovereign genius, as itself also a sovereign. If Æschylus be that man he is taken for, he has not yet done his office, when he has educated the learned of Europe for a thousand years. He is now to approve himself a master of delight to me also. If he cannot do that, all his fame shall avail him nothing with me. I were a fool not to sacrifice a thousand Æschyluses to my intellectual integrity. Especially take the same ground in regard to abstract truth, the science of the mind. The Bacon, the Spinoza, the Hume, Schelling, Kant, or whosoever propounds to you a philosophy of the mind, is only a more or less awkward translator of things in your consciousness, which you have also your way of seeing, perhaps of denominating. Say then, instead of too timidly poring into his obscure sense, that he has not succeeded in rendering back to you your consciousness. He has not succeeded; now let another try. If Plato cannot, perhaps Spinoza will. If Spinoza cannot, then perhaps Kant. Any how, when at last it is done, you will find it is no recondite, but a simple, natural, common state, which the writer restores to you.

But let us end these didactics. I will not, though the subject might provoke it, speak to the open question between Truth and Love. I shall not presume to interfere in the old politics of the skies; " The cherubim know most; the seraphim love most." The gods shall settle their own quarrels. But I cannot recite, even thus rudely, laws of the intellect, without remembering that lofty and sequestered class of men who have been its prophets and oracles, the high priesthood of the pure reason, the *Trismegisti*, the expounders of the principles of thought from age to age. When at long intervals, we turn over their abstruse pages, wonderful seems the calm and grand air of these few, these great spiritual lords, who have walked in the world, — these of the old religion, — dwelling in a worship which makes the sanctities of christianity look *parvenues* and popular; for " persuasion is in soul, but necessity is in intellect." This band of grandees, Hermes, Heraclitus, Empedocles,

Plato, Plotinus, Olympiodorus, Proclus, Synesius,
and the rest, have somewhat so vast in their logic, so
primary in their thinking, that it seems antecedent to
all the ordinary distinctions of rhetoric and literature,
and to be at once poetry, and music, and dancing,
and astronomy, and mathematics. I am present at
the sowing of the seed of the world. With a geometry of sunbeams, the soul lays the foundations of
nature. The truth and grandeur of their thought is
proved by its scope and applicability, for it commands
the entire schedule and inventory of things, for its
illustration. But what marks its elevation, and has
even a comic look to us, is the innocent serenity with
which these babe-like Jupiters sit in their clouds, and
from age to age prattle to each other, and to no contemporary. Well assured that their speech is intelligible, and the most natural thing in the world, they
add thesis to thesis, without a moment's heed of
the universal astonishment of the human race below,
who do not comprehend their plainest argument ; nor
do they ever relent so much as to insert a popular or
explaining sentence ; nor testify the least displeasure
or petulance at the dulness of their amazed auditory.
The angels are so enamored of the language that is
spoken in heaven, that they will not distort their lips
with the hissing and unmusical dialects of men, but
speak their own, whether there be any who understand
it or not.

ART.

ESSAY XII.

ART.

———

BECAUSE the soul is progressive, it never quite repeats itself, but in every act attempts the production of a new and fairer whole. This appears in works both of the useful and the fine arts, if we employ the popular distinction of works according to their aim, either at use or beauty. Thus in our fine arts, not imitation, but creation is the aim. In landscapes, the painter should give the suggestion of a fairer creation than we know. The details, the prose of nature he should omit, and give us only the spirit and splendor. He should know that the landscape has beauty for his eye, because it expresses a thought which is to him good : and this, because the same power which sees through his eyes, is seen in that spectacle ; and he will come to value the expression of nature, and not nature itself, and so exalt in his copy, the features that please him. He will give the gloom of gloom,

13

and the sunshine of sunshine. In a portrait, he must inscribe the character, and not the features, and must esteem the man who sits to him as himself only an imperfect picture or likeness of the aspiring original within.

What is that abridgment and selection we observe in all spiritual activity, but itself the creative impulse? for it is the inlet of that higher illumination which teaches to convey a larger sense by simpler symbols. What is a man but nature's finer success in self-explication? What is a man but a finer and compacter landscape, than the horizon figures; nature's eclecticism? and what is his speech, his love of painting, love of nature, but a still finer success? all the weary miles and tons of space and bulk left out, and the spirit or moral of it contracted into a musical word, or the most cunning stroke of the pencil?

But the artist must employ the symbols in use in his day and nation, to convey his enlarged sense to his fellow-men. Thus the new in art is always formed out of the old. The Genius of the Hour always sets his ineffaceable seal on the work, and gives it an inexpressible charm for the imagination. As far as the spiritual character of the period overpowers the artist, and finds expression in his work, so far it will always retain a certain grandeur, and will represent to future beholders the Unknown, the Inevitable, the Divine. No man can quite exclude this element of Necessity from his labor. No man can quite emancipate himself from his age and country, or produce a model in which the education,

the religion, the politics, usages, and arts, of his times
shall have no share. Though he were never so original, never so wilful and fantastic, he cannot wipe
out of his work every trace of the thoughts amidst
which it grew. The very avoidance betrays the
usage he avoids. Above his will, and out of his sight,
he is necessitated, by the air he breathes, and the idea
on which he and his contemporaries live and toil,
to share the manner of his times, without knowing
what that manner is. Now that which is inevitable
in the work, has a higher charm than individual talent
can ever give, inasmuch as the artist's pen or chisel
seems to have been held and guided by a gigantic
hand to inscribe a line in the history of the human
race. This circumstance gives a value to the Egyptian hieroglyphics, to the Indian, Chinese, and Mexican
idols, however gross and shapeless. They denote the
height of the human soul in that hour, and were not
fantastic, but sprung from a necessity as deep as the
world. Shall I now add that the whole extant product
of the plastic arts has herein its highest value, *as history ;* as a stroke drawn in the portrait of that fate,
perfect and beautiful, according to whose ordinations
all beings advance to their beatitude.

Thus, historically viewed, it has been the office
of art to educate the perception of beauty. We are
immersed in beauty, but our eyes have no clear vision.
It needs, by the exhibition of single traits, to assist and
lead the dormant taste. We carve and paint, or we
behold what is carved and painted, as students of the
mystery of Form. The virtue of art lies in detach-

ment, in sequestering one object from the embarrassing variety.   Until one thing comes out from the
connection of things, there can be enjoyment, contemplation, but no thought.   Our happiness and un-
happiness are unproductive.   The infant lies in a
pleasing trance, but his individual character, and his
practical power depend on his daily progress in the
separation of things, and dealing with one at a time.
Love and all the passions concentrate all existence
around a single form.   It is the habit of certain minds
to give an all-excluding fulness to the object, the thought,
the word, they alight upon, and to make that for the
time the deputy of the world.   These are the artists,
the orators, the leaders of society.   The power to
detach, and to magnify by detaching, is the essence
of rhetoric in the hands of the orator and the poet.
This rhetoric, or power to fix the momentary emi-
nency of an object, so remarkable in Burke, in Byron, in Carlyle, — the painter and sculptor exhibit in
color and in stone.   The power depends on the depth
of the artist's insight of that object he contemplates.
For every object has its roots in central nature, and
may of course be so exhibited to us as to represent
the world.   Therefore, each work of genius is the
tyrant of the hour, and concentrates attention on
itself.   For the time, it is the only thing worth naming,
to do that, — be it a sonnet, an opera, a landscape, a
statue, an oration, the plan of a temple, of a cam-
paign, or of a voyage of discovery.   Presently we
pass to some other object, which rounds itself into a
whole, as did the first ; for example, a well laid gar-

den : and nothing seems worth doing but the laying out of gardens. I should think fire the best thing in the world, if I were not acquainted with air, and water, and earth. For it is the right and property of all natural objects, of all genuine talents, of all native properties whatsoever, to be for their moment the top of the world. A squirrel leaping from bough to bough, and making the wood but one wide tree for his pleasure, fills the eye not less than a lion, is beautiful, self-sufficing, and stands then and there for nature. A good ballad draws my ear and heart whilst I listen, as much as an epic has done before. A dog, drawn by a master, or a litter of pigs, satisfies, and is a reality not less than the frescoes of Angelo. From this succession of excellent objects, learn we at last the immensity of the world, the opulence of human nature, which can run out to infinitude in any direction. But I also learn that what astonished and fascinated me in the first work, astonished me in the second work also, that excellence of all things is one.

The office of painting and sculpture seems to be merely initial. The best pictures can easily tell us their last secret. The best pictures are rude draughts of a few of the miraculous dots and lines and dyes which make up the ever-changing " landscape with figures " amidst which we dwell. Painting seems to be to the eye what dancing is to the limbs. When that has educated the frame to self-possession, to nimbleness, to grace, the steps of the dancing-master are better forgotten ; so painting teaches me the splendor of color and the expression of form, and, as

I see many pictures and higher genius in the art, I
see the boundless opulence of the pencil, the indifferency in which the artist stands free to choose out of
the possible forms.   If he can draw every thing, why
draw any thing ? and then is my eye opened to the
eternal picture which nature paints in the street with
moving men and children, beggars, and fine ladies,
draped in red, and green, and blue, and gray ; long-
haired, grizzled, white-faced, black-faced, wrinkled,
giant, dwarf, expanded, elfish, — capped and based
by heaven, earth, and sea.

A gallery of sculpture teaches more austerely the
same lesson.   As picture teaches the coloring, so
sculpture the anatomy of form.   When I have seen
fine statues, and afterwards enter a public assembly,
I understand well what he meant who said, " When
I have been reading Homer, all men look like giants."
I too see that painting and sculpture are gymnastics
of the eye, its training to the niceties and curiosities
of its function.   There is no statue like this living
man, with his infinite advantage over all ideal sculpture, of perpetual variety.   What a gallery of art
have I here !   No mannerist made these varied groups
and diverse original single figures.   Here is the artist
himself improvising, grim and glad, at his block.
Now one thought strikes him, now another, and with
each moment he alters the whole air, attitude and
expression of his clay.   Away with your nonsense of
oil and easels, of marble and chisels : except to open
your eyes to the witchcraft of eternal art, they are
hypocritical rubbish.

The reference of all production at last to an Aboriginal Power, explains the traits common to all works of the highest art, that they are universally intelligible ; that they restore to us the simplest states of mind ; and are religious. Since what skill is therein shown is the reappearance of the original soul, a jet of pure light; it should produce a similar impression to that made by natural objects. In happy hours, nature appears to us one with art ; art perfected, — the work of genius. And the individual in whom simple tastes and susceptibility to all the great human influences, overpowers the accidents of a local and special culture, is the best critic of art. Though we travel the world over to find the beautiful, we must carry it with us, or we find it not. The best of beauty is a finer charm than skill in surfaces, in outlines, or rules of art can ever teach, namely, a radiation from the work of art, of human character, — a wonderful expression through stone or canvass or musical sound of the deepest and simplest attributes of our nature, and therefore most intelligible at last to those souls which have these attributes. In the sculptures of the Greeks, in the masonry of the Romans, and in the pictures of the Tuscan and Venetian masters, the highest charm is the universal language they speak. A confession of moral nature, of purity, love, and hope, breathes from them all. That which we carry to them, the same we bring back more fairly illustrated in the memory. The traveller who visits the Vatican, and passes from chamber to chamber through galleries of statues, vases, sarcophagi, and candelabra, through all forms of beauty, cut in the richest materials, is in danger of forgetting the simplicity of the principles out of which they all sprung, and that they had their origin from thoughts and laws in his own breast. He studies the technical rules on these wonderful remains, but forgets that these works were not always thus constellated ; that they are the contributions of many ages, and many countries ; that each came out of the solitary workshop of one artist, who toiled perhaps in ignorance of the existence of other sculpture, created his work without other model, save life, household life, and the sweet and smart of personal relations, of beating hearts, and meeting eyes, of poverty, and necessity, and hope, and fear. These were his inspirations, and these are the effects he carries home to your heart and mind. In proportion to his force, the artist will find in his work an outlet for his proper character. He must not be in any manner pinched or hindered by his material, but through his necessity of imparting himself, the adamant will be wax in his hands, and will allow an adequate communication of himself in his full stature and proportion. Not a conventional nature and culture need he cumber himself with, nor ask what is the mode in Rome or in Paris, but that house, and weather, and manner of living, which poverty and the fate of birth have made at once so odious and so dear, in the gray, unpainted wood cabin, on the corner of a New Hampshire farm, or in the log hut of the backwoods, or in the narrow lodging where he has endured the constraints and seeming of a city poverty, — will serve as well as any other condition, as the symbol of a thought which pours itself indifferently through all

I remember, when in my younger days, I had heard of the wonders of Italian painting, I fancied the great pictures would be great strangers ; some surprising combination of color and form ; a foreign wonder, barbaric pearl and gold, like the spontoons and standards of the militia, which play such pranks in the eyes and imaginations of school-boys. I was to see and acquire I knew not what. When I came at last to Rome, and saw with eyes the pictures, I found that genius left to novices the gay and fantastic and ostentatious, and itself pierced directly to the simple and true ; that it was familiar and sincere ; that it was the old, eternal fact I had met already in so many forms ; unto which I lived ; that it was the plain *you and me* I knew so well, — had left at home in so many conversations. I had the same experience already in a church at Naples. There I saw that nothing was changed with me but the place, and said to myself, — ' Thou foolish child, hast thou come out hither, over four thousand miles of salt water, to find that which was perfect to thee, there at home ? ' — that fact I saw again in the Academmia at Naples, in the chambers of sculpture, and yet again when I came to Rome, and to the paintings of Raphael, Angelo, Sacchi, Titian, and Leonardo da Vinci. " What old mole ! workest thou in the earth so fast ? " It had travelled by my side : that which I fancied I had left in Boston, was here in the Vatican, and again at Milan, and at Paris, and made all travelling ridiculous as a treadmill. I now require this of all pictures, that they domesticate me, not that they dazzle me. Pictures must not be too picturesque. Nothing astonishes men so much as common sense and plain dealing. All great actions have been simple, and all great pictures are.

The Transfiguration, by Raphael, is an eminent example of this peculiar merit. A calm, benignant beauty shines over all this picture, and goes directly to the heart. It seems almost to call you by name. The sweet and sublime face of Jesus is beyond praise, yet how it disappoints all florid expectations! This familiar, simple, home-speaking countenance, is as if one should meet a friend. The knowledge of picture-dealers has its value, but listen not to their criticism when your heart is touched by genius. It was not painted for them, it was painted for you; for such as had eyes capable of being touched by simplicity and lofty emotions.

Yet when we have said all our fine things about the arts, we must end with a frank confession, that the arts, as we know them, are but initial. Our best praise is given to what they aimed and promised, not to the actual result. He has conceived meanly of the resources of man, who believes that the best age of production is past. The real value of the Iliad, or the Transfiguration, is as signs of power; billows or ripples they are of the great stream of tendency; tokens of the everlasting effort to produce, which even in its worst estate, the soul betrays. Art has not yet come to its maturity, if it do not put itself abreast with the most potent influences of the world, if it is not practical and moral, if it do not stand in connection with the conscience, if it do not make the poor and uncultivated feel that it addresses them with a voice of lofty cheer. There is higher work for Art than the arts. They are abortive births of an imperfect or vitiated instinct. Art is the need to create ; but in its essence, immense and universal, it is impatient of working with lame or tied hands, and of making cripples and monsters, such as all pictures and statues are. Nothing less than the creation of man and nature is its end. A man should find in it an outlet for his whole energy. He may paint and carve only as long as he can do that. Art should exhilarate, and throw down the walls of circumstance on every side, awakening in the beholder the same sense of universal relation and power which the work evinced in the artist, and its highest effect is to make new artists.

Already History is old enough to witness the old age and disappearance of particular arts. The art of sculpture is long ago perished to any real effect. It was originally an useful art, a mode of writing, a savage's record of gratitude or devotion, and among a people possessed of a wonderful perception of form, this childish carving was refined to the utmost splendor of effect. But it is the game of a rude and youthful people, and not the manly labor of a wise and spiritual nation. Under an oak tree loaded with leaves and nuts, under a sky full of eternal eyes, I stand in a thoroughfare ; but in the works of our plastic arts, and especially of sculpture, creation is driven into a corner. I cannot hide from myself that there is a certain appearance of paltriness, as of toys, and the trumpery of a theatre, in sculpture. Nature transcends all our moods of thought, and its secret we do not yet find. But the gallery stands at the mercy of our moods, and there is a moment when it becomes frivolous. I do not wonder that Newton, with an attention habitually engaged on the path of planets and suns, should have wondered what the Earl of Pembroke found to admire in " stone dolls." Sculpture may serve to teach the pupil how deep is the secret of form, how purely the spirit can translate its meanings into that eloquent dialect. But the statue will look cold and false before that new activity which needs to roll through all things, and is impatient of counterfeits, and things not alive. Picture and sculpture are the celebrations and festivities of form. But true art is never fixed, but always flowing. The sweetest music is not in the oratorio, but in the human voice when it speaks from its instant life, tones of tenderness, truth, or courage. The oratorio has already lost its relation to the morning, to the sun, and the earth, but that persuading voice is in tune with these. All works of art should not be detached, but extempore performances. A great man is a new statue in every attitude and action. A beautiful woman is a picture which drives all beholders nobly mad. Life may be lyric or epic, as well as a poem or a romance.

A true announcement of the law of creation, if a

man were found worthy to declare it, would carry
art up into the kingdom of nature, and destroy its
separate and contrasted existence. The fountains of
invention and beauty in modern society are all but
dried up.   A popular novel, a theatre, or a ball-room
makes us feel that we are all paupers in the alms-
house of this world, without dignity, without skill, or
industry. Art is as poor and low.   The old tragic
Necessity, which lowers on the brows even of the
Venuses and the Cupids of the antique, and furnishes
the sole apology for the intrusion of such anomalous
figures into nature, — namely, that they were inevitable ; that the artist was drunk with a passion for form
which he could not resist, and which vented itself in these
fine extravagancies, — no longer dignifies the chisel or
the pencil. But the artist, and the connoisseur, now seek
in art the exhibition of their talent, or an asylum from
the evils of life. Men are not well pleased with the figure they make in their own imagination, and they flee
to art, and convey their better sense in an oratorio, a
statue, or a picture.   Art makes the same effort
which a sensual prosperity makes, namely, to detach
the beautiful from the useful, to do up the work as
unavoidable, and hating it, pass on to enjoyment.
These solaces and compensations, this division of
beauty from use, the laws of nature do not permit.
As soon as beauty is sought not from religion and
love, but for pleasure, it degrades the seeker.   High
beauty is no longer attainable by him in canvass or in
stone, in sound, or in lyrical construction ; an effemi-
nate prudent, sickly beauty, which is not beauty, is all

that can be formed ; for the hand can never execute any thing higher than the character can inspire.

The art that thus separates, is itself first separated. Art must not be a superficial talent, but must begin farther back in man. Now men do not see nature to be beautiful, and they go to make a statue which shall be. They abhor men as tasteless, dull, and inconvertible, and console themselves with color-bags, and blocks of marble. They reject life as prosaic, and create a death which they call poetic. They despatch the day's weary chores, and fly to voluptuous reveries. They eat and drink, that they may afterwards execute the ideal. Thus is art vilified ; the name conveys to the mind its secondary and bad senses ; it stands in the imagination, as somewhat contrary to nature, and struck with death from the first. Would it not be better to begin higher up, — to serve the ideal before they eat and drink ; to serve the ideal in eating and drinking, in drawing the breath, and in the functions of life ? Beauty must come back to the useful arts, and the distinction between the fine and the useful arts be forgotten. If history were truly told, if life were nobly spent, it would be no longer easy or possible to distinguish the one from the other. In nature, all is useful, all is beautiful. It is therefore beautiful, because it is alive, moving, reproductive ; it is therefore useful, because it is symmetrical and fair. Beauty will not come at the call of a legislature, nor will it repeat in England or America, its history in Greece. It will come, as always, unannounced, and spring up between the feet of brave and earnest

men. It is in vain that we look for genius to reiterate
its miracles in the old arts ; it is its instinct to find
beauty and holiness in new and necessary facts, in
the field and roadside, in the shop and mill. Proceeding from a religious heart it will raise to a
divine use, the railroad, the insurance office, the
joint stock company, our law, our primary assemblies,
our commerce, the galvanic battery, the electric jar,
the prism, and the chemist's retort, in which we seek
now only an economical use. Is not the selfish, and
even cruel aspect which belongs to our great mechanical works, to mills, railways, and machinery, the
effect of the mercenary impulses which these works
obey ? When its errands are noble and adequate, a
steamboat bridging the Atlantic between Old and New
England, and arriving at its ports with the punctuality
of a planet, — is a step of man into harmony with
nature. The boat at St. Petersburgh, which plies
along the Lena by magnetism, needs little to make it
sublime. When science is learned in love, and its
powers are wielded by love, they will appear the
supplements and continuations of the material creation.

THE END.

ESSAYS:

SECOND SERIES.

BY

R. W. EMERSON.

———◆———

BOSTON:
JAMES MUNROE AND COMPANY.
———
MDCCCXLIV.

BOSTON:
PRINTED BY THURSTON, TORRY, AND CO.
31 Devonshire Street.

CONTENTS.

THE POET.

A moody child and wildly wise
Pursued the game with joyful eyes,
Which chose, like meteors, their way,
And rived the dark with private ray :
They overleapt the horizon's edge,
Searched with Apollo's privilege ;
Through man, and woman, and sea, and star,
Saw the dance of nature forward far ;
Through worlds, and races, and terms, and times,
Saw musical order, and pairing rhymes.

Olympian bards who sung
Divine ideas below,
Which always find us young,
And always keep us so.

ESSAY I.

THE POET.

———

THOSE who are esteemed umpires of taste, are often persons who have acquired some knowledge of admired pictures or sculptures, and have an inclination for whatever is elegant; but if you inquire whether they are beautiful souls, and whether their own acts are like fair pictures, you learn that they are selfish and sensual. Their cultivation is local, as if you should rub a log of dry wood in one spot to produce fire, all the rest remaining cold. Their knowledge of the fine arts is some study of rules and particulars, or some limited judgment of color or form, which is exercised for amusement or for show. It is a proof of the shallowness of the doctrine of beauty, as it lies in the minds of our amateurs, that men seem to have lost the perception of the instant dependence of form upon soul.

There is no doctrine of forms in our philosophy. We were put into our bodies, as fire is
put into a pan, to be carried about; but there
is no accurate adjustment between the spirit
and the organ, much less is the latter the germination of the former. So in regard to other
forms, the intellectual men do not believe in
any essential dependence of the material world
on thought and volition. Theologians think
it a pretty air-castle to talk of the spiritual
meaning of a ship or a cloud, of a city or a
contract, but they prefer to come again to the
solid ground of historical evidence; and even
the poets are contented with a civil and con-
formed manner of living, and to write poems
from the fancy, at a safe distance from their
own experience. But the highest minds of
the world have never ceased to explore the
double meaning, or, shall I say, the quadruple,
or the centuple, or much more manifold meaning, of every sensuous fact: Orpheus, Empedocles, Heraclitus, Plato, Plutarch, Dante,
Swedenborg, and the masters of sculpture,
picture, and poetry. For we are not pans and
barrows, nor even porters of the fire and torch-
bearers, but children of the fire, made of it,

and only the same divinity transmuted, and at two or three removes, when we know least about it. And this hidden truth, that the fountains when all this river of Time, and its creatures, floweth, are intrinsically ideal and beautiful, draws us to the consideration of the nature and functions of the Poet, or the man of Beauty, to the means and materials he uses, and to the general aspect of the art in the present time.

The breadth of the problem is great, for the poet is representative. He stands among partial men for the complete man, and apprises us not of his wealth, but of the commonwealth. The young man reveres men of genius, because, to speak truly, they are more himself than he is. They receive of the soul as he also receives, but they more. Nature enhances her beauty, to the eye of loving men, from their belief that the poet is beholding her shows at the same time. He is isolated among his contemporaries, by truth and by his art, but with this consolation in his pursuits, that they will draw all men sooner or later. For all men live by truth, and stand in need of expression. In love, in art, in avarice, in politics, in labor, in games, we study to utter our painful secret. The man is only half himself, the other half is his expression.

Notwithstanding this necessity to be published, adequate expression is rare. I know not how it is that we need an interpreter; but the great majority of men seem to be minors, who have not yet come into possession of their own, or mutes, who cannot report the conversation they have had with nature. There is no man who does not anticipate a supersensual utility in the sun, and stars, earth, and water. These stand and wait to render him a peculiar service. But there is some obstruction, or some excess of phlegm in our constitution, which does not suffer them to yield the due effect. Too feeble fall the impressions of nature on us to make us artists. Every touch should thrill. Every man should be so much an artist, that he could report in conversation what had befallen him. Yet, in our experience, the rays or appulses have sufficient force to arrive at the senses, but not enough to reach the quick, and compel the reproduction of themselves in speech. The poet is the person in whom these powers are in balance, the man without impediment, who sees and handles that which others dream of, traverses the whole scale of experience, and its representative of man, in virtue of being the largest power to receive and to impart.

For the Universe has three children, born at one time, which reappear, under different names, in every system of thought, whether they be called cause, operation, and effect; or, more poetically, Jove, Pluto, Neptune; or, theologically, the Father, the Spirit, and the Son; but which we will call here, the Knower, the Doer, and the Sayer. These stand respectively for the love of truth, for the love of good, and for the love of beauty. These three are equal. Each is that which he is essentially, so that he cannot be surmounted or analyzed, and each of these three has the power of the others latent in him, and his own patent.

The poet is the sayer, the namer, and represents beauty. He is a sovereign, and stands on the centre. For the world is not painted, or adorned, but is from the beginning beautiful; and God has not made some beautiful things, but Beauty is the creator of the universe.　Therefore the poet is not any permissive potentate, but is emperor in his own right.　Criticism is infested with a cant of materialism, which assumes that manual skill and activity is the first merit of all men, and disparages such as say and do not, overlooking the fact, that some men, namely, poets, are natural sayers, sent into the world to the end of expression, and confounds them with those whose province is action, but who quit it to imitate the sayers.　But Homer's words are as costly and admirable to Homer, as Agamemnon's victories are to Agamemnon.　The poet does not wait for the hero or the sage, but, as they act and think primarily, so he writes primarily what will and must be spoken, reckoning the others, though primaries also, yet, in respect to him, secondaries and servants; as sitters or models in the studio of a painter, or as assistants who bring building materials to an architect.

For poetry was all written before time was, and whenever we are so finely organized that we can penetrate into that region where the air is music, we hear those primal warblings, and attempt to write them down, but we lose

ever and anon a word, or a verse, and substitute something of our own, and thus miswrite
the poem. The men of more delicate ear
write down these cadences more faithfully,
and these transcripts, though imperfect, become the songs of the nations. For nature is
as truly beautiful as it is good, or as it is reasonable, and must as much appear, as it must
be done, or be known. Words and deeds are
quite indifferent modes of the divine energy.
Words are also actions, and actions are a kind
of words.

The sign and credentials of the poet are,
that he announces that which no man foretold.
He is the true and only doctor ; he knows and
tells ; he is the only teller of news, for he was
present and privy to the appearance which he
describes. He is a beholder of ideas, and an
utterer of the necessary and causal. For we
do not speak now of men of poetical talents,
or of industry and skill in metre, but of the
true poet. I took part in a conversation the
other day, concerning a recent writer of lyrics,
a man of subtle mind, whose head appeared to
be a music-box of delicate tunes and rhythms,
and whose skill, and command of language,

we could not sufficiently praise. But when
the question arose, whether he was not only a
lyrist, but a poet, we were obliged to confess
that he is plainly a contemporary, not an eternal man. He does not stand out of our low
limitations, like a Chimborazo under the line,
running up from the torrid base through all
the climates of the globe, with belts of the
herbage of every latitude on its high and
mottled sides ; but this genius is the landscape-
garden of a modern house, adorned with fountains and statues, with well-bred men and
women standing and sitting in the walks and
terraces. We hear, through all the varied
music, the ground-tone of conventional life.
Our poets are men of talents who sing, and
not the children of music. The argument is
secondary, the finish of the verses is primary.

For it is not metres, but a metre-making
argument, that makes a poem, — a thought
so passionate and alive, that, like the spirit of
a plant or an animal, it has an architecture of
its own, and adorns nature with a new thing.
The thought and the form are equal in the
order of time, but in the order of genesis the
thought is prior to the form. The poet has a

new thought : he has a whole new experience
to unfold ; he will tell us how it was with
him, and all men will be the richer in his
fortune. For, the experience of each new age
requires a new confession, and the world seems
always waiting for its poet. I remember, when
I was young, how much I was moved one
morning by tidings that genius had appeared
in a youth who sat near me at table. He had
left his work, and gone rambling none knew
whither, and had written hundreds of lines,
but could not tell whether that which was in
him was therein told : he could tell nothing
but that all was changed, — man, beast,
heaven, earth, and sea. How gladly we listened! how credulous! Society seemed to
be compromised. We sat in the aurora of a
sunrise which was to put out all the stars.
Boston seemed to be at twice the distance it
had the night before, or was much farther than
that. Rome, — what was Rome ? Plutarch
and Shakspeare were in the yellow leaf, and
Homer no more should be heard of. It is
much to know that poetry has been written
this very day, under this very roof, by your
side. What ! that wonderful spirit has not

expired! these stony moments are still sparkling and animated! I had fancied that the
oracles were all silent, and nature had spent
her fires, and behold! all night, from every
pore, these fine auroras have been streaming.
Every one has some interest in the advent of
the poet, and no one knows how much it may
concern him. We know that the secret of
the world is profound, but who or what shall
be our interpreter, we know not. A mountain
ramble, a new style of face, a new person, may
put the key into our hands. Of course, the
value of genius to us is in the veracity of its
report. Talent may frolic and juggle ; genius
realizes and adds. Mankind, in good earnest,
have availed so far in understanding themselves and their work, that the foremost
watchman on the peak announces his news.
It is the truest word ever spoken, and the
phrase will be the fittest, most musical, and
the unerring voice of the world for that time.

All that we call sacred history attests that
the birth of a poet is the principal event in
chronology. Man, never so often deceived,
still watches for the arrival of a brother who
can hold him steady to a truth, until he has

made it his own. With what joy I begin to read a poem, which I confide in as an inspiration! And now my chains are to be broken; I shall mount above these clouds and opaque airs in which I live, — opaque, though they seem transparent, — and from the heaven of truth I shall see and comprehend my relations. That will reconcile me to life, and renovate nature, to see trifles animated by a tendency, and to know what I am doing. Life will no more be a noise; now I shall see men and women, and know the signs by which they may be discerned from fools and satans. This day shall be better than my birth-day: then I became an animal: now I am invited into the science of the real. Such is the hope, but the fruition is postponed. Oftener it falls, that this winged man, who will carry me into the heaven, whirls me into the clouds, then leaps and frisks about with me from cloud to cloud, still affirming that he is bound heavenward; and I, being myself a novice, am slow in perceiving that he does not know the way into the heavens, and is merely bent that I should admire his skill to rise, like a fowl or a flying fish, a little way from the ground or the water; but the all-piercing, all-feeding, and ocular air of heaven, that man shall never inhabit. I tumble down again soon into my old nooks, and lead the life of exaggerations as before, and have lost my faith in the possibility of any guide who can lead me thither where I would be.

But leaving these victims of vanity, let us, with new hope, observe how nature, by worthier impulses, has ensured the poet's fidelity to his office of announcement and affirming, namely, by the beauty of things, which becomes a new, and higher beauty, when expressed. Nature offers all her creatures to him as a picture-language. Being used as a type, a second wonderful value appears in the object, far better than its old value, as the carpenter's stretched cord, if you hold your ear close enough, is musical in the breeze. " Things more excellent than every image," says Jamblichus, " are expressed through images." Things admit of being used as symbols, because nature is a symbol, in the whole, and in every part. Every line we can draw in the sand, has expression; and there is no body without its spirit or genius. All form is

an effect of character : all condition, of the
quality of the life ; all harmony, of health ;
(and, for this reason, a perception of beauty
should be sympathetic, or proper only to the
good.) The beautiful rests on the foundations
of the necessary. The soul makes the body,
as the wise Spenser teaches : —

> " So every spirit, as it is most pure,
> And hath in it the more of heavenly light,
> So it the fairer body doth procure
> To habit in, and it more fairly dight,
> With cheerful grace and amiable sight.
> For, of the soul, the body form doth take,
> For soul is form, and doth the body make."

Here we find ourselves, suddenly, not in a
critical speculation, but in a holy place, and
should go very warily and reverently. We
stand before the secret of the world, there
where Being passes into Appearance, and Unity
into Variety.

The Universe is the externisation of the
soul. Wherever the life is, that bursts into
appearance around it. Our science is sensual,
and therefore superficial. The earth, and the
heavenly bodies, physics, and chemistry, we
sensually treat, as if they were self-existent ;

but these are the retinue of that Being we have.
" The mighty heaven," said Proclus, " exhibits, in its transfigurations, clear images of
the splendor of intellectual perceptions; being
moved in conjunction with the unapparent
periods of intellectual natures." Therefore,
science always goes abreast with the just elevation of the man, keeping step with religion
and metaphysics; or, the state of science is
an index of our self-knowledge. Since everything in nature answers to a moral power, if
any phenomenon remains brute and dark, it is
that the corresponding faculty in the observer
is not yet active.

No wonder, then, if these waters be so deep,
that we hover over them with a religious regard. The beauty of the fable proves the
importance of the sense; to the poet, and to
all others; or, if you please, every man is so
far a poet as to be susceptible of these enchantments of nature: for all men have the
thoughts whereof the universe is the celebration. I find that the fascination resides in the
symbol. Who loves nature? Who does not?
Is it only poets, and men of leisure and cultivation, who live with her? No; but also

hunters, farmers, grooms, and butchers, though they express their affection in their choice of life, and not in their choice of words. The writer wonders what the coachman or the hunter values in riding, in horses, and dogs. It is not superficial qualities. When you talk with him, he holds these at as slight a rate as you. His worship is sympathetic ; he has no definitions, but he is commanded in nature, by the living power which he feels to be there present. No imitation, or playing of these things, would content him ; he loves the earnest of the northwind, of rain, of stone, and wood, and iron. A beauty not explicable, is dearer than a beauty which we can see to the end of. It is nature the symbol, nature certifying the supernatural, body overflowed by life, which he worships, with coarse, but sincere rites.

The inwardness, and mystery, of this attachment, drives men of every class to the use of emblems. The schools of poets, and philosophers, are not more intoxicated with their symbols, than the populace with theirs. In our political parties, compute the power of badges and emblems. See the great ball

2

which they roll from Baltimore to Bunker hill! In the political processions, Lowell goes in a loom, and Lynn in a shoe, and Salem in a ship. Witness the cider-barrel, the log-cabin, the hickory-stick, the palmetto, and all the cognizances of party. See the power of national emblems. Some stars, lilies, leopards, a crescent, a lion, an eagle, or other figure, which came into credit God knows how, on an old rag of bunting, blowing in the wind, on a fort, at the ends of the earth, shall make the blood tingle under the rudest, or the most conventional exterior. The people fancy they hate poetry, and they are all poets and mystics!

Beyond this universality of the symbolic language, we are apprised of the divineness of this superior use of things, whereby the world is a temple, whose walls are covered with emblems, pictures, and commandments of the Deity, in this, that there is no fact in nature which does not carry the whole sense of nature; and the distinctions which we make in events, and in affairs, of low and high, honest and base, disappear when nature is used as a symbol. Thought makes every thing fit for use. The vocabulary of an omniscient man

would embrace words and images excluded
from polite conversation. What would be base,
or even obscene, to the obscene, becomes illustrious, spoken in a new connexion of thought.
The piety of the Hebrew prophets purges
their grossness. The circumcision is an example of the power of poetry to raise the low
and offensive. Small and mean things serve
as well as great symbols. The meaner the
type by which a law is expressed, the more
pungent it is, and the more lasting in the
memories of men : just as we choose the smallest box, or case, in which any needful utensil
can be carried. Bare lists of words are found
suggestive, to an imaginative and excited mind ;
as it is related of Lord Chatham, that he was
accustomed to read in Bailey's Dictionary,
when he was preparing to speak in Parliament.
The poorest experience is rich enough for all
the purposes of expressing thought. Why
covet a knowledge of new facts? Day and
night, house and garden, a few books, a few
actions, serve us as well as would all trades
and all spectacles. We are far from having
exhausted the significance of the few symbols
we use. We can come to use them yet with

a terrible simplicity. It does not need that a poem should be long. Every word was once a poem. Every new relation is a new word. Also, we use defects and deformities to a sacred purpose, so expressing our sense that the evils of the world are such only to the evil eye. In the old mythology, mythologists observe, defects are ascribed to divine natures, as lameness to Vulcan, blindness to Cupid, and the like, to signify exuberances.

For, as it is dislocation and detachment from the life of God, that makes things ugly, the poet, who re-attaches things to nature and the Whole,—re-attaching even artificial things, and violations of nature, to nature, by a deeper insight,—disposes very easily of the most disagreeable facts. Readers of poetry see the factory-village, and the railway, and fancy that the poetry of the landscape is broken up by these; for these works of art are not yet consecrated in their reading; but the poet sees them fall within the great Order not less than the bee-hive, or the spider's geometrical web. Nature adopts them very fast into her vital circles, and the gliding train of cars she loves like her own. Besides, in a centred mind, it

signifies nothing how many mechanical inventions you exhibit. Though you add millions, and never so surprising, the fact of
mechanics has not gained a grain's weight.
The spiritual fact remains unalterable, by
many or by few particulars; as no mountain
is of any appreciable height to break the curve
of the sphere. A shrewd country-boy goes to
the city for the first time, and the complacent
citizen is not satisfied with his little wonder.
It is not that he does not see all the fine
houses, and know that he never saw such before, but he disposes of them as easily as the
poet finds place for the railway. The chief
value of the new fact, is to enhance the great
and constant fact of Life, which can dwarf
any and every circumstance, and to which the
belt of wampum, and the commerce of America, are alike.

The world being thus put under the mind
for verb and noun, the poet is he who can
articulate it. For, though life is great, and
fascinates, and absorbs, — and though all men
are intelligent of the symbols through which
it is named, — yet they cannot originally use
them. We are symbols, and inhabit symbols;

workman, work, and tools, words and things,
birth and death, all are emblems; but we
sympathize with the symbols, and, being infatuated with the economical uses of things,
we do not know that they are thoughts. The
poet, by an ulterior intellectual perception,
gives them a power which makes their old use
forgotten, and puts eyes, and a tongue, into
every dumb and inanimate object. He perceives the independence of the thought on the
symbol, the stability of the thought, the ac-
cidency and fugacity of the symbol. As the
eyes of Lynkæus were said to see through the
earth, so the poet turns the world to glass, and
shows us all things in their right series and
procession. For, through that better perception, he stands one step nearer to things, and
sees the flowing or metamorphosis; perceives
that thought is multiform; that within the
form of every creature is a force impelling it
to ascend into a higher form; and, following
with his eyes the life, uses the forms which
express that life, and so his speech flows with
the flowing of nature. All the facts of the
animal economy, sex, nutriment, gestation,
birth, growth, are symbols of the passage of

the world into the soul of man, to suffer there a change, and reappear a new and higher fact. He uses forms according to the life, and not according to the form. This is true science. The poet alone knows astronomy, chemistry, vegetation, and animation, for he does not stop at these facts, but employs them as signs. He knows why the plain, or meadow of space, was strown with these flowers we call suns, and moons, and stars; why the great deep is adorned with animals, with men, and gods; for, in every word he speaks he rides on them as the horses of thought.

By virtue of this science the poet is the Namer, or Language-maker, naming things sometimes after their appearance, sometimes after their essence, and giving to every one its own name and not another's, thereby rejoicing the intellect, which delights in detachment or boundary. The poets made all the words, and therefore language is the archives of history, and, if we must say it, a sort of tomb of the muses. For, though the origin of most of our words is forgotten, each word was at first a stroke of genius, and obtained currency, because for the moment it symbolized

the world to the first speaker and to the
hearer. The etymologist finds the deadest
word to have been once a brilliant picture.
Language is fossil poetry. As the limestone
of the continent consists of infinite masses of
the shells of animalcules, so language is made
up of images, or tropes, which now, in their
secondary use, have long ceased to remind us
of their poetic origin. But the poet names
the thing because he sees it, or comes one step
nearer to it than any other. This expression,
or naming, is not art, but a second nature,
grown out of the first, as a leaf out of a tree.
What we call nature, is a certain self-regulated
motion, or change; and nature does all things
by her own hands, and does not leave another
to baptise her, but baptises herself; and this
through the metamorphosis again. I remember that a certain poet described it to me
thus:

Genius is the activity which repairs the de-
cays of things, whether wholly or partly of a
material and finite kind. Nature, through all
her kingdoms, insures herself. Nobody cares
for planting the poor fungus: so she shakes

down from the gills of one agaric countless
spores, any one of which, being preserved,
transmits new billions of spores to-morrow or
next day. The new agaric of this hour has a
chance which the old one had not. This atom
of seed is thrown into a new place, not subject to the accidents which destroyed its parent two rods off. She makes a man; and
having brought him to ripe age, she will no
longer run the risk of losing this wonder at a
blow, but she detaches from him a new self,
that the kind may be safe from accidents to
which the individual is exposed. So when
the soul of the poet has come to ripeness of
thought, she detaches and sends away from it
its poems or songs, — a fearless, sleepless,
deathless progeny, which is not exposed to
the accidents of the weary kingdom of time:
a fearless, vivacious offspring, clad with wings
(such was the virtue of the soul out of which
they came), which carry them fast and far,
and infix them irrecoverably into the hearts of
men. These wings are the beauty of the
poet's soul. The songs, thus flying immortal
from their mortal parent, are pursued by clam-
orous flights of censures, which swarm in far

greater numbers, and threaten to devour them; but these last are not winged. At the end of a very short leap they fall plump down, and rot, having received from the souls out of which they came no beautiful wings. But the melodies of the poet ascend, and leap, and pierce into the deeps of infinite time.

So far the bard taught me, using his freer speech. But nature has a higher end, in the production of new individuals, than security, namely, *ascension*, or, the passage of the soul into higher forms. I knew, in my younger days, the sculptor who made the statue of the youth which stands in the public garden. He was, as I remember, unable to tell directly, what made him happy, or unhappy, but by wonderful indirections he could tell. He rose one day, according to his habit, before the dawn, and saw the morning break, grand as the eternity out of which it came, and, for many days after, he strove to express this tranquillity, and, lo! his chisel had fashioned out of marble the form of a beautiful youth, Phosphorus, whose aspect is such, that, it is said, all persons who look on it become silent. The poet also resigns himself to his mood, and that thought which agitated him is expressed, but *alter idem*, in a manner totally new. The expression is organic, or, the new type which things themselves take when liberated. As, in the sun, objects paint their images on the retina of the eye, so they, sharing the aspiration of the whole universe, tend to paint a far more delicate copy of their essence in his mind. Like the metamorphosis of things into higher organic forms, is their change into melodies. Over everything stands its dæmon, or soul, and, as the form of the thing is reflected by the eye, so the soul of the thing is reflected by a melody. The sea, the mountain-ridge, Niagara, and every flower-bed, pre-exist, or super-exist, in pre-cantations, which sail like odors in the air, and when any man goes by with an ear sufficiently fine, he overhears them, and endeavors to write down the notes, without diluting or depraving them. And herein is the legitimation of criticism, in the mind's faith, that the poems are a corrupt version of some text in nature, with which they ought to be made to tally. A rhyme in one of our sonnets should not be less pleasing than the iterated nodes of a sea-shell, or the resembling difference of a group of flowers. The pairing of the birds is an idyl, not tedious as our idyls are ; a tempest is a rough ode, without falsehood or rant : a summer, with its harvest sown, reaped, and stored, is an epic song, subordinating how many admirably executed parts. Why should not the symmetry and truth that modulate these, glide into our spirits, and we participate the invention of nature ?

This insight, which expresses itself by what is called Imagination, is a very high sort of seeing, which does not come by study, but by the intellect being where and what it sees, by sharing the path, or circuit of things through forms, and so making them translucid to others. The path of things is silent. Will they suffer a speaker to go with them ? A spy they will not suffer ; a lover, a poet, is the transcendency of their own nature, — him they will suffer. The condition of true naming, on the poet's part, is his resigning himself to the divine *aura* which breathes through forms, and accompanying that.

It is a secret which every intellectual man

quickly learns, that, beyond the energy of his possessed and conscious intellect, he is capable of a new energy (as of an intellect doubled on itself), by abandonment to the nature of things; that, beside his privacy of power as an individual man, there is a great public power, on which he can draw, by unlocking, at all risks, his human doors, and suffering the ethereal tides to roll and circulate through him : then he is caught up into the life of the Universe, his speech is thunder, his thought is law, and his words are universally intelligible as the plants and animals. The poet knows that he speaks adequately, then, only when he speaks somewhat wildly, or, " with the flower of the mind ; " not with the intellect, used as an organ, but with the intellect released from all service, and suffered to take its direction from its celestial life ; or, as the ancients were wont to express themselves, not with intellect alone, but with the intellect inebriated by nectar. As the traveller who has lost his way, throws his reins on his horse's neck, and trusts to the instinct of the animal to find his road, so must we do with the divine animal who carries us through this world. For if in any

manner we can stimulate this instinct, new
passages are opened for us into nature, the
mind flows into and through things hardest
and highest, and the metamorphosis is possible.

This is the reason why bards love wine,
mead, narcotics, coffee, tea, opium, the fumes
of sandal-wood and tobacco, or whatever other
species of animal exhilaration. All men avail
themselves of such means as they can, to add
this extraordinary power to their normal powers ; and to this end they prize conversation, music, pictures, sculpture, dancing, thea-
tres, travelling, war, mobs, fires, gaming,
politics, or love, or science, or animal intoxi-
cation, which are several coarser or finer *quasi-*
mechanical substitutes for the true nectar,
which is the ravishment of the intellect by
coming nearer to the fact. These are auxiliaries to the centrifugal tendency of a man, to
his passage out into free space, and they help
him to escape the custody of that body in
which he is pent up, and of that jail-yard of
individual relations in which he is enclosed.
Hence a great number of such as were pro-
fessionally expressors of Beauty, as painters,

poets, musicians, and actors, have been more than others wont to lead a life of pleasure and indulgence; all but the few who received the true nectar; and, as it was a spurious mode of attaining freedom, as it was an emancipation not into the heavens, but into the freedom of baser places, they were punished for that advantage they won, by a dissipation and deterioration. But never can any advantage be taken of nature by a trick. The spirit of the world, the great calm presence of the creator, comes not forth to the sorceries of opium or of wine. The sublime vision comes to the pure and simple soul in a clean and chaste body. That is not an inspiration which we owe to narcotics, but some counterfeit excitement and fury. Milton says, that the lyric poet may drink wine and live generously, but the epic poet, he who shall sing of the gods, and their descent unto men, must drink water out of a wooden bowl. For poetry is not 'Devil's wine,' but God's wine. It is with this as it is with toys. We fill the hands and nurseries of our children with all manner of dolls, drums, and horses, withdrawing their eyes from the plain face and sufficing objects

of nature, the sun, and moon, the animals, the
water, and stones, which should be their toys.
So the poet's habit of living should be set on
a key so low and plain, that the common influences should delight him. His cheerfulness
should be the gift of the sunlight; the air
should suffice for his inspiration, and he should
be tipsy with water. That spirit which suffices quiet hearts, which seems to come forth
to such from every dry knoll of sere grass,
from every pine-stump, and half-imbedded
stone, on which the dull March sun shines,
comes forth to the poor and hungry, and such
as are of simple taste. If thou fill thy brain
with Boston and New York, with fashion and
covetousness, and wilt stimulate thy jaded
senses with wine and French coffee, thou shalt
find no radiance of wisdom in the lonely
waste of the pinewoods.

If the imagination intoxicates the poet, it is
not inactive in other men. The metamorphosis excites in the beholder an emotion of
joy. The use of symbols has a certain power
of emancipation and exhilaration for all men.
We seem to be touched by a wand, which
makes us dance and run about happily, like

children. We are like persons who come out
of a cave or cellar into the open air. This is
the effect on us of tropes, fables, oracles, and
all poetic forms. Poets are thus liberating gods.
Men have really got a new sense, and found
within their world, another world, or nest of
worlds ; for, the metamorphosis once seen, we
divine that it does not stop. I will not now
consider how much this makes the charm of
algebra and the mathematics, which also have
their tropes, but it is felt in every definition ;
as, when Aristotle defines *space* to be an immovable vessel, in which things are contained ; — or, when Plato defines a *line* to be
a flowing point; or, *figure* to be a bound of
solid; and many the like. What a joyful
sense of freedom we have, when Vitruvius
announces the old opinion of artists, that no
architect can build any house well, who does
not know something of anatomy. When
Socrates, in Charmides, tells us that the soul
is cured of its maladies by certain incantations, and that these incantations are beautiful
reasons, from which temperance is generated
in souls ; when Plato calls the world an animal ; and Timæus affirms that the plants also

3

are animals; or affirms a man to be a heavenly
tree, growing with his root, which is his head,
upward; and, as George Chapman, following
him, writes, —

> " So in our tree of man, whose nervie root
> Springs in his top ; "

when Orpheus speaks of hoariness as "that
white flower which marks extreme old age;"
when Proclus calls the universe the statue of
the intellect; when Chaucer, in his praise
of 'Gentilesse,' compares good blood in mean
condition to fire, which, though carried to the
darkest house betwixt this and the mount of
Caucasus, will yet hold its natural office, and
burn as bright as if twenty thousand men did
it behold; when John saw, in the apocalypse,
the ruin of the world through evil, and the stars
fall from heaven, as the figtree casteth her un-
timely fruit; when Æsop reports the whole
catalogue of common daily relations through
the masquerade of birds and beasts; — we
take the cheerful hint of the immortality of
our essence, and its versatile habit and escapes,
as when the gypsies say, "it is in vain to hang
them, they cannot die."

The poets are thus liberating gods. The ancient British bards had for the title of their order, " Those who are free throughout the world." They are free, and they make free. An imaginative book renders us much more service at first, by stimulating us through its tropes, than afterward, when we arrive at the precise sense of the author. I think nothing is of any value in books, excepting the transcendental and extraordinary. If a man is inflamed and carried away by his thought, to that degree that he forgets the authors and the public, and heeds only this one dream, which holds him like an insanity, let me read his paper, and you may have all the arguments and histories and criticism. All the value which attaches to Pythagoras, Paracelsus, Cornelius Agrippa, Cardan, Kepler, Swedenborg, Schelling, Oken, or any other who introduces questionable facts into his cosmogony, as angels, devils, magic, astrology, palmistry, mesmerism, and so on, is the certificate we have of departure from routine, and that here is a new witness. That also is the best success in conversation, the magic of liberty, which puts the world, like a ball, in our hands. How cheap even the liberty then seems; how mean to study, when an emotion communicates to the intellect the power to sap and upheave nature: how great the perspective! nations, times, systems, enter and disappear, like threads in tapestry of large figure and many colors; dream delivers us to dream, and, while the drunkenness lasts, we will sell our bed, our philosophy, our religion, in our opulence.

There is good reason why we should prize this liberation. The fate of the poor shepherd, who, blinded and lost in the snowstorm, perishes in a drift within a few feet of his cottage door, is an emblem of the state of man. On the brink of the waters of life and truth, we are miserably dying. The inaccessibleness of every thought but that we are in, is wonderful. What if you come near to it,— you are as remote, when you are nearest, as when you are farthest. Every thought is also a prison; every heaven is also a prison. Therefore we love the poet, the inventor, who in any form, whether in an ode, or in an action, or in looks and behavior, has yielded us a new thought. He unlocks our chains, and admits us to a new scene.

This emancipation is dear to all men, and the power to impart it, as it must come from greater depth and scope of thought, is a measure of intellect. Therefore all books of the imagination endure, all which ascend to that truth, that the writer sees nature beneath him, and uses it as his exponent. Every verse or sentence, possessing this virtue, will take care of its own immortality. The religions of the world are the ejaculations of a few imaginative men.

But the quality of the imagination is to flow, and not to freeze. The poet did not stop at the color, or the form, but read their meaning; neither may he rest in this meaning, but he makes the same objects exponents of his new thought. Here is the difference betwixt the poet and the mystic, that the last nails a symbol to one sense, which was a true sense for a moment, but soon becomes old and false. For all symbols are fluxional; all language is vehicular and transitive, and is good, as ferries and horses are, for conveyance, not as farms and houses are, for homestead. Mysticism consists in the mistake of an accidental and individual symbol for an universal one.

The morning-redness happens to be the favorite meteor to the eyes of Jacob Behmen, and comes to stand to him for truth and faith ; and he believes should stand for the same realities to every reader. But the first reader prefers as naturally the symbol of a mother and child, or a gardener and his bulb, or a jeweller polishing a gem. Either of these, or of a myriad more, are equally good to the person to whom they are significant. Only they must be held lightly, and be very willingly translated into the equivalent terms which others use. And the mystic must be steadily told, — All that you say is just as true without the tedious use of that symbol as with it. Let us have a little algebra, instead of this trite rhetoric, — universal signs, instead of these village symbols,— and we shall both be gainers. The history of hierarchies seems to show, that all religious error consisted in making the symbol too stark and solid, and, at last, nothing but an excess of the organ of language.

Swedenborg, of all men in the recent ages, stands eminently for the translator of nature into thought. I do not know the man in history to whom things stood so uniformly for

words. Before him the metamorphosis continually plays. Everything on which his eye
rests, obeys the impulses of moral nature.
The figs become grapes whilst he eats them.
When some of his angels affirmed a truth, the
laurel twig which they held blossomed in their
hands. The noise which, at a distance, appeared like gnashing and thumping, on coming
nearer was found to be the voice of disputants.
The men, in one of his visions, seen in heavenly light, appeared like dragons, and seemed
in darkness : but, to each other, they appeared
as men, and, when the light from heaven
shone into their cabin, they complained of the
darkness, and were compelled to shut the window that they might see.

There was this perception in him, which
makes the poet or seer, an object of awe and
terror, namely, that the same man, or society
of men, may wear one aspect to themselves
and their companions, and a different aspect
to higher intelligences. Certain priests, whom
he describes as conversing very learnedly together, appeared to the children, who were at
some distance, like dead horses : and many the
like misappearances. And instantly the mind

inquires, whether these fishes under the bridge, yonder oxen in the pasture, those dogs in the yard, are immutably fishes, oxen, and dogs, or only so appear to me, and perchance to themselves appear upright men ; and whether I appear as a man to all eyes. The Bramins and Pythagoras propounded the same question, and if any poet has witnessed the transformation, he doubtless found it in harmony with various experiences. We have all seen changes as considerable in wheat and caterpillars. He is the poet, and shall draw us with love and terror, who sees, through the flowing vest, the firm nature, and can declare it.

I look in vain for the poet whom I describe. We do not, with sufficient plainness, or sufficient profoundness, address ourselves to life, nor dare we chaunt our own times and social circumstance. If we filled the day with bravery, we should not shrink from celebrating it. Time and nature yield us many gifts, but not yet the timely man, the new religion, the reconciler, whom all things await. Dante's praise is, that he dared to write his autobiography in colossal cipher, or into universality. We have yet had no genius in America, with tyrannous eye, which knew the value of our incomparable materials, and saw, in the barbarism and materialism of the times, another carnival of the same gods whose picture he so much admires in Homer; then in the middle age; then in Calvinism. Banks and tariffs, the newspaper and caucus, methodism and unitarianism, are flat and dull to dull people, but rest on the same foundations of wonder as the town of Troy, and the temple of Delphos, and are as swiftly passing away. Our logrolling, our stumps and their politics, our fisheries, our Negroes, and Indians, our boats, and our repudiations, the wrath of rogues, and the pusillanimity of honest men, the northern trade, the southern planting, the western clearing, Oregon, and Texas, are yet unsung. Yet America is a poem in our eyes; its ample geography dazzles the imagination, and it will not wait long for metres. If I have not found that excellent combination of gifts in my countrymen which I seek, neither could I aid myself to fix the idea of the poet by reading now and then in Chalmers's collection of five centuries of English poets. These are wits, more than poets, though there have been poets among them. But when we adhere to the ideal of the poet, we have our difficulties even with Milton and Homer. Milton is too literary, and Homer too literal and historical.

But I am not wise enough for a national criticism, and must use the old largeness a little longer, to discharge my errand from the muse to the poet concerning his art.

Art is the path of the creator to his work. The paths, or methods, are ideal and eternal, though few men ever see them, not the artist himself for years, or for a lifetime, unless he come into the conditions. The painter, the sculptor, the composer, the epic rhapsodist, the orator, all partake one desire, namely, to express themselves symmetrically and abundantly, not dwarfishly and fragmentarily. They found or put themselves in certain conditions, as, the painter and sculptor before some impressive human figures; the orator, into the assembly of the people; and the others, in such scenes as each has found exciting to his intellect; and each presently feels the new desire. He hears a voice, he sees a beckoning. Then he is apprised, with won-

der, what herds of dæmons hem him in. He
can no more rest; he says, with the old
painter, "By God, it is in me, and must go
forth of me." He pursues a beauty, half seen,
which flies before him. The poet pours out
verses in every solitude. Most of the things
he says are conventional, no doubt; but by and
by he says something which is original and
beautiful. That charms him. He would say
nothing else but such things. In our way of
talking, we say, 'That is yours, this is mine;'
but the poet knows well that it is not his;
that it is as strange and beautiful to him as
to you; he would fain hear the like eloquence
at length. Once having tasted this immortal
ichor, he cannot have enough of it, and, as an
admirable creative power exists in these intellections, it is of the last importance that these
things get spoken. What a little of all we
know is said! What drops of all the sea of
our science are baled up! and by what accident it is that these are exposed, when so many
secrets sleep in nature! Hence the necessity
of speech and song; hence these throbs and
heart-beatings in the orator, at the door of the
assembly, to the end, namely, that thought
may be ejaculated as Logos, or Word.

Doubt not, O poet, but persist. Say, 'It is in me, and shall out.' Stand there, baulked and dumb, stuttering and stammering, hissed and hooted, stand and strive, until, at last, rage draw out of thee that *dream*-power which every night shows thee is thine own; a power transcending all limit and privacy, and by virtue of which a man is the conductor of the whole river of electricity. Nothing walks, or creeps, or grows, or exists, which must not in turn arise and walk before him as exponent of his meaning. Comes he to that power, his genius is no longer exhaustible.. All the creatures, by pairs and by tribes, pour into his mind as into a Noah's ark, to come forth again to people a new world. This is like the stock of air for our respiration, or for the combustion of our fireplace, not a measure of gallons, but the entire atmosphere if wanted. And therefore the rich poets, as Homer, Chaucer, Shakspeare, and Raphael, have obviously no limits to their works, except the limits of their lifetime, and resemble a mirror carried through the street, ready to render an image of every created thing.

O poet! a new nobility is conferred in

groves and pastures, and not in castles, or by the sword-blade, any longer. The conditions are hard, but equal. Thou shalt leave the world, and know the muse only. Thou shalt not know any longer the times, customs, graces, politics, or opinions of men, but shalt take all from the muse. For the time of towns is tolled from the world by funereal chimes, but in nature the universal hours are counted by succeeding tribes of animals and plants, and by growth of joy on joy. God wills also that thou abdicate a manifold and duplex life, and that thou be content that others speak for thee. Others shall be thy gentlemen, and shall represent all courtesy and worldly life for thee; others shall do the great and resounding actions also. Thou shalt lie close hid with nature, and canst not be afforded to the Capitol or the Exchange. The world is full of renunciations and apprenticeships, and this is thine: thou must pass for a fool and a churl for a long season. This is the screen and sheath in which Pan has protected his well-beloved flower, and thou shalt be known only to thine own, and they shall console thee with tenderest love. And thou shalt not be able to rehearse the names of thy friends in thy verse, for an old shame before the holy ideal. And this is the reward : that the ideal shall be real to thee, and the impressions of the actual world shall fall like summer rain, copious, but not troublesome, to thy invulnerable essence. Thou shalt have the whole land for thy park and manor, the sea for thy bath and navigation, without tax and without envy ; the woods and the rivers thou shalt own ; and thou shalt possess that wherein others are only tenants and boarders. Thou true land-lord ! sea-lord ! air-lord ! Whereve snow falls, or water flows, or birds fly, wherever day and night meet in twilight, wherever the blue heaven is hung by clouds, or sown with stars, wherever are forms with transparent boundaries, wherever are outlets into celestial space, wherever is danger, and awe, and love, there is Beauty, plenteous as rain, shed for thee, and though thou shouldest walk the world over, thou shalt not be able to find a condition inopportune or ignoble.

EXPERIENCE.

THE lords of life, the lords of life, —
I saw them pass,
In their own guise,
Like and unlike,
Portly and grim,
Use and Surprise,
Surface and Dream,
Succession swift, and spectral Wrong,
Temperament without a tongue,
And the inventor of the game
Omnipresent without name ; —
Some to see, some to be guessed,
They marched from east to west :
Little man, least of all,
Among the legs of his guardians tall,
Walked about with puzzled look : —
Him by the hand dear nature took ;
Dearest nature, strong and kind,
Whispered, ' Darling, never mind !
Tomorrow they will wear another face,
The founder thou ! these are thy race ! '

ESSAY II.

EXPERIENCE.

———

WHERE do we find ourselves? In a series
of which we do not know the extremes, and
believe that it has none. We wake and find
ourselves on a stair; there are stairs below us,
which we seem to have ascended; there are
stairs above us, many a one, which go upward
and out of sight. But the Genius which,
according to the old belief, stands at the door
by which we enter, and gives us the lethe to
drink, that we may tell no tales, mixed the
cup too strongly, and we cannot shake off the
lethargy now at noonday. Sleep lingers all
our lifetime about our eyes, as night hovers
all day in the boughs of the fir-tree. All
things swim and glitter. Our life is not so
much threatened as our perception. Ghostlike we glide through nature, and should not
know our place again. Did our birth fall in

4

some fit of indigence and frugality in nature, that she was so sparing of her fire and so liberal of her earth, that it appears to us that we lack the affirmative principle, and though we have health and reason, yet we have no superfluity of spirit for new creation? We have enough to live and bring the year about, but not an ounce to impart or to invest. Ah that our Genius were a little more of a genius! We are like millers on the lower levels of a stream, when the factories above them have exhausted the water. We too fancy that the upper people must have raised their dams.

If any of us knew what we were doing, or where we are going, then when we think we best know! We do not know today whether we are busy or idle. In times when we thought ourselves indolent, we have afterwards discovered, that much was accomplished, and much was begun in us. All our days are so unprofitable while they pass, that 'tis wonderful where or when we ever got anything of this which we call wisdom, poetry, virtue. We never got it on any dated calendar day. Some heavenly days must have been intercalated somewhere, like those that Hermes

won with dice of the Moon, that Osiris might
be born. It is said, all martyrdoms looked
mean when they were suffered. Every ship is a
romantic object, except that we sail in. Embark, and the romance quits our vessel, and
hangs on every other sail in the horizon. Our
life looks trivial, and we shun to record it.
Men seem to have learned of the horizon the
art of perpetual retreating and reference.
' Yonder uplands are rich pasturage, and my
neighbor has fertile meadow, but my field,'
says the querulous farmer, ' only holds the
world together.' I quote another man's saying; unluckily, that other withdraws himself
in the same way, and quotes me. 'Tis the
trick of nature thus to degrade today; a good
deal of buzz, and somewhere a result slipped
magically in. Every roof is agreeable to the
eye, until it is lifted; then we find tragedy
and moaning women, and hard-eyed husbands,
and deluges of lethe, and the men ask, ' What's
the news?' as if the old were so bad. How
many individuals can we count in society?
how many actions? how many opinions? So
much of our time is preparation, so much is
routine, and so much retrospect, that the pith

of each man's genius contracts itself to a very few hours.   The history of literature — take the net result of Tiraboschi, Warton, or Schlegel, — is a sum of very few ideas, and of very few original tales,— all the rest being variation of these.   So in this great society wide lying around us, a critical analysis would find very few spontaneous actions.   It is almost all custom and gross sense.   There are even few opinions, and these seem organic in the speakers, and do not disturb the universal necessity.

What opium is instilled into all disaster!   It shows formidable as we approach it, but there is at last no rough rasping friction, but the most slippery sliding surfaces.   We fall soft on a thought.   *Ate Dea* is gentle,

> " Over men's heads walking aloft,
>   With tender feet treading so soft."

People give and bemoan themselves, but it is not half so bad with them as they say. There are moods in which we court suffering, in the hope that here, at least, we shall find reality, sharp peaks and edges of truth.   But it turns out to be scene-painting and counterfeit. The only thing grief has taught me, is to know how shallow it is. That, like all the rest, plays about the surface, and never introduces me into the reality, for contact with which, we would even pay the costly price of sons and lovers. Was it Boscovich who found out that bodies never come in contact? Well, souls never touch their objects. An innavigable sea washes with silent waves between us and the things we aim at and converse with. Grief too will make us idealists. In the death of my son, now more than two years ago, I seem to have lost a beautiful estate, — no more. I cannot get it nearer to me. If tomorrow I should be informed of the bankruptcy of my principal debtors, the loss of my property would be a great inconvenience to me, perhaps, for many years ; but it would leave me as it found me, — neither better nor worse. So is it with this calamity : it does not touch me : some thing which I fancied was a part of me, which could not be torn away without tearing me, nor enlarged without enriching me, falls off from me, and leaves no scar. It was caducous. I grieve that grief can teach me nothing, nor carry me one step into real nature. The Indian who was laid under a curse, that the wind should not blow on him, nor water flow to him, nor fire burn him, is a type of us all. The dearest events are summer-rain, and we the Para coats that shed every drop. Nothing is left us now but death. We look to that with a grim satisfaction, saying, there at least is reality that will not dodge us.

I take this evanescence and lubricity of all objects, which lets them slip through our fingers then when we clutch hardest, to be the most unhandsome part of our condition. Nature does not like to be observed, and likes that we should be her fools and playmates. We may have the sphere for our cricket-ball, but not a berry for our philosophy. Direct strokes she never gave us power to make; all our blows glance, all our hits are accidents. Our relations to each other are oblique and casual.

Dream delivers us to dream, and there is no end to illusion. Life is a train of moods like a string of beads, and, as we pass through them, they prove to be many-colored lenses

which paint the world their own hue, and
each shows only what lies in its focus. From
the mountain you see the mountain. We animate what we can, and we see only what we
animate. Nature and books belong to the eyes
that see them. It depends on the mood of the
man, whether he shall see the sunset or the
fine poem. There are always sunsets, and
there is always genius ; but only a few hours
so serene that we can relish nature or criticism.
The more or less depends on structure or temperament. Temperament is the iron wire on
which the beads are strung. Of what use is
fortune or talent to a cold and defective nature ?
Who cares what sensibility or discrimination a
man has at some time shown, if he falls asleep
in his chair ? or if he laugh and giggle ? or if
he apologize ? or is affected with egotism ? or
thinks of his dollar ? or cannot go by food ?
or has gotten a child in his boyhood ? Of what
use is genius, if the organ is too convex or too
concave, and cannot find a focal distance within the actual horizon of human life ? Of what
use, if the brain is too cold or too hot, and the
man does not care enough for results, to stimulate him to experiment, and hold him up in it ?

or if the web is too finely woven, too irritable by pleasure and pain, so that life stagnates from too much reception, without due outlet?   Of what use to make heroic vows of amendment, if the same old law-breaker is to keep them? What cheer can the religious sentiment yield, when that is suspected to be secretly dependent on the seasons of the year, and the state of the blood?   I knew a witty physician who found theology in the biliary duct, and used to affirm that if there was disease in the liver, the man became a Calvinist, and if that organ was sound, he became a Unitarian. Very mortifying is the reluctant experience that some unfriendly excess or imbecility neutralizes the promise of genius. We see young men who owe us a new world, so readily and lavishly they promise, but they never acquit the debt; they die young and dodge the account: or if they live, they lose themselves in the crowd.

Temperament also enters fully into the system of illusions, and shuts us in a prison of glass which we cannot see. There is an optical illusion about every person we meet. In truth, they are all creatures of given temperament, which will appear in a given character, whose boundaries they will never pass : but we look at them, they seem alive, and we presume there is impulse in them. In the moment it seems impulse ; in the year, in the lifetime, it turns out to be a certain uniform tune which the revolving barrel of the music-box must play. Men resist the conclusion in the morning, but adopt it as the evening wears on, that temper prevails over everything of time, place, and condition, and is inconsumable in the flames of religion. Some modifications the moral sentiment avails to impose, but the individual texture holds its dominion, if not to bias the moral judgments, yet to fix the measure of activity and of enjoyment.

I thus express the law as it is read from the platform of ordinary life, but must not leave it without noticing the capital exception. For temperament is a power which no man will-ingly hears any one praise but himself. On the platform of physics, we cannot resist the contracting influences of so-called science. Temperament puts all divinity to rout. I know the mental proclivity of physicians. I hear the chuckle of the phrenologists. Theoretic

kidnappers and slave-drivers, they esteem each
man the victim of another, who winds him
round his finger by knowing the law of his
being, and by such cheap signboards as the
color of his beard, or the slope of his occiput,
reads the inventory of his fortunes and character.   The grossest ignorance does not disgust like this impudent knowingness.   The
physicians say, they are not materialists; but
they are : — Spirit is matter reduced to an extreme thinness: O *so* thin! — But the definition of *spiritual* should be, *that which is its
own evidence.*   What notions do they attach
to love! what to religion!   One would not
willingly pronounce these words in their hearing, and give them the occasion to profane
them.   I saw a gracious gentleman who adapts
his conversation to the form of the head of
the man he talks with!   I had fancied that
the value of life lay in its inscrutable possibilities; in the fact that I never know, in
addressing myself to a new individual, what
may befall me.   I carry the keys of my castle
in my hand, ready to throw them at the feet
of my lord, whenever and in what disguise soever he shall appear.   I know he is in the

neighborhood hidden among vagabonds. Shall
I preclude my future, by taking a high seat, and
kindly adapting my conversation to the shape
of heads? When I come to that, the doctors
shall buy me for a cent. —— 'But, sir, medical
history; the report to the Institute; the proven
facts!' — I distrust the facts and the inferences.
Temperament is the veto or limitation-power
in the constitution, very justly applied to restrain an opposite excess in the constitution,
but absurdly offered as a bar to original equity.
When virtue is in presence, all subordinate
powers sleep. On its own level, or in view of
nature, temperament is final. I see not, if one
be once caught in this trap of so-called sciences, any escape for the man from the links
of the chain of physical necessity. Given
such an embryo, such a history must follow.
On this platform, one lives in a sty of sensualism, and would soon come to suicide. But it
is impossible that the creative power should
exclude itself. Into every intelligence there
is a door which is never closed, through which
the creator passes. The intellect, seeker of
absolute truth, or the heart, lover of absolute
good, intervenes for our succor, and at one

whisper of these high powers, we awake from ineffectual struggles with this nightmare. We hurl it into its own hell, and cannot again contract ourselves to so base a state.

The secret of the illusoriness is in the necessity of a succession of moods or objects. Gladly we would anchor, but the anchorage is quicksand. This onward trick of nature is too strong for us : *Pero si muove.* When, at night, I look at the moon and stars, I seem stationary, and they to hurry.   Our love of the real draws us to permanence, but health of body consists in circulation, and sanity of mind in variety or facility of association. We need change of objects.   Dedication to one thought is quickly odious.   We house with the insane, and must humor them ; then conversation dies out. Once I took such delight in Montaigne, that I thought I should not need any other book; before that, in Shakspeare ; then in Plutarch ; then in Plotinus; at one time in Bacon ; afterwards in Goethe ; even in Bettine ; but now I turn the pages of either of them languidly, whilst I still cherish their genius.   So with pictures ; each will bear an emphasis of attention

once, which it cannot retain, though we fain
would continue to be pleased in that manner.
How strongly I have felt of pictures, that
when you have seen one well, you must take
your leave of it ; you shall never see it again.
I have had good lessons from pictures, which
I have since seen without emotion or remark.
A deduction must be made from the opinion,
which even the wise express of a new book or
occurrence. Their opinion gives me tidings
of their mood, and some vague guess at the
new fact, but is nowise to be trusted as the
lasting relation between that intellect and that
thing. The child asks, ' Mamma, why don't I
like the story as well as when you told it me
yesterday ? ' Alas, child, it is even so with
the oldest cherubim of knowledge. But will
it answer thy question to say, Because thou
wert born to a whole, and this story is a particular? The reason of the pain this discovery
causes us (and we make it late in respect to
works of art and intellect), is the plaint of
tragedy which murmurs from it in regard to
persons, to friendship and love.

That immobility and absence of elasticity
which we find in the arts, we find with more

pain in the artist. There is no power of expansion in men. Our friends early appear to us as representatives of certain ideas, which they never pass or exceed. They stand on the brink of the ocean of thought and power, but they never take the single step that would bring them there. A man is like a bit of Labrador spar, which has no lustre as you turn it in your hand, until you come to a particular angle ; then it shows deep and beautiful colors. There is no adaptation or universal applicability in men, but each has his special talent, and the mastery of successful men consists in adroitly keeping themselves where and when that turn shall be oftenest to be practised. We do what we must, and call it by the best names we can, and would fain have the praise of having intended the result which ensues. I cannot recall any form of man who is not superfluous sometimes. But is not this pitiful? Life is not worth the taking, to do tricks in.

Of course, it needs the whole society, to give the symmetry we seek. The parti-colored wheel must revolve very fast to appear white. Something is learned too by conversing with so much folly and defect. In fine, whoever loses, we are always of the gaining party. Divinity is behind our failures and follies also. The plays of children are nonsense, but very educative nonsense. So it is with the largest and solemnest things, with commerce, government, church, marriage, and so with the history of every man's bread, and the ways by which he is to come by it. Like a bird which alights nowhere, but hops perpetually from bough to bough, is the Power which abides in no man and in no woman, but for a moment speaks from this one, and for another moment from that one.

But what help from these fineries or pedantries? What help from thought? Life is not dialectics. We, I think, in these times, have had lessons enough of the futility of criticism. Our young people have thought and written much on labor and reform, and for all that they have written, neither the world nor themselves have got on a step. Intellectual tasting of life will not supersede muscular activity. If a man should consider the nicety of the passage of a piece of bread down his throat, he would starve. At Education-Farm, the noblest theory of life sat on the noblest figures of young men and maidens, quite powerless and melancholy. It would not rake or pitch a ton of hay ; it would not rub down a horse ; and the men and maidens it left pale and hungry. A political orator wittily compared our party promises to western roads, which opened stately enough, with planted trees on either side, to tempt the traveller, but soon became narrow and narrower, and ended in a squirrel-track, and ran up a tree. So does culture with us ; it ends in head-ache. Unspeakably sad and barren does life look to those, who a few months ago were dazzled with the splendor of the promise of the times. "There is now no longer any right course of action, nor any self-devotion left among the Iranis." Objections and criticism we have had our fill of. There are objections to every course of life and action, and the practical wisdom infers an indifferency, from the omnipresence of objection. The whole frame of things preaches indifferency. Do not craze yourself with thinking, but go about your business anywhere. Life is not intellectual or critical, but sturdy. Its chief good is for well-mixed people who can enjoy what they find, without question. Nature hates peeping, and our mothers speak her very sense when they say, "Children, eat your victuals, and say no more of it." To fill the hour, — that is happiness ; to fill the hour, and leave no crevice for a repentance or an approval. We live amid surfaces, and the true art of life is to skate well on them. Under the oldest mouldiest conventions, a man of native force prospers just as well as in the newest world, and that by skill of handling and treatment. He can take hold anywhere. Life itself is a mixture of power and form, and will not bear the least excess of either. To finish the moment, to find the journey's end in every step of the road, to live the greatest number of good hours, is wisdom. It is not the part of men, but of fanatics, or of mathematicians, if you will, to say, that, the shortness of life considered, it is not worth caring whether for so short a duration we were sprawling in want, or sitting high. Since our office is with moments, let us husband them. Five minutes of today are worth as much to me, as five minutes in the

5

next millennium.   Let us be poised, and wise,
and our own, today.   Let us treat the men
and women well : treat them as if they were
real : perhaps they are.   Men live in their
fancy, like drunkards whose hands are too
soft and tremulous for successful labor.   It is
a tempest of fancies, and the only ballast I
know, is a respect to the present hour.   Without any shadow of doubt, amidst this vertigo of
shows and politics, I settle myself ever the
firmer in the creed, that we should not postpone
and refer and wish, but do broad justice where
we are, by whomsoever we deal with, accepting our actual companions and circumstances,
however humble or odious, as the mystic
officials to whom the universe has delegated
its whole pleasure for us.   If these are mean
and malignant, their contentment, which is the
last victory of justice, is a more satisfying
echo to the heart, than the voice of poets and
the casual sympathy of admirable persons.   I
think that however a thoughtful man may
suffer from the defects and absurdities of his
company, he cannot without affectation deny
to any set of men and women, a sensibility to
extraordinary merit.   The coarse and friv-

olous have an instinct of superiority, if they have not a sympathy, and honor it in their blind capricious way with sincere homage.

The fine young people despise life, but in me, and in such as with me are free from dyspepsia, and to whom a day is a sound and solid good, it is a great excess of politeness to look scornful and to cry for company. I am grown by sympathy a little eager and sentimental, but leave me alone, and I should relish every hour and what it brought me, the potluck of the day, as heartily as the oldest gossip in the bar-room. I am thankful for small mercies. I compared notes with one of my friends who expects everything of the universe, and is disappointed when anything is less than the best, and I found that I begin at the other extreme, expecting nothing, and am always full of thanks for moderate goods. I accept the clangor and jangle of contrary tendencies. I find my account in sots and bores also. They give a reality to the circumjacent picture, which such a vanishing meteorous appearance can ill spare. In the morning I awake, and find the old world, wife, babes, and mother, Concord and Boston, the dear old spiritual world, and even the dear old devil not far off. If we will take the good we find, asking no questions, we shall have heaping measures. The great gifts are not got by analysis. Everything good is on the highway. The middle region of our being is the temperate zone. We may climb into the thin and cold realm of pure geometry and life-less science, or sink into that of sensation. Between these extremes is the equator of life, of thought, of spirit, of poetry,—a narrow belt. Moreover, in popular experience, everything good is on the highway. A collector peeps into all the picture-shops of Europe, for a landscape of Poussin, a crayon-sketch of Salvator; but the Transfiguration, the Last Judgment, the Communion of St. Jerome, and what are as transcendent as these, are on the walls of the Vatican, the Uffizii, or the Louvre, where every footman may see them ; to say nothing of nature's pictures in every street, of sunsets and sunrises every day, and the sculpture of the human body never absent. A collector recently bought at public auction, in London, for one hundred and fifty-seven guineas, an autograph of Shakspeare: but for nothing a school-boy can read Hamlet, and can detect secrets of highest concernment yet unpublished therein. I think I will never read any but the commonest books,— the Bible, Homer, Dante, Shakspeare, and Milton. Then we are impatient of so public a life and planet, and run hither and thither for nooks and secrets. The imagination delights in the wood-craft of Indians, trappers, and bee-hunters. We fancy that we are strangers, and not so intimately domesticated in the planet as the wild man, and the wild beast and bird. But the exclusion reaches them also ; reaches the climbing, flying, gliding, feathered and four-footed man. Fox and woodchuck, hawk and snipe, and bittern, when nearly seen, have no more root in the deep world than man, and are just such superficial tenants of the globe. Then the new molecular philosophy shows astronomical interspaces betwixt atom and atom, shows that the world is all outside : it has no inside.

The mid-world is best. Nature, as we know her, is no saint. The lights of the church, the ascetics, Gentoos and Grahamites, she does not distinguish by any favor. She comes eating and drinking and sinning. Her darlings, the great, the strong, the beautiful, are not children of our law, do not come out of the Sunday School, nor weigh their food, nor punctually keep the commandments. If we will be strong with her strength, we must not harbor such disconsolate consciences, borrowed too from the consciences of other nations. We must set up the strong present tense against all the rumors of wrath, past or to come. So many things are unsettled which it is of the first importance to settle, — and, pending their settlement, we will do as we do. Whilst the debate goes forward on the equity of commerce, and will not be closed for a century or two, New and Old England may keep shop. Law of copyright and international copyright is to be discussed, and, in the interim, we will sell our books for the most we can. Expediency of literature, reason of literature, lawfulness of writing down a thought, is questioned; much is to say on both sides, and, while the fight waxes hot, thou, dearest scholar, stick to thy foolish task, add a line every hour, and between whiles add a line. Right to hold land, right of property, is disputed, and the conventions convene, and before the vote is taken, dig away in your garden, and spend your earnings as a waif or godsend to all serene and beautiful purposes. Life itself is a bubble and a skepticism, and a sleep within a sleep. Grant it, and as much more as they will, — but thou, God's darling! heed thy private dream: thou wilt not be missed in the scorning and skepticism: there are enough of them: stay there in thy closet, and toil, until the rest are agreed what to do about it. Thy sickness, they say, and thy puny habit, require that thou do this or avoid that, but know that thy life is a flitting state, a tent for a night, and do thou, sick or well, finish that stint. Thou art sick, but shalt not be worse, and the universe, which holds thee dear, shall be the better.

Human life is made up of the two elements, power and form, and the proportion must be invariably kept, if we would have it sweet and sound. Each of these elements in excess makes a mischief as hurtful as its defect. Everything runs to excess: every good quality is noxious, if unmixed, and, to carry the danger to the edge of ruin, nature causes each man's peculiarity to superabound.   Here, among the farms, we adduce the scholars as examples of this treachery.   They are nature's victims of expression.   You who see the artist, the orator, the poet, too near, and find their life no more excellent than that of mechanics or farmers, and themselves victims of partiality, very hollow and haggard, and pronounce them failures, — not heroes, but quacks, — conclude very reasonably, that these arts are not for man, but are disease.   Yet nature will not bear you out.   Irresistible nature made men such, and makes legions more of such, every day.   You love the boy reading in a book, gazing at a drawing, or a cast : yet what are these millions who read and behold, but incipient writers and sculptors ?   Add a little more of that quality which now reads and sees, and they will seize the pen and chisel.   And if one remembers how innocently he began to be an artist, he perceives that nature joined with his enemy.   A man is a golden impossibility. The line he must walk is a hair's breadth. The wise through excess of wisdom is made a fool.

How easily, if fate would suffer it, we might keep forever these beautiful limits, and adjust ourselves, once for all, to the perfect calculation of the kingdom of known cause and effect. In the street and in the newspapers, life appears so plain a business, that manly resolution and adherence to the multiplication-table through all weathers, will insure success. But ah! presently comes a day, or is it only a a half-hour, with its angel-whispering,— which discomfits the conclusions of nations and of years! Tomorrow again, everything looks real and angular, the habitual standards are reinstated, common sense is as rare as genius,— is the basis of genius, and experience is hands and feet to every enterprise ; — and yet, he who should do his business on this understanding, would be quickly bankrupt. Power keeps 'quite another road thàn the turnpikes of choice and will, namely, the subterranean and invisible tunnels and channels of life. It is ridiculous that we are diplomatists, and doctors, and considerate people : there are no dupes like these. Life is a series of surprises, and would not be worth taking or keeping, if it were not. God delights to isolate us every day, and hide

from us the past and the future. We would
look about us, but with grand politeness he
draws down before us an impenetrable screen
of purest sky, and another behind us of purest
sky. 'You will not remember,' he seems to
say, 'and you will not expect.' All good
conversation, manners, and action, come from
a spontaneity which forgets usages, and makes
the moment great. Nature hates calculators;
her methods are saltatory and impulsive. Man
lives by pulses; our organic movements are
such; and the chemical and ethereal agents
are undulatory and alternate; and the mind
goes antagonizing on, and never prospers but
by fits. We thrive by casualties. Our chief
experiences have been casual. The most attractive class of people are those who are powerful obliquely, and not by the direct stroke :
men of genius, but not yet accredited : one
gets the cheer of their light, without paying
too great a tax. Theirs is the beauty of the
bird, or the morning light, and not of art. In
the thought of genius there is always a surprise ; and the moral sentiment is well called
" the newness," for it is never other ; as new
to the oldest intelligence as to the young

child, — "the kingdom that cometh without observation." In like manner, for practical success, there must not be too much design. A man will not be observed in doing that which he can do best. There is a certain magic about his properest action, which stupefies your powers of observation, so that though it is done before you, you wist not of it. The art of life has a pudency, and will not be exposed. Every man is an impossibility, until he is born ; every thing impossible, until we see a success. The ardors of piety agree at last with the coldest skepticism, — that nothing is of us or our works, — that all is of God. Nature will not spare us the smallest leaf of laurel. All writing comes by the grace of God, and all doing and having. I would gladly be moral, and keep due metes and bounds, which I dearly love, and allow the most to the will of man, but I have set my heart on honesty in this chapter, and I can see nothing at last, in success or failure, than more or less of vital force supplied from the Eternal. The results of life are uncalculated and uncalculable. The years teach much which the days never know. The persons who compose our company, con-

verse, and come and go, and design and execute many things, and somewhat comes of it
all, but an unlooked for result.   The individual is always mistaken.   He designed many
things, and drew in other persons as coadjutors,
quarrelled with some or all, blundered much,
and something is done ; all are a little advanced,
but the individual is always mistaken.   It turns
out somewhat new, and very unlike what he
promised himself.

The ancients, struck with this irreducible-
ness of the elements of human life to calculation, exalted Chance into a divinity, but that
is to stay too long at the spark, — which glitters truly at one point, — but the universe is
warm with the latency of the same fire.   The
miracle of life which will not be expounded,
but will remain a miracle, introduces a new
element.   In the growth of the embryo, Sir
Everard Home, I think, noticed that the evo-
lution was not from one central point, but co-
active from three or more points.   Life has no
memory.   That which proceeds in succession
might be remembered, but that which is co-
existent, or ejaculated from a deeper cause, as

yet far from being conscious, knows not its own tendency. So is it with us, now skeptical, or without unity, because immersed in forms and effects all seeming to be of equal yet hostile value, and now religious, whilst in the reception of spiritual law. Bear with these distractions, with this coetaneous growth of the parts: they will one day be *members*, and obey one will. On that one will, on that secret cause, they nail our attention and hope. Life is hereby melted into an expectation or a religion. Underneath the inharmonious and trivial particulars, is a musical perfection, the Ideal journeying always with us, the heaven without rent or seam. Do but observe the mode of our illumination. When I converse with a profound mind, or if at any time being alone I have good thoughts, I do not at once arrive at satisfactions, as when, being thirsty, I drink water, or go to the fire, being cold: no! but I am at first apprised of my vicinity to a new and excellent region of life. By persisting to read or to think, this region gives further sign of itself, as it were in flashes of light, in sudden discoveries of its profound beauty and repose, as if the clouds that cov-

ered it parted at intervals, and showed the
approaching traveller the inland mountains,
with the tranquil eternal meadows spread at
their base, whereon flocks graze, and shepherds
pipe and dance.   But every insight from this
realm of thought is felt as initial, and promises
a sequel.   I do not make it ; I arrive there, and
behold what was there already.   I make !   O
no !   I clap my hands in infantine joy and
amazement, before the first opening to me of
this august magnificence, old with the love and
homage of innumerable ages, young with the
life of life, the sunbright Mecca of the desert.
And what a future it opens !   I feel a new
heart beating with the love of the new beauty.
I am ready to die out of nature, and be born
again into this new yet unapproachable America I have found in the West.

> " Since neither now nor yesterday began
>   These thoughts, which have been ever, nor yet can
>   A man be found who their first entrance knew."

If I have described life as a flux of moods, I
must now add, that there is that in us which
changes not, and which ranks all sensations
and states of mind.   The consciousness in
each man is a sliding scale, which identifies

him now with the First Cause, and now with
the flesh of his body ; life above life, in infinite degrees. The sentiment from which it
sprung determines the dignity of any deed,
and the question ever is, not, what you have
done or forborne, but, at whose command you
have done or forborne it.

Fortune, Minerva, Muse, Holy Ghost, —
these are quaint names, too narrow to cover
this unbounded substance. The baffled intellect must still kneel before this cause, which
refuses to be named, — ineffable cause, which
every fine genius has essayed to represent by
some emphatic symbol, as, Thales by water,
Anaximenes by air, Anaxagoras by ($Nου\varsigma$)
thought, Zoroaster by fire, Jesus and the mod-
erns by love : and the metaphor of each has
become a national religion. The Chinese Mencius has not been the least successful in his
generalization. " I fully understand language,"
he said, " and nourish well my vast-flowing
vigor." — " I beg to ask what you call vast-
flowing vigor ? " — said his companion. " The
explanation," replied Mencius, " is difficult.
This vigor is supremely great, and in the highest degree unbending. Nourish it correctly, and

do it no injury, and it will fill up the vacancy
between heaven and earth.   This vigor accords with and assists justice and reason, and
leaves no hunger." — In our more correct
writing, we give to this generalization the
name of Being, and thereby confess that we
have arrived as far as we can go.   Suffice it
for the joy of the universe, that we have not
arrived at a wall, but at interminable oceans.
Our life seems not present, so much as prospective ; not for the affairs on which it is
wasted, but as a hint of this vast-flowing
vigor.   Most of life seems to be mere advertisement of faculty : information is given us
not to sell ourselves cheap ; that we are very
great.   So, in particulars, our greatness is always in a tendency or direction, not in an
action.   It is for us to believe in the rule, not
in the exception.   The noble are thus known
from the ignoble.   So in accepting the leading
of the sentiments, it is not what we believe
concerning the immortality of the soul, or the
like, but *the universal impulse to believe,* that
is the material circumstance, and is the principal fact in the history of the globe.   Shall
we describe this cause as that which works

directly? The spirit is not helpless or needful of mediate organs. It has plentiful powers
and direct effects. I am explained without
explaining, I am felt without acting, and
where I am not. Therefore all just persons
are satisfied with their own praise. They refuse to explain themselves, and are content
that new actions should do them that office.
They believe that we communicate without
speech, and above speech, and that no right
action of ours is quite unaffecting to our
friends, at whatever distance; for the influence
of action is not to be measured by miles.
Why should I fret myself, because a circumstance has occurred, which hinders my presence
where I was expected? If I am not at the
meeting, my presence where I am, should be
as useful to the commonwealth of friendship
and wisdom, as would be my presence in that
place. I exert the ·same quality of power in
all places. Thus journeys the mighty Ideal
before us; it never was known to fall into the
rear. No man ever came to an experience
which was satiating, but his good is tidings of
a better. Onward and onward! In liberated
moments, we know that a new picture of life

6

and duty is already possible; the elements already exist in many minds around you, of a doctrine of life which shall transcend any written record we have.   The new statement will comprise the skepticisms, as well as the faiths of society, and out of unbeliefs a creed shall be formed.   For, skepticisms are not gratuitous or lawless, but are limitations of the affirmative statement, and the new philosophy must take them in, and make. affirmations outside of them, just as much as it must include the oldest beliefs.

It is very unhappy, but too late to be helped, the discovery we have made, that we exist.   That discovery is called the Fall of Man. Ever afterwards, we suspect our instruments. We have learned that we do not see directly, but mediately, and that we have no means of correcting these colored and distorting lenses which we are, or of computing the amount of their errors.   Perhaps these subject-lenses have a creative power; perhaps there are no objects.   Once we lived in what we saw; now, the rapaciousness of this new power, which threatens to absorb all things, engages

us.   Nature, art, persons, letters, religions, —
objects, successively tumble in, and God is
but one of its ideas.   Nature and literature are
subjective phenomena; every evil and every
good thing is a shadow which we cast.   The
street is full of humiliations to the proud.   As
the fop contrived to dress his bailiffs in his
livery, and make them wait on his guests at
table, so the chagrins which the bad heart
gives off as bubbles, at once take form as ladies
and gentlemen in the street, shopmen or bar-
keepers in hotels, and threaten or insult whatever is threatenable and insultable in us.   'Tis
the same with our idolatries.   People forget
that it is the eye which makes the horizon, and
the rounding mind's eye which makes this or
that man a type or representative of humanity
with the name of hero or saint.   Jesus the
" providential man," is a good man on whom
many people are agreed that these optical laws
shall take effect.   By love on one part, and by
forbearance to press objection on the other
part, it is for a time settled, that we will look
at him in the centre of the horizon, and ascribe to him the properties that will attach to
any man so seen.   But the longest love or aver-

sion has a speedy term. The great and cres-
cive self, rooted in absolute nature, supplants
all relative existence, and ruins the kingdom of
mortal friendship and love. Marriage (in what
is called the spiritual world) is impossible, because of the inequality between every subject
and every object. The subject is the receiver
of Godhead, and at every comparison must feel
his being enhanced by that cryptic might.
Though not in energy, yet by presence, this
magazine of substance cannot be otherwise
than felt: nor can any force of intellect at-
tribute to the object the proper deity which
sleeps or wakes forever in every subject.
Never can love make consciousness and ascrip-
tion equal in force. There will be the same
gulf between every me and thee, as between
the original and the picture. The universe is
the bride of the soul. All private sympathy is
partial. Two human beings are like globes,
which can touch only in a point, and, whilst
they remain in contact, all other points of each
of the spheres are inert; their turn must also
come, and the longer a particular union lasts,
the more energy of appetency the parts not in
union acquire.

Life will be imaged, but cannot be divided nor doubled. Any invasion of its unity would be chaos. The soul is not twin-born, but the only begotten, and though revealing itself as child in time, child in appearance, is of a fatal and universal power, admitting no co-life. Every day, every act betrays the ill-concealed deity. We believe in ourselves, as we do not believe in others. We permit all things to ourselves, and that which we call sin in others, is experiment for us. It is an instance of our faith in ourselves, that men never speak of crime as lightly as they think : or, every man thinks a latitude safe for himself, which is nowise to be indulged to another. The act looks very differently on the inside, and on the outside ; in its quality, and in its consequences. Murder in the murderer is no such ruinous thought as poets and romancers will have it ; it does not unsettle him, or fright him from his ordinary notice of trifles : it is an act quite easy to be contemplated, but in its sequel, it turns out to be a horrible jangle and confounding of all relations. Especially the crimes that spring from love, seem right and fair from the actor's

point of view, but, when acted, are found destructive of society.   No man at last believes
that he can be lost, nor that the crime in him
is as black as in the felon.   Because the intellect qualifies in our own case the moral
judgments.   For there is no crime to the
intellect.   That is antinomian or hypernomian,
and judges law as well as fact.   "It is worse
than a crime, it is a blunder," said Napoleon,
speaking the language of the intellect.   To it,
the world is a problem in mathematics or the
science of quantity, and it leaves out praise
and blame, and all weak emotions.   All steal-
ing is comparative.   If you come to absolutes,
pray who does not steal?   Saints are sad,
because they behold sin, (even when they
speculate,) from the point of view of the conscience, and not of the intellect ; a confusion
of thought.   Sin seen from the thought, is a
diminution or *less :* seen from the conscience
or will, it is pravity or *bad.*   The intellect
names it shade, absence of light, and no
essence.   The conscience must feel it as
essence, essential evil.   This it is not: it has
an objective existence, but no subjective.

Thus inevitably does the universe wear our

color, and every object fall successively into
the subject itself. The subject exists, the
subject enlarges; all things sooner or later fall
into place. As I am, so I see; use what language we will, we can never say anything but
what we are; Hermes, Cadmus, Columbus,
Newton, Buonaparte, are the mind's ministers.
Instead of feeling a poverty when we encounter a great man, let us treat the new
comer like a travelling geologist, who passes
through our estate, and shows us good slate, or
limestone, or anthracite, in our brush pasture.
The partial action of each strong mind in one
direction, is a telescope for the objects on
which it is pointed. But every other part of
knowledge is to be pushed to the same extrav-
agance, ere the soul attains her due spheric-
ity. Do you see that kitten chasing so prettily
her own tail? If you could look with her
eyes, you might see her surrounded with hundreds of figures performing complex dramas,
with tragic and comic issues, long conversations, many characters, many ups and downs
of fate, — and meantime it is only puss and
her tail. How long before our masquerade
will end its noise of tamborines, laughter, and

shouting, and we shall find it was a solitary performance ? — A subject and an object, — it takes so much to make the galvanic circuit complete, but magnitude adds nothing.   What imports it whether it is Kepler and the sphere ; Columbus and America; a reader and his book ; or puss with her tail ?

It is true that all the muses and love and religion hate these developments, and will find a way to punish the chemist, who publishes in the parlor the secrets of the laboratory. And we cannot say too little of our constitutional necessity of seeing things under private aspects, or saturated with our humors.   And yet is the God the native of these bleak rocks. That need makes in morals the capital virtue of self-trust.   We must hold hard to this poverty, however scandalous, and by more vigorous self-recoveries, after the sallies of action, possess our axis more firmly.   The life of truth is cold, and so far mournful ; but it is not the slave of tears, contritions, and perturbations.   It does not attempt another's work, nor adopt another's facts.   It is a main lesson of wisdom to know your own from another's. I have learned that I cannot dispose of other people's facts ; but I possess such a key to my own, as persuades me against all their denials, that they also have a key to theirs.   A sympathetic person is placed in the dilemma of a swimmer among drowning men, who all catch at him, and if he give so much as a leg or a finger, they will drown him.   They wish to be saved from the mischiefs of their vices, but not from their vices.   Charity would be wasted on this poor waiting on the symptoms. A wise and hardy physician will say, *Come out of that,* as the first condition of advice.

In this our talking America, we are ruined by our good nature and listening on all sides. This compliance takes away the power of being greatly useful.   A man should not be able to look other than directly and forthright.   A preoccupied attention is the only answer to the importunate frivolity of other people : an attention, and to an aim which makes their wants frivolous.   This is a divine answer, and leaves no appeal, and no hard thoughts.   In Flaxman's drawing of the Eumenides of Æschylus, Orestes supplicates Apollo, whilst the Furies sleep on the threshold.   The face of the god expresses a shade of regret and compassion, but calm with the conviction of the irreconcilableness of the two spheres. He is born into other politics, into the eternal and beautiful. The man at his feet asks for his interest in turmoils of the earth, into which his nature cannot enter. And the Eumenides there lying express pictorially this disparity. The god is surcharged with his divine destiny.

Illusion, Temperament, Succession, Surface, Surprise, Reality, Subjectiveness, — these are threads on the loom of time, these are the lords of life. I dare not assume to give their order, but I name them as I find them in my way. I know better than to claim any completeness for my picture. I am a fragment, and this is a fragment of me. I can very confidently announce one or another law, which throws itself into relief and form, but I am too young yet by some ages to compile a code. I gossip for my hour concerning the eternal politics. I have seen many fair pictures not in vain. A wonderful time I have lived in. I am not the novice I was fourteen, nor yet seven years ago. Let who will

ask, where is the fruit? I find a private fruit
sufficient. This is a fruit, — that I should not
ask for a rash effect from meditations, counsels, and the hiving of truths. I should feel
it pitiful to demand a result on this town
and county, an overt effect on the instant
month and year. The effect is deep and secular as the cause. It works on periods in
which mortal lifetime is lost. All I know is
reception; I am and I have: but I do not
get, and when I have fancied I had gotten
anything, I found I did not. I worship
with wonder the great Fortune. My reception has been so large, that I am not annoyed
by receiving this or that superabundantly. I
say to the Genius, if he will pardon the proverb, *In for a mill, in for a million.* When
I receive a new gift, I do not macerate my
body to make the account square, for, if I
should die, I could not make the account
square. The benefit overran the merit the
first day, and has overran the merit ever since.
The merit itself, so-called, I reckon part of
the receiving.

Also, that hankering after an overt or practical effect seems to me an apostasy. In good

earnest, I am willing to spare this most unnecessary deal of doing. Life wears to me a
visionary face. Hardest, roughest action is
visionary also. It is but a choice between
soft and turbulent dreams. People disparage
knowing and the intellectual life, and urge
doing. I am very content with knowing, if
only I could know. That is an august entertainment, and would suffice me a great while.
To know a little, would be worth the expense
of this world. I hear always the law of
Adrastia, "that every soul which had acquired
any truth, should be safe from harm until
another period."

I know that the world I converse with in
the city and in the farms, is not the world I
think. I observe that difference, and shall
observe it. One day, I shall know the value
and law of this discrepance. But I have not
found that much was gained by manipular
attempts to realize the world of thought.
Many eager persons successively make an experiment in this way, and make themselves
ridiculous. They acquire democratic manners,
they foam at the mouth, they hate and deny.
Worse, I observe, that, in the history of man-

kind, there is never a solitary example of success, — taking their own tests of success. I say this polemically, or in reply to the inquiry, why not realize your world ? But far be from me the despair which prejudges the law by a paltry empiricism, — since there never was a right endeavor, but it succeeded. Patience and patience, we shall win at the last. We must be very suspicious of the deceptions of the element of time. It takes a good deal of time to eat or to sleep, or to earn a hundred dollars, and a very little time to entertain a hope and an insight which becomes the light of our life. We dress our garden, eat our dinners, discuss the household with our wives, and these things make no impression, are forgotten next week ; but in the solitude to which every man is always returning, he has a sanity and revelations, which in his passage into new worlds he will carry with him. Never mind the ridicule, never mind the defeat : up again, old heart ! — it seems to say, — there is victory yet for all justice ; and the true romance which the world exists to realize, will be the transformation of genius into practical power.

CHARACTER.

The sun set ; but set not his hope :
Stars rose ; his faith was earlier up :
Fixed on the enormous galaxy,
Deeper and older seemed his eye :
And matched his sufferance sublime
The taciturnity of time.
He spoke, and words more soft than rain
Brought the Age of Gold again :
His action won such reverence sweet,
As hid all measure of the feat.

Work of his hand
He nor commends nor grieves:
Pleads for itself the fact;
As unrepenting Nature leaves
Her every act.

ESSAY III.

CHARACTER.

———

I have read that those who listened to Lord Chatham felt that there was something finer in the man, than anything which he said. It has been complained of our brilliant English historian of the French Revolution, that when he has told all his facts about Mirabeau, they do not justify his estimate of his genius. The Gracchi, Agis, Cleomenes, and others of Plutarch's heroes, do not in the record of facts equal their own fame. Sir Philip Sidney, the Earl of Essex, Sir Walter Raleigh, are men of great figure, and of few deeds. We cannot find the smallest part of the personal weight of Washington, in the narrative of his exploits. The authority of the name of Schiller is too great for his books. This inequality of the reputation to the works or the anecdotes, is not accounted for by saying that the reverberation is longer than the thunder-clap; but somewhat resided in these men which begot an expectation that outran all their performance. The largest part of their power was latent. This is that which we call Character, — a reserved force which acts directly by presence, and without means. It is conceived of as a certain undemonstrable force, a Familiar or Genius, by whose impulses the man is guided, but whose counsels he cannot impart; which is company for him, so that such men are often solitary, or if they chance to be social, do not need society, but can entertain themselves very well alone. The purest literary talent appears at one time great, at another time small, but character is of a stellar and undiminishable greatness. What others effect by talent or by eloquence, this man accomplishes by some magnetism. "Half his strength he put not forth." His victories are by demonstration of superiority, and not by crossing of bayonets. He conquers, because his arrival alters the face of affairs. '"O Iole! how did you know that Hercules was a god?" "Because," answered Iole, "I was content the moment my eyes fell on him.

When I beheld Theseus, I desired that I might see him offer battle, or at least guide his horses in the chariot-race ; but Hercules did not wait for a contest ; he conquered whether he stood, or walked, or sat, or whatever thing he did." ' Man, ordinarily a pendant to events, only half attached, and that awkwardly, to the world he lives in, in these examples appears to share the life of things, and to be an expression of the same laws which control the tides and the sun, numbers and quantities.

But to use a more modest illustration, and nearer home, I observe, that in our political elections, where this element, if it appears at all, can only occur in its coarsest form, we sufficiently understand its incomparable rate. The people know that they need in their representative much more than talent, namely, the power to make his talent trusted. They cannot come at their ends by sending to Congress a learned, acute, and fluent speaker, if he be not one, who, before he was appointed by the people to represent them, was appointed by Almighty God to stand for a fact, — invincibly persuaded of that fact in himself, — so that the most confident and the most violent

persons learn that here is resistance on which
both impudence and terror are wasted, namely,
faith in a fact. The men who carry their
points do not need to inquire of their constitu-
ents what they should say, but are themselves
the country which they represent: nowhere
are its emotions or opinions so instant and true
as in them; nowhere so pure from a selfish
infusion. The constituency at home hearkens
to their words, watches the color of their
cheek, and therein, as in a glass, dresses its
own. Our public assemblies are pretty good
tests of manly force. Our frank countrymen
of the west and south have a taste for character, and like to know whether the New Eng-
lander is a substantial man, or whether the
hand can pass through him.

The same motive force appears in trade.
There are geniuses in trade, as well as in war,
or the state, or letters; and the reason why this
or that man is fortunate, is not to be told. It
lies in the man : that is all anybody can tell
you about it. See him, and you will know as
easily why he succeeds, as, if you see Napoleon, you would comprehend his fortune. In
the new objects we recognize the old game, the

habit of fronting the fact, and not dealing with it at second hand, through the perceptions of somebody else. Nature seems to authorize trade, as soon as you see the natural merchant, who appears not so much a private agent, as her factor and Minister of Commerce. His natural probity combines with his insight into the fabric of society, to put him above tricks, and he communicates to all his own faith, that contracts are of no private interpretation. The habit of his mind is a reference to standards of natural equity and public advantage; and he inspires respect, and the wish to deal with him, both for the quiet spirit of honor which attends him, and for the intellectual pastime which the spectacle of so much ability affords. This immensely stretched trade, which makes the capes of the Southern Ocean his wharves, and the Atlantic Sea his familiar port, centres in his brain only; and nobody in the universe can make his place good. In his parlor, I see very well that he has been at hard work this morning, with that knitted brow, and that settled humor, which all his desire to be courteous cannot shake off. I see plainly how many firm acts have been done;

how many valiant *noes* have this day been spoken, when others would have uttered ruinous *yeas*. I see, with the pride of art, and skill of masterly arithmetic and power of remote combination, the consciousness of being an agent and playfellow of the original laws of the world. He too believes that none can supply him, and that a man must be born to trade, or he cannot learn it.

This virtue draws the mind more, when it appears in action to ends not so mixed. It works with most energy in the smallest companies and in private relations. In all cases, it is an extraordinary and incomputable agent. The excess of physical strength is paralyzed by it. Higher natures overpower lower ones by affecting them with a certain sleep. The faculties are locked up, and offer no resistance. Perhaps that is the universal law. When the high cannot bring up the low to itself, it benumbs it, as man charms down the resistance of the lower animals. Men exert on each other a similar occult power. How often has the influence of a true master realized all the tales of magic! A river of command seemed to run down from his eyes into all those who beheld him, a torrent of strong sad light, like an Ohio or Danube, which pervaded them with his thoughts, and colored all events with the hue of his mind. "What means did you employ?" was the question asked of the wife of Concini, in regard to her treatment of Mary of Medici; and the answer was, "Only that influence which every strong mind has over a weak one." Cannot Cæsar in irons shuffle off the irons, and transfer them to the person of Hippo or Thraso the turnkey? Is an iron handcuff so immutable a bond? Suppose a slaver on the coast of Guinea should take on board a gang of negroes, which should contain persons of the stamp of Toussaint L'Ouverture: or, let us fancy, under these swarthy masks he has a gang of Washingtons in chains. When they arrive at Cuba, will the relative order of the ship's company be the same? Is there nothing but rope and iron? Is there no love, no reverence? Is there never a glimpse of right in a poor slave-captain's mind; and cannot these be supposed available to break, or elude, or in any manner overmatch the tension of an inch or two of iron ring?

This is a natural power, like light and heat,

and all nature coöperates with it. The reason
why we feel one man's presence, and do not
feel another's, is as simple as gravity. Truth
is the summit of being : justice is the application of it to affairs. All individual natures
stand in a scale, according to the purity of this
element in them. The will of the pure runs
down from them into other natures, as water
runs down from a higher into a lower vessel.
This natural force is no more to be withstood,
than any other natural force. We can drive a
stone upward for a moment into the air, but it
is yet true that all stones will forever fall;
and whatever instances can be quoted of un-
punished theft, or of a lie which somebody
credited, justice must prevail, and it is the
privilege of truth to make itself believed.
Character is this moral order seen through the
medium of an individual nature. An individual is an encloser. Time and space, liberty
and necessity, truth and thought, are left at
large no longer. Now, the universe is a close
or pound. All things exist in the man tinged
with the manners of his soul. With what
quality is in him, he infuses all nature that he
can reach ; nor does he tend to lose himself in

vastness, but, at how long a curve soever, all his regards return into his own good at last. He animates all he can, and he sees only what he animates. He encloses the world, as the patriot does his country, as a material basis for his character, and a theatre for action. A healthy soul stands united with the Just and the True, as the magnet arranges itself with the pole, so that he stands to all beholders like a transparent object betwixt them and the sun, and whoso journeys towards the sun, journeys towards that person. He is thus the medium of the highest influence to all who are not on the same level. Thus, men of character are the conscience of the society to which they belong.

The natural measure of this power is the resistance of circumstances. Impure men consider life as it is reflected in opinions, events, and persons. They cannot see the action, until it is done. Yet its moral element pre-existed in the actor, and its quality as right or wrong, it was easy to predict. Everything in nature is bipolar, or has a positive and negative pole. There is a male and a female, a spirit and a fact, a north and a south. Spirit is the positive, the event is the negative. Will is the north, action the south pole. Character may be ranked as having its natural place in the north. It shares the magnetic currents of the system. The feeble souls are drawn to the south or negative pole. They look at the profit or hurt of the action. They never behold a principle until it is lodged in a person. They do not wish to be lovely, but to be loved. The class of character like to hear of their faults: the other class do not like to hear of faults; they worship events; secure to them a fact, a connexion, a certain chain of circumstances, and they will ask no more. The hero sees that the event is ancillary: it must follow *him.* A given order of events has no power to secure to him the satisfaction which the imagination attaches to it; the soul of goodness escapes from any set of circumstances, whilst prosperity belongs to a certain mind, and will introduce that power and victory which is its natural fruit, into any order of events. No change of circumstances can repair a defect of character. We boast our emancipation from many superstitions; but if we have broken any idols, it is through a transfer of the idolatry. What have I gained, that I no longer immolate a bull to Jove, or to Neptune, or a mouse to Hecate ; that I do not tremble before the Eumenides, or the Catholic Purgatory, or the Calvinistic Judgment-day, — if I quake at opinion, the public opinion, as we call it ; or at the threat of assault, or contumely, or bad neighbors, or poverty, or mutilation, or at the rumor of revolution, or of murder ? If I quake, what matters it what I quake at ? Our proper vice takes form in one or another shape, according to the sex, age, or temperament of the person, and, if we are capable of fear, will readily find terrors. The covetousness or the malignity which saddens me, when I ascribe it to society, is my own. I am always environed by myself. On the other part, rectitude is a perpetual victory, celebrated not by cries of joy, but by serenity, which is joy fixed or habitual. It is disgraceful to fly to events for confirmation of our truth and worth. The capitalist does not run every hour to the broker, to coin his advantages into current money of the realm ; he is satisfied to read in the quotations of the market, that his stocks have risen.

The same transport which the occurrence of
the best events in the best order would occasion me, I must learn to taste purer in the
perception that my position is every hour
meliorated, and does already command those
events I desire. That exultation is only to be
checked by the foresight of an order of things
so excellent, as to throw all our prosperities
into the deepest shade.

The face which character wears to me is
self-sufficingness. I revere the person who is
riches; so that I cannot think of him as alone,
or poor, or exiled, or unhappy, or a client, but
as perpetual patron, benefactor, and beatified
man. Character is centrality, the impossibility of being displaced or overset. A man
should give us a sense of mass. Society is
frivolous, and shreds its day into scraps, its
conversation into ceremonies and escapes.
But if I go to see an ingenious man, I shall
think myself poorly entertained if he give me
nimble pieces of benevolence and etiquette;
rather he shall stand stoutly in his place, and
let me apprehend, if it were only his resistance; know that I have encountered a new and
positive quality; — great refreshment for both

of us. It is much, that he does not accept the conventional opinions and practices. That nonconformity will remain a goad and remembrancer, and every inquirer will have to dispose of him, in the first place. There is nothing real or useful that is not a seat of war. Our houses ring with laughter and personal and critical gossip, but it helps little. But the uncivil, unavailable man, who is a problem and a threat to society, whom it cannot let pass in silence, but must either worship or hate, — and to whom all parties feel related, both the leaders of opinion, and the obscure and eccentric, — he helps; he puts America and Europe in the wrong, and destroys the skepticism which says, 'man is a doll, let us eat and drink, 'tis the best we can do,' by illuminating the untried and unknown. Acquiescence in the establishment, and appeal to the public, indicate infirm faith, heads which are not clear, and which must see a house built, before they can comprehend the plan of it. The wise man not only leaves out of his thought the many, but leaves out the few. Fountains, fountains, the self-moved, the absorbed, the commander because he is commanded, the assured, the primary, — they are good; for these announce the instant presence of supreme power.

Our action should rest mathematically on our substance. In nature, there are no false valuations. A pound of water in the ocean-tempest has no more gravity than in a mid-summer pond. All things work exactly according to their quality, and according to their quantity; attempt nothing they cannot do, except man only. He has pretension : he wishes and attempts things beyond his force. I read in a book of English memoirs, "Mr. Fox (afterwards Lord Holland) said, he must have the Treasury; he had served up to it, and would have it." — Xenophon and his Ten Thousand were quite equal to what they attempted, and did it; so equal, that it was not suspected to be a grand and inimitable exploit. Yet there stands that fact unrepeated, a high-water-mark in military history. Many have attempted it since, and not been equal to it. It is only on reality, that any power of action can be based. No institution will be better than the institutor. I knew an amiable and accomplished person who undertook a practical reform, yet I was

never able to find in him the enterprise of
love he took in hand. He adopted it by ear
and by the understanding from the books
he had been reading. All his action was
tentative, a piece of the city carried out
into the fields, and was the city still, and
no new fact, and could not inspire enthusiasm. Had there been something latent in
the man, a terrible undemonstrated genius
agitating and embarrassing his demeanor, we
had watched for its advent. It is not enough
that the intellect should see the evils, and their
remedy. We shall still postpone our existence, nor take the ground to which we are
entitled, whilst it is only a thought, and not a
spirit that incites us. We have not yet served
up to it.

These are properties of life, and another
trait is the notice of incessant growth. Men
should be intelligent and earnest. They must
also make us feel, that they have a controlling
happy future, opening before them, which
sheds a splendor on the passing hour. The
hero is misconceived and misreported : he cannot therefore wait to unravel any man's
blunders : he is again on his road, adding new

powers and honors to his domain, and new claims on your heart, which will bankrupt you, if you have loitered about the old things, and have not kept your relation to him, by adding to your wealth. New actions are the only apologies and explanations of old ones, which the noble can bear to offer or to receive. If your friend has displeased you, you shall not sit down to consider it, for he has already lost all memory of the passage, and has doubled his power to serve you, and, ere you can rise up again, will burden you with blessings.

We have no pleasure in thinking of a benevolence that is only measured by its works. Love is inexhaustible, and if its estate is wasted, its granary emptied, still cheers and enriches, and the man, though he sleep, seems to purify the air, and his house to adorn the landscape and strengthen the laws. People always recognize this difference. We know who is benevolent, by quite other means than the amount of subscription to soup-societies. It is only low merits that can be enumerated. Fear, when your friends say to you what you have done well, and say it through ; but when they stand with uncertain timid looks of respect and half-dislike, and must suspend their judgment for years to come, you may begin to hope. Those who live to the future must always appear selfish to those who live to the present. Therefore it was droll in the good Riemer, who has written memoirs of Goethe, to make out a list of his donations and good deeds, as, so many hundred thalers given to Stilling, to Hegel, to Tischbein: a lucrative place found for Professor Voss, a post under the Grand Duke for Herder, a pension for Meyer, two professors recommended to foreign universities, &c. &c. The longest list of specifications of benefit, would look very short. A man is a poor creature, if he is to be measured so. For, all these, of course, are exceptions; and the rule and hodiernal life of a good man is benefaction. The true charity of Goethe is to be inferred from the account he gave Dr. Eckermann, of the way in which he had spent his fortune. " Each bon-mot of mine has cost a purse of gold. Half a million of my own money, the fortune I inherited, my salary, and the large income derived from my writings for fifty years back,

8

have been expended to instruct me in what I now know. I have besides seen," &c.

I own it is but poor chat and gossip to go to enumerate traits of this simple and rapid power, and we are painting the lightning with charcoal; but in these long nights and vacations, I like to console myself so. Nothing but itself can copy it. A word warm from the heart enriches me. I surrender at discretion. How death-cold is literary genius before this fire of life! These are the touches that reanimate my heavy soul, and give it eyes to pierce the dark of nature. I find, where I thought myself poor, there was I most rich. Thence comes a new intellectual exaltation, to be again rebuked by some new exhibition of character. Strange alternation of attraction and repulsion! Character repudiates intellect, yet excites it; and character passes into thought, is published so, and then is ashamed before new flashes of moral worth.

Character is nature in the highest form. It is of no use to ape it, or to contend with it. Somewhat is possible of resistance, and of persistence, and of creation, to this power, which will foil all emulation.

This masterpiece is best where no hands but nature's have been laid on it. Care is taken that the greatly-destined shall slip up into life in the shade, with no thousand-eyed Athens to watch and blazon every new thought, every blushing emotion of young genius. Two persons lately, — very young children of the most high God, — have given me occasion for thought. When I explored the source of their sanctity, and charm for the imagination, it seemed as if each answered, 'From my nonconformity: I never listened to your people's law, or to what they call their gospel, and wasted my time. I was content with the simple rural poverty of my own : hence this sweetness : my work never reminds you of that ; — is pure of that.' And nature advertises me in such persons, that, in democratic America, she will not be democratized. How cloistered and constitutionally sequestered from the market and from scandal ! It was only this morning, that I sent away some wild flowers of these wood-gods. They are a relief from literature, — these fresh draughts from the sources of thought and sentiment ; as we read, in an age of polish and criticism, the first lines

of written prose and verse of a nation. How
captivating is their devotion to their favorite
books, whether Æschylus, Dante, Shakspeare,
or Scott, as feeling that they have a stake in
that book : who touches that, touches them ; —
and especially the total solitude of the critic,
the Patmos of thought from which he writes,
in unconsciousness of any eyes that shall ever
read this writing. Could they dream on still,
as angels, and not wake to comparisons, and
to be flattered! Yet some natures are too
good to be spoiled by praise, and wherever the
vein of thought reaches down into the profound, there is no danger from vanity.
Solemn friends will warn them of the danger
of the head's being turned by the flourish
of trumpets, but they can afford to smile.
I remember the indignation of an eloquent
Methodist at the kind admonitions of a
Doctor of Divinity, — 'My friend, a man can
neither be praised nor insulted.' But forgive
the counsels ; they are very natural. I remember the thought which occurred to me
when some ingenious and spiritual foreigners
came to America, was, Have you been victim-
ized in being brought hither ? — or, prior ot
that, answer me this, 'Are you victimizable ? '

As I have said, nature keeps these sovereignties in her own hands, and however pertly our sermons and disciplines would divide some share of credit, and teach that the laws fashion the citizen, she goes her own gait, and puts the wisest in the wrong. She makes very light of gospels and prophets, as one who has a great many more to produce, and no excess of time to spare on any one. There is a class of men, individuals of which appear at long intervals, so eminently endowed with insight and virtue, that they have been unanimously saluted as *divine*, and who seem to be an accumulation of that power we consider. Divine persons are character born, or, to borrow a phrase from Napoleon, they are victory organized. They are usually received with ill-will, because they are new, and because they set a bound to the exaggeration that has been made of the personality of the last divine person. Nature never rhymes her children, nor makes two men alike. When we see a great man, we fancy a resemblance to some historical person, and predict the sequel of his character and fortune, a result which he is sure to disappoint. None will ever solve the problem of his character according to our prejudice, but only in his own high unprecedented way. Character wants room; must not be crowded on by persons, nor be judged from glimpses got in the press of affairs or on few occasions. It needs perspective, as a great building. It may not, probably does not, form relations rapidly; and we should not require rash explanation, either on the popular ethics, or on our own, of its action.

I look on Sculpture as history. I do not think the Apollo and the Jove impossible in flesh and blood. Every trait which the artist recorded in stone, he had seen in life, and better than his copy. We have seen many counterfeits, but we are born believers in great men. How easily we read in old books, when men were few, of the smallest action of the patriarchs. We require that a man should be so large and columnar in the landscape, that it should deserve to be recorded, that he arose, and girded up his loins, and departed to such a place. The most credible pictures are those of majestic men who prevailed at their entrance, and convinced the senses; as happened to the eastern magian who was sent to test the merits of Zertusht or Zoroaster. When the Yunani sage arrived at Balkh, the Persians tell us, Gushtasp appointed a day on which the Mobeds of every country should assemble, and a golden chair was placed for the Yunani sage. Then the beloved of Yezdam, the prophet Zertusht, advanced into the midst of the assembly. The Yunani sage, on seeing that chief, said, " This form and this gait cannot lie, and nothing but truth can proceed from them." Plato said, it was impossible not to believe in the children of the gods, " though they should speak without probable or necessary arguments." I should think myself very unhappy in my associates, if I could not credit the best things in history. " John Bradshaw," says Milton, " appears like a consul, from whom the fasces are not to depart with the year; so that not on the tribunal only, but throughout his life, you would regard him as sitting in judgment upon kings." I find it more credible, since it is anterior information, that one man should *know heaven*, as the Chinese say, than that so many men should know the world. " The virtuous prince confronts the gods, without any misgiving. He waits a hundred ages till a sage comes, and does not doubt. He who confronts the gods, without any misgiving, knows heaven ; he who waits a hundred ages until a sage comes, without doubting, knows men. Hence the virtuous prince moves, and for ages shows empire the way." But there is no need to seek remote examples. He is a dull observer whose experience has not taught him the reality and force of magic, as well as of chemistry. The coldest precisian cannot go abroad without encountering inexplicable influences. One man fastens an eye on him, and the graves of the memory render up their dead ; the secrets that make him wretched either to keep or to betray, must be yielded ; — another, and he cannot speak, and the bones of his body seem to lose their cartilages ; the entrance of a friend adds grace, boldness, and eloquence to him ; and there are persons, he cannot choose but remember, who gave a transcendant expansion to his thought, and kindled another life in his bosom.

What is so excellent as strict relations of amity, when they spring from this deep root? The sufficient reply to the skeptic, who doubts the power and the furniture of man, is in that possibility of joyful intercourse with persons, which makes the faith and practice of all reasonable men. I know nothing which life has to offer so satisfying as the profound good understanding, which can subsist, after much exchange of good offices, between two virtuous men, each of whom is sure of himself, and sure of his friend. It is a happiness which postpones all other gratifications, and makes politics, and commerce, and churches, cheap. For, when men shall meet as they ought, each a benefactor, a shower of stars, clothed with thoughts, with deeds, with accomplishments, it should be the festival of nature which all things announce. Of such friendship, love in the sexes is the first symbol, as all other things are symbols of love. Those relations to the best men, which, at one time, we reckoned the romances of youth, become, in the progress of the character, the most solid enjoyment.

If it were possible to live in right relations with men! — if we could abstain from asking anything of them, from asking their praise, or help, or pity, and content us with compelling them through the virtue of the eldest laws! Could we not deal with a few persons, — with one person, — after the unwritten statutes, and make an experiment of their efficacy? Could we not pay our friend the compliment of truth, of silence, of forbearing? Need we be so eager to seek him? If we are related, we shall meet. It was a tradition of the ancient world, that no metamorphosis could hide a god from a god; and there is a Greek verse which runs,

" The Gods are to each other not unknown."

Friends also follow the laws of divine necessity; they gravitate to each other, and cannot otherwise : —

When each the other shall avoid,
Shall each by each be most enjoyed.

Their relation is not made, but allowed. The gods must seat themselves without seneschal in our Olympus, and as they can instal themselves by seniority divine. Society is spoiled, if pains are taken, if the associates are brought a mile to meet. And if it be not society, it is a mischievous, low, degrading jangle, though made up of the best. All the greatness of each is kept back, and every foible in painful activity, as if the Olympians should meet to exchange snuff-boxes.

Life goes headlong. We chase some flying scheme, or we are hunted by some fear or command behind us. But if suddenly we encounter a friend, we pause; our heat and hurry look foolish enough; now pause, now possession, is required, and the power to swell the moment from the resources of the heart. The moment is all, in all noble relations.

A divine person is the prophecy of the mind; a friend is the hope of the heart. Our beatitude waits for the fulfilment of these two in one. The ages are opening this moral force. All force is the shadow or symbol of that. Poetry is joyful and strong, as it draws its inspiration thence. Men write their names on the world, as they are filled with this. History has been mean; our nations have been mobs; we have never seen a man : that divine form we do not yet know, but only the dream and prophecy of such : we do not know the majestic manners which belong to him, which appease and exalt the beholder. We shall one day see that the most private is the most public energy, that quality atones for quantity, and grandeur of character acts in the dark, and succors them who never saw it. What greatness has yet appeared, is beginnings and encouragements to us in this direction. The history of those gods and saints which the world has written, and then worshipped, are documents of character. The ages have exulted in the manners of a youth who owed nothing to fortune, and who was hanged at the Tyburn of his nation, who, by the pure quality of his nature, shed an epic splendor around the facts of his death, which has transfigured every particular into an universal symbol for the eyes of mankind. This great defeat is hitherto our highest fact. But the mind requires a victory to the senses, a force of character which will convert judge, jury, soldier, and king ; which will rule animal and mineral virtues, and blend with the courses of sap, of rivers, of winds, of stars, and of moral agents.

If we cannot attain at a bound to these grandeurs, at least, let us do them homage. In society, high advantages are set down to the possessor, as disadvantages. It requires the more wariness in our private estimates.

I do not forgive in my friends the failure to know a fine character, and to entertain it with thankful hospitality. When, at last, that which we have always longed for, is arrived, and shines on us with glad rays out of that far celestial land, then to be coarse, then to be critical, and treat such a visitant with the jabber and suspicion of the streets, argues a vulgarity that seems to shut the doors of heaven. This is confusion, this the right insanity, when the soul no longer knows its own, nor where its allegiance, its religion, are due. Is there any religion but this, to know, that, wherever in the wide desert of being, the holy sentiment we cherish has opened into a flower, it blooms for me ? if none sees it, I see it ; I am aware, if I alone, of the greatness of the fact. Whilst it blooms, I will keep sabbath or holy time, and suspend my gloom, and my folly and jokes. Nature is indulged by the presence of this guest. There are many eyes that can detect and honor the prudent and household virtues ; there are many that can discern Genius on his starry track, though the mob is incapable ; but when that love which is all-suffering, all-abstaining, all-aspiring, which has vowed to itself, that it will be a wretch and also a fool in this world, sooner than soil its white hands by any compliances, comes into our streets and houses, — only the pure and aspiring can know its face, and the only compliment they can pay it, is to own it.

MANNERS.

———

" How near to good is what is fair!
  Which we no sooner see,
But with the lines and outward air
  Our senses taken be.

  Again yourselves compose,
And now put all the aptness on
Of Figure, that Proportion
  Or Color can disclose;
That if those silent arts were lost,
Design and Picture, they might boast
  From you a newer ground,
Instructed by the heightening sense
Of dignity and reverence
  In their true motions found."

BEN JONSON.

ESSAY IV.

MANNERS.

———

HALF the world, it is said, knows not how the other half live. Our Exploring Expedition saw the Feejee islanders getting their dinner off human bones; and they are said to eat their own wives and children. The husbandry of the modern inhabitants of Gournou (west of old Thebes) is philosophical to a fault. To set up their housekeeping, nothing is requisite but two or three earthern pots, a stone to grind meal, and a mat which is the bed. The house, namely, a tomb, is ready without rent or taxes. No rain can pass through the roof, and there is no door, for there is no want of one, as there is nothing to lose. If the house do not please them, they walk out and enter another, as there are several hundreds at their command. "It is somewhat singular," adds Belzoni, to whom we owe this ac-

9

count, "to talk of happiness among people
who live in sepulchres, among the corpses and
rags of an ancient nation which they know
nothing of." In the deserts of Borgoo, the
rock-Tibboos still dwell in caves, like cliff-
swallows, and the language of these negroes is
compared by their neighbors to the shrieking
of bats, and to the whistling of birds. Again,
the Bornoos have no proper names ; individuals
are called after their height, thickness, or other
accidental quality, and have nicknames merely.
But the salt, the dates, the ivory, and the gold,
for which these horrible regions are visited,
find their way into countries, where the pur-
chaser and consumer can hardly be ranked
in one race with these cannibals and man-
stealers; countries where man serves himself
with metals, wood, stone, glass, gum, cotton,
silk, and wool ; honors himself with architecture ; writes laws, and contrives to execute
his will through the hands of many nations ;
and, especially, establishes a select society,
running through all the countries of intelligent
men, a self-constituted aristocracy, or fraternity
of the best, which, without written law or
exact usage of any kind, perpetuates itself,

colonizes every new-planted island, and adopts and makes its own whatever personal beauty or extraordinary native endowment anywhere appears.

What fact more conspicuous in modern history, than the creation of the gentleman? Chivalry is that, and loyalty is that, and, in English literature, half the drama, and all the novels, from Sir Philip Sidney to Sir Walter Scott, paint this figure. The word *gentleman*, which, like the word Christian, must hereafter characterize the present and the few preceding centuries, by the importance attached to it, is a homage to personal and incommunicable properties. Frivolous and fantastic additions have got associated with the name, but the steady interest of mankind in it must be attributed to the valuable properties which it designates. An element which unites all the most forcible persons of every country; makes them intelligible and agreeable to each other, and is somewhat so precise, that it is at once felt if an individual lack the masonic sign, cannot be any casual product, but must be an average result of the character and faculties universally found in men. It seems a certain permanent average ; as the atmosphere is a permanent composition, whilst so many gases are combined only to be decompounded. *Comme il faut*, is the Frenchman's description of good society, *as we must be*. It is a spontaneous fruit of talents and feelings of precisely that class who have most vigor, who take the lead in the world of this hour, and, though far from pure, far from constituting the gladdest and highest tone of human feeling, is as good as the whole society permits it to be. It is made of the spirit, more than of the talent of men, and is a compound result, into which every great force enters as an ingredient, namely, virtue, wit, beauty, wealth, and power.

There is something equivocal in all the words in use to express the excellence of manners and social cultivation, because the quantities are fluxional, and the last effect is assumed by the senses as the cause. The word *gentleman* has not any correlative abstract to express the quality. *Gentility* is mean, and *gentilesse* is obsolete. But we must keep alive in the vernacular, the distinction between *fashion*, a word of narrow and often sinister meaning, and the heroic character which the gentleman imports. The usual words, however, must be respected : they will be found to contain the root of the matter. The point of distinction in all this class of names, as courtesy, chivalry, fashion, and the like, is, that the flower and fruit, not the grain of the tree, are contemplated. It is beauty which is the aim this time, and not worth. The result is now in question, although our words intimate well enough the popular feeling, that the appearance supposes a substance. The gentleman is a man of truth, lord of his own actions, and expressing that lordship in his behavior, not in any manner dependent and servile either on persons, or opinions, or possessions. Beyond this fact of truth and real force, the word denotes good-nature or benevolence : manhood first, and then gentleness. The popular notion certainly adds a condition of ease and fortune ; but that is a natural result of personal force and love, that they should possess and dispense the goods of the world. In times of violence, every eminent person must fall in with many opportunities to approve his stoutness and worth ; therefore every man's name that emerged at all from the mass in the feudal ages, rattles in our ear like a flourish of trumpets. But personal force never goes out of fashion. That is still paramount today, and, in the moving crowd of good society, the men of valor and reality are known, and rise to their natural place. The competition is transferred from war to politics and trade, but the personal force appears readily enough in these new arenas.

Power first, or no leading class. In politics and in trade, bruisers and pirates are of better promise than talkers and clerks. God knows that all sorts of gentlemen knock at the door; but whenever used in strictness, and with any emphasis, the name will be found to point at original energy. It describes a man standing in his own right, and working after untaught methods. In a good lord, there must first be a good animal, at least to the extent of yielding the incomparable advantage of animal spirits. The ruling class must have more, but they must have these, giving in every company the sense of power, which makes things easy to be done which daunt the wise. The society of the energetic class, in their friendly and festive meetings, is full of courage, and of attempts, which intimidate the pale scholar. The courage which girls exhibit is like a battle of Lundy's Lane, or a sea-fight. The intellect relies on memory to make some supplies to face these extemporaneous squadrons. But memory is a base mendicant with basket and badge, in the presence of these sudden masters. The rulers of society must be up to the work of the world, and equal to their versatile office: men of the right Cæsarian pattern, who have great range of affinity. I am far from believing the timid maxim of Lord Falkland, ("that for ceremony there must go two to it; since a bold fellow will go through the cunningest forms,") and am of opinion that the gentleman is the bold fellow whose forms are not to be broken through; and only that plenteous nature is rightful master, which is the complement of whatever person it converses with. My gentleman gives the law where he is; he will outpray saints in chapel, outgeneral veterans in the field, and outshine all courtesy in the hall. He is good company for pirates, and good with academicians; so that it is useless to fortify yourself against him ; he has the private entrance to all minds, and I could as easily exclude myself, as him. The famous gentlemen of Asia and Europe have been of this strong type : Saladin, Sapor, the Cid, Julius Cæsar, Scipio, Alexander, Pericles, and the lordliest personages. They sat very carelessly in their chairs, and were too excellent themselves, to value any condition at a high rate.

A plentiful fortune is reckoned necessary, in the popular judgment, to the completion of this man of the world : and it is a material deputy which walks through the dance which the first has led. Money is not essential, but this wide affinity is, which transcends the habits of clique and caste, and makes itself felt by men of all classes. If the aristocrat is only valid in fashionable circles, and not with truckmen, he will never be a leader in fashion ; and if the man of the people cannot speak on equal terms with the gentleman, so that the gentleman shall perceive that he is already really of his own order, he is not to be feared. Diogenes, Socrates, and Epaminondas, are gentlemen of the best blood, who have chosen the condition of poverty, when that of wealth was equally open to them. I use these old names, but the men I speak of are my contemporaries. Fortune will not supply to every generation one of these well-appointed knights, but every collection of men furnishes some example of the class : and the politics of this country, and the trade of every town, are controlled by these hardy and irresponsible doers, who have invention to take the lead, and a broad sympathy which puts them in fellowship with crowds, and makes their action popular.

The manners of this class are observed and caught with devotion by men of taste. The association of these masters with each other, and with men intelligent of their merits, is mutually agreeable and stimulating. The good forms, the happiest expressions of each, are repeated and adopted. By swift consent, everything superfluous is dropped, everything graceful is renewed. Fine manners show themselves formidable to the uncultivated man. They are a subtler science of defence to parry and intimidate ; but once matched by the skill of the other party, they drop the point of the sword, — points and fences disappear, and the youth finds himself in a more transparent atmosphere, wherein life is a less troublesome game, and not a misunderstanding rises between the players. Manners aim to facilitate life, to get rid of impediments, and bring the man pure to energize. They aid our dealing and conversation, as a railway aids travelling, by getting rid of all avoidable obstructions of the road, and leaving nothing to be conquered but pure space. These forms very soon become fixed, and a fine sense of propriety is cultivated with the more heed, that it becomes a badge of social and civil distinctions. Thus grows up Fashion, an equivocal semblance, the most puissant, the most fantastic and frivolous, the most feared and followed, and which morals and violence assault in vain.

There exists a strict relation between the class of power, and the exclusive and polished circles. The last are always filled or filling from the first. The strong men usually give some allowance even to the petulances of fashion, for that affinity they find in it. Napoleon, child of the revolution, destroyer of the old noblesse, never ceased to court the

Faubourg St. Germain: doubtless with the feeling, that fashion is a homage to men of his stamp. Fashion, though in a strange way, represents all manly virtue. It is virtue gone to seed : it is a kind of posthumous honor. It does not often caress the great, but the children of the great : it is a hall of the Past. It usually sets its face against the great of this hour. Great men are not commonly in its halls : they are absent in the field : they are working, not triumphing. Fashion is made up of their children; of those, who, through the value and virtue of somebody, have acquired lustre to their name, marks of distinction, means of cultivation and generosity, and, in their physical organization, a certain health and excellence, which secures to them, if not the highest power to work, yet high power to enjoy. The class of power, the working heroes, the Cortez, the Nelson, the Napoleon, see that this is the festivity and permanent celebration of such as they; that fashion is funded talent; is Mexico, Marengo, and Trafalgar beaten out thin; that the brilliant names of fashion run back to just such busy names as their own, fifty or sixty years ago. They are the sowers, their sons shall be the reapers, and *their* sons, in the ordinary course of things, must yield the possession of the harvest to new competitors with keener eyes and stronger frames. The city is recruited from the country. In the year 1805, it is said, every legitimate monarch in Europe was imbecile. The city would have died out, rotted, and exploded, long ago, but that it was reinforced from the fields. It is only country which came to town day before yesterday, that is city and court today.

Aristocracy and fashion are certain inevitable results. These mutual selections are indestructible. If they provoke anger in the least favored class, and the excluded majority revenge themselves on the excluding minority, by the strong hand, and kill them, at once a new class finds itself at the top, as certainly as cream rises in a bowl of milk : and if the people should destroy class after class, until two men only were left, one of these would be the leader, and would be involuntarily served and copied by the other. You may keep this minority out of sight and out of mind, but it is tenacious of life, and is one of the estates of the realm. I am the more struck with this tenacity, when I see its work. It respects the administration of such unimportant matters, that we should not look for any durability in its rule. We sometimes meet men under some strong moral influence, as, a patriotic, a litera-ry, a religious movement, and feel that the moral sentiment rules man and nature. We think all other distinctions and ties will be slight and fugitive, this of caste or fashion, for example ; yet come from year to year, and see how permanent that is, in this Boston or New York life of man, where, too, it has not the least countenance from the law of the land. Not in Egypt or in India a firmer or more im-passable line. Here are associations whose ties go over, and under, and through it, a meet-ing of merchants, a military corps, a college-class, a fire-club, a professional association, a political, a religious convention ; — the persons seem to draw inseparably near ; yet, that assembly once dispersed, its members will not in the year meet again. Each returns to his degree in the scale of good society, porcelain remains porcelain, and earthen earthen. The objects of fashion may be frivolous, or fashion may be objectless, but the nature of this union and selection can be neither frivolous nor accidental. Each man's rank in that perfect graduation depends on some symmetry in his structure, or some agreement in his structure to the symmetry of society. Its doors unbar instantaneously to a natural claim of their own kind. A natural gentleman finds his way in, and will keep the oldest patrician out, who has lost his intrinsic rank. Fashion understands itself; good-breeding and personal superiority of whatever country readily fraternize with those of every other. The chiefs of savage tribes have distinguished themselves in London and Paris, by the purity of their tournure.

To say what good of fashion we can, — it rests on reality, and hates nothing so much as pretenders ; — to exclude and mystify pretenders, and send them into everlasting 'Coventry,' is its delight. We contemn, in turn, every other gift of men of the world ; but the habit even in little and the least matters, of not appealing to any but our own sense of propriety, constitutes the foundation of all chivalry. There is almost no kind of self-reliance, so it be sane and proportioned, which fashion does not occasionally adopt, and give it the freedom of its saloons. A sainted soul is always elegant, and, if it will, passes unchallenged into the most guarded ring. But so will Jock the teamster pass, in some crisis that brings him thither, and find favor, as long as his head is not giddy with the new circumstance, and the iron shoes do not wish to dance in waltzes and cotillons. For there is nothing settled in manners, but the laws of behavior yield to the energy of the individual. The maiden at her first ball, the countryman at a city dinner, believes that there is a ritual according to which every act and compliment must be performed, or the failing party must be cast out of this presence. Later, they learn that good sense and character make their own forms every moment, and speak or abstain, take wine or refuse it, stay or go, sit in a chair or sprawl with children on the floor, or stand on their head, or what else soever, in a new and aboriginal way : and that strong will is always in fashion, let who will be unfashionable. All that fashion demands is composure, and self-content. A

circle of men perfectly well-bred would be a
company of sensible persons, in which every
man's native manners and character appeared.
If the fashionist have not this quality, he is
nothing. We are such lovers of self-reliance,
that we excuse in a man many sins, if he will
show us a complete satisfaction in his position,
which asks no leave to be, of mine, or any
man's good opinion. But any deference to
some eminent man or woman of the world,
forfeits all privilege of nobility. He is an
underling : I have nothing to do with him ; I
will speak with his master. A man should
not go where he cannot carry his whole sphere
or society with him, — not bodily, the whole
circle of his friends, but atmospherically. He
should preserve in a new company the same
attitude of mind and reality of relation, which
his daily associates draw him to, else he is
shorn of his best beams, and will be an orphan
in the merriest club. " If you could see Vich
Ian Vohr with his tail on ! —— " But Vich
Ian Vohr must always carry his belongings in
some fashion, if not added as honor, then
severed as disgrace.

There will always be in society certain per-

sons who are mercuries of its approbation, and
whose glance will at any time determine for
the curious their standing in the world.
These are the chamberlains of the lesser gods.
Accept their coldness as an omen of grace
with the loftier deities, and allow them all
their privilege. They are clear in their office,
nor could they be thus formidable, without
their own merits. But do not measure the
importance of this class by their pretension,
or imagine that a fop can be the dispenser of
honor and shame. They pass also at their
just rate; for how can they otherwise, in circles which exist as a sort of herald's office for
the sifting of character?

As the first thing man requires of man,
is reality, so, that appears in all the forms of
society. We pointedly, and by name, introduce the parties to each other. Know you
before all heaven and earth, that this is An-
drew, and this is Gregory; — they look each
other in the eye; they grasp each other's hand,
to identify and signalize each other. It is a
great satisfaction. A gentleman never dodges:
his eyes look straight forward, and he assures

10

the other party, first of all, that he has been met. For what is it that we seek, in so many visits and hospitalities? Is it your draperies, pictures, and decorations? Or, do we not insatiably ask, Was a man in the house? I may easily go into a great household where there is much substance, excellent provision for comfort, luxury, and taste, and yet not encounter there any Amphitryon, who shall subordinate these appendages. I may go into a cottage, and find a farmer who feels that he is the man I have come to see, and fronts me accordingly. It was therefore a very natural point of old feudal etiquette, that a gentleman who received a visit, though it were of his sovereign, should not leave his roof, but should wait his arrival at the door of his house. No house, though it were the Thuilleries, or the Escurial, is good for anything without a master. And yet we are not often gratified by this hospitality. Every body we know surrounds himself with a fine house, fine books, conservatory, gardens, equipage, and all manner of toys, as screens to interpose between himself and his guest. Does it not seem as if man was of a very sly, elusive nature, and dreaded nothing so much as a full rencontre front to front with his fellow ? It were unmerciful, I know, quite to abolish the use of these screens, which are of eminent convenience, whether the guest is too great, or too little. We call together many friends who keep each other in play, or, by luxuries and ornaments we amuse the young people, and guard our retirement. Or if, perchance, a searching realist comes to our gate, before whose eye we have no care to stand, then again we run to our curtain, and hide ourselves as Adam at the voice of the Lord God in the garden. Cardinal Caprara, the Pope's legate at Paris, defended himself from the glances of Napoleon, by an immense pair of green spectacles. Napoleon remarked them, and speedily managed to rally them off: and yet Napoleon, in his turn, was not great enough with eight hundred thousand troops at his back, to face a pair of freeborn eyes, but fenced himself with etiquette, and within triple barriers of reserve : and, as all the world knows from Madame de Stael, was wont, when he found himself observed, to discharge his face of all expression. But emperors and rich men are by no means the most skilful masters of good manners. No rentroll nor army-list can dignify skulking and dissimulation : and the first point of courtesy must always be truth, as really all the forms of good-breeding point that way.

I have just been reading, in Mr. Hazlitt's translation, Montaigne's account of his journey into Italy, and am struck with nothing more agreeably than the self-respecting fashions of the time. His arrival in each place, the arrival of a gentleman of France, is an event of some consequence. Wherever he goes, he pays a visit to whatever prince or gentleman of note resides upon his road, as a duty to himself and to civilization. When he leaves any house in which he has lodged for a few weeks, he causes his arms to be painted and hung up as a perpetual sign to the house, as was the custom of gentlemen.

The complement of this graceful self-respect, and that of all the points of good breeding I most require and insist upon, is deference. I like that every chair should be a throne, and hold a king. I prefer a tendency to stateliness, to an excess of fellowship. Let the incommunicable objects of nature and the metaphysical isolation of man teach us independence. Let us not be too much acquainted. I would have a man enter his house through a hall filled with heroic and sacred sculptures, that he might not want the hint of tranquillity and self-poise. We should meet each morning, as from foreign countries, and spending the day together, should depart at night, as into foreign countries. In all things I would have the island of a man inviolate. Let us sit apart as the gods, talking from peak to peak all round Olympus. No degree of affection need invade this religion. This is myrrh and rosemary to keep the other sweet. Lovers should guard their strangeness. If they forgive too much, all slides into confusion and meanness. It is easy to push this deference to a Chinese etiquette ; but coolness and absence of heat and haste indicate fine qualities. A gentleman makes no noise: a lady is serene. Proportionate is our disgust at those invaders who fill a studious house with blast and running, to secure some paltry convenience. Not less I dislike a low sympathy of each with his neighbor's needs. Must we have a good understanding with one another's palates? as foolish people who have lived long together, know when each wants salt or sugar. I pray my companion, if he wishes for bread, to ask me for bread, and if he wishes for sassafras or arsenic, to ask me for them, and not to hold out his plate, as if I knew already. Every natural function can be dignified by deliberation and privacy. Let us leave hurry to slaves. The compliments and ceremonies of our breeding should signify, however remotely, the recollection of the grandeur of our destiny.

The flower of courtesy does not very well bide handling, but if we dare to open another leaf, and explore what parts go to its conformation, we shall find also an intellectual quality. To the leaders of men, the brain as well as the flesh and the heart must furnish a proportion. Defect in manners is usually the defect of fine perceptions. Men are too coarsely made for the delicacy of beautiful carriage and customs. It is not quite sufficient to good-breeding, a union of kindness and independence. We imperatively require a perception of, and a homage to beauty in our companions. Other virtues are in request in the field and workyard, but a certain degree of taste is not to be spared in those we sit with. I could better eat with one who did not respect the truth or the laws, than with a sloven and unpresentable person. Moral qualities rule the world, but at short distances, the senses are despotic. The same discrimination of fit and fair runs out, if with less rigor, into all parts of life. The average spirit of the energetic class is good sense, acting under certain limitations and to certain ends. It entertains every natural gift. Social in its nature, it respects everything which tends to unite men. It delights in measure. The love of beauty is mainly the love of measure or proportion. The person who screams, or uses the superlative degree, or converses with heat, puts whole drawing-rooms to flight. If you wish to be loved, love measure. You must have genius, or a prodigious usefulness, if you will hide the want of measure. This perception comes in to polish and perfect the parts of the social instrument. Society will pardon much to genius and special gifts, but, being in its nature a convention, it loves what is conventional, or what belongs to coming together. That makes the good and bad of manners, namely, what helps or hinders fellowship. For, fashion is not good sense absolute, but relative ; not good sense private, but good sense entertaining company. It hates corners and sharp points of character, hates quarrelsome, egotistical, solitary, and gloomy people ; hates whatever can interfere with total blending of parties ; whilst it values all peculiarities as in the highest degree refreshing; which can consist with good fellowship. And besides the general infusion of wit to heighten civility, the direct splendor of intellectual power is ever welcome in fine society as the costliest addition to its rule and its credit.

The dry light must shine in to adorn our festival, but it must be tempered and shaded, or that will also offend. Accuracy is essential to beauty, and quick perceptions to politeness, but not too quick perceptions. One may be too punctual and too precise. He must leave the omniscience of business at the door, when he comes into the palace of beauty. Society loves creole natures, and sleepy, languishing manners, so that they cover sense, grace, and good-will; the air of drowsy strength, which disarms criticism; perhaps, because such a person seems to reserve himself for the best of the game, and not spend himself on surfaces; an ignoring eye, which does not see the annoyances, shifts, and inconveniences, that cloud the brow and smother the voice of the sensitive.

Therefore, besides personal force and so much perception as constitutes unerring taste, society demands in its patrician class, another element already intimated, which it significantly terms good-nature, expressing all degrees of generosity, from the lowest willingness and faculty to oblige, up to the heights of magnanimity and love. Insight we must have, or we shall run against one another, and miss the way to our food; but intellect is selfish and barren. The secret of success in society, is a certain heartiness and sympathy. A man who is not happy in the company, cannot find any word in his memory that will fit the occasion. All his information is a little impertinent. A man who is happy there, finds in every turn of the conversation equally lucky occasions for the introduction of that which he has to say. The favorites of society, and what it calls *whole souls*, are able men, and of more spirit than wit, who have no uncomfortable egotism, but who exactly fill the hour and the company, contented and contenting, at a marriage or a funeral, a ball or a jury, a water-party or a shooting-match. England, which is rich in gentlemen, furnished, in the beginning of the present century, a good model of that genius which the world loves, in Mr. Fox, who added to his great abilities the most social disposition, and real love of men. Parliamentary history has few better passages than the debate, in which Burke and Fox separated in the House of Commons; when Fox urged on his old friend the claims of old friendship with such tenderness, that the house was moved to tears. Another anecdote is so close to my matter, that I must hazard the story. A tradesman who had long dunned him for a note of three hundred guineas, found him one day counting gold, and demanded payment: "No," said Fox, "I owe this money to Sheridan: it is a debt of honor: if an accident should happen to me, he has nothing to show." " Then," said the creditor, " I change my debt into a debt of honor," and tore the note in pieces. Fox thanked the man for his confidence, and paid him, saying, " his debt was of older standing, and Sheridan must wait." Lover of liberty, friend of the Hindoo, friend of the African slave, he possessed a great personal popularity ; and Napoleon said of him on the occasion of his visit to Paris, in 1805, " Mr. Fox will always hold the first place in an assembly at the Thuilleries."

We may easily seem ridiculous in our eulogy of courtesy, whenever we insist on benevolence as its foundation. The painted phantasm Fashion rises to cast a species of derision on what we say. But I will neither be driven from some allowance to Fashion as a symbolic institution, nor from the belief that love is the basis of courtesy. We must obtain *that*, if we can ; but by all means we must affirm *this*. Life owes much of its spirit to these sharp contrasts. Fashion which affects to be honor, is often, in all men's experience, only a ballroom-code. Yet, so long as it is the highest circle, in the imagination of the best heads on the planet, there is something necessary and excellent in it; for it is not to be supposed that men have agreed to be the dupes of anything preposterous; and the respect which these mysteries inspire in the most rude and sylvan characters, and the curiosity with which details of high life are read, betray the universality of the love of cultivated manners. I know that a comic disparity would be felt, if we should enter the acknowledged 'first circles,' and apply these terrific standards of justice, beauty, and benefit, to the individuals actually found there. Monarchs and heroes, sages and lovers, these gallants are not. Fashion has many classes and many rules of probation and admission; and not the best alone. There is not only the right of conquest, which genius pretends,— the individual, demonstrating his natural aristocracy best of the best; — but less claims will pass for the time; for Fashion loves lions, and points, like Circe, to her horned company. This gentleman is this afternoon arrived from Denmark; and that is my Lord Ride, who came yesterday from Bagdat; here is Captain Friese, from Cape Turnagain; and Captain Symmes, from the interior of the earth; and

Monsieur Jovaire, who came down this morning in a balloon; Mr. Hobnail, the reformer;
and Reverend Jul Bat, who has converted the
whole torrid zone in his Sunday school; and
Signor Torre del Greco, who extinguished
Vesuvius by pouring into it the Bay of Naples; Spahi, the Persian ambassador; and
Tul Wil Shan, the exiled nabob of Nepaul,
whose saddle is the new moon.—But these are
monsters of one day, and tomorrow will be
dismissed to their holes and dens; for, in
these rooms, every chair is waited for. The
artist, the scholar, and, in general, the clerisy,
wins its way up into these places, and gets
represented here, somewhat on this footing of
conquest. Another mode is to pass through
all the degrees, spending a year and a day in
St. Michael's Square, being steeped in Cologne
water, and perfumed, and dined, and introduced, and properly grounded in all the biography, and politics, and anecdotes of the boudoirs.

Yet these fineries may have grace and wit.
Let there be grotesque sculpture about the
gates and offices of temples. Let the creed
and commandments even have the saucy hom-

age of parody. The forms of politeness universally express benevolence in superlative
degrees. What if they are in the mouths of
selfish men, and used as means of selfishness?
What if the false gentleman almost bows the
true out of the world? What if the false gentleman contrives so to address his companion,
as civilly to exclude all others from his discourse, and also to make them feel excluded?
Real service will not lose its nobleness. All
generosity is not merely French and sentimental; nor is it to be concealed, that living
blood and a passion of kindness does at last
distinguish God's gentleman from Fashion's.
The epitaph of Sir Jenkin Grout is not wholly
unintelligible to the present age. "Here lies
Sir Jenkin Grout, who loved his friend, and
persuaded his enemy: what his mouth ate,
his hand paid for: what his servants robbed,
he restored: if a woman gave him pleasure,
he supported her in pain: he never forgot his
children: and whoso touched his finger, drew
after it his whole body." Even the line of
heroes is not utterly extinct. There is still
ever some admirable person in plain clothes,
standing on the wharf, who jumps in to rescue

a drowning man; there is still some absurd inventor of charities; some guide and comforter
of runaway slaves; some friend of Poland;
some Philhellene; some fanatic who plants
shade-trees for the second and third generation, and orchards when he is grown
old; some well-concealed piety; some just
man happy in an ill-fame; some youth
ashamed of the favors of fortune, and impa-
tiently casting them on other shoulders. And
these are the centres of society, on which it
returns for fresh impulses. These are the
creators of Fashion, which is an attempt to
organize beauty of behavior. The beautiful
and the generous are, in the theory, the doctors
and apostles of this church : Scipio, and the
Cid, and Sir Philip Sidney, and Washington, and every pure and valiant heart, who
worshipped Beauty by word and by deed.
The persons who constitute the natural aristocracy, are not found in the actual aristocracy,
or, only on its edge; as the chemical energy of
the spectrum is found to be greatest just outside of the spectrum. Yet that is the infirmity
of the seneschals, who do not know their
sovereign, when he appears. The theory of

society supposes the existence and sovereignty of these. It divines afar off their coming. It says with the elder gods, —

> " As Heaven and Earth are fairer far
> Than Chaos and blank Darkness, though once chiefs ;
> And as we show beyond that Heaven and Earth,
> In form and shape compact and beautiful ;
> So, on our heels a fresh perfection treads ;
> A power, more strong in beauty, born of us,
> And fated to excel us, as we pass
> In glory that old Darkness :
> ———————   for, 't is the eternal law,
> That first in beauty shall be first in might."

Therefore, within the ethnical circle of good society, there is a narrower and higher circle, concentration of its light, and flower of courtesy, to which there is always a tacit appeal of pride and reference, as to its inner and imperial court, the parliament of love and chivalry. And this is constituted of those persons in whom heroic dispositions are native, with the love of beauty, the delight in society, and the power to embellish the passing day. If the individuals who compose the purest circles of aristocracy in Europe, the guarded blood of centuries, should pass in review, in such manner as that we could, at leisure, and critically inspect their behavior, we might find no gentleman, and no lady ; for, although excellent specimens of courtesy and high-breeding would gratify us in the assemblage, in the particulars, we should detect offence. Because, elegance comes of no breeding, but of birth. There must be romance of character, or the most fastidious exclusion of impertinencies will not avail. It must be genius which takes that direction : it must be not courteous, but courtesy. High behavior is as rare in fiction, as it is in fact. Scott is praised for the fidelity with which he painted the demeanor and conversation of the superior classes. Certainly, kings and queens, nobles and great ladies, had some right to complain of the absurdity that had been put in their mouths, before the days of Waverley ; but neither does Scott's dialogue bear criticism. His lords brave each other in smart epigramatic speeches, but the dialogue is in costume, and does not please on the second reading : it is not warm with life. In Shakspeare alone, the speakers do not strut and bridle, the dialogue is easily great, and he adds to so many titles that of being the best-bred man in Eng-

11

land, and in Christendom. Once or twice in a lifetime we are permitted to enjoy the charm of noble manners, in the presence of a man or woman who have no bar in their nature, but whose character emanates freely in their word and gesture. A beautiful form is better than a beautiful face ; a beautiful behavior is better than a beautiful form : it gives a higher pleasure than statues or pictures ; it is the finest of the fine arts. A man is but a little thing in the midst of the objects of nature, yet, by the moral quality radiating from his countenance, he may abolish all considerations of magnitude, and in his manners equal the majesty of the world. I have seen an individual, whose manners, though wholly within the conventions of elegant society, were never learned there, but were original and commanding, and held out protection and prosperity ; one who did not need the aid of a court-suit, but carried the holiday in his eye ; who exhilarated the fancy by flinging wide the doors of new modes of existence ; who shook off the captivity of etiquette, with happy, spirited bearing, good-natured and free as Robin Hood ; yet with the port of an emperor, — if need be, calm, serious, and fit to stand the gaze of millions.

The open air and the fields, the street and public chambers, are the places where Man executes his will ; let him yield or divide the sceptre at the door of the house. Woman, with her instinct of behavior, instantly detects in man a love of trifles, any coldness or imbecility, or, in short, any want of that large, flowing, and magnanimous deportment, which is indispensable as an exterior in the hall. Our American institutions have been friendly to her, and at this moment, I esteem it a chief felicity of this country, that it excels in women. A certain awkward consciousness of inferiority in the men, may give rise to the new chivalry in behalf of Woman's Rights. Certainly, let her be as much better placed in the laws and in social forms, as the most zealous reformer can ask, but I confide so entirely in her inspiring and musical nature, that I believe only herself can show us how she shall be served. The wonderful generosity of her sentiments raises her at times into heroical and godlike regions, and verifies the pictures of Minerva, Juno, or Polymnia; and, by the firmness with which she treads her up-

ward path, she convinces the coarsest calculators
that another road exists, than that which their
feet know. But besides those who make good
in our imagination the place of muses and of
Delphic Sibyls, are there not women who fill our
vase with wine and roses to the brim, so that
the wine runs over and fills the house with
perfume ; who inspire us with courtesy ; who
unloose our tongues, and we speak ; who
anoint our eyes, and we see ? We say things
we never thought to have said ; for once,
our walls of habitual reserve vanished, and
left us at large ; we were children playing
with children in a wide field of flowers.
Steep us, we cried, in these influences,
for days, for weeks, and we shall be sunny
poets, and will write out in many-colored
words the romance that you are. Was it
Hafiz or Firdousi that said of his Persian
Lilla, She was an elemental force, and astonished me by her amount of life, when I saw
her day after day radiating, every instant,
redundant joy and grace on all around her.
She was a solvent powerful to reconcile all
heterogeneous persons into one society : like
air or water, an element of such a great range

of affinities, that it combines readily with a thousand substances. Where she is present, all others will be more than they are wont. She was a unit and whole, so that whatsoever she did, became her. She had too much sympathy and desire to please, than that you could say, her manners were marked with dignity, yet no princess could surpass her clear and erect demeanor on each occasion. She did not study the Persian grammar, nor the books of the seven poets, but all the poems of the seven seemed to be written upon her. For, though the bias of her nature was not to thought, but to sympathy, yet was she so perfect in her own nature, as to meet intellectual persons by the fulness of her heart, warming them by her sentiments ; believing, as she did, that by dealing nobly with all, all would show themselves noble.

I know that this Byzantine pile of chivalry or Fashion, which seems so fair and picturesque to those who look at the contemporary facts for science or for entertainment, is not equally pleasant to all spectators. The constitution of our society makes it a giant's castle to the ambitious youth who have not found their names enrolled in its Golden Book, and whom it has excluded from its coveted honors and privileges. They have yet to learn that its seeming grandeur is shadowy and relative : it is great by their allowance : its proudest gates will fly open at the approach of their courage and virtue. For the present distress, however, of those who are predisposed to suffer from the tyrannies of this caprice, there are easy remedies. To remove your residence a couple of miles, or at most four, will commonly relieve the most extreme susceptibility. For, the advantages which fashion values, are plants which thrive in very confined localities, in a few streets, namely. Out of this precinct, they go for nothing; are of no use in the farm, in the forest, in the market, in war, in the nuptial society, in the literary or scientific circle, at sea, in friendship, in the heaven of thought or virtue.

But we have lingered long enough in these painted courts. The worth of the thing signified must vindicate our taste for the emblem. Everything that is called fashion and courtesy humbles itself before the cause and fountain of honor, creator of titles and dignities, namely, the heart of love. This is the royal blood, this the fire, which, in all countries and contingencies, will work after its kind, and conquer and expand all that approaches it. This gives new meanings to every fact. This impoverishes the rich, suffering no grandeur but its own. What *is* rich? Are you rich enough to help anybody? to succor the unfashionable and the eccentric? rich enough to make the Canadian in his wagon, the itinerant with his consul's paper which commends him "To the charitable," the swarthy Italian with his few broken words of English, the lame pauper hunted by overseers from town to town, even the poor insane or besotted wreck of man or woman, feel the noble exception of your presence and your house, from the general bleakness and stoniness; to make such feel that they were greeted with a voice which made them both remember and hope? What is vulgar, but to refuse the claim on acute and conclusive reasons? What is gentle, but to allow it, and give their heart and yours one holiday from the national caution? Without the rich heart, wealth is an ugly beggar. The

king of Schiraz could not afford to be so bountiful as the poor Osman who dwelt at his gate.
Osman had a humanity so broad and deep, that
although his speech was so bold and free with
the Koran, as to disgust all the dervishes, yet
was there never a poor outcast, eccentric, or
insane man, some fool who had cut off his beard.
or who had been mutilated under a vow, or
had a pet madness in his brain, but fled at
once to him, — that great heart lay there so
sunny and hospitable in the centre of the
country, — that it seemed as if the instinct of
all sufferers drew them to his side.   And the
madness which he harbored, he did not share.
Is not this to be rich? this only to be rightly
rich?

But I shall hear without pain, that I play
the courtier very ill, and talk of that which I
do not well understand.   It is easy to see, that
what is called by distinction society and fashion, has good laws as well as bad, has much
that is necessary, and much that is absurd.
Too good for banning, and too bad for blessing, it reminds us of a tradition of the pagan
mythology, in any attempt to settle its character.   'I overheard Jove, one day,' said

Silenus, 'talking of destroying the earth ; he said, it had failed; they were all rogues and vixens, who went from bad to worse, as fast as the days succeeded each other. Minerva said, she hoped not; they were only ridiculous little creatures, with this odd circumstance, that they had a blur, or indeterminate aspect, seen far or seen near; if you called them bad, they would appear so ; if you called them good, they would appear so ; and there was no one person or action among them, which would not puzzle her owl, much more all Olympus, to know whether it was fundamentally bad or good.'

GIFTS

Gifts of one who loved me, —
'T was high time they came ;
When he ceased to love me,
Time they stopped for shame.

ESSAY V.

GIFTS.

Iт is said that the world is in a state of bankruptcy, that the world owes the world more than the world can pay, and ought to go into chancery, and be sold. I do not think this general insolvency, which involves in some sort all the population, to be the reason of the difficulty experienced at Christmas and New Year, and other times, in bestowing gifts; since it is always so pleasant to be generous, though very vexatious to pay debts. But the impediment lies in the choosing. If, at any time, it comes into my head, that a present is due from me to somebody, I am puzzled what to give, until the opportunity is gone. Flowers and fruits are always fit presents; flowers, because they are a proud assertion that a ray of beauty outvalues all the utilities of the world. These gay natures contrast with the somewhat stern countenance of ordinary nature : they are like music heard out of a work-house. Nature does not cocker us : we are children, not pets : she is not fond : everything is dealt to us without fear or favor, after severe universal laws. Yet these delicate flowers look like the frolic and interference of love and beauty. Men use to tell us that we love flattery, even though we are not deceived by it, because it shows that we are of importance enough to be courted. Something like that pleasure, the flowers give us : what am I to whom these sweet hints are addressed ? Fruits are acceptable gifts, because they are the flower of commodities, and admit of fantastic values being attached to them. If a man should send to me to come a hundred miles to visit him, and should set before me a basket of fine summer-fruit, I should think there was some proportion between the labor and the reward.

For common gifts, necessity makes pertinences and beauty every day, and one is glad when an imperative leaves him no option, since if the man at the door have no shoes, you have not to consider whether you could procure him a paint-

box. And as it is always pleasing to see a man
eat bread, or drink water, in the house or out
of doors, so it is always a great satisfaction to
supply these first wants. Necessity does
everything well. In our condition of universal dependence, it seems heroic to let the
petitioner be the judge of his necessity, and to
give all that is asked, though at great inconvenience. If it be a fantastic desire, it is better
to leave to others the office of punishing him.
I can think of many parts I should prefer
playing to that of the Furies. Next to things
of necessity, the rule for a gift, which one of
my friends prescribed, is, that we might convey to some person that which properly belonged to his character, and was easily associated with him in thought. But our tokens
of compliment and love are for the most part
barbarous. Rings and other jewels are not
gifts, but apologies for gifts. The only gift is
a portion of thyself. Thou must bleed for me.
Therefore the poet brings his poem; the shep-
herd, his lamb; the farmer, corn; the miner, a
gem; the sailor, coral and shells; the painter,
his picture; the girl, a handkerchief of her
own sewing. This is right and pleasing, for

it restores society in so far to its primary basis, when a man's biography is conveyed in his gift, and every man's wealth is an index of his merit. But it is a cold, lifeless business when you go to the shops to buy me something, which does not represent your life and talent, but a goldsmith's. This is fit for kings, and rich men who represent kings, and a false state of property, to make presents of gold and silver stuffs, as a kind of symbolical sin-offering, or payment of black-mail.

The law of benefits is a difficult channel, which requires careful sailing, or rude boats. It is not the office of a man to receive gifts. How dare you give them? We wish to be self-sustained. We do not quite forgive a giver. The hand that feeds us is in some danger of being bitten. We can receive anything from love, for that is a way of receiving it from ourselves; but not from any one who assumes to bestow. We sometimes hate the meat which we eat, because there seems something of degrading dependence in living by it.

" Brother, if Jove to thee a present make,
　Take heed that from his hands thou nothing take."

We ask the whole. Nothing less will content us. We arraign society, if it do not give us besides earth, and fire, and water, opportunity, love, reverence, and objects of veneration.

He is a good man, who can receive a gift well. We are either glad or sorry at a gift, and both emotions are unbecoming. Some violence, I think, is done, some degradation borne, when I rejoice or grieve at a gift. I am sorry when my independence is invaded, or when a gift comes from such as do not know my spirit, and so the act is not supported; and if the gift pleases me overmuch, then I should be ashamed that the donor should read my heart, and see that I love his commodity, and not him. The gift, to be true, must be the flowing of the giver unto me, correspondent to my flowing unto him. When the waters are at level, then my goods pass to him, and his to me. All his are mine, all mine his. I say to him, How can you give me this pot of oil, or this flagon of wine, when all your oil and wine is mine, which belief of mine this gift seems to deny? Hence the fitness of beautiful, not useful things for gifts. This giving is flat usurpation, and therefore

12

when the beneficiary is ungrateful, as all bene-
ficiaries hate all Timons, not at all considering
the value of the gift, but looking back to the
greater store it was taken from, I rather sympathize with the beneficiary, than with the
anger of my lord Timon. For, the expectation of gratitude is mean, and is continually
punished by the total insensibility of the
obliged person. It is a great happiness to get
off without injury and heart-burning, from one
who has had the ill luck to be served by you.
It is a very onerous business, this of being
served, and the debtor naturally wishes to give
you a slap. A golden text for these gentlemen
is that which I so admire in the Buddhist,
who never thanks, and who says, "Do not
flatter your benefactors."

The reason of these discords I conceive to
be, that there is no commensurability between a
man and any gift. You cannot give anything
to a magnanimous person. After you have
served him, he at once puts you in debt by his
magnanimity. The service a man renders his
friend is trivial and selfish, compared with the
service he knows his friend stood in readiness
to yield him, alike before he had begun to

serve his friend, and now also. Compared with that good-will I bear my friend, the benefit it is in my power to render him seems small. Besides, our action on each other, good as well as evil, is so incidental and at random, that we can seldom hear the acknowledgments of any person who would thank us for a benefit, without some shame and humiliation. We can rarely strike a direct stroke, but must be content with an oblique one; we seldom have the satisfaction of yielding a direct benefit, which is directly received. But rectitude scatters favors on every side without knowing it, and receives with wonder the thanks of all people.

I fear to breathe any treason against the majesty of love, which is the genius and god of gifts, and to whom we must not affect to prescribe. Let him give kingdoms or flower-leaves indifferently. There are persons, from whom we always expect fairy tokens; let us not cease to expect them. This is prerogative, and not to be limited by our municipal rules. For the rest, I like to see that we cannot be bought and sold. The best of hospitality and of generosity is also not in the will, but in fate. I find that I am not much to you ; you do not need me ; you do not feel me ; then am I thrust out of doors, though you proffer me house and lands. No services are of any value, but only likeness. When I have attempted to join myself to others by services, it proved an intellectual trick, — no more. They eat your service like apples, and leave you out. But love them, and they feel you, and delight in you all the time.

NATURE.

The rounded world is fair to see,
Nine times folded in mystery :
Though baffled seers cannot impart
The secret of its laboring heart,
Throb thine with Nature's throbbing breast,
And all is clear from east to west.
Spirit that lurks each form within
Beckons to spirit of its kin ;
Self-kindled every atom glows,
And hints the future which it owes.

ESSAY VI.

NATURE.

———

THERE are days which occur in this climate, at almost any season of the year, wherein the world reaches its perfection, when the air, the heavenly bodies, and the earth, make a harmony, as if nature would indulge her offspring; when, in these bleak upper sides of the planet, nothing is to desire that we have heard of the happiest latitudes, and we bask in the shining hours of Florida and Cuba; when everything that has life gives sign of satisfaction, and the cattle that lie on the ground seem to have great and tranquil thoughts. These halcyons may be looked for with a little more assurance in that pure October weather, which we distinguish by the name of the Indian Summer. The day, immeasurably long, sleeps over the broad hills and warm wide fields. To have lived through

all its sunny hours, seems longevity enough.
The solitary places do not seem quite lonely.
At the gates of the forest, the surprised man of
the world is forced to leave his city estimates
of great and small, wise and foolish. The
knapsack of custom falls off his back with the
first step he makes into these precincts. Here
is sanctity which shames our religions, and
reality which discredits our heroes. Here
we find nature to be the circumstance
which dwarfs every other circumstance,
and judges like a god all men that come
to her. We have crept out of our close
and crowded houses into the night and morning, and we see what majestic beauties daily
wrap us in their bosom. How willingly we
would escape the barriers which render them
comparatively impotent, escape the sophistica-
tion and second thought, and suffer nature to
intrance us. The tempered light of the
woods is like a perpetual morning, and is stimulating and heroic. The anciently reported
spells of these places creep on us. The stems
of pines, hemlocks, and oaks, almost gleam
like iron on the excited eye. The incommunicable trees begin to persuade us to live with

them, and quit our life of solemn trifles. Here no history, or church, or state, is interpolated on the divine sky and the immortal year. How easily we might walk onward into the opening landscape, absorbed by new pictures, and by thoughts fast succeeding each other, until by degrees the recollection of home was crowded out of the mind, all memory obliterated by the tyranny of the present, and we were led in triumph by nature.

These enchantments are medicinal, they sober and heal us. These are plain pleasures, kindly and native to us. We come to our own, and make friends with matter, which the ambitious chatter of the schools would persuade us to despise. We never can part with it; the mind loves its old home: as water to our thirst, so is the rock, the ground, to our eyes, and hands, and feet. It is firm water: it is cold flame: what health, what affinity! Ever an old friend, ever like a dear friend and brother, when we chat affectedly with strangers, comes in this honest face, and takes a grave liberty with us, and shames us out of our nonsense. Cities give not the human senses room enough. We go out daily and nightly to feed the eyes on the horizon, and require so much scope, just as we need water for our bath. There are all degrees of natural influence, from these quarantine powers of nature, up to her dearest and gravest ministrations to the imagination and the soul. There is the bucket of cold water from the spring, the wood-fire to which the chilled traveller rushes for safety, — and there is the sublime moral of autumn and of noon. We nestle in nature, and draw our living as parasites from her roots and grains, and we receive glances from the heavenly bodies, which call us to solitude, and foretell the remotest future. The blue zenith is the point in which romance and reality meet. I think, if we should be rapt away into all that we dream of heaven, and should converse with Gabriel and Uriel, the upper sky would be all that would remain of our furniture.

It seems as if the day was not wholly profane, in which we have given heed to some natural object. The fall of snowflakes in a still air, preserving to each crystal its perfect form ; the blowing of sleet over a wide sheet of water, and over plains, the waving ryefield, the mimic waving of acres of houstonia, whose innumerable florets whiten and ripple before the eye; the reflections of trees and and flowers in glassy lakes; the musical steaming odorous south wind, which converts all trees to windharps; the crackling and spurting of hemlock in the flames; or of pine logs, which yield glory to the walls and faces in the sittingroom, — these are the music and pictures of the most ancient religion. My house stands in low land, with limited outlook, and on the skirt of the village. But I go with my friend to the shore of our little river, and with one stroke of the paddle, I leave the village politics and personalities, yes, and the world of villages and personalities behind, and pass into a delicate realm of sunset and moonlight, too bright almost for spotted man to enter without noviciate and probation. We penetrate bodily this incredible beauty : we dip our hands in this painted element : our eyes are bathed in these lights and forms. A holiday, a villeggiatura, a royal revel, the proudest, most heart-rejoicing festival that valor and beauty, power and taste, ever decked and enjoyed, establishes itself on the instant.

These sunset clouds, these delicately emerging stars, with their private and ineffable glances, signify it and proffer it. I am taught the poorness of our invention, the ugliness of towns and palaces. Art and luxury have early learned that they must work as enhancement and sequel to this original beauty. I am over-instructed for my return. Henceforth I shall be hard to please. I cannot go back to toys. I am grown expensive and sophisticated. I can no longer live without elegance: but a countryman shall be my master of revels. He who knows the most, he who knows what sweets and virtues are in the ground, the waters, the plants, the heavens, and how to come at these enchantments, is the rich and royal man. Only as far as the masters of the world have called in nature to their aid, can they reach the height of magnificence. This is the meaning of their hanging-gardens, villas, garden-houses, islands, parks, and preserves, to back their faulty personality with these strong accessories. I do not wonder that the landed interest should be invincible in the state with these dangerous auxiliaries. These bribe and invite; not kings, not palaces, not

men, not women, but these tender and poetic
stars, eloquent of secret promises. We heard
what the rich man said, we knew of his villa,
his grove, his wine, and his company, but the
provocation and point of the invitation came
out of these beguiling stars. In their soft
glances, I see what men strove to realize in
some Versailles, or Paphos, or Ctesiphon. Indeed, it is the magical lights of the horizon,
and the blue sky for the background, which
save all our works of art, which were otherwise bawbles. When the rich tax the poor
with servility and obsequiousness, they should
consider the effect of men reputed to be the possessors of nature, on imaginative minds. Ah!
if the rich were rich as the poor fancy riches!
A boy hears a military band play on the field
at night, and he has kings and queens, and
famous chivalry palpably before him. He
hears the echoes of a horn in a hill country,
in the Notch Mountains, for example, which
converts the mountains into an Æolian harp,
and this supernatural *tiralira* restores to him
the Dorian mythology, Apollo, Diana, and all
divine hunters and huntresses. Can a musical
note be so lofty, so haughtily beautiful! To

the poor young poet, thus fabulous is his picture of society; he is loyal; he respects the rich; they are rich for the sake of his imagination; how poor his fancy would be, if they were not rich! That they have some high-fenced grove, which they call a park; that they live in larger and better-garnished saloons than he has visited, and go in coaches, keeping only the society of the elegant, to watering-places, and to distant cities, are the groundwork from which he has delineated estates of romance, compared with which their actual possessions are shanties and paddocks. The muse herself betrays her son, and enhances the gifts of wealth and well-born beauty, by a radiation out of the air, and clouds, and forests that skirt the road, — a certain haughty favor, as if from patrician genii to patricians, a kind of aristocracy in nature, a prince of the power of the air.

The moral sensibility which makes Edens and Tempes so easily, may not be always found, but the material landscape is never far off. We can find these enchantments without visiting the Como Lake, or the Madeira Islands. We exaggerate the praises of local scenery. In every landscape, the point of astonishment is the meeting of the sky and the earth, and that is seen from the first hillock as well as from the top of the Alleghanies. The stars at night stoop down over the brownest, homeliest common, with all the spiritual magnificence which they shed on the Campagna, or on the marble deserts of Egypt. The uprolled clouds and the colors of morning and evening, will transfigure maples and alders. The difference between landscape and landscape is small, but there is great difference in the beholders. There is nothing so wonderful in any particular landscape, as the necessity of being beautiful under which every landscape lies. Nature cannot be surprised in undress. Beauty breaks in everywhere.

But it is very easy to outrun the sympathy of readers on this topic, which schoolmen called *natura naturata*, or nature passive. One can hardly speak directly of it without excess. It is as easy to broach in mixed companies what is called " the subject of religion." A susceptible person does not like to indulge his tastes in this kind, without the apology of some trivial necessity : he goes to see a wood-

lot, or to look at the crops, or to fetch a plant
or a mineral from a remote locality, or he carries a fowling piece, or a fishing-rod. I suppose this shame must have a good reason. A
dilettantism in nature is barren and unworthy.
The fop of fields is no better than his brother
of Broadway. Men are naturally hunters and
inquisitive of wood-craft, and I suppose that
such a gazetteer as wood-cutters and Indians
should furnish facts for, would take place in
the most sumptuous drawingrooms of all the
" Wreaths " and " Flora's chaplets " of the
bookshops ; yet ordinarily, whether we are too
clumsy for so subtle a topic, or from whatever
cause, as soon as men begin to write on nature,
they fall into euphuism. Frivolity is a most
unfit tribute to Pan, who ought to be represented in the mythology as the most continent of
gods. I would not be frivolous before the admirable reserve and prudence of time, yet I
cannot renounce the right of returning often
to this old topic. The multitude of false
churches accredits the true religion. Literature, poetry, science, are the homage of man to
this unfathomed secret, concerning which no
sane man can affect an indifference or incuri-

osity. Nature is loved by what is best in us. It is loved as the city of God, although, or rather because there is no citizen. The sunset is unlike anything that is underneath it : it wants men. And the beauty of nature must always seem unreal and mocking, until the landscape has human figures, that are as good as itself. If there were good men, there would never be this rapture in nature. If the king is in the palace, nobody looks at the walls. It is when he is gone, and the house is filled with grooms and gazers, that we turn from the people, to find relief in the majestic men that are suggested by the pictures and the architecture. The critics who complain of the sickly separation of the beauty of nature from the thing to be done, must consider that our hunting of the picturesque is inseparable from our protest against false society. Man is fallen ; nature is erect, and serves as a differential thermometer, detecting the presence or absence of the divine sentiment in man. By fault of our dulness and selfishness, we are looking up to nature, but when we are convalescent, nature will look up to us. We see the foaming brook with compunction : if our own

13

life flowed with the right energy, we should shame the brook. The stream of zeal sparkles with real fire, and not with reflex rays of sun and moon. Nature may be as selfishly studied as trade. Astronomy to the selfish becomes astrology ; psychology, mesmerism (with intent to show where our spoons are gone); and anatomy and physiology, become phrenology and palmistry.

But taking timely warning, and leaving many things unsaid on this topic, let us not longer omit our homage to the Efficient Nature, *natura naturans*, the quick cause, before which all forms flee as the driven snows, itself secret, its works driven before it in flocks and multitudes, (as the ancient represented nature by Proteus, a shepherd,) and in undescribable variety. It publishes itself in creatures, reaching from particles and spicula, through transformation on transformation to the highest symmetries, arriving at consummate results without a shock or a leap. A little heat, that is, a little motion, is all that differences the bald, dazzling white, and deadly cold poles of the earth from the prolific tropical climates. All changes pass without violence, by reason of the two cardinal conditions of boundless space and boundless time. Geology has initiated us into the secularity of nature, and taught us to disuse our dame-school measures, and exchange our Mosaic and Ptolemaic schemes for her large style. We knew nothing rightly, for want of perspective. Now we learn what patient periods must round themselves before the rock is formed, then before the rock is broken, and the first lichen race has disintegrated the thinnest external plate into soil, and opened the door for the remote Flora, Fauna, Ceres, and Pomona, to come in. How far off yet is the trilobite! how far the quadruped! how inconceivably remote is man! All duly arrive, and then race after race of men. It is a long way from granite to the oyster; farther yet to Plato, and the preaching of the immortality of the soul. Yet all must come, as surely as the first atom has two sides.

Motion or change, and identity or rest, are the first and second secrets of nature: Motion and Rest. The whole code of her laws may be written on the thumbnail, or the signet of a ring. The whirling bubble on the surface of a brook, admits us to the secret of the mechanics of the sky. Every shell on the beach is a key to it. A little water made to rotate in a cup explains the formation of the simpler shells; the addition of matter from year to year, arrives at last at the most complex forms; and yet so poor is nature with all her craft, that, from the beginning to the end of the universe, she has but one stuff, — but one stuff with its two ends, to serve up all her dream-like variety. Compound it how she will, star, sand, fire, water, tree, man, it is still one stuff, and betrays the same properties.

Nature is always consistent, though she feigns to contravene her own laws. She keeps her laws, and seems to transcend them. She arms and equips an animal to find its place and living in the earth, and, at the same time, she arms and equips another animal to destroy it. Space exists to divide creatures; but by clothing the sides of a bird with a few feathers, she gives him a petty omnipresence. The direction is forever onward, but the artist still goes back for materials, and begins again with the first elements on the most advanced stage : otherwise, all goes to ruin. If we look at her

work, we seem to catch a glance of a system
in transition. Plants are the young of the
world, vessels of health and vigor ; but they
grope ever upward towards consciousness ; the
trees are imperfect men, and seem to bemoan
their imprisonment, rooted in the ground.
The animal is the novice and probationer of a
more advanced order. The men, though
young, having tasted the first drop from the
cup of thought, are already dissipated : the
maples and ferns are still uncorrupt ; yet no
doubt, when they come to consciousness, they
too will curse and swear. Flowers so strictly
belong to youth, that we adult men soon
come to feel, that their beautiful generations
concern not us : we have had our day ; now
let the children have theirs. The flowers
jilt us, and we are old bachelors with our
ridiculous tenderness.

Things are so strictly related, that according to the skill of the eye, from any one object
the parts and properties of any other may be
predicted. If we had eyes to see it, a bit of
stone from the city wall would certify us of
the necessity that man must exist, as readily
as the city. That identity makes us all one,

and reduces to nothing great intervals on our customary scale. We talk of deviations from natural life, as if artificial life were not also natural. The smoothest curled courtier in the boudoirs of a palace has an animal nature, rude and aboriginal as a white bear, omnipotent to its own ends, and is directly related, there amid essences and billetsdoux, to Himmaleh mountain-chains, and the axis of the globe. If we consider how much we are nature's, we need not be superstitious about towns, as if that terrific or benefic force did not find us there also, and fashion cities. Nature who made the mason, made the house. We may easily hear too much of rural influences. The cool disengaged air of natural objects, makes them enviable to us, chafed and irritable creatures with red faces, and we think we shall be as grand as they, if we camp out and eat roots; but let us be men instead of wood-chucks, and the oak and the elm shall gladly serve us, though we sit in chairs of ivory on carpets of silk.

This guiding identity runs through all the surprises and contrasts of the piece, and characterizes every law. Man carries the world in his head, the whole astronomy and chemistry suspended in a thought. Because the history of nature is charactered in his brain, therefore is he the prophet and discoverer of her secrets. Every known fact in natural science was divined by the presentiment of somebody, before it was actually verified. A man does not tie his shoe without recognising laws which bind the farthest regions of nature : moon, plant, gas, crystal, are concrete geometry and numbers. Common sense knows its own, and recognises the fact at first sight in chemical experiment. The common sense of Franklin, Dalton, Davy, and Black, is the same common sense which made the arrangements which now it discovers.

If the identity expresses organized rest, the counter action runs also into organization. The astronomers said, ' Give us matter, and a little motion, and we will construct the universe. It is not enough that we should have matter, we must also have a single impulse, one shove to launch the mass, and generate the harmony of the centrifugal and centripetal forces. Once heave the ball from the hand, and we can show how all this mighty order grew.' — 'A very unreasonable postulate,' said the metaphysicians, 'and a plain begging of the question. Could you not prevail to know the genesis of projection, as well as the continuation of it?' Nature, meanwhile, had not waited for the discussion, but, right or wrong, bestowed the impulse, and the balls rolled. It was no great affair, a mere push, but the astronomers were right in making much of it, for there is no end to the consequences of the act. That famous aboriginal push propagates itself through all the balls of the system, and through every atom of every ball, through all the races of creatures, and through the history and performances of every individual. Exaggeration is in the course of things. Nature sends no creature, no man into the world, without adding a small excess of his proper quality. Given the planet, it is still necessary to add the impulse; so, to every creature nature added a little violence of direction in its proper path, a shove to put it on its way; in every instance, a slight generosity, a drop too much. Without electricity the air would rot, and without this violence of direction, which men and women have, without a spice

of bigot and fanatic, no excitement, no efficiency. We aim above the mark, to hit the
mark. Every act hath some falsehood of
exaggeration in it. And when now and then
comes along some sad, sharp-eyed man, who
sees how paltry a game is played, and refuses
to play, but blabs the secret ; — how then ? is
the bird flown ? O no, the wary Nature sends
a new troop of fairer forms, of lordlier youths,
with a little more excess of direction to hold
them fast to their several aim ; makes them a
little wrongheaded in that direction in which
they are rightest, and on goes the game again
with new whirl, for a generation or two more.
The child with his sweet pranks, the fool of
his senses, commanded by every sight and
sound, without any power to compare and rank
his sensations, abandoned to a whistle or a
painted chip, to a lead dragoon, or a ginger-
bread-dog, individualizing everything, generalizing nothing, delighted with every new
thing, lies down at night overpowered by the
fatigue, which this day of continual pretty
madness has incurred. But Nature has answered her purpose with the curly, dimpled
lunatic. She has tasked every faculty, and

has secured the symmetrical growth of the bodily frame, by all these attitudes and exertions, — an end of the first importance, which could not be trusted to any care less perfect than her own. This glitter, this opaline lustre plays round the top of every toy to his eye, to ensure his fidelity, and he is deceived to his good. We are made alive and kept alive by the same arts. Let the stoics say what they please, we do not eat for the good of living, but because the meat is savory and the appetite is keen. The vegetable life does not content itself with casting from the flower or the tree a single seed, but it fills the air and earth with a prodigality of seeds, that, if thousands perish, thousands may plant themselves, that hundreds may come up, that tens may live to maturity, that, at least, one may replace the parent. All things betray the same calculated profusion. The excess of fear with which the animal frame is hedged round, shrinking from cold, starting at sight of a snake, or at a sudden noise, protects us, through a multitude of groundless alarms, from some one real danger at last. The lover seeks in marriage his private felicity and perfection, with no prospective end; and nature hides in his happiness her own end, namely, progeny, or the perpetuity of the race.

But the craft with which the world is made, runs also into the mind and character of men. No man is quite sane; each has a vein of folly in his composition, a slight determination of blood to the head, to make sure of holding him hard to some one point which nature had taken to heart. Great causes are never tried on their merits; but the cause is reduced to particulars to suit the size of the partizans, and the contention is ever hottest on minor matters. Not less remarkable is the overfaith of each man in the importance of what he has to do or say. The poet, the prophet, has a higher value for what he utters than any hearer, and therefore it gets spoken. The strong, self-complacent Luther declares with an emphasis, not to be mistaken, that "God himself cannot do without wise men." Jacob Behmen and George Fox betray their egotism in the pertinacity of their controversial tracts, and James Naylor once suffered himself to be worshipped as the Christ. Each prophet comes presently to identify himself with his thought, and to esteem his hat and shoes sacred. However this may discredit such persons with the judicious, it helps them with the people, as it gives heat, pungency, and publicity to their words. A similar experience is not infrequent in private life. Each young and ardent person writes a diary, in which, when the hours of prayer and penitence arrive, he inscribes his soul. The pages thus written are, to him, burning and fragrant: he reads them on his knees by midnight and by the morning star; he wets them with his tears: they are sacred; too good for the world, and hardly yet to be shown to the dearest friend. This is the man-child that is born to the soul, and her life still circulates in the babe. The umbilical cord has not yet been cut. After some time has elapsed, he begins to wish to admit his friend to this hallowed experience, and with hesitation, yet with firmness, exposes the pages to his eye. Will they not burn his eyes? The friend coldly turns them over, and passes from the writing to conversation, with easy transition, which strikes the other party with astonishment and vexation. He cannot suspect the writing itself. Days and

nights of fervid life, of communion with
angels of darkness and of light, have engraved
their shadowy characters on that tear-stained
book. He suspects the intelligence or the
heart of his friend. Is there then no friend?
He cannot yet credit that one may have impressive experience, and yet may not know how
to put his private fact into literature; and perhaps the discovery that wisdom has other
tongues and ministers than we, that though
we should hold our peace, the truth would not
the less be spoken, might check injuriously
the flames of our zeal. A man can only speak,
so long as he does not feel his speech to be
partial and inadequate. It is partial, but he
does not see it to be so, whilst he utters it.
As soon as he is released from the instinctive
and particular, and sees its partiality, he shuts
his mouth in disgust. For, no man can write
anything, who does not think that what he
writes is for the time the history of the world;
or do anything well, who does not esteem his
work to be of importance. My work may be
of none, but I must not think it of none, or I
shall not do it with impunity.

In like manner, there is throughout nature

something mocking, something that leads us on and on, but arrives nowhere, keeps no faith with us. All promise outruns the performance. We live in a system of approximations. Every end is prospective of some other end, which is also temporary; a round and final success nowhere. We are encamped in nature, not domesticated. Hunger and thirst lead us on to eat and to drink; but bread and wine, mix and cook them how you will, leave us hungry and thirsty, after the stomach is full. It is the same with all our arts and performances. Our music, our poetry, our language itself are not satisfactions, but suggestions. The hunger for wealth, which reduces the planet to a garden, fools the eager pursuer. What is the end sought? Plainly to secure the ends of good sense and beauty, from the intrusion of deformity or vulgarity of any kind. But what an operose method! What a train of means to secure a little conversation! This palace of brick and stone, these servants, this kitchen, these stables, horses and equipage, this bank-stock, and file of mortgages; trade to all the world, country-house and cottage by the waterside, all for a little conversation, high, clear, and spiritual ! Could it not be had as well by beggars on the highway ? No, all these things came from successive efforts of these beggars to remove friction from the wheels of life, and give opportunity. Conversation, character, were the avowed ends; wealth was good as it appeased the animal cravings, cured the smoky chimney, silenced the creaking door, brought friends together in a warm and quiet room, and kept the children and the dinner-table in a different apartment. Thought, virtue, beauty, were the ends; but it was known that men of thought and virtue sometimes had the headache, or wet feet, or could lose good time whilst the room was getting warm in winter days. Unluckily, in the exertions necessary to remove these inconveniences, the main attention has been diverted to this object; the old aims have been lost sight of, and to remove friction has come to be the end. That is the ridicule of rich men, and Boston, London, Vienna, and now the governments generally of the world, are cities and governments of the rich, and the masses are not men, but *poor men*, that is, men who would be rich ; this is the ridicule of the class, that they arrive with pains and sweat and fury nowhere; when all is done, it is for nothing. They are like one who has interrupted the conversation of a company to make his speech, and now has forgotten what he went to say. The appearanec strikes the eye everywhere of an aimless society, of aimless nations. Were the ends of nature so great and cogent, as to exact this immense sacrifice of men?

Quite analogous to the deceits in life, there is, as might be expected, a similar effect on the eye from the face of external nature. There is in woods and waters a certain enticement and flattery, together with a failure to yield a present satisfaction. This disappointment is felt in every landscape. I have seen the softness and beauty of the summer-clouds floating feathery overhead, enjoying, as it seemed, their height and privilege of motion, whilst yet they appeared not so much the drapery of this place and hour, as forelooking to some pavilions and gardens of festivity beyond. It is an odd jealousy: but the poet finds himself not near enough to his object. The pine-tree, the river, the bank of flowers before him, does not seem to be nature. Nature is still elsewhere. This or this is but outskirt and far-off reflection and echo of the triumph that has passed by, and is now at its glancing splendor and heyday, perchance in the neighboring fields, or, if you stand in the field, then in the adjacent woods. The present object shall give you this sense of stillness that follows a pageant which has just gone by. What splendid distance, what recesses of ineffable pomp and loveliness in the sunset! But who can go where they are, or lay his hand or plant his foot thereon? Off they fall from the round world forever and ever. It is the same among the men and women, as among the silent trees; always a referred existence, an absence, never a presence and satisfaction. Is it, that beauty can never be grasped? in persons and in landscape is equally inaccessible? The accepted and betrothed lover has lost the wildest charm of his maiden in her acceptance of him. She was heaven whilst he pursued her as a star: she cannot be heaven, if she stoops to such a one as he.

What shall we say of this omnipresent ap-

14

pearance of that first projectile impulse, of this flattery and baulking of so many well-meaning creatures? Must we not suppose somewhere in the universe a slight treachery and derision? Are we not engaged to a serious resentment of this use that is made of us? Are we tickled trout, and fools of nature? One look at the face of heaven and earth lays all petulance at rest, and soothes us to wiser convictions. To the intelligent, nature converts itself into a vast promise, and will not be rashly explained. Her secret is untold. Many and many an Œdipus arrives: he has the whole mystery teeming in his brain. Alas! the same sorcery has spoiled his skill; no syllable can he shape on his lips. Her mighty orbit vaults like the fresh rainbow into the deep, but no archangel's wing was yet strong enough to follow it, and report of the return of the curve. But it also appears, that our actions are seconded and disposed to greater conclusions than we designed. We are escorted on every hand through life by spiritual agents, and a beneficent purpose lies in wait for us. We cannot bandy words with nature, or deal with her as we deal with persons. If we measure our individual forces against hers, we may easily feel as if we were the sport of an insuperable destiny. But if, instead of identifying ourselves with the work, we feel that the soul of the workman streams through us, we shall find the peace of the morning dwelling first in our hearts, and the fathomless powers of gravity and chemistry, and, over them, of life, preëxisting within us in their highest form.

The uneasiness which the thought of our helplessness in the chain of causes occasions us, results from looking too much at one condition of nature, namely, Motion. But the drag is never taken from the wheel. Wherever the impulse exceeds, the Rest or Identity insinuates its compensation. All over the wide fields of earth grows the prunella or self-heal. After every foolish day we sleep off the fumes and furies of its hours; and though we are always engaged with particulars, and often enslaved to them, we bring with us to every experiment the innate universal laws. These, while they exist in the mind as ideas, stand around us in nature forever embodied, a present sanity to expose and cure the insanity of men.　Our servitude to particulars betrays into a hundred foolish expectations.　We anticipate a new era from the invention of a locomotive, or a balloon; the new engine brings with it the old checks.　They say that by electro-magnetism, your sallad shall be grown from the seed, whilst your fowl is roasting for dinner: it is a symbol of our modern aims and endeavors, — of our condensation and acceleration of objects: but nothing is gained: nature cannot be cheated: man's life is but seventy sallads long, grow they swift or grow they slow.　In these checks and impossibilities, however, we find our advantage, not less than in the impulses.　Let the victory fall where it will, we are on that side.　And the knowledge that we traverse the whole scale of being, from the centre to the poles of nature, and have some stake in every possibility, lends that sublime lustre to death, which philosophy and religion have too outwardly and literally striven to express in the popular doctrine of the immortality of the soul.　The reality is more excellent than the report.　Here is no ruin, no discontinuity, no spent ball.　The divine circulations never rest nor linger.　Nature is the incarnation of a thought, and turns to a thought again, as ice becomes water and gas. The world is mind precipitated, and the volatile essence is forever escaping again into the state of free thought. Hence the virtue and pungency of the influence on the mind, of natural objects, whether inorganic or organized. Man imprisoned, man crystallized, man vegetative, speaks to man impersonated. That power which does not respect quantity, which makes the whole and the particle its equal channel, delegates its smile to the morning, and distils its essence into every drop of rain. Every moment instructs, and every object : for wisdom is infused into every form. It has been poured into us as blood; it convulsed us as pain ; it slid into us as pleasure ; it enveloped us in dull, melancholy days, or in days of cheerful labor ; we did not guess its essence, until after a long time.

POLITICS.

Gold and iron are good
To buy iron and gold ;
All earth's fleece and food
For their like are sold.
Boded Merlin wise,
Proved Napoleon great, —
Nor kind nor coinage buys
Aught above its rate.
Fear, Craft, and Avarice
Cannot rear a State.
Out of dust to build
What is more than dust, —
Walls Amphion piled
Phœbus stablish must.
When the Muses nine
With the Virtues meet,
Find to their design
An Atlantic seat,
By green orchard boughs
Fended from the heat,
Where the statesman ploughs
Furrow for the wheat ;
When the Church is social worth,
When the state-house is the hearth,
Then the perfect State is come,
The republican at home.

ESSAY VII.

POLITICS.

In dealing with the State, we ought to remember that its institutions are not aboriginal, though they existed before we were born : that they are not superior to the citizen : that every one of them was once the act of a single man : every law and usage was a man's expedient to meet a particular case : that they all are imitable, all alterable ; we may make as good ; we may make better. Society is an illusion to the young citizen. It lies before him in rigid repose, with certain names, men, and institutions, rooted like oak-trees to the centre, round which all arrange themselves the best they can. But the old statesman knows that society is fluid ; there are no such roots and centres ; but any particle may suddenly become the centre of the movement, and compel

the system to gyrate round it, as every man of
strong will, like Pisistratus, or Cromwell, does
for a time, and every man of truth, like Plato,
or Paul, does forever. But politics rest on
necessary foundations, and cannot be treated
with levity. Republics abound in young
civilians, who believe that the laws make the
city, that grave modifications of the policy
and modes of living, and employments of the
population, that commerce, education, and
religion, may be voted in or out; and that
any measure, though it were absurd, may be
imposed on a people, if only you can get sufficient voices to make it a law. But the wise
know that foolish legislation is a rope of sand,
which perishes in the twisting; that the State
must follow, and not lead the character and
progress of the citizen; the strongest usurper
is quickly got rid of; and they only who
build on Ideas, build for eternity; and that
the form of government which prevails, is the
expression of what cultivation exists in the
population which permits it. The law is
only a memorandum. We are superstitious,
and esteem the statute somewhat: so much
life as it has in the character of living men, is

its force. The statute stands there to say, yesterday we agreed so and so, but how feel ye this article today? Our statute is a currency, which we stamp with our own portrait: it soon becomes unrecognizable, and in process of time will return to the mint. Nature is not democratic, nor limited-monarchical, but despotic, and will not be fooled or abated of any jot of her authority, by the pertest of her sons: and as fast as the public mind is opened to more intelligence, the code is seen to be brute and stammering. It speaks not articulately, and must be made to. Meantime the education of the general mind never stops. The reveries of the true and simple are prophetic. What the tender poetic youth dreams, and prays, and paints today, but shuns the ridicule of saying aloud, shall presently be the resolutions of public bodies, then shall be carried as grievance and bill of rights through conflict and war, and then shall be triumphant law and establishment for a hundred years, until it gives place, in turn, to new prayers and pictures. The history of the State sketches in coarse outline the progress of thought, and follows at a distance the delicacy of culture and of aspiration.

The theory of politics, which has possessed the mind of men, and which they have expressed the best they could in their laws and in their revolutions, considers persons and property as the two objects for whose protection government exists. Of persons, all have equal rights, in virtue of being identical in nature. This interest, of course, with its whole power demands a democracy. Whilst the rights of all as persons are equal, in virtue of their access to reason, their rights in property are very unequal. One man owns his clothes, and another owns a county. This accident, depending, primarily, on the skill and virtue of the parties, of which there is every degree, and, secondarily, on patrimony, falls unequally, and its rights, of course, are unequal. Personal rights, universally the same, demand a government framed on the ratio of the census : property demands a government framed on the ratio of owners and of owning. Laban, who has flocks and herds, wishes them looked after by an officer on the frontiers, lest the Midianites shall drive them off, and pays a tax to that end. Jacob has no flocks or herds, and no fear of the Midianites, and pays no tax to the officer. It seemed fit that Laban and Jacob should have equal rights to elect the officer, who is to defend their persons, but that Laban, and not Jacob, should elect the officer who is to guard the sheep and cattle. And, if question arise whether additional officers or watch-towers should be provided, must not Laban and Isaac, and those who must sell part of their herds to buy protection for the rest, judge better of this, and with more right, than Jacob, who, because he is a youth and a traveller, eats their bread and not his own.

In the earliest society the proprietors made their own wealth, and so long as it comes to the owners in the direct way, no other opinion would arise in any equitable community, than that property should make the law for property, and persons the law for persons.

But property passes through donation or inheritance to those who do not create it. Gift, in one case, makes it as really the new owner's, as labor made it the first owner's: in the other case, of patrimony, the law makes an ownership, which will be valid in each man's view according to the estimate which he sets on the public tranquillity.

It was not, however, found easy to embody the readily admitted principle, that property should make law for property, and persons for persons : since persons and property mixed themselves in every transaction. At last it seemed settled, that the rightful distinction was, that the proprietors should have more elective franchise than non-proprietors, on the Spartan principle of "calling that which is just, equal; not that which is equal, just."

That principle no longer looks so self-evident as it appeared in former times, partly, because doubts have arisen whether too much weight had not been allowed in the laws, to property, and such a structure given to our usages, as allowed the rich to encroach on the poor, and to keep them poor; but mainly, because there is an instinctive sense, however obscure and yet inarticulate, that the whole constitution of property, on its present tenures, is injurious, and its influence on persons deteriorating and degrading; that truly, the only interest for the consideration of the State, is persons: that property will always follow persons; that the highest end of government is the culture of men : and if men can be educated, the institutions will share their improvement, and the moral sentiment will write the law of the land.

If it be not easy to settle the equity of this question, the peril is less when we take note of our natural defences. We are kept by better guards than the vigilance of such magistrates as we commonly elect. Society always consists, in greatest part, of young and foolish persons. The old, who have seen through the hypocrisy of courts and statesmen, die, and leave no wisdom to their sons. They believe their own newspaper, as their fathers did at their age. With such an ignorant and deceivable majority, States would soon run to ruin, but that there are limitations, beyond which the folly and ambition of governors cannot go. Things have their laws, as well as men ; and things refuse to be trifled with. Property will be protected. Corn will not grow, unless it is planted and manured ; but the farmer will not plant or hoe it, unless the chances are a hundred to one, that he will cut and harvest it. Under any forms, persons and property must and will have their just sway. They exert their power, as steadily as matter its attraction. Cover up a pound of earth never so cunningly, divide and subdivide it; melt it to liquid, convert it to gas ; it will always weigh a pound : it will always attract and resist other matter, by the full virtue of one pound weight ; — and the attributes of a person, his wit and his moral energy, will exercise, under any law or extinguishing tyranny, their proper force, — if not overtly, then covertly ; if not for the law, then against it; with right, or by might.

The boundaries of personal influence it is impossible to fix, as persons are organs of moral or supernatural force. Under the dominion of an idea, which possesses the minds of multitudes, as civil freedom, or the religious sentiment, the powers of persons are no longer subjects of calculation. A nation of men unanimously bent on freedom, or conquest, can easily confound the arithmetic of statists, and achieve extravagant actions, out of all proportion to their means ; as, the Greeks, the Saracens, the Swiss, the Americans, and the French have done.

In like manner, to every particle of property belongs its own attraction. A cent is the representative of a certain quantity of corn or other commodity. Its value is in the necessities of the animal man. It is so much warmth, so much bread, so much water, so much land. The law may do what it will with the owner of property, its just power will still attach to the cent. The law may in a mad freak say, that all shall have power except the owners of property : they shall have no vote. Nevertheless, by a higher law, the property will, year after year, write every statute that respects property. The non-proprietor will be the scribe of the proprietor. What the owners wish to do, the whole power of property will do, either through the law, or else in defiance of it. Of course, I speak of all the property, not merely of the great estates. When the rich are outvoted, as frequently happens, it is the joint treasury of the poor which exceeds their accumulations. Every man owns something, if it is only a cow, or a wheelbarrow, or his arms, and so has that property to dispose of.

The same necessity which secures the rights of person and property against the malignity or folly of the magistrate, determines the

15

form and methods of governing, which are proper to each nation, and to its habit of thought, and nowise transferable to other states of society. In this country, we are very vain of our political institutions, which are singular in this, that they sprung, within the memory of living men, from the character and condition of the people, which they still express with sufficient fidelity, — and we ostentatiously prefer them to any other in history. They are not better, but only fitter for us. We may be wise in asserting the advantage in modern times of the democratic form, but but to other states of society, in which religion consecrated the monarchical, that and not this was expedient. Democracy is better for us, because the religious sentiment of the present time accords better with it. Born democrats, we are nowise qualified to judge of monarchy, which, to our fathers living in the monarchical idea, was also relatively right. But our institutions, though in coincidence with the spirit of the age, have not any exemption from the practical defects which have discredited other forms. Every actual State is corrupt. Good men must not obey the laws too well. What satire on government can equal the severity of censure conveyed in the word *politic*, which now for ages has signified *cunning*, intimating that the State is a trick ?

The same benign necessity and the same practical abuse appear in the parties into which each State divides itself, of opponents and defenders of the administration of the government. Parties are also founded on instincts, and have better guides to their own humble aims than the sagacity of their leaders. They have nothing perverse in their origin, but rudely mark some real and lasting relation. We might as wisely reprove the east wind, or the frost, as a political party, whose members, for the most part, could give no account of their position, but stand for the defence of those interests in which they find themselves. Our quarrel with them begins, when they quit this deep natural ground at the bidding of some leader, and, obeying personal considerations, throw themselves into the maintenance and defence of points, nowise belonging to their system. A party is perpetually corrupted by personality. Whilst we absolve the association from dishonesty, we cannot extend the same charity to their leaders. They reap the rewards of the docility and zeal of the masses which they direct. Ordinarily, our parties are parties of circumstance, and not of principle; as, the planting interest in conflict with the commercial; the party of capitalists, and that of operatives; parties which are identical in their moral character, and which can easily change ground with each other, in the support of many of their measures. Parties of principle, as, religious sects, or the party of free-trade, of universal suffrage, of abolition of slavery, of abolition of capital punishment, degenerate into personalities, or would inspire enthusiasm. The vice of our leading parties in this country (which may be cited as a fair specimen of these societies of opinion) is, that they do not plant themselves on the deep and necessary grounds to which they are respectively entitled, but lash themselves to fury in the carrying of some local and momentary measure, nowise useful to the commonwealth. Of the two great parties, which, at this hour, almost share the nation between them, I should say, that, one has the best cause, and the other contains the best men. The philosopher, the poet, or the religious man, will, of course, wish to cast his vote with the democrat, for free-trade, for wide suffrage, for the abolition of legal cruelties in the penal code, and for facilitating in every manner the access of the young and the poor to the sources of wealth and power. But he can rarely accept the persons whom the so-called popular party propose to him as representatives of these liberalities. They have not at heart the ends which give to the name of democracy what hope and virtue are in it. The spirit of our American radicalism is destructive and aimless : it is not loving ; it has no ulterior and divine ends ; but is destructive only out of hatred and selfishness. On the other side, the conservative party, composed of the most moderate, able, and cultivated part of the population, is timid, and merely defensive of property. It vindicates no right, it aspires to no real good, it brands no crime, it proposes no generous policy, it does not build, nor write, nor cherish the arts, nor foster religion, nor establish schools, nor encourage science, nor emancipate the slave, nor befriend the poor, or the Indian, or the immigrant. From neither party, when in power, has the world any benefit to expect in science, art, or humanity, at all commensurate with the resources of the nation.

I do not for these defects despair of our republic. We are not at the mercy of any waves of chance. In the strife of ferocious parties, human nature always finds itself cherished, as the children of the convicts at Botany Bay are found to have as healthy a moral sentiment as other children. Citizens of feudal states are alarmed at our democratic institutions lapsing into anarchy; and the older and more cautious among ourselves are learning from Europeans to look with some terror at our turbulent freedom. It is said that in our license of construing the Constitution, and in the despotism of public opinion, we have no anchor; and one foreign observer thinks he has found the safeguard in the sanctity of Marriage among us; and another thinks he has found it in our Calvinism. Fisher Ames expressed the popular security more wisely, when he compared a monarchy and a republic, saying, " that a monarchy is a merchantman, which sails well, but will sometimes strike on a rock, and go to the bottom ; whilst a republic is a raft, which would never sink, but then your feet are always in water." No forms can have any dangerous importance, whilst we are befriended by the laws of things. It makes no difference how many tons weight of atmosphere presses on our heads, so long as the same pressure resists it within the lungs. Augment the mass a thousand fold, it cannot begin to crush us, as long as reaction is equal to action. The fact of two poles, of two forces, centripetal and centrifugal, is universal, and each force by its own activity develops the other. Wild liberty develops iron conscience. Want of liberty, by strengthening law and decorum, stupefies conscience. ' Lynch-law ' prevails only where there is greater hardihood and self-subsistency in the leaders. A mob cannot be a permanency : everybody's interest requires that it should not exist, and only justice satisfies all.

We must trust infinitely to the beneficent necessity which shines through all laws. Human nature expresses itself in them as characteristically as in statues, or songs, or railroads, and an abstract of the codes of nations would be a transcript of the common conscience. Governments have their origin in the moral identity of men. Reason for one is seen to be reason for another, and for every other. There is a middle measure which satisfies all parties, be they never so many, or so resolute for their own. Every man finds a sanction for his simplest claims and deeds in decisions of his own mind, which he calls Truth and Holiness. In these decisions all the citizens find a perfect agreement, and only in these ; not in what is good to eat, good to wear, good use of time, or what amount of land, or of public aid, each is entitled to claim. This truth and justice men presently endeavor to make application of, to the measuring of land, the apportionment of service, the protection of life and property. Their first endeavors, no doubt, are very awkward. Yet absolute right is the first governor ; or, every government is an impure theocracy. The idea, after which each community is aiming to make and mend its law, is, the will of the wise man. The wise man, it cannot find in nature, and it makes awkward but earnest efforts to secure his government by contrivance ; as, by causing the entire people to give their voices on every measure ; or, by a double choice to get the representation of the whole ; or, by a selection of the best citizens; or, to secure the advantages of efficiency and internal peace, by confiding the government to one, who may himself select his agents. All forms of government symbolize an immortal government, common to all dynasties and independent of numbers, perfect where two men exist, perfect where there is only one man.

Every man's nature is a sufficient advertisement to him of the character of his fellows. My right and my wrong, is their right and their wrong. Whilst I do what is fit for me, and abstain from what is unfit, my neighbor and I shall often agree in our means, and work together for a time to one end. But whenever I find my dominion over myself not sufficient for me, and undertake the direction of him also, I overstep the truth, and come into false relations to him. I may have so much more skill or strength than he, that he cannot express adequately his sense of wrong, but it is a lie, and hurts like a lie both him and me. Love and nature cannot maintain the assump-

tion : it must be executed by a practical lie,
namely, by force. This undertaking for
another, is the blunder which stands in colossal
ugliness in the governments of the world. It
is the same thing in numbers, as in a pair,
only not quite so intelligible. I can see well
enough a great difference between my setting
myself down to a self-control, and my going
to make somebody else act after my views :
but when a quarter of the human race assume
to tell me what I must do, I may be too much
disturbed by the circumstances to see so clearly the absurdity of their command. Therefore, all public ends look vague and quixotic
beside private ones. For, any laws but
those which men make for themselves, are
laughable. If I put myself in the place
of my child, and we stand in one thought,
and see that things are thus or thus, that
perception is law for him and me. We are
both there, both act. But if, without carrying him into the thought, I look over into
his plot, and, guessing how it is with him, or-
dain this or that, he will never obey me. This
is the history of governments, — one man does
something which is to bind another. A man

who cannot be acquainted with me, taxes me;
looking from afar at me, ordains that a part of
my labor shall go to this or that whimsical
end, not as I, but as he happens to fancy.
Behold the consequence. Of all debts, men
are least willing to pay the taxes. What a
satire is this on government! Everywhere
they think they get their money's worth, except for these.

Hence, the less government we have,
the better, — the fewer laws, and the less
confided power. The antidote to this abuse
of formal Government, is, the influence of
private character, the growth of the Individual; the appearance of the principal
to supersede the proxy; the appearance of
the wise man, of whom the existing government, is, it must be owned, but a shab-
by imitation. That which all things tend
to educe, which freedom, cultivation, intercourse, revolutions, go to form and deliver, is
character; that is the end of nature, to reach
unto this coronation of her king. To educate
the wise man, the State exists; and with the
appearance of the wise man, the State expires.
The appearance of character makes the State

unnecessary.   The wise man is the State.
He needs no army, fort, or navy, — he loves
men too well ; no bribe, or feast, or palace,
to draw friends to him ; no vantage ground,
no favorable circumstance.   He needs no
library, for he has not done thinking ; no
church, for he is a prophet ; no statute book,
for he has the lawgiver ; no money, for he is
value ; no road, for he is at home where he is ;
no experience, for the life of the creator shoots
through him, and looks from his eyes.   He
has no personal friends, for he who has the
spell to draw the prayer and piety of all men
unto him, needs not husband and educate a
few, to share with him a select and poetic life.
His relation to men is angelic ; his memory is
myrrh to them ;   his presence, frankincense
and flowers.

    We think our civilization near its meridian,
but we are yet only at the cock-crowing and
the morning star.   In our barbarous society the
influence of character is in its infancy.   As a
political power, as the rightful lord who is to
tumble all rulers from their chairs, its presence
is hardly yet suspected.   Malthus and Ricardo
quite omit it ; the Annual Register is silent ;

in the Conversations' Lexicon, it is not set
down; the President's Message, the Queen's
Speech, have not mentioned it; and yet it is
never nothing. Every thought which genius
and piety throw into the world, alters the
world. The gladiators in the lists of power
feel, through all their frocks of force and simu-
lation, the presence of worth. I think the
very strife of trade and ambition are confession of this divinity; and successes in those
fields are the poor amends, the fig-leaf with
which the shamed soul attempts to hide its
nakedness. I find the like unwilling homage
in all quarters. It is because we know how
much is due from us, that we are impatient to
show some petty talent as a substitute for
worth. We are haunted by a conscience of
this right to grandeur of character, and are
false to it. But each of us has some talent,
can do somewhat useful, or graceful, or formidable, or amusing, or lucrative. That we do,
as an apology to others and to ourselves, for
not reaching the mark of a good and equal
life. But it does not satisfy *us*, whilst we
thrust it on the notice of our companions. It
may throw dust in their eyes, but does not

smooth our own brow, or give us the tranquillity of the strong when we walk abroad. We do penance as we go. Our talent is a sort of expiation, and we are constrained to reflect on our splendid moment, with a certain humiliation, as somewhat too fine, and not as one act of many acts, a fair expression of our permanent energy. Most persons of ability meet in society with a kind of tacit appeal. Each seems to say, 'I am not all here.' Senators and presidents have climbed so high with pain enough, not because they think the place specially agreeable, but as an apology for real worth, and to vindicate their manhood in our eyes. This conspicuous chair is their compensation to themselves for being of a poor, cold, hard nature. They must do what they can. Like one class of forest animals, they have nothing but a prehensile tail : climb they must, or crawl. If a man found himself so rich-natured that he could enter into strict relations with the best persons, and make life serene around him by the dignity and sweetness of his behavior, could he afford to circumvent the favor of the caucus and the press, and covet relations so hollow and pompous, as those of a

politician ? Surely nobody would be a charla-
tan, who could afford to be sincere.

The tendencies of the times favor the idea
of self-government, and leave the individual,
for all code, to the rewards and penalties of his
own constitution, which work with more energy than we believe, whilst we depend on
artificial restraints. The movement in this direction has been very marked in modern
history. Much has been blind and discredita-
ble, but the nature of the revolution is not
affected by the vices of the revolters; for this
is a purely moral force. It was never adopted
by any party in history, neither can be. It
separates the individual from all party, and
unites him, at the same time, to the race. It
promises a recognition of higher rights than
those of personal freedom, or the security of
property. A man has a right to be employed,
to be trusted, to be loved, to be revered. The
power of love, as the basis of a State, has
never been tried. We must not imagine that
all things are lapsing into confusion, if every
tender protestant be not compelled to bear his
part in certain social conventions : nor doubt
that roads can be built, letters carried, and

the fruit of labor secured, when the government of force is at an end. Are our methods now so excellent that all competition is hopeless ? Could not a nation of friends even devise better ways ? On the other hand, let not the most conservative and timid fear anything from a premature surrender of the bayonet, and the system of force. For, according to the order of nature, which is quite superior to our will, it stands thus ; there will always be a government of force, where men are selfish ; and when they are pure enough to abjure the code of force, they will be wise enough to see how these public ends of the post-office, of the highway, of commerce, and the exchange of property, of museums and libraries, of institutions of art and science, can be answered.

We live in a very low state of the world, and pay unwilling tribute to governments founded on force. There is not, among the most religious and instructed men of the most religious and civil nations, a reliance on the moral sentiment, and a sufficient belief in the unity of things to persuade them that society can be maintained without artificial restraints, as well as the solar system ; or that the private citizen might be reasonable, and a good neighbor, without the hint of a jail or a confiscation. What is strange too, there never was in any man sufficient faith in the power of rectitude, to inspire him with the broad design of renovating the State on the principle of right and love. All those who have pretended this design, have been partial reformers, and have admitted in some manner the supremacy of the bad State. I do not call to mind a single human being who has steadily denied the authority of the laws, on the simple ground of his own moral nature. Such designs, full of genius and full of fate as they are, are not entertained except avowedly as air-pictures. If the individual who exhibits them, dare to think them practicable, he disgusts scholars and churchmen; and men of talent, and women of superior sentiments, cannot hide their contempt. Not the less does nature continue to fill the heart of youth with suggestions of this enthusiasm, and there are now men, — if indeed I can speak in the plural number, — more exactly, I will say, I have just been conversing with one man, to whom no weight of adverse experience will make it

16

for a moment appear impossible, that thousands of human beings might exercise towards each other the grandest and simplest sentiments, as well as a knot of friends, or a pair of lovers.

NOMINALIST AND REALIST.

In countless upward-striving waves
The moon-drawn tide-wave strives ;
In thousand far-transplanted grafts
The parent fruit survives ;
So, in the new-born millions,
The perfect Adam lives.
Not less are summer-mornings dear
To every child they wake,
And each with novel life his sphere
Fills for his proper sake.

ESSAY VIII.

NOMINALIST AND REALIST.

I CANNOT often enough say, that a man is only a relative and representative nature. Each is a hint of the truth, but far enough from being that truth, which yet he quite newly and inevitably suggests to us. If I seek it in him, I shall not find it. Could any man conduct into me the pure stream of that which he pretends to be! Long afterwards, I find that quality elsewhere which he promised me. The genius of the Platonists, is intoxicating to the student, yet how few particulars of it can I detach from all their books. The man momentarily stands for the thought, but will not bear examination; and a society of men will cursorily represent well enough a certain quality and culture, for example, chivalry or beauty of manners, but separate them, and there is no gentleman and no lady in the group. The least hint sets us on the pursuit of a character, which no man realizes. We have such exorbitant eyes, that on seeing the smallest arc, we complete the curve, and when the curtain is lifted from the diagram which it seemed to veil, we are vexed to find that no more was drawn, than just that fragment of an arc which we first beheld. We are greatly too liberal in our construction of each other's faculty and promise. Exactly what the parties have already done, they shall do again; but that which we inferred from their nature and inception, they will not do. That is in nature, but not in them. That happens in the world, which we often witness in a public debate. Each of the speakers expresses himself imperfectly: no one of them hears much that another says, such is the preoccupation of mind of each; and the audience, who have only to hear and not to speak, judge very wisely and superiorly how wrongheaded and unskilful is each of the debaters to his own affair. Great men or men of great gifts you shall easily find, but symmetrical men never. When I meet a pure intellectual force, or a

generosity of affection, I believe, here then is
man ; and am presently mortified by the discovery, that this individual is no more available to his own or to the general ends, than his
companions ; because the power which drew
my respect, is not supported by the total symphony of his talents. All persons exist to
society by some shining trait of beauty or
utility, which they have. We borrow the
proportions of the man from that one fine feature, and finish the portrait symmetrically ;
which is false ; for the rest of his body is
small or deformed. I observe a person who
makes a good public appearance, and conclude
thence the perfection of his private character,
on which this is based ; but he has no private
character. He is a graceful cloak or lay-figure
for holidays. All our poets, heroes, and saints,
fail utterly in some one or in many parts to
satisfy our idea, fail to draw our spontaneous
interest, and so leave us without any hope of
realization but in our own future. Our exaggeration of all fine characters arises from the
fact, that we identify each in turn with the
soul. But there are no such men as we fable ;
no Jesus, nor Pericles, nor Cæsar, nor Angelo,

nor Washington, such as we have made. We consecrate a great deal of nonsense, because it was allowed by great men. There is none without his foible. I verily believe if an angel should come to chaunt the chorus of the moral law, he would eat too much ginger-bread, or take liberties with private letters, or do some precious atrocity. It is bad enough, that our geniuses cannot do anything useful, but it is worse that no man is fit for society, who has fine traits. He is admired at a dis-tance, but he cannot come near without appearing a cripple. The men of fine parts protect themselves by solitude, or by courtesy, or by satire, or by an acid worldly manner, each concealing, as he best can, his incapacity for useful association, but they want either love or self-reliance.

Our native love of reality joins with this experience to teach us a little reserve, and to dissuade a too sudden surrender to the brilliant qualities of persons. Young people admire talents or particular excellences ; as we grow older, we value total powers and effects, as, the impression, the quality, the spirit of men and things. The genius is all. The man, —

it is his system : we do not try a solitary
word or act, but his habit. The acts which
you praise, I praise not, since they are depar-
tures from his faith, and are mere compliances.
The magnetism which arranges tribes and
races in one polarity, is alone to be respected ;
the men are steel-filings. Yet we unjustly
select a particle, and say, ' O steel-filing number one ! what heart-drawings I feel to thee !
what prodigious virtues are these of thine !
how constitutional to thee, and incommunicable.' Whilst we speak, the loadstone is withdrawn ; down falls our filing in a heap with
the rest, and we continue our mummery to
the wretched shaving. Let us go for universals; for the magnetism, not for the needles.
Human life and its persons are poor empirical
pretensions. A personal influence is an *ignis
fatuus.* If they say, it is great, it is great ; if
they say, it is small, it is small ; you see it,
and you see it not, by turns ; it borrows all its
size from the momentary estimation of the
speakers : the Will-of-the-wisp vanishes, if
you go too near, vanishes if you go too far,
and only blazes at one angle. Who can tell if
Washington be a great man, or no ? Who can

tell if Franklin be ? Yes, or any but the twelve, or six, or three great gods of fame ? And they, too, loom and fade before the eternal.

We are amphibious creatures, weaponed for two elements, having two sets of faculties, the particular and the catholic. We adjust our instrument for general observation, and sweep the heavens as easily as we pick out a single figure in the terrestrial landscape. We are practically skilful in detecting elements, for which we have no place in our theory, and no name. Thus we are very sensible of an atmospheric influence in men and in bodies of men, not accounted for in an arithmetical addition of all their measurable properties. There is a genius of a nation, which is not to be found in the numerical citizens, but which characterizes the society. England, strong, punctual, practical, well-spoken England, I should not find, if I should go to the island to seek it. In the parliament, in the playhouse, at dinner-tables, I might see a great number of rich, ignorant, book-read, conventional, proud men, — many old women, — and not anywhere the Englishman who made the good speeches, combined the accurate engines, and did the bold and nervous deeds. It is even worse in America, where, from the intellectual quickness of the race, the genius of the country is more splendid in its promise, and more slight in its performance. Webster cannot do the work of Webster. We conceive distinctly enough the French, the Spanish, the German genius, and it is not the less real, that perhaps we should not meet in either of those nations, a single individual who corresponded with the type. We infer the spirit of the nation in great measure from the language, which is a sort of monument, to which each forcible individual in a course of many hundred years has contributed a stone. And, universally, a good example of this social force, is the veracity of language, which cannot be debauched. In any controversy concerning morals, an appeal may be made with safety to the sentiments, which the language of the people expresses. Proverbs, words, and grammar inflections convey the public sense with more purity and precision, than the wisest individual.

In the famous dispute with the Nominalists, the Realists had a good deal of reason. General ideas are essences. They are our gods: they round and ennoble the most partial and sordid way of living. Our proclivity to details cannot quite degrade our life, and divest it of poetry. The day-laborer is reckoned as standing at the foot of the social scale, yet he is saturated with the laws of the world. His measures are the hours; morning and night, solstice and equinox, geometry, astronomy, and all the lovely accidents of nature play through his mind. Money, which represents the prose of life, and which is hardly spoken of in parlors without an apology, is, in its effects and laws, as beautiful as roses. Property keeps the accounts of the world, and is always moral. The property will be found where the labor, the wisdom, and the virtue have been in nations, in classes, and (the whole life-time considered, with the compensations) in the individual also. How wise the world appears, when the laws and usages of nations are largely detailed, and the completeness of the municipal system is considered! Nothing is left out. If you go into the markets, and the custom-houses, the insurers' and notaries' offices, the offices of sealers of weights and measures, of inspection of provisions, — it will appear as if one man had made it all. Wherever you go, a wit like your own has been before you, and has realized its thought. The Eleusinian mysteries, the Egyptian architecture, the Indian astronomy, the Greek sculpture, show that there always were seeing and knowing men in the planet. The world is full of masonic ties, of guilds, of secret and public legions of honor; that of scholars, for example; and that of gentlemen fraternizing with the upper class of every country and every culture.

I am very much struck in literature by the appearance, that one person wrote all the books; as if the editor of a journal planted his body of reporters in different parts of the field of action, and relieved some by others from time to time; but there is such equality and identity both of judgment and point of view in the narrative, that it is plainly the work of one all-seeing, all-hearing gentleman. I looked into Pope's Odyssey yesterday: it is as correct and elegant after our canon of today, as if it were newly written. The modernness of all good books seems to give me an existence as

wide as man. What is well done, I feel as if
I did; what is ill-done, I reck not of. Shakspeare's passages of passion (for example, in
Lear and Hamlet) are in the very dialect of
the present year. I am faithful again to the
whole over the members in my use of books.
I find the most pleasure in reading a book in a
manner least flattering to the author. I read
Proclus, and sometimes Plato, as I might read
a dictionary, for a mechanical help to the
fancy and the imagination. I read for the
lustres, as if one should use a fine picture in a
chromatic experiment, for its rich colors. 'Tis
not Proclus, but a piece of nature and fate that
I explore. It is a greater joy to see the
author's author, than himself. A higher pleasure of the same kind I found lately at a concert, where I went to hear Handel's Messiah.
As the master overpowered the littleness and
incapableness of the performers, and made them
conductors of his electricity, so it was easy to
observe what efforts nature was making
through so many hoarse, wooden, and imperfect persons, to produce beautiful voices, fluid
and soul-guided men and women. The
genius of nature was paramount at the oratorio.

This preference of the genius to the parts is the secret of that deification of art, which is found in all superior minds. Art, in the artist, is proportion, or, a habitual respect to the whole by an eye loving beauty in details. And the wonder and charm of it is the sanity in insanity which it denotes. Proportion is almost impossible to human beings. There is no one who does not exaggerate. In conversation, men are encumbered with personality, and talk too much. In modern sculpture, picture, and poetry, the beauty is miscellaneous ; the artist works here and there, and at all points, adding and adding, instead of unfolding the unit of his thought. Beautiful details we must have, or no artist : but they must be means and never other. The eye must not lose sight for a moment of the purpose. Lively boys write to their ear and eye, and the cool reader finds nothing but sweet jingles in it. When they grow older, they respect the argument.

We obey the same intellectual integrity, when we study in exceptions the law of the world. Anomalous facts, as the never quite obsolete rumors of magic and demonology, and the new allegations of phrenologists and neurologists, are of ideal use. They are good indications. Homœopathy is insignificant as an art of healing, but of great value as criticism on the hygeia or medical practice of the time. So with Mesmerism, Swedenborgism, Fourierism, and the Millennial Church ; they are poor pretensions enough, but good criticism on the science, philosophy, and preaching of the day. For these abnormal insights of the adepts, ought to be normal, and things of course.

All things show us, that on every side we are very near to the best. It seems not worth while to execute with too much pains some one intellectual, or æsthetical, or civil feat, when presently the dream will scatter, and we shall burst into universal power. The reason of idleness and of crime is the deferring of our hopes. Whilst we are waiting, we beguile the time with jokes, with sleep, with eating, and with crimes.

Thus we settle it in our cool libraries, that all the agents with which we deal are subalterns, which we can well afford to let pass, and life will be simpler when we live at the

centre, and flout the surfaces. I wish to speak with all respect of persons, but sometimes I must pinch myself to keep awake, and preserve the due decorum. They melt so fast into each other, that they are like grass and trees, and it needs an effort to treat them as individuals. Though the uninspired man certainly finds persons a conveniency in household matters, the divine man does not respect them : he sees them as a rack of clouds, or a fleet of ripples which the wind drives over the surface of the water. But this is flat rebellion. Nature will not be Buddhist : she resents generalizing, and insults the philosopher in every moment with a million of fresh particulars. It is all idle talking : as much as a man is a whole, so is he also a part ; and it were partial not to see it. What you say in your pompous distribution only distributes you into your class and section. You have not got rid of parts by denying them, but are the more partial. You are one thing, but nature is *one thing and the other thing*, in the same moment. She will not remain orbed in a thought, but rushes into persons ; and when each person, inflamed to a fury of personality,

17

would conquer all things to his poor crotchet, she raises up against him another person, and by many persons incarnates again a sort of whole. She will have all. Nick Bottom cannot play all the parts, work it how he may : there will be somebody else, and the world will be round. Everything must have its flower or effort at the beautiful, coarser or finer according to its stuff. They relieve and recommend each other, and the sanity of society is a balance of a thousand insanities. She punishes abstractionists, and will only forgive an induction which is rare and casual. We like to come to a height of land and see the landscape, just as we value a general remark in conversation. But it is not the intention of nature that we should live by general views. We fetch fire and water, run about all day among the shops and markets, and get our clothes and shoes made and mended, and are the victims of these details, and once in a fortnight we arrive perhaps at a rational moment. If we were not thus infatuated, if we saw the real from hour to hour, we should not be here to write and to read, but should have been burned or frozen long ago. She would never get anything done, if she suffered admirable Crichtons, and universal geniuses. She loves better a wheelwright who dreams all night of wheels, and a groom who is part of his horse : for she is full of work, and these are her hands. As the frugal farmer takes care that his cattle shall eat down the rowan, and swine shall eat the waste of his house, and poultry shall pick the crumbs, so our economical mother despatches a new genius and habit of mind into every district and condition of existence, plants an eye wherever a new ray of light can fall, and gathering up into some man every property in the universe, establishes thousandfold occult mutual attractions among her offspring, that all this wash and waste of power may be imparted and exchanged.

Great dangers undoubtedly accrue from this incarnation and distribution of the godhead, and hence nature has her maligners, as if she were Circe ; and Alphonso of Castille fancied he could have given useful advice. But she does not go unprovided ; she has hellebore at the bottom of the cup. Solitude would ripen a plentiful crop of despots. The recluse

thinks of men as having his manner, or as
not having his manner; and as having degrees of it, more and less. But when he
comes into a public assembly, he sees that
men have very different manners from his
own, and in their way admirable. In his
childhood and youth, he has had many checks
and censures, and thinks modestly enough of
his own endowment. When afterwards he
comes to unfold it in propitious circumstance,
it seems the only talent: he is delighted with
his success, and accounts himself already the
fellow of the great. But he goes into a mob,
into a banking-house, into a mechanic's shop,
into a mill, into a laboratory, into a ship, into
a camp, and in each new place he is no better
than an idiot: other talents take place, and rule
the hour. The rotation which whirls every
leaf and pebble to the meridian, reaches to every
gift of man, and we all take turns at the top.

For nature, who abhors mannerism, has set
her heart on breaking up all styles and tricks,
and it is so much easier to do what one has
done before, than to do a new thing, that
there is a perpetual tendency to a set mode.
In every conversation, even the highest, there

is a certain trick, which may be soon learned by an acute person, and then that particular style continued indefinitely. Each man, too, is a tyrant in tendency, because he would impose his idea on others; and their trick is their natural defence. Jesus would absorb the race; but Tom Paine or the coarsest blasphemer helps humanity by resisting this exuberance of power. Hence the immense benefit of party in politics, as it reveals faults of character in a chief, which the intellectual force of the persons, with ordinary opportunity, and not hurled into aphelion by hatred, could not have seen. Since we are all so stupid, what benefit that there should be two stupidities! It is like that brute advantage so essential to astronomy, of having the diameter of the earth's orbit for a base of its triangles. Democracy is morose, and runs to anarchy, but in the state, and in the schools, it is indispensable to resist the consolidation of all men into a few men. If John was perfect, why are you and I alive? As long as any man exists, there is some need of him; let him fight for his own. A new poet has appeared; a new character approached us; why should we refuse to eat bread, until we have found his regiment and section in our old army-files? Why not a new man? Here is a new enterprise of Brook Farm, of Skeneateles, of Northampton: why so impatient to baptise them Essenes, or Port-Royalists, or Shakers, or by any known and effete name? Let it be a new way of living. Why have only two or three ways of life, and not thousands? Every man is wanted, and no man is wanted much. We came this time for condiments, not for corn. We want the great genius only for joy; for one star more in our constellation, for one tree more in our grove. But he thinks we wish to belong to him, as he wishes to occupy us. He greatly mistakes us. I think I have done well, if I have acquired a new word from a good author; and my business with him is to find my own, though it were only to melt him down into an epithet or an image for daily use.

" Into paint will I grind thee, my bride! "

To embroil the confusion, and make it impossible to arrive at any general statement, when we have insisted on the imperfection of indi-

viduals, our affections and our experience urge
that every individual is entitled to honor, and
a very generous treatment is sure to be repaid.
A recluse sees only two or three persons, and
allows them all their room ; they spread themselves at large. The man of state looks at
many, and compares the few habitually with
others, and these look less. Yet are they not
entitled to this generosity of reception ? and is
not munificence the means of insight ? For
though gamesters say, that the cards beat all
the players, though they were never so skilful,
yet in the contest we are now considering,
the players are also the game, and share the
power of the cards. If you criticise a fine
genius, the odds are that you are out of your
reckoning, and, instead of the poet, are censuring your own caricature of him. For there
is somewhat spheral and infinite in every man,
especially in every genius, which, if you can
come very near him, sports with all your
limitations. For, rightly, every man is a
channel through which heaven floweth, and,
whilst I fancied I was criticising him, I was
censuring or rather terminating my own soul.
After taxing Goethe as a courtier, artificial,

unbelieving, worldly,—I took up this book of Helena, and found him an Indian of the wilderness, a piece of pure nature like an apple or an oak, large as morning or night, and virtuous as a briar-rose.

But care is taken that the whole tune shall be played. If we were not kept among surfaces, every thing would be large and universal : now the excluded attributes burst in on us with the more brightness, that they have been excluded. "Your turn now, my turn next," is the rule of the game. The universality being hindered in its primary form, comes in the secondary form of *all sides :* the points come in succession to the meridian, and by the speed of rotation, a new whole is formed. Nature keeps herself whole, and her representation complete in the experience of each mind. She suffers no seat to be vacant in her college. It is the secret of the world that all things subsist, and do not die, but only retire a little from sight, and afterwards return again. Whatever does not concern us, is concealed from us. As soon as a person is no longer related to our present well-being, he is concealed, or *dies*, as we say. Really, all things and persons are related to us, but according to our nature, they act on us not at once, but in succession, and we are made aware of their presence one at a time. All persons, all things which we have known, are here present, and many more than we see; the world is full. As the ancient said, the world is a *plenum* or solid; and if we saw all things that really surround us, we should be imprisoned and unable to move. For, though nothing is impassable to the soul, but all things are pervious to it, and like highways, yet this is only whilst the soul does not see them. As soon as the soul sees any object, it stops before that object. Therefore, the divine Providence, which keeps the universe open in every direction to the soul, conceals all the furniture and all the persons that do not concern a particular soul, from the senses of that individual. Through solidest eternal things, the man finds his road, as if they did not subsist, and does not once suspect their being. As soon as he needs a new object, suddenly he beholds it, and no longer attempts to pass through it, but takes another way. When he has exhausted for the time the nourishment to be drawn from any one person or thing, that object is withdrawn from his observation, and though still in his immediate neighborhood, he does not suspect its presence.

Nothing is dead : men feign themselves dead, and endure mock funerals and mournful obituaries, and there they stand looking out of the window, sound and well, in some new and strange disguise. Jesus is not dead : he is very well alive : nor John, nor Paul, nor Mahomet, nor Aristotle ; at times we believe we have seen them all, and could easily tell the names under which they go.

If we cannot make voluntary and conscious steps in the admirable science of universals, let us see the parts wisely, and infer the genius of nature from the best particulars with a becoming charity. What is best in each kind is an index of what should be the average of that thing. Love shows me the opulence of nature, by disclosing to me in my friend a hidden wealth, and I infer an equal depth of good in every other direction. It is commonly said by farmers, that a good pear or apple costs no more time or pains to rear, than a poor one ; so I would have no work of art,

no speech, or action, or thought, or friend, but
the best.

The end and the means, the gamester
and the game, — life is made up of the
intermixture and reaction of these two ami-
cable powers, whose marriage appears beforehand monstrous, as each denies and tends
to abolish the other. We must reconcile the
contradictions as we can, but their discord
and their concord introduce wild absurdities
into our thinking and speech. No sentence
will hold the whole truth, and the only way
in which we can be just, is by giving ourselves the lie ; Speech is better than silence ;
silence is better than speech ; — All things are
in contact ; every atom has a sphere of repulsion ; — Things are, and are not, at the same
time ; — and the like. All the universe over,
there is but one thing, this old Two-Face,
creator-creature, mind-matter, right-wrong, of
which any proposition may be affirmed or
denied. Very fitly, therefore, I assert, that
every man is a partialist, that nature secures
him as an instrument by self-conceit, prevent-
ing the tendencies to religion and science ; and
now further assert, that, each man's genius

being nearly and affectionately explored, he is justified in his individuality, as his nature is found to be immense; and now I add, that every man is a universalist also, and, as our earth, whilst it spins on its own axis, spins all the time around the sun through the celestial spaces, so the least of its rational children, the most dedicated to his private affair, works out, though as it were under a disguise, the universal problem. We fancy men are individuals; so are pumpkins; but every pumpkin in the field, goes through every point of pumpkin history. The rabid democrat, as soon as he is senator and rich man, has ripened beyond possibility of sincere radicalism, and unless he can resist the sun, he must be conservative the remainder of his days. Lord Eldon said in his old age, "that, if he were to begin life again, he would be damned but he would begin as agitator."

We hide this universality, if we can, but it appears at all points. We are as ungrateful as children. There is nothing we cherish and strive to draw to us, but in some hour we turn and rend it. We keep a running fire of sarcasm at ignorance and the life of the senses;

then goes by, perchance, a fair girl, a piece of
life, gay and happy, and making the commonest offices beautiful, by the energy and heart
with which she does them, and seeing this,
we admire and love her and them, and say,
" Lo ! a genuine creature of the fair earth,
not dissipated, or too early ripened by books,
philosophy, religion, society, or care ! " insin-
uating a treachery and contempt for all we
had so long loved and wrought in ourselves
and others.

If we could have any security against
moods ! If the profoundest prophet could be
holden to his words, and the hearer who is
ready to sell all and join the crusade, could
have any certificate that tomorrow his prophet
shall not unsay his testimony ! But the Truth
sits veiled there on the Bench, and never in-
terposes an adamantine syllable ; and the most
sincere and revolutionary doctrine, put as if
the ark of God were carried forward some
furlongs, and planted there for the succor of
the world, shall in a few weeks be coldly set
aside by the same speaker, as morbid ; " I
thought I was right, but I was not," — and the
same immeasurable credulity demanded for

new audacities. If we were not of all opinions! if we did not in any moment shift the
platform on which we stand, and look and
speak from another! if there could be any
regulation, any 'one-hour-rule,' that a man
should never leave his point of view, without
sound of trumpet. I am always insincere, as
always knowing there are other moods.

How sincere and confidential we can be,
saying all that lies in the mind, and yet go
away feeling that all is yet unsaid, from the
incapacity of the parties to know each other,
although they use the same words! My companion assumes to know my mood and habit
of thought, and we go on from explanation to
explanation, until all is said which words can,
and we leave matters just as they were at
first, because of that vicious assumption. Is
it that every man believes every other to be
an incurable partialist, and himself an universalist? I talked yesterday with a pair of philosophers: I endeavored to show my good men
that I love everything by turns, and nothing
long; that I loved the centre, but doated on
the superficies; that I loved man, if men
seemed to me mice and rats; that I revered

saints, but woke up glad that the old pagan world stood its ground, and died hard ; that I was glad of men of every gift and nobility, but would not live in their arms. Could they but once understand, that I loved to know that they existed, and heartily wished them Godspeed, yet, out of my poverty of life and thought, had no word or welcome for them when they came to see me, and could well consent to their living in Oregon, for any claim I felt on them, it would be a great satisfaction.

NEW ENGLAND REFORMERS.

18

NEW ENGLAND REFORMERS.

A LECTURE READ BEFORE THE SOCIETY IN AMORY HALL,
ON SUNDAY, 3 MARCH, 1844.

WHOEVER has had opportunity of acquaintance with society in New England, during the last twenty-five years, with those middle and with those leading sections that may constitute any just representation of the character and aim of the community, will have been struck with the great activity of thought and experimenting. His attention must be commanded by the signs that the Church, or religious party, is falling from the church nominal, and is appearing in temperance and non-resistance societies, in movements of abolitionists and of socialists, and in very significant assemblies, called Sabbath and Bible Conventions, — composed of ultraists, of seekers, of all the soul of the soldiery of dissent, and meeting to call in question the authority of the Sabbath, of the priesthood, and of the church. In these movements, nothing was more remarkable than the discontent they begot in the movers. The spirit of protest and of detachment, drove the members of these Conventions to bear testimony against the church, and immediately afterward, to declare their discontent with these Conventions, their independence of their colleagues, and their impatience of the methods whereby they were working. They defied each other, like a congress of kings, each of whom had a realm to rule, and a way of his own that made concert unprofitable. What a fertility of projects for the salvation of the world! One apostle thought all men should go to farming; and another, that no man should buy or sell: that the use of money was the cardinal evil; another, that the mischief was in our diet, that we eat and drink damnation. These made unleavened bread, and were foes to the death to fermentation. It was in vain urged by the housewife, that God made yeast, as well as dough, and loves fermentation just as dearly as he loves vegetation ; that fermentation develops the saccharine element in the grain, and makes it more palatable and more digestible. No ; they wish the pure wheat, and will die but it shall not ferment. Stop, dear nature, these incessant advances of thine ; let us scotch these ever-rolling wheels! Others attacked the system of agriculture, the use of animal manures in farming ; and the tyranny of man over brute nature ; these abuses polluted his food. The ox must be taken from the plough, and the horse from the cart, the hundred acres of the farm must be spaded, and the man must walk wherever boats and locomotives will not carry him. Even the insect world was to be defended, — that had been too long neglected, and a society for the protection of ground-worms, slugs, and mosquitos was to be incorporated without delay. With these appeared the adepts of homœopathy, of hydropathy, of mesmerism, of phrenology, and their wonderful theories of the Christian miracles ! Others assailed particular vocations, as that of the lawyer, that of the merchant, of the manufacturer, of the clergyman, of the scholar. Others attacked the institution of marriage, as the fountain of social evils. Others devoted themselves to the worrying of churches and meetings for public worship; and the fertile forms of antinomianism among the elder puritans, seemed to have their match in the plenty of the new harvest of reform.

With this din of opinion and debate, there was a keener scrutiny of institutions and domestic life than any we had known, there was sincere protesting against existing evils, and there were changes of employment dictated by conscience. No doubt, there was plentiful vaporing, and cases of backsliding might occur. But in each of these movements emerged a good result, a tendency to the adoption of simpler methods, and an assertion of the sufficiency of the private man. Thus it was directly in the spirit and genius of the age, what happened in one instance, when a church censured and threatened to excommunicate one of its members, on account of the somewhat hostile part to the church, which his conscience led him to take in the anti-slavery business; the threatened individual immediately excommunicated the church in a public and formal process. This has been several times repeated: it was excellent when it was done the first time, but, of course, loses all value when it is copied. Every project in the history of reform, no matter how violent and surprising, is good, when it is the dictate of a man's genius and constitution, but very dull and suspicious when adopted from another. It is right and beautiful in any man to say, 'I will take this coat, or this book, or this measure of corn of yours,' — in whom we see the act to be original, and to flow from the whole spirit and faith of him ; for then that taking will have a giving as free and divine : but we are very easily disposed to resist the same generosity of speech, when we miss originality and truth to character in it.

There was in all the practical activities of New England, for the last quarter of a century, a gradual withdrawal of tender consciences from the social organizations. There is observable throughout, the contest between mechanical and spiritual methods, but with a steady tendency of the thoughtful and virtuous to a deeper belief and reliance on spiritual facts.

In politics, for example, it is easy to see the

progress of dissent. The country is full of rebellion ; the country is full of kings. Hands off! let there be no control and no interference in the administration of the affairs of this kingdom of me. Hence the growth of the doctrine and of the party of Free Trade, and the willingness to try that experiment, in the face of what appear incontestable facts. I confess, the motto of the Globe newspaper is so attractive to me, that I can seldom find much appetite to read what is below it in its columns, " The world is governed too much." So the country is frequently affording solitary examples of resistance to the government, solitary nullifiers, who throw themselves on their reserved rights ; nay, who have reserved all their rights ; who reply to the assessor, and to the clerk of court, that they do not know the State ; and embarrass the courts of law, by non-juring, and the commander-in-chief of the militia, by non-resistance.

The same disposition to scrutiny and dissent appeared in civil, festive, neighborly, and domestic society. A restless, prying, conscientious criticism broke out in unexpected quarters. Who gave me the money with which I bought my coat? Why should professional labor and that of the counting-house be paid so disproportionately to the labor of the porter, and woodsawyer? This whole business of Trade gives me to pause and think, as it constitutes false relations between men; inasmuch as I am prone to count myself relieved of any responsibility to behave well and nobly to that person whom I pay with money, whereas if I had not that commodity, I should be put on my good behavior in all companies, and man would be a benefactor to man, as being himself his only certificate that he had a right to those aids and services which each asked of the other. Am I not too protected a person? is there not a wide disparity between the lot of me and the lot of thee, my poor brother, my poor sister? Am I not defrauded of my best culture in the loss of those gymnastics which manual labor and the emergencies of poverty constitute? I find nothing healthful or exalting in the smooth conventions of society; I do not like the close air of saloons. I begin to suspect myself to be a prisoner, though treated with all this courtesy and luxury. I pay a destructive tax in my conformity.

The same insatiable criticism may be traced in the efforts for the reform of Education. The popular education has been taxed with a want of truth and nature. It was complained that an education to things was not given. We are students of words: we are shut up in schools, and colleges, and recitation-rooms, for ten or fifteen years, and come out at last with a bag of wind, a memory of words, and do not know a thing. We cannot use our hands, or our legs, or our eyes, or our arms. We do not know an edible root in the woods, we cannot tell our course by the stars, nor the hour of the day by the sun. It is well if we can swim and skate. We are afraid of a horse, of a cow, of a dog, of a snake, of a spider. The Roman rule was, to teach a boy nothing that he could not learn standing. The old English rule was, 'All summer in the field, and all winter in the study.' And it seems as if a man should learn to plant, or to fish, or to hunt, that he might secure his subsistence at all events, and not be painful to his friends and fellow men. The lessons of science should be experimental also. The sight of the planet through a telescope, is worth all the course on astronomy : the shock of the electric spark in the elbow, out-values all the theories ; the taste of the nitrous oxide, the firing of an artificial volcano, are better than volumes of chemistry.

One of the traits of the new spirit, is the inquisition it fixed on our scholastic devotion to the dead languages. The ancient languages, with great beauty of structure, contain wonderful remains of genius, which draw, and always will draw, certain likeminded men, — Greek men, and Roman men, in all countries, to their study ; but by a wonderful drowsiness of usage, they had exacted the study of *all* men. Once (say two centuries ago), Latin and Greek had a strict relation to all the science and culture there was in Europe, and the Mathematics had a momentary importance at some era of activity in physical science. These things became stereotyped as *education*, as the manner of men is. But the Good Spirit never cared for the colleges, and though all men and boys were now drilled in Latin, Greek, and Mathematics, it had quite left these shells high and dry on the beach, and was now creating and feeding other matters at other ends of the world. But in a hundred high schools and colleges, this warfare against common sense still goes on. Four, or six, or ten years, the pupil is parsing Greek and Latin, and as soon as he leaves the University, as it is ludicrously called, he shuts those books for the last time. Some thousands of young men are graduated at our colleges in this country every year, and the persons who, at forty years, still read Greek, can all be counted on your hand. I never met with ten. Four or five persons I have seen who read Plato.

But is not this absurd, that the whole liberal talent of this country should be directed in its best years on studies which lead to nothing? What was the consequence? Some intelligent persons said or thought ; ' Is that Greek and Latin some spell to conjure with, and not words of reason? If the physician, the lawyer, the divine, never use it to come at their ends, I need never learn it to come at mine. Conjuring is gone out of fashion, and I will omit this conjugating, and go straight to affairs.' So they jumped the Greek and Latin, and read law, medicine, or sermons, without it. To the astonishment of all, the self-made men took even ground at once with the oldest of the regular graduates, and in a few months the most conservative circles of Boston and New York had quite forgotten who of their gownsmen was college-bred, and who was not.

One tendency appears alike in the philosophical speculation, and in the rudest democratical movements, through all the petulance and all the puerility, the wish, namely, to cast aside the superfluous, and arrive at short methods, urged, as I suppose, by an intuition that the human spirit is equal to all emergencies, alone, and that man is more often injured than helped by the means he uses.

I conceive this gradual casting off of material aids, and the indication of growing trust in the private, self-supplied powers of the individual, to be the affirmative principle of the recent philosophy : and that it is feeling its own profound truth, and is reaching forward at this very hour to the happiest conclusions. I readily concede that in this, as in every period of intellectual activity, there has been a noise of denial and protest ; much was to be resisted, much was to be got rid of by those who were reared in the old, before they could begin to affirm and to construct. Many a reformer perishes in his removal of rubbish, — and that makes the offensiveness of the class. They are partial; they are not equal to the work they pretend. They lose their way; in the assault on the kingdom of darkness, they expend all their energy on some accidental evil, and lose their sanity and power of benefit. It is of little moment that one or two, or twenty errors of our social system be corrected, but of much that the man be in his senses.

The criticism and attack on institutions which we have witnessed, has made one thing plain, that society gains nothing whilst a man, not himself renovated, attempts to renovate things around him: he has become tediously good in some particular, but negligent or narrow in the rest; and hypocrisy and vanity are often the disgusting result.

It is handsomer to remain in the establishment better than the establishment, and conduct that in the best manner, than to make a sally against evil by some single improvement, without supporting it by a total regeneration. Do not be so vain of your one objection. Do you think there is only one ? Alas! my good friend, there is no part of society or of life better than any other part. All our things are right and wrong together. The wave of evil washes all our institutions alike. Do you complain of our Marriage ? Our marriage is no worse than our education, our diet, our trade, our social customs. Do you complain of the laws of Property ? It is a pedantry to give such importance to them. Can we not play the game of life with these counters, as well as with those ; in the institution of property, as well as out of it. Let into it the new and renewing principle of love, and property will be universality. No one gives the impression of superiority to the institution, which he must give who will reform it. It makes no difference what you say : you must make me feel that you are aloof from it ; by your natural and supernatural advantages, do easily see to the end of it, — do see how man can do without it. Now all men are on one side. No man deserves to be heard against property. Only Love, only an Idea, is against property, as we hold it.

I cannot afford to be irritable and captious, nor to waste all my time in attacks. If I should go out of church whenever I hear a false sentiment, I could never stay there five minutes. But why come out? the street is as false as the church, and when I get to my house, or to my manners, or to my speech, I have not got away from the lie. When we see an eager assailant of one of these wrongs, a special reformer, we feel like asking him, What right have you, sir, to your one virtue? Is virtue piecemeal? This is a jewel amidst the rags of a beggar.

In another way the right will be vindicated. In the midst of abuses, in the heart of cities, in the aisles of false churches, alike in one place and in another, — wherever, namely, a just and heroic soul finds itself, there it will do what is next at hand, and by the new quality of character it shall put forth, it shall abrogate that old condition, law or school in which it stands, before the law of its own mind.

If partiality was one fault of the movement party, the other defect was their reliance on Association. Doubts such as those I have intimated, drove many good persons to agitate the questions of social reform. But the revolt against the spirit of commerce, the spirit of aristocracy, and the inveterate abuses of cities, did not appear possible to individuals ; and to do battle against numbers, they armed themselves with numbers, and against concert, they relied on new concert.

Following, or advancing beyond the ideas of St. Simon, of Fourier, and of Owen, three communities have already been formed in Massachusetts on kindred plans, and many more in the country at large. They aim to give every member a share in the manual labor, to give an equal reward to labor and to talent, and to unite a liberal culture with an education to labor. The scheme offers, by the economies of associated labor and expense, to make every member rich, on the same amount of property, that, in separate families, would leave every member poor. These new associations are composed of men and women of superior talents and sentiments: yet it may easily be questioned, whether such a community will draw, except in its beginnings, the able and the good ; whether those who have energy, will not prefer their chance of superiority and power in the world,

19

to the humble certainties of the association; whether such a retreat does not promise to become an assylum to those who have tried and failed, rather than a field to the strong; and whether the members will not necessarily be fractions of men, because each finds that he cannot enter it, without some compromise. Friendship and association are very fine things, and a grand phalanx of the best of the human race, banded for some catholic object: yes, excellent; but remember that no society can ever be so large as one man. He in his friendship, in his natural and momentary associations, doubles or multiplies himself; but in the hour in which he mortgages himself to two or ten or twenty, he dwarfs himself below the stature of one.

But the men of less faith could not thus believe, and to such, concert appears the sole specific of strength. I have failed, and you have failed, but perhaps together we shall not fail. Our housekeeping is not satisfactory to us, but perhaps a phalanx, a community, might be. Many of us have differed in opinion, and we could find no man who could make the truth plain, but possibly a college, or an ecclesiasti-

cal council might. I have not been able
either to persuade my brother or to prevail on
myself, to disuse the traffic or the potation of
brandy, but perhaps a pledge of total abstinence might effectually restrain us. The
candidate my party votes for is not to be
trusted with a dollar, but he will be honest in
the Senate, for we can bring public opinion to
bear on him. Thus concert was the specific
in all cases. But concert is neither better nor
worse, neither more nor less potent than individual force. All the men in the world cannot
make a statue walk and speak, cannot make a
drop of blood, or a blade of grass, any more
than one man can. But let there be one man,
let there be truth in two men, in ten men, then
is concert for the first time possible, because
the force which moves the world is a new
quality, and can never be furnished by adding
whatever quantities of a different kind. What
is the use of the concert of the false and
the disunited? There can be no concert
in two, where there is no concert in one.
When the individual is not *individual*, but is
dual; when his thoughts look one way, and
his actions another; when his faith is traversed

by his habits; when his will, enlightened by
reason, is warped by his sense; when with one
hand he rows, and with the other backs water,
what concert can be ?

I do not wonder at the interest these projects inspire. The world is awaking to the
idea of union, and these experiments show
what it is thinking of. It is and will be
magic. Men will live and communicate, and
plough, and reap, and govern, as by added
ethereal power, when once they are united;
as in a celebrated experiment, by expiration
and respiration exactly together, four persons
lift a heavy man from the ground by the little
finger only, and without sense of weight.
But this union must be inward, and not one of
covenants, and is to be reached by a reverse of
the methods they use. The union is only
perfect, when all the uniters are isolated. It is
the union of friends who live in different
streets or towns. Each man, if he attempts to
join himself to others, is on all sides cramped
and diminished of his proportion; and the
stricter the union, the smaller and the more
pitiful he is. But leave him alone, to recognize in every hour and place the secret soul, he

will go up and down doing the works of a
true member, and, to the astonishment of all,
the work will be done with concert, though
no man spoke. Government will be adamantine without any governor. The union must
be ideal in actual individualism.

I pass to the indication in some particulars
of that faith in man, which the heart is
preaching to us in these days, and which
engages the more regard, from the consideration, that the speculations of one generation
are the history of the next following.

In alluding just now to our system of education, I spoke of the deadness of its details.
But it is open to graver criticism than the
palsy of its members : it is a system of despair.
The disease with which the human mind now
labors, is want of faith. Men do not believe
in a power of education. We do not think
we can speak to divine sentiments in man,
and we do not try. We renounce all high
aims. We believe that the defects of so
many perverse and so many frivolous people,
who make up society, are organic, and society
is a hospital of incurables. A man of good
sense but of little faith, whose compassion

seemed to lead him to church as often as he went there, said to me ; " that he liked to have concerts, and fairs, and churches, and other public amusements go on." I am afraid the remark is too honest, and comes from the same origin as the maxim of the tyrant, " If you would rule the world quietly, you must keep it amused." I notice too, that the ground on which eminent public servants urge the claims of popular education is fear : ' This country is filling up with thousands and millions of voters, and you must educate them to keep them from our throats.' We do not believe that any education, any system of philosophy, any influence of genius, will ever give depth of insight to a superficial mind. Having settled ourselves into this infidelity, our skill is expended to procure alleviations, diversion, opiates. We adorn the victim with manual skill, his tongue with languages, his body with inoffensive and comely manners. So have we cunningly hid the tragedy of limitation and inner death we cannot avert. Is it strange that society should be devoured by a secret melancholy, which breaks through all its smiles, and all its gayety and games ?

But even one step farther our infidelity has gone. It appears that some doubt is felt by good and wise men, whether really the happiness and probity of men is increased by the culture of the mind in those disciplines to which we give the name of education. Unhappily, too, the doubt comes from scholars, from persons who have tried these methods. In their experience, the scholar was not raised by the sacred thoughts amongst which he dwelt, but used them to selfish ends. He was a profane person, and became a showman, turning his gifts to a marketable use, and not to his own sustenance and growth. It was found that the intellect could be independently developed, that is, in separation from the man, as any single organ can be invigorated, and the result was monstrous. A canine appetite for knowledge was generated, which must still be fed, but was never satisfied, and this knowledge not being directed on action, never took the character of substantial, humane truth, blessing those whom it entered. It gave the scholar certain powers of expression, the power of speech, the power of poetry, of literary art, but it did not bring him to peace, or to beneficence.

When the literary class betray a destitution of faith, it is not strange that society should be disheartened and sensualized by unbelief. What remedy? Life must be lived on a higher plane. We must go up to a higher platform, to which we are always invited to ascend; there, the whole aspect of things changes. I resist the skepticism of our education, and of our educated men. I do not believe that the differences of opinion and character in men are organic. I do not recognize, beside the class of the good and the wise, a permanent class of skeptics, or a class of conservatives, or of malignants, or of materialists. I do not believe in two classes. You remember the story of the poor woman who importuned King Philip of Macedon to grant her justice, which Philip refused: the woman exclaimed, "I appeal": the king, astonished, asked to whom she appealed: the woman replied, "from Philip drunk to Philip sober." The text will suit me very well. I believe not in two classes of men, but in man in two moods, in Philip drunk and Philip sober. I think, according to the good-hearted word of Plato, "Unwillingly the soul is deprived of truth."

Iron conservative, miser, or thief, no man is, but by a supposed necessity, which he tolerates by shortness or torpidity of sight. The soul lets no man go without some visitations and holydays of a diviner presence. It would be easy to show, by a narrow scanning of any man's biography, that we are not so wedded to our paltry performances of every kind, but that every man has at intervals the grace to scorn his performances, in comparing them with his belief of what he should do, that he puts himself on the side of his enemies, listening gladly to what they say of him, and accusing himself of the same things.

What is it men love in Genius, but its infinite hope, which degrades all it has done? Genius counts all its miracles poor and short. Its own idea it never executed. The Iliad, the Hamlet, the Doric column, the Roman arch, the Gothic minster, the German anthem, when they are ended, the master casts behind him. How sinks the song in the waves of melody which the universe pours over his soul! Before that gracious Infinite, out of which he drew these few strokes, how mean they look, though the praises of the world attend them. From the triumphs of his art, he turns with desire to this greater defeat. Let those admire who will. With silent joy he sees himself to be capable of a beauty that eclipses all which his hands have done, all which human hands have ever done.

Well, we are all the children of genius, the children of virtue, — and feel their inspirations in our happier hours. Is not every man sometimes a radical in politics? Men are conservatives when they are least vigorous, or when they are most luxurious. They are conservatives after dinner, or before taking their rest; when they are sick, or aged: in the morning, or when their intellect or their conscience have been aroused, when they hear music, or when they read poetry, they are radicals. In the circle of the rankest tories that could be collected in England, Old or New, let a powerful and stimulating intellect, a man of great heart and mind, act on them, and very quickly these frozen conservators will yield to the friendly influence, these hopeless will begin to hope, these haters will begin to love, these immovable statues will begin to spin and revolve. I cannot help recalling the fine anec-

dote which Warton relates of Bishop Berkeley,
when he was preparing to leave England,
with his plan of planting the gospel among
the American savages. " Lord Bathurst told
me, that the members of the Scriblerus club,
being met at his house at dinner, they agreed
to rally Berkeley, who was also his guest, on
his scheme at Bermudas. Berkeley, having
listened to the many lively things they had to
say, begged to be heard in his turn, and dis-
played his plan with such an astonishing and
animating force of eloquence and enthusiasm,
that they were struck dumb, and, after some
pause, rose up all together with earnestness,
exclaiming, ' Let us set out with him immediately.' " Men in all ways are better than
they seem. They like flattery for the moment, but they know the truth for their own.
It is a foolish cowardice which keeps us from
trusting them, and speaking to them rude
truth. They resent your honesty for an
instant, they will thank you for it always.
What is it we heartily wish of each other?
Is it to be pleased and flattered? No, but to
be convicted and exposed, to be shamed out
of our nonsense of all kinds, and made men of,

instead of ghosts and phantoms. We are weary
of gliding ghostlike through the world, which
is itself so slight and unreal. We crave a sense
of reality, though it come in strokes of pain. I
explain so, — by this manlike love of truth, —
those excesses and errors into which souls of
great vigor, but not equal insight, often fall.
They feel the poverty at the bottom of all the
seeming affluence of the world. They know
the speed with which they come straight
through the thin masquerade, and conceive a
disgust at the indigence of nature : Rousseau,
Mirabeau, Charles Fox, Napoleon, Byron, —
and I could easily add names nearer home, of
raging riders, who drive their steeds so hard,
in the violence of living to forget its illusion :
they would know the worst, and tread the
floors of hell. The heroes of ancient and
modern fame, Cimon, Themistocles, Alcibiades, Alexander, Cæsar, have treated life and
fortune as a game to be well and skilfully
played, but the stake not to be so valued,
but that any time, it could be held as a
trifle light as air, and thrown up. Cæsar, just
before the battle of Pharsalia, discourses with
the Egyptian priest, concerning the fountains

of the Nile, and offers to quit the army, the empire, and Cleopatra, if he will show him those mysterious sources.

The same magnanimity shows itself in our social relations, in the preference, namely, which each man gives to the society of superiors over that of his equals. All that a man has, will he give for right relations with his mates. All that he has, will he give for an erect demeanor in every company and on each occasion. He aims at such things as his neighbors prize, and gives his days and nights, his talents and his heart, to strike a good stroke, to acquit himself in all men's sight as a man. The consideration of an eminent citizen, of a noted merchant, of a man of mark in his profession; naval and military honor, a general's commission, a marshal's baton, a ducal coronet, the laurel of poets, and, anyhow procured, the acknowledgment of eminent merit, have this lustre for each candidate, that they enable him to walk erect and unashamed, in the presence of some persons, before whom he felt himself inferior. Having raised himself to this rank, having established his equality with class after class, of those with whom

he would live well, he still finds certain
others, before whom he cannot possess himself, because they have somewhat fairer, somewhat grander, somewhat purer, which extorts
homage of him. Is his ambition pure ? then,
will his laurels and his possessions seem
worthless : instead of avoiding these men who
make his fine gold dim, he will cast all behind
him, and seek their society only, woo and
embrace this his humiliation and mortification,
until he shall know why his eye sinks, his
voice is husky, and his brilliant talents are
paralyzed in this presence. He is sure that
the soul which gives the lie to all things, will
tell none. His constitution will not mislead
him. If it cannot carry itself as it ought, high
and unmatchable in the presence of any man,
if the secret oracles whose whisper makes the
sweetness and dignity of his life, do here
withdraw and accompany him no longer, it is
time to undervalue what he has valued, to
dispossess himself of what he has acquired, and
with Cæsar to take in his hand the army, the
empire, and Cleopatra, and say, ' All these will
I relinquish, if you will show me the fountains
of the Nile.' Dear to us are those who love us,

the swift moments we spend with them are a compensation for a great deal of misery; they enlarge our life; — but dearer are those who reject us as unworthy, for they add another life : they build a heaven before us, whereof we had not dreamed, and thereby supply to us new powers out of the recesses of the spirit, and urge us to new and unattempted performances.

As every man at heart wishes the best and not inferior society, wishes to be convicted of his error, and to come to himself, so he wishes that the same healing should not stop in his thought, but should penetrate his will or active power. The selfish man suffers more from his selfishness, than he from whom that selfishness withholds some important benefit. What he most wishes is to be lifted to some higher platform, that he may see beyond his present fear the transalpine good, so that his fear, his coldness, his custom may be broken up like fragments of ice, melted and carried away in the great stream of good will. Do you ask my aid? I also wish to be a benefactor. I wish more to be a benefactor and servant, than you wish to be served by me, and surely the greatest good fortune that could befall me, is precisely to be so moved by you that I should say, ' Take me and all mine, and use me and mine freely to your ends ' ! for, I could not say it, otherwise than because a great enlargement had come to my heart and mind, which made me superior to my fortunes. Here we are paralyzed with fear; we hold on to our little properties, house and land, office and money, for the bread which they have in our experience yielded us, although we confess, that our being does not flow through them. We desire to be made great, we desire to be touched with that fire which shall command this ice to stream, and make onr existence a benefit. If therefore we start objections to your project, O friend of the slave, or friend of the poor, or of the race, understand well, that it is because we wish to drive you to drive us into your measures. We wish to hear ourselves confuted. We are haunted with a belief that you have a secret, which it would highliest advantage us to learn, and we would force you to impart it to us, though it should bring us to prison, or to worse extremity.

Nothing shall warp me from the belief, that every man is a lover of truth. There is no pure lie, no pure malignity in nature. The entertainment of the proposition of depravity is the last profligacy and profanation. There is no skepticism, no atheism but that. Could it be received into common belief, suicide would unpeople the planet. It has had a name to live in some dogmatic theology, but each man's innocence and his real liking of his neighbor, have kept it a dead letter. I remember standing at the polls one day, when the anger of the political contest gave a certain grimness to the faces of the independent electors, and a good man at my side looking on the people, remarked, " I am satisfied that the largest part of these men, on either side, mean to vote right." I suppose, considerate observers looking at the masses of men, in their blameless, and in their equivocal actions, will assent, that in spite of selfishness and frivolity, the general purpose in the great number of persons is fidelity. The reason why any one refuses his assent to your opinion, or his aid to your benevolent design, is in you: he refuses to accept you as a bringer of

20

truth, because, though you think you have it, he feels that you have it not. You have not given him the authentic sign.

If it were worth while to run into details this general doctrine of the latent but ever soliciting Spirit, it would be easy to adduce illustration in particulars of a man's equality to the church, of his equality to the state, and of his equality to every other man. It is yet in all men's memory, that, a few years ago, the liberal churches complained, that the Calvinistic church denied to them the name of Christian. I think the complaint was confession : a religious church would not complain. A religious man like Behmen, Fox, or Swedenborg, is not irritated by wanting the sanction of the church, but the church feels the accusation of his presence and belief.

It only needs, that a just man should walk in our streets, to make it appear how pitiful and inartificial a contrivance is our legislation. The man whose part is taken, and who does not wait for society in anything, has a power which society cannot choose but feel. The familiar experiment, called the hydrostatic paradox, in which a capillary column of water balances the ocean, is a symbol of the relation of one man to the whole family of men. The wise Dandini, on hearing the lives of Socrates, Pythagoras, and Diogenes read, "judged them to be great men every way, excepting, that they were too much subjected to the reverence of the laws, which to second and authorize, true virtue must abate very much of its original vigor."

And as a man is equal to the church, and equal to the state, so he is equal to every other man. The disparities of power in men are superficial; and all frank and searching conversation, in which a man lays himself open to his brother, apprizes each of their radical unity. When two persons sit and converse in a thoroughly good understanding, the remark is sure to be made, See how we have disputed about words! Let a clear, apprehensive mind, such as every man knows among his friends, converse with the most commanding poetic genius, I think, it would appear that there was no inequality such as men fancy between them; that a perfect understanding, a like receiving, a like perceiving, abolished differences, and the poet would confess, that his creative imagination gave him no deep advantage, but only the superficial one, that he could express himself, and the other could not ; that his advantage was a knack, which might impose on indolent men, but could not impose on lovers of truth ; for they know the tax of talent, or, what a price of greatness the power of expression too often pays. I believe it is the conviction of the purest men, that the net amount of man and man does not much vary. Each is incomparably superior to his companion in some faculty. His want of skill in other directions, has added to his fitness for his own work. Each seems to have some compensation yielded to him by his infirmity, and every hindrance operates as a concentration of his force.

These and the like experiences intimate, that man stands in strict connexion with a higher fact never yet manifested. There is power over and behind us, and we are the channels of its communications. We seek to say thus and so, and over our head some spirit sits, which contradicts what we say. We would persuade our fellow to this or that ; another self within our eyes dissuades him.

That which we keep back, this reveals. In vain we compose our faces and our words; it holds uncontrollable communication with the enemy, and he answers civilly to us, but believes the spirit. We exclaim, 'There's a traitor in the house!' but at last it appears that he is the true man, and I am the traitor. This open channel to the highest life is the first and last reality, so subtle, so quiet, yet so tenacious, that although I have never expressed the truth, and although I have never heard the expression of it from any other, I know that the whole truth is here for me. What if I cannot answer your questions? I am not pained that I cannot frame a reply to the question, What is the operation we call Providence? There lies the unspoken thing, present, omnipresent. Every time we converse, we seek to translate it into speech, but whether we hit, or whether we miss, we have the fact. Every discourse is an approximate answer : but it is of small consequence, that we do not get it into verbs and nouns, whilst it abides for contemplation forever.

If the auguries of the prophesying heart shall make themselves good in time, the man

who shall be born, whose advent men
and events prepare and foreshow, is one
who shall enjoy his connexion with a higher life, with the man within man; shall
destroy distrust by his trust, shall use his
native but forgotten methods, shall not
take counsel of flesh and blood, but shall
rely on the Law alive and beautiful, which
works over our heads and under our feet.
Pitiless, it avails itself of our success, when
we obey it, and of our ruin, when we contravene it. Men are all secret believers in it,
else, the word justice would have no meaning: they believe that the best is the true;
that right is done at last; or chaos would
come. It rewards actions after their nature,
and not after the design of the agent. 'Work,'
it saith to man, 'in every hour, paid or unpaid,
see only that thou work, and thou canst not
escape the reward: whether thy work be fine
or coarse, planting corn, or writing epics, so
only it be honest work, done to thine own
approbation, it shall earn a reward to the
senses as well as to the thought: no matter,
how often defeated, you are born to victory.

The reward of a thing well done, is to have done it.'

As soon as a man is wonted to look beyond surfaces, and to see how this high will prevails without an exception or an interval, he settles himself into serenity. He can already rely on the laws of gravity, that every stone will fall where it is due ; the good globe is faithful, and carries us securely through the celestial spaces, anxious or resigned : we need not interfere to help it on, and he will learn, one day, the mild lesson they teach, that our own orbit is all our task, and we need not assist the administration of the universe. Do not be so impatient to set the town right concerning the unfounded pretensions and the false reputation of certain men of standing. They are laboring harder to set the town right concerning themselves, and will certainly succeed. Suppress for a few days your criticism on the insufficiency of this or that teacher or experimenter, and he will have demonstrated his insufficiency to all men's eyes. In like manner, let a man fall into the divine circuits, and he is enlarged. Obedience to his genius is the only liberating influence. We wish to escape from subjection, and a sense of inferiority, — and we make self-denying ordinances, we drink water, we eat grass, we refuse the laws, we go to jail: it is all in vain ; only by obedience to his genius; only by the freest activity in the way constitutional to him, does an angel seem to arise before a man, and lead him by the hand out of all the wards of the prison.

That which befits us, embosomed in beauty and wonder as we are, is cheerfulness and courage, and the endeavor to realize our aspirations. The life of man is the true romance, which, when it is valiantly conducted, will yield the imagination a higher joy than any fiction. All around us, what powers are wrapped up under the coarse mattings of custom, and all wonder prevented. It is so wonderful to our neurologists that a man can see without his eyes, that it does not occur to them, that it is just as wonderful, that he should see with them ; and that is ever the difference between the wise and the unwise: the latter wonders at what is unusual, the wise man wonders at the usual. Shall not the heart which has received so much, trust the Power by which it lives? May it not quit other leadings, and listen to the Soul that has guided it so gently, and taught it so much, secure that the future will be worthy of the past?

★ MUSIC FOR YOUNG AMERICANS

TEACHER'S ANNOTATED EDITION

This edition is planned to be of special assistance to the teacher, providing aids which will make the teacher's task easier and more productive, and offering suggestions which will enhance the value of the work in music for pupils. Below are given features of this annotated edition.

PUPIL'S BOOK The pupil's book is presented exactly as it appears in the Pupil's Edition.

TEACHER'S GUIDE A complete Teacher's Guide is included following the pupil's book. This guide includes information for the teacher and suggestions for teaching each song to make learning interesting, meaningful, and valuable to pupils.

ANNOTATION Overprinted in color on the pages of the pupil's book are annotations that provide handy references to the pages in the Teacher's Guide and in the Guide and Accompaniments book. These references relate to each musical selection. Annotations also highlight points about each song that can be emphasized in class. They frequently supply added information and insight. References to recordings of the songs are also indicated.

Auxiliary Materials

GUIDE AND ACCOMPANIMENTS In addition to the Teacher's Annotated Edition, this music series offers a Guide and Accompaniments book for each grade. This book presents guide material plus piano accompaniment for every selection in the series.

RECORDINGS Recordings are available for a number of the songs in each book of this series. In preparing the recordings, a great variety in instrumentation has been used, and singers have been carefully selected for different qualities. Specific directions for locating songs on records are clearly given in the Teacher's Annotated Edition accompanying each pupil's book of the series.

MUSIC ★ FOR

ABC MUSIC SERIES

★ BOOK SIX ★

Explanation of Symbols:

◉ — Recording: side, section, number
(example) 4 - 3 - 2

G — Guide page number (ex. G-11)

A — Accompaniment book page
number (ex. A-12)

⬚ ○○○ ○○○○ — Melody instruments:
(tonettes, flutophones, etc.)

G, D_7, etc., indicate chords for piano, autoharp,
ukulele

★ YOUNG ★ AMERICANS

RICHARD C. BERG
DIRECTOR OF MUSIC EDUCATION, YONKERS, N. Y.

DANIEL S. HOOLEY
PROFESSOR OF MUSIC EDUCATION
GEORGIA SOUTHERN COLLEGE, COLLEGEBORO, GEORGIA

JOSEPHINE WOLVERTON
ASSISTANT SUPERVISOR OF MUSIC, EVANSTON PUBLIC SCHOOLS
AND ASSISTANT PROFESSOR OF MUSIC
NORTHWESTERN UNIVERSITY, EVANSTON, ILLINOIS

CLAUDEANE BURNS
CONSULTANT, AMERICAN BOOK COMPANY, CHICAGO, ILLINOIS

AMERICAN BOOK COMPANY ©

CONTENTS

Winter Holidays PAGES 66—84

Songs to Sing in the Keys of A♭ and D♭ PAGES 85—93

Songs to Sing and Play in Various Keys PAGES 94—102

Songs to Sing and Play in the Keys of E and G PAGES 102—115

Spring Holidays and Listening PAGES 116—130

1-1-1   G-7   A-6

Lift Up Your Voice and Sing!

Words and Music by Richard C. Berg

Key: G JOYFULLY, TWO BEATS TO A MEASURE

Starts: 1. A song is a won-der-ful kind of thing, So lift up your voice — and sing! —
D-5-So 2. A song lifts the heart in a care-free way, So lift up your voice — and sing! —

Just start a glad song, let it float, let it ring, And lift up your voice and sing! —
You'll find it will help you chase blues far a-way, So lift up your voice and sing! —

Refrain

We shall make mu-sic to bright-en the day, Mu-sic will help us to light-en the way;

Lift up your voice! Lift up your voice! Lift up your voice — and sing! —

Expressive singing
Rhythm

1

1-1-2   G-7   A-7

● We're All Together Again

Key: G

GAILY, TWO BEATS TO A MEASURE

Adapted Words   Traditional **Tune**

Creative activities
Rhythm
Tie

Starts:
D-5-So

1. We're all to-geth-er a - gain, We're here, we're here! ___
2. Al - though we have-n't been part - ed long or far, ___

We're all to-geth-er a - gain, We're here, we're here! ___
We're all to-geth-er a - gain, Yes, here we are! ___

Refrain

Here we are sing-ing all to-geth-er a - gain,

Sing-ing all to-geth-er a-gain, We're here, we're here! ___

Encourage children to make additional
stanzas.

2

Clap, snap fingers, or slap knees on the rests, marked ⨯.

Chumbara

Key: D

Nonsense song

French-Canadian Folk Song

RAPIDLY

Starts:
D-1-Do

1. Chum-ba-ra,   chum-ba-ra,   chum-ba-ra,   chum-ba-ra,
2. Chow-ber-ski, chow-ber-ski, chow-ber-ski, chow-ber-ski,

Descending scale in D major

Chum-ba-ra,   chum-ba-ra, chum chum chum chum   chum chum chum chum,
Chow-ber-ski, chow-ber-ski, chow chow chow chow   chow chow chow chow,

Chum-ba-ra,   chum-ba-ra,   chum-ba-ra,   chum-ba-ra,
Chow-ber-ski, chow-ber-ski, chow-ber-ski, chow-ber-ski,

Chum-ba-ra,   chum-ba-ra,   chum, chum.
Chow-ber-ski, chow-ber-ski, chow, chow.

3. Fee-do-lee, fee-do-lee, fee-do-lee, fee-do-lee,
Fee-do-lee, fee-do-lee, fee fee fee fee fee fee fee fee,
Fee-do-lee, fee-do-lee, fee-do-lee, fee-do-lee,
Fee-do-lee, fee-do-lee, fee, fee.

Make up extra stanzas. For instance, you might sing "rum-dee-dum" or "yo-de-lay."

Try playing different instruments: the triangle on one stanza; wood blocks on another, etc., at the places marked ⨯.

Creative activities   Rhythm activities

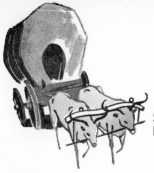

G-8 A-9.

Sweet Betsy from Pike

American Folk Song

Key: D   GAILY

Starts:
D-1-Do

1. Did you ev - er   hear of sweet Bet - sy from   Pike,
2. The al - ka - li   des - ert was   burn - ing and   bare,
3. They swam the wide   riv - ers and crossed the tall   peaks,

Rhythmic unity
Harmony
Correlation

Who crossed the wide   prai - rie   with her hus - band, Ike,
And   Ike cried in   fear, "We   are lost, I de - clare!
They camped on the   prai - rie   for weeks and for   weeks;

With two   yoke of   cat - tle   and one spot - ted   hog,
My dear   old Pike   Coun - ty,   I'll go back to   you."
They fought off the   In - dians with mus - ket and   ball,

A   tall Shang - hai   roost - er, and an old yal - ler   dog?
Said Bet - sy, "You'll   go by your - self, if   you   do."
And reached Cal - i - for - nia in __ spite of   it   all.

Refrain

Sing __ too ra   li   oo ra   li   oo ra   li   ay,

Sing __ too ra   li   oo ra   li   oo ra   li   ay.

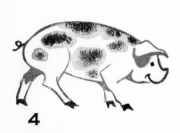

4

Verses might be sung by various small groups.
Notice repetition of the rhythm pattern in verse.

1-4-3   G-8   A-10

🎵 Keep in the Middle of the Road

Solo singing
Part-singing
Enunciation

Spiritual

Key: E♭

WITH SPIRIT

Starts:
G-3-Mi

1. I hear the an - gels call - ing loud, } Keep in the mid-dle of the road;
2. I don't have time to stop and talk, } Keep in the mid-dle of the road.

They're __ wait-ing there in a great big crowd, } Keep in the mid-dle of the road.
'Cause the road is rough and __ hard to walk, } Keep in the mid-dle of the road.

I see them stand-ing 'round a big white gate, Now __ move a - long, __ it's get-ting late,
I fix my eye __ on the gold-en stair, And I'll keep on go-ing till I get there,

For it does-n't make sense just to sit and wait, } Keep in the mid-dle of the road.
A __ gold - en crown I __ know I'll wear, } Keep in the mid-dle of the road.

Refrain

Then, chil-dren, keep in the mid-dle of the road; Then, chil-dren, keep in the

mid - dle of the road; Don't you look to the right, don't you

look to the left, But keep in the mid - dle of the road.

Bracketed passages are all the same.

5

Clap this rhythm pattern:

Syncopated rhythm

1-2-2 G-8 A-12

There's Work to be Done

Words and Music by Richard C. Berg

Key: C IN CALYPSO RHYTHM

Starts:
C-1-Do

1. Hur - ry, hur - ry, hur - ry, hur - ry, come on the run;
2. Get a - long, you sleep - y - head, and come on the run;

Hur - ry, hur - ry, hur - ry, hur - ry, day is be - gun;
Must you be so slow and la - zy? Day is be - gun.

Come a - long and hur - ry now, there's work to be done;
If you do not fin - ish with the work to be done,

When you have fin - ished there'll be time for fun.
You can't go out and play and have some fun.

Accompaniment L—left hand R—right hand

Play this on the claves
for measures 1-7.

Play this on the bongo drums
and maracas for measures 1-7.

Play this for the
last measure.

Companion song
This song can be sung together with "No Need to Hurry," on the next page.
The girls may sing this song, and the boys may sing the other one.

Stress the desirability of good musical quality when singing combined songs.

6

Clap this rhythm pattern:

How many times do you find this syncopated rhythm pattern in the song?

1-2-2   G-9   A-13

● No Need to Hurry

Words and Music by Richard C. Berg

Children may be familiar with Harry Belafonte
and his calypso singing.

Key: C   IN CALYPSO RHYTHM

Starts: 1. All right, I come now; all right, I come; No need to hur-ry, no need to run.
E-3-Mi 2. Don't be so nois-y, my lit-tle one, You'll wake the town be-fore you are done.

It is too ear-ly, where is the sun? I am so tired that I can-not run.
If I should work hard out in the sun, I'll be so tired that I'll have no fun.

Similar or nearly similar phrases make this song easy to learn.

G-9   A-17

Red River Valley

American Folk Song

Interpretation
Part-singing

Key: G   SMOOTHLY, RATHER SLOWLY

Starts: 1. From this val-ley they say you are go-ing,— We will miss your bright eyes and sweet smile,—
D-5-So 2. Come and sit by my side if you love me,— Do not has-ten to bid me a-dieu,—

For they say you are tak-ing the sun-shine— That— bright-ens our path-way a while.
But re-mem-ber the Red Riv-er Val-ley,— And the girl that has loved you so true.

3. Won't you think of the valley you're leaving?
Oh, how lonely, how sad it will be!
Oh, think of the fond heart you're breaking
And the grief you are causing to me!

4. From this valley they say you are going;
When you go, may your darling go too?
Would you leave her behind, unprotected,
When she loves no one else but you?

Guitar accompaniment would be suitable for this song.
Encourage children to work for excellence of singing quality.

Hiking Song

IN MARCHING RHYTHM

Adapted Words   Old English Tune

Key: C

(A) Descant

We hike a - long,   long,   long, So keep mov- ing a- long;

Melody

A - hik- ing we go on a   long, wind-ing trail, So keep on mov-ing a- long;

Starts:
G-5-
So

(A)

We hike a - long,   long,   long, So keep mov - ing a - long.

We'll soon reach the end of a long, long ___ trail, So keep on mov - ing a - long.

(B)

Look   up, not down, wear a   smile, not a   frown, Raise your voice in a hap - py song.

Look   up, not down, wear a   smile, not a   frown, Raise your voice in a hap - py song.

(A)

We hike a - long,   long,   long, So keep mov - ing a - long.

A - hik - ing we go on a   long, wind - ing trail, So keep on mov - ing a - long.

[The form of this song is AABA: Phrases **1, 2,** and **4** are similar and Phrase **3** is different from the others.

8

Clap this rhythm:

Notice the way in which this rhythm pattern is repeated throughout the song; the repetition helps to provide rhythmic unity.

3-2-2   G-10   A-16

Harvest Ball

Key: C

Adapted Words   Polish Tune

Starts:
C-1-Do

1. Said the farm-er, said the farm-er, "Come and join in the fun,
2. So the folks came on the dou-ble, Yes, they came on the run,

Now that har-vest time is o - ver And our work __ is all done."
Did - n't want to miss a min - ute,'Cause the par - ty had be - gun.

3. Oh, the music that was playing
   Was the prettiest tune;
   And it sounded all the better
   'Neath the bright and shiny moon.

4. Work's a hard thing, yes, a hard thing,
   But we don't mind at all,
   'Cause we celebrate together
   At the annual Harvest Ball.

This song can be sung at sight.

9

Keep America Free and Strong

Expressive singing
Two-part development

Words and Music by Richard C. Berg

Key: F

WITH SPIRIT

mf Descant

Our coun-try was found-ed   on   jus-tice and free-dom

f Melody

Starts:
C-5-So

By   men __ who would strive a-gainst op-pres-sion and wrong.

di   *do*

With   cour-age and   vi-sion, they made their de-ci-sion

To   fight __ for the right to build a   coun-try free and strong.

di   *do*

Boys who play drums in band could accompany this song.

10

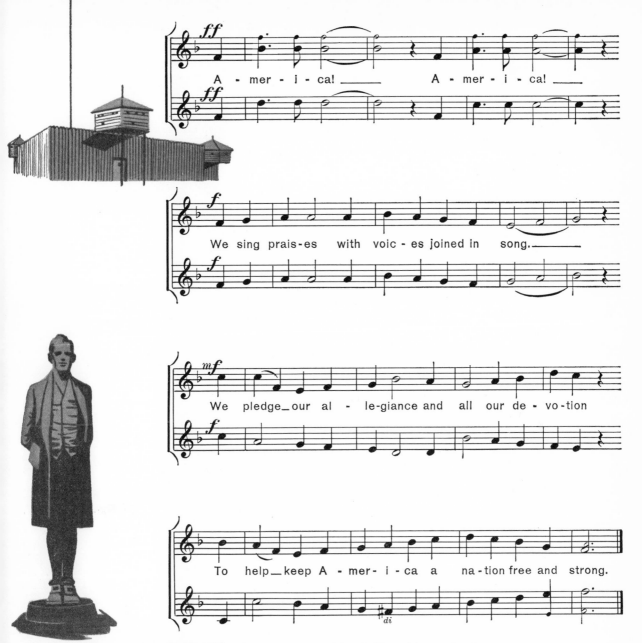

A - mer - i - ca! _____ A - mer - i - ca! _____

We sing prais-es with voic - es joined in song. _____

We pledge _ our al - le-giance and all our de - vo-tion

To help _ keep A - mer - i - ca a na -tion free and strong.

Call children's attention to skips followed by scalewise
passages in melody portion of song.

11

1-3-1   G-10   A-22

A Merry Life

Key: E♭

Words and Music by Luigi Denza

Expressive singing
Two-part development

LIVELY

mf

B♭-5-So

1. Some think — the world is made for fun and frol-ic,—
2. Ah, me! — 'tis strange that some should take to sigh-ing,—

And so do I! — And so do I! —
And like it well! — And like it well! —

Some think — it well to be all mel-an-chol-ic,—
For me, — I have not thought it worth the try-ing,—

To pine and sigh, — To pine and sigh. —
So can-not tell, — So can-not tell. —

But I, — I love to spend my time in sing-ing —
With laugh — and dance and song the day soon pass-es,—

Some joy-ous song, — Some joy-ous song; —
Full soon is gone, — Full soon is gone; —

12

To set ___ the air with mu-sic brave-ly ring-ing ___
For mirth ___ was made for joy-ous lads and las-ses ___

Is far from wrong, ___ Is far from wrong! ___
To call their own, ___ To call their own! ___

Refrain
f
Hark - en! Hark - en! Mu-sic sounds a-far! ___

Hark - en! Hark - en! Mu-sic sounds a - far!

mp
Fu - ni - cu - li, fu - ni - cu - la,

fu - ni - cu - li, fu - ni - cu - la!

f
Joy is ev-'ry-where, Fu-ni-cu-li, fu-ni-cu-la!

The expression marks used in this song are explained in the Glossary at the back of the book.

THE MAJOR SCALE

One of the scales most frequently used in music is the major scale.

C MAJOR SCALE

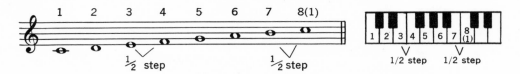

All of the intervals except those from 3 to 4 and 7 to 8 are whole steps.

As you sing and play this major scale, notice that 3 and 4, and 7 and 8 sound closer together than the other intervals.

KEY OF C MAJOR

Divide the class into 3 groups, letting each group sing one note of the chord.

Practice sustaining the chord so they actually <u>hear</u> all the parts of it before moving to the next chord.

Such practice is excellent training for 3-part singing.

The V_7 chord is purposely incomplete as shown above, so that the three chords can be sung in three parts.

The complete V_7 (G_7) chord is:

G-10   A-26
Down by the River
Folk Song of the West Indies

Key: C
IN CALYPSO RHYTHM
Reading Song

Play this accompaniment on the bongo drums:

Desk tops also make good drums.

1. Down by the riv-er Ma-ma wash-es my shirt,
2. Down by the riv-er there's a good fish-ing hole

G-5-So

She likes to use a stone to knock out the dirt.
Down by the riv-er cut a big bam-boo pole.

The riv-er is shal-low, the kids jump a-bout,
When Pa-pa gets time off so he can be free;

And when it's time for sup-per, Ma-ma has to pull them out.
He comes down by the riv-er 'cause he likes to fish with me.

Refrain

Don't go 'way, don't go 'way, Mis-ter Riv-er,

Can't you stop and play, as you trav-el out to sea?

Emphasize the importance of rhythm in the reading of this song.

15

A Capital Ship

Key: C

Words and Music by Charles E. Carryl

LIVELY
_mf_

G-5-So

1. A cap-i-tal ship for an o-cean trip Was the Wal-lop-ing__ Win-dow Blind;
2. The boat-swain's mate was__ ver-y se-date Yet__ fond__ of a-muse-ment, too;

No__ gale that blew dis-mayed her crew, Or__ trou-bled the cap-tain's mind.
And he played hop-scotch with the star-board watch While the cap-tain tick-led the crew.

The__ man__ at the wheel was taught to feel Con-tempt__ for the wild-est blow-ow-ow,
And the gun-ner we__ had was ap-par-ent-ly mad For he sat__ on the aft-er ra-a-ail,

And it of-ten ap-peared, when the wea-ther had cleared, That he'd been in his bunk be-low.
And__ fired__ sa-lutes with the cap-tain's boots, In the teeth of the rag-ing gale.

16 The frequent use of the tie is explained in the Guide.

Refrain

G7 C | C | F | C

Then blow, ye winds, heigh - ho! A - rov - ing I will go!

G7 C | F C | F | G7

I'll stay no more on Eng-land's shore, So let the mu-sic play-ay-ay!

C | C | F | C

I'm off for the morn-ing train! I'll cross the rag-ing main!

G7 C | F C | F *ritard.* G7 | C

I'm off to my love with a box-ing glove, Ten thou-sand miles a - way

[The small notes are to be sung if three-part harmony is desired.]

3. The captain sat on the commodore's hat,   But the cook was new and burned the stew
    And dined in a royal way,   And other food he served the crew-ew-ew,
    On roasted pigs and pickled figs   And he gave them tons of soggy buns
    And apple pie each day.   That tasted just like glue.

The Parrot
Key: C

Independent part-singing
Enunciation

Venezuelan Game Song

Latin American rhythms lend themselves to accompaniment with instruments.
Children might devise their own "orchestration."

Why all the chat-ter? What is the mat-ter?

Qua qua! Qua qua qua qua qua qua! Qua qua qua qua qua!

Upper Staff 2. When a parrot pays attention To a lady we could mention,
Polly sheds her feathers olden For some new ones green and golden.

3. When two parrots live together, Dining is for them a pleasure;
Without knife or fork they're skillful, All they do is take a bill full.

Lower Staff 2. When a parrot pays attention To a lady we could mention,
Polly sheds her feathers, olden, golden.

3. When two parrots live together, Dining is for them a pleasure;
Without knife or fork they're skillful, bill full.

Good-by, Old Paint
G-12   A-33

Cowboy Song

Key: C
SMOOTHLY

Sustained tones emphasize necessity
of good singing quality.

1-3. Good - by, old Paint, I'm a - leav-ing Chey-enne,

A-6-La

1. My foot in the stir-rup, my po - ny won't stand;
2. I'm rid-ing old Paint and a - lead-ing old Fan;
3. Go hitch up your hors-es and give them some hay,

I'm a - leav-ing Chey-enne and I'm off to Mon - tan'.
Good - by, lit - tle An - nie, I'm off to Mon - tan'.
And seat your-self by me as long as you stay.

1-3. Good - by, old Paint, I'm a - leav-ing Chey - enne.

Paper cups might be used to imitate sound of horses' hooves.

[Clap this rhythm:]

Call attention to the meter signature, 3/8

G-12   A-34

Buy a Tamale

Adapted Words   Mexican Folk Tune

Key: C
ENTHUSIASTICALLY   Two-part singing
                          Chromatics

E-3-Mi
C-1-Do

1-2. Buy a ta - ma - le! Buy a ta - ma - le!

1. Step up and get one, they're read - y to eat.
2. Please, se - ño - ri - ta, se - ño - ra, se - ñor!

1-2. Buy a ta - ma - le! Buy a ta - ma - le!

1. Hot and so tast - y, you're in for a treat.
2. When you have tried them you'll come back for more.

1-2. Buy a ta - ma - le! Buy a ta - ma - le!

Steamed to a gold - en brown; ___ Eat a ta - ma - le,

red-hot and good, The fin - est ta - ma - les in town! ___

For a detailed explanation of chromatics, see Guide.

20

For an accompaniment, play this rhythm on wood blocks: ♩♪ ♩ ♩♪ ♩ ♩♪ ♩ ♩♪ ♩ ‖

3-2-3 [The descant in this song consists of the descending and ascending C major scale.]

● Hayride   G-12   A-35   Words and Music by Richard C. Berg
Key: C

RHYTHMICALLY

C Descant   F   C   F   C   G7   C

C-1-Do We are go - ing for a hay - ride,

Melody

E-3-Mi Come on a-long, we're go-ing for a hay-ride, Fill up the wag-on with a load of hay;

C   F   C   F   C   G7   C

Au - tumn days are on their way.—

Come on a-long, we're go-ing for a hay-ride, Frost's on the pump-kin, autumn's on its way.

G7   C   G7   C   G7   C   F   G7

We'll go jog - ging far a - way,—

Gid-dy up, Dob-bin, oh, here we go a-jog-ging O-ver the hills and far a-way.

C   F   C   F   C   G7   C

Sing and have a hap - py day.—

Come on a-long, we're go-ing for a hay-ride; Sing and be mer-ry, have a hap-py day.

For suggested performance ideas, consult Guide.

21

Santa Lucia

Encourage a legato (flowing) style for this melody.   Italian Folk Song

Key: C FLOWINGLY

G-5-So   Now 'neath the   sil-ver moon   o-cean   is   glow-ing,
E-3-Mi   Here balm-y   breez-es blow,   pure joys   in-vite ___ us,

O'er the   calm   bil-   low   soft wind   is   blow-ing;
And   as   we   gen-tly row,   all things de-   light   us.

Refrain

Hark how the   sail-or's cry   joy-ous-ly   ech-oes nigh;

San-ta   Lu-ci-   a,   San-ta   Lu-ci-a!   San-ta   Lu-ci-a!

Chromatics: F#   F♮

Can you find any other chromatics in this song?
The class should sing the chromatic passages correctly before singing the entire song.

1.   2.   These signs indicate first and second endings.

When you have sung through the first ending, go back and repeat from the preceding double bar (‖:); this time, skip the first ending and sing the second ending.

22

KEY OF F MAJOR

1	2	3	4	5	6	7	8(1)
F	G	A	B♭	C	D	E	F
do	re	mi	fa	so	la	ti	do

See page 14.

These chords may be sung by the class or played on autoharp. Try playing them on resonator bells, using 5 children — one for each tone.

Clap this rhythm:

Bells in the Steeple

Three-part Round by Diana Christy

Key: F

MODERATELY

Hear the bells in the stee-ple ring, Hear the or-gan play and the choir — sing; Hear the bells in the stee-ple — ring.

Using the melody bells, play this measure twice as an introduction; then continue to play it throughout the song as an accompaniment.

Autoharp chords will be F and C7.

This tune might also be sung by a few children.

23

Clap this pattern or play it on your rhythm instruments as an accompaniment throughout the song:

G-13   A-39

Cumberland Gap Adapted Words   American Folk Tune

Key: F   LIVELY

C-5-So 1. O, Cum-ber-land Gap is a ver-y fine place,
2. Old Dan-iel Boone stood on a rock,
3. Then Dan-iel with the crit-ter fought,

With lots of wa-ter for to wash your face,—
And load-ed up his old flint-lock,—
The bear cried, "Ouch,— I've just been shot!"—

La-dies there in silk and lace,
Looked a bear right in the face,
Dan-iel looked him in the face,

In Cum-ber-land Gap, a right fine place!
In Cum-ber-land Gap, a right fine place!
Said, "Cum-ber-land Gap's a right fine place!"

1-3. Hi-did-dle dum dum, did-dle dum dee!

The mark // tells you to take a quick breath.

Since this tune has a square dance "flavor" the class may be interested in making up its own dance.

24

RHYTHM CHALLENGE

To play in a band or orchestra, or to sing in a chorus, it is important to be able to read rhythmic notation quickly and accurately. Here are some rhythmic patterns commonly used in the music you play and sing. How well can you read them? Start at a moderate speed, and then challenge yourself to see how well you can read these rhythms at quicker tempos.

For a class game, all stand and clap the rhythms together. When a player makes an error, he sits down. The last player on his feet is the winner.

After everyone in the class has learned the rhythms in 1 and 2, try them together, letting part of the class clap the first rhythm while the rest claps the second.

After everyone in the class has learned the rhythms in 3 and 4, try them together as you did with 1 and 2.

After everyone in the class has learned the rhythms in 5 and 6, try them together as you did with 1 and 2.

Home on the Range

Cowboy Song

Key: F

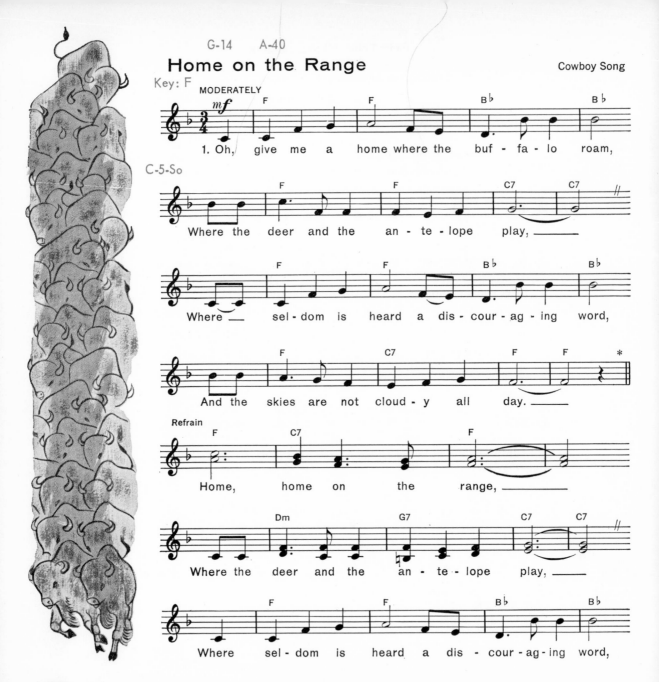

MODERATELY

mf

1. Oh, give me a home where the buf - fa - lo roam,

C-5-So

Where the deer and the an - te - lope play, ____

Where ____ sel - dom is heard a dis - cour - ag - ing word,

And the skies are not cloud - y all day. ____

Refrain

Home, home on the range, ____

Where the deer and the an - te - lope play, ____

Where sel - dom is heard a dis - cour - ag - ing word,

And the skies are not cloud-y all day. _____

[If you sing this song with "My Home's in Montana," sing only to*. *]

2. How often at night when the heavens are bright
With the lights from the glittering stars,
Have I stood there amazed and asked as I gazed,
If their glory exceeds that of ours.

My Home's in Montana

Cowboy Song

Key: F   MODERATELY

1. My home's in Mon-tan-a, I wear a ban-dan-na,
2. When val-leys are dust-y, my po-ny is trust-y,
3. When far from the ranch-es, I chop the pine branch-es

My spurs are of sil-ver, my po-ny is gray;
He lopes through the bliz-zard, the snow in his ears;
To heap on my camp-fire as day-light grows pale;

When rid-ing the rang-es my luck nev-er chang-es,
The cat-tle may scat-ter, but what does it mat-ter?
When I have par-tak-en of beans and of ba-con,

With foot in the stir-rup, I'll gal-lop a-way.
My rope is a hal-ter for pig-head-ed steers.
I whis-tle a mer-ry old song of the trail.

[Try singing this song with "Home on the Range." When two separate tunes
are sung together we call the combination "counterpoint."]

Bless Us, Lord

Words and Music by Margaret Hurley

Key: F

REVERENTLY

Reading song

mf

1-2. Oh, bless us, Lord, to Thee we ___ pray; ___

C-5-So   *mf*

C-5-So

1. Bless these, Thy gifts, most gra-cious God, from Whom all good-ness springs; ___
2. We thank Thee for the har-vest time, we thank Thee for Thy love; ___

Observation of expression marks leads to better musical interpretation.

Oh, keep us safe through ev-'ry day.

Make pure our hearts and feed our souls with good and ho-ly things.
Thy boun-teous gifts sur-round us new, we praise Thee, Lord a-bove.

Children will need little help with this song if they observe
the stepwise pattern of the melody.

Autumn Is Here

Words and Music by Frederica Reynolds

Key: F

RHYTHMICALLY

Part-singing
Chromatics

mf   F   Melody
A-3-Mi

C7   C7   F

1-2. Sum-mer's o-ver and the fall is here, But I don't mind, it's a good time of year;

mp   Harmony

F-1-Do

28

Call attention to places where melody goes below the harmony so the
children will be prepared for them.

The natural (♮) followed by the flat (b) is explained in the Guide.

Clap and chant this rhythm:

Fresh po-ta-toes, ripe to-ma-toes

3-3-1   G-15   A-46

● At the Market Place (Three-part Round)

Words and Music by Robert Edwards

Key: F

IN CALYPSO RHYTHM

1

C-5-So   Fresh po-ta-toes, ripe to-ma-toes, Nic-est you've ev-er seen!

2

Cau-li-flow-er picked this hour,— Let-tuce so crisp and green!

3

Come and take a look a-round, Best place to buy in town!

You may play this rhythm accompaniment on the bongo drums, or you may experiment and play it on the top of your desk.

L L   L L
R R   R R

The rhythm patterns of parts 1 and 2 are exactly the same.

This song is real fun to sing and lends itself to additional original verses.

FRUITS

HOME—GROWN VEGETABLES

30

This meter is sung with three beats to a measure:

Clap and chant this rhythm before singing.

Autoharp chords are F and C₇.

G-15   A-46

Down in the Valley

American Folk Song

Key: F

SMOOTHLY, THREE BEATS TO A MEASURE

A-3-Mi
C-5-So

1. Down in the val - ley, the val - ley so low,
2. Ros - es love sun - shine, __ vi' - lets love dew, __
3. Build me a cas - tle __ for - ty feet high, __

Hang your head o - ver, hear the wind blow; __
An - gels in heav - en know I love you; __
So I can see him as he rides by; __

Hear the wind blow, dear, hear the wind blow; __
Know I love you, dear, know I love you, __
As he rides by, dear, as he rides by, __

Hang your head o - ver, hear the wind blow. __
An - gels in heav - en know I love you. __
So I can see him as he rides by. __

Using two chords, F and C₇, someone may accompany this song on autoharp. Encourage the class to change chords by ear.

Friendship Song

Key: F

WITH SPIRIT

Adapted Words   Danish Student Song

Excellent helps for teaching found in Guide.

Fine

Here's to   you, friend! And to you, friend! Here's to friends so good and   true!

F-1-Do

Hur - rah, hur-rah, hur - rah, hur-rah, hur-rah, Hur - rah, hur-rah, hur - rah, hur-rah, hur-rah,

Here's to   you, friend! And to   you, friend! To your health and hap-pi-ness.

Note the change of meter at this point.

Bra - vo,   bra - vo,   bra - vo, bra - vis - si - mo!   Bra - vo,

bra - vo,   bra - vis - si -   mo!   Bra - vo, bra - vis - si - mo,

D.C. al Fine

bra - vo, bra - vis - si - mo,   Bra - vo,   bra - vo, bra - vis - si - mo!

All Through the Night

Welsh Folk Song

This makes a fine program number.

Children know the melody of this song from earlier grades. Adding parts is easier when the class discovers the form: AABA.

One More River

American Folk Song

Key: F

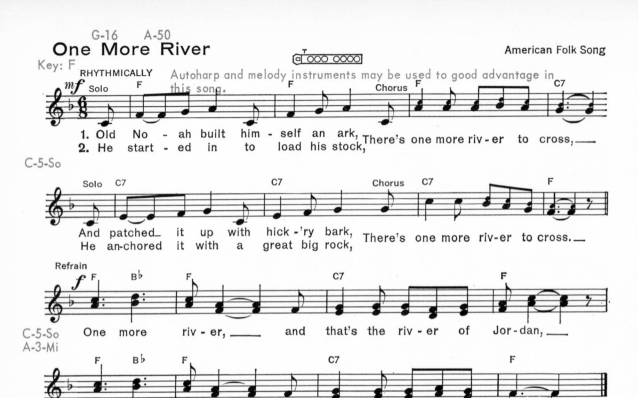

RHYTHMICALLY

Autoharp and melody instruments may be used to good advantage in this song.

mf Solo   F   F   Chorus   F   C7

1. Old No - ah built him - self an ark, There's one more riv - er to cross, ___
2. He start - ed in to load his stock,

C-5-So

Solo   C7   C7   Chorus   C7   F

And patched it up with hick -'ry bark, There's one more riv - er to cross. ___
He an-chored it with a great big rock,

Refrain

f   F   B♭   F   C7   F

C-5-So   One more riv - er, ___ and that's the riv - er of Jor - dan, ___
A-3-Mi

F   B♭   F   C7   F

One more riv - er, ___ There's one more riv - er to cross. ___

3. The animals entered one by one, etc.,
   The elephant chewed a toasted bun, etc.

4. The animals entered two by two, etc.,
   The tiger and the kangaroo, etc.

5. The animals entered three by three, etc.,
   The bear, the flea, the bumble bee, etc.

6. The animals entered four by four, etc.,
   The goat knocked down the galley door, etc.

7. The animals entered five by five, etc.,
   Said Noah, "Bring them back alive," etc.

8. The animals entered six by six, etc.,
   The monkey started playing tricks, etc.

9. The animals entered sev'n by sev'n, etc.,
   The clock began to strike elev'n, etc.

10. The animals entered eight by eight, etc.,
    The lion growled, "It's getting late," etc.

11. The animals entered nine by nine, etc.,
    And Noah said, "We're doing fine," etc.

12. The animals entered ten by ten, etc.,
    The thunder roared, the rain began, etc.

Children should be made aware that in each verse melody, words and rhythm must fit together.

Clap this rhythm: **4/4**

G-16   A-52

There's a Little Wheel

Key: F

Children could select a different instrument for each verse.

Spiritual

LIVELY
mp

F-1-Do
1. There's a lit-tle wheel a-turn-ing in my heart,—
2. There's a lit-tle song a-sing-ing in my heart,—
3. Oh, I feel so ver-y hap-py in my heart,—

There's a lit-tle wheel a-turn-ing in my heart,
There's a lit-tle song a-sing-ing in my heart,
Oh, I feel so ver-y hap-py in my heart,

1-3. In my heart,——— in my heart,———

There's a lit-tle wheel a-turn-ing in my heart.
There's a lit-tle song a-sing-ing in my heart.
Oh, I feel so ver-y hap-py in my heart.

Songs are always easier to sing when similarities in melody or rhythm are pointed out, as in phrases 1, 2, and 4.

35

MINER SCALES

First 5 tones of the C Major scale:

First 5 tones of the C minor scale:

G-17   A-53   Combined modes

Erie Canal
MODERATELY
Key: D minor

Note this rhythm pattern (♩ ♩) which appears repeatedly.

American Folk Song

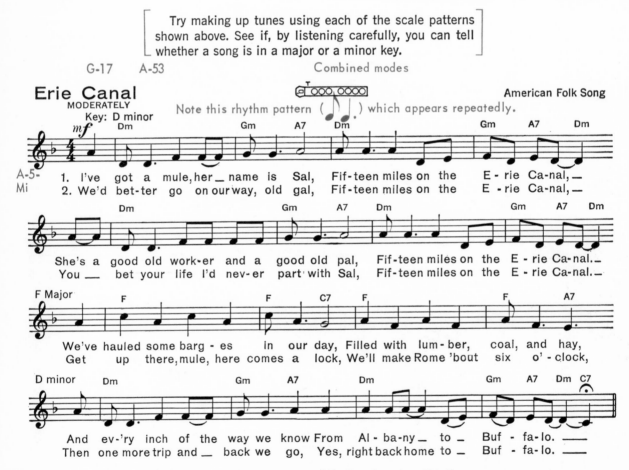

A-5-
Mi

1. I've got a mule, her name is Sal, Fif-teen miles on the E - rie Ca-nal,—
2. We'd bet-ter go on our way, old gal, Fif-teen miles on the E - rie Ca-nal,—

She's a good old work-er and a good old pal, Fif-teen miles on the E - rie Ca-nal.—
You — bet your life I'd nev-er part with Sal, Fif-teen miles on the E - rie Ca-nal.—

We've hauled some barg - es in our day, Filled with lum - ber, coal, and hay,
Get up there, mule, here comes a lock, We'll make Rome 'bout six o' - clock,

And ev-'ry inch of the way we know From Al - ba-ny— to — Buf - fa-lo. ——
Then one more trip and — back we go, Yes, right back home to — Buf - fa-lo. ——

Think of the minor scale as starting on "la" rather than "do".

Refrain F Major

Low bridge! Ev-'ry-bod-y down! Low bridge, for we're go-ing thro' a town!

Low_ bridge!_ Ev-'ry-bod-y down!_ Low_bridge, for we're go-ing thro' a town!

And you'll al-ways know your neigh-bor, you'll al-ways know your pal

And you'll al-ways know your neigh-bor, you'll al-ways know your pal

If you've ev-er nav-i-gat-ed on the E-rie Ca-nal. _

If you've ev-er nav-i-gat-ed on the E-rie Ca-nal. _

37

This 5-tone scale is called the pentatonic scale. Play these notes, which are the tones on which this song is built. Notice that E and Bb are not used.

keynote

Pentatonic scale may also be played on the black keys of the piano.

G-17   A-56

Wayfaring Stranger

Spiritual

MODERATELY SLOW

Key: D minor

Note meter signature

D-1-La

I'm just a poor way-far-ing stran-ger A-trav-'ling thro' this world of woe,

But there's no sick-ness, toil, nor dan-ger In that bright world to which I go;

I'm go-ing there to see my fa-ther, I'm go-ing there no more to roam,
(mother)
(brother)

ritard.

I'm just a-go-ing o-ver Jor-dan, I'm just a-go-ing o-ver home.

Try making up tunes on the pentatonic scale. It's easy.

38

Group 1

4/4 Here comes the el - e - phant,

Here comes the el - e - phant,

Here comes the el - e - phant,

Here he comes now.

Group 2 (start on Group 1 chant when Group 1 completes its first four lines)

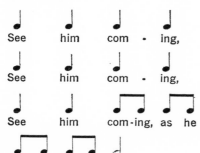

See him com - ing,

See him com - ing,

See him com-ing, as he

Swings his heav - y trunk.

Group 3 (start on Group 1 chant when Group 2 completes the first four lines of the chant)

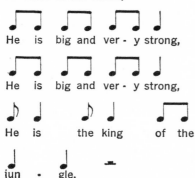

He is big and ver - y strong,

He is big and ver - y strong,

He is the king of the

jun - gle.

RHYTHM ROUND

Divide the class into three groups. Each group chants the entire selection in the manner of a round. Chant rhythmically, at moderate speed.

For variation, clap or play this rhythm round. Try making up chants similar to this one, using your own words and ideas. You might also try making up a melody to this chant.

Why not combine some of these rhythms with the tones of the pentatonic scale and see what happens?

39

4. At last they reached an island shore,
   An island they called San Salvador,
   In fourteen hundred ninety-two,
   In fourteen hundred ninety-two!
   Columbus and his little band
   Had led the way to our native land!

5. Then hail Columbus! Let his name
   Be written large in the hall of fame.
   Sing hey, sing ho, and hey-i-o,
   Sing hey, sing ho, and hey-i-o!
   Hail men on land, on sea, in air
   Who, like Columbus, will do and dare.

G-17   A-58

Singin' Johnny

Key: E♭

This might be a good time to review chanteys learned in other grades.

Sailor Chantey

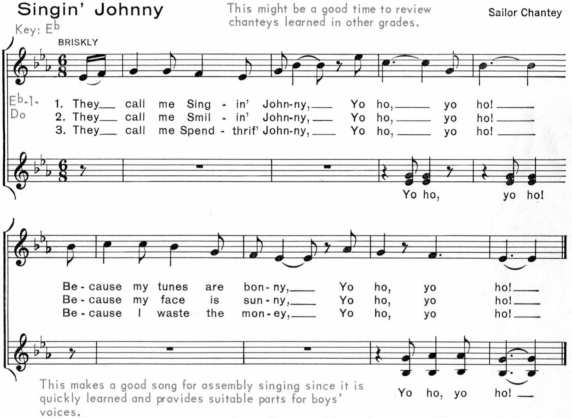

1. They___ call me Sing - in' John-ny,___ Yo ho,___ yo ho! ___
2. They___ call me Smil - in' John-ny,___ Yo ho,___ yo ho! ___
3. They___ call me Spend - thrif' John-ny,___ Yo ho,___ yo ho! ___

Yo ho,   yo ho!

Be - cause my tunes are bon - ny,___ Yo ho, yo ho!___
Be - cause my face is sun - ny,___ Yo ho, yo ho!___
Be - cause I waste the mon - ey,___ Yo ho, yo ho!___

Yo ho, yo ho! ___

This makes a good song for assembly singing since it is quickly learned and provides suitable parts for boys' voices.

Chanteys are work songs that sailors used to make up on sailing vessels many years ago. They were usually sung in rhythm with some particular job. A leader (chanteyman) and the crew took turns singing in solo and chorus fashion.

This is a "long haul chantey." The sailors hauled the ropes twice during each chorus, pulling strongly on the accented beats in swinging rhythm. The chanteyman often made up new verses for the solo parts.

Clap or play an accompaniment:

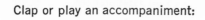

4-1-2   G-18   A-59

Mountain Climbers

Adapted Words   Mexican Folk Tune

SLOWLY AND RHYTHMICALLY
Key: D minor.

Help the class to select suitable rhythm
instruments to accompany this song.

A-5-
Mi

1. The moun-tain sum-mit _____ is high a - bove them, _____
2. The val - ley fer - tile _____ lies far be - low them, _____
3. Though weak and wea - ry, _____ so ver - y wea - ry, _____

As they go climb - ing high - er, climb - ing up ___ in - to the sky. ___
As they go climb - ing high - er, climb - ing up ___ in - to the sky. ___
They keep on climb - ing high - er, climb - ing up ___ in - to the sky. ___

The winds are blow - ing, _____ it's cold and snow - ing, _____
The moun - tain climb - ers _____ ig - nore all dan - ger, _____
Some-times they stum - ble, _____ they of - ten stum - ble, _____

But they go climb - ing high-er, climb-ing up ___ in - to the sky. ___
To reach the sum - mit is to them a case ___ of do or die. ___
But then at last they're on the moun-tain top and reach the sky. ___

After the class has learned the song they may enjoy listening
to the lovely recording of it.

G-18   A-60

Thanksgiving

Program number

Adapted Words   Welsh Hymn Tune

Key: A♭

MODERATELY

mp Harmony

1. Let us give our thanks to-day, For all our bless-ings let us pray;
2. God is good and God is great, He guides our coun-try's des-ti-ny and fate;

mf Melody

mf Melody

There in Plym-outh long a-go, Aft-er the hard-ships, ice, and snow,
For our na-tion, strong and free, We give our thanks for lib-er-ty,

mp Harmony

mp Harmony

ritard.

Pil-grim fa-thers to the Lord did pray And gave Him thanks on that first Thanks-giv-ing Day.
Let us with a joy-ful heart now pray, And give our thanks for that first Thanks-giv-ing Day.

mf Melody

Notice that the melody shifts from one part to the other.
When your part carries the harmony, sing softly, so that the
melody can be plainly heard.

This song and the one on p. 44 make two excellent program songs. Both are
effective without being too difficult.

43

G-18   A-62

Song of Thanksgiving

Anonymous Words   Flemish Tune

MODERATELY

Key: G

Encourage children to read phrasewise instead of note by note.

mf

G-1-Do

A
1. Give thanks for the corn and the wheat that are reaped,
2. Give thanks for the homes that with kind-ness are blessed,

(optional)

A
For la-bor well done and for barns that are heaped,
For sea-sons of plen-ty and well-de-served rest,

B
For the sun and the rain and the sweet hon-ey-comb,
For our coun-try, our own land, that ev-er will be

B₁
For the rose and the song and the har-vest brought home.
The __ Home of the Brave and the Land of the Free.

The form of this song is A A B B₁: the first two phrases are alike, and the last two are almost alike. How do the last two phrases differ from each other?

44

See page 14.

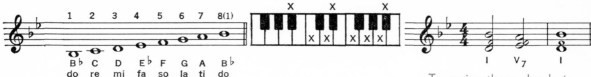

Try using these chords in the new key as was done on p. 23.

G-18   A-64

Great-Grandad

Key: Bb

On the autoharp you would need C and G₇ chords.

Adapted American Frontier Song

JOVIALLY

Bb-1-Do 1. Great - gran - dad, when the land was young, Barred his door with a wag-on tongue,

And the times were rough as a hoot owl's screech, So he kept his shot-gun with-in his reach.

2. He was tough, and he could be grim,
   Danger was nothing new to him,
   For he ate corn pone fried in bacon fat;
   It's a fact he ate nothing more than that.

3. Twenty-one sons, not a-one was bad,
   Always minded their great-grandad;
   'Cause if they'd been bad he'd have been right glad
   Just to tan their hides with a hick'ry gad.

4. He had sons, twenty-one, it's true,
   Tall and strong on the bacon grew;
   And they hunted game in their coonskin hats,
   And they slept all night with the dogs and cats.

5. They grew strong in heart and hand,
   Kind of stock that has built this land;
   For they learned to take and they learned to give,
   Great-grandad taught them the way to live.

45

Sing this song with "We'll Dance to the Fiddler" on the opposite page.
When sung together, the melodies produce contrapuntal music.

G-19   A-65

Harvest Time

Words and Music by Richard C. Berg

Key: B♭ WELL ACCENTED

The frost is on the mead-ow-land, the stars are shin-ing bright;
Now all the barns are full of hay, the si-lo's filled with corn;

F-5-So

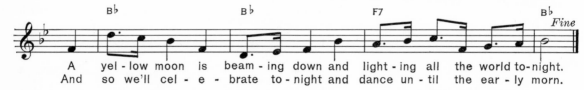

A yel-low moon is beam-ing down and light-ing all the world to-night.
And so we'll cel-e-brate to-night and dance un-til the ear-ly morn.

G Minor

Oh, it's har-vest time, har-vest time, har-vest time in fall;

D.C. al Fine

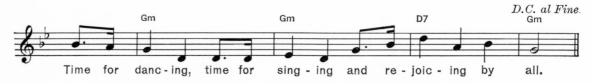

Time for danc-ing, time for sing-ing and re-joic-ing by all.

"D.C. al Fine" tells you to go back to the beginning of the song
and repeat until you come to the place marked "Fine."

46

We'll Dance to the Fiddler

Key: B♭

Words and Music by Richard C. Berg

WELL ACCENTED

mf

F-5-So   Oh, we'll dance and we'll sing, and we'll

prom - e - nade the hall To the tune of the

Fine

fid - dler at the gold - en har - vest ball.

G minor

Take your __ part - ner by the hand,

As we cir - cle a - round

D.C. al Fine

to the rhy - thm of the band.

Notice the change from major to minor. These are rousing songs and while one group sings another might be doing a dance.

so mi do mi
5 3 8(1) 3
F D Bb D

G-19   A-66

The Young Voyageur

American Folk Song

Key: Bb

WITH MOTION

Keep this very smooth by breathing only at the end of the phrase.

F-5-So

1. From the wilds of the North comes the young voy-a-geur,
2. There's a song on the lips of the young voy-a-geur,

With his stur-dy ca-noe well - lad-en with fur.
And his voice, sound-ing far, sets the for-est a-stir.

1-2. Hap-py is he, with a spir-it that's free,

There is joy in the heart of the young voy-a-geur.

Can the class decide why the form is A B C A ?

48

The Gallant Victory

G-19 A-68

Clap the rhythm:

Chantey

Key: Bb WITH VIGOR

F-5-So

1. The cap-tain had a ship in the north __ coun-try,
2. But up then spoke our Jack, he __ was the cab-in boy,

She went __ by the name of the Gal-lant Vic-to-ry.
Says he, "What will you give me if them I will de-stroy?"

Says he, "I am a-fraid of the en-e-my I see,
"Tis gold and sil-ver store and my daugh-ter dear for you,

As she sails up-on the Low-lands, Low-lands, Low-lands,
If you sink them in the Low-lands, Low-lands, Low-lands,

As she sails up-on the Low-lands low."
If you sink them in the Low-lands low."

3. Then Jack he took his ax and overboard
   went he,
   And swam very fast till he reached
   the enemy;
   He put out all her lights, and he let the
   water in,
   And he sank her in the Lowlands,
   Lowlands, Lowlands,
   And he sank her in the Lowlands low.

4. The boy, he bent his arms, swam to his
   own vessel's side,
   "Oh, shipmates, take me in, I am going
   with the tide."
   His captain pulled him out, and then on
   the decks he died,
   And they sank him in the Lowlands,
   Lowlands, Lowlands,
   And they sank him in the Lowlands low.

The children will enjoy this song if the rhythm is strictly observed.
Fit the words to the tune.

The picture illustrates the formation for this dance.

G-19   A-69

Havah Nagilah (Hora)

Adapted Words   Palestinian Folk Dance

LIVELY
Key: G minor

D-5-Mi

Out in the mead-ow mu-sic is play-ing; Peo-ple are danc-ing,

They cir-cle a-bout. Arms linked with one an-oth-er, They dance the

ho-ra   And while they dance mer-ri-ly shout: "Come, do the ho-ra now,

Watch, and we'll show you how; Step, hop, and once a-gain. See how it is done.

Hear how we keep the beat, Step-ping with live-ly feet; Come, join our cir-cle now;

Come, dance with your friends! Now that we're to-geth-er,

Ev-'ry-one steps a lit-tle fast-er, Ev-'ry-one hops a lit-tle fast-er;

See how the cir-cle's turn-ing fast-er, See how the cir-cle's turn-ing fast-er!

Now it is done; rest, ev-'ry-one. We've danced the ho-ra joy-ful-ly!

The melody is recorded in MYA, grade 8. Perhaps your class could listen and dance to it. This is not a difficult dance and children find it exciting.

Dance Formation: One big circle; hands around each other's shoulders. If the group is large, form 2 circles, one inside the other and moving in the opposite direction.

Dance Steps: Step on R foot to R; step on L foot backwards to R; step on R foot to R again; kick L foot across R and hop on R foot at the same time; step with L foot (which is in the air) to L; kick R foot across L and hop on L foot at the same time. This step takes 6 beats and is repeated throughout the dance. Start the dance slowly and gradually increase the tempo.

Go Down, Moses

G-20 A-73

Three-part harmony

Spiritual

Note rhythm.

Note meter signature.

EXPRESSIVELY
Key: G minor

D-5-Mi

1. When Is-rael was in E-gypt's land, Let my peo-ple go,

Op-pressed so hard they could not stand, Let my peo-ple go.

Refrain

Go down, Mo-ses, 'way down in E-gypt's land,—

ritard.

Tell old Pha-raoh, — Let my peo-ple go.

2. "Thus saith the Lord," bold Moses said,
   "Let my people go,
   If not I'll smite your first-born dead,
   Let my people go."

3. No more shall they in bondage toil,
   "Let my people go,
   Let them come out with Egypt's spoil,
   Let my people go."

52

La Raspa

G-20 A-76

Key: A NOT TOO FAST

Try claves on this pattern.

Maracas on this pattern

Adapted Words Mexican Folk Dance

E-5-So

1. In old Mex-i-co they sing, Tra la la la la la la,
2. Now hum it or sing it low, Tra la la la la la la,

A song bright-ens ev-'ry-thing, Tra la la la la la la.
Wher-ev-er you chance to go, Tra la la la la la la.

Refrain

So let the ma-ra-cas and cla-ves play, Click click-a-click click click.

Keep time to the tune as the danc-ers sway, Boom chick-a-boom chick chick.

Formation: A circle of partners.

Your class may have additional ideas for steps they can try with this music.

M 1: Partners face, holding hands, and jump lightly, starting with R foot: R heel forward, L heel forward; repeat.

M 2: Each dancer makes a complete turn in place to the left, starting with L foot.

M 3, 4: Same as M 1, 2 but starting with L foot and turning in place to the right, starting with R foot.

M 5, 6: Partners link R arms and turn in place.

M 7, 8: Partners link L arms and turn in opposite direction. Repeat the dance several times.

53

2-4-3   G-20   A-75

◑ Please, Señorita!

Adapted Words   Spanish Folk Tune

LILTINGLY

Key: G   Introduction (bells)

B-3-Mi

Other suitable instruments may be substituted.

Tambourine or castanets

1. Come with   me, please, Se - ño - ri - ta! _____
2. Dance with   me, please, Se - ño - ri - ta! _____

Come, pret-ty one,   fair - est   of   all! _____
Come, pret-ty one,   fair - est   of   all! _____

Come with   me, please, Se - ño - ri - ta! _____
Dance with   me, please, Se - ño - ri - ta! _____

You'll be   the Queen   of   the Ball. _____
Come, dance with   me   at   the Ball. _____

3.
Sing for me, please, Señorita,
Come, pretty one, fairest of all;
Sing for me, please, Señorita,
Sing as we dance at the Ball!

4.
Thank you, my dear Señorita,
Thanks, pretty one, fairest of all;
Thank you, my dear Señorita,
For a good time at the Ball!

With some children playing instruments and a small group
singing this makes a very effective program number.

KEY OF Eb MAJOR

(See page 14.)

Hey Diddle Dum (Round)

Words and Music by Erica Grober

Key: Eb GAILY

For best results sing this round through just once.

G-3-Mi

1. Hey did-dle dum, hey did-dle dum, hey did-dle dum dan-dy,

2. Hey did-dle dum, my sug-ar plum, sweet-er than can-dy,

3. Come and dance with me at the ball, We'll be the hand-som-est cou-ple of all.

Accompaniment for clarinet or trumpet:

Autoharp chords are F and C7.

Repeat to end of song.

This same rhythm pattern could be played on rhythm instruments.

This round is based on sequences: the little tune in the first measure is repeated over and over, sometimes higher, sometimes lower.

55

Improvise new verses based on school life.

Claves
Bongo

L R R L R L R R L R

4-1-1   G-21   A-78

I Build Me a Little House

The charm of this song lies in
the rhythm and the accents.
Help children to observe
both carefully.

Jamaican Folk Song

Key: E♭

IN CALYPSO RHYTHM

mf

B♭-5-So

1. I build me   a   lit-tle house, Oh!__ I build me a   lit-tle   house, Oh!__
2. I build me   a   lit-tle house, Oh!__ I build me a   lit-tle   house, Oh!__

I build me   a   lit-tle house, Oh!__ I build it   on the sand-y ground.
I build me   a   lit-tle house, Oh!__ I build it   on the sol-id ground.

My   house   built on   a   sand-y ground,   It will fall,   you   see.
My   house   built on   a   sol-id ground,   It will stand, you   see.

The   rain   will   wet it   up, Ha! Ha! The   sun will burn   it   up, Ha! Ha!
The   rain   can't wet it   up, Ha! Ha! The   sun can't burn   it   up, Ha! Ha!

The breeze will shake it   up, Ha! Ha! The storm come blow it down, Ha! Ha!
The breeze can't shake it   up, Ha! Ha! The storm can't blow it down, Ha! Ha!

My   house   can nev-er   be, No! No! My house too weak, you   see, No! No!
My   house   will ev-er   stand, Yes! Yes! It's built on sol-id   land, Ha! Ha!

56

G-21   A-84

Zum Gali Gali

Adapted Words   Palestinian Folk Tune

STEADILY
Key: E minor

G-3-Do

As we work we sing a — song, — We — sing it all day — long.
When we reach the end of the day, — We will dance, and sing, and be gay.

E-1-La

Zum — ga-li ga-li ga-li, Zum ga-li ga-li, Zum ga-li ga-li ga-li, Zum ga-li ga-li.

One group may sing "Zum" at the beginning of each measure, holding
a half note on E.

57

Tide of Sleep

Words by Clare Giffin   Music by Johannes Brahms

Key: E♭

MODERATELY

The melody of this song is from Brahms Waltz No. 15, which can be heard on a recording.

Tide, O flow-ing tide, Re-turn-ing dark from the deep,

G-3-Mi

From wan-d'ring wide where winds a-bide With-in the sing-ing hall of sleep,

The hid-den hall where wa-ters fall In mur-m'ring foun-tains of sleep,

Their qui-et call re-peat-ing all The rest-less cry-ing of the deep!

Your rip-pling waves so light-ly beat The peb-bly shore with run-ning feet,

The lit-tle birds are un-a-wak-ened and at rest.

The lit-tle winds are qui-et all_____ on your breast.

O flow-ing tide, O flow-ing tide, Bring me your mur-mured charm of sleep!

Most children know the Lullaby by Brahms, but they may not be so familiar with his vigorous Hungarian Dances. Much of Brahms' piano music appeals to children of this age, also, and many fine recordings are available.

G-22 A-81

Our Door Is Always Open (Round)

Adapted Words French Folk Tune

Key: Eb MODERATELY

Once the rhythm pattern is established, children should be able to read this.

Eb-1-Do

Our door is al-ways o-pen To our friends who pass this way,

We are al-ways glad to wel-come a friend When he pass-es a-long our way.

Crawdad

American Folk Song

Key: E♭
LIVELY

Notice the unusual 3-measure phrases.

E♭-1-Do 1. Stand-ing on the ice till my feet got cold, Sug-ar Babe;

Stand-ing on the ice till my feet got cold, Sug-ar Babe;

Stand-ing on the ice till my feet got cold,

Watch-ing that craw-dad go to his hole, Sug-ar Babe.

Sixth-grade children will have many ideas for rhythmic accompaniment, with hands, feet, and instruments.

2. Standing on the ice till my feet got cold, Sugar Babe, etc.,
   Watching that crawdad dig his hole, Sugar Babe.

3. Standing on the ice till my feet got hot, Sugar Babe, etc.,
   Watching that crawdad rock and trot, Sugar Babe.

4. Standing on the ice till my feet got numb, Sugar Babe, etc.,
   Watching that crawdad go and come, Sugar Babe.

A crawdad (crayfish) is a very small fresh-water lobster.

60

2-4-2   G-22   A-85

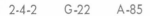 **The Alphabet**

Key: Eb

Practice clapping this pattern before singing.
The expression marks will help in the interpretation of the music.

Music by W. A. Mozart

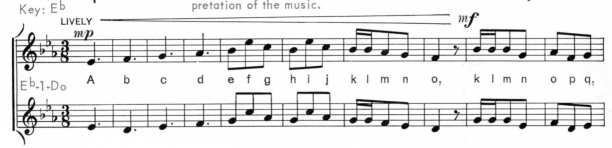

A b c d e f g h i j k l m n o, k l m n o p q,

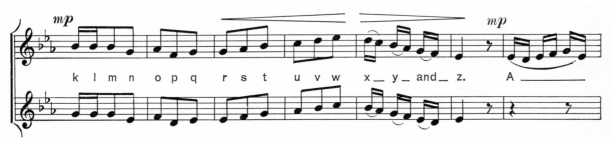

k l m n o p q r s t u_ v w x_ y_ and_ z.   A _____

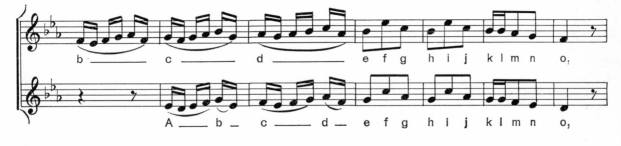

b _____ c d _____ e f g h i j k l m n o,

A ___ b_ c ___ d_ e f g h i j k l m n o,

k l m n o p q, k l m n o p q r s t u v w x_ y_ and_ z.

Your class might like to listen to "The Magic Flute" by Mozart.

Here Comes the Band (Round)

Key: E♭

English Folk Tune

Adapted Words

LIVELY

Descending scale in E♭ Major.

E♭-1-Do Here is the way that a band does play:

The clar-i-nets mel-low, doo-dle doo-dle dee-ay.

Trum-pets go ta-ta-ta-ta-ta-ta-ta-ta, hear them play;

And the trom-bones go slid-ing, too-wah,— too-way.

Bass, the bass, the sou-sa-phone,

Goes oom-pah-pah, oom-pah-pah-pah-pah poom-poom-poom.

This round has a great deal of appeal and the children will enjoy working to perfect it. Try choosing a leader for each group.

Drill, Ye Tarriers

Words by Thomas Casey   Music by Charles Connolly

HEAVILY ACCENTED
Key: C minor

The Guide contains much good help for presenting this song.

C-1-La

1. Ev -'ry morn-ing at sev-en o'-clock There's twen-ty tar-ri-ers a-
2. Our new fore-man is Dan Mc-Cann, I'll tell you sure __ he's a
3. Next time pay-day __ came a-round Jim Goff was short __ one __

work-ing at the rock, And the boss comes a-long and he
mean __ old __ man. Last __ week a __ fault-y __
buck __ he __ found. "What __ for?" says __ he, Then __

says,"Keep still and __ come down __ heav-y on the cast-iron drill."
blast went off and a mile in the air __ went __ big Jim Goff.
this re-ply, "You're docked for the time __ you were in the sky."

Refrain

And drill, ye tar-ri-ers, drill; And drill, ye tar-ri-ers, drill!

Oh! it's work all day for sug-ar in your "tay"

Down be-yond the rail-way; And drill, ye tar-ri-ers, drill!

The men who laid the rails and helped build the railroads across our country called themselves "tarriers." They often sang as they worked, in rhythm with their movements.

Clap and chant this rhythm, making the ♪ notes very short.

Men of Har - lech, on to glo - ry.

♩·· is called a double-dotted quarter note. It gets 1¾ beats in this music.

G-23   A-90

Men of Harlech

Additional helps with rhythm are found in the Guide.

Words by Thomas Oliphant   Old Welsh Tune

Key: Eb   WITH SPIRIT

Eb-1-Do

1. Hark! I hear the foe ad - vanc - ing, War - rior steeds are proud - ly pranc - ing;
2. 'Mid the fray, see dead and dy - ing, Friend and foe to - geth - er ly - ing;

Hel - mets, in the sun - beams glanc - ing, Glit - ter through the trees.
All a - round the ar - rows, fly - ing, Scat - ter sud - den death.

Men of Har - lech, lie you dream - ing? See you not their lanc - es gleam - ing,
Fright-ened steeds are wild - ly neigh - ing, Bra - zen trum-pets hoarse - ly bray - ing,

While their pen - nants, gai - ly stream - ing, Flut - ter in the breeze?
Wound - ed men for mer - cy pray - ing With their part - ing breath!

From the rocks re - bound - ing, Let the war cry, sound - ing,
See, they're in dis - or - der! Com - rades, keep close or - der!

64

Sum - mon all at Cam - bria's call, The haugh - ty___ foe___ sur - round-ing.
Ev - er they shall rue the day They ven - tured o'er___ the___ bor-der!

Men of Har - lech, on to glo - ry! See, your___ ban - ner famed in sto - ry
Now the Sax - on flees be - fore us; Vic - t'ry's___ ban - ner floats a - bove us!

Waves these burn - ing words be - fore you: "Brit - ain scorns to yield!"
Raise the loud ex - ult - ing cho - rus, "Brit - ain wins the field!"

"Cambria" is another name for Wales. "Harlech" was the name of a castle in Wales.

Drummers in your class might work out some patterns for this song.

Rock of Ages (Hanukkah Song)

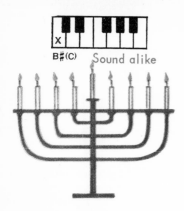

Key: E

MODERATELY

Traditional Words　Hebrew Melody

The words suggest singing this on one breath.

B♯(C)　Sound alike

E-1-Do　　1. Rock of A-ges, let our song Praise Thy sav-ing pow - er;
　　　　　　2. Kin-dling new the ho- ly lamps, Priests, ap-proved in suf - f'ring,

Thou, a - midst the rag-ing foes, Was our shel-t'ring tow - er.
Pur - i - fied the na-tion's shrine, Gave to God their of - f'ring.

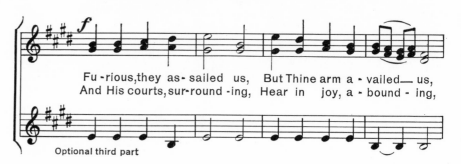

Fu - rious, they as- sailed us, But Thine arm a - vailed— us,
And His courts, sur-round -ing, Hear in   joy, a - bound - ing,

Optional third part

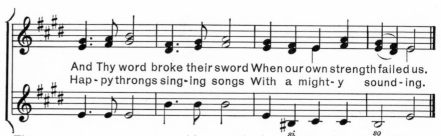

And Thy word broke their sword When our own strength failed us.
Hap - py throngs sing-ing songs With a might-y   sound - ing.

si　　*so*

This song presents no new problems in rhythm, so the class should be
encouraged to sing it with musical style.

Hanukkah (hah-noo-kah) is a festival celebrated each year to commemmorate the
victory of the Maccabees over opposing armies in Old Testament Days. By this
victory the Maccabees won independence for their people, the Judeans.

66

● Happy Holiday! (Canon)

Words and Music by Frederica Reynolds

BRIGHTLY
Key: A minor

An easy descant may be found in the Guide.

B-2-Ti Hap - py hol - i - day to you!   Hap - py hol - i - day!

Hap - py hol - i - day to you!

Hap - py hol. - i - day to you!   Hap - py hol - i - day!   Hap - py hol - i - day!

Hap - py hol - i - day!   Hap - py hol - i - day to you!   Hap - py hol - i - day!

Call attention to expression marks. The last phrase could be repeated, pp.

This song can be used for various special occasions, such as:

Happy Hanukkah to you! Happy Hanukkah!   Happy New Year, everyone! Happy, safe New Year!

Happy Easter time to you! Happy Easter time!   Happy birthday, here's to you! Happy birthday, John!

67

The First Noel

Key: D

Old English Carol

1. The first Noel the angels did say
2. They looked up and saw a star

Was to certain poor shepherds in fields as they lay,
Shining in the East beyond them far,

Help the children fit the words to the music here.

In fields where they lay keeping their sheep
And to the earth it gave great light;

On a cold winter's night that was so deep.
And so it continued both day and night.

Refrain
Descant

A violinist in your class could play this descant.

No - el, No - el, No - el, No - el! No -

Melody
No - el, No - el, No - el, No - el!

el, _____ No - el, __ No - el!

Born is the King__ of Is - ra - el!

3. And by the light of that same star,
   Three Wise Men came from country far;
   To seek for a king was their intent
   And to follow the star, wherever it went.

4. This star drew nigh to the northwest,
   O'er Bethlehem it took its rest;
   And there it did both stop and stay
   Right over the place where Jesus lay.

5. Then entered in those Wise Men three
   Full reverently upon their knee,
   And offered there, in His presence,
   Their gold and myrrh and frankincense.

6. Then let us all with one accord
   Sing praises to our heavenly Lord
   That hath made Heaven and earth of nought
   And with His blood mankind hath bought.

G-25   A-95

Merry Christmas! (Round)
Words and Music by Erica Grober

Key: E♭

WITH SPIRIT

While this is ¾ meter it has a martial air about it
which might be helped along by drummer boys.

B♭-5-So

Mer - ry Christ-mas! Mer-ry Christ-mas! And a Hap-py New Year!

Oh, we wish you! Oh, we wish you Hap - pi - ness and good cheer!

This song can be sung as a two- or three-part round.

2-3-2   G-25   A-99

◗This Wond'rous Night

Adapted Words   Old English Tune

Key: E♭ SMOOTHLY

Descant (voice, or violin or flute)

1, 3. La la la la la la la la la la, La la la la la.
2. Ah _____   Ah _____

E♭-1-Do   mp Melody

1. This won - d'rous night an awe-some sight, A Star as bright as day! __
2. Three Wise Men, bear - ing gifts for Him, Had come from far a - way; __
3. We cel - e - brate His birth-day still On ev - 'ry Christ-mas Day __

La la la la la la la la la la La la la la la la la la la.
Ah _____   Ah _____

And in His crib in Beth - le - hem, The In - fant Je - sus lay. __
They gazed with love up - on this Child Who in the man - ger lay. __
Though man - y cen - t'ries now have passed Since in the crib He lay. __

Because of the stepwise movement of this melody, it is easy to read. As is the case with many Christmas songs, the children need help with phrasing, with breathing, and with expression.

70

Notice that, in one measure, the meter changes from 3/4 to 4/4.

Count steadily:
G-25 A-96

Foom! Foom! Foom!

This is a very lively carol which calls for instrumental accompaniment. The Guide offers good suggestions.

Spanish Folk Song

RHYTHMICALLY
Key: A minor
mf

A-1-La

1. On De - cem - ber twen - ty - five, foom, foom, foom!
2. All the stars up in the sky, foom, foom, foom!

On De - cem - ber twen - ty - five, foom, foom, foom! In a
All the stars up in the sky; foom, foom, foom! As they

man - ger low - ly there was born a babe, the Ho - ly Child, Of___
twin - kle bright - ly, glit - ter light - ly, danc - ing in the sky, O'er the

Note the change of meter.

Ma - ry born a - live this cold De - cem - ber twen - ty - five, foom, foom, foom!
man - ger they do shine and light the way of all man - kind, foom, foom, foom!

71

Angels We Have Heard

Words by Bishop Chadwick   Traditional French Tune

Key: G

JOYOUSLY

mf

B-3-Mi

1. An - gels we have heard on high,   Sweet - ly sing - ing o'er the plains;
2. Shep-herds, why this ju - bi - lee?   Why your glad - some strain pro - long?
3. Come to Beth - l'hem, come and see   Him whose birth the an - gels sing;

And the moun-tains in re - ply   Ech - o still their joy - ous strains.
Say, what may the ti - dings be   Which in-spire your heav'n - ly song?
Come, a - dore on bend - ed knee   The In-fant Christ, the new - born King.

Refrain

Glo - - - - - - - - - - ri - a

Children can sing this phrase on one breath if they try — and they like to try!

in ex - cel - sis De - o,   Glo - - - - - - - - -

- - - - - - ri - a   in ex - cel - sis De - - o.

Emphasize the need for listening to each part. When children become conscious
of the overall effect they begin to see a need for blending voices.

72

Wassail Song

English Carol

Key: F

WITH SPIRIT

mf

F-1-Do

1. Here we come a - was - sail-ing   a - mong the leaves so green;___
2. We are not dai - ly   beg - gars that beg from door to door,___
3. God bless the mas - ter   of this house, God bless the mis-tress, too,___

This type of song lends itself to solo or small-group singing on the verses.

___ Here we come a - wan-der-ing   so   fair___ to   be   seen.
But we are neigh-bors' chil - dren whom you have seen be - fore.
And all the lit - tle chil - dren that round the ta - ble go.

The meter signature changes but the speed of singing stays the same.

Refrain *f*

Love and joy___ come to   you, and to   you your was-sail too,

And God bless___ you and send___ you a   Hap - py New Year,___

di

And God   send___ you   a   Hap - py New ___ Year.

di

Wassail (wos"l) means "Here's to your good health!"

73

⦿ O Come, All Ye Faithful

Key: Ab

Traditional Words   Music by John Reading

Descant *mf*

Eb-5-So

1.   O come, ye faith-ful, Joy-ful and tri - um-phant,
2. Sing, choirs of an-gels, Sing in ex - ul - ta-tion,

Melody *f*

1.   O come, all ye faith-ful, Joy-ful and tri - um-phant,
Ab-1-Do 2. _ Sing, choirs of an - gels, Sing in ex - ul - ta-tion,

Since most of the children already know the melody, it might be well to spend time teaching the descant. Observe that it weaves around the melody — sometimes above, sometimes below.

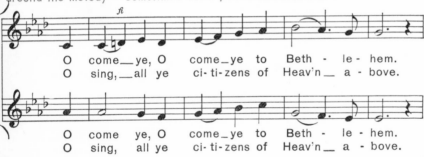

f

O come_ye, O   come_ye to Beth - le - hem.
O sing,_all ye ci-ti-zens of Heav'n_ a - bove.

O come ye, O   come_ye to Beth - le - hem.
O sing, all ye ci-ti-zens of Heav'n_ a - bove.

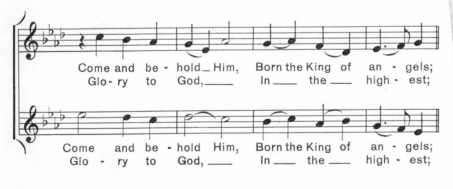

Come and be - hold_ Him, Born the King of an - gels;
Glo - ry   to God,_   In _ the _ high - est;

Come and be - hold Him, Born the King of an - gels;
Glo - ry   to God, _   In _ the _ high - est;

74

O come, let us a - dore Him; O come, let us a - dore — Him;

O come, let us a - dore Him; O come, let us a - dore Him;

O come, let us a - dore — Him, — Christ, — the Lord.

O come, let us a - dore Him, — Christ, — the Lord.

G-26   A-95

Here's to Friends (Round)

Adapted Words   English Folk Tune

LIVELY
Key: F minor

F-1-La   Here's to friends, both old — and — new, — Here's to friends that are ev - er — true!

This can be sung at a slow tempo until the children become used to the minor tonality.

Auld Lang Syne

Words by Robert Burns   Old Scottish Air

Key: G

SMOOTHLY

G   **D7**   **G**   **C**

1. Should auld ac-quaint-ance be for-got And nev-er brought to mind?
2. And here's a hand, my trust-y friend, And gie's a hand o' thine;

D-5-So

G   **D7**   **G**   **C   D7   G**

Should auld ac-quaint-ance be for-got And days of auld lang syne?
We'll take a cup o' kind-ness yet For auld___ lang___ syne.

Refrain

C   G   **D7**   **G**   **C**

For auld___ lang___ syne, my dear, For auld___ lang___ syne;

Optional third part

The optional part may be learned later in the year and added to the song for a spring program number.

G   **D7**   **C   D7   G**

We'll take a cup o' kind-ness yet For auld___ lang___ syne.

"Auld lang syne" means "old time's sake." The song is sung on New Year's Eve and on occasions when people bid one another farewell with the hope that they will meet again.

This makes a very appropriate program number any time.

RHYTHM CANON

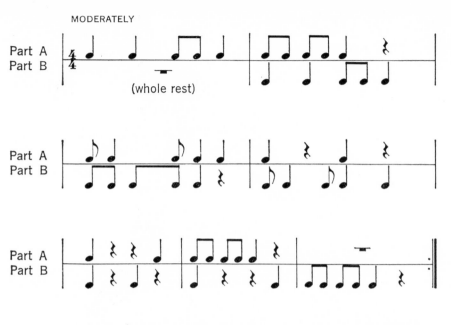

Divide the class into two sections, one section clapping Part A, the other clapping Part B. If rhythm instruments are used, divide and play in the same manner.

Notice that Parts A and B are exactly alike, except that Part B begins one measure later than Part A. When the second part in a two-part composition exactly imitates the first part, the whole piece is called a "canon."

Help the children be discriminate in their choice of instruments. Contrasting sounds give the best effects — as A might be played on sticks, B on maracas; A on bells, B on drums. They will enjoy discovering a variety of possible combinations.

77

Children might like to
make up their own words
about the other seasons,
drawing or painting pic-
tures to illustrate the
theme.

2-3-1   G-26   A-104

Creative activity

Winter's Best For Me

Words and Music by Robert Edwards

Key: C RHYTHMICALLY

mf   C   Chromatics   G7 Rhythm pattern

C-1-Do

Oh, it's nice in the spring and it's fine in the fall,

G7   *fi*   C   *fi*

It's pleas-ant in the sum-mer, but the best time of all

F   C

Is the time when there's ice up-on the lake in the park;

Skate till it's late, lights are twin - kling in the dark.

Fire burn - ing bright - ly on a bank o - ver there,

The voic - es of the crowd float - ing through the win - ter air.

As they sing a jol - ly song, I feel as hap - py as a lark,

'Cause there's ice on the lake, and the lake is in the park,

And the lights are glow - ing bright - ly as they twin - kle in the dark.

Don't you see, win - ter's best!

So, you see, win - ter's best, So you see win - ter's best for me!

Here, again, we have a song with an easy melody line, so the first
emphasis should be on the repeated rhythm pattern —

79

The First Snowfall

The snow had begun in the gloaming,
And busily all the night
Had been heaping field and highway
With a silence deep and white.

Every pine and fir and hemlock
Wore ermine too dear for an earl,
And the poorest twig on the elm tree
Was ridged inch deep with pearl.

—James Russell Lowell

80

Let's Skate Today (Round)

Key: F

Words and Music by Brian Merrell

WALTZ TEMPO

C-5-So

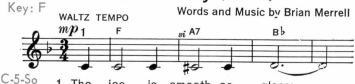

1. The ice is smooth as glass;_____
2. The wind is freez-ing cold,_____

Come on, let's skate to - day!
But we don't care a lick;

Put on your heav - y wool - en things;
We like the weath- er as it is

Let's hur - ry on our way._____
Be - cause the ice is thick._____

We'll skim a - cross the ice,_____
We'll have a jol - ly time,_____

Come on, let's skate to - day._____
Come on, let's skate to - day._____

Autoharp accompaniment is lovely with this very melodic
round. Work for good tone quality and appreciation for
the mood.

Sleighbell accompaniment:

G-27   A-110

Troika Riding

RAPIDLY
Key: A minor   Am

Adapted Words   Ukrainian Folk Tune

Try an accompaniment of bells with this.

1. O'er the ground we   go   a - fly - ing,   Far   be - yond the   cit - y   ply - ing;
2. 'Round us swirls the   snow a - fly - ing,   Ice   be - neath the   snow   is   ly - ing;

A-1-La

How   I   love to   go   a - rid - ing,   Rid - ing   in   a   troi - ka!
Bun - dled   up, don't   mind the weath - er,   Snug - gled   in   a   troi - ka!

Hors - es three, with   hooves a - pound - ing,   Pull   us   on;   a   curve we're round - ing!
Ev - 'ry - one   is   out   a - sleigh - ing,   Skat - ing, slid - ing,   or   just   play - ing.

1-2. Win - ter's   lots   of   fun   for   me   When   rid - ing   in   a   troi - ka!

A troika (troy-kah) is a vehicle drawn by three horses abreast.

This is a fine example of a minor song which is gay and lively.

81

We're Heading Home (Canon)

Words and Music by Peter McCormick

Key: G

G-1-Do

IN JOGGING RHYTHM

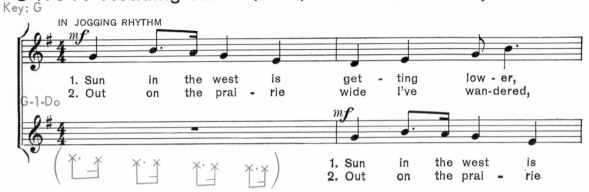

1. Sun in the west is get - ting low - er,
2. Out on the prai - rie wide I've wan-dered,

1. Sun in the west is
2. Out on the prai - rie

Repeat this pattern throughout the song, using temple blocks or other sound effects.

Come on a - long, we're head - ing home.
Rid - ing up - on my trust - y roan.

get - ting low-er,
wide I've wan-dered,

Come on a - long, we're head-ing
Rid - ing up - on my trust - y

Round up the strays and lit - tle do - gies,
"Come on a - long, old pal, get start-ed,

home.
roan.

Round up the strays and
"Come on a - long, old

Sing this lazily — and enjoy it!

82

'Fore they get lost and start to roam.
Come on a - long, we're head-ing home."

lit - tle do - gies, 'Fore they get lost and start to roam.
pal, get start-ed, Come on a - long, we're head-ing home."

G-27   A-109

Arirang

Key: G

NOT TOO FAST

Korean Folk Song

Social studies correlation.
Rhythm accompaniment may be found in the Guide.

mp

D-5-So

1. A - ri - rang,__ A - ri - rang,__ A - ra - ri - yo, O - ver the
2. A - ri - rang,__ A - ri - rang,__ A - ra - ri - yo, O - ver the

Altered tone gives a minor effect.

me

A - ri - rang__ Pass I go. I know not how__ my
A - ri - rang__ Hills I go. Flow-ers are bloom-ing, a

me

jour - ney__ will __ be, If it will end on the__ moun-tain or sea.
lone - ly__ bird__ trills, This is my home-land: the__ A - ri - rang Hills.

The children might compare the mood of this song with the one on p. 82.

83

Steal Away

Key: F

SLOWLY

Help the children observe the fermatas [𝄐] and other marks of expression in order to bring out the beauty of this song.

Spiritual

F-1-Do 1-3. Steal a-way, steal a-way, steal a-way to Je - sus.

Steal a-way, steal a-way home, I don't have long to stay here.

Fine

Optional third part

Some of your good soloists or small groups will have a chance to perform here.

Solo   *faster*

1. My Lord _____ calls me, He calls me by the thun - der;
2. Green trees _____ are bend - ing, Poor sin - ners stand ____ trem - bling;
3. My Lord _____ calls me, He calls me by the light - ning;

Chorus

p *ritard.*

D.C. al Fine

1-3. The trum-pet sounds with - in - a my soul; I don't have long to stay here.

See page 14.

Ab Bb C Db Eb F G Ab
do re mi fa so la ti do

1 2 3 4 5 6 7 8(1)

I   V7   I

G-28   A-107

Soldier, Soldier

American Folk Song

Key: Ab   RATHER FAST   Reading song

Ab-1-Do

1. "Sol-dier,— sol-dier, will you mar-ry me With your mus-ket, fife, and drum?" "How can I mar-ry such a pret-ty lit-tle girl When I have no hat to put on?"

2. Off to the hatter she did go
   As hard as she could run,
   Brought him back the finest that was there.
   "Now, soldier, put it on."

3. "Soldier, soldier, will you marry me
   With your musket, fife, and drum?"
   "How can I marry such a pretty little girl
   When I have no coat to put on?"

4. Off to the tailor she did go
   As hard as she could run,
   Brought him back the finest that was there.
   "Now, soldier, put it on."

5. "Soldier, soldier, will you marry me
   With your musket, fife, and drum?"
   "How can I marry such a pretty little girl
   When I have no shoes to put on?"

6. Off to the shoe shop she did go
   As hard as she could run,
   Brought him back the finest that were there.
   "Now, soldier, put them on."

7. "Soldier, soldier, will you marry me
   With your musket, fife, and drum?"
   "How can I marry such a pretty little girl
   With a wife and child at home?"

The dramatic quality of this song appeals to the boys and girls so they need little urging to act it out. Solo voices may be featured.

Jolly Wee Miner Men G-28   A-114 Old English Song   Canadian Version

Key: A♭

WITH VIGOR

Notice that the rhythm pattern of each line is different.

E♭-5-So

1. We're all___ jol-ly good min-er men, We're min-er men to stay;___
2. Some-times there's mon-ey for ev-'ry-one, And some-times none at all.___

We have trav-eled through Can-a-da For man-y's the long,___long day.___
When we strike___ it rich, it's fun And plen-ty for___ us all,___

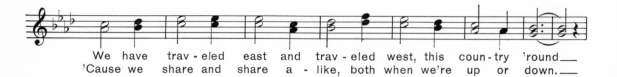

We have trav-eled east and trav-eled west, this coun-try 'round___
'Cause we share and share a-like, both when we're up or down.___

For to dig___ and find___ the wealth That lies be-low the ground.___
Here's my health___ to all you good men That work be-low the ground.___

The children may be surprised at the forcefulness of this song in $\frac{3}{4}$ meter.

86

Oh, Worship the King

Key: A♭

Words by Sir Robert Grant   Music by Joseph Haydn

WITH SPIRIT

E♭-5-So

1. Oh, wor-ship the King, all glo-rious a - bove!
2. Oh, tell of His might, oh, tell of His grace,

Oh, grate-ful-ly sing His pow-er and His love!
Whose robe is the light, whose can - o - py space!

Our shield and de - fend-er, the An-cient of Days,
His char-iots of wrath the deep thun-der-clouds form,

Pa - vil-ioned in splen-dor and gird - ed with praise.
And dark is His path on the wings— of the storm.

Suggestions for correct breathing may be found in the Guide.

Children may be interested in con-trasting this melody with themes from Haydn's "Surprise Symphony," with which they may be familiar.

87

Rowing Song

Adapted Words   Southern Folk Tune

ROWING MOTION AND SPEED

[Hey!]

Key: F minor

F-1-La

1. Pull, pull on the oars, Pull! __ Pull, my heart-y boys, Pull!
2. Pull, hard on the oars, Pull! __ Pull, my heart-y boys, Pull!
3. Pull, bend on the oars, Pull! __ Pull, my heart-y boys, Pull!

[Hey!]

Go, lit-tle boat, through that wa-ter, __ Go, lit-tle boat, __ Go!
Fast, lit-tle boat, slice that wa-ter, __ Make waves a foot __ high!
Speed, lit-tle boat, hur-ry, hur-ry, __ Go, lit-tle boat, __ Go!

This tune is based on just 3 tones, so the rests, accent marks, and rhythm one might expect it to be monotonous. However, give it an unusual quality.

KEY OF Db MAJOR

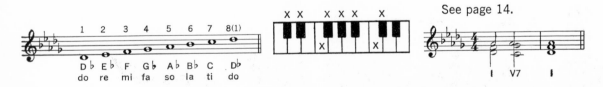

See page 14.

1 2 3 4 5 6 7 8(1)

Db Eb F Gb Ab Bb C Db
do re mi fa so la ti do

I   V7   I

The pattern ♩. ♪ is not new but it should be carefully noted in learning the song.

G-29   A-116
Dabbling in the Dew

Old Cornish Song

Key: Db LIVELY

1. "Where be you a-go-ing, my dear lit-tle maid-en,
2. "Say,___ shall I wed you, my dear lit-tle maid-en,

Db-1-Do

1-2. With your red, ros-y cheeks and your black, curl-y hair?"

"I be go-ing a-milk-ing, kind lit-tle man," she said,
"Oh, with that I a-gree, my kind lit-tle man," she said,

1-2. "It's dab-bling in the dew makes the milk-maid___ fair."

The phrases containing Cb should be learned first by rote.

89

How many times is this rhythm repeated?   [Seven times]

G-29   A-117

Londonderry Air

Adapted Words   Old Irish Tune

Key: Db   EXPRESSIVELY, WITH MOTION

mp

C-7-Ti

1. I like to sing this love-ly I-rish mel-o-dy
2. There's "Dan-ny Boy" and sweet "Kath-leen Ma - vour - neen,"

That comes from far a - way a - cross the sea;
From Don-e - gal to Gal - way Bay they sing

90

And when I hear its lilt - ing tune and har - mo - ny,
Of all they've seen of life be - neath the harp of green,

It's like a breath of Ire - land come to me.
Of that dear land to which their hearts e'er cling.

mf

To dear old Ire - land, far a - way a - cross the sea,
O land of lakes, O love - ly land of sto - ry,

I'm tak - en back on wings of mem - o - ry;
Land of the lep - re - chaun and Blar - ney Stone,

f

Each time I hear its lilt - ing tune and har - mo - ny,
Land of brave kings who ruled in an - cient glo - ry!

mf

It's like a breath of dear old Ire - land come to me.
Sure, all these things are dear old Ire - land's ver - y own.

Part of this may be combined with "Annie Laurie," found on p. 92.

Clap this rhythm:

This pattern occurs 5 times in the song.

G-29   A-119

Annie Laurie

Words by William Douglass   Music by Lady John Scott

Key: D♭

MODERATELY

The Scottish words are explained in the Guide.

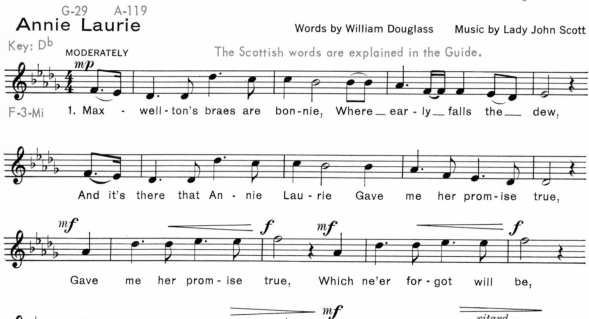

F-3-Mi   *mp*   1. Max - well-ton's braes are bon-nie, Where __ ear-ly __ falls the __ dew,

And it's there that An - nie Lau - rie Gave me her prom-ise true,

mf   *f*   *mf*   *f*
Gave me her prom-ise true, Which ne'er for-got will be,

mf   ritard.
And for bon - nie An - nie __ Lau - rie I'd __ lay __ me doon and dee.

See Guide for combining this song with "Londonderry Air."

2. Her brow is like the snowdrift,
   Her throat is like the swan,
   Her face it is the fairest
   That e'er the sun shone on,
   That e'er the sun shone on,
   And dark blue is her e'e, etc.

3. Like dew on gowan lying
   Is the fall of her fairy feet,
   And like winds in summer sighing,
   Her voice is low and sweet,
   Her voice is low and sweet,
   She's all the world to me, etc.

92

RHYTHM GAMES

Try these rhythm games by:

1. dividing the class into two groups, one section clapping the upper part and the other tapping feet on the lower.

2. having the entire group clap the upper part and tap feet on the lower part.

Use rhythm instruments for variation.

1. After you have learned this rhythmic pattern, try using it as a rhythm accompaniment to "Oh! Susanna." As you sing the song, repeat this rhythm throughout.

You might also use other familiar songs having $\frac{4}{4}$ meter.

MODERATELY (then vary speeds when you repeat the games)

Hand clap (or high drum)

Foot tap (or low drum)

2. Surprise ending (wait for the quarter rests on the first beat):

Children can make up their own rhythm patterns using these same note and rest values.

Tune Ukulele

G C E A   F   C7   B♭

Clapping or drum accompaniment:

Social studies correlation

1-3-3   G-30   A-120

Lovely Islands of Hawaii

Key: F

LEISURELY
mp

Adapted Words   Hawaiian Folk Song

A-3-Mi
F-1-Do

1. Oh, love - ly Is - lands of Ha - wa - ii,
2. Oh, love - ly Is - lands of Ha - wa - ii,

Where the bril - liant red hi - bis - cus* grow,
With your state - ly peaks and moun - tains high,

With the blue Pa - ci - fic all a - round you,
Foam - ing surf pounds gen - tly on your beach - es,

You are cooled by winds that gen - tly blow.
'Neath a blue and ev - er sun - ny sky.

*The hibiscus (high-bis-kus), the state flower of Hawaii, grows wild throughout the Islands. The flower is showy and brilliant in color. Hawaii, our fiftieth state, consists of a group of islands. Honolulu is the capital.

This song, with the ones on the following pages, would make an interesting contribution to an assembly program.

94

Tune
Ukulele

G-30   A-121 GCEA   G   C   D7

Aloha Oe

Adapted Words   Music by Queen Liliuokalani

Key: G

DREAMILY

Note chromatic tone.

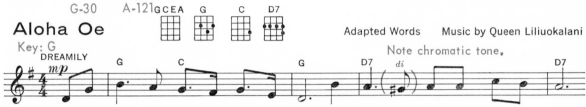

D-5-So

1. Love-ly is-lands far a-cross the sea Keep call-ing out, "Come back to me!"
2. Land of fra-grant bush and flow'-ring tree, Soft breez-es sweep-ing 'cross the sea,

I a-wait the day when I'll re-turn To my is-land par-a-dise a-cross the sea.
How I long to see your shores a-gain, Say your per-fumed par-a-dise will wel-come me!

Refrain

Fare-well to thee, Fare-well to thee, Oh, is-lands filled with charm and rar-est beau-ty.

We sail a-way, but I'll re-turn some day, And so, "A-lo-ha!" to you.

If at all possible, use ukulele with the song; however, autoharp sounds fine.
Practice different ways of strumming it, for variety.

95

Drum introduction and accompaniment

G-30   A-122

Hawaiian Chant

Key: B♭

Hawaiian Folk Song

Counter rhythms.

RHYTHMICALLY, WITH ACCENT

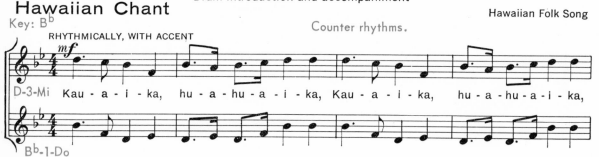

D-3-Mi Kau - a - i - ka, hu - a - hu - a - i - ka, Kau - a - i - ka, hu - a - hu - a - i - ka,

B♭-1-Do

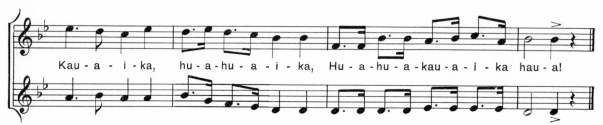

Kau - a - i - ka, hu - a - hu - a - i - ka, Hu - a - hu - a - kau - a - i - ka hau - a!

While the drummers play the pattern above, other instruments, chosen by the class,
could play the rhythm pattern of the melody.

4-3-3   G-31   A-123

🔴 Alaska, We Salute You!

Key: F

Words and Music by Richard C. Berg

MARCH TEMPO

Social studies correlation

C-5-So 1. A - las - ka, A - las - ka, We sa - lute you as the for - ty - ninth state,
        2. A - las - ka, A - las - ka, With your lore ___ and ___ his - to - ry,

C-5-So Optional third part

96

The big-gest, most north-ern, in the whole U - nit - ed States.
A land of ad - ven - ture and a land of in - dus - try,

From Maine to Ha - wa - ii, To the straits of the Be - ring___ Sea,
You join in a na - tion built by men with a will to be free,

1-2. A - mer - i - ca is hold - ing the torch of lib - er - ty!

The children should be able to see at once the form of the song, A B A C.

1-4-1   G-31   A-125

● Chopsticks

Key: C

Words and Music by Diana Christy

WITH A SWING   Program novelty

G7 Descant   C

1. Play   for   me   my   fa - v'rite mel - o - dy,
2. Right   hand   up   and   left   hand down, __ down,

B-7-Ti

1-2. One, two, three, stead-i-ly,   let's hear the   mel - o - dy,

G-5-So
F-4-Fa

G7   C

You   know   how   it   goes. _____
That's   the   way   it   goes. _____

This   is   the   way __   that   "Chop - sticks" goes. _____

G7   C

Don't   for - get   the   tune   and   rhy - thm
One   tune   up,   the   oth - er   down, __ down,

Be   sure   to   give them   that   reg - u - lar   rhy - thm and

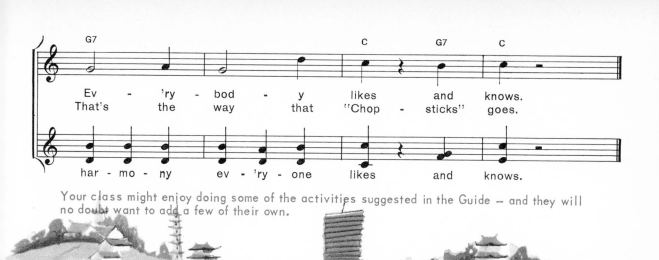

Ev - 'ry - bod - y likes and knows.
That's the way that "Chop - sticks" goes.

har - mo - ny ev - 'ry - one likes and knows.

Your class might enjoy doing some of the activities suggested in the Guide — and they will no doubt want to add a few of their own.

4-1-3   G-31   A-130

Sail On, Little Boat

Adapted Words   Ancient Chinese Tune

Key: D minor
GENTLY, RATHER SLOWLY   (wood block)   Social studies correlation

1. Sail on, lit - tle boat,   Far a - cross the peace - ful wa - ters blue;
2. Come back, lit - tle boat,   From a - far a - cross the deep blue sea;

A-5-Mi

Gen - tle winds that blow   To a dis - tant shore will car - ry you.
Bring the sail - or home   To his wife and lit - tle chil - dren, three.

1-2. Sail a - long, now,   lit - tle boat, sail on, far a - cross the wa - ters blue.

If a gong is available you might find effective use for it in this charming song.
Finger cymbals are also especially good.

99

The Leaving of My Love

Adapted Words   English Capstan Chantey

Key: Db   LONGINGLY   Expressive singing

mp

Db-1-Do

1. I must say good - by, my love, and leave you now;
2. I have signed a - board a Yan - kee clip - per ship,
3. We are bound a - way up - on the o - cean wide,

I must leave, the time has come to go.
She's a ves - sel fast and safe, I know.
And the storm - y winds do fierce - ly blow.

1-3. I'm on my way to Cal - i - for - ni - a,

Fare thee well, for I must go.

Refrain *mf*

Fare thee well, my dar - ling, my own true love,

I'll re - turn and we'll be mar - ried some fine day;

And so the leav-ing of you, my love, won't make me sad,

1,2. Since I know that we'll mar-ry some fine day! **3.** Since I know that we'll mar-ry some fine day!

ritard.

Help the children observe the marks of expression.

Notice that this is a capstan chantey. In the old days, capstan chanties were sung in marching rhythm, as the crew walked around and "wound the capstan." The capstan was a vertical, drumlike cylinder. Around it there was a cable attached to some heavy object on board which had to be moved, or to the ship's anchor in the water below. By winding the capstan, the crew could move the heavy object or raise the anchor.

[Play the first two measures on a melody instrument as an introduction.]

1-3-5   G-32   A-129

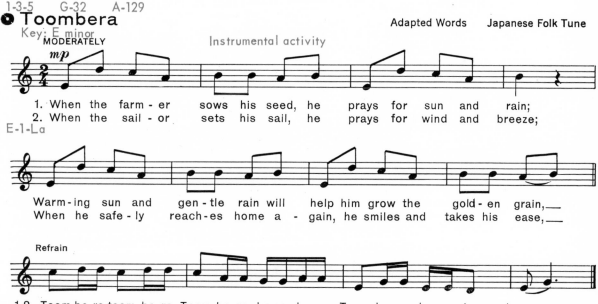

● **Toombera**

Key: E minor

MODERATELY

Adapted Words   Japanese Folk Tune

Instrumental activity

mp

1. When the farm-er sows his seed, he prays for sun and rain;
2. When the sail-or sets his sail, he prays for wind and breeze;

E-1-La

Warm-ing sun and gen-tle rain will help him grow the gold-en grain,___
When he safe-ly reach-es home a-gain, he smiles and takes his ease,___

Refrain

1-2. Toom-be-ra, toom-be-ra, Toom-be-ra-be-ra-be-ra, Toom-be-ra-be-ra-toom-toom.___

Ideas for instrumental accompaniment might be suggested after listening to the recording.

Alouette

French-Canadian Folk Song

Key: G

Social studies correlation

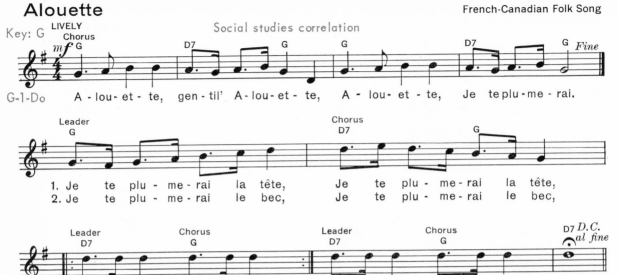

A - lou-et - te, gen - til' A - lou-et - te, A - lou - et - te, Je te plu - me - rai.

G-1-Do

1. Je te plu - me - rai la tête, Je te plu - me - rai la tête,
2. Je te plu - me - rai le bec, Je te plu - me - rai le bec,

1. Et la tête, et la tête, A - lou - ette, A - lou - ette, O!
2. Et le bec, et le bec, A - lou - ette, A - lou - ette, O!
   Et la tête, et la tête,

"Gentil Alouette" means "pretty meadow lark." "Je te plumerai" means "I shall pick off your feathers." 1. La tête: head. 2. Le bec: beak. 3. Le cou: neck. 4. Le dos: back. 5. Les pattes: feet.

In this action song, when you sing "la tête" touch your head; when you sing "le bec" touch your nose; when you sing "le cou" touch your neck; when you sing "le dos" touch your back; when you sing "les pattes" touch your feet.

After the first stanza, repeat the measure between the repeat bars with the words in reverse order. For example, the last stanza is: Et les pattes, et les pattes; Et le dos, et le dos; Et le cou, et le cou; Et le bec, et le bec; Et la tête, et la tête, Alouette, Alouette, O!

Foreign language songs are much more effective if the words are pronounced correctly. Consult someone who can help with pronunciation.

KEY OF E MAJOR

See page 14.

1 2 3 4 5 6 7 8(1)
E F# G# A B C# D# E
do re mi fa so la ti do

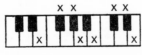

I IV I V7 I

After these skips at the beginning, this song moves smoothly by steps to the end of the phrase.

do do so mi
1 1 5 3

G-32   A-130

Praise to the Lord

German Hymn Tune

Key: E   FERVENTLY   Reading song in E

E-1-Do
1. Praise to the Lord, the Al-might-y, the King of cre -
2. Praise to the Lord, oh, let all that is in me a -

a - tion! Oh, my soul, praise Him for He is thy
dore Him! All that hath life and breath, come now with

health and sal - va - tion! All ye who hear, now to His
prais - es be - fore Him! Let the A - men sound from His

tem - ple draw near; Join me in glad ad - o - ra - tion.
peo - ple a - gain. Glad-ly for aye we a - dore Him.

This song is in AABC form.

[Find other places in which the tune moves by skips, and those in which it moves by steps.]

The class will be able to choose instruments suitable for this rhythm pattern.

The Guide gives a suggestion for how to start a song on the second beat of the measure.

Rhythm accompaniment:

A double sharp ✕ raises the pitch of a note one whole step. Can you find F ✕ in the song?

F✕(G)

4-3-4   G-33   A-132

El Sombrero Blanco

Adapted Words   Old California Tune

Key: E Major

WITH MOTION

mf

G-3-Mi

What a love-ly hat is my fine new som-bre-ro,_____ Oh, I would-n't

trade for a ver-y big sum,_____When I take a ride on my faith-ful bur-ro,_____

Nev-er wor-ry what kind of wea-ther will come; I won't mind rain or sun. _____

Oh, my hand-some, my hand-some som-bre-ro,

Optional third part

sharp
double sharp

El som-bre-ro blan-co es-ta bue-no,

With a wide, wide brim to pro-tect me

From the rain or glar-ing sun.

"El sombrero blanco esta bueno" means "the white hat is good."

Notice that the optional third part uses only two tones - Do and So.

Raccoon Hunt

Key: E

Southern Folk Song

Hand-clapping and foot-tapping might accompany this song.

LIVELY

mf Harmony

G-3-Mi

1. As I walked out by the light of the moon, So mer-ri-ly sing-ing
2. I at the rac-coon___ take a ___ peep, And then so___ soft-ly
3. Of all the songs that___ I ev-er sing, The Rac-coon Hunt's the

Melody

E-1-Do

this old tune, I came a-cross a big rac-coon a-sit-ting on a rail.
to him creep, I find the rac-coon fast a-sleep and pull him off the rail.
great-est thing, It al-ways pleas-es old and young, and then they cry, "En-core."

Refrain

These chromatics could be played on bells or piano before being sung.

te   *si*   *fi*

Sit-ting on a rail, Sit-ting on a rail, Sit-ting on a rail, Sleep-ing ver-y sound.

106

KEY OF G MAJOR

See page 14.

G-33   A-135

Sing Your Way Home

This is a good song on which to try
a little impromptu harmonizing "by ear."

Campers' Song

Key: G   SMOOTHLY

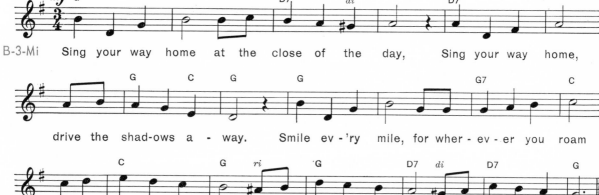

B-3-Mi   Sing your way home at the close of the day, Sing your way home,

drive the shad-ows a - way.   Smile ev-'ry mile, for wher-ev-er you roam

It will bright-en your road, It will light-en your load If you sing your way home.

Special attention should be paid to singing the chromatic tones accurately.

This song uses only two chords, tonic (I) and domi-nant seventh (V_7). Try these chords on the piano; then try making up an accompaniment to "The Lone Prairie."

Try these chords on resonator bells!

I

V_7

G-33   A-140

The Lone Prairie

This makes a good song for assembly singing. The repeated phrases are easily learned and the melody may be sung by a small group.

Cowboy Song

Key: G IN JOGGING RHYTHM

Introduction

B-3-Mi

D-5-So

1-2. Won't you lis-ten to my plea?   Won't you lis-ten to my plea?

1. Oh, bur-y me not _____ on the lone prai-rie, _____

Won't you lis-ten to my plea?   Won't you lis-ten to my plea?

These words came low _____ and _____ mourn-ful-ly, _____

chord changes

Won't you lis-ten to my plea?   Won't you lis-ten to my plea?

From the pal-lid lips _____ of a youth who lay _____

Don't you ev-er bur-y me, Don't you ev-er bur-y me,

On his dy-ing bed _____ at the close of day. _____

(optional ending)

V7 V7

chord changes

Out up-on the lone prai-rie, Out up-on the lone prai-rie.

(extended ending)

(Hum) _____ (Hum) _____ Out up-on the lone prai-rie.

Out up-on the lone prai-rie, Out up-on the lone prai-rie.

If the optional ending is used, the class might like to experiment with different dynamics than those suggested.

2. They buried him there on the lone prairie,
   Where coyotes howl and the wind blows free,
   In a narrow grave just six by three,
   In a narrow grave on the lone prairie.
   (Out upon the lone prairie.)

109

Sweet Sally Sue

Adapted Words   American Folk Tune

Key: G

This song should be sung in a very simple style.

FLOWINGLY
mf

D-5-So

1. In some lone-ly val-ley a ___ girl I once knew
2. The cit-y is lone-ly, and the cit-y is cold,
3. Some day to my dar-ling I will sure-ly re-turn,

Is think-ing of me, and to ___ me will be true;
But here I must stay 'til I've ___ plen-ty of gold
For lights of the cit-y I ___ nev-er will yearn,

I went ___ to the ___ cit-y, a trade to pur-sue,
To pur-chase a ___ ring and a dress trimmed in blue
To the-a-ter and ___ res-t'rant I'll bid fair a-dieu,

But some day I'll re-turn to my ___ sweet Sal-ly Sue.
For my dar-ling, my sweet-heart, my ___ sweet Sal-ly Sue.
Just to be once a-gain with my ___ sweet Sal-ly Sue.

For suggested helps in the reading of this song see the Guide.

3-4-1   G-34   A-136

The Lumberjack's Song

American Folk Song

Key: G   VIGOROUSLY

D-5-So

Social studies correlation

1. Come, all you sons of free-dom who log the land___ with glee,
2. When white frost paints the val-ley, and snow con-ceals___ the ground,
3. With ax-es on our shoul-ders, we'll make the woods___ re-sound,

Syncopated pattern

Come, all you rov-ing lum-ber-jacks, and lis-ten now to me.
The ax-es ring and saws do sing as tim-ber crash-es down.
No bet-ter bunch of lum-ber-jacks can an-y-where be found.

We'll cross the roar-ing riv-er where an-gry wa-ters flow,
We'll take the logs and sled them down to the stream be-low,
We work through heat and driz-zle, we work in storm or snow,

1-3. And we'll range the wild woods o-ver, a-log-ging we___ will go;

Oh, we'll range the wild woods o-ver, a-log-ging we will go.

111

3-4-2   G-34   A-145

A Bicycle Built for Two

If the recording is used keep in mind that this is a finished product. Children will have to learn at a much slower tempo.

Words and Music by Henry Dacre

Key: G   GAILY

Descant: Pret-ty Dai-sy, an-swer me! Will you mar-ry me? Will you mar-ry me?

Melody: Dai — sy,

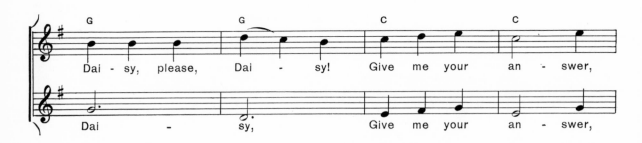

Dai-sy, please, Dai — sy! Give me your an-swer,

Dai — sy, Give me your an-swer,

do! How I love you, Dai — sy! I am go-ing, I am go-ing

do! I'm half

Singers on the descant will have to wake up their "lazy tongues" if they wish to be understood. This demands crisp pronunciation.

cra - zy, half cra - zy, All for the love ___ of you, of you.

cra - zy, All for the love of you. ___

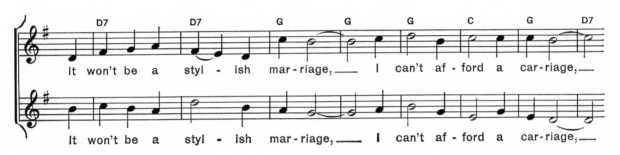

It won't be a styl - ish mar - riage, ___ I can't af - ford a car - riage, ___

It won't be a styl - ish mar - riage, ___ I can't af - ford a car - riage, ___

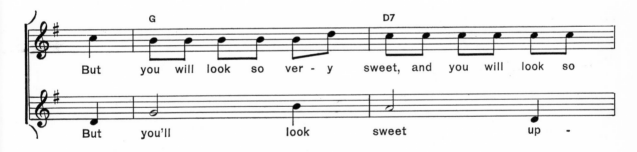

But you will look so ver - y sweet, and you will look so

But you'll look sweet up -

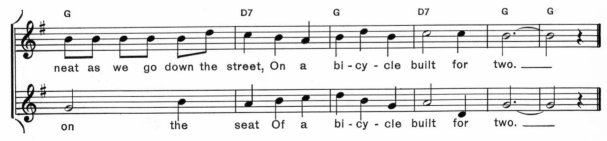

neat as we go down the street, On a bi - cy - cle built for two. ___

on the seat Of a bi - cy - cle built for two. ___

113

Riddle Song

American Folk Song from the Southern Highlands

Notice the pattern ♪♩ found in each phrase.

ABBA, form

Key: G PLAINTIVELY

mp

1. I gave my love a cher-ry that has no__stone,
2. How can there be a cher-ry that has no__stone?
3. A cher-ry when it's bloom-ing it has no__stone,

D-5-So

I gave my love a chick-en that has no__bone,
How can there be a chick-en that has no__bone?
A chick-en when it's peep-in' it has no__bone,

I gave my love a ring___ that has no__ end,
How can there be a ring___ that has no__ end?
A ring when it's a-roll-in' it has no__ end,

I gave my love a ba-by that's no cry-in'.
How can there be a ba-by that's no cry-in'?
A ba-by when it's sleep-in' is no cry-in'.

This is another example of a song which uses the pentatonic scale. (See p. 38.) After the class learns the song, some of them might play the melody on the black keys of the piano.

The form of this song is AABB: the first two phrases are alike, and the last two phrases are alike.

G-35   A-150

The Viking Ship

Adapted Words   Norwegian Folk Tune

Because of the repeated phrases, this song is easy to play on melody instruments.

VIGOROUSLY
Key: E minor

(A)
1. The Vi-king ship put out to sea, her he-roes raised their song;
2. Then fare you well, you Norse-men bold, who plowed the an-gry seas

(A) B-5-Mi
The months went by, but where was she, due home for o-ver-long?
And brought to na-tions far a-way the sto-ry of your deeds!

(B)
The "Sea Wolf" of the Norse-men lies a wreck on Dev-on strand;
No long-er do you set your sails for coun-tries far a-way,

(B)
Her he-ro crew, the o-cean's pride, will ne'er see Nor-way's land.
But leg-ends of your val-iant trips come down to us to-day.

115

Some of the children may be encouraged to try the autoharp accompaniment which uses more chords than the usual 2 or 3.

G-35   A-151

To Washington and Lincoln

Adapted Words   American Folk Tune

Key: F MODERATELY

C-5-So George Wash-ing-ton, first of our lead-ers,__ And Lin-coln, an-oth-er great man,__

Are hon-ored each year by our na-tion;__ In love and re-spect we all stand.__

They led us in times that were trou-bled,__ With cour-age that nev-er did sway.__

With men such as these we have build-ed__ A coun-try of free men to-day.__

Here's to America!

Key: F   MODERATELY   Adapted Words   Silesian Folk Tune (Crusader's Hymn)

F-1-Do

1. Here's__ to A - mer - i - ca! Here's to A - mer - i - ca!
2. Na - tion so boun-ti - ful, Na - tion so beau-ti - ful,

Found - ed by men who were brave and true;
Moun - tains ma - jes - tic and o - ceans blue;

Cra - dle of lib - er - ty, Land__ of de - moc - ra - cy,
We give our thanks to thee, Land__ of de - moc - ra - cy,

We pledge our loy - al - ty to you!
We pledge our loy - al - ty to you!

This song should be sung smoothly. Breathing only at end of
phrases will help in singing expressively.

117

⊙ POLOVTSIAN DANCES

by Alexander Borodin

Alexander Borodin, who lived in Russia a hundred years ago, was a very successful scientist. Yet he loved music and spent much of his spare time composing and talking about music and listening to it with his friends.

One of his most popular compositions is the "Polovtsian Dances" from his opera Prince Igor. This opera tells the story of a young prince who was captured many centuries ago by the Tartars, a tribe of warriors in central Asia. Prince Igor and his son were not treated as ordinary prisoners but were entertained royally by the "Polovtsian Dances."

In the first dance, a beautiful melody is played by flute and oboe, as accompaniment to the procession of the royal captives:

The second dance is performed by a group of savage men; the clarinet introduces the melody:

In the third dance, boys act out war games to a lively tune played by strings, with cymbals entering as the dance grows wilder and wilder:

In the last, very exciting dance, the music grows faster and more furious until it finally ends with cymbals crashing and brasses blowing wildly.

● THE SYMPHONY

A composer can write music in many forms for an orchestra. Some of these are overtures, suites, and symphonies. The symphony is perhaps the most challenging form, and it has been used by the world's greatest composers to express their musical ideas.

Usually, a symphony consists of four movements which are so closely related to one another that they are played successively to make one long, unified composition.

3-1-1

First Movement of Beethoven's Fifth Symphony

The first movement of a symphony is often longer and more complicated than the movements which follow. It is usually written in what is called "sonata form," in which several themes, or tunes, are introduced and developed.

A famous first movement is the one in Beethoven's Fifth Symphony. As you listen to it, notice that this rhythm, introduced at the very beginning, is heard over and over again:

Ludwig van Beethoven, born in Bonn, Germany nearly two hundred years ago, wrote nine symphonies, the last one when he was totally deaf. He was one of the greatest composers of all times, and his symphonies are still considered some of the finest ever written.

2-1-2

Second Movement of Dvořák's New World Symphony

The second movement of a symphony is generally a slow, melodious piece of music. This beautiful theme, played by the English horn, is heard in the second movement of Dvořák's New World Symphony.

Antonin Dvořák was a Bohemian, born a little over a hundred years ago. He wrote this symphony after a long visit to our country. For three years he was head of the National Conservatory in New York City. He also spent some time in Iowa, where many of his fellow countrymen had settled. It was there that he wrote most of this symphony.

Twilight G-36   A-154

Adapted Words   Music by W. A. Mozart

Encourage the class to sing this in their very best style; observing all marks of expression.

Key: G   MODERATELY   *mp*

When the dark'ning shad-ows fall, o'er the val-ley steal - ing,

B-3-Mi

When the dark'ning shad-ows fall, o'er the val-ley steal - ing,

G-1-Do

di   *p*

Far-off church bells slow - ly call, soft their mes-sage peal-ing.

te   *di*

Far-off church bells slow - ly call, soft their mes-sage peal-ing.

mf

Hear the ring-ing, sing-ing bells, qui-et night the sound fore-tells.

Hear the ring-ing, sing-ing bells, qui-et night the

fi   *di*   *fi*

Ring, ding dong! How sweet their part-ing song!

sound fore-tells. Ring, ding dong! Their part - ing song!

Round the pleas-ant coun-try-side shad-ows dark are fall-ing,

Round the pleas-ant coun-try-side shad-ows dark are fall-ing,

di

Ves-per bells at e-ven-tide men to rest are call-ing.

te *fi* *fa*

Ves-per bells at e-ven-tide men to rest are call-ing.

This beautiful song by a master composer makes a very fine program number.

G-36 A-157

To Spring! (Round)

Adapted Words   English Tune

Key: D JOYFULLY

D-1-Do Spring is the time when ev-'ry liv-ing thing

Will join in na-ture's cho-rus and be-gin to sing.

Each phrase of this round has a different rhythm pattern.

121

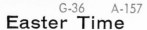

Easter Time

Words by Julie Gibault   Music by Ludwig van Beethoven

Key: B♭

JOYFULLY

Program number

F-5-So

1. Re-joice, O world, re - joice in spring's birth! East-er a - gain has come to the earth!
2. Sun shines on high and green grass-es grow, Lil - ies gleam white and soft breez-es blow,

So-Do   So-Mi   Ti-Fa

The birds are sing-ing, the flow'rs in bloom, And gone is win - ter's cold and gloom.
The brooks are sparkling, the skies are clear, Re - joice, re-joice for East - er's here!

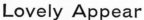

Lovely Appear

Words Adapted from the Bible   Music by Charles Gounod

Key: E♭

MODERATELY

Group 1

Program number

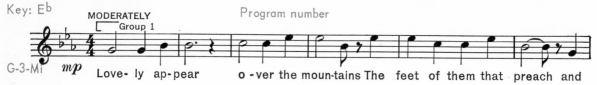

G-3-Mi   mp   Love- ly ap-pear   o - ver the moun-tains The feet of them that preach and

bring good news of peace, — The feet of them that preach and bring good news of peace.

122

This selection is from the oratorio "The Redemption."

An oratorio is a dramatic work similar to an opera but performed without costumes and scenery. It is religious in nature. The music given here is part of a longer section. The words are few and are repeated over and over. Such repetition is typical of the oratorio, in which many songs are used to tell the complete story of the work.

Notice that Group 2 sings the same melody as Group 1 but at a lower pitch.

Detailed suggestions will be found in the Guide.

123

Alleluia (Canon)

G-37   A-162

Words by Isaac Watts   Old German Air

Key: E♭

JOYFULLY

Program number

E♭-1-Do

From all that dwell be-low the skies   Let the Cre - a-tor's praise a-

From   all that dwell be-low the skies   Let

rise,   Al - le - lu - ia! Al - le - lu - ia! Let the Re-deem-er's name be

the Cre - a - tor's praise a - rise,   Al - le - lu - ia!   Let

sung   Through ev -'ry land, by ev -'ry tongue,   Al - le - lu - ia!

the Re-deem-er's name be sung   Through ev -'ry land, by ev -'ry tongue!

Al-le - lu - ia! Al - le - lu - ia! Al-le - lu - ia! Al-le - lu — ia!

Al-le - lu - ia! Al - le - lu - ia! Al-le - lu - ia! Al-le - lu — ia!

124   Before singing the song it might be well to have the class compare the two parts to find
likenesses and differences.

Spring Is a Wonderful Time

Key: G

WALTZ TEMPO   Adapted Words   American Folk Tune

(melody instruments or bells)

This little melody can be played as an interlude between verses.

1. The spring is a won-der-ful time of the year!
2. All na-ture is call-ing,"Come out in the sun!
3. The flow-ers are bloom-ing, the grass is all green,

D-5-So

Now win-ter is o-ver, va-ca-tion is near;
The cold days are o-ver, for spring has be - gun!"
Loo loo loo loo loo loo, loo loo loo loo loo,

The flow-ers are bloom-ing, the bees start to hum,
Birds sing in the tree-tops,fish swim in the pool;
The earth has a look that is fresh and all clean,

The spring-time has fi - nal - ly come. ____
It's hard to stay in-doors in school. ____
Loo loo loo loo loo loo loo loo. ____

125

🔾 Lovely Messengers

Words Adapted from the Bible   Music by Felix Mendelssohn

Key: G

SLOWLY, WITH MOTION   Program number

How   love - ly   are   the   mes - sen - gers that preach us the gos - pel of   peace,

D-5-So

How   love - ly   are   the   mes - sen - gers that preach us the gos - pel of   peace,

The   gos - pel   of   peace,____   The   mes - sen - gers that preach____ us   the

How love - ly are   the   mes - sen - gers that preach us the gos-pel of

gos-pel of peace, How love -

peace, How love - ly are the mes - sen - gers that

- ly are they that preach us the gos-pel of peace.

preach us the gos- pel of peace, the gos - pel of peace.

See if the class can create a real feeling of <u>peace</u> in their singing of this song.

This selection is from the oratorio "St. Paul."

G-38   A-166

A Prayer of Thanks

Traditional Hymn

SLOWLY
Key: A minor

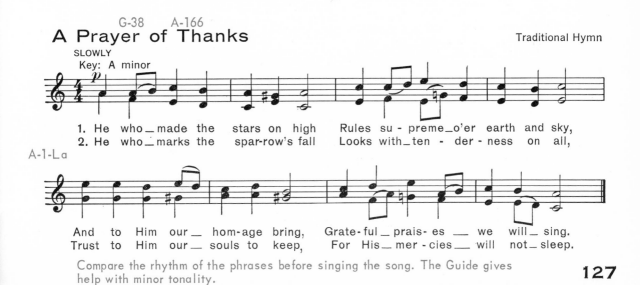

1. He who — made the stars on high   Rules su - preme — o'er earth and sky,
2. He who — marks the spar-row's fall   Looks with — ten - der - ness on all,

A-1-La

And to Him our — hom-age bring,   Grate- ful — prais- es — we will — sing.
Trust to Him our — souls to keep,   For His — mer - cies — will not — sleep.

Compare the rhythm of the phrases before singing the song. The Guide gives
help with minor tonality.

127

Maple Sugar Time

Social studies correlation

Adapted Words   Vermont Folk Tune

Key: G

1. When you see the farm-er car-ry ma-ple pails a-cross the land,
2. Then we'll take a scoop or two of clean and new-ly fall-en snow,

Then you know the time for sug-ar mak-ing once more is at hand,
Pour the hot and boil-ing sap up-on it; tastes good, don't you know?

As the fra-grant o-dors pour through the o-pen shan-ty door,
Make a ma-ple su-gar sun-dae as good as you can buy,

How the ea-ger chil-dren ral-ly, ev-er loud-ly call-ing, "More!"
It's a hab-it that we have in su-gar time that you should try.

Oh, bub-ble, bub-ble, bub-ble, bub-ble, bub-ble goes the pan, Fur-nish sweet-er

mu-sic for the sea-son if you can; Oh, see the gold-en bil-low,

Watch its ebb and flow, Sweet-est joys in-deed that su-gar mak-ers know.

"Sugarin' time" is a sure sign of spring in New England, especially in Vermont, one of the leading producers of maple syrup in the country. Maple syrup is made by "tapping" the sap from sugar trees in the spring and boiling it. It takes many buckets of sap to make a small quantity of pure, delicious maple syrup.

129

Cuckoo Bird

Key: F

Adapted Words   Austrian Folk Tune

Fun song

LIVELY

A-3-Mi

1. Oh, I went down to the mill-er's pond and I si-lent-ly stood
2. When you hear that sweet mel-o-dy, it's a sure sign of spring;

When I heard there a cuck-oo bird as she called from the wood.
So keep war-bling, my cuck-oo bird, in the wood gai-ly sing!

Refrain   Each time the refrain is sung, add another "cuckoo."

Ho - lee - ah, ho - la - rah - ha - hee - ah, ho - la - rah, cuck-oo!

Ho - la - rah - ha - hee - ah, ho - la - rah, cuck-oo! Ho - la - rah - ha - hee - ah,

ho - la - rah, cuck-oo! Ho - la - rah - ha - hee - ah ho - la!

Good suggestions for performing this song may be found in the Guide.

KEY OF D MAJOR

D E F# G A B C# D
do re mi fa so la ti do

See page 14.

I IV I V7 I

G-38   A-173

Kookaburra

Key: D LIVELY

This is a fun song which children will like to sing. Australian Round
Some of them will think of extra verses.

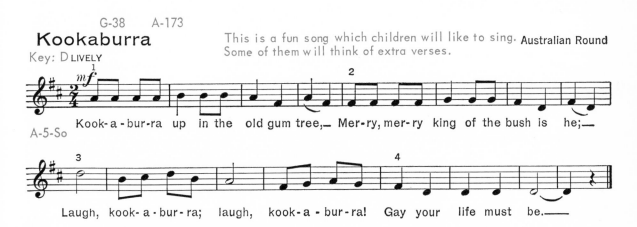

Kook-a-bur-ra up in the old gum tree,— Mer-ry, mer-ry king of the bush is he;—

A-5-So

Laugh, kook-a-bur-ra; laugh, kook-a-bur-ra! Gay your life must be.—

The kookaburra is an Australian bird that makes a laughing sound when it sings.

131

Sacramento

American Sea Chantey

Key: D LIVELY

Social studies correlation

1. As I was walk-ing on the quay, Hoo-dah, to my hoo-dah,
2. Her hair was brown, her eyes were blue, Hoo-dah, to my hoo-dah,

A-5-So

A pret-ty girl I chanced to meet, Hoo-dah hoo-dah day.
Her lips were red and sweet to view, Hoo-dah hoo-dah day.

Refrain

Blow, boys, blow for Cal-i-for-ni-o! There's plen-ty of gold, so

I've been told, On the banks of the Sac-ra-men-to.

3. I raised my hat and said, "How do?"
   She bowed and said, "Quite well, thank you."

4. I asked her then to come with me,
   Down to the docks my ship to see.

5. She quickly answered, "Oh, dear, no,
   I thank you, but I cannot go."

6. "I have a sweetheart young and true,
   And cannot give my love to you."

7. I said, "Good-by" and strode away,
   Although with her I longed to stay.

8. And as I bade this girl adieu,
   I said that girls like her were few.

Consult Guide for material about the Gold Rush.

The form of this song is AABBC: the first two phrases are alike, the third and fourth phrases are alike, and the fifth phrase is different.

1-4-2   G-39   A-177

The Fiddler

Norwegian Folk Song

Key: D GAILY, TWO BEATS TO A MEASURE   For review of $\frac{6}{8}$ meter, consult Guide.

A-5-So

A

1. There once was a fid - dler with on - ly one cow;
2. He res - ined his bow and he tuned ev - 'ry string,

A

To get him some mu - sic, he did not care how;
He scraped on the fid - dle, and how it did sing!

B

He trad - ed the cow for a fid - dle, and then
As boys and their maid - ens went danc - ing a - round,

B

With mu - sic at hand he was hap - py a - gain.
The coun - try - side ech - oed the rol - lick - ing sound.

C

1-2. "Old vi - o - lin, go fid - dle um dum, fid - dle um dum dum dum do."

3. "If I grow as old as the moss on the tree,"
The fiddler exclaimed, "I shall never agree
To barter my fiddle for cattle or sheep,
For music is better than critters to keep.
Old violin, go fiddle um dum, fiddle um dum dum dum do."

133

The Keeper

Social studies correlation

Key: D   MODERATELY

1. The keep-er did a-shoot-ing go, And   un-der his cloak he car-ried a bow,
2. The   first doe she did cross the plain, The   keep-er_ fetched her back_ a-gain,

A-5-So   3. The   sec-ond doe, she crossed the brook, The   keep-er_ fetched her with_ a hook,

All for to shoot at the mer-ry lit-tle doe, A-mong the leaves so_ green-o.
Where she is now she_ may_ re-main, A-mong the leaves so_ green-o.
Where she is now you can go_ and_ look, A-mong the leaves so_ green-o.

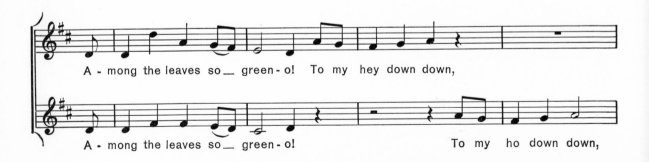

Jack-y boy!   Sing ye well?   Hey down!   Der-ry, der-ry down,

Mas-ter!   Ver-y well!   Ho down!

A-mong the leaves so_ green-o! To my hey down down,

A-mong the leaves so_ green-o!   To my ho down down,

134

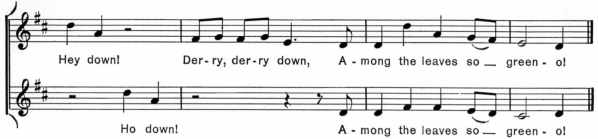

Hey down! Der-ry, der-ry down, A-mong the leaves so __ green-o!

Ho down! A-mong the leaves so __ green-o!

Help the children keep up the tempo in the question-answer parts of the song because quite often there is a tendency to slow down.

3-4-3   G-40   A-175

Further explanation of the meter is found in the Guide.

❶Beautiful Dreamer

Words and Music by Stephen Foster

Key: D

SMOOTHLY

1. Beau-ti-ful dream-er, wake un-to me, __ Star-light and dew-drops are wait-ing for
D-1-Do 2. Beau-ti-ful dream-er, out on the sea __ Mer-maids are chant-ing the wild Lor-e-

thee; _____ Sounds of the rude world, heard in the day, _____
lei; _____ O-ver the stream-let va-pors are borne, _____

Lulled by the moon-light have all passed a-way. _____ Beau-ti-ful dream-er,
Wait-ing to fade at the bright com-ing morn. _____ Beau-ti-ful dream-er,

queen of my song, __ List while I woo thee with soft mel-o-dy; ____
beam on my heart __ E'en as the morn on the stream-let and sea; ____

di

Gone are the cares of life's bus - y throng. __
Then will all clouds of sor - row de - part. __

1-2. Beau - ti - ful dream-er, a - wake un - to me! __

ritard.

Beau - ti - ful dream-er, a - wake un - to me! __

Some very helpful suggestions on legato singing may be found in the Guide.

This song is in AABB form: the first two phrases are alike, and the last two phrases are alike.

4-1-4   G-40   A-180

Robin Hood

Adapted Words   Old English Tune

Key: D   MODERATELY   See p. 192 for another English tune.

1. Bold Rob - in Hood and his band of mer - ry men
2. Bold Rob - in Hood and his com-rade Lit - tle John

D-1-Do

Lived a - way down deep __ in a for - est glen,
Roamed the for - est, mead-ow-land, and lit - tle town

(A)

And they went a-hunt-ing with noth - ing but a bow,
To right all the wrongs that the poor were suf - fer-ing;

They would all give chase to catch a buck or doe.
'Round the camp-fire they were al - ways heard to sing.

Refrain (B)

In Sher-wood For - est these mer - ry, mer - ry men

Would __ feast and sing a jol - ly song, __

(B)

In Sher-wood For - est these mer - ry, mer - ry men

Would __ feast and sing a jol - ly song. __

This is an excellent song for boys' voices.

137

KEY OF A MAJOR

See page 14.

1-3-4   G-40   A-181

Toviska

✗ slap knee   ✗ clap

Fun song

Moravian Folk Song

Key: A

BRISKLY

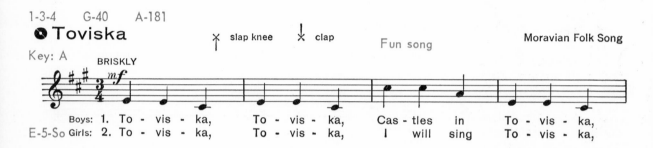

Boys: 1. To - vis - ka,   To - vis - ka,   Cas - tles   in   To - vis - ka,
E-5-So Girls: 2. To - vis - ka,   To - vis - ka,   I   will   sing   To - vis - ka,

Were there no   las - sies I'd   not   be   a   sol - dier.
If   you leave now, I   am   sure   to   for - get ____ you.

Hoo-ya hoo-ya-ya, Hoo-ya hoo-ya-ya, Hoo-ya hoo-ya-ya - ya, Ya - ya!

3. Boys: Toviska, Toviska, Hear me sing Toviska!
There is no hurry, I might change my mind for you.

4. Girls: Toviska, Toviska, Who's singing Toviska?
Are you still here though I've said my good-by to you?

5. All: Toviska, Toviska, Castles in Toviska!
We'll go a-walking and talking together.

Toviska = toh-vish-kah

This song should be sung with a very firm accent on the first beat of measure.

138

Over the Hills and Far Away

English Army Song, 1719

Key: A   LIVELY   Consult the Guide for suggested activities.

1. Hark! now the drums beat up a-gain, For all true_sol - diers and gen-tle-men,

A-1-Do 2. Here's for-ty shill - ings__on the drum For those that__vol - un - teers do come,

Then let's en - list_and_march, I   say,   O - ver the hills and   far   a - way.

With shirts and clothes and__ pres - ent   pay,   O - ver the hills and   far   a - way.

Refrain

O - ver the hills and   o - ver the main To_ Flan-ders, Por - tu - gal, and Spain;

Queen_ Anne com-mands, and we'll o - bey   O - ver the hills and   far   a - way,

Sing - ing,   o   ver   the   hills   and   far   a - way.

The boys in the class may enjoy comparing this "service song" with the familiar
ones which are found on pp. 152-157.

3. Come on then, boys, and you shall see,
We ev'ryone shall captains be,
To dress and strut as well as they
Over the hills and far away.

4. What though our friends our absence mourn,
We with all honor shall return;
And then we'll sing both night and day,
Over the hills and far away.

Every Pull of the Oar

Key: A SMOOTHLY   Adapted Words   Scottish Folk Tune

Reading song

1. We will row 'cross the lake to a place that I know,
2. We will swim for a while, and then rest in the shade,

A-1-Do

Where the trees give you shade and the wild flow-ers grow,
Then we'll head back for home   as the sun starts to fade,

Where the wa - ter is warm and as clear__ as glass,
We will row 'cross the lake in the gold-en sun-set,

And the ground is   all cov-ered with vel-vet - y grass.
With __ mem -'ries of sum-mer we'll nev-er for-get.

1-2. So,   row a-way, row, for it's nev-er a chore,__

Ev - 'ry pull of the oar brings us clos-er to shore.

This song presents no problem either in rhythm or in melody and
should therefore be fairly easy for the class to sight read. Let
them try it.

Down at the Barber Shop

Words and Music by J. Berli

Key: F MODERATELY

Three-part "fun" song

The Guide gives very helpful suggestions for teaching this song.

Clap the rhythm:

G-42   A-187

Little David

Spiritual

Key: G   Chorus   QUICKLY

Program number
clap

mf

Lit - tle Da - vid,

p   Notice that this pattern is repeated throughout the chorus.

B-3-Mi
D-5-So   Play on   your   harp!   Play on   your harp!

The clap may also be repeated.

play   on   your   harp, hal - le - lu! Hal - le - lu! Lit - tle Da - vid,

mp

Play   on   your   harp!   Play   on   your   harp!

1.   2.

play   on   your   harp, hal - le - lu! _____   lu! _____

Play   on   your   harp!   Play   on   your   harp! Play on your harp!

Leader

1. Lit - tle   Da - vid was   a   shep-herd boy; He   slew Go - li - ath and sang for joy. ___
2. Old __ Dan - iel   in   the   li - on's den; But   he came out __ all whole a - gain. ___
3. Lit - tle   Da - vid was   a   might - y King; And   all   the peo - ple came to sing. ___

142

Chorus

Lit - tle Da - vid, play on your harp, hal - le - lu! Hal - le - lu!

Play on your harp! Play on your harp!

1-2. | 3.

Lit - tle Da - vid, play on your harp, hal - le - lu! ————— lu! —————

Play on your harp! Play on your harp! Play on your harp!

Soloists and small groups have a wonderful opportunity to perform in this song.

The halyard chantey was used for long, heavy pulls, such as hauling up the mainsail.

So Handy

G-42   A-190

Halyard Chantey

Key: F LUSTILY, NOT TOO FAST

Solo f F   B♭   F   Chorus F   C₇   F

F-1-Do

1. Hand - y high and hand - y low,
2. Growl you must, but go you must!
3. Climb a - loft from down be - low,
4. We are bound a - round Cape Horn,

Hand - y, me boys, so hand - y, ———

Solo   Dm   B♭   Chorus C₇   F

Oh, it's hand - y high and a - way we go,
In your sea - man - ship just __ put your trust,
Up __ high a - loft that __ sail must go,
We'll __ round it by the __ ear - ly morn,

Hand - y, me boys, so hand - y! __

After the song is learned the class might enjoy reviewing some of the other
chanteys sung so far this year.

143

Legend

Key: E minor
SMOOTHLY

Clap the rhythm.

Ancient Finnish Song

mf

E-1-La   Although this is an uncommon meter, you will note that every phrase

1. Broth-ers, join our tri-bal sing-ing, Tell-ing o'er the old-en sto - ry,

is the same.

All our an-cient leg-ends bring-ing, All our tale of by-gone glo - ry.

2. Songs our honored fathers taught us,
From the mystic runes beginning,
Tales our gentle mothers brought us,
By the fireside deftly spinning.

3. Legends of the field and meadow,
Chanted oft by Wai-na-moi-nen,
Minstrel of the Kalevala,
Known thro' all the mighty Northland.

The short-haul chantey was used for jobs in which short, quick pulls
were made rather than the steady, slow kind used in hoisting the mainsail.

Haul Away, Joe

Key: Eb

Ideas for an assembly program number using
chanteys may be found in the Guide.

Short-haul Chantey

ACCENTED

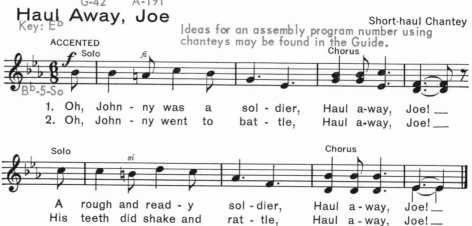

Solo   *f*   *fi*   Chorus

Bb-5-So

1. Oh, John - ny was a sol - dier, Haul a-way, Joe! __
2. Oh, John - ny went to bat - tle, Haul a-way, Joe! __

Solo   *si*   Chorus

A rough and read - y sol - dier, Haul a-way, Joe! __
His teeth did shake and rat - tle, Haul a-way, Joe! __

Solo: 3. And when the shooting started,
He found himself faint-hearted.

4. So Johnny quick retreated,
And ran back home, defeated.

5. Then Johnny got his shotgun,
The battle he had soon won.

6. They made of him a captain,
And now he winds the capstan.

Rio Grande

Key: C

Sea Chantey

IN A ROLLICKING MANNER

1. Oh, say, were you ev - er in Ri - o Grande?
2. Oh, New York town is no place for me,
3. Good - by, all you girls, I will be true,

A - way, you Ri-o!

C-1-Do

Oh, say, were you ev - er out there on the strand?
I'll pack up my bags and go to sea,
My thoughts will be on - ly for each of you,

1-3. For we're bound for the Ri - o Grande!

And a - way, you Ri - o, 'Way, you Ri - o!

Sing fare you well, my pret - ty young girls,

For we're bound for the Ri - o Grande!

Everyone who wants to sing a solo should have a
chance on this song.

Bendemeer's Stream

Key: F   SMOOTHLY   Words by Thomas Moore   Irish Folk Tune

1. There's a bow-er of ros-es by Ben-de-meer's stream,
2. No, the ros-es soon with-ered that hung o'er the wave,

And the night-in-gale sings 'round it all the day long;
But some blos-soms were gath-ered while fresh-ly they shone,

In the time of my child-hood 'twas like a sweet dream,
And a dew was dis-tilled from their flow-ers that gave

To __ sit in the ros-es and hear the bird's song.
All the fra-grance of sum-mer when sum-mer was gone.

Most children are very fond of this song. They should work toward a suitable balance between melody and harmony.

146

That bow'r and its mu-sic I'll nev-er for-get,
Thus mem-o-ry draws from de-light ere it dies

But oft when a-lone in the bloom of the year,
An es-sence that breathes of it man-y a year;

I think, "Is the night-in-gale sing-ing there yet?
Thus bright to my soul, as 'twas then to my eyes,

Are the ros-es still bright by the calm Ben-de-meer?"
Is that bow'r on the banks of the calm Ben-de-meer.

The Guide offers some specific help in interpretation.
Some member of the class may work out a harplike
accompaniment on the autoharp.

147

The Band

Key: C   IN MARCH TEMPO

Words and Music by Stephen Anderson

Program number

1. Here comes the band ___ with mu-sic loud and gay,

1-4. We are march-ing, we are march-ing

Too too too too too too too, ___ The trom-bones lead the way.

To the drum-mer's stead-y beat; ___

Drum-mers play a stead-y beat to set the pace for march-ing feet.

We are march-ing, we are march-ing,

Rat-tat-a-tat-a-tat-tat, ___ Pa-rad-ing down the street.

We are march-ing down the street.

148   The Guide lists several suggestions for additional activities.

2. Here comes the band with music loud and gay,
   Ta ta ta ta ta ta ta! Oh, hear the trumpets play.
   Drummers play a steady beat
   To set the pace for marching feet,
   Rat-tat-a-tat-a-tat-tat,
   Parading down the street.

3. Here comes the band with music loud and gay,
   Dee dee-dle dee-dle dee dee, the clarinets do play.
   Drummers play, etc.

4. Here comes the band with music loud and gay,
   Dee dee-dle dee-dle dee dee, the piccolos do play.
   Drummers play, etc.

   Add stanzas about other instruments in the band.
   As you sing about each instrument, imitate the way
   in which it is played.

149

Loch Lomond

Key: F

WITH SPIRIT

C-5-So

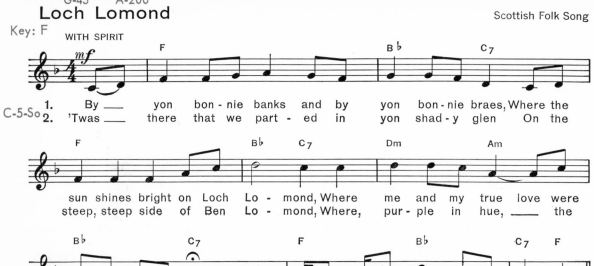

1. By ___ yon bon-nie banks and by yon bon-nie braes, Where the
2. 'Twas ___ there that we part-ed in yon shad-y glen On the

sun shines bright on Loch Lo - mond, Where me and my true love were
steep, steep side of Ben Lo - mond, Where, pur-ple in hue, ___ the

ev - er wont to gae On the bon-nie, bon-nie banks of Loch Lo - mond.
High-land hills we view And the moon ___ com-ing out in the gloam-ing.

150

Someone may play a bagpipe "drone" as suggested in the Guide.

151

2-2-1   G-44   A-202

● United States Armed Forces

Adapted Words   "The British Grenadiers"

Key: F   IN SLOW, STATELY MARCH TEMPO
Counter-melody (imitate bugle call)

Girls might sing the counter-melody while boys sing the melody.

C-5-So
Melody

Ta   ta   ta   ta   ta   ta   ta   ta   ta   ta,

The   sol-diers and the   sail-ors march a-long   in   u-ni-forms __ neat;

Ta   ta   ta   ta   ta   ta   ta   ta   ta   ta.

And   next, Ma-rines and   Air Corps come a-march-ing, march-ing down the   street;

Ta ta ta ta ta ta ta ta ta ta,

Of all the he - roes in the world no oth - ers can com - pare

Ta ta ta ta ta ta ta ta.

With U - nit - ed States Armed Forc - es on land, on sea, and in the air.

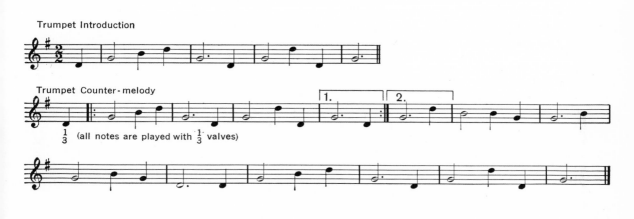

Trumpet Introduction

Trumpet Counter - melody

$\frac{1}{3}$ (all notes are played with $\frac{1}{3}$ valves)

Play on the snare drum (or clap knees):

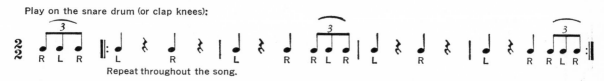

R L R L R L R R L R L R L R R L R

Repeat throughout the song.

Encourage your students who are in the band to play these instrumental parts.

● Field Artillery Song

Words and Music by Brig. Gen. E. L. Gruber

Key: C

IN MARCH TEMPO

Descant *mf*

C-1-Do

Keep them roll-ing, roll-ing on,

f Melody

O-ver hill, o-ver dale, we will hit the dust-y trail,

G-5-So Up and down, in and out, coun-ter-march and left a-bout,

Keep on roll-ing a-long, a-long.

And those cais-sons go roll-ing a-long. ____
And those cais-sons go roll-ing a-long. ____

Hi hi hee! Hi ___ hi ___ hee!

For it's hi hi hee in the Field Ar-til-ler-y,

Shout out your num-ber loud and strong, ___ Keep them roll-ing,

1-2-3-4

Shout out your num-ber loud and strong, ___ For wher-e'er we go

154   A small group of boys could call out the numbers, "1-2-3-4."

roll - ing a - long, Roll a - long, a - long,

You will al-ways know That those cais-sons go roll-ing a - long,

(Keep them roll-ing!) Roll a - long, a - long. —

(Keep them roll-ing!) And those cais-sons go roll-ing a - long. —

2-2-3   G-44   A-207

The Marines' Hymn

Words and Music by L. Z. Phillips

Key: C IN MARCH TEMPO

mf Descant

1. From the halls of Mon-te-zu-ma To the shores of Trip-o-li, Trip-o-li,

G-5-So

f Melody

1. From the halls of Mon-te-zu-ma To the shores of Trip-o-li,

C-1-Do

We__ fight our coun-try's__ bat-tles In the air, on land, and sea, land and sea;

We__ fight our coun-try's bat-tles In the air, on land, and sea;

First to fight for right and free - dom And to keep our hon- or clean; hon- or clean,

First to fight for right and free - dom And to keep our hon- or clean, _____

We are proud to claim _the _ ti - tle of U - nit - ed States Ma - rine. __

We are proud to claim the ti - tle of U - nit- ed States Ma - rine. __

2. Our flag's unfurled to ev'ry breeze
    From dawn to setting sun; (setting sun;)
    We have fought in ev'ry clime and place
    Where we could take a gun, (take a gun,)
    In the snow of far-off northern lands
    And in sunny tropic scenes; (tropic scenes;)
    You will find us always on the job:
    The United States Marines.

3. Here's health to you and to our Corps,
    Which we are proud to serve; (proud to serve;)
    In many a strife we've fought for life
    And never lost our nerve. (lost our nerve.)
    If the Army and the Navy
    Ever look on Heaven's scenes, (Heaven's scenes,)
    They will find the streets are guarded
    By United States Marines.

Descant singers should be reminded not to sing louder than the melody.

157

America the Beautiful
Words by Katherine Lee Bates   Music by Samuel A. Ward

Key: D   REVERENTLY

A-5-So
F-3-Mi
1. O   beau-ti-ful for   spa-cious skies, For am-ber waves of   grain,
2. O   beau-ti-ful for   pil-grim feet, Whose stern im-pas-sioned stress

For   pur-ple moun-tain   maj-es-ties A-bove the fruit-ed   plain. __
A   thor-ough-fare for   free-dom beat A-cross the wil-der-ness. __

A-mer-i-ca! A-mer-i-ca! God   shed His grace on   thee,
A-mer-i-ca! A-mer-i-ca! God   mend thine ev-'ry   flaw,

And   crown thy good with   broth-er-hood From   sea to shin-ing   sea!
Con-firm thy soul in   self-con-trol, Thy   lib-er-ty in   law!

Listening should be a part of every music lesson. Remind the children to blend
the second part with the melody.

3. O beautiful for heroes proved
   In liberating strife,
   Who more than self their country loved,
   And mercy more than life.
   America! America! May God thy gold refine
   Till all success be nobleness
   And ev'ry gain divine.

4. O beautiful for patriot dream
   That sees beyond the years
   Thine alabaster cities gleam
   Undimmed by human tears.
   America! America! God shed His grace on thee,
   And crown thy good with brotherhood
   From sea to shining sea.

Dona Nobis Pacem (Grant Us Peace)

Old German Canon

Key: F

Program number

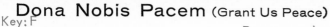
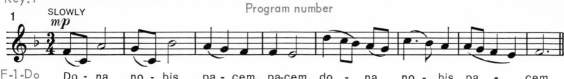

SLOWLY
mp

1

F-1-Do　Do - na　no - bis　pa - cem, pa-cem, do - na ‿ no - bis pa - cem.

2

Do - na　no - bis　pa - cem,　do - na　no - bis　pa - cem.

3

Do - na　no - bis ‿ pa - cem;　do - na　no - bis　pa - cem.

For best results with this lovely song be very sure that everyone knows the entire song well before attempting it as a round.

Tallis's Canon

Words by Thomas Ken　　Music by Thomas Tallis (1567)

Key: G

MODERATELY AND SMOOTHLY

1　　　　　　　2

G-1-Do　Glo - ry　to Thee, my　God, this night, For　all　the bless-ings　of　the light;

3　　　　　　　4

Keep　me,　oh, keep me,　King　of kings, Be - neath Thine own al - might-y　wings.

Most children are already familiar with the song. Their attention should be called to the fact that there is time for only the quickest of breaths between phrases.

Thomas Tallis was organist of the Chapel Royal of Queen Elizabeth I. He wrote much church music which is still played at services today.

Thomas Ken was an English bishop. He wrote the words of this evening hymn and set them to Tallis's music for the boys at Winchester College.

We Sing of Golden Mornings

The form of this song is AABA.

Key: F MODERATELY

Anonymous Words

Music by William Walker

C-5
So

1. We sing of gold-en morn-ings, We sing of spar-kling seas,
2. We sing the heart cou-ra-geous, The youth-ful, ea-ger mind!

Optional third part

Of prai-ries, val-leys, moun-tains, And state-ly for-est trees.
We sing of hopes un-daunt-ed, Of friend-ly ways and kind.

We sing of flash-ing sun-shine And life-be-stow-ing rain,
We sing of ros-es wait-ing Be-neath the deep-piled snow;

Of birds a-mong the branch-es, And spring-time come a-gain.
We sing, when night is dark-est, The day's re-turn-ing glow.

Some of the boys can sing the optional third part with very little help since it uses only two tones, Do and So.

160

The Band Concert

Adapted Words   Brazilian Folk Song arranged by Villa-Lobos

Key: F   RHYTHMICALLY   Instrumental activity

C-5-So

Down in the park on the band-stand, ____ Hear the rol-lick-ing, rhyth-mi-cal
Cor-net and trom-bone and tu-ba, _____ Mel-low bar-i-tone, pic-co-lo

Oom-pa-pa oom-pa-pa oom-pa-pa oom-pa-pa oom-pa-pa oom-pa-pa

F-1-Do   Suggestions for instrumental accompaniment may be found in the Guide.

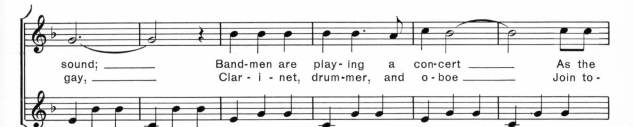

sound; _____ Band-men are play-ing a con-cert _____ As the
gay, _____ Clar-i-net, drum-mer, and o-boe _____ Join to-

oom-pa-pa oom-pa-pa oom-pa-pa oom-pa-pa oom-pa-pa oom-pa-pa

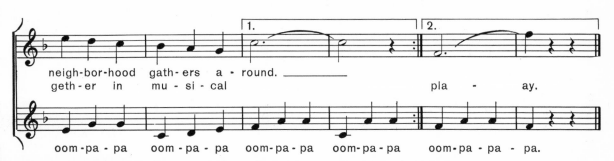

1.   2.

neigh-bor-hood gath-ers a-round. _____
geth-er in mu-si-cal   pla - ay.

oom-pa-pa oom-pa-pa oom-pa-pa oom-pa-pa oom-pa-pa-pa.

Some of the class may be interested in hearing other music by Villa-Lobos. He is
a contemporary composer and many of his works are available on recordings.

The Trout

Words by C. F. D. Schubart   Music by Franz Schubert

Key: Bb MODERATELY FAST

mp

Art song

F-5-So

In yon-der brook-let stream-ing, Ap-peared a play-ful _ trout;
With rod and silk line run-ning, An an-gler came that _ way

Like some bright ar-row gleam-ing, It dart-ed _ in and out.
And saw with cru-el cun-ning The trout be-low him play.

A-bove I watched_with_ pleas-ure, Con-tent to lie_ and_look
I turned my thoughts_to _ wish-ing That in a brook_so_clear

At such a sil-ver treas-ure Go swim-ming in the brook;
No lure would help the fish-ing, The trout would not go near;

At such _ a sil-ver _ treas-ure Go swim-ming in the brook.
No lure_would help_the _ fish-ing, The trout would not go near.

At last the an-gler wil-y,   as time went by,

The sixteenth-note passages require some careful attention but
with practice the class should be able to sing them correctly.

Made that clear brook-let dim and roil - y, And then __ I gave a cry—

mf

The rod and line were shak-en: The trout, O the trout was firm-ly caught

And from the brook-let tak - en, Quite shame-ful-ly, I thought;

mp

And from __ the brook-let __ tak - en, Quite shame-ful-ly, I thought.

You may refer to the Guide for further suggestions.

The Linden Tree

Adapted Words   Music by Franz Schubert

Key: F

1. Be - side the might-y riv - er there stands a lin - den tree,
2. And when I cease my rov - ing and live a - cross the sea,

I sit be - neath its shade watch-ing ships sail out to sea.
Fond mem - o - ries will haunt me of days that used to be,

I dream a - bout ad - ven - ture in lands so far a - way,
When seat - ed 'neath the lin - den I watched the ships sail by,

And hope a ship will car - ry me a - cross the sea some day,
I'll won - der if an - oth - er dreams dreams there the same as I,

164

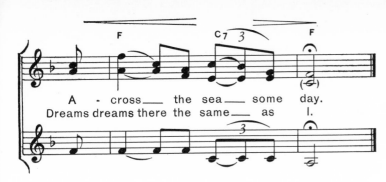

A - cross___ the sea___ some day.
Dreams dreams there the same___ as I.

If only two parts are sung, the second part should omit the notes in parentheses and double the first-part notes instead.

The Guide gives very helpful ideas for teaching the <u>triplet.</u>

My Island

G-47   A-225

Philippine Folk Song

Key: E   SMOOTHLY   Social studies correlation

mp

B-5-So
G-3-Mi

1. The sun is ris - ing high a - bove the
2. The sea comes rid - ing o'er the reef with
3. The gen - tle breez-es car - ry on the

moun-tains green___ To light a crown of
spar - kling foam___ A - long the cor - al
soft warm air___ The scent of fruit and

beau - ty___ up - on my is - land queen.___
beach-es___ a - round my is - land home.___
blos-soms___ thro all my is - land fair.___

165

4-3-2   G-47   A-224

Now the Day Is Over

Interpretation

Key: Eb

Words by Sabine Baring-Gould   Music by Joseph Barnby

MODERATELY, WITH EXPRESSION

Bb-5-So

1.   Now the day is— o-ver, Night is draw-ing— nigh,—
2.   Lord, please give the— wea-ry Calm and sweet re - pose;—

G-3-Mi

Eb-1-Do

1.   Now the day is   o-ver, Night is draw-ing— nigh,—
2.   Lord, please give the wea-ry Calm and sweet re - pose;—

Shad-ows of the   eve-ning— Steal a-cross the sky.
With Thy ten-d'rest bless - ing— May our eye-lids close.

Shad-ows of the   eve-ning Steal a-cross the sky.
With Thy ten-d'rest bless - ing May our eye-lids close.

Both of these songs
demand good breath
control for smooth,
legato singing.

3. When the morning wakens,
Then may we arise
Pure and fresh and worthy
In Thy holy eyes.

G-48   A-225

The Children's Prayer Operatic selection

Key: D

MODERATELY

Words by A. Wette   Music by E. Humperdinck

D-1-Do When at night I   go to sleep, Four-teen an-gels round me creep,—

When at night I   go to sleep, Four-teen an-gels round me creep,—

166

Two my head com-mand-ing, Two be-low me stand-ing,

Two my head com-mand-ing, Two be-low me stand-ing,

mp
Two my right se-lect-ing, Two my left pro-tect-ing,

mp
Two my right se-lect-ing, Two my left pro-

p   *mp*
Two_ give me cov-er, Two_ o'er me hov-er,

p   *mp*
tect-ing, Two_ give me cov-er, Two_ o'er me

mf   *ritard.*
Two_ near me bid-ing, My heav'n-ly jour-ney guid-ing.

mf
hov-er, Two my heav'n-ly jour-ney guid-ing.

This song is from Humperdinck's opera "Hänsel and Gretel," which has long been a favorite of young people everywhere. In the opera it is sung by the two children, Hänsel and Gretel, when they lose their way in the woods as night comes upon them.

If a recording of this opera is available, play it for the class. Many of the melodies will be familiar to the children.

Night Time

SLOWLY
Key: A minor

Program song

Words by Maria Rindelli   Music by Margaret Hurley

mp

1. Mur-m'ring breeze,_____ m, Mur-m'ring breeze,_____ m,
2. Shin - y moon, _____ m; Shin - y moon, _____ m;

A-1-La

mp

1. Mur-m'ring breeze, m, Mur-m'ring breeze, m,
2. Shin - y moon, m, Shin - y moon, m,

F-6-Fa

mp

1. Mur - m'ring breeze, Mur-m'ring breeze,
2. Shin - y moon, Shin - y moon,

D-4-Re

Lull me to sleep with your faint ser-e-nade, Rust-ling the leaves of the slum-ber-ing trees,
Lull me to sleep with your sil-ver-y light, Shed-ding your qui-et beams down on my dreams,

1-2. Loo (or hum) _____ Loo _____

1-2. Loo (or hum) _____ Loo _____

168 This is another song requiring careful breathing. By now, children should be aware of the importance of proper breath control in legato singing.

Jacob's Ladder

Spiritual

4-3-1 G-48 A-230

Key: F

WITH DIGNITY

1. We are climb-ing Ja-cob's lad-der, We are climb-ing Ja-cob's lad-der,
2. Ev-'ry round goes high-er, high-er, Ev-'ry round goes high-er, high-er,

A-3-Mi
F-1-Do

Optional third part

1. We are climb-ing Ja-cob's lad-der, We are climb-ing Ja-cob's lad-der,
2. Ev-'ry round goes high-er, high-er, Ev-'ry round goes high-er, high-er,

C-5-So

(Part 2 sing small notes if Part 3 is omitted)

We are climb-ing Ja-cob's lad-der, Sol-diers of the Cross._____
Ev-'ry round goes high-er, high-er, Sol-diers of the Cross._____

We are climb-ing Ja-cob's lad-der, Sol-diers of the Cross._____
Ev-'ry round goes high-er, high-er, Sol-diers of the Cross._____

Children may know this song from some other source, so they need to pay special attention to the parts which might be slightly different in this version.

169

do	mi	so	mi	so	do	so	do	mi	do
1	3	5	3	5	8(1)	5	8(1)	3	1
C	E	G	E	G	C	G	C	E	C

When you read new songs, always look for chord and scale passages. It is more musicianly, and easier, to read music in this way than note by note.

G-49   A-231

My Ukulele

Adapted Words   Music by W. A. Mozart

Key: C RHYTHMICALLY

1. Oh, just give me a small u - ku - le - le   And I'll strum while you sing to me gai - ly,
2. When I play on my small u - ku - le - le   Loud or soft, or how - ev - er it may be,

G-5-So

Just the same as they do   in Ha - wa - ii   Where they play by the light of the moon.
I can pic - ture the shores of Ha - wa - ii   With the green palms be - side blue la - goons.

It's the way that they play   in Ha - wa - ii   By the light of the stars and the moon.
It's a scene from the isles   of Ha - wa - ii   With its palms, foam - ing surf, blue la - goons.

Some of the children might think of a new way to strum the autoharp in this song.

170

Operatic selection

Anvil Chorus (from the opera "Il Trovatore")   Adapted Words   Giuseppi Verdi (Adapted)

Key: F **IN MARCH TEMPO**

mf (Start at the chorus if no accompaniment is used, omitting this section.)

F-1-Do   God of all na-tions, in glo-ry en-thron-éd, Up-on our lov'd coun-try Thy bless-ings pour!

Guide us and guard us from strife in the fu-ture, Let peace dwell a-mong us for-ev-er more.

Chorus *f*

Proud-ly our Stars and Stripes now glows with gold-en lus-ter,   Bright-ly each

star shines forth with-in the glo-rious clus-ter!   Lib-er-ty for-ev-er

more!   And peace with free-dom, and peace with free-dom, Let ring through-out our land!

The class will be able to find phrases which are similar.

Verdi was an Italian composer. He lived in the nineteenth century. His operas combine beautiful music with stirring drama, and they are often performed today. You can also hear them on records. "Il Trovatore," "Rigoletto," "La Traviata," and "Aida" are perhaps the most popular. Verdi also wrote fine church music.

For teaching purposes it is well to have the children hear the recording, if at all possible, in order to feel the vigorous mood of the selection.

Dance Together

Adapted Words   Italian Folk Tune

QUICKLY
Key: D minor

Creative activity

E-2-Ti All to-geth-er, dance to-geth-er, bring the girls, come dance to-geth-er! Round the

G-4-Re

ends and down the mid-dle! Quick, or I'll put up my fid-dle! All to-

1.

2.

fid-dle! Ha, ha, ha! What a fine lot of girls you are! Look a-live now,

what's the mat-ter? Join the line and stop your chat-ter! All to-geth-er!

Children might create a dance, letting the words of the song suggest the activity —
"Join the line," "Round the ends and down the middle," etc.

Now we're spin-ning, don't give up, it's just be-gin-ning! gin-ning!

4-2-3   G-49   A-237

Four in a Boat

American Singing Game

Rhythm pattern in the Guide may
be used as a clapping accompaniment.

Key: F   LIVELY

F-1-Do

1. Four in a boat — and the tide rolls high, Four in a boat — and the tide rolls high,
2. Get me a pret-ty one — by and by, Get me a pret-ty one — by and by,
3. Eight in a boat — and it won't go 'round, Eight in a boat — and it won't go 'round,

Four in a boat — and the tide rolls high, You get a pret-ty one — by and by.
Get me a pret-ty one — by and by, We don't — care — what the old folks say.
Eight in a boat — and it won't go 'round, Swing that — pret-ty one — you've just found.

Join hands in a large circle and face center. Four boys stand in the middle of the
circle, with hands joined. The circle moves to the right, and the boys in the center
move to the left as the first stanza is sung. At the start of the second stanza, the four
boys each choose a partner from the circle and move again to the left, hands joined
to their partner's. The big circle stops moving on the third stanza and claps hands
as the partners in the middle swing each other around with hooked elbows.

When the song is repeated, the four girls remain in the center and the four boys
join the big circle. Repeat the dance, with the four girls in the center.

Skip to the Fiddle

Adapted Words   Music by H. G. Nägeli

Key: D   GAILY

F-3-Mi   Skip, skip to the fid - dle, Skip, skip all a - round in a ring.

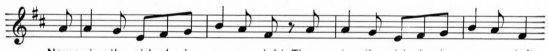

Free boy in the mid - dle, Link your arms as we sing.___

Now swing the girl who is on your right, Then swing the girl who is on your left,

Re - peat to right and hi - dee - ho, And swing once a - gain to your left, O!

Skip, skip to the fid - dle, Skip, now to the three just a - head.

Dance all of it o - ver, Hi - dee - ho, hi - dee - hee!___

Before the class sings the song, time may be well spent in finding the similar phrases. Staffs 1 and 2 are like 5 and 6. Staffs consists of a phrase which is repeated.

Form a triple circle consisting of sets of three (boy with a girl on each arm) facing clockwise. Then let each alternate group of three face the opposite direction.

M stands for measure.

M 1-4:   Each group of three skips 4 steps forward to its opposite group of three; then back 4 steps.

M 5-8:   Repeat steps for M 1-4.

M 9-10:   Boy links right elbow with girl on right and swings around 4 steps. Girl on left skips around in place, 4 steps.

M 11-12: Repeat M 9-10 with girl on boy's left. Girl on his right skips around in place, 4 steps.

M 13-16: Repeat steps for M 9-12.

M 17-20: Repeat M 1-4.

M 21-24: Each group of three skips 4 steps forward to its opposite group of three. Each group then goes forward 4 steps more, going through the opposite group (passing left shoulders) to meet a new set of three. Repeat the entire dance with the new set.

Have someone with a clear voice "call" the dance with some square dance calls worked out by the class.

SQUARE DANCE

175

● Fiesta

Key: G

Adapted Words   Mexican Folk Tune

LIVELY

D-5-
So

1. O - le!   O - le!   Fi - es - ta be-gins to - day;
2. O - le!   O - le!   Gui - tar and a vi - o - lin,

O - le!   O - le!   We'll dance and we'll sing and play;
O - le!   O - le!   Ma - ra - cas and man - do - lin;

O - le!   O - le!   Our trou-bles we'll throw a - way;
O - le!   O - le!   The mar-ket place rings with sound,

O - le!   O - le!   We'll dance to the mu - sic gay.
O - le!   O - le!   Come dance all a-round and 'round.

Refrain   Chromatics

Oh, what fun to go danc - ing to - geth - er,

With a swing and a sway and a twirl!___

Form a circle of couples, girls on the outside. Partners face each other and join both hands.

M stands for measure.

M 1:
Spring on left foot, bringing right heel forward at the same time (heel on floor, toe pointing up).

M 2:
Repeat above step, springing on right foot and bringing left heel forward.

M 3:
Continue above steps; spring on left foot, then on right.

M 4:
Same step, spring on left foot.

M 5-8:
Same as M 1-4, starting on right foot.

The steps for M 1-8 are these:
L—R—L R L;
R—L—R L R.

M 9-16:
Repeat steps for M 1-8.

M 17-20:
Partners link right elbows and circle in place moving clockwise.

M 21-24:
Partners link left elbows and circle in place moving counterclockwise.

176

Ev-'ry step is as light as a feath-er, Oh, what fun to go round in a whirl!

Dancers and singers should take turns, since it is very difficult to do both at the same time.

177

⊘Caller's Song

American Singing Game

Key: A♭

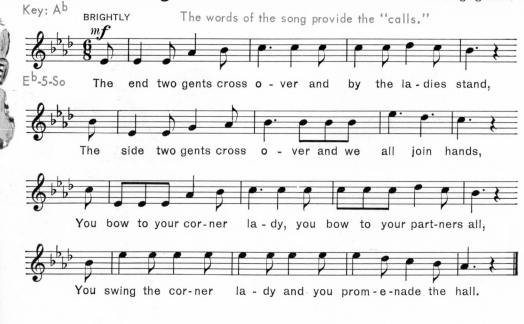

BRIGHTNESS / BRIGHTLY

The words of the song provide the "calls."

E♭-5-So   The   end two gents cross o - ver and   by   the la - dies stand,

The   side two gents cross o - ver and we   all   join   hands,

You bow to your cor - ner   la - dy, you bow to your part - ners all,

You swing the cor - ner   la - dy and you prom - e - nade the hall.

[Form a square of four couples with the girl to the right of the boy. The first and third couples are the "end couples." The "corner lady" is the lady at the left of each boy. The song tells what to do.   Choose a "caller" from the class.

Sing the song a second time for the promenade so that the couples can circle twice.

The girl leads her new partner back to her place in the square. Repeat the dance until the original partners are back together again.]

The five dances on these pages would make a very colorful contribution to an assembly program. The children would enjoy adding simple costumes, also.

The Fisherman's Farewell

Adapted Words　　Bohemian Folk Tune

Key: C
FLOWINGLY

Analysis of structure

E-3-Mi
1. Strong is the beat of the win-ter rain, And long the cry of the sea;
2. Spring-time is here and the win-ter's past, Oh, hear the call of the sea!

C-1-Do

Optional third part

I must go back to the sea a-gain, Back home, back home to the sea.
I shall go back to the sea at last, Back home, back home to the sea.

Day and night I can hear ____ Sound of waves break-ing near; ____
Loud and clear, all day long ____ Wave and wind chant their song; ____

ritard.

I must go back to the sea a-gain, ⎱
I shall go back to the sea at last, ⎰ Fare-well, my love, to thee. ____

As is the case in most songs, time will be saved if the music is analyzed first.
The Guide contains an analysis of this song.

179

A Life on the Ocean Wave

Words by Henry Russell   Music by Epes Sargent

Key: G

chromatic

chromatic tones

180

The refrain is exactly like the first two lines of the song.

Refrain

A life on the o-cean wave, — A — home on the roll - ing deep, — Where the

scat - tered wa - ters rave, — And the winds their rev - els keep! —

This makes a wonderful program song for boys. The chromatic tones may be played first on a melody instrument to insure accuracy of pitch.

181

G-51   A-248

We Sail the Ocean Blue

Words by W. S. Gilbert   Music by Sir Arthur Sullivan

Key: C

MODERATELY   You may refer to the Guide for material about Gilbert and Sullivan.

C-1-Do   We—— sail the o - cean blue, And our sau - cy ship's a beau - ty;

We're—— so - ber men and true, And at - ten - tive to our du - ty;

When the shots whis-tle free o'er the bright— blue sea, We stand to our guns all day,

When at an - chor we ride on the Ports-mouth tide, We've plen - ty of time for play,

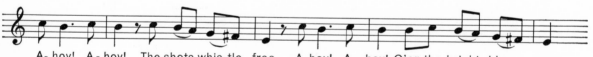

A - hoy! A - hoy! The shots whis-tle free, A - hoy! A - hoy! O'er the bright— blue— sea;

We stand to our guns, to our guns all day.——

We—— sail the o - cean blue, And our sau - cy ship's a beau - ty;

182

We're___ so-ber men and true, And at-ten-tive to our du-ty;

Our sau-cy ship's a beau-ty; We're at-ten-tive to our du-ty;

We're so-ber men and true, We sail the o - cean blue.

From the light opera "H. M. S. Pinafore."

G-52   A-252

The Mermaid

Sailor Chantey

Key: B♭

STEADILY

Three-part "fun" song

F-5-So

1. 'Twas Fri-day morn when we set sail and were
2. Then up spoke the cap-tain of our gal - lant ship, and a

not far out from land, When the cap-tain spied a
well-spo-ken man was he: "I left a wife in

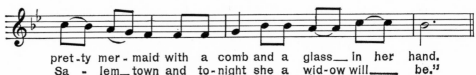

pret-ty mer - maid with a comb and a glass in her hand.
Sa - lem town and to-night she a wid-ow will be."

Refrain

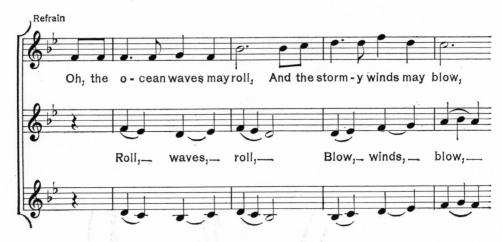

Oh, the o - cean waves may roll, And the storm - y winds may blow,

Roll, waves, roll, Blow, winds, blow,

The second and third parts have a similar rhythm pattern but you will
observe that it differs from that of the melody.

184

While we poor sail-ors go skip-ping to the tops, And the land-lub-bers lie down be-

While we poor sail-ors go skip-ping to the tops, And the land-lub-bers lie down be-

low, be-low, be-low, And the land-lub-bers lie down be-low.

low, be-low, be-low, And the land-lub-bers lie down be-low.___

The children will want to sing all the stanzas of this silly song!

3. Then up spoke the cook of our gallant ship,
   And a red-hot cook was he:
   "I care much more for my pots and pans
   Than I do for the bottom of the sea."

4. Then three times 'round went our gallant ship,
   And three times 'round went she;
   Then three times 'round went our gallant ship,
   And she sank to the bottom of the sea.

185

Find Work, My Daughter

French Folk Song

LIVELY
Key: A minor

Analysis of structure

mf

A-1-La

1. "Find work, my daugh-ter, You can milk a   cow, dee-dle-dum-dum,
2. "Well, then, my daugh-ter, Choose a stead-y   man, dee-dle-dum-dum,
3. "Daugh-ter, a farm-er's bet-ter than a   king, dee-dle-dum-dum,

C-3-Do

Find work, my   daugh-ter,   You can milk a   cow."
Well, then, my   daugh-ter,   Choose a stead-y   man."
Daugh-ter, a   farm-er's   bet-ter than a   king."

"No, no, my   moth-er,   Let me mar-ry   now, dee-dle-dum-dum,
"Moth-er, I   want a   prop-er gen-tle - man, dee-dle-dum-dum,
"Give me a   hus-band   who can dance and   sing, dee-dle-dum-dum,

No, no, my   moth-er,   Let me mar-ry   now."
Moth-er, I   want a   prop-er gen-tle - man."
Give me a   hus-band   who can dance and   sing."

186

The analysis of the song is given in the Guide. However, the
class should be able to analyze it without help.

Cockles and Mussels

Key: G

$\frac{3}{4}$ Note the repetition of the rhythmic pattern.

Irish Folk Song

NOT TOO FAST

mf

D-5-So

1. In___ Dub-lin's fair cit- y, where girls are so   wit- ty, 'Twas there that I   met her, sweet
2. She___ was a fish-mong-er, and sure 'twas no won-der, For   so were her moth-er and
3. But she died of the "fa-ver," and noth-ing could save her, And   that was the   end of poor

Mol - ly Ma - lone; She___wheeled her wheel - bar-row thro' streets broad and nar - row,
fa - ther be - fore; They___ each wheeled their   bar-row thro' streets broad and nar - row,
Mol - ly Ma - lone; But her ghost wheels her   bar-row thro' streets broad and nar - row,

Cry-ing: "Cock-les and mus-sels, a - live, a-live, O! A- live, a-live, O!___

Children may need practice in reading the chords.

A - live, a - live,   O!"___   Cry-ing: "Cock-les and mus-sels, a - live, a - live, O!"

"Faver" means "fever."   The autoharp sounds especially good with
this type of tune.

187

The Nightingale

Kentucky Folk Song

Key: C   SMOOTHLY

The Guide offers good suggestions for teaching this song.

C   G7   C   G7 (continue)   mp

C-1-Do

1. One morn-ing, one morn-ing, one morn-ing in May,
2. "Good morn-ing, good morn-ing, good morn-ing to thee,

Doo doo doo doo doo doo doo doo, etc.
(Use "Ah" or hum, if you prefer.)

E-3-Mi
C-1-Do

I met a fair cou-ple a-mak-ing their way, And one was a la-dy so
O where are you go-ing, my pret-ty la-dy?" "O I am a-goin' to the

neat and so fair, The oth-er a sol-dier, a brave vol-un-teer.
banks of the sea, To hear___ the night-in-gale sing___ for me."

The melody should be thoroughly learned before the other parts are added.

3. We hadn't been standing but one hour or two,
   When from his knapsack a fiddle he drew,
   The tune that he played made the valleys ring
   With sounds such as nightingales surely would sing.

4. "O lady, fair lady, it's time to return."
   "No, wait, for another tune do I yearn,
   I'd much rather hear just a tune on one string
   Than all of the songs that the nightingales sing."

Make up a rhythm accompaniment on the drum and claves.

G-53   A-260

Ring the Banjo

Words and Music by Stephen Foster

Key: E♭

BRIGHTLY

Rhythmic activity

mf

B♭-5-
So

1. The time is nev-er drear-y   If a   fel-low nev-er
2. Oh, nev-er count the bub-bles While there's wa-ter in the

groans,   A par-ty's nev-er wea-ry With the rat-tle of the bones.
spring,   A man can have no trou-bles While he's got this song to sing.

Then come a-gain, Su - san-na,   By the gas-light of the moon,
The beau-ties of cre - a-tion Will___ nev - er lose their charm,

We'll___ turn the old pi - an - o When the ban-jo's out of tune.
While I roam the old plan - ta-tion With my true love on my arm.

Refrain

Ring, ring the ban - jo!   I   like that good old   song.

Come a - gain, my   true love, Oh, where you been   so long?

The Guide offers suggestions for rhythmic accompaniment, but the class should
be encouraged to try out their own ideas.

189

G-53   A-262

Happy Village

Old French Song

Key: F   The beauty of this song lies in its simplicity.

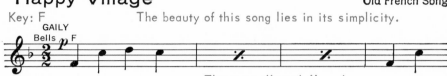

These are "simile" marks.

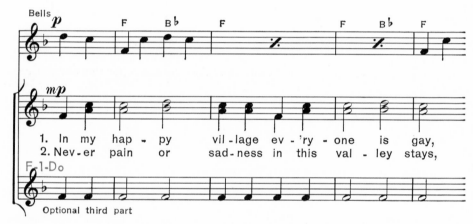

1. In my hap - py vil - lage ev - 'ry - one is gay,
2. Nev - er pain or sad - ness in this val - ley stays,

F-1-Do

Optional third part

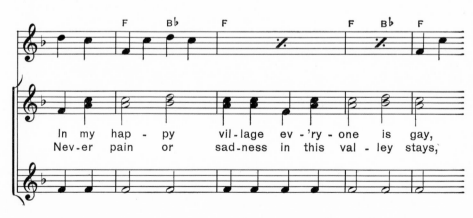

In my hap - py vil - lage ev - 'ry - one is gay,
Nev - er pain or sad - ness in this val - ley stays,

190

Sweet the shep-herd's song, At eve when all his toil is end-ed,
Here life seems at rest, Here love-ly laugh-ter has its dwell-ing,

Sweet the shep-herd's song, At eve when all his toil is end-ed,
Here life seems at rest, Here love-ly laugh-ter has its dwell-ing,

At the day's soft close To his hearth he goes.
In my vil-lage home On-ly joy is known.

The Guide contains some very specific ideas for ways to make this
into an interesting program number.

Walk into the Spring

Key: C

Old English Words   English Morris Dance

BRIGHTLY
mp

1. Come, let's walk in - to the spring Where we may hear the
2. Yon-der dale has glow-ing flow'rs And many pleas-ant

C-1-Do

blue - bird sing! Rob - in Red-breast and the thrush, The
shad - y bow'rs; Purl - ing brooks with sil - ver streams, All

night - in - gale in thorn - y bush, The ma - vis sweet-ly
beau - ti - fied by gold - en beams, Come steal-ing thro' the

car - ol - ing, These to my love con - tent will bring!
trees for fear, Be - cause Di - an - a wan - ders here.

192

Rob - in Red-breast and — the — thrush, The — night-in-gale in
Purl -ing brooks with sil - ver — streams, All — beau -ti -fied by

thorn - y bush, Ma- vis sweet-ly car - ol - ing, These —
gold - en beams, Steal-ing thro' the trees for — fear, Be -

to my love con - tent will bring. Come, let's — walk in -
cause Di - an - a wan - ders here. Come, let's — walk in -

to the — spring, Where — we may hear the blue - birds sing.
to the — spring, Where — we may hear the blue - birds sing.

Some of the class will recognize this tune as part of
"Country Gardens." See Guide for further details.

Going to Shout

Spiritual

1-3. Heav'n,_____ heav'n,_____ Ev - 'ry - bod - y talk - ing 'bout

1-3. Heav'n,_____ heav'n,_____ Ah_____

heav'n's not goin'_ there; Heav'n,_____ heav'n,_____ Goin' to
heav'n's not goin'_ there; Heav'n,_____ heav'n,_____ Goin' to
heav'n's not goin'_ there; Heav'n,_____ heav'n,_____ Goin' to

1., 2.
shout all o - ver God's heav'n._____
walk all o - ver God's heav'n._____

3.
Note the crescendo ending.
play all o - ver God's heav'n._____

195

On a Fine Summer Day

G-54   A-274

Adapted Words   French Folk Tune

MARCH TEMPO   Drum patterns would emphasize the march tempo.

Key: C

1. Where trails are the rough-est and moun-tains rise the high-est,
2. The hills and the val-leys lie spread-ing out be-fore us,

Optional third part

1-2. We like to go out hik-ing on a fine sum-mer day;

For we are just a jol-ly band, a jol-ly band of hik-ers,
The air is clear and brac-ing, and the sun is shin-ing bright-ly,

We go hik-ing on a fine sum-mer day.

Some of the boys may be able to sing these low tones.

[Whistle a
third stanza.]

197

Streets of Laredo

Cowboy Song

Key: F   SADLY   Each phrase of the descant should be sung on one breath.

Descant

A-3-Mi   Ah

Melody

1. As I walked out on the streets of La - re - do, As
2. "I see by your out - fit that you are a cow-boy," These

C-5-So

Ah

I walked out in La - re - do one day, I
words he did say as I bold - ly walked by; "Come

Ah

spied a young cow-boy all wrapped in white lin - en, All
sit down be - side me and hear my sad sto - ry, I'm

Ah

wrapped in white lin - en and cold as the clay.
shot in the chest and I know I must die."

3. "Get six jolly cowboys to carry my coffin,
Get six pretty maidens to sing me a song,
Take me to the valley and lay the sod o'er me,
For I'm a young cowboy and know I've done wrong."

4. "Oh, beat the drum slowly and play the fife lowly,
While sounding the dead march o'er my fun'ral pall;
Put bunches of roses all over my coffin,
The roses will deaden the clods as they fall."

A small group may sing the descant, or play it on bells or melody instruments. Notice that it uses only three tones.

Try harmonizing the song with the chords given above. Play this accompaniment on the piano, or sing it.

Guitar accompaniment would also be suitable.

Notice that all but one of the phrases are 3 measures in length, instead of the usual 4. Which phrase is not 3 measures long?

[The third phrase is 4 measures long.]

G-55   A-278

Farewell Song

Key: E♭

Czechoslovakian Folk Song

MODERATELY   This song has an unusual "flavor" which appeals to children.

1. Where the grass is grow-ing I'll go mow-ing,
2. I must leave my sweet-heart now for - ev - er;

E♭-1-Do

Watch the wa - ter, cool - ing wa - ter, flow - ing,
Part - ing, that's a sick - ness worse than fe - ver,

Note the chromatics.

Hear the wa - ter flow-ing on, o - ver shin-ing grav - el,
When you find the heal-ing herb, fe - ver soon is end - ed,

Hear the wa - ter flow-ing on, o - ver shin-ing grav - el,
When you find the heal-ing herb, fe - ver soon is end - ed,

Optional third part

Think that from my home-land I__ must__ trav - el.
Bro - ken hearts are nev - er, nev - er__ mend - ed.

G-55   A-280

Praise Ye the Lord

Key: F

Words by Cecil Cowdrey   Polish Folk Tune

MODERATELY
mp   Special day song

C-5-So

1. Praise ye the Lord! Oh, come to - day with sing - ing! Bless ye the
2. Bow in His pres - ence, ask that He may guide you; Still, day and

A-3-Mi

Optional third part

F-1-Do

Lord, all hon - or to Him bring - ing! Come, all ye peo - ple,
night, He ev - er walks be - side you. Come, all ye peo - ple,

His great love pro - claim, _ Kneel and a - dore Him, Ho - ly is His name! _
here His love pro - claim, _ Kneel and a - dore Him, Ho - ly is His name! _

The piano accompaniment for this song can be played by one of the class members. Or, the class might sing unaccompanied with a simple bell melody as an interlude.

The Star - Spangled Banner

Interpretation

Key: B♭ MODERATELY

Words by Francis Scott Key   Music by John Stafford Smith

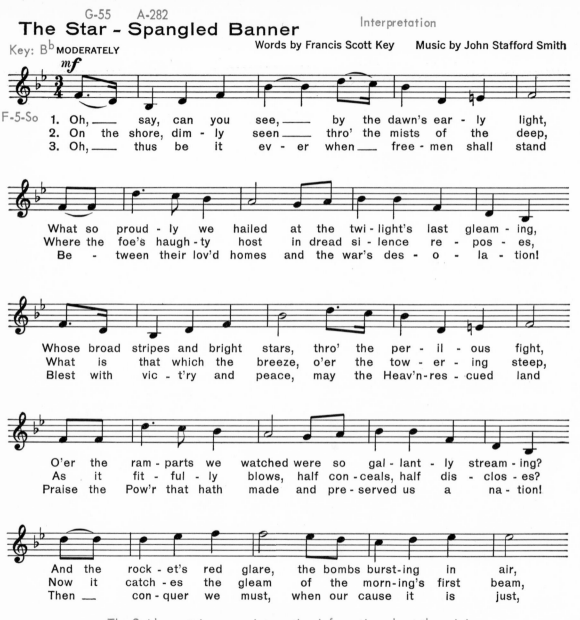

F-5-So

1. Oh,— say, can you see,— by the dawn's ear - ly light,
2. On the shore, dim - ly seen— thro' the mists of the deep,
3. Oh,— thus be it ev - er when— free - men shall stand

What so proud - ly we hailed at the twi - light's last gleam - ing,
Where the foe's haugh - ty host in dread si - lence re - pos - es,
Be - tween their lov'd homes and the war's des - o - la - tion!

Whose broad stripes and bright stars, thro' the per - il - ous fight,
What is that which the breeze, o'er the tow - er - ing steep,
Blest with vic - t'ry and peace, may the Heav'n-res - cued land

O'er the ram - parts we watched were so gal - lant - ly stream - ing?
As it fit - ful - ly blows, half con - ceals, half dis - clos - es?
Praise the Pow'r that hath made and pre - served us a na - tion!

And the rock - et's red glare, the bombs burst-ing in air,
Now it catch - es the gleam of the morn-ing's first beam,
Then — con - quer we must, when our cause it is just,

The Guide contains some interesting information about the origin
of the song.

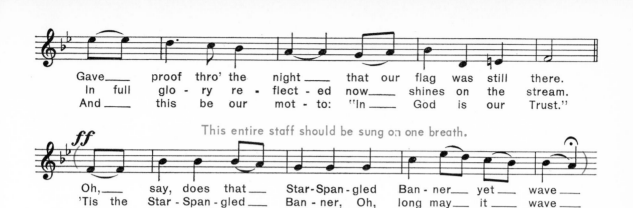

Gave____ proof thro' the night ____ that our flag was still there.
In full glo - ry re - flect - ed now____ shines on the stream.
And ____ this be our mot - to: "In ____ God is our Trust."

This entire staff should be sung on one breath.

ff

Oh,____ say, does that ____ Star - Span - gled Ban - ner____ yet ____ wave ____
'Tis the Star - Span - gled ____ Ban - ner, Oh, long may ____ it ____ wave ____
And the Star - Span - gled ____ Ban - ner in tri - umph____shall ____ wave ____

O'er the land _____ of the free and the home of the brave?
O'er the land _____ of the free and the home of the brave!
O'er the land _____ of the free and the home of the brave.

This is, of course, a very familiar song, but children of this age should be urged to improve their interpretation by practicing what they have learned about breathing and by observing carefully the various expression marks.

203

A REVIEW OF MUSICAL TERMS AND SYMBOLS

Staff

The staff is the set of five horizontal lines on which music is written.

Clef

A clef is a symbol which appears at the beginning of every staff of music. It identifies the pitch of the notes on the staff.

 The G clef, or treble clef, tells us that G is located on the second line.

 The F clef, or bass clef, tells us that F is located on the fourth line.

Key Signature

A key signature consists of the sharp(s) or flat(s) which may appear on the staff directly following the clef symbol. It tells us that these notes should be played as sharps or flats throughout the piece.

Time Signature

The time signature (or meter signature) consists of two numbers and appears right after the key signature at the beginning of a piece. The upper number tells us how many beats are in each measure; the lower number tells us what kind of note gets one beat.

Cut Time ¢

In this type of meter there are two beats to each measure, and a half note or rest gets one beat instead of the usual two beats.

Measure

A measure is a short section of music enclosed within two vertical lines on the staff. It must contain the number of beats called for in the time signature.

Notes and Rests

Sixteenth	♪	4 equal 1 beat	
Eighth	♪	2 equal 1 beat	
Quarter	♩	equals 1 beat	
Half	♩	equals 2 beats	
Whole	o	equals 4 beats	

Leger Line

A leger line is a short, horizontal line used to indicate the pitch of notes that are too high or too low to appear on the staff.

Bar

A bar is a single, vertical line used to separate measures. The first beat in a measure comes right after the bar.

Double Bar

Two thin bars indicate the end of a section. A thin plus a heavy bar indicates the end of the piece.

Down Beat

The first beat, or count, in a measure is called the down beat.

Half-step

When two notes are directly next to each other on the piano keyboard without either a black or a white key between them, they are said to be a half-step apart. Any black key is a half-step higher or lower than its adjacent white keys. Some half-steps are E to F, C to C#, and A# to B.

Whole Step

Two consecutive half-steps equal one whole step. Some whole steps are C to D, Bb to C, F# to G#, and E to F#.

Octave

In naming notes by letter names, we use only seven letters of the alphabet: A, B, C, D, E, F, and G. Then we begin all over again with A. The reason for this is plain if you sound on the piano any two notes of the same name (two consecutive C's, for instance). The upper C simply duplicates the sound of the lower C at a higher pitch. The eighth note upward or downward from any starting note is called the "octave" of the original note. The whole span of eight notes is also called an "octave."

Sharp ♯

A sharp sign before a note tells us to raise that note one half-step. If it appears in the key signature, it applies throughout the song. If it appears within the piece, it means for that measure only.

Double Sharp ✖

A double sharp sign before a note tells us to raise that note one *whole* step.

Flat ♭

A flat sign before a note tells us to lower that note one half-step. If it appears in the key signature, it applies throughout the song. If it appears within the piece, it means for that measure only.

Natural ♮

A natural sign before a note cancels the previous sharp, flat, or double sharp.

Slur

A slur is a curved line connecting two or more notes of different pitch that are sung to the same syllable of text.

Tie

A tie is a curved line linking two notes of the same pitch. It indicates that the notes are to be held for the combined value of both.

Dot

A dot placed after a note or rest increases the value of that note or rest by one half.

A dot placed above or below a note tells us to sing or play that note very short and to come off it quickly.

Triplet

A triplet is a group of three notes linked by a curved line and the number three. It is given the same number of beats, or rhythmic value, as two of those notes would ordinarily get. Therefore, you must sing triplet notes a little faster.

Fermata 𝄐

A fermata placed over a note or rest tells us to pause and hold that note or rest a little longer.

Accent >

An accent (*sforzando*) over or under a note tells us to sing or play that note with more emphasis.

Syncopation

This term describes a rhythm in which the accent falls on what would ordinarily be an unaccented, or weak, beat. In 4 meter, for example, the accents
4
usually fall on 1 and 3:

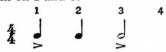

The following rhythm would be considered syncopated:

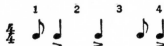

Breath Marks

Two short lines as shown here tell us to take a quick breath at this point.

Dynamics

In music we use expression marks to indicate loudness or softness, or dynamics. These Italian terms are used by musicians of all nations.

pp	*pianissimo*	very soft
p	*piano*	soft
mp	*mezzo piano*	moderately soft
mf	*mezzo forte*	moderately loud
f	*forte*	loud
ff	*fortissimo*	very loud

Repeat

This symbol tells us to repeat from the previous repeat sign, or, if there is none, to repeat from the beginning.

This symbol *Z.* tells us to repeat the previous measure.

1st & 2nd Endings

These numbered brackets tell us to sing or play through the first ending to the repeat sign. Then we are to go back to the beginning of the section and sing or play it through again, this time skipping the first ending and taking the second ending instead.

Da Capo al Fine or *D. C. al Fine*

This Italian musical term indicates the end of a section and is shown by two thin bars. It tells us to go back to the beginning and sing through to the place marked *Fine*.

Fine (fee'nay)

Fine is an Italian word which indicates the end of a piece of music. It is shown by a thin and a heavy double bar.

Crescendo

The term *crescendo*, abbreviated *"cresc.,"* or shown by the above sign tells us to sing or play louder.

Decrescendo

The term *decrescendo*, abbreviated *"decresc.,"* or shown by the above sign tells us to sing or play softer.

Ritardando

This word is abbreviated *"ritard."* or *"rit.,"* and it means "slower."

Poco Accelerando

In Italian *poco* means "a little"; *accelerando* means "faster." This term tells us to sing or play a little faster.

A tempo

Tempo is an Italian term meaning "rate of speed." *A tempo* tells us to go back to the original tempo, or speed, in a piece of music.

Phrase

A phrase is a short section consisting of one musical idea. Often we take a breath at the end of a phrase.

Sequence

The repetition of a short musical idea on different levels of pitch is called a sequence.

Descant

A descant is an extra, separate piece of music which makes an interesting combination when sung or played with the original melody.

Coda

This is a short section of music added at the end of a piece to make a more interesting and effective closing.

Round

A round is a type of song in which two or more groups sing the same melody starting and ending at different times.

Canon

A canon is a type of song like a round, in which several groups imitate each other by starting the same melody at different times. In a canon, some of the parts are changed at the end so that all groups end the song together.

Counterpoint

When two or more melodies are sung or played simultaneously, we call the combination counterpoint.

Orchestral Choirs

The various instruments in the modern symphony orchestra are grouped together into families, or choirs, according to the way in which they are played or the materials from which they are made.

String Choir

The instruments in the string choir are: Violin, Viola, Violoncello (or Cello), and Double Bass.

Wood-wind Choir

The instruments in the wood-wind choir are: Piccolo, Flute, Oboe, Clarinet, Bassoon, and English Horn.

Brass Choir

The instruments in the brass choir are: French Horn, Trumpet, Trombone, and Tuba.

Percussion Choir

Some percussion instruments are: Kettledrums, Bass Drum, Snare Drum, Bells, Tambourines, Cymbals, and Rhythm Sticks, among others.

Flute Fingerings

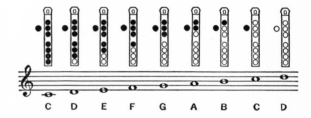

Chromatic Tones

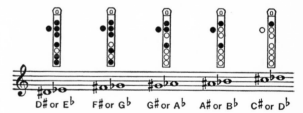

Alphabetical Index of Recordings

One album of two LP recordings
Produced by Audio Education, Inc., distributed by American Book Company

CLASSIFIED INDEX

211

ALPHABETICAL INDEX OF SONGS

MUSIC FOR YOUNG AMERICANS

☆ ABC MUSIC SERIES ☆

MUSIC ★ FOR

ABC MUSIC SERIES

☆

**GUIDE TO
BOOK SIX**

★ **YOUNG** ★ **AMERICANS**

RICHARD C. BERG
DIRECTOR OF MUSIC EDUCATION, YONKERS, N. Y.

DANIEL S. HOOLEY
PROFESSOR OF MUSIC EDUCATION
GEORGIA SOUTHERN COLLEGE, COLLEGEBORO, GEORGIA

JOSEPHINE WOLVERTON
ASSISTANT SUPERVISOR OF MUSIC, EVANSTON PUBLIC SCHOOLS
AND ASSISTANT PROFESSOR OF MUSIC
NORTHWESTERN UNIVERSITY, EVANSTON, ILLINOIS

CLAUDEANE BURNS
CONSULTANT, AMERICAN BOOK COMPANY, CHICAGO, ILLINOIS

AMERICAN BOOK COMPANY ©

MUSIC EDUCATION IN THE SIXTH GRADE

A Comprehensive Music Program

Music education in the Sixth Grade should consist of a comprehensive program aimed at developing each pupil's musical skill, knowledge, and enjoyment to his fullest capacity. In addition to continuing the activities begun in earlier grades in singing, playing instruments, reading music, creative experiences, rhythmic development, and listening, the Sixth Grade should offer extended opportunities in part-singing. In this grade, the children are at an age when, with proper previous preparation in the grades below, they respond to and find satisfaction in the challenge of two- and three-part songs, in descants, and in rounds. BOOK SIX of *Music for Young Americans* contains a wide variety of material designed to implement the objectives stated above. In this Guide, the teacher is offered suggestions for the use of each song found in the child's book.

The enthusiasm and resourcefulness of the teacher are the primary assets of any music program in the elementary schools, and the material and suggestions offered in this Guide are intended to assist her in administering a program based on her creative abilities and on her intimate knowledge of the needs of her pupils.

Music Reading

The preceding books in the series provide a music-reading program which systematically develops music-reading skills from reading readiness in the primary grades to integrated tonal and rhythmic reading in BOOKS THREE, FOUR, and FIVE. In BOOK SIX, the songs have been carefully selected to provide additional experiences based on tonal and rhythmic patterns previously introduced and lying within the framework of keys and meters already familiar. The keys of C, Db, D, Eb, E, F, G, Ab, A, and Bb major have already been presented. In addition to a review of basic reading skills and concepts, the minor mode, chromatics, and harmony are presented in a manner which is intended to broaden and extend the pupil's reading ability.

Music-reading skill is acquired through the assimilation of a number of separate learning pro-

1

cesses. In BOOK SIX, as in the other books of the series, constant attention is given to developing each skill as a unit integrated in the total reading process. Attention is called to the following reading elements:

1. identical, similar, or contrasting phrases.
2. unusual or characteristic rhythmic patterns.
3. noteworthy tonal patterns or intervals.
4. scalewise, chordal, or other melodic features.
5. differentiation between major and minor tonalities.

The development of reading ability depends largely on the child's interest. Therefore, reading skills are introduced within the context of songs chosen for their musical merit and suitability to the interests of the age group.

Learning to read music becomes more interesting and attainable when both vocal and instrumental media are used. The child's book uses keyboard illustrations to highlight important teaching points; to facilitate clear visualization of scales, intervals, and tonal patterns; and to enable the child to play and hear these features on the piano or chromatic bells. Many songs playable on melody instruments are included as reading reinforcements and for the interest and variety they lend to a program of classroom music.

Several systems are used in this country for naming scale tones; so-fa syllables, numbers, and letter names are all employed. In this series, each of these systems is used to illustrate teaching points. Choice of note name should be based on whatever practice is considered suitable in your school system.

The Music Period

The ideal use of music in the elementary-school program depends upon enthusiastic teaching and adequate time allotment. Pupil progress and musical enjoyment are directly related to the effectiveness in planning and the skill in presenting lessons. Enthusiasm on the part of the teacher, or the lack of it, is transmitted to the pupils; their response reflects the manner of presentation. Adequate time allotment refers to the planning of regularly scheduled lessons which are of sufficient length to permit teaching fundamental skills and to provide time for singing, playing, and listening for enjoyment. In addition, music can also serve to enrich other areas of the curriculum.

Thus, a desirable program is one that accounts for the proper development of musical skills and insights during fixed music periods and, at the same time, is sufficiently flexible to include songs and other musical activities as they support and enhance other subject areas.

The music period should be a time for serious, challenging effort, but always in an atmosphere which makes music learning a pleasurable experience. Music is a disciplined art requiring concentration and teamwork; but as an expressive art it must allow pupils a certain degree of individual freedom. Skilled teaching involves the careful balancing of emotional, creative responses with disciplined, controlled pupil action.

Lesson Planning

Every music lesson should have a period of singing for sheer enjoyment; there should be a period devoted to reading new music and to learning and perfecting new skills. Among the latter might be the learning of a new rhythmic pattern or a new tonal pattern, or perhaps the introduction of a new classroom instrument. Then there should be a period in which pupils have an opportunity to sing or play for one another. A single music lesson, of course, is not long enough to include all of the desirable activities of a comprehensive music program. It is necessary, therefore, to plan a series of lessons which, as a unit, will provide a broad, balanced program.

Lesson planning includes providing listening lessons and creative activities as well as a consideration of seasons, holidays, and special occasions. The Classified Index near the end of the child's book will aid you in planning lessons incorporating the various activities. There you will also find lists of songs according to country of origin and subject, which will assist you in selecting music to be used in social-studies units.

Planning a music lesson should include a consideration of:

1. variety in each music period, in order to add enjoyment and to insure covering and reinforcing the several areas of a comprehensive program.

2. the maturity and musical abilities and limitations of the pupils for whom the lessons are being planned.

3. the needs and interests of the gifted as well as the average and slow children, so that the talented pupil does not go unchallenged or deprived of creative and performing opportunities.

4. variety in the format of the lessons, so that the music periods do not become stereotyped and dull.

5. long-range objectives to insure that each lesson is clearly directed toward a goal.

Interpretation and Tone Quality

Expressive singing should be one of the primary goals in teaching music to children. To sing expressively, children must understand the meaning of the words and convey the thoughts and mood of the song through their own interpretation.

Sixth-graders are capable of highly artistic, expressive singing. A discussion of the thought conveyed by the song is valuable: "Is this a sad song?

a happy one? Is it a song of loneliness? of love for one's country?" Pupils should then decide, under the teacher's guidance, how the mood can best be expressed musically; that is, whether the song should be fast, slow, loud, soft, and so on. Until a singer, whether he is a sixth-grader or an adult, sings a song expressively, it remains a pedantic exercise for him. And he will not sing it expressively until it becomes meaningful to him.

In BOOK SIX, expression marks are used in all songs. They should be observed or modified according to the teacher's musical judgment. The following symbols indicate loudness or softness:

pp	pianissimo	very soft
p	piano	soft
mp	mezzo piano	rather soft, but slightly louder than *p*
mf	mezzo forte	slightly louder than *mp*
f	forte	loud, but not raucous
ff	fortissimo	very loud, but with controlled tone

Pupils should be taught to produce tones by sustaining vowels with an open, free tone. Vocal technique is a subject beyond the scope of the ordinary classroom lesson. However, by encouraging pupils to sit erect, to breathe deeply enough to sustain their tones through a normal phrase, and to open their mouths when singing vowels, tone quality can be considerably improved. Perhaps the two most important things to remember are: (1) get the children to sing in the way most pleasing to yourself and themselves; and (2) avoid songs that tire and strain their voices.

Introducing a New Song

There is no single procedure that should be followed in introducing a song to the pupils for the first time. A song to be learned without reading (sometimes referred to as a "rote song") can be taught by having the melody sung by the teacher or played on the piano or heard on a phonograph recording. In the Sixth Grade, it would seem advisable to teach as many songs as possible by having pupils read them. Even songs too difficult to read in their entirety can usually be read in part, with pupils receiving assistance only when they need it. This, incidentally, is the way in which professional, experienced singers learn new songs, using the piano or other aid only when it is necessary.

But even with a song to be read, it is good practice, occasionally, to hear it first played on a recording or performed by the teacher. When this procedure is used, pupils should follow the music in their books, observing features of the melodic line, the rhythm, the tempo, and the like.

At other times, the challenge of reading the song in its entirety should be presented, thus permitting the pupils to experience the adventure of discovering new tunes for themselves rather than having to follow the route already explored. In reading songs, it is important to establish the key, the meter, and the tempo, and to direct the class so that all start the song together.

Sometimes it is a good practice to anticipate rhythms or tonal patterns which may cause reading problems, and to master these problems before reading the song. This should not become an established procedure, however. Many songs should be read without prior analysis or study, and the class should continue singing until a problem is encountered which completely blocks its progress. Then, when the problem is studied, pupils will see and hear it in context, and they will be aware of the need to work on it until it is solved. In this way, the class works with a real, not a synthetic, problem, and the class can see it in its musical setting.

In introducing a song to the pupils, make them aware of its mood and meaning and explain unfamiliar words. If the song is written by a famous composer, or if it is representative of a certain country, information should be given which will enhance enjoyment and understanding.

Whenever possible, songs should be learned in their entirety, but if they are long and difficult or if time does not permit, they can be taught by phrases. Many songs are based on repeated or similar phrases and can therefore be learned nearly as quickly as one learns a single phrase, since the learning of this phrase offers a key to unlocking the entire melody.

Rhythm and Melody Instruments

Suggestions for the use of specific instruments are made in many songs contained in the child's book; further suggestions are offered in this Guide. In addition, creative efforts should be encouraged, for these give pupils an opportunity to experiment with various rhythm patterns and various combinations of rhythm instruments.

BOOK SIX contains a series of rhythm games and studies; these can be clapped and chanted, and they can also be used with rhythm instruments.

Autoharp chords are indicated for all songs suitable to the key or chord limitations of this instrument. Pupils should be encouraged to experiment with different ways of strumming the chords, so that the accompaniments are played in a manner best suited to each song. In some songs, strumming on every beat will be appropriate; in others, strumming only on the first beat of the measure will be best.

Many songs in this book are playable on tonettes, flutophones, and song flutes. The Guide material for the individual songs indicates which ones can be used in this way. Any songs or descants listed for melody instruments can be played on the violin as well as the instruments cited above. The same songs can be played on the trumpet and clarinet; but if either of these instruments is used, it must read the descant one whole step higher. This will allow for the difference between the written note and the actual tone produced by these transposing instruments.

Ukulele chords are included in several selections; and the guitar and accordion can play accompaniments to those songs for which autoharp chords are shown.

The Listening Program

Listening should be an important part of the over-all music program. It provides an opportunity for the children to hear music that is far beyond their performance level; thus, it gives them a total experience which offers immediate satisfaction coupled with the development of an appreciation and enjoyment which will endure for a lifetime.

Listening to recorded music or to a live performance is a highly personalized experience. This is an activity in which a pupil can truly assert his independence, because nobody can dictate that he must enjoy a piece of music; he either likes or dislikes it on his own terms. Unconsciously, however, he will tend to like many pieces simply because they are familiar. If he repeatedly hears good music, appropriate to his experience and maturity, under pleasant conditions, the chances are that he will come to enjoy it.

Guidance is also needed, the kind of guidance which is not arbitrary but which directs attention to features of a piece upon which the child can build his own creative ideas. It is important and valuable, for example, to point out a solo by the English horn, showing him the way the notation of the theme being heard looks in a book or on a blackboard. He will find this knowledge helpful in developing a discriminating musical awareness. At the same time, he needs to be permitted to enjoy music for its emotional appeal, for its appeal to his imagination, and just for the sheer delight that the melody or rhythm of a certain piece gives him.

A Sixth-grade pupil with a reasonably good background in listening is ready to hear a great variety of recorded music with understanding and enjoyment. With the wealth of new recordings that are available, teachers have a wide range from which to choose music for listening. The following suggestions are inadequate, as is any arbitrary list, but may indicate the kinds of recordings that are useful:

Arioso *(Cantata No. 156)*	J. S. Bach
Essay for Orchestra	Barber
Habanera *(Carmen)*	Bizet
Polonaise in Ab Major	Chopin
Appalachian Spring	Copland
Billy the Kid	Copland
El Salón México	Copland
Afternoon of a Faun	Debussy
Ritual Fire Dance	De Falla
The Sorcerer's Apprentice	Dukas
Second Movement *(From the New World)*	Dvořák
An American in Paris	Gershwin
The White Peacock	Griffes
Grand Canyon Suite	Grofé
Symphony No. 3	Harris
Caucasian Sketches	Ippolitov-Ivanov
Malagueña *(Suite Andalucia)*	Lecuona
March *(Love of Three Oranges)*	Prokofieff
Bolero	Ravel
The Pines of Rome	Respighi
Finlandia	Sibelius
Dance of the Comedians *(The Bartered Bride)*	Smetana
Anvil Chorus *(Il Trovatore)*	Verdi

Recordings designed to enforce the material in the *Music for Young Americans* series have been produced by Audio Educaion, Inc. and are distributed by American Book Company. The album accompanying BOOK SIX contains the following material:

1. unison, two-part, and three-part songs.
2. selections featuring the various brass, woodwind, string, and percussion instruments of the orchestra.
3. selections for listening lessons.
4. folk dances.

These recorded songs are listed in an index near the end of this Guide. Also, for additional convenience, a small black disc drawing has been placed next to the titles of the recorded songs on the pages which follow.

The listening lessons based on Borodin's "Dance of the Polovtsian Maidens" from the opera *Prince Igor,* the first movement of Beethoven's Fifth Symphony, and the second movement of Dvořák's symphony *From the New World* are implemented by the discussions given in the text of the child's book.

Recordings are an important teaching tool, but they must be used with discretion. They can make the singing of a song an exciting experience when used as an accompaniment, and they can aid in learning a song; but if they are used indiscriminately, they can interfere with music-reading experience, eliminate creative interpretation, and, finally, become monotonous. One of the chief attributes of a dynamic, successfully conducted music lesson is the use of multiple, well-chosen, and well-timed approaches. Recordings are a tremendous asset when used judiciously.

○ Lift Up Your Voice and Sing! (PAGE 1)
KEY OF G
STARTS ON D (5—SO)

✔ EXPRESSIVE SINGING ✔ RHYTHM

Above all else, singing should be an enjoyable experience. In this song, emphasis should be on singing expressively, with a lively rhythm and controlled but jubilant tone quality. Sing with two swings to a measure:

The first note, called a "pick-up" note or "anacrusis," does not come on an accented beat, the first accented word being "song." To begin the song so that pupils start precisely together and sing the rhythm at the same speed, count:

The speed at which you count "1, 2" will set the tempo (speed). With consistent practice in using this procedure in establishing the tempo of a song, false starts will be avoided and time will be saved.

○ We're All Together Again (PAGE 2)
KEY OF G
STARTS ON D (5—SO)

✔ CREATIVE ACTIVITIES ✔ TIE ✔ RHYTHM

Boys and girls enjoy singing songs that they can teach to their friends at Scout meetings, summer camps, on hikes, and so on. Added stanzas can be created to this tune, suited to the activities and interests of class members. For instance, a stanza similar to this one might be added:

> We'll rake the leaves and we'll pile them high,
> high, high;
> We'll rake the leaves and we'll pile them high,
> high, high.
> Here we are working all together again,
> Working all together again to pile them high.

Pupils should be asked to point out the ties in the song. How many ties are there? (3) What does a tie do? (It connects two or more notes of the same pitch. The rhythmic value is found by counting the value of each note within the tie and totaling them.) How many beats do the ties at the end of the first, second, and fourth lines receive? (5)

Sing the song with two swings to each measure. Chant and clap the rhythm to gain familiarity with the characteristics of this meter and tempo. The children will find it in many songs.

○ Chumbara (PAGE 3)
KEY OF D
STARTS ON D (1—DO)

✔ "FUN" SONG ✔ CREATIVE ACTIVITIES
✔ RHYTHM ACTIVITIES

"Chumbara," a favorite with children, is a nonsense title, a word without meaning, as are all the words in this song. Pupils might enjoy making up extra stanzas, as is suggested in their books.

Instruments may be used at the places in the music marked ♪, instead of the clapping, finger-snapping, and knee-slapping actions indicated. For instance, one stanza could use a triangle, the second a wood block, the third a gong, etc. If desired, after they have learned the song, the class may remain silent on the eighth rests and not clap. But in learning it, it is helpful to clap to establish the basic rhythmic pattern.

Sweet Betsy from Pike (PAGE 4)
KEY OF D
STARTS ON D (1—DO)

✔ HARMONY ✔ RHYTHMIC UNITY ✔ CORRELATION

Have your pupils take turns singing the upper (small) notes of the refrain. Or you could have small groups take turns singing the harmony and the melody of the refrain, thus providing yourself with an opportunity to check each pupil's ability in carrying a second part and to assist those needing help. Also, pupils would benefit by hearing one another in small-group singing.

Every acceptable piece of music contains certain unifying features. Often unity is attained through similar phrases. An interesting observation to be made of this piece is that the first four phrases are all different melodically but are given unity by exact repetition of the rhythmic pattern. Melodic unity is gained by a refrain which repeats the last line melodically and verbally.

While this is a humorous song, it illustrates the ability of the early settlers in America, who "crossed the wide prairie," to maintain a sense of humor in spite of hardships and dangers. The song could be correlated with a pioneer unit in the social studies.

◯ Keep in the Middle of the Road (PAGE 5)
KEY OF Eb
STARTS ON G (3—MI)

✔ SOLO SINGING ✔ PART-SINGING ✔ ENUNCIATION

Occasional short solos offer variety. When they are wisely used, they are a means of encouraging rather shy singers to develop self-confidence. One soloist might be used here for the entire song, or one on each stanza. You might prefer to use as many as six, one on each short solo.

Before teaching the second part, let the entire class learn and sing the song in unison. Then, slow down the tempo from the lively speed at which the song normally should be sung to a speed at which the two parts are sung clearly and correctly. When accuracy has been attained, increase the tempo to one which you consider appropriate.

On this and all part-songs (unless one part goes out of range for some pupils), have the two parts alternate so that all pupils have ample experience in singing harmony as well as melody.

An excellent chance to stress enunciation is given in the rapid chorus passages, "Keep in the middle of the road." Practice chanting this rhythm and these words, urging pupils to pronounce each word clearly and with precision.

◯ There's Work to be Done (PAGE 6)
KEY OF C
STARTS ON C (8—DO)

✔ COMPANION SONG ✔ RHYTHM ACTIVITIES

Ask your pupils to count and clap the rhythm pattern shown at the top of the page in their books, noting that the second measure is a syncopated rhythm. Let them examine the song, noting how many times this two-measure rhythm pattern is used. (3 times)

Call attention to the accent marks (*sforzando*) on the last three notes. What do these marks indicate? (Extra stress on the notes)

To accompany the singing, a calypso rhythm is suggested in the child's book, to be played on bongo drums, with maracas, and with claves. (The bongo-drum part may be imitated by slapping the knees; and the claves, by clapping.)

This song and "No Need to Hurry," on the facing page, are companion songs; that is, they can be sung together because the harmony is the same in each.

● No Need to Hurry (PAGE 7)
KEY OF C
STARTS ON E (3—MI)

✔ COMPANION SONG ✔ DRAMATIZATION ✔ RHYTHM

Let the children count and clap the familiar rhythm pattern which appears at the top of the page in their books. Since Phrases 1 and 3 are alike, and Phrases 2 and 4 almost alike, in both melody and rhythm, the class should be able to sing the song at sight.

After the song has been learned and sung, let the boys sing it while the girls sing "There's Work to be Done." Be sure that the boys' voices do not over-balance the girls', but blend into a unified effect. Songs sung together, as well as rounds and canons, are examples of a type of music which was popular in the time of J. S. Bach. This music is called "counterpoint." It is the weaving-together of two or more independent melodies.

In singing the two songs together, it is suggested that the following procedure be used:
Girls: Stanza 1 of "There's Work to be Done"
Boys: Stanza 1 of "No Need to Hurry"
Girls: Stanza 2 of "There's Work to be Done"
Boys: Stanza 2 of "No Need to Hurry"
All:　Stanzas 1 and 2 of the combined songs
By action and vocal expression, act out the pleading of the girls to hurry and the boys' unhurried reaction.

Red River Valley (PAGE 7)
KEY OF G
STARTS ON D (5—SO)

✔ INTERPRETATION ✔ PART-SINGING

This beautiful melody challenges us to see how excellent the quality of our singing can be. It moves sufficiently slowly to allow careful attention to be given to sustaining all vowels with purity of tone. For instance, on "val-" our mouths should be open wide enough to produce a free, resonant vowel sound. Lead your pupils to listen carefully to each phrase, matching rhythm, and consonants at the ends of words.

Discuss interpretation of the song to add meaning to the text. Cowboys, it should be noted, even when singing sad songs, do not sing in a "tear-jerking" manner but in a simple straight-forward style.

When the class sings the song in two parts, be sure that they carefully blend and balance the lower part with the melody.

Melody instruments can play either part of the song if the following fingering for the note F# is taught:

● Hiking Song (PAGE 8)
KEY OF C
STARTS ON G (5—SO)

✔ DESCANT ✔ FORM

Teach the class the melody first and then the descant. (A descant is a secondary melody that adds embellishment to a principal melody.) When the class is secure in both parts, divide it into two groups which alternate in singing the melody and the descant at subsequent music periods. The descant is to be sung slightly softer than the melody.

Melody instruments might play the song as a second stanza; or, if you prefer, let them occasionally play the descant while the class sings the melody. The flute fingering for F# is found in the teaching instruction for "Red River Valley," given immediately above.

"Form" is the term used to describe the structure of a piece of music. In this song, the first, second, and fourth phrases of the melody are alike (except for the last note in Phrase 1). The third phrase is different. Therefore the form of the song is AABA.

9

To stress the idea of this form, it is suggested that you divide the class into 3 groups, each singing "A": Group 1 sings Phrase 1; Group 2, Phrase 2; and Group 3, Phrase 4. All simultaneously sing their phrase with "loo," so that the words will not conflict.

◑ Harvest Ball (PAGE 9)
KEY OF C
STARTS ON C (1—DO)

✔ TONIC CHORD ✔ RHYTHM

Both phrases start with tones of the tonic chord: do mi so so do (C E G G C; 1 3 5 5 8). The children have had experience with this chord in earlier books of the series. They have also had experience with the only rhythmic problem

Let them try to read the song at sight. If they have difficulty with the second part in the last two and half measures, teach it separately.

Keep America Free and Strong (PAGE 10)
KEY OF F
DESCANT STARTS ON C (5—SO)
MELODY STARTS ON C (5—SO)

✔ EXPRESSIVE SINGING ✔ TWO-PART DEVELOPMENT

Performed in unison or with the descant, this song may be used for assemblies and special occasions as well as for classroom singing. The words should be discussed, with emphasis on attaining the larger concepts in the text, as well as an understanding of the meaning of individual words. The implications of such phrases as "on justice and freedom" and "strive against oppression and wrong" need to be understood in terms meaningful to Sixth-grade pupils, if the song is to have significance to the performers.

2/2 meter is sung in the same manner as ₵, the two meter symbols being used interchangeably.

The melody should be sung a trifle louder than the descant. Syllable names of chromatic tones (F#) are given in the child's book, to be used only if your school uses the syllable system of reading. Teach the melody first, and the descant next; then combine the two parts.

◑ A Merry Life (PAGE 12)
KEY OF Eb
STARTS ON Bb (5—SO)

✔ EXPRESSIVE SINGING ✔ TWO-PART DEVELOPMENT

In no country do people sing with more warmth and spirit than in Italy. This favorite melody reflects that exuberance and needs to be sung joyously. Its tempo should be moderately fast, with two beats to each measure. The dynamic marks do not show the delicate variations that are needed; these will come as the singers' volume rises and falls with the contours of the melodic line. For example, the second phrase, pitched lower than the first, should be sung more softly. Observing the crescendo indicated in the refrain will add to the effectiveness of the interpretation.

The harmony part in the refrain should be sung lightly to balance and blend with the melody.

Denza wrote this song to celebrate the opening of cable-car (funicular) service up Mt. Vesuvius in Italy (1880). The words in the refrain, "Funiculi, funicula," would appear therefore to be a play on the Italian word for cable-car instead of nonsense syllables with no meaning.

Down by the River (PAGE 15)
KEY OF C
STARTS ON G (5—SO)

✔ READING SONG ✔ RHYTHM ✔ CALYPSO

This is the first reading song in the key of C, which is presented on the facing page in the pupil's book, page 14. To introduce the key of C, or to review it, correlate the sound and the appearance of the scale. As the class sing it, have them follow the notation in their books. They should also locate the notation on the keyboard printed there. They will thus hear the sounds of the scale, see them as they appear on the staff, and locate them on the keyboard.

In the Sixth Grade, pupils should become aware of the sight and the sound of tonic and dominant chords. Have them sing these two chords in two parts, one part on the upper notes and the other on the lower. If the class can sing the chords in three-part harmony, assign a third group to the small top notes. Then let all sing the chords a few times to attune their ears to the sounds.

The skips in the first measure are based on tones of the tonic chord. Perhaps the biggest reading problem lies in the rhythm of the song. But if your pupils examine the rhythm, they will observe that it is based on a syncopated figure:

This figure, which they often hear in West Indian music on the radio and TV, sets the pattern for the rest of the song.

A Capital Ship (PAGE 16)
KEY OF C
STARTS ON G (5—SO)

✔ READING ✔ PART-SINGING

Whenever songs include several stanzas, an added reading problem is introduced because the rhythm of the words of each stanza needs to be notated accurately, making it frequently necessary in printed music to use tied notes. Handling the problem, however, is a normal part of sight-singing and must be learned.

In this song, for example, the opening measures in the child's book indicate the following rhythm for each of the two stanzas:

In reading the song before words are introduced, chant the rhythm of the first stanza. Once this is firmly established, there will be little difficulty in chanting Stanza 2.

Have the children examine the melody phrase by phrase, noting stepwise and skipwise passages. Then, as the class reads the song, stop on any phrase which causes difficulty, isolate the problem, repeat the phrase until it flows smoothly, and continue to the next phrase.

The refrain may be sung in unison but offers possibilities for a good two-part climax. For classes ready to sing three-part songs, a third part, written in small notes has been added.

The Parrot (PAGE 18)
KEY OF C
BOTH PARTS START ON E (3—MI)

✔ INDEPENDENT PART-SINGING ✔ ENUNCIATION

There are several ways in which songs are harmonized. One way is to have the rhythm of the parts move simultaneously. A second way is to have one part "chase" another, as in rounds and canons. Here we have a song which combines these two ways. The stanzas are written in modified canon style; that is, the lower part in general follows the melody of the upper part, entering one measure after the upper part has begun the tune. The refrain brings the two parts together.

11

Let the children compare the stanza section of the song, noting where the lower part follows the upper one (a measure behind). The second and third measures of the lower part are the same as the first and second measures of the upper part; the sixth and seventh measures of the lower part are the same as the fifth and sixth measures of the upper part.

The tempo should be fairly lively, with one swing to a measure. Singing at this tempo requires energetic tongue and lip movements for clear enunciation. Stress precision and clarity in enunciation by having the class chant the words, exaggerating mouth movements until the desired results are attained.

Good-by, Old Paint (PAGE 19)
KEY OF C
STARTS ON A (6—LA)

⤝ TONE QUALITY

This two-part arrangement of an old favorite should present no difficulty. The children most likely know the melody; they need learn only two phrases for the second part.

Tone quality should be stressed in the performance of every song, but a song such as this one, which includes many sustained tones, provides an exceptionally good opportunity to concentrate on the production of proper voice quality. In the word "good-by," for instance, the second syllable (by) is held for two beats, during which time the sound "ah" is the point of tonal emphasis. Pupils will tend to sing "good-bah-ee," holding the tone on "ee." Instead, the mouth should be held open more widely on the sustained tone, emphasizing "bah" and then completing the word by moving to the "ee" sound.

Buy a Tamale (PAGE 20)
KEY OF C
UPPER PART STARTS ON E (3—MI)
LOWER PART STARTS ON C (1—DO)

⤝ TWO-PART SINGING ⤝ CHROMATICS

Let the class clap and chant the pattern at the top of the page in their books until the rhythm is well-established. They then learn the melody by reading it. After singing the song in unison, they learn the lower part together. (If you like, call the upper part in all two-part songs the "soprano part;" and the lower part, the "alto part." Take care, however, that no pupils always sing the upper part and thereby become inflexibly soprano-minded. Singing harmony should be an important part of the musical experiences of all pupils, making them better sight-readers and more easily adjustable to later demands of choral singing.

Chromatics are tones which are not in the diatonic scale in which a piece is written; that is, they are tones which require modification in the score by having a sharp ♯, a flat ♭, or a natural sign ♮ placed before them to alter their pitch from that indicated by the key signature. Before calling attention to the chromatics in the song, demonstrate the sound and structure of the chromatic scale on the piano by starting on C and playing every white and every black key up to the next C. Then let the class find the chromatic passages in the song and sing them slowly, repeating them until they are sung correctly. Assistance should be given on all chromatic passages until the class has gained facility in reading them.

⊙ Hayride (PAGE 21)
KEY OF C
MELODY STARTS ON E (3—MI)
DESCANT STARTS ON C (8—DO)

⤝ DESCANT ⤝ INSTRUMENTAL ACTIVITIES

The descant in this song consists of the descending and ascending C major scale and provides a sustained harmonic part to accompany the rhythmic, faster-flowing melody. Teach the melody first, adding the descant without teaching it separately because it is merely the scale.

Ask the class what the rhythm of the first three notes of the melody is called. (Syncopation) Then have them clap and chant the rhythm of the first two measures. Once the rhythm is established, teach the melody.

For performance, you may want to add melody instruments and proceed as follows:

1. the class sings the melody with autoharp accompaniment.

2. the class plays the melody on available instruments.

3. the class sings the melody with the descant, or sings the melody while a few play the descant on an instrument other than the flute.

For a rhythmic accompaniment, see the child's book.

● Santa Lucia (PAGE 22)
KEY OF C
MELODY (UPPER PART) STARTS ON G (5—SO)
HARMONY (LOWER PART) STARTS ON E (3—MI)

✔ PHRASING   ✔ CHROMATICS

This melody requires *legato* (smooth, flowing) phrasing to achieve the correct interpretation. Pupils ordinarily breathe too frequently in legato singing, partly because their breathing capacity is not fully developed and partly because their attention has not been called to the habit. Phrasing in this song requires singing four measures on a breath. Use a moderately paced tempo to achieve good results.

Call attention to the chromatic passages and ask the class to sing them correctly before attempting the song as a whole.

● Bells in the Steeple (PAGE 23)
KEY OF F
STARTS ON C (5—SO)

✔ THREE-PART ROUND   ✔ BELL DESCANT

This is the first reading song in the key of F, which is presented immediately before this song. See the directions for "Down by the River," page 10 of this Guide, for the presentation of a new key.

Read the song in unison, stressing accuracy in rhythmic as well as tonal reading. Make certain that the dotted quarter-eighth-note figures are sung precisely. Ask the children to count and clap the figure.

This round includes a variation, consisting of a one-measure bell part which can be played either along with the round sung in unison or with the complete three voice parts. If the bell measure is used, play it twice as an introduction to the round and continue to repeat it throughout the song.

If you wish to keep the song purely vocal, use a few voices on the bell part singing "Bells are ringing" for each measure.

Cumberland Gap (PAGE 24)
KEY OF F
STARTS ON C (5—SO)

✔ DRAMATIZATION   ✔ RHYTHM ACTIVITIES

This is a rollicking, humorous song that calls for spirited interpretation through dramatization. After the children have chanted the words together and learned the melody so that they can sing the song accurately, let them suggest dramatization. For example, they might suggest something like the following:

Stanza 1. "With lots of water for to wash your face" (wash face)
"Ladies there in silk and lace" (girls preen)

13

Stanza 2. "And loaded up his old flintlock" (load rifle)

"Looked a bear right in the face" (stare at bear)

Stanza 3. "Then Daniel with the critter fought" (fight bear)

The bear cried, 'Ouch, I've just been shot!'" (bear staggers)

"Cumberland Gap's a right fine place" (swing right arm sweepingly)

As an accompaniment, clap or play on rhythm instruments the pattern printed in the child's book.

Home on the Range (PAGE 26)
KEY OF F
STARTS ON C (5—SO)

✓ COMPANION SONG ✓ EXPRESSIVE SINGING

This familiar and well-liked song offers variation in treatment which children enjoy. The variation consists in combining the song with "My Home's in Montana" as a companion song. Use only the stanzas of "Home on the Range" when singing the two songs together, for the harmonies will conflict if the refrain is also used. The whole class (both groups) may continue with the refrain of "Home on the Range" to the end. Or you may decide to let the group which has been singing "Home on the Range" continue with one part of the refrain while the group originally assigned to "My Home's in Montana" sings the other part. Try different ways of combining the songs for variety at subsequent music periods.

Both songs should be sung smoothly, so that the parts blend.

My Home's in Montana (PAGE 27)
KEY OF F
STARTS ON C (5—SO)

✓ COMPANION SONG ✓ EXPRESSIVE SINGING

Directions for singing this song as a companion piece to "Home on the Range" are given with the latter song. The class will also want to sing each song separately on occasions.

Note that both songs start on a "pick-up" note; that is, a quarter note starting on the third beat of the measure. To start precisely, count:

$$\frac{3}{4} \quad \underset{>}{1} \quad 2 \quad 3 \quad \bigg| \quad \underset{>}{1} \quad 2 \quad \text{(sing)}$$

Bless Us, Lord (PAGE 28)
KEY OF F
UPPER PART STARTS ON THIRD-SPACE C (5—SO)
LOWER PART STARTS ON MIDDLE C (5—SO)

✓ READING ✓ TONE QUALITY ✓ PHRASING

The two parts are easy enough to challenge an alert class to attempt to read them simultaneously. If the children decide to do so, let each part first test the first two notes by having the top part sing 5-3 (so-mi) alone; the lower part, 5-1 (so-do) alone; and then the two parts together. These two notes in each part should be sung slowly at first and then in tempo.

Stress tone quality in this song. The sustained, flowing melodic line, particularly in the upper part, offers a chance for concentration on voice production. Pupils should listen carefully to the quality of vowel sounds which they produce when singing the upper part, opening their mouths wide enough to attain a resonant tone.

Phrasing should be in long, flowing lines, made possible by breathing only at the ends of phrases. The tempo should be at a moderate speed, and the dynamic markings should be observed.

For assembly or concert use, flutes or violins (or flute on one part and violin on the other) might play the song between stanzas and accompany the singers on the second stanza. The flute fingering for Bb is as follows:

● Autumn Is Here (PAGE 28)
KEY OF F
MELODY STARTS ON A (3—MI)
HARMONY STARTS ON F (1—DO)

✔ PART-SINGING ✔ CHROMATICS

Ask the class to find the chromatic tone in the melody (B natural). This tone is the raised fourth degree of the scale, called "fi" if syllables are used. It is also found in the harmony part in the same measure. Explain that the B-flat sign is placed in the following measure to remind singers that the natural sign used in the previous measure is no longer in effect. Such a reminder is not necessary, as the key signature automatically cancels the effect of a chromatic sign when a new measure is reached; but it is often used as an aid to insuring the return to the scale tonality.

The chromatic in the harmony part at the beginning of the last line, F#, is called "di" if syllables are used.

In part-singing, balancing and blending the parts is of utmost importance, the harmony part supporting and blending but not covering the sound of the melody. In this arrangement, the lower part rises above the melody in several measures, at which times careful attention should be given to holding the volume of the harmony below the level of the melody.

Both parts are playable by melody instruments, or by violins and flutes. For an instrumental introduction, begin at "It's a very good time..." and play to the end, voices beginning the first stanza immediately after the introduction.

● At the Market Place (PAGE 30)
KEY OF F
STARTS ON C (5—SO)

✔ THREE-PART SINGING ✔ CREATIVE ACTIVITIES

To learn this round, the children first chant and clap the rhythm pattern printed at the top of the page in their books. They then chant and clap the words in unison. Next, they read the song with syllables, letter names, numbers, or "loo," and then sing it with the words.

When they can sing the song in unison, divide the class into three groups and sing it as a round three times.

As a creative activity, ask your pupils to make up additional stanzas. Here is an example:

> Peanuts, popcorn, tender hot corn,
> Step up and buy them here;
> So delicious, so nutritious;
> Come, try our cold root beer.
> Come and take a look around,
> Best place to buy in town.

A rhythm accompaniment, appropriate for a calypso song, is given in the child's book.

Down in the Valley (PAGE 31)
KEY OF F
STARTS ON C (5—SO)
HARMONY PART STARTS ON A (3—MI)

9/8 meter is sung with three beats to a measure:

Let the class chant and clap the rhythm before singing the song.

The melody should present no difficulty. Each phrase follows an up-and-down pattern; Phrases 1 and 3 are the same, and Phrases 2 and 4 are the same. After the class has established the rhythm, let them sing the melody in unison at sight. Later add the harmony part.

Friendship Song (PAGE 32)
KEY OF F
STARTS ON F (1—DO)

✔ METER CHANGE ✔ CREATIVE ACTIVITIES

Sometimes a song changes meters, as does this composition. Call attention to the change from 4/4 to 3/4. Change the tempo, also, speeding up slightly on the section starting with the words "Hurrah, hurrah." At the meter change, the tempo remains steady even though there is one less beat to each measure. The quarter notes are still sung at the same pace. At the *D.C. al Fine,* the meter returns to 4/4 but is slowed down to the tempo at which this section was previously sung.

Ask the class to exercise their ingenuity in making up additional verses to suit other occasions. "Happy birthday, happy birthday, happy birthday now to you," "Here's to springtime, here's to springtime, to the merry month of May," "Here's to our school, here's to our school, sing a song about our school," may start them off.

All Through the Night (PAGE 33)
KEY OF F
MELODY STARTS ON F (1—DO)
UPPER HARMONY STARTS ON C (5—SO)
LOWER HARMONY STARTS ON A (3—MI)

✔ THREE-PART SINGING

Let the class first sing the melody in unison. Then teach the lower harmony part and combine it with the melody. If only two-part singing is desired, these two parts will suffice. For three-part singing, add the upper harmony part after it has been taught separately.

Many music educators consider it desirable to teach all three parts of a three-part song simultaneously either without assistance or with the aid of a piano. This method of teaching a song as a complete harmonic unit is an ideal toward which to strive. It can be used only when a class has had much experience in reading and in part-singing.

One More River (PAGE 34)
KEY OF F
STARTS ON C (5—SO)

✔ PART-SINGING ✔ INSTRUMENTAL ACTIVITIES

Songs about Noah and his ark have a great appeal for children, probably because they tell a story and sometimes are quite long, as is this one. Use a few voices on the solo parts and the rest of the class on the chorus. Divide the voices on the chorus into two groups, with the group singing the melody slightly larger than the group singing the harmony.

Both parts of the song may be played on melody instruments.

There's a Little Wheel (PAGE 35)
KEY OF F
STARTS ON F (1—DO)

✔ RHYTHM ✔ INTERPRETATION

This spiritual, like all spirituals, should be sung with feeling. It is a simple, happy song.

The children should count and clap the rhythm pattern printed at the top of the page in their books. Make certain that the rhythm is clapped precisely as it is written, the first note very short, accenting the second, longer note:

Next, the children should chant the words to establish the rhythm firmly, and then add the melody.

Notice that the first, second, and fourth phrases are alike rhythmically; the second and fourth phrases are also alike melodically.

Erie Canal (PAGE 36)

STANZAS IN THE KEY OF D MINOR
REFRAIN IN THE KEY OF F MAJOR
STARTS ON A (5—MI)

✔ COMBINED MODES ✔ RELATIVE MINOR

In some tunes, an interesting variation is obtained by the combination of the major and the minor mode. This song illustrates such variation effectively. As the children sing or listen to the song, have them observe the mode markings in their books and note the contrast and interest provided by these mode changes.

The stanzas begin in the key of D minor, and the refrain begins in the key of F Major. The key signature (one flat) is the same for both, the key of D minor being the *relative minor* of F Major. The relative minor centers its tonality on the sixth degree (la) of its related major key, which in this tune is D. Reading music depends on more than a mechanical process; it is the development of a feeling for tonality, both major and minor, that facilitates skillful reading.

Wayfaring Stranger (PAGE 38)

KEY OF D MINOR
STARTS ON D (1—LA)

✔ 3/2 METER ✔ MINOR TONALITY

In 3/2 meter, the half note receives one beat:

Let the children count and clap the above rhythm to become accustomed to the note values found in this song. Next, count and clap and then chant the rhythm of the first phrase. When this is well established, let the class try the rest of the song.

Note the minor tonality of the song. Note, also, that the piece is built on the pentatonic (5-tone) scale; Bb and E are not used:

Keynote

Columbus (PAGE 40)

KEY OF F# MINOR
STARTS ON E (7—SO)

✔ MINOR TONALITY ✔ SOCIAL STUDIES

The tune of this song is a robust chantey and should therefore be sung vigorously. The tempo is moderately fast, with two beats to each measure.

The song tells in rather complete detail the story of Columbus's first voyage. Improvised dramatization of the words heightens the interpretation of the often-repeated tale.

On a map placed on the bulletin board, have the children trace the route which Columbus sailed on his first voyage to the New World and locate San Salvador (present-day Watling Island in the Bahamas).

The fifth stanza invites a discussion of the contributions made by "men on land, on sea, in air," in which the pupils may be urged to offer original ideas.

Singin' Johnny (PAGE 41)

KEY OF Eb
STARTS ON Eb (1—DO)

✔ THREE-PART SINGING

This song might be included in a Columbus Day program. It is a favorite of most boys. The class may sing the song as a whole, or a solo voice (or small group) may sing the text with the rest of the class joining in on the "Yo ho's."

Sing the chantey briskly at a steady tempo.

● Mountain Climbers (PAGE 42)
KEY OF D MINOR
STARTS ON A (5—MI)

✔ **MINOR TONALITY** ✔ **RHYTHM ACTIVITIES**

Have the class chant and clap the rhythm pattern printed in their books, and then locate it in the song. When they are thoroughly familiar with it, let them chant the words of the song, for the other rhythm patterns should present no difficulty.

Do the children hear the minor tonality in the song? Direct their attention to it. Note that the song ends on *la* (D, 1).

Phrases 1 and 3 are alike, and Phrases 2 and 4 are almost alike; the song is consequently melodically easy to read.

Thanksgiving (PAGE 43)
KEY OF Ab
MELODY PART STARTS ON Eb (5—SO)
HARMONY PART STARTS ON C (3—MI)

✔ **SHIFT OF MELODY FROM ONE PART TO ANOTHER**

Two-part reading should be used in learning this song, since both parts are simple melodically and rhythmically. Have your pupils first read the melody, which begins in the lower part. After the first two phrases have been read satisfactorily, continue with the third phrase, in which the melody shifts to the upper part. At the fifth phrase it again shifts to the lower part. The class should have no difficulty, since the melody part is plainly labeled in their books.

After all the children have sung the melody and know the tune, let them sing the upper part through to the end as printed in their books; then they sing the lower part as printed. Next, divide the class into two groups, one singing the upper part throughout and the other singing the lower part. At all times the melody should predominate slightly, just enough to be clearly heard without losing the harmonic balance. Therefore, as each part shifts from melody to

harmony, or vice versa, each singer must carefully modulate his voice as the transfer of melody is made.

Song of Thanksgiving (PAGE 44)
KEY OF G
STARTS ON G (1—DO)

✔ **FORM** ✔ **OPTIONAL THREE-PART SONG**

For classes prepared to sing three-part music, an optional third part is offered in this song. The arrangement is complete harmonically, however, for those wishing to use only the upper two parts.

Have the class study the structure of the song. The first two phrases are exactly alike; the second two phrases are almost alike. The form is therefore AABB₁. Help your class to establish the habit of analyzing a song briefly before attempting to sing it. This habit will encourage them to read phrasewise instead of note by note (a most undesirable practice).

Great-Grandad (PAGE 45)
KEY OF Bb
STARTS ON Bb (1—DO)

✔ **MUSIC READING**

This is the first reading song in the key of Bb Major. To review the key, see the directions for the key of C under "Down by the River," page 10.

The song is easy to read, as it moves for the most part in steps. Give pupils the starting tone, set the tempo, and let them see how well they can read it. If they encounter difficulty, isolate the problem, drill on it, and then return to the beginning of the phrase in which it occurs and sing it again.

Creativity could take the form of adding verses to the song, dramatizing it as the words suggest action. You might also add a rhythm accompaniment by clapping or using rhythm instruments.

Harvest Time (PAGE 46)
KEY OF Bb
STARTS ON F (5—SO)

✓ COMPANION SONG ✓ COUNTERPOINT

This song can be sung simultaneously with "We'll Dance to the Fiddler." Two separate tunes sung together make what is called "contrapuntal music." Sixth-grade pupils should become aware of the different kinds of textures found in music, including unison melodies (in which there is no harmonic part); harmony of the kind provided by chording on the piano or autoharp (and heard in much of the music played on radio and television); and counterpoint, or the weaving-together of different melodies (as in this song).

Sing the song separately before combining it. Phrases 3 and 4 are in the minor mode. The rest of the piece is in the major mode.

We'll Dance to the Fiddler (PAGE 47)
KEY OF Bb
STARTS ON F (5—SO)

✓ COMPANION SONG ✓ CREATIVE ACTIVITIES

Before the class combine this song with "Harvest Time" let them sing it independently, paying particular attention to singing the chromatic passage just before the *D.C. al Fine.* If they have difficulty, play it on the piano or melody bells. The first phrase should present no difficulty, since it starts out like "The Star-Spangled Banner."

For a program, sing one song, then the other, and finally both together. Perhaps a dance could be added as a creative project.

The Young Voyageur (PAGE 48)
KEY OF Bb
STARTS ON F (5—SO)

✓ ABCA₁ FORM ✓ READING

"Voyageur" (vwà-yà-zhûr) was the term used in the pioneering days of Canada to indicate a man employed by the fur companies to transport goods and men to and from remote stations by boat.

The wide skip in the second phrase, from 3 to 8, has been singled out as a tonal pattern for the class to drill on, and has therefore been placed at the top of the page. Phrasewise reading is always the goal, but there are occasions when even experienced, expert sight-readers must take a small section apart, work it out, and then put it back in its proper setting. Note that this particular problem is based on the tonic chord.

The Gallant Victory (PAGE 49)
KEY OF Bb
STARTS ON F (5—SO)

✓ READING ✓ DOTTED EIGHTH AND SIXTEENTH NOTES

First, establish rhythmic accuracy by having the children count and clap the dotted-eighth-and-sixteenth-note pattern shown at the top of the page in their books. Next, chant the words "The captain had a ship," following this same rhythm.

After the rhythm is well established, let the children sing the first phrase with attention to both melodic and rhythmic accuracy. Let them then learn the rest of the melody phrase by phrase.

When the complete melody has been learned, teach the harmony part to the entire class. Then divide the group into two parts for singing the complete arrangement of the song.

Havah Nagilah (PAGE 50)
KEY OF G MINOR
STARTS ON D (5—MI)

✓ RHYTHM ACTIVITIES

This dance (hora) is a favorite with young people because it is gay and graceful. Up to the last phrase it increases in tempo and intensity, as is indicated in the words which have been set to it. Let some of the class sing and clap while the rest dance. Be sure to alternate the groups.

If the group is large, form two circles, one inside the other and moving in the opposite direction.

Step: Step on R foot to R; step on L foot backwards to R; step on R foot to R again; kick L foot across R and hop on R foot at the same time; step with L foot, which is in air, to L; kick R foot across L and hop on L foot. (This step takes 6 beats and is repeated throughout the dance.) Start the dance slowly and gradually increase the tempo.

Formation: One big circle of dancers, with their right arms around the shoulders of the person to the right, and their left arms around the shoulders of the person to the left.

Go Down, Moses (PAGE 52)
KEY OF G MINOR
STARTS ON D (5—MI)

✔ INTERPRETATION   ✔ THREE-PART HARMONY

A spiritual, to be sung effectively, demands a sensitive interpretation. This song should not be sung in a tempo too fast or a tone quality too bright; yet it should not be given a heavy, slow, unrhythmic rendition. Sixth-grade children are capable of singing a song of this type with great beauty and expression when they understand the spirit it embodies.

If desired, the first two phrases may be sung by a soloist, the class entering on the chords sung with "Let my people go." If a piano is available, play the chords first, so that your pupils may hear their sounds before singing.

La Raspa (PAGE 53)
KEY OF A
STARTS ON E (5—SO)

✔ DANCE   ✔ INSTRUMENTAL ACTIVITY

Divide the class into two groups and let one group sing while the other dances, and then alternate the two. Chant and clap the rhythm pattern at the top of the page in the child's book to establish a sure feeling for the pulse. This is the way Mexicans dance the number:

Formation: A circle of partners, the girl to the right of the boy. M stands for measure.

M 1: Partners face, holding hands, and jump lightly from foot to foot 4 times, one jump on each beat, starting with R foot: R heel forward, L heel forward, and repeat.

M 2: Each makes a complete turn in place to the left, starting with L foot.

M 3, 4: Same as M 1, 2 but starting with L foot and turning in place to the right, starting with R foot.

M 5, 6: Partners link R arms and turn in place.

M 7, 8: Partners link L arms and turn in opposite direction.

Repeat the dance several times.

A good accompaniment can be furnished by maracas and claves. They play the pattern printed in the child's book twice as an introduction and continue it throughout the song.

◑ Please, Señorita (PAGE 54)
KEY OF G
MELODY STARTS ON B (3—MI)
HARMONY STARTS ON G (1—DO)

✔ RHYTHM ACCOMPANIMENT   ✔ TWO-PART HARMONY

An introduction for bells and an accompaniment for tambourines, castanets, or other rhythm instruments are included in the score in the child's book. Omit them, if you so desire, but their inclusion enhances the arrangement and makes the song an attractive program number.

The song itself is in an easy two-part arrangement, allowing concentration on reading and good blending of voices. Since the parts move in such smooth harmony (in thirds largely, typical of much Spanish music), a gifted class might try reading the parts together at the outset rather than learning one part at a time. Before attempting to do so, they should establish the rhythm by counting and clapping.

● Hey Diddle Dum (PAGE 55)
KEY OF Eb
STARTS ON G (3—MI)

✔ KEY OF Eb ✔ THREE-PART HARMONY ✔ SEQUENCES

This is the first reading song in the key of Eb, which is presented at the top of the page in the pupil's book. See the directions for "Down by the River," page 10 of this Guide, for the presentation of a new key.

The song should be sung first in unison, and later as a round in three parts. Notice that it is based on sequences. The little tune in the first measure is repeated several times, sometimes higher and sometimes lower.

If any of your children are studying the clarinet or trumpet, let them play the accompaniment in their books. It is only four measures long and is repeated throughout the song.

● I Build Me a Little House (PAGE 56)
KEY OF Eb
STARTS ON Bb (5—SO)

✔ CALYPSO RHYTHM ✔ RHYTHM ACCOMPANIMENT

The calypso comes to us from the West Indies, where it is sung to the accompaniment of drums and whatever other instruments are available. It is music that is strongly rhythmic, and it needs to be sung with rhythmic accent even when unaccompanied. Calypso words are improvised, singers earning their reputations by their creative ability to make up stanza after stanza on any kind of subject, often topical in nature. After this song has been learned, let your pupils add stanzas of their own improvisation.

In teaching the song, have the class clap the first pattern in their books and chant the words until the rhythm pattern is firmly established. Then let them attempt singing the song with words.

When they can sing the song in good, steady calypso rhythm, add the accompaniment as given in the second pattern in their books. If you do not have a bongo drum, a small group may clap the pattern.

Zum Gali Gali (PAGE 57)
KEY OF E MINOR
UPPER PART STARTS ON G (3—DO)
LOWER PART STARTS ON E (1—LA)

✔ RHYTHMIC CHANT ✔ CREATIVE ACTIVITY

The entire class should learn each part separately and then take turns, divided into two groups, in singing the parts. The upper part should be sung in a flowing manner, while the lower part is sung with accent and staccato rhythm. The lower part is a two-measure chant, repeated, as an accompaniment to the tune.

For performance, try adding a short introduction by having the lower part sing its first two measures before going into the song. For an ending, the lower part could continue repeating its chant several times, gradually fading away until the sound disappears completely.

Drumming the chant with the fingertips on a book or the desk top makes a nice accompaniment.

Tide of Sleep (PAGE 58)
KEY OF Eb
STARTS ON G (3—MI)

✔ MUSIC OF BRAHMS

Pupils should become familiar with great music written by master composers. Singing words to a melody by Brahms, one of the masters of musical composition, will not by itself alone develop a love and understanding of his music. It should serve as an introduction and be followed by playing recordings of some of his works appropriate to the age of the pupils listening, and by library reading of books written about him. It is the broad acquaintance with music by great composers and familiarity with their lives and times that gradually develop the enjoyment and appreciation which endures for a lifetime.

This melody, from Op. 39, Waltz No. 15, reveals Brahms's gift for writing beautiful tunes. It should be sung in a light, lilting manner, with flowing phrases, to capture the quality of the song. Tone quality should be stressed, pupils being encouraged to sing as freely and beautifully as possible.

Our Door Is Always Open (PAGE 59)
KEY OF Eb
STARTS ON Eb (1—DO)

✔ ROUND

Rounds have been a favorite form of social singing for many generations, lending themselves equally well to classroom use, community singing in the assembly, or at Scout meetings, summer camps, and other places where young people gather for recreation.

A round has added value in the classroom, as it provides an interesting and not difficult experience in part-singing. Singing a harmony part depends on learning a melody or supporting harmony and holding it against another one or several parts, so that the combined parts sound well together. A round provides this practice in maintaining an independent part and at the same time gives everyone a chance to sing the tune.

This round is a good one for reading at sight, since the rhythms and melodic features are of a simple nature.

Crawdad (PAGE 60)
KEY OF Eb
STARTS ON Eb (1—DO)

✔ TONAL PATTERNS   ✔ IRREGULAR PHRASES

Accurate reading requires accuracy in singing the rhythm as well as the tune of a song. Have pupils chant and clap the rhythm; then add the melody by reading it. In preparation for reading the melody, the two tonal patterns shown in the pupil's book should be learned. Then the song should be read phrase by phrase until it is sung perfectly.

In using tonal patterns, throughout the book, vary the approach from song to song whenever they are included. Sometimes start with the tonal patterns, and then sing the song. At other times, permit a song to be read first, practicing the tonal patterns only if it is necessary.

Most songs with which we are familiar are based on phrases of four measures. An interesting feature of this folk song is that its phrases do not follow this standard pattern. The first two phrases are each only three measures long. Therefore the dotted half notes need to be counted carefully to adhere to the notated rhythm.

● The Alphabet (PAGE 61)
KEY OF Eb
BOTH PARTS START ON Eb (1—DO)

✔ METER   ✔ MUSIC OF MOZART   ✔ TWO-PART SINGING

The rhythmic pattern shown at the top of the page in the pupil's book provides a study of 3/8 meter, in which meter this song is written. Have your pupils clap and count the pattern to become accustomed to the duration values when an eighth note receives one beat (quarter note, two beats; dotted quarter note, three beats, etc.).

The song moves at a tempo of one beat to a measure. This tempo will come naturally and easily after the parts have been learned slowly enough to be sung with care and accuracy. When the melody and harmony sound well together, speed up the tempo to one that provides the light, lively quality intended by Mozart.

Diction is important in this song, as the letters of the alphabet must be pronounced clearly and crisply to give the rhythm and momentum the song needs for good performance. Observe the dynamic markings, increasing the volume as the phrases rise and decreasing it as they descend melodically.

Mozart's name is undoubtedly familiar to most of your pupils, but as a review it would be well to take time to discuss him, his music, and his masterly contributions to the world of music.

Here Comes the Band (PAGE 62)
KEY OF Eb
STARTS ON Eb (8—DO)

✔ READING ✔ ROUND ✔ THREE-PART SINGING

This song offers, in its first phrase, an opportunity to sing the Eb major descending scale in the musical setting of an English folk song. Even though your pupils have been singing and reading songs in the various keys as they were introduced in earlier grades, a review of the keys now will strengthen them in their musical abilities.

After the song has been learned, divide the class into three groups and let them sing it as a round, each part singing the song three times.

Drill, Ye Tarriers (PAGE 63)
KEY OF C MINOR
STARTS ON C (1—LA)

✔ SIXTEENTH NOTES ✔ SOCIAL STUDIES RELATIONSHIP

Have pupils count and clap the rhythm pattern at the top of the page in their books and then chant the words of the first phrase. The words of the song

are direct aids in demonstrating the rhythm of the sixteenth notes, and of sixteenth notes related to eighth notes. As phrases are chanted, pupils should give careful attention to the way the words are represented by rhythmic notation. For example,

Drill, ye   tar - ri - ers,   drill

illustrates the sound of this grouping of rhythmic values clearly and precisely. In the same way, treat four sixteenth notes to a beat:

sug - ar in your "tay"

Place the notation for these words on the blackboard and ask your pupils to clap them, adding the words if assistance is needed.

The song should be sung in a rhythmic, accented style appropriate to the way in which a group of men, hard at work, would sing it. It is a good-natured piece.

Men of Harlech (PAGE 64)
KEY OF Eb
STARTS ON Eb (1—DO)

✔ THE DOUBLE-DOTTED QUARTER NOTE

The double-dotted quarter note is not often used in vocal music, but pupils should be familiar with its appearance and name so that they will know how to deal with it when it occurs. In 4/4 meter, it receives one and three-fourths beats. This seeming rhythmic complexity, in terms of usage, is much simpler to execute than it seems. In the first words of the song, "Hark! I hear the foe..." the words "I" and "the" are sung very fast, moving quickly to and accenting the words that follow them.

Have your pupils count and chant:

Then count and chant:

Later in the song the figure is reversed:

The double-dotted rhythm is used to produce the crisp, martial spirit of this robust marching song.

Rock of Ages (PAGE 66)
KEY OF E
STARTS ON E (1—DO)

✔ ENHARMONICS

The tempo (speed) should be moderate but not slow enough to become ponderous. Each tone should be sung firmly, without sliding from one to the next. The phrases should be flowing in style. The first phrase should not be broken by taking a breath after the half note on the word "song," as the break would destroy the continuity of the phrase of the text. The words demand that only one breath be used to sing "Rock of Ages, let our song Praise Thy saving power."

The third part is optional. If it is used, call attention to the B♯ in the next to the last measure. It is enharmonic with C natural, and therefore it is sung on the same pitch as C natural, as illustrated in the pupil's book.

◉ Happy Holiday (PAGE 67)
KEY OF A MINOR
STARTS ON B (2—TI)

✔ CANON   ✔ SPECIAL-OCCASION SONG   ✔ DESCANT

Suggestions are given in the children's book for using this canon for various special occasions.

The lower part repeats identically the melody of the upper part, starting two measures later than the upper part. (It stops two measures short of the upper part.) The canon should be sung at a lively tempo in a bright, gay manner.

For variety, the girls might sing one part, the boys the other; or small groups might take turns and come to the front of the room and sing the canon for their classmates. You might add the following descant, played on bells or sung with "Ah" by several singers. Repeat the two measures throughout the song.

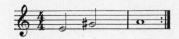

The First Noel (PAGE 68)
KEY OF D
STARTS ON F♯ (3—MI)

✔ PROGRAM SONG   ✔ DESCANT

This old English carol is a perennial favorite at Christmas time and is often heard on special programs. It looks more difficult than it really is. The melodies for Phrases 1 and 2 are repeated in Phrases 3 and 4; the refrain is short.

When the class can sing the melody well, add the descant. Teach it separately. You might let a small group sing it on the odd-numbered stanzas and play it on bells on the even-numbered stanzas. Let the class experiment with the song and instruments to attain an effective rendition.

Merry Christmas (PAGE 69)
KEY OF Eb
STARTS ON Bb (5—SO)

⌐ **THREE-PART ROUND**

If you prefer, have your pupils sing this round in two parts instead of three. It is a happy little number of no great consequence, but young people like to sing it at Christmas time.

In singing in three parts, be sure that each of the three groups comes in exactly on time.

◉ This Wond'rous Night (PAGE 70)
KEY OF Eb
MELODY STARTS ON Eb (1—DO)
DESCANT STARTS ON Eb (8—DO)

⌐ **PROGRAM SONG** ⌐ **DESCANT** ⌐ **INSTRUMENTAL ACTIVITY**

The tempo should be one beat to a measure, not too fast. The song should be sung in flowing phrases with a light, lyric quality.

The descant can be sung by a few voices or played by the flute or violin. A transposed part for the clarinet is printed in the pupil's book in case you have a young clarinetist in your class.

This song, with instrumental accompaniment, might well be a featured selection in a Christmas program.

Foom! Foom! Foom (PAGE 71)
KEY OF A MINOR
STARTS ON A (1—LA)

⌐ **CHRISTMAS SONG** ⌐ **CHANGING METER**

This Spanish carol is sung in a rhythmic style, in contrast to the quieter style used for many carols. The minor tonality also differentiates it from the usual mode used in carols. It might be interesting to note that carols originally were dances and therefore in the lively mood found here.

The one-measure change from 4/4 meter to 3/4 and then back to 4/4 should be performed accurately. Give it special attention if you find your class having difficulty with it. Let your pupils count and clap the two-measure pattern shown on the page of their books, repeating it until they have perfected it. The speed of the quarter-note basic beat (common to both 4/4 and 3/4) should not vary with the meter changes.

A rhythmic accompaniment could be added by having rhythm sticks or high-pitched instruments play the rhythm of the song, except on the words "foom, foom, foom!" Each time these words occur, play the quarter-note rhythm to which they are sung on a tom-tom or other low-pitched instrument.

Angels We Have Heard (PAGE 72)
KEY OF G
STARTS ON B (3—MI)

⌐ **CHRISTMAS SONG** ⌐ **PART-SONG**

The beauty of this traditional French carol can be brought out by singing triumphantly and joyously. Do not let the tempo of the stanzas drag, and note that the first two staffs in the pupils' books are the same melodically. Your class should be able to read them at sight.

Teach the two parts of the refrain separately and then combine them. Here, again, note that the first six measures of the refrain are almost exactly repeated in the last seven measures.

Wassail Song (PAGE 73)
KEY OF F
STARTS ON F (1—DO)

⌐ **NEW YEAR'S SONG** ⌐ **CHANGING METER**

This well-known song which celebrates the coming of the New Year should be sung in a joyful, lively manner. For variety, the stanzas could be sung by three different groups or by three soloists, the entire class joining in on the refrain each time through.

25

The meter used (2/2) is identical with *alla breve* (cut time), ₵. The half note serves as the basic beat, making two quarter notes equal to one beat, and so on.

The tempo at the beginning of the song is the speed of a lively march, which gives two beats to a measure in 6/8 meter. When the refrain, changing to 2/2 meter, is sung, maintain the same speed per beat as you used in the beginning of the stanza.

● O Come, All Ye Faithful (PAGE 74)
KEY OF Ab
MELODY STARTS ON Ab (1—DO)
DESCANT STARTS ON Eb (5—SO)

✔ **CHRISTMAS SONG** ✔ **DESCANT**

Sing this popular carol at a moderate tempo in a spirited manner. The addition of the descant makes it suitable for use at a school assembly or on a Christmas Program.

The descant crosses above and below the melody, making it necessary to give attention to a careful balancing of parts so that the melody is clearly heard at all times.

Here's to Friends (PAGE 75)
KEY OF F MINOR
STARTS ON F (1—LA)

✔ **MINOR TONALITY** ✔ **ROUND**

This short, two-part round offers experience in singing harmony in minor tonality. Although the tempo should be quite lively, let the class occasionally sing the song at a slower tempo so that they can clearly hear the sound of the minor tonality.

Auld Lang Syne (PAGE 76)
KEY OF G
STARTS ON D (5—SO)

✔ **NEW YEAR'S SONG** ✔ **THREE-PART OPTIONAL HARMONY**

"Auld Lang Syne" can be sung and enjoyed at any time, although it is particularly appropriate at the close of the year. Its graceful, flowing phrases should be sung expressively, with good quality, and rather softly. Let voices rise with the rise of the melody and become more subdued in volume as the melody gently descends at phrase endings.

The third part in the refrain is optional. If your class is not yet ready to use it, come back to the song later in the year, adding the third part for a spring assembly or other program.

● Winter's Best for Me (PAGE 78)
KEY OF C
STARTS ON C (1—DO)

✔ **CHROMATICS** ✔ **CREATIVE ACTIVITY**

As an aid in teaching this song, use the recording of it or play it on the piano. Pay particular attention to the many chromatic tones found in the melody and make certain that they are heard and sung accurately.

Near the end of the song there is an echo part of two measures (Don't you see, winter's best!) which can be sung by a small group of singers as the rest of the class sings the melody. The small group may also sing the two optional harmony notes at the end.

Added stanzas could be written as a creative project. The class might be encouraged to choose another season of the year to write about.

● Let's Skate Today (PAGE 80)
KEY OF F
STARTS ON C (5—SO)

✔ **THREE-PART HARMONY** ✔ **ACTION SONG**

The tempo for this song should be waltz tempo, with a strong accent on the first beat of the measure, at a speed appropriate for graceful ice skating. The tone should be flowing in order to give the smooth effect demanded by the text.

After the song has been learned in unison, divide the class into three groups, each group singing its part three times.

Action may be added by arm movements or skating pantomime. Various members of the class may suggest dramatization, such as donning coats, caps, and mufflers; shivering in the cold; etc.

Troika Riding (PAGE 81)
KEY OF A MINOR
STARTS ON (1—LA)

✓ MINOR TONALITY ✓ RHYTHM ACTIVITIES

Ukrainian tunes are often in the minor mode, as is this song. It is gay and lively and should be sung as rapidly as good enunciation permits. A slight increase in volume should occur in every two measures as the high note is sung.

Sleighbells (any type of bells that give a jingling sound) add a happy sound effect if played in the rhythm printed in the child's book.

⬤ We're Heading Home (PAGE 82)
KEY OF G
STARTS ON G (1—DO)

✓ CANON ✓ RHYTHM ACTIVITIES

Teach the upper part first and let the class sing it in unison. Then call attention to the fact that the song is a canon, the lower part being exactly the same as the upper and following the upper by one measure. Let the class then sing the song as a canon.

The tempo should be rather lazy, somewhat like a horse's gait at the end of a long day. To add to the effect of a jogging horse rhythm, use upturned paper cups, temple blocks, or other sound effects in this rhythm:

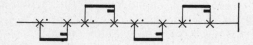

Start the rhythm accompaniment before the melody begins and continue it at the end of the second stanza, gradually fading out in volume as though the horse and rider were moving off into the distance.

Arirang (PAGE 83)
KEY OF G
STARTS ON D (5—SO)

✓ SOCIAL STUDIES RELATIONSHIP
✓ ALTERED THIRD SCALE DEGREE

Locate Korea on a map and discuss the text of the song. This selection is suitable for use in a unit on the Islands of the Pacific, along with the other songs on Hawaii, Japan, and China.

An interesting feature of the melody is that, while it stays within the bounds of our Western major scale in most instances, it alters the third degree in two places, giving a minor-tonality effect as measured by our familiar scale patterns.

The tempo should be not too fast, and the song should be sung in a quiet, even voice with little change in volume from high to low tones. The phrases should be *legato* (smooth).

Try the following accompaniment or another using a similar combination of sticks and triangle:

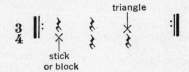

Steal Away (PAGE 84)
KEY OF F
STARTS ON F (1—DO)

✓ OPTIONAL THIRD PART ✓ INCIDENTAL SOLO
✓ TONE QUALITY

The slow tempo and sustained tones in this spiritual permit concentration on good tone quality. Be sure that the children sound the vowels properly.

The solo passage offers an outlet for the talents of the gifted singers in the class. You might use several voices singing the solo passage in unison if you use the song as a program number.

An optional third part is included. It is especially effective when the class, without piano or other accompaniment, sings the number on a special program.

Soldier, Soldier (PAGE 85)
KEY OF Ab
STARTS ON Ab (1—DO)

✔ KEY OF Ab ✔ READING SONG

This is the first of the reading songs in the key of Ab. Review the key with the material immediately preceding the song in the child's book. See "Down by the River," page 10 of this book for suggestions on presenting keys.

You might like to dramatize the song. Divide the class into three groups. Group 1, consisting of several boys and girls, sings the narrative. Group 2, made up of girls, sings the girl's questions. Group 3, composed of boys, sings the soldier's answers. Sixth-graders like a dialogue song such as this one.

Jolly Wee Miner Men (PAGE 86)
KEY OF Ab
STARTS ON Eb (5—SO)

✔ TWO-PART SINGING ✔ SOCIAL STUDIES RELATIONSHIP

"Jolly miner men" would sing this song of good fellowship vigorously in a moderately fast tempo, with a strong accent on the first beat of each measure. Their tone would be robust without being raucous.

Much of our American folk music came originally from Europe, brought here by immigrants and adapted to our ways of living and interests. This song came to Canada and our country from England and has long been a favorite in mining sections. It reveals the spirit of cooperation which prevails among men of like occupations, as expressed in such phrases "'cause we share and share alike, both when we're up or down."

● Oh, Worship the King (PAGE 87)
KEY OF Ab
STARTS ON Eb (5—SO)

✔ TWO-PART SINGING ✔ VOICE QUALITY

The tempo and movements of the two parts make this a good number for emphasizing part-singing. The two parts should move very precisely together, each chord controlled so that it is well-tuned and properly balanced. Since the speed at which the hymn is sung is spirited, the quality of the singing can be listened to with care and corrected if necessary.

The words should be pronounced clearly, with the active jaw, tongue, and lip movement necessary to attain good diction and at the same time resonant tone quality. Breath should be taken at the end of each four-measure phrase, *not* in the middle. By continuing the phrase to the end, the volume can increase toward the middle of it, as it should in an ascending line, and taper off toward the ending.

Rowing Song (PAGE 88)
KEY OF F MINOR
STARTS ON F (1—LA)

✔ THREE-TONE CHANT ✔ RHYTHMIC ACTION

Rhythm forms the basis of this song, derived from the motion of the oarsman as he pulls on the oars. The tempo should be regulated to the rhythm used in rowing.

This chant is based on just three tones:

Let the class imitate a steady rowing motion as they sing.

Dabbling in the Dew (PAGE 89)
KEY OF Db
STARTS ON Db (1—DO)

✓ **KEY OF Db** ✓ **LOWERED SEVENTH DEGREE**

This is the first reading song in the key of Db Major. See "Down by the River," page 10 of this book, for suggestions on presenting new keys.

Breathing is a special problem in this song because there are no long, held tones at the ends of the phrases, where one normally is able to catch a breath to begin a new phrase. Only one breath should be taken during the course of each stanza, after the second phrase. It must be taken quickly so that the next phrase will start without breaking and interrupting the steady rhythm of the song. If the tempo is lively, with a lilt, it will aid in mastering the breathing problem.

Folk music of various countries is often distinguished by certain rhythmic or melodic features. This Cornish tune gains an interesting, characteristic sound by the use of Cb (lowered 7; te). Have the pupils sing by rote "Where be you a-going," which progresses up the Db scale until it skips to Cb. Sing "I be going a-milking" in the same way, hearing the sound of the Cb in relation to the other tones in this passage before singing it.

Londonderry Air (PAGE 90)
KEY OF Db
STARTS ON C (7—TI)

✓ **PICK-UP NOTES** ✓ **RHYTHM PATTERN**

To start a group singing this song together with accuracy, it is necessary to indicate precisely when the first pick-up note starts. Pick-up notes are unaccented tones that begin songs with an incomplete measure, in contrast to other songs which begin on the first beat of a measure. The three pick-up notes here begin on the last half of the third beat. Start the singing by counting as follows: One, two, three, "I like to sing," etc.

A characteristic pattern, repeated over and over, is found in this tune:

So that pupils will learn to scan a song to pick out distinguishing features, ask them to examine the selection to see how many times this basic rhythm pattern is found. (Seven times. Only the last phrase varies.)

Good tone quality and smooth, expressive phrasing are essential to a worthy performance of this beautiful Irish tune. The volume of tone should be controlled for loveliness of sound, increasing slightly with the rise of a melodic line and decreasing with the downward direction of a phrase. Follow the dynamic markings in the score tempered with the shadings that seem appropriate while singing.

Annie Laurie (PAGE 92)
KEY OF Db
STARTS ON F (3—MI)

✓ **RHYTHM PATTERN** ✓ **SING-TOGETHER SONGS**

Ask the class to find how many times the following rhythm pattern occurs in the song: (Five times)

After your class has sung this Scottish song satisfactorily, try combining it with "Londonderry Air." Only the first four phrases of each song are compatible harmonically; so "Londonderry Air" must be discontinued at the end of the fourth phrase.

Finish by singing "Annie Laurie" alone to the end or by ending both songs at the end of the fourth phrase.

For assembly singing, one song could be sung alone, then the other, and then the two could be combined for the four phrases as an ending. Be sure to start the two songs so that they are sung in precise rhythm together, else they will not sound harmonious with one another.

Explain the Scottish terms: braes=hillsides; doon =down; dee=die; e'e=eye; gowan=daisy.

⊙ Lovely Islands of Hawaii (PAGE 94)
KEY OF F
UPPER PART STARTS ON A (3—MI)
LOWER PART STARTS ON F (1—DO)

✔ SOCIAL STUDIES RELATIONSHIP ✔ ACCOMPANIMENTS

Discuss the words of the song, using a map of the Hawaiian Islands to locate the scene of the text. Pictures aid in completing the visualization of Hawaii. Show a picture of the hibiscus, the Hawaian state flower.

Ukulele chords are included in the pupil's book. They give pupils who play this instrument an opportunity to display their talents and at the same time aid in presenting a Hawaiian song in an authentic setting, as the Hawaiians use the ukulele with much of their singing.

A drum accompaniment is also included, L indicating the use of the left hand and R the use of the right hand. Begin the accompaniment several measures before starting the singing, as an introduction. Ukulele or autoharp may play an F chord during the introduction.

Aloha Oe (PAGE 95)
KEY OF G
STARTS ON D (5—SO)

✔ UKULELE ACCOMPANIMENT ✔ PHRASING ✔ CHROMATICS

Ukulele chords are printed in the pupil's book in order to provide a characteristic Hawaiian setting.

If no ukuleles are available, use an autoharp, piano, or other chording instrument.

The phrasing should be *legato* (smooth), and the voices should be controlled to sing easy, floating tones in a soft, lyrical manner. The tempo is a relaxed, drifting-along pace, suited to the mood of the text.

Call attention to the chromatic tones.

Hawaiian Chant (PAGE 96)
KEY OF Bb
MELODY STARTS ON D (3—MI)
LOWER PART STARTS ON Bb (1—DO)

✔ RHYTHMIC CHANT ✔ DRUM ACCOMPANIMENT
✔ CREATIVE ACTIVITY

Make sure that the class sings this chant in a steady, strongly accented rhythm, at a moderate tempo. Teach one part at a time, then combine the two, letting the children take turns on each part for reading practice.

For the rhythm accompaniment, a low-pitched drum should be used and played with the hands rather than with sticks. The rhythm pattern shown in the pupil's book should be repeated throughout the song. It can be used alone as a short introduction. Play the rhythm as follows:

R means right hand; L means left hand.

As a creative activity, words could be added and drum beats could be varied or expanded to include several instruments playing counter rhythms (two separate rhythms that follow the basic beat of the song).

● Alaska, We Salute You (PAGE 96)

KEY OF F
STARTS ON C (5—SO)

✔ SPECIAL-OCCASION SONG ✔ ABAC FORM

This song could be used in an assembly presentation as a culminating activity in a unit study of Alaska. It should be sung in the style of a spirited march, with sturdy tone and in a steady rhythm emphasized by detached, accented phrases.

The third part is optional, to be used by classes prepared for three-part singing.

The form of the song is ABAC: the first and third phrases are alike melodically; the second and fourth phrases differ from each other and from the first and third.

● Chopsticks (PAGE 98)

KEY OF C
UPPER PART STARTS ON B (7—TI)
MIDDLE PART STARTS ON G (5—SO)
LOWER PART STARTS ON F (4—FA)

✔ "FUN" SONG ✔ PROGRAM NOVELTY

It seems that every boy and girl who has had access to a piano has tried to play "Chopsticks" with two fingers. In this arrangement of the tune, a melody (descant) and words have been added to the two-finger version. Use bells or piano to play the original tune. After the class has heard and recognized it, let them try to read the middle and lower parts, one part at a time and then together, adding words when they are ready.

Sing the upper part next, and when it is learned combine the three parts.

For a novelty number on a program, try the following:

1. The two-finger version is played on piano or bells.

2. This is repeated with the middle and lower parts joining in.

3. The three parts are sung without accompaniment.

4. The voices and piano (or bells) perform Stanza 2.

● Sail On, Little Boat (PAGE 99)

KEY OF D MINOR
STARTS ON A (5—MI)

✔ PENTATONIC SCALE ✔ INSTRUMENTAL ACTIVITY

Like most Oriental music, this ancient Chinese tune is based on a scale not customarily used in music familiar to us. In indicating that the tune is in the key of D minor, we are merely expressing tonality as closely as it can be stated in terms related to our major and minor modes. Oriental music is based on the pentatonic scale, a five-toned scale using the intervals heard if only the black keys on the piano are played. Encourage your pupils to experiment with these tones.

Melody instruments can play this melody. The flute would be especially effective, as its tone is appropriate to the quality of sound used in Oriental music. If a member of the class plays the violin, let him use the instrument without *vibrato,* imitating the sound of a Chinese one-string fiddle. Use wood blocks (or sticks) as indicated in the pupil's book.

The Leaving of My Love (PAGE 100)

KEY OF Db
STARTS ON Db (1—DO)

✔ READING ✔ EXPRESSIVE SINGING

Before reading this song, it would be helpful to familiarize your pupils again with the appearance of Db notation by placing the scale on the blackboard and spending a few minutes in having the class sing various intervals as you point to them.

Two intervals (skips) which might cause reading problems are (1) the octave skip at the end of the first phrase

1	8	6	5
do	do	la	so
and	leave	you	now

and (2) the skip at the end of the fourth phrase:

4	7	1
fa	ti	do
I	must	go.

Have the class read the phrases, one at a time, going back to perfect these intervals only if it is necessary.

The melody of this English chantey is particularly lyrical and should be sung in a light, flowing manner.

● Toombera (PAGE 101)
KEY OF E MINOR
STARTS ON E (1—LA)

↙ **ORIENTAL MUSIC** ↙ **INSTRUMENTAL ACTIVITY**

Oriental music differs from ours not only by its use of the pentatonic scale but also by the fact that it does not use harmony as we are accustomed to use it. As you listen to Oriental music, you will hear voices and instruments often following the same melody.

Bells, melody instruments, flutes, or violins could play the melody as it is sung in "Toombera." For additional instrumentation, add a gong or cymbal struck with a mallet on the beat on which a quarter rest appears. Also add sticks or wood blocks during the last phrase, having them play the rhythm. Sing in a light, sing-songy style, increasing the volume slightly while singing "Toombera," etc.

Alouette (PAGE 102)
KEY OF G
STARTS ON G (1—DO)

↙ **"FUN" SONG**

This popular French song, brought to the New World by early settlers in French Canada, is sung and enjoyed by school children, college students, and adults who enjoy the fun of a rousing action song. The actions are indicated in the pupil's book.

For classes using conversational French as part of their curricular activities, the song will have added use in expanding their French vocabulary and giving interesting practice to words already learned.

A lively tempo and a robust voice quality go with this type of song, to achieve the gay, animated spirit which it expresses.

Praise to the Lord (PAGE 103)
KEY OF E
STARTS ON E (1—DO)

↙ **KEY OF E** ↙ **AABC FORM**

This is the first reading song in the key of E Major. See "Down by the River," page 10 of this book, for suggestions on presenting or reviewing keys.

Before reading this song, let your group examine it to locate the stepwise and skipwise passages. Notice that Measures 2-6 consist entirely of stepwise intervals, moving directly down the E scale, starting on 3 (mi), down to low 5 (so), then back up to the keynote.

The wider interval found in the first measure is an easy one because it is based on the tonic chord, moving from 1 (do) to 5 (so); on the second measure, it moves to 3 (mi), another note of the tonic chord.

The form is AABC, because the first and second phrases are alike, while the third and fourth are both different.

⬤ El Sombrero Blanco (PAGE 104)
KEY OF E
STARTS ON G# (3—MI)

✔ **DOUBLE SHARP** ✔ **RHYTHM ACCOMPANIMENT**

The melody begins on the second beat of the measure. To begin with precision and to indicate the tempo (moderate speed), count:

The double sharp is explained in the pupil's book, and it is suggested that pupils examine it carefully to become acquainted with this symbol which, although they may not use it frequently in singing, is part of the musical vocabulary.

For optional use, a rhythm accompaniment is shown in the pupil's book, to be played by tambourine, castanets, or other instruments judged appropriate by the teacher and the class.

Raccoon Hunt (PAGE 106)
KEY OF E
MELODY STARTS ON E (1—DO)
HARMONY STARTS ON G# (3—MI)

✔ **CHROMATICS**

This is a rollicking, lively tune that should be sung in the spirit of fun. Sing the refrain slightly louder than the stanzas.

The chromatics in the refrain should be learned by hearing the melody played or sung. Let your pupils observe the effects produced by the chromatic tones as the melody is played quite slowly at first, and then at the proper tempo.

Sing Your Way Home (PAGE 107)
KEY OF G
STARTS ON B (3—MI)

✔ **KEY OF G** ✔ **CHROMATICS**

To review the key of G Major, proceed as you did in reviewing the key of E in connection with "Praise to the Lord."

The chromatics in the melody should be sung carefully, so that they are accurate in pitch. It is a good idea to play the tune on the piano or a melody instrument, stressing these passages in order to attain good tuning of the tones.

This is a favorite camp song and is often sung at the end of a hike or after the campfire.

The Lone Prairie (PAGE 108)
KEY OF G
MELODY STARTS ON D (5—SO)
UPPER HARMONY PART STARTS ON B (3—MI)
LOWER HARMONY PART STARTS ON D (5—SO)

✔ **RHYTHMIC VOCAL ACCOMPANIMENT**
✔ **PIANO CHORDS I AND V₇**

This arrangement is suitable for an assembly community sing or for other occasions when a simple harmony part, taught without music, is desired. If only the large notes of the accompanying vocal part are used, it is not necessary to read music at all since the seven-note figure, "Won't you listen to my plea," is repeated over and over throughout the song. The part needs to be followed only for the sake of the changing words. For assembly, with no books used, the same words could be chanted repeatedly without change.

Adding the small notes provides a more complete and full-sounding accompaniment. This part, too, is simple and easy to learn, making only one easy change from the pattern sung in most of the arrangement.

The melody should be sung in a smooth, flowing manner, whereas the accompaniment should be sung in short, detached tones to provide a steady, accented rhythm.

Sweet Sally Sue (PAGE 110)
KEY OF G
STARTS ON D (5—SO)

✔ READING IN THE KEY OF G

Write the G scale on the blackboard and let your pupils sing intervals as you point them out. This procedure aids in orienting the class to the position of notes on the staff when this key is used.

In reading the song, make certain that the class knows the pitch names and the names used in reading (syllables, numbers, or whatever system you use). The first phrase should be checked by asking your class to name the notes according to the reading system used:

D	G	E	D	G	A	B	A	G	E	G	D
5	1	6	5	1	2	3	2	1	6	1	5
so	do	la	so	do	re	mi	re	do	la	do	so

Continue this procedure only until your pupils know the correct names, for the goal to reach (as quickly as they are ready) is to sing the correct pitches simultaneously without recognizing and identifying them by name. Reading is not true reading until the melody is sung with pitch and rhythm performed as indicated by the notation. Therefore, steps leading to this goal should be only as many and as long as absolutely essential.

The tune is playable by melody instruments. An arrangement for performance could include vocal and instrumental choruses, singing the first stanza, playing a chorus, singing the next stanza, and so on.

⬤ The Lumberjack's Song (PAGE 111)
KEY OF G
STARTS ON D (5—SO)

✔ SOCIAL STUDIES RELATIONSHIP

The story of lumbering forms part of our country's history. The lumberjack, or logger as he is often called today, was a hardy, colorful man who carried his songs with him as he moved from logging camp to logging camp, cutting down the timber, hauling it to the mills, and providing the lumber to build our homes and factories. Lumberjack songs from various parts of our country and Canada bear a close resemblance, having been carried from one section to another with slight modifications to fit particular local scenes.

As for all songs originally sung by the sturdy men who sailed our ships, built our railroads, and worked in mines, the interpretation must keep these original singers in mind and be jolly and virile.

⬤ A Bicycle Built for Two (PAGE 112)
KEY OF G
MELODY STARTS ON D (5—SO)
DESCANT STARTS ON D (5—SO)

✔ "FUN" SONG   ✔ DESCANT   ✔ DICTION

The descant begins two measures before the melody, thus providing an introduction. If you prefer to omit the introduction, start at the double bar and begin the descant on B (3—mi).

As the descant moves rather quickly, it should be practiced more slowly than it will be sung in performance and then gradually speeded up until it goes at the right speed in relation to the tempo for the melody, which is moderate, with one beat to each measure.

The descant offers a good exercise in improving diction, because the words must be enunciated carefully and crisply to be heard clearly and to move at the correct tempo.

To make a longer arrangement for effective program use, you might consider the following routine:
First time through: melody only.
Second time through: melody played by melody instruments alone.
Third time through: melody and descant sung together.

Riddle Song (PAGE 114)
KEY OF G
STARTS ON D (5—SO)

☛ PENTATONIC SCALE   ☛ ABBA₁ FORM

This plaintive, pleasing melody should be sung smoothly and flowingly, in a quiet, restful voice. It begins softly, grows slightly louder as the melody ascends in the second and third phrases, then diminishes in volume as the last phrase descends to an unusual ending on the fifth tone of the scale below the keynote.

The plaintive quality comes, in part, from the use of the pentatonic scale (see notes on "Sail On, Little Boat"). Pupils should become aware, as they sing Oriental, Scottish, and certain American folk songs, that the pentatonic scale is used by many people throughout the world. In fact, it has a far greater world-wide use than our major and minor scales.

Encourage your pupils to attempt, in their free time, to play this tune "by ear," transposing it to the black keys. The starting tone will be Db.

The form of the song is ABBA₁, since the second and third phrases are alike, and the first and fourth phrases nearly alike. Call attention to the form after the song has been learned and let the class note the features of similarity and contrast.

The Viking Ship (PAGE 115)
KEY OF E MINOR
STARTS ON B (5—MI)

☛ AABB FORM   ☛ MINOR TONALITY

A discussion of Viking explorations would add interest to the song. Leif Ericson and Eric the Red are usually of interest to boys and girls in this age group because of their discoveries on the North American coasts. Sing the song vigorously in character with the virility of these explorers.

The form of the song, AABB, is marked in the pupil's book. Call attention to it to develop an awareness of this feature of musical composition. Knowledge of form makes the learning of new songs easier when it is realized that learning the tune of one phrase often spells the learning of another simultaneously.

To Washington and Lincoln (PAGE 116)
KEY OF F
STARTS ON C (5—SO)

☛ SONG FOR SPECIAL DAY

You might add other patriotic songs from this book to make a unit of songs to use for an assembly program. "Keep America Free and Strong," "United States Armed Forces," "Field Artillery Song," "The Marines' Hymn," and our national anthem would be suitable. Or you might add familiar songs, such as "Yankee Doodle," as representative of Washington's time, and "Battle Hymn of the Republic" or "Dixie," as representative of Lincoln's time.

This song can be played by melody instruments.

Here's to America (PAGE 117)
KEY OF F
STARTS ON F (1—DO)

☛ PATRIOTIC SELECTION   ☛ THREE-PART SINGING

The words set to this very old Silesian tune make it suitable for patriotic programs. For festivals, it is most effective when all three parts are used. In classroom singing, two or three parts may be used as preferred.

The tempo should be very steady, at a slow walking speed. Breaths should be taken only every four measures, since long phrasing gives the song a flowing motion. Encourage full-throated singing, with ringing, open tones.

Twilight (PAGE 120)
KEY OF G
MELODY STARTS ON B (3—MI)
LOWER PART STARTS ON G (1—DO)

⌐ ENSEMBLE SINGING

First teach the melody to everyone, and then the harmony (lower part). Let the class read as much as possible independently and refer to the piano or other assistance only when it is necessary. The first four measures are not difficult, but the next phrase will require help since it employs the use of chromatic tones. Review the meaning of the *fermata* (hold) in the sixth measure, and when this measure is sung indicate the length of the hold by holding your right hand up until you wish the class to move to the next measure.

This song, with music by one of the great composers, offers possibilities for an excellent program or festival number. The two parts should be sung with close attention to balance and blend of voices. Ensemble (group singing in parts) training provides important immediate experience, and, in addition, prepares pupils for later participation in choruses and glee clubs.

To Spring (PAGE 121)
KEY OF D
STARTS ON D (1—DO)

⌐ ROUND

Sing this three-part round in a joyful spirit at a moderately fast tempo. Sing each part through three times, entering as indicated by an interval of two measures. The third part will sing the last two measures of the third chorus alone.

Easter Time (PAGE 122)
KEY OF Bb
STARTS ON F (5—SO)

⌐ PROGRAM SONG

This happy Easter song is a good number for a spring festival. It should be sung joyfully with good enunciation and one swing to a measure. To make it more effective, let someone play the melody on bells between the two stanzas.

Note the chromatic tone in the second phrase. It should present no difficulty; but if it does, drill on so-fi-so briefly.

Lovely Appear (PAGE 122)
KEY OF Eb
STARTS ON G (3—MI)

⌐ PROGRAM SONG ⌐ ORATORIO

One group may sing the entire song, although suggestions in the pupil's book call for two groups. Group 1 should include singers who sing easily and well in the higher range of the first section of the song, while Group 2 should include singers with a naturally lower voice quality (alto), as this section repeats the melody sung by the first group (sopranos) in a lower range. The entire song is within the normal range of most sixth-graders, but a division into parts is desirable in achieving a difference in voice quality between the two sections.

If selective grouping on the two parts is not feasible or practical, divide the class by rows as a quicker method of grouping. The register in which each of the two sections is sung will provide a limited change in voice quality.

Discuss the meaning of "oratorio" with the class.

This song is good for program use and could be used effectively by a large festival group as well as by a class-size chorus. It should be sung with light, clear tone quality in *legato* style.

Alleluia (PAGE 124)
KEY OF Eb
STARTS ON Eb (1—DO)

✓ CANON ✓ 3/2 METER ✓ PHRASING

Have the class count and clap the rhythm pattern:

With the half note as the basic beat, two quarter notes are sounded to comprise one full beat, and a whole note is held for two counts.

Chant the rhythm of the first phrase next, and then teach the upper part phrase by phrase. The lower part will be easy to learn, as it repeats the melody one measure behind the upper part until the last few measures. At this point the two parts move in unison until the last two measures, when the lower part moves in harmony with the melody.

The tempo should be moderately fast, just fast enough to give motion and smooth phrasing to the interpretation without losing the stately mood which the song expresses. Children tend to breathe too frequently while singing a song of this type, in which sustained, flowing phrases are necessary for good interpretation. Ask them if they can sing "From all that dwell below the skies Let the Creator's praise arise" on one breath. Pupils often respond more successfully to a challenge than to a direction.

● Spring Is a Wonderful Time (PAGE 125)
KEY OF G
STARTS ON D (5—SO)

✓ INSTRUMENTAL ACTIVITY ✓ PROGRAM SONG

Here is another good song for a spring program. To enhance it, have bells, melody instruments, or flutes play the introduction and interludes during the song. If singing alone is preferred, the class may sing the introduction with "la."

As a creative activity, your pupils might add stanzas describing the things they like to do on a warm, sunny spring day.

The tempo should be in a swinging, relaxed rhythm, with one beat to each measure. The tone should be light and expressive of a happy, carefree mood.

● Lovely Messengers (PAGE 126)
KEY OF G
STARTS ON D (5—SO)

✓ PROGRAM SONG ✓ INTERPRETATION

Sung by a class or by a special chorus, this two-part song makes an excellent selection for program or festival use.

The intervals of melody move quite smoothly in most places; but on intervals such as the one moving from the first to the second measure, your class may require assistance:

The rhythm should move in two beats to a measure to achieve flowing phrases, and these two beats in each measure should be sung at a slow, steady tempo.

Sing the song softly, with a slight increase in volume as the melodic line ascends. Stress voice quality, as this beautiful melody requires well-controlled singing to achieve the best results.

37

A Prayer of Thanks (PAGE 127)
KEY OF A MINOR
STARTS ON A (1—LA)

✔ MINOR TONALITY ✔ TWO-PART SINGING

When songs in the minor mode are sung, re-emphasize the fact that every key signature indicates *two* key possibilities. In the major mode, tones of the tonic chord (1-3-5; do-mi-so) are generally used in the very beginning and ending notes of a tune. Tunes that start and end on what would be 6 (la) of the related major key are in the minor mode.

If this song is played on a piano or other instrument capable of playing the two parts together, pupils will have an opportunity to hear the characteristic sounds of minor tonality. If you have no such instrument, after the song has been learned, let groups of pupils perform for other members of the class so that all can hear the effect of the minor tonality.

Sing the song slowly and with *legato* (smooth) phrasing. Blend and balance the parts carefully.

Maple Sugar Time (PAGE 128)
KEY OF G
UPPER PART STARTS ON B (3—MI)
LOWER PART STARTS ON G (1—DO)

✔ TWO-PART SONG ✔ SOCIAL STUDIES RELATIONSHIP

The stanzas should be sung at a moderate tempo, in a steady rhythm. The refrain goes a little faster. The tone should be light and gay, with good diction emphasized to make the words clearly understandable.

Teach the upper part (melody) first. If both parts are used, try having the lower part sung simultaneously with the upper without teaching it separately. If this procedure does not work out well, teach it separately, and then combine the two parts.

If yours is one of the several states which produce maple syrup and maple sugar, you might use the song on a spring program. If any of your pupils has been in a sugar bush or sugar camp during the sugaring season, he might tell the class about his experiences.

Cuckoo Bird (PAGE 130)
KEY OF F
STARTS ON A (3—MI)

✔ INSTRUMENTAL ACTIVITY ✔ INTERPRETATION

For performance, singing and playing on melody instruments could be combined. One possibility is to sing the first stanza and chorus, then to play the song through, and to end by singing the second stanza and chorus, or by singing and playing it.

The rhythm should be accented at the beginning of each measure in a moderately fast tempo, one beat to each measure.

This is a yodeling song and should be sung in imitation of the style and tone quality of a yodel. The refrain could be sung by two groups, the second pretending to be on a mountain slope farther off than the first group. The first group would therefore sing in full voice, and the second softly to give a far-away effect. If two groups are used on the refrain (starting immediately following the three held tones), Group 1 sings two measures, Group 2 sings two measures, etc. to the end. There will thus be two calls and two answers (echoes) in the refrain.

Kookaburra (PAGE 131)
KEY OF D
STARTS ON A (5—SO)

✔ KEY OF D ✔ FOUR-PART ROUND

This is the first reading song in the key of D Major. See "Down by the River," page 10 of this book, for suggestions on presenting or reviewing scales.

Sing "Kookaburra" in a lively tempo, lightly and gaily. After the tune has been well learned, divide the class into four groups and sing it as a round, each group entering as indicated and singing the song three times.

Sacramento (PAGE 132)
KEY OF D
STARTS ON A (5—SO)

✔ SOCIAL STUDIES RELATIONSHIP

The days of the California Gold Rush were times of exciting adventure on the high seas as well as in the mining camps, since many prospectors traveled west by ship. Some sailed to Panama, crossed the isthmus, and re-embarked on the Pacific coast. Others sailed from the east coast all the way around Cape Horn at the southern tip of South America to reach their destination in California. This is why a ballad of gold-mining days often has a salty flavor and the tune of a sea chantey.

Discuss the gold-mining days in California in order to give fuller meaning to this song. On a map trace the various routes from the east to the west coast.

◐ The Fiddler (PAGE 133)
KEY OF D
STARTS ON A (5—SO)

✔ AABBC FORM ✔ 6/8 METER IN DUPLE RHYTHM

Many songs written in 6/8 meter are sung in two beats to a measure. Fast 6/8 meter is always sung this way, as is a march written in this meter. Pupils should learn to read such rhythm correctly whenever it is encountered. Place various patterns of notes on the board and let your class count and clap for practice in developing ability to read quickly and accurately. The eye needs to be trained to see measures in two-beats-to-the-measure groupings:

The intervals in the first measure of the song are rather difficult and need to be learned carefully before proceeding to the following measures.

The form of the song is AABBC, the first two phrases being alike, the third and fourth alike, with a three-measure contrasting phrase added at the end of each stanza, a device quite frequently used in folk songs.

The Keeper (PAGE 134)
KEY OF D
STARTS ON A (5—SO)

✔ TWO-PART SINGING ✔ SOCIAL STUDIES RELATIONSHIP

Although this is a two-part song, most of the measures do not use harmony. In many of these measures, the melody shifts back and forth between the upper and lower parts. Ask your pupils to find the two-part measures in which there is no harmony.

In teaching the song, let everyone sing the melody, shifting from the upper part to the lower when the melody shifts and then moving back to the upper when the melody shifts back. Next, add the harmony to those measures which have it. Finally sing the song with the parts divided as printed. The tempo should be moderately fast, and the diction crisp and clear.

This song and "Robin Hood" might serve to introduce a unit on the Elizabethan period in England.

⊙ Beautiful Dreamer (PAGE 135)
KEY OF D
STARTS ON D (8—DO)

➤ 9/8 METER ➤ EXPRESSIVE SINGING

9/8 meter is sung in three swings to a measure in a smooth-flowing melodic line. The first two measures are counted as follows:

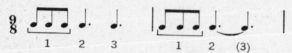

The next two measures ("starlight and dewdrops are waiting for thee") are counted:

This very tuneful melody should be sung with a light and floating tone, with *legato* phrasing emphasized. The phrases end on tones that are held long enough to stress tone quality. Vowels should be sustained, as for example: on "throng" and "song" the open "aw" sound should be held; the mouth should be closed for "ng" only when it is time to breathe and begin the next phrase. The tendency, unless checked, is to change from the vowel to a consonant too quickly on held tones.

⊙ Robin Hood (PAGE 136)
KEY OF D
STARTS ON D (1—DO)

➤ AABB FORM ➤ DOTTED EIGHTH AND SIXTEENTH NOTES
➤ RHYTHM

The second phrase repeats the tune of the first, and the fourth is like the third. The form is therefore AABB. Call attention to the form, so that your pupils will develop an awareness of this interesting and important aspect of musical composition.

The dotted eighth note followed by the sixteenth is a rhythm which occurs frequently in music yet needs constant attention. Sometimes there is a tendency to sing this grouping as two even notes rather than as a long-short rhythmic pattern.

Sing the song at a spirited tempo in a precise manner. The voice quality should be robust and firm.

The introduction to this song as played on the recording is the opening measures of "Country Gardens," the tune to which the text "Walk into the Spring," page 192 of the pupil's book, is set.

⊙ Toviska (PAGE 138)
KEY OF A
STARTS ON E (5—SO)

➤ KEY OF A ➤ RHYTHMIC ACTIVITY

This is the first reading song in the key of A Major. See "Down by the River," page 10 of this book for presenting or reviewing scales.

"Toviska" is a favorite at social meetings, community sings, and summer camps. The lively tune, the shouted "hoo-ya" of the refrain, and the clapping accompaniment add life and gaiety to any informal social gathering where singing for fun is in order.

The tempo should be lively, one beat to a measure. Tone quality should be robust but not ponderous, and words should be sung crisply.

After the song has been learned, add the rhythm accompaniment printed in the pupil's book.

Over the Hills and Far Away (PAGE 139)
KEY OF A
STARTS ON A (1—DO)

➤ PHRASE COMPARISON

Count, clap, and chant the words of the first phrase to establish the correct rhythm. When two notes are used for a single-vowel word, as in "drums" and "beat," chant as follows to make the second eighth note in each case sound:

Hark! now the dru-hums be-heat up a - gain.

When the tune is added, the "h" is discarded in each word, as the changed pitch brings in the second eighth note of each slurred word.

Compare the second phrase with the first. How are they alike? How do they differ? The third phrase is like the first, except that it (1) adds a pick-up note on the word "Then" and (2) has a different last note.

Note other similarities and contrasts in other phrases. This kind of observation aids reading, as it develops an awareness of melodic direction, repetition of rhythmic and tonal patterns, and note groups rather than individual notes.

Every Pull of the Oar (PAGE 140)
KEY OF A
STARTS ON A (1—DO)

✔ TWO-PART SINGING ✔ READING

Every song in the book that your pupils can read should be read, but some are better suited to completely independent reading than others. When certain intervals or rhythms are difficult, read what is within practical limits, give assistance in the difficult passages, and then complete the learning of the song.

This song is well suited to independent reading because both rhythm and intervals are quite easy, the melody being largely composed of scalewise steps. Give the starting tone and count 1, 2, 3, 1, 2. The singers start on 3. Let them see how far they can keep going without faltering. If minor errors occur but tonality and rhythm remain steady, permit the class to continue. On the other hand, if the reading becomes confused and disintegrated, stop the group and go back to the beginning of whatever phrase causes difficulty and have it read correctly. Finally proceed to sing the song correctly from beginning to end.

Teach the melody first, next the harmony part, and then sing them together.

Ⓞ Down at the Barber Shop (PAGE 141)
KEY OF F
LOWER PART STARTS ON F (1—DO)
MIDDLE PART STARTS ON A (3—MI)
UPPER PART STARTS ON C (5—SO)

✔ THREE-PART SINGING ✔ DRAMATIZATION

The first three measures provide a means of introducing and tuning three-part singing, as each part sings its starting tone alone and then joins on the tonic chord (1-3-5; do-mi-so).

Try teaching the three parts simultaneously, perfecting the first four measures, then the next four, similar in treatment to the first three except that the three parts combine to form the dominant chord (7-2-5; ti-re-so). If a piano is available, it could be used to aid in supporting the voice parts, although it is not necessary and is even considered a hindrance to independent part-singing by some educators.

If certain passages cause problems that are difficult to solve by the three-part approach, take parts one at a time over the difficult spot and then combine them again.

For assembly performance, the boys might dramatize the song. They might make themselves up as Gay Nineties barber-shop singers, parting their hair straight down the middle and wearing handle-bar moustaches. A leader could dress as a barber and wave a comb to direct the singing. A customer could sit (lathered) in a simulated barber chair and be "shaved" by the barber-leader while the others sit in the "waiting customer" chairs.

41

Little David (PAGE 142)
KEY OF G
UPPER PART IN INTRODUCTION STARTS ON B (3—MI)
LOWER PART IN INTRODUCTION STARTS ON D (5—SO)
MELODY STARTS ON B (3—MI)

☞ THREE-PART SINGING ☞ RHYTHM ACCOMPANIMENT
☞ SOLO SINGING

The simplicity of the accompanying vocal parts makes this a suitable number for assembly singing as well as for classroom use. The parts can be taught quickly and without books.

The upper harmony part repeats over and over just two tones, B and C. The lower part repeats over and over just two tones also, D and E. In teaching the harmony, give the pitches of the tones; have them held until they are accurate and secure (in tune with each other); and then have the figure "Play on your harp" sung in rhythm, first at a rather slow tempo and then at the speed appropriate for the interpretation of the song.

Have the entire class learn the melody together, including all three stanzas; then divide the class into three groups to sing the arrangement as printed.

If you like, add the clapping rhythm shown in the pupil's book. You may prefer to use rhythm instruments instead.

So Handy (PAGE 143)
KEY OF F
STARTS ON F (1—DO)

☞ INCIDENTAL SOLOS ☞ SOCIAL STUDIES RELATIONSHIP

Use four soloists, one on each stanza, and permit all your pupils to sing a solo part at some time or other, if they want to, when the song is sung.

This and other chanties should be sung in a robust style. Have your pupils read the explanation in their books concerning the nature of this chantey and let them imitate the actions used in pulling up the mainsail of a sailing ship.

Secure pictures of sailing vessels and urge your pupils to read about sea transportation in the early years of our country.

Legend (PAGE 144)
KEY OF E MINOR
STARTS ON E (1—LA)

☞ 5/4 METER ☞ MINOR TONALITY

In most songs familiar to us, 5/4 meter is uncommon. Have your pupils count and clap the illustration of 5/4 meter shown in their books. Then chant the words of the song, and it will be noticed that every measure follows precisely the rhythm found in the first measure. This is the meter found in the Kalevala of the Finnish people, one of the oldest heroic poems known to man.

Haul Away, Joe (PAGE 144)
KEY OF Eb
STARTS ON Bb (5—SO)

☞ SOLO AND CHORUS ☞ DRAMATIZATION

The chanties in *Book Six* could be used as the basis of a unit on sailing-vessel transportation, in which some of the history of our country could be related by a study of such events as the War of 1812, the Barbary Wars, the California Gold Rush, and so on.

The chanties could also be used for a dramatic presentation, for which a simple backdrop showing a deck and sails might serve as a setting for pupils dressed like sailors.

Rio Grande (PAGE 145)
KEY OF C
STARTS ON C (1—DO)

☞ CHANTEY ☞ SOLO AND CHORUS

"Rio Grande" has remained one of the most popular of all chanties. Select soloists to sing the incidental solos indicated in the score, using one throughout the song or selecting one for the solo in each stanza. For programs, it is desirable to use outstanding singers in the class, but for classroom performance give everyone wanting a chance to sing a solo the opportunity to do so. On the other hand, do not force a pupil against his wishes to sing alone, for the embarrassment to a person who is highly sensitive could do serious psychological harm by destroying his pleasure in being a member of the group.

Bendemeer's Stream (PAGE 146)
KEY OF F
MELODY STARTS ON C (5—SO)
HARMONY (UPPER STAFF) STARTS ON A (3—MI)

✓ TWO-PART SINGING ✓ INTERPRETATION

Sing the melody (lower staff) first at a moderate tempo with *legato* phrasing, regarding changes in volume and speed as indicated in the score.

Next teach the harmony part, stressing light, good voice quality as each of the two parts is sung. Have your pupils observe the dynamic (volume) symbols used, including the "swell" (crescendo and decrescendo) used in two places. Have them practice these dynamic changes, in both melody and harmony, until the change is smooth, never becoming strident as the volume increases or flat and lifeless in pitch and tone as the volume decreases.

Then let the class sing the two parts together. Caution the singers to maintain a balance in which the melody is heard clearly and call attention to the *mf* direction for the melody and the *mp* direction for the harmony. The final check as to the proper volume for each part is the judgment of the teacher as she listens carefully and adjusts the volume of each part until the two sound well together, with the melody distinctly heard.

The Band (PAGE 148)
KEY OF C
UPPER PART STARTS ON C (8—DO)
MIDDLE PART STARTS ON E (3—MI)
LOWER PART STARTS ON C (1—DO)

✓ THREE-PART SINGING ✓ ACTION SONG
✓ INSTRUMENTAL ACTIVITY

This is a very easy three-part song, the two harmony parts repeating a scalewise four-note pattern throughout the arrangement. Have everyone learn the melody and then divide the class into three groups and teach the two harmony parts simultaneously.

Imitate the action used in playing the instruments named in the text. For further action, have the class march by marking time (stepping in place) or by parading around the room if space permits. Add stanzas about other instruments.

All three parts are playable by melody instruments and band instruments. If transposing instruments are used, make certain that they all sound in the same key. By using trumpets and clarinets or C instruments together (melody instruments, flute, violin), a program number could be devised consisting of a vocal chorus, an instrumental chorus, a vocal chorus singing a second stanza, and so on.

For an introduction, have the harmony parts sing (or play) the first four measures only.

Loch Lomond (PAGE 150)
KEY OF F
STARTS ON C (5—SO)

✓ TWO-PART SINGING ✓ INSTRUMENTAL ACTIVITY

After the class has learned to sing the song in unison, teach the harmony part (upper part in the refrain). Take care to balance the parts so that the melody is heard distinctly. It must be sung slightly louder than the harmony to compensate for its being sung below the pitch of the harmony.

Sing in a spirited tempo, with animated tone, observing the *fermatas* by sustaining them a little beyond the normal value of the notes over which they are placed. To keep the class together on the *fermatas,* direct these places by holding up your hand for the desired length of the hold and then dropping it to signal the start, in tempo, of the next tone.

The melody can be played by melody instruments along with the singing or to provide an extra chorus between the first and second stanzas.

For an imitation bagpipe accompaniment, have a pupil play this part on the piano. If this drone effect seems too monotonous to use throughout the song, use it for an introduction, during the stanzas only, or during the refrain, as preferred:

◉ United States Armed Forces (PAGE 152)
KEY OF F
STARTS ON C (5—SO)

⤳ PATRIOTIC SELECTION ⤳ INSTRUMENTAL ACTIVITY

This is an adaptation of a famous English military song, "The British Grenadiers." It is in march tempo in 2/2 meter. This meter is performed the same way as *alla breve* (cut time, ₵), in two beats to a measure with a half note receiving one beat. Have your pupils chant the words of the first phrase until the rhythm is well established.

The counter-melody may be sung by imitating the sounds of a bugle call, or a trumpet may play the special part printed in the pupil's book. If there is a drummer in the class, let him play the drum part;

if not, try having pupils play the rhythm by slapping their knees as they sing, following the drum score shown in their book.

The tune is playable on melody instruments.

◉ Field Artillery Song (PAGE 154)
KEY OF C
MELODY STARTS ON G (5—SO)
DESCANT STARTS ON C (8—DO)

⤳ MILITARY SONG ⤳ DESCANT ⤳ INSTRUMENTAL ACTIVITY

This continues to be one of the most popular songs with boys and girls, even though the rocket-missile age has more or less outmoded the field artillery and horse-drawn caisson. The spirit and vitality of the words and music remain as effective today as when the song was written many years ago.

Explain to your pupils that the word "caisson" means "ammunition wagon," at one time drawn by horses.

The use of the descant adds variety and interest to a song already familiar to most pupils, serving to illustrate how a familiar tune can be treated in various ways, from singing it in unison to performing it in other ways, to provide variety.

◉ The Marines' Hymn (PAGE 156)
KEY OF C
MELODY STARTS ON C (1—DO)
DESCANT STARTS ON G (5—SO)

⤳ MILITARY SONG ⤳ DESCANT ⤳ INSTRUMENTAL ACTIVITY

This arrangement of another military song popular with boys and girls likewise adds a descant to a melody with which they are already familiar.

Review the melody, having everyone sing it together; then teach the descant to everyone. Divide the class into two groups to take turns singing the melody and the descant. Do not sing the marching tempo too quickly, keeping the speed steady and accented. To be heard distinctly, the melody should be sung slightly louder than the descant.

Melody instruments can play both parts, or can be used on the descant as the melody is sung. On the phrase "First to fight for right and freedom," on the word "freedom" play C for both syllables, as E is above the playing range of many melody instruments.

America the Beautiful (PAGE 158)
KEY OF D
MELODY (UPPER PART) STARTS ON A (5—SO)
LOWER PART STARTS ON F# (3—MI)

✔ **TWO-PART SINGING** ✔ **PATRIOTIC SONG**

"America the Beautiful" is one of our most inspiring patriotic songs because of its broad visionary scope and deep-rooted love for our country. Miss Bates, a professor of English at Wellesley College, wrote the text in 1893. It was set to this hymn tune, originally written for "O Mother Dear, Jerusalem" by Samuel A. Ward.

The song should be sung with ringing, clear tones, and in flowing phrases. The tempo should be moderate.

Dona Nobis Pacem (PAGE 159)
KEY OF F
STARTS ON F (1—DO)

✔ **CANON** ✔ **PROGRAM SONG**

As is apparent in the score, a round and a canon are performed in the same way, the same melody being repeated identically by several voices, with an interval of space between each entrance. This canon can be sung in the traditional way in which rounds are sung, three times by each part, the first part starting alone, and the third part ending alone.

If you prefer a harmonic final phrase, have each part sing the canon three times, the first part starting, the second entering when Part 1 begins the second line, and so on. When the first part completes the third time through, the singers on this part again repeat the first two lines; the second part,

after three times through the canon, again repeats the first line. Then the third part, singing through the canon three times and stopping, will end with the other two parts. Try the canon both ways and use the arrangement you prefer.

Sung with expression, good tone quality, and smooth phrasing, this is a fine program number.

Tallis's Canon (PAGE 159)
KEY OF G
STARTS ON G (1—DO)

✔ **CANON**

Although this canon was written four hundred years ago, it is still very popular in England, especially at Winchester College, an institution for boys. Bishop Thomas Ken wrote the words as an evening hymn for Winchester students.

We Sing of Golden Mornings (PAGE 160)
KEY OF F
STARTS ON C (5—SO)

✔ **THIRD PART OPTIONAL** ✔ **AABA FORM**

This song may be sung in unison, two parts, or three parts. Teach the melody (upper part) first; then add the second (middle) part. The third part, on the lower staff, is optional, as the song will sound satisfactory if only the two upper parts are used. But the bass part, using only F and C (1 and 5) is easy and gives experience to boys in the kind of singing many of them will do when they become full-fledged basses.

The song is in AABA form, common to many familiar pieces. This form gives strong emphasis to its principal melody through repetitions which make it easy to remember. The melody of the first phrase is repeated identically in the second phrase, then a contrasting phrase appears, and, finally, in the fourth phrase the melody of the first phrase is again repeated.

45

The Band Concert (PAGE 161)
KEY OF F
UPPER PART (MELODY) STARTS ON C (5—SO)
LOWER PART STARTS ON F (1—DO)

✔ TWO-PART SINGING ✔ INSTRUMENTAL ACTIVITY
✔ CREATIVE ACTIVITY

In "The Band Concert" we have a two-part song that is easy to read and to adapt for varied use. Melody instruments might play both parts by changing one note in their melody part (play C instead of E on "neigh-" at the beginning of the last line) and staying on the last dotted half note F of the melody, rather than going up to the high F.

Trumpets and clarinets can play the two parts by reading the music as it is printed.

Stanzas could be added, bringing in other instruments or fitting added words to instruments played by pupils in the class, as, for instance:

> Johnny can play on the trumpet,
> Tommy plays on the shining trombone;
> Sally can play on the piano,
> Mary plays on a big xylophone.

● The Trout (PAGE 162)
KEY OF Bb
STARTS ON F (5—SO)

✔ ART SONG ✔ EXPRESSIVE SINGING

During the course of their experiences in singing, pupils should become familiar with a great variety of music, including folk songs of many countries and art songs, which represent the music of master composers. Folk songs are more easily sung than art songs, partly because their vocal demands are usually less and partly because the texts and music are easier. Nevertheless, pupils will gain the greatest insight into the art songs of such masters as Franz Schubert by singing them rather than only hearing others sing them.

The tempo should be moderately fast, but never faster than a class can sing easily and accurately. The kind of music boys and girls hear in such overabundance on radio and TV, in which sliding from note to note with heavy tone quality is considered appropriate, makes it all the more important that the kind of music represented by "The Trout" is learned and sung properly.

"The Trout" can be sung beautifully by pupils when they have learned it well and sing it in a light, flowing manner. The passages that move quickly and delicately must be sung lightly, in precise rhythm. Do not let your pupils merely slide over an approximation of these tones. They should, for example, hear and repeat a good rendition of the first phrase ending, on the words "a playful trout." Each phrase should be worked out carefully in the same way, giving attention to sixteenth-note figures to see that they are done lightly and with precision.

The Linden Tree (PAGE 164)
KEY OF F
UPPER PART (MELODY) STARTS ON C (5—SO)
MIDDLE PART STARTS ON A (3—MI)
LOWER PART STARTS ON F (1—DO)

✔ THREE-PART SINGING ✔ FRANZ SCHUBERT ✔ TRIPLETS

The three parts should be learned, if it is at all feasible; if it is not, use the two upper parts, having singers on the harmony part omit the notes in parentheses, singing the melody notes at those points. When three parts are sung, have the singers on the middle part sing the notes in parentheses, as they will provide a more complete harmonic structure.

In three places, near the end of the first and second phrases, and near the end of the very last phrase, triplet rhythm occurs. The triplets are sung within the space of one beat, the third beat of the measure in the three examples in this song. Repeating the word "merrily" gives a natural triplet rhythm:

Have pupils repeat this rhythm while looking at the appearance of the rhythmic figure, which has been placed on the blackboard. Next, have them sing:

When the triplet figure has been learned, place it in the context of the phrases in which it occurs in the song, starting with the first phrase:

Let your pupils read an account of the life and music of Franz Schubert in books in the school or public library. If pictures are available, place them on the bulletin board. Also, play recordings of the "Unfinished Symphony" or other Schubert works which may be in your record library.

My Island (PAGE 165)

KEY OF E
MELODY STARTS ON B (5—SO)
HARMONY (LOWER) PART STARTS ON G# (3—MI)

✔ TWO-PART SINGING   ✔ SOCIAL STUDIES RELATIONSHIP

The tempo should be moderate, the 6/8 meter performed in two beats to a measure. Phrases should be flowing, and tone quality should be light.

Let your pupils read the parts simultaneously, after tuning and establishing the pitch of the first tones. If they cannot, teach the melody first, with everyone singing it. Then let everyone learn the harmony. Finally, divide the class into two groups to sing the song in harmony.

This selection could be used as part of a unit on the Philippine Islands, or as part of a unit on Islands of the Pacific.

● Now the Day Is Over (PAGE 166)

KEY OF Eb
UPPER PART STARTS ON Bb (5—SO)
MIDDLE PART STARTS ON G (3—MI)
LOWER PART STARTS ON Eb (1—DO)

✔ THREE-PART SINGING   ✔ INTERPRETATION

The harmonies in this arrangement move partly in unison rhythm and partly (e.g., the middle part at the end of the first phrase on the word "nigh") by motion in which one part holds as another moves. The effect can be very pleasing if the chords are well tuned and if the sustained parts hold their tones until the moving voices are ready to move to the next measure or phrase.

The song should be sung legato. Instead of permitting your pupils to breathe at the end of the second measure (after the word "over"), challenge them to continue on one breath to the end of the phrase, through the word "nigh."

The tempo may be varied to slow down slightly at the end of the fourth measure and again at the end of each stanza.

The Children's Prayer (PAGE 166)

KEY OF D
UPPER PART (MELODY) STARTS ON D (1—DO)
LOWER PART STARTS ON D (1—DO)

✔ OPERATIC SELECTION ✔ TWO-PART SINGING

This well-known melody from the popular children's opera "Hänsel and Gretel" is a lovely tune that merits special attention to good phrasing and tone quality. The tempo should be moderate, and the mood should be a quiet, peaceful one. Singing should be light, with a floating quality. Phrases should be sung very smoothly. The first phrase of four measures should be sung on one breath, avoiding the tendency to breathe after the word "sleep."

The part-singing in this song is interesting to do and to hear, as it changes from unison rhythm at the beginning to independent rhythms in each part, starting with the melody on the phrase "Two my right selecting." In this section, make certain that groups singing each part are very accurate in their rhythm as well as melody, so that the two parts will move precisely and smoothly when sung together.

Chromatic tones are used throughout the melody and harmony. They can be learned easily with the aid of a piano. Using the piano accompaniment, after the song has been learned, also aids the singers in maintaining accurate tonality and makes the performance more effective.

Briefly review the story of Hänsel and Gretel.

Night Time (PAGE 168)

KEY OF A MINOR
UPPER PART STARTS ON A (1—LA)
MIDDLE PART STARTS ON F (6—FA)
LOWER PART STARTS ON D (4—RE)

✔ PROGRAM SONG ✔ THREE-PART SONG

The three parts should be used as an effective concert or festival number. They are interdependent, all being required to complete the harmony on which the arrangement is based.

Teach the first four measures first, waiting in moving on to the next phrase until each part is securely learned and sung well in tune. The next four measures are identical except for the last tone of the upper part.

Next, have the singers on the upper part learn the melody which begins on the ninth measure and continues for eight measures. Teach the two lower parts together (the dotted half notes), as they move together harmonically and rhythmically to form an accompaniment to the melody sung by the upper-part voices.

When this main section of the number has been learned, teach the ending section (the last eight measures). Here again the upper part enters, followed by the middle voice and then the lower voice, to form a three-part chord.

The tempo should be rather slow, yet the song should be sung with quiet, flowing motion.

● Jacob's Ladder (PAGE 169)

KEY OF F
MELODY STARTS ON A (3—MI)
MIDDLE PART STARTS ON F (1—DO)
LOWER PART STARTS ON C (5—SO)

✔ THREE-PART SINGING

As an effective program number, let your class sing this selection in three parts or use the upper two parts only, if you prefer. For a festival, it is desirable to use all three parts without accompaniment.

The tempo should be moderate, and the phrasing smooth and flowing. The volume should grow gradually until the melody reaches its highest tones (F, top line of the staff) and then gradually diminish toward the end of the song.

My Ukulele (PAGE 170)
KEY OF C
STARTS ON G (5—SO)

✔ TONIC CHORD ✔ INSTRUMENTAL ACCOMPANIMENT

Be sure that your pupils read the teaching material printed above the song in their books. Let them sing, several times, the passage given there. They should then have no difficulty in reading the second and third staffs. The first staff is equally simple, for it is built on a sequence.

Anvil Chorus (PAGE 171)
KEY OF F
STARTS ON F (1—DO)

✔ OPERATIC SELECTION

This excerpt from a well-known opera can be used as an introduction to a brief study of opera, including listening to other operatic excerpts on records, looking at pictures of scenes from operas, and watching and hearing TV opera productions.

"Anvil Chorus" from the opera "Il Trovatore" is sung by a chorus, whereas many of the musical dialogues are sung by individual performers. These solo numbers are called "arias." Play recordings, if any are available, to illustrate operatic choruses and arias.

Opera, even when performed in this country, is often sung in the language in which the opera was originally written. Since many operas are of Italian origin, much of the beautiful music available on recordings and heard in our opera houses is sung in Italian. Since translations are necessary for singing this music in schools, many text versions are encountered. The text used here is an adaptation providing a patriotic setting.

Encourage your pupils to read about the life and works of Verdi in books in the school or public library, for he was one of the giants of operatic composition.

Dance Together (PAGE 172)
KEY OF D MINOR
UPPER PART STARTS ON E (2—TI)
LOWER PART STARTS ON G (4—RE)

✔ CREATIVE ACTIVITY ✔ MINOR TONALITY

Here is a happy dance tune in minor tonality. It is quite simple, since the harmony part (lower staff) is in the main one third lower than the melody and moves in parallel motion with it.

Divide your class into two groups, one for each part, and let them try to sing the song at sight. If they have difficulty, isolate the phrase in which the error occurs and resing it until it is correct.

You might consider the song an introduction to the dances which follow in the pupil's book; but if you wish to assign a creative activity, let your class make up a dance to it. The song contains cue words to help them: "Round the ends and down the middle," "Join the line," and "spinning."

If you use the song as a dance, divide the class into three groups, two groups to sing and the third to dance.

⬤ Four in a Boat (PAGE 173)
KEY OF F
STARTS ON F (1—DO)

✔ SINGING GAME ✔ RHYTHMIC ACTIVITY

Chant and clap the rhythm, repeating it several times, before you teach the song:

When the tune has been learned, divide the class into two groups, one to sing and one to dance. Alternate the groups at later singings.

An autoharp accompaniment using only three different chords adds color.

Dance directions: Join hands in a large circle and face center. Four boys stand in the middle of the circle, with hands joined. The circle moves to the right, and the boys in the center move to the left as the first stanza is sung. At the start of the second stanza, the four boys each choose a partner from the circle and move again to the left, hands joined to their partner's. The big circle stops moving on the third stanza and claps hands as the partners in the middle swing each other with hooked elbows.

When the song is repeated, the four girls remain in the center and the four boys join the big circle.

⦿ Skip to the Fiddle (PAGE 174)
KEY OF D
STARTS ON F♯ (3—MI)

✔ DANCE

The works of this composer (1773-1836), a well-known Swiss music educator and publisher, greatly influenced our own Lowell Mason, "the father of public-school music."

Your class should be able to sing the song at sight. Help them to discover that Staffs 1 and 2 in their books are melodically like Staffs 5 and 6. Staff 3 consists of a phrase and its repetition. There are two swings to a measure.

Let groups alternate in singing and dancing.

Dance directions: Form a triple circle consisting of sets of three (boy with a girl on each arm) facing clockwise. Then let each alternate group of three face the opposite direction.

M stands for measure.

M 1-4:　Each group of three skips 4 steps forward to its opposite group of three; then back 4 steps.

M 5-8:　Repeat steps for M 1-4.

M 9-10:　Boy links right elbow with girl on right and swings around 4 steps. Girl on left skips around in place, 4 steps.

M 11-12:　Repeat M 9-10 with girl on boy's left. Girl on his right skips around in place, 4 steps.

M 13-16:　Repeat steps for M 9-12.

M 17-20:　Repeat M 1-4.

M 21-24:　Each group of three skips 4 steps forward to its opposite group of three. Each group then goes forward 4 steps more, going through the opposite group (passing left shoulders) to meet a new set of three. Repeat the entire dance with the new set.

⦿ Fiesta (PAGE 176)
KEY OF G
STARTS ON D (5—SO)

✔ DANCE　　✔ CHROMATICS

Here is another circle dance in 6/8 meter, a favorite in Mexico. It is a good selection for a Pan American Day Program, especially if the singers and dancers wear simple but vivid Mexican costumes. Latin-American instruments might be played in accompaniment.

"Ole" is pronounced "oh-lay" and means "bravo," an ejaculation of approval.

Dance directions: Form a circle of couples, girls on the outside. Partners face each other and join both hands.

M stands for measure.

M 1:　　Spring on left foot, bringing right heel forward at the same time (heel on floor; toe pointing up).

M 2:　　Repeat above step, springing on right foot and bringing left heel forward.

M 3:　　Continue above steps; spring on left foot, then on right.

M 4:　　Same step, spring on left foot.

M 5-8:　Same as M 1-4, starting on right foot.
　　　　　　　　L—R—L R L;
The steps for M 1-8 are these:R—L—R L R.

M 9-16:　Repeat steps for M 1-8.

M 17-20:　Partners link right elbows and circle in place moving clockwise.

M 21-24:　Partners link left elbows and circle in place moving counter-clockwise.

● Caller's Song (PAGE 178)
KEY OF Ab
STARTS ON Eb (5—SO)

✔ SQUARE DANCE ✔ SOLO SINGING

Square dancing, dating back to Colonial America, has again become popular with our young people. They are most likely familiar with this tune, for it is often heard on TV "folk" programs. Individual pupils or a small group might be the "caller" and sing the song, while the rest of the class dances.

Dance directions: Form a square of four couples with the girl to the right of the boy. The first and third couples are the "end couples." The "corner lady" is the lady at the left of each boy. The song tells what to do.

Sing the song a second time for the promenade, so that the couples can circle twice.

The girl leads her new partner back to her place in the square. Repeat the dance until the original partners are back together again.

Occasionally do the dance to the recording instead of the singing accompaniment to add variety.

The Fisherman's Farewell (PAGE 179)
KEY OF C
UPPER PART STARTS ON E (3—MI)
MIDDLE PART STARTS ON C (1—DO)
LOWER PART STARTS ON C (1—DO)

✔ THREE-PART SINGING ✔ STRUCTURE ANALYSIS

If your class cannot as yet sing in three parts, let them sing the upper two parts, which are complete in themselves.

The song is not so difficult as it looks. Analyze it and help the class find the melodic phrases that are exactly alike (1 and 2) and those that are nearly alike (1 and 4). Notice that Phrase 3 consists of a repeated figure.

Although the autoharp is not associated with sea songs, it can be used to good effect with this selection.

A Life on the Ocean Wave (PAGE 180)
KEY OF G
ALL PARTS START ON D (5—SO)

✔ THREE-PART SONG ✔ PROGRAM SONG

This song is a favorite of boys' glee clubs and is often performed on special programs. It should be sung robustly and at a moderately fast tempo, two swings to a measure.

Teach each part separately and then put them together. The phrases containing chromatics may need special attention. Note that Staffs 1 and 2 in the pupil's book are melodically almost like Staffs 5 and 6.

We Sail the Ocean Blue (PAGE 182)
KEY OF C
STARTS ON C (1—DO)

✔ "FUN" SONG ✔ LIGHT OPERA

What adult person has not chuckled over the light operas of Gilbert and Sullivan? These two Englishmen teamed up in the late nineteenth century, much as our own Rodgers and Hammerstein, to write delightful musical plays. Many of their works are still in great vogue, especially in the larger cities, Little Theaters, and college centers.

"We Sail the Ocean Blue" is from "H.M.S. Pinafore." (H.M.S. means "His Majesty's Ship.") This light opera is staged on the deck of a ship of the Royal Navy. It has an involved, humorously melodramatic plot and abounds in tuneful numbers, for Sullivan had a good sense of fun, a strong feeling for rhythm, and a gift for melody. Recordings of the entire light opera and of abridged versions are available. Perhaps you can get one to play for your class, to interest them in light operas and operettas.

Other popular Gilbert and Sullivan works are "The Pirates of Penzance," "The Mikado," "Patience," "Iolanthe," and "The Yeomen of the Guard."

The Mermaid (PAGE 184)
KEY OF Bb
STARTS ON F (5—SO)

✔ "FUN" SONG   ✔ THREE-PART SONG

This is a forecastle chantey, since it tells a story and was sung to pass the time during leisure hours on deck.

The unison part is simple, because it consists of only two phrases, melodically alike. The three-part section starts out with the tonic chord. If the class has difficulty with the parts, teach each separately and then combine them.

The song should be sung steadily at a moderate tempo, with a light tone. Be sure that the class observes the *fermata,* working up to it with a lilt.

You might like to have an Assembly Program of chanties and sea songs. There are thirteen such songs in the child's book.

Cockles and Mussels (PAGE 187)
KEY OF G
STARTS ON D (5—SO)

✔ UNISON AND THREE-PART SINGING

Sing this popular Irish folk song at a moderate pace with clear enunciation. The unison section should cause no difficulty, but the class may have to practice singing the chords.

Be sure that the dotted quarter notes followed by eighth notes, and the eighth notes followed by dotted quarter notes are given their true values, for they furnish the song its characteristic lilt. You might have the class chant and clap the first phrase before attempting to sing.

G, D7, and C are the three accompanying chords. Playing them lightly on the autoharp makes a nice accompaniment.

Find Work, My Daughter (PAGE 186)
KEY OF A MINOR
UPPER PART STARTS ON A (1—LA)
LOWER PART STARTS ON C (3—DO)

✔ DIALOGUE SONG   ✔ STRUCTURE ANALYSIS

Here is a song for the girls. If the boys want to join in, the "daughter" should sing "my father" instead of "my mother" wherever the words occur.

Notice that Phrases 1 and 2 are almost alike and Phrases 3 and 4 are almost alike. The form is therefore AA_1BB_1. The song is simple.

Divide the class into four groups. Group 1 sings the upper staff of the mother's part, and Group 2 sings the lower staff of that part. Group 3 sings the upper staff of the daughter's part, and Group 4 sings the lower staff of that part. Before the class sings the song in dialogue form, let all learn both staffs of the entire song.

Sing the song in a light and lively fashion.

The Nightingale (PAGE 188)
KEY OF C
UPPER PART STARTS ON C (1—DO)
MIDDLE PART STARTS ON E (3—MI)
LOWER PART STARTS ON C (1—DO)

✔ THREE-PART SINGING   ✔ DIALOGUE

Let the class sing up and down the tonic chord to establish the tonality before they sing the song. Then let all sing the melody (upper part) at sight. When they can do so successfully, form three groups. The large Group 1 sings the melody. Groups 2 and 3 are smaller, and sing the two-toned accompaniment lightly. Group 2 has only three tones to repeat over and over: E, F, and G; Group 3 has likewise only three: C, D, and E.

For variety, you might divide Group 1 into two sections, to sing the melody in dialogue form. Both of these sections sing Stanzas 1 and 3. The first section sings the soldier's words, and the second section sings the lady's words in Stanzas 2 and 4.

Ring the Banjo (PAGE 189)
KEY OF Eb
STARTS ON Bb (5—SO)

✔ UNISON AND TWO-PART SINGING
✔ RHYTHM ACCOMPANIMENT

"Ring the Banjo" is one of the most popular of Stephen Foster's humorous songs. It should be sung brightly, with strict attention to the meter. Notice that the two voices in the refrain are, in the main, a third apart and move in parallel motion.

A rhythm accompaniment is suggested in the pupil's book. You might help the class by proposing the following for the claves:

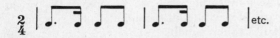

Then let the class experiment with the drums until they have created a satisfactory accompanying rhythm.

Happy Village (PAGE 190)
KEY OF F
BELLS AND VOICES START ON F (1—DO)

✔ BELL ACCOMPANIMENT ✔ PROGRAM SONG

This happy French song can be beautifully presented on a spring program or some other festive occasion, if the bell accompaniment is used and the song is performed in three parts. The selection is not so difficult as it may seem. The form is AABBC, and therefore there are only three different melodic phrases. The third part consists of only two tones: F and C. The bell accompaniment consists of only three different tones: F, C, and D.

When the class can sing the upper two parts well, play F and low C on the bells so that those who will sing the lowest part can attune their ears to the only two tones on their staff. Then combine the three parts and add the bell accompaniment, played lightly.

The *simile* (literally, "in like manner") mark is explained in the pupil's book. It means "Repeat the previous measure."

Walk into the Spring (PAGE 192)
KEY OF C
UPPER PART STARTS ON C (1—DO)
LOWER PART STARTS ON C (1—LOW DO)

✔ TWO-PART SINGING ✔ LISTENING

The melody of this song is a Morris Dance tune of Old England. Morris dancers were a sprightly lot, wearing bells on their legs and carrying large handkerchiefs or sticks which they waved. They often performed at May Day festivals. So the music to which they danced was equally sprightly and gay.

Percy Grainger, an Australian-born American musician, used this tune in his composition "Country Gardens." Recordings of it for the piano and also for orchestra are available. Your class might be interested in listening to them.

A few measures of the tune are used as an introduction to our recorded "Robin Hood," page 136 of the pupil's book.

Sing the song smoothly at a moderately fast tempo with an accent on the first beat and only a slight stress on the third beat.

If the second part goes too low in range for your particular class, let all sing the melody in unison.

Going to Shout (PAGE 194)
KEY OF Ab
BOTH PARTS START ON Ab (1—DO)

✔ SPIRITUAL ✔ RHYTHM ACCOMPANIMENT

Because of its appealing simplicity, this is one of our best-loved spirituals. It should be sung happily and brightly at a moderate tempo and in strict rhythm. Your class is most likely familiar with the melody through repeated hearings on the radio and TV.

Let the class all learn the melody. When they can sing it well, choose a group to sing the second part. Teach this part separately. Be sure that both parts observe the rhythm punctiliously, for the syncopation is one of the charms of this spiritual. The clapping and tapping accompaniment suggested in the pupil's book aids in keeping to strict rhythm.

Listen to the Lambs (PAGE 196)
KEY OF D MINOR
STARTS ON A (5—MI)

✔ THREE-PART SINGING ✔ CREATIVE RHYTHM ACTIVITY

In contrast to "Going to Shout," this is a rather pleading spiritual. It should be sung at a moderate tempo and not be allowed to "drag." The last two staffs in the pupil's book may even be speeded up a little. Call attention to the *fermatas* and see that they are observed in the interest of good interpretation.

Teach the melody first, and when the entire class is familiar with it, add the other two parts.

The class may wish to make up a rhythm accompaniment, tapping their feet or clapping their hands as they sing. Encourage them to do so, being sure to keep any accompaniment light and delicate, in keeping with the tone of the spiritual.

The autoharp accompaniment, utilizing three different chords, adds to the effectiveness of performance.

On a Fine Summer Day (PAGE 197)
KEY OF C
THREE PARTS START ON G (5—SO)

✔ THREE-PART SINGING ✔ WHISTLING

This jolly spring song may be sung in two or three parts, depending on the abilities of a specific class. It is a robust number, to be sung in march rhythm with a steady beat.

The last four measures of the optional third part offer a choice of tones to be sung. If any of your boys can sing the low G, encourage them to do so in order to get the effect of four-part singing.

Let the class whistle a third stanza.

Streets of Laredo (PAGE 198)
KEY OF F
DESCANT STARTS ON A (3—MI)
MELODY STARTS ON C (5—SO)

✔ INSTRUMENTATION ✔ INTERPRETATION

Like many cowboy songs, "Streets of Laredo" has a plaintive, rather sad touch, which should be brought out in the interpretation of the piece.

The melody is a simple tune that can be read at sight. The descant uses only three different tones: A, Bb, C.

In performance, the boys might sing the melody while the girls softly sing the descant. Or have the descant played on bells or melody instruments, while the entire class sings the tune.

The pupil's book suggests harmonizing the song with the chords that are printed below the text:

There are a variety of activities that may be performed with the song. Let the class experiment with as many of them as they have time for.

Farewell Song (PAGE 200)
KEY OF Eb
BOTH PARTS START ON Eb (1—DO)

✔ PHRASING ✔ CHROMATICS

The note in the pupil's book calls attention to the fact that all but one of the phrases in this song are 3 measures long. The third phrase is 4 measures long, adding a touch of individuality to this Czechoslovak folk song.

Sing the song smoothly at a moderate tempo. Call attention to the chromatics in the second phrase of the lower part and be sure that they are sung correctly.

The third phrase may be sung in three parts, if you like. Divide the pupils who are singing the lower part into two groups, one group to stay on the lower part and the other group to sing the third part on Phrase 3 and return to the lower part on Phrase 4.

Praise Ye the Lord (PAGE 201)
KEY OF F
UPPER PART STARTS ON C (5—SO)
MIDDLE PART STARTS ON A (3—MI)
LOWER PART STARTS ON F (1—DO)

✔ SPECIAL DAY SONG ✔ BELL INTERLUDE

This hymn is excellent for performance at Easter, Christmas, or any other time of religious significance.

It should be sung reverently and rather exultantly at a moderate tempo. It is good in either two or three parts, but for public performance the three-part arrangement is more effective.

The melody may be played on bells as an interlude between stanzas.

The Star-Spangled Banner (PAGE 202)
KEY OF Bb
STARTS ON F (5—SO)

✔ ASSEMBLY SONG

The melody of our national anthem is that of "To Anacreon in Heaven," composed by John Stafford Smith (1750-1836) and used as the club song of the Anacreontic Society, a group of wealthy amateur musicians. The music had been well-known in the Colonies, where sets of words, among them "Adams and Liberty," were sung to it. The words of "The Star-Spangled Banner" were written during the War of 1812.

On September 13, 1814, Francis Scott Key, a young Baltimore lawyer, obtained permission to visit the English fleet to sue for the release of a physician friend who had been captured during the hostilities. He rowed out under a flag of truce and, while his mission was successful, he was not allowed to leave the boat that night because the bombardment of Fort McHenry had begun. All night long he anxiously awaited the result of the battle and when the first rays of the sun showed the Stars and Stripes still floating over the fort, he wrote the first stanza of this song. The other stanzas were completed on shore, and the song was published in *The Baltimore Patriot* a week later.

"The Star-Spangled Banner" was made the official national anthem of the United States by a Bill which passed the Senate on March 3, 1931.

Index of Recordings

One album of two LP recordings
Produced by Audio Education, Inc., distributed by American Book Company

*These are orchestral selections and have no piano accompaniments. The page numbers are those in the children's book.

INDEX OF SONGS